The Complete Guide
to
Lincoln
Cents

By

David W. Lange

Bowers and Merena Galleries, Inc.

Wolfeboro, New Hampshire

The origin, concept, typography and layout of this volume were
by the author, David W. Lange, and by David and John Feigenbaum of DLRC Press.

Bowers and Merena Galleries, Inc.
Box 1224
Wolfeboro, New Hampshire
(603) 569-5095 • fax (603) 569-5319

Printed in the United States of America

Look for these and other great titles from Bowers and Merena Galleries, Inc.

Collecting Coins and Making Money: A Peek at the 19th Century, edited by Q. David Bowers

A Buyers' Guide to Silver Dollars and Trade Dollars of the United States, by Q. David Bowers

Buyers' Guide to United States Gold Coins, by Q. David Bowers

Commemorative Coins of the United States: A Complete Encyclopedia, by Q. David Bowers

The History of United States Coinage, by Q. David Bowers

Louis E. Eliasberg, Sr.: King of Coins, by Q. David Bowers

United States Gold Coins: An Illustrated History, by Q. David Bowers

The Cherrypickers' Guide to Rare Die Varieties, by Bill Fivaz and J.T. Stanton

A Basic Guide to United States Commemorative Coins, by Michael Hodder and Q. David Bowers

The Norweb Collection: An American Legacy, by Michael Hodder and Q. David Bowers

United States Pattern and Related Issues, by Andrew W. Pollock, III

Walter Breen's Encyclopedia of United States and Colonial Proof Coins

The United States Clad Coinage, by Ginger Rapsus

Encyclopedia of United States Silver and Gold Commemorative Coins, by Anthony Swiatek and Walter Breen

And coming soon from Bowers and Merena Galleries, Inc.

A Buyer's and Enthusiast's Guide to Flying Eagle and Indian Cents, by Q. David Bowers

This book is dedicated to the steadfast trio
who have have unfailingly enabled me to do my best work . . .

Tom Mulvaney, superb photographer and friend,
and the team of Bill Fivaz and J. T. Stanton,
advisors . . . critics . . . comrades

This book is dedicated also to
the Old San Francisco Mint Museum,
within whose historic walls
so much of my research was performed

. . . and finally,
this book is dedicated to F. and N.
for minding their P's and Q's

Acknowledgements

This book is in many respects a collaborative effort. A number of persons contributed unwittingly by virtue of their excellent published research, and the author took every opportunity to use this material when applicable. Others, however, contributed materially by offering their time, skill, knowledge and collections without restriction so that this work might be everything its author intended.

The layout and design of this book was performed by John A. Feigenbaum of DLRC Press.

A major debt is owed to those who reviewed all or part of the first draft of the author's manuscript with critical and constructive eyes. These include Steve Benson, Stewart Blay, J. T. Stanton and Phelps Dean Witter. Their experience and expertise was crucial to providing further perspective to the author's own experience with the Lincoln series.

Additional consultation was provided by Thomas K. DeLorey, Michael L. Ellis, Kevin Flynn, William T. Gibbs, Ronald L. Hickman, Marion Krause, Eric M. Larson and Ken Potter.

The superb photography presented in this volume was also the product of several key individuals. First and foremost of these is Tom Mulvaney, whose skill is represented in the many photos which appear without specific credits. His work is particularly evident within Chapters 7 and 8, where each particular coin issue is illustrated. The task of shooting varieties was shared between Tom and the prolific team of Bill Fivaz and J. T. Stanton. Their skill in maintaining clarity, even in extreme close-up, is greatly appreciated, as is their generosity in sharing the results with the readers of this book.

Additional photographic credits include Dawn Hencinsky, Ralph Iacobelli, Cathy Dumont Wilson, Doug Plasencia, and Allan Willits.

At times, photography is effective only when the desired coins are made available as needed. While many of the coins illustrated are from the author's collection, critical gaps were filled by several individuals, businesses and institutions. Those persons who generously loaned items for photographing or provided photographic prints include Ken Barr, Steve Benson, Stewart Blay, Fred J. Borgmann, Q. David Bowers, David F. Cieniewicz, Timothy Claire, Beth Deisher, Bill Fivaz, Frank Gasparro, John Klosowski, Eric M. Larson, Arnold Margolis, Harry Miller, Tom Miller, Ken Potter, William Shamhart, Jr., Marian A. Sinton, Mike Sulak, Sam Thurman and Robert Van Ryzin. Businesses furnishing coins or photographs include Auctions by Bowers & Merena, Bara-King Photographic, Numismatic Guaranty Corporation, The Scotsman Coins and Stack's. Non-profit institutions which provided photographs include the American Numismatic Association, the American Numismatic Society, the National Archives, the Saint-Gaudens National Historic Site, the Smithsonian Institution's National Museums of American Art and American History and the United States Mint. Publications furnishing coins or photographs include *The Coin Collector, Coin World, Error Trends Coin Magazine, The Numismatist, Numismatic News* and *The Standard Catalog of World Coins*.

Data was reprinted with permission from *ANACS Population Report, NGC Census Report and PCGS Population Report*. Major portions of Chapter 6 were reprinted with permission from *The Official American Numismatic Association Grading Standards for United States Coins*. Reference works were provided by the American Numismatic Association Library, the Drew University Library, the Morristown Library, the Old San Francisco Mint Museum Library and the Pacific Coast Numismatic Society Library.

Individuals who assisted in multiple small ways to facilitate the production of this book include Augustine A. Albino, Betsy Burstein, Lynn Chen, Dr. Richard Doty, Leslie A. Elam, David Feigenbaum, Barbara Gregory, Elizabeth L. Hill, Herbie Lam, Michael Levin, Jane Merritt, William E. Metcalf, Edward Metzger, Douglas A. Mudd, Korin Rosencrantz, Gregory C. Schwarz, William F. Sherman, Annie Smith, Dr. Alan M. Stahl, Joan Stahl, Michael Turoff and Olga Widness.

Foreword

by J.T. Stanton

When David Lange asked whether I would write the foreword to his new book, it took me but a second to answer. To be associated with him and the book, which will undoubtedly be a mainstay for years to come, is indeed an honor.

The Lincoln Cent is certainly the most widely collected coinage series in history. This lowly coin is very likely responsible for more collectors entering the hobby than any other series. It is what sparked my collecting interest some 37 years ago.

Lange has left no coin unturned in his research. His unique and enjoyable writing style makes the history of the design, the designer, and the object of the Lincoln Cent so interesting, it is difficult to put the book down. His detail of the controversies relating to the coin makes the reference even *more* enjoyable.

Interesting facts abound as Lange follows the production of the Lincoln Cent through the years. He emphasizes change has been the norm for the Lincoln Cent. The designer's initials being removed in 1909, to be restored again in 1918, and a change in alloy in 1943, 1944, 1947, 1962 and finally in 1982 are among the modifications that have taken place. Strikings of test alloys are chronicled. As Lange relates, design changes have also contributed to the popularity of the Lincoln Cent. Very interesting research into the coin shortages during the past 87 years exhibits the effects on the design--and on collecting interest.

Of particular benefit to the collector is the extent to which Lange goes to provide as much historical information as possible to exhibit collecting interest, price changes through the years, and availability of each mint-marked date. He also depicts many error coins, which are gaining in popularity, as well as all major varieties of the series, of which there are many.

The date-and-mint analysis is unsurpassed by that contained in any other book. High-quality photographs start each date, followed by rarity, values, varieties, comments, and populations for those Mint State examples.

This is a book I can't wait to add to my numismatic library. In fact, I know I will be referring to it frequently, whether for authentication, values, or general information. *The Complete Guide to Lincoln Cents* is needed by every serious collector who wants to be informed as fully as possible regarding this coin. It is the best book I have read on a single series.

David Lange has created a new standard for a numismatic reference work.

J.T. Stanton

J. T. Stanton

Introduction

A penny saved is a penny earned

Mind your pennies and the dollars mind themselves

See a penny
Pick it up . . .
All that day
You'll have good luck

Abe Lincoln frowns on this oversize novelty coin, a common fixture in gift shops around the country. (Actual size: 77mm)

Such sentiments, while at one time spoken with conviction and a certain regularity, have largely become obsolete as the United States of America approaches the 21st Century. Yet until it was rendered practically useless by inflation during the 1970s and '80s, the one-cent piece represented the lowest common denominator of our society. It provided the simplest link between the consumer and the nation's economy. When in the possession of just a single cent, even a child could participate in the American dream in his or her own small way through the purchase of a gumball. As the embodiment of this shared experience for most of the present century, the humble Lincoln Cent occupies a unique place in American culture that transcends its value as both a piece of money and a numismatic object.

Sadly, in the United States of the 1990s there is not a single object which can be purchased with a cent. This coin exists today solely as an antiquated unit of measure, unable to command attention except when presented in multiples and even then subject to a negative response. The Treasury Department continues to favor production of the one-cent piece for the seigniorage that it provides. This seigniorage is accrued as profit to the Federal Government, and as long as materials may be found from which to coin cents at a cost below their face value this peculiar practice will continue. It's ironic that the Treasury Department and the United States Mint point to the almost unfathomable numbers being minted each and every year as proof of the coin's usefulness, failing to note that the reason so many replacement cents are

needed is that no one bothers to recirculate the ones they receive!

This situation cannot be sustained much longer, however, as the cost of producing one-cent pieces is already approaching their face value, and no solution's in sight. Regardless of its material value, the cost of producing one unit of any object, whether it be a coin, a stamp or a gumball, is likely to soon exceed one cent, given the continued effects of inflation. In short, there may be no substance left from which to make cents that won't still produce a loss to the United States. Of course, the prospect of wasting taxpayers' money has never stopped the Federal Government in the past, but it will likely stir up those members of Congress who are already questioning the usefulness of our smallest coin. This pressure is sure to increase along with the rising mintage of cents, since additional space and equipment will be needed within the mint structures to expand such activity.

* * *

Though the Lincoln Cent is now an object of derision, except among coin collectors, it was not always so. This coin debuted to much acclaim in 1909, the centennial year of Abraham Lincoln's birth. There were then persons still living who could recall his presidency, and the sentimental appeal of this humble yet distinguished figure appearing on the nation's most humble coin was intense. Despite a flap over the presence of the artist's initials on the first issue of Lincoln Cents, coins of this type were warmly received.

There were then many useful objects and services which could be provided in exchange for a single cent. Daily newspapers were commonly priced at this figure, as were many confections. A cent could provide flights of fancy at the Penny Arcade, where numerous mechanical amusements awaited both child and adult. As amazing as it may seem to Americans of the 1990s, there were yet a

The Illinois commemorative half dollar. Issued in 1918.

number of items which could be purchased in quantity for a single cent; candy is one example which comes to mind.

Though for quite a few years they circulated side-by-side with the Indian Head Cents of 1859-1909, Lincoln Cents quickly came to predominate by their sheer numbers. This trend accelerated during the period of America's involvement in World War I, as wartime taxes on a wide variety of products dramatically increased the need for making change in odd figures and led to record mintages. Though this activity subsided shortly afterward, so many Lincolns were then in circulation that by the end of the 1920s collectors were remarking how scarce the old Indians had become.

This medal was issued in aluminum and nickel by Krause Publications to celebrate the 30th anniversary of its flagship periodical, Numismatic News. It was sculpted by former U.S. Mint Chief Engraver Frank Gasparro, who also created the reverse of the Lincoln Memorial Cent. (actual size: 39mm)

For at least three generations now the Lincoln Cent has been the only coin of this value in general circulation. It has been produced for a longer time than any other coin type in the history of the United States. Though Victor D. Brenner's original heraldic reverse of 1909 was supplanted by Frank Gasparro's depiction of the Lincoln Memorial beginning in 1959, the profile of Abraham Lincoln has become perhaps the most universally known image in our entire culture. It's safe to say that every person who has lived in the United States since 1909 has at one time or another held an example of this coin in his or her hands, and the number of people included in this population is simply staggering. So too is the number of Lincoln Cents minted from 1909 through 1995—-more than 330 billion!

* * *

The place which the Lincoln Cent occupies in America's history must be measured in more than sheer numbers, for this coin is as familiar a cultural icon as our popular television characters, the brands of our consumer goods and the names of our towns and cities. Ever since its debut, advertisers have enlisted this instantly recognizable coin in every conceivable promotion and enticement. There have been innumerable graphic representations of the Lincoln Cent, often with Lincoln smiling at some bargain offering of a second item priced at only one cent when purchased with the first item at full price. The sizes of these representations have also varied; there have been quite a few big pennies to advertise big bargains. With the advent of television there have been animated heads of Honest Abe emerging from his circular home to tell of the "honest" trading at so-and-so's car dealership or mattress warehouse.

Consider for just a moment the number of times a Lincoln Cent or two has been received in the mail, pasted to some offering of a new detergent or a book club membership. Then multiply this figure by the number of households in the United States and it becomes evident how countless millions of these coins have been consumed. While many may have been pried loose and deposited in one's cookie jar, desk drawer or five-gallon jug, in recent decades most have simply been discarded with the rest of the "junk mail."

The Lincoln Cent has been the coin of choice for generations of wishing-well tossers, and there's no telling how many have been swallowed by children, pets and vacuum cleaners. A child of 1910, or even one of 1960 would not have ignored a penny found on the street, but when was the last time a young boy or girl expressed delight at finding a one-cent piece? Ask yourself too how many years it has been since the last time you bothered to pick one up from the sidewalk. Several times weekly we are posed with such a dilemma, yet our

The designer of Guatemala's one-peso and five-peso coins dated 1923 was obviously influenced by the Lincoln Cent in laying out the portraits and legends. (Standard Catalog of World Coins)

Proof that the Lincoln Cent is still a fixture in advertising.

choice is invariably the same.

* * *

Since the 1960s we've been accustomed to receiving cents which have no value, whether as money or as numismatic pieces, yet would a coin collector living in 1940 or 1950 have overlooked a cent lying in the street knowing that there might yet be key and semi-key dates in circulation? The chance finding of a cent in the street was at one time a cause for anticipation in the mind of a collector, yet this allure has become only a treasured memory for the lucky few who remember.

Since the collecting of coins from circulation first became popular in the 1930s, the traditional avenue of entry for the budding collector has been Lincoln Cents. Offering a wide variety of date-and-mint combinations at little cost to the saver, this series has brought out the collecting instinct in millions of Americans, a mania which peaked during the late 1950s and early '60s. This time saw a flourishing of assorted albums and folders for collecting coins from circulation, yet it was the Lincoln Cent series which formed the one universal link between all the different brands and styles. No company produced a coin album without including this title, for it was the most commonly collected series both then and now.

The advent of the Lincoln Memorial design in 1959 hastened the withdrawal of all older cents, including ones which will never be rare or valuable. While this has greatly reduced the allure of collecting Lincolns from circulation, inexpensive folders are still being produced for the novice and the casual collector, as there are yet many different dates to be found within the unsorted bags and junk boxes offered by coin dealers. For the serious collector the emphasis has shifted toward the slow and meticulous assembling of a set in higher grades. He or she may continue to favor albums, but recent generations of collectors are increasingly drawn toward the gathering of individual pieces that have been graded and encapsulated by professionals. Though something magical has been lost with the decline of circulation finds, hobbyists are today being created who will become superbly knowledgeable and who will find the pursuit of quality every bit as satisfying as those of previous generations did their simple treasure hunt.

It's been my good fortune to taste both of these eras. As with countless others, my discovery of coin collecting began with a Whitman folder for Lincoln Cents. This was in 1965, at a time when I was just learning to read and knew nothing of numismatics beyond the overwhelming compulsion to fill holes. Such activity was pursued solely with the coins found in my own limited pocket change as well as that of any willing participant in my mania. While all the really valuable dates were long gone by then, I was blissfully unaware of this at the time. After all, a penny dated 1935 was already quite ancient to a seven-year-old in 1965, and the discovery of many coins dating from the 1930s, '40s and '50s was enough to seize and retain my interest until other avenues of acquisition opened to me.

Lincoln has long been a fixture on our paper money.

There is simply no way to convey in words the sense of anticipation and adventure that existed for a young child at a time when old coins of obsolete types were still circulating. Even so, the fact that you have picked up this book and have read this far indicates that, whatever your age or experience in the hobby, you have come to understand the timeless appeal of the Lincoln Cent. If the pages which follow serve to speed you on your journey of discovery and impart to you some of the delight that I've found in this long-running series it will prove a complete vindication of the many weekends lost in their preparation.

THE LINCOLN CENT

The Lincoln cent is the first United States coin made for general circulation that has an actual person depicted. It was first produced in 1909 for the 100th anniversary of Lincoln's birth.

"ENRICHING COIN COLLECTING THROUGH KNOWLEDGE."
1-800-253-4555

No. 1 in a Series

A recent Coin World promotional item

David W. Lange
June, 1996

P. O. Box 288
Morris Plains, NJ 07950

Table of Contents

Chapter 1

History of the Lincoln Cent

•

Abraham Lincoln

•

Victor D. Brenner

•

Frank Gasparro

Bronze galvano of Brenner's obverse model (United States Mint)

Galvano of Brenner's original reverse model with his name spelled in full (U. S. Mint)

Galvano of Gasparro's model for the Memorial reverse (U. S. Mint)

What might have been

As the 19th Century dissolved into the 20th, the United States Mint was an institution bound by tradition. Employment there was often for one's lifetime, and it was not unusual for a job title to pass from father to son to grandson (the few female employees enjoyed no such privileges). In such an atmosphere, conventional thinking and practices were the order of the day, and there was little incentive for technical innovation and even less for artistic experimentation. When it came to preparing new coin designs, the man who held the title of Chief Engraver had a virtual monopoly. Of the designs then current, all but one were the work of the incumbent Chief Engraver, Charles E. Barber, or one of his predecessors in that role. The sole exception was the silver dollar, which was the design of Assistant Engraver George T. Morgan. Barber and Morgan enjoyed a congenial rivalry, but a rivalry nonetheless. Morgan ultimately succeeded Barber in the role of Chief Engraver upon the latter's death in 1917, just as Barber had succeeded his father, William, in 1880.

It was into this closed society that one man intruded in the Spring of 1905. Perhaps no other figure would have dared tread on such private ground, but then Theodore Roosevelt was no ordinary man. Having been tacked onto the Republican ticket for the election of 1900 without much forethought by party elders, Roosevelt shocked them by succeeding to the Presidency following the assassination of William McKinley in 1901. He further stunned his Republican bosses by proving a dynamic and popular leader, albeit one with an alarming propensity for reforming corrupt industries. No mere politician, however, "Teddy" Roosevelt was a champion of education and the arts, as well.

This interest in fine arts came to a head in 1905 over the preparation of a medal commemorating his second term. Finding the official government medal designed by Barber (obverse) and Morgan (reverse) too unimaginative, Roosevelt sought America's pre-eminent sculptor, Augustus Saint-Gaudens, to create something special for his privately-funded inaugural committee. The artist modeled Roosevelt in a high-relief, profile view, in the style of the great Renaissance medallists of the 16th Century. This portrait was mated to a reverse which featured a

Plaster models for the cent by Augustus Saint-Gaudens (Saint-Gaudens National Historic Site)

striding eagle, the same bird which would later grace the reverse of the ten-dollar piece in 1907.

So pleased was President Roosevelt with the result that he enlisted Saint-Gaudens to redesign all of America's current coins, which both men agreed were inferior to similar work being done in Europe. Though the two ruffled a few feathers within the United States Mint's establishment, they were ultimately successful in getting Saint-Gaudens' models adopted for the eagle (ten dollars) and double eagle (twenty dollars). Sadly, the great sculptor died before his work was complete, and it was left to others to carry it forward.

Medal commemorating Augustus St. Gaudens

Roosevelt remained undaunted, however, and on the recommendation of Dr. William Sturgis Bigelow he commissioned Boston sculptor Bela Lyon Pratt to rework the quarter eagle (two-and-one-half dollars) and half eagle (five dollars). These handsome coins debuted late in 1908, though they were not as widely acclaimed as the Saint-Gaudens pieces of 1907.

This work accomplished, Roosevelt's term as President was now coming to a close. Among the projects left on the drawing board was a complete redesign of the one-cent piece. It was reported in *The Numismatist* for May of 1906 that "A change in the design of the small bronze cent . . . is being considered by a Congressional committee." Not content to wait for government wheels to turn, Roosevelt and Saint-Gaudens had already discussed new models for the cent, and some initial work was performed until Saint-Gaudens was redirected toward completing the gold coins. Models dated 1907 were prepared featuring the head of Nike (Victory) which Saint-Gaudens had originally created for the monument to General William Tecumseh Sherman in New York City's Central Park. This was mated to a simple wreath design, with a bundle of arrows below. No pattern coins were ever struck from these models.

It seems that Saint-Gaudens' earliest plan for the cent did not include either of the above models, but rather was the revival of a design from the nation's past. Reference to it survives in a letter from him to President Roosevelt, dated June 28, 1906:

> Now I am attacking the cent. It may interest you to know that on the "Liberty" side of the cent I am using a flying eagle, a modification of the device which was used on the cent of 1857. I had not seen that coin for many years, and was so impressed by it, that I thought if carried out with some modifications, nothing better could be done. It is by all odds the best design on any American coin.[1]

Apparently, Roosevelt did not agree with the artist's assessment of the flying eagle design, as it was quietly dropped from the cent sometime during the following months, only to re-emerge as the adopted reverse for the double eagle of 1907. The next surviving communication from Saint-Gaudens to Roosevelt is dated February 11, 1907:

> I have received your letter of February the eighth regarding the Indian feather headdress in its application to the one-cent piece
>
> I have already begun the trial in the way you suggest, so it should not be long before I will be able to tell you of the result. I shall endeavor to let you know with the utmost possible dispatch.[2]

Roosevelt seemed obsessed with the concept of the goddess Liberty adorned in a feathered headdress, as each model Saint-Gaudens prepared for the various coin denominations was at some point refitted with this feature, though it ultimately survived only on the ten-dollar piece. Evidently, the President's insistence on the headdress was questioned by Saint-Gaudens, as Roosevelt's letter of February 16 reveals his growing self-consciousness:

> I wonder if I am one of those people of low appreciation of artistic things, against whom I have been inveighing! I like that feather head-dress so much that I have accepted that design of yours. Of course all the designs are conventional, as far as head-dresses go, because Liberty herself is conventional when embodied in a woman's head; and I don't see why we should not have a conventional head-dress of purely American type for the Liberty figure.[3]

After reworking his models again to the President's satisfaction, Saint-Gaudens forwarded them to the U. S. Mint in Philadelphia on March 12, 1907. That same day, he again wrote to Roosevelt confessing "I like so much the head with the headdress (and by the way, I am very glad you suggested doing the head in that manner) that I should like very much to see it tried not only on the the one-cent piece but also on the twenty-dollar gold piece, instead of the figure of Liberty."[4] It seems that this addition was never made to the cent, as the only surviving models by Saint-Gaudens portray a laureate head. The feathered headdress was used on pattern coins of the double eagle, but the circulating version utilized a standing figure instead. The final reference to the Saint-Gaudens cent is found in his letter to Roosevelt of May 11, 1907:

> Greatly as I should like to please you, I feel that I cannot now model another design in profile for the Twenty Dollar gold piece. Indeed, as far as I am concerned, I should prefer seeing the head of Liberty in place of any figure of Liberty on the Twenty Dollar coin as well as on the One

Cent.[5]

At the time this letter was penned, Augustus Saint-Gaudens was already quite ill with cancer. His death in August of 1907 seemed to conclude any question of redesigning the cent in the near future. Still, Roosevelt was determined, and fate held for him a most fruitful acquaintance in the person of one Victor D. Brenner.

The right man for the job

One of the great undertakings of Theodore Roosevelt's administration was the building of a canal linking the Atlantic and Pacific Oceans through the Isthmus of Panama. A miracle of diplomacy, medical science and engineering, the Panama Canal was built during the years 1904-14. In that time, countless workers died or were maimed for life by both industrial injuries and disease. To honor those individuals who worked at least two years on the project, the Isthmian Canal Commission was directed by President Roosevelt to present each one with a medal commemorating his service.[6] Roosevelt himself would adorn its obverse, yet the models for this medal were to be sculpted not by the U. S. Mint's own staff but rather by an outsider. His adopted name was Victor D. Brenner, though he had been born Viktoras Barnauskas.

When Roosevelt sat for Brenner in the Summer of 1908, the two men talked of the fine arts in general and of Roosevelt's struggle in achieving new coin designs. The President's attention was drawn to a plaque by Brenner featuring a profile bust of Abraham Lincoln. This was modeled from a recently discovered photograph of Lincoln taken February 9, 1864 by Anthony Berger, a member of Mathew Brady's team of photographers.[7] The plaque was dated 1907, and Brenner had since devised several other medallic works from the same original models.

It's not certain which party originally suggested the transformation of this portrait into a coin, but with the centennial of Lincoln's birth approaching in 1909 it seemed a worthy scheme. Researcher Don Taxay credits Brenner with this inspiration, as the artist was later quoted as saying that his head was then "full of Lincoln."[8]

Though Roosevelt may have revealed to him that the one-cent piece was due for a new design, it was evidently Brenner who favored this coin to bear his work. In a let-

The original 1907 edition of Brenner's Abraham Lincoln plaque which caught the eye of President Roosevelt. (ANA)

ter dated January 4, 1909 from Brenner to Mint Director Frank A. Leach, Brenner noted "I was thinking of embodying the portrait of Mr. Lincoln in the cent piece, and find that it will compose very well."[9] Two days later, Brenner again wrote to Leach:

Many thanks for your letter of yesterday. I am glad to say that the President has a copy of my Lincoln medal and likes it very much.

On several occasions I noticed the knowledge of art the President has, and feel sure that with your appreciation and his we will arrive to have in art of coins [sic] that will be a pleasure to all.[10]

The long and winding road

Brenner's work progressed quickly, and on January 18 he sent his models to Director Leach:

Please receive plaster models for the Lincoln cent which if it pleases you and the President as it is, or with some changes it could be ready for a formal acceptance for the 12th of Feb. the date of Mr. Lincoln's birth.

I am working on the other models, and improving them, and they will be posted very soon.[11]

It's not clear what the "other models" were, though Brenner had already sketched a standing figure of Liberty which he proposed for the reverse. This was obviously borrowed from the current coinage of France which depicted a striding figure of *Le Semeuse*, or "the sower," sculpted by the great Louis Oscar Roty. Another sketch of Brenner's depicted a single branch of olive or laurel, this copied from the reverse of Roty's coin. Such plagiarism was not detected by government officials until after Brenner had submitted plaster models of both the Lincoln and striding Liberty themes.

In the meantime his work continued, as noted in the following letter to Director Leach, dated February 1, 1909:

I have Ex. [expressed] to you four plaster casts to day, one is a new Lincoln head just finished resembling the one you have only in the reverse. The model of the

Frank A. Leach

Eagel [sic] is inspired by the engraving you gave me, and if my last Lincoln head is adopted the Eagel could well [be] made for the other side. I think that a half dollar would be more suitable for the Lincoln coin than a penny?

In a day or so, I shall send on to you a helmeted head of Liberty to go for one side of the cent or nickel. The other figure in this model seems, are [illegible] for each of the cent and nickel, so that with this head I am to send, I think the models for the three coins would be completed, except the changing of the denominations, and final finishing of detail in faces and otherwise. I would also finish the Hubs so as to get all I want in the ultimate size.

I should consider it a privilege to have the cent and nickel adopted during the President's administration, whose time expires but too soon.[12]

It's clear that Brenner's vision of his role in redesigning the nation's coinage had expanded greatly, though how much Roosevelt knew of this is uncertain. Now a lame duck, Roosevelt had little hope of seeing the Lincoln coin through to completion before leaving office on March 4. Unfortunately, there is no correspondence from him relating to these matters, so his side of the story remains untold.

The helmeted head and eagle models to which Brenner refers are now untraced, but it's clear that Leach was becoming nervous with all of these additional schemes. The very next day he wrote to Brenner informing him of certain limitations:

Your letter of the first instant just received. It is useless at this time to make any attempt to change the designs of the subsidiary coins [dime through half dollar], as no change in these coins can be made for seven years yet without permission of Congress. We have only two coins on which we can make a change now, the penny and the nickel. For one of these coins I had already requested Mr. Barber to submit a design, and therefore I can only use your design, if it [is] accepted, on the penny or the nickel.[13]

After providing a status report on the matter of Brenner's fee for performing this work, a recurring theme in several of their letters, Leach added "If we can settle this matter and it should be decided that we can use the design, it will be possible to complete the work before the expiration of this administration. All engraving must be done by the engravers at the Philadelphia Mint. I think we all prefer the second model of Lincoln which you sent."[14]

Revealing the confused state of affairs which existed at this point in the process, Brenner replied cryptically "Since learning that a Lincoln coin could not be adopted, I stayed on the modeling of the head of which I spoke in my last letter."[15]

Also joining the debate was William Loeb, Jr., Roosevelt's secretary, who wrote to Director Leach on February 4 inquiring "The President understands that Brenner's design is to be used for the penny. Is this correct?"[16]

Choosing to stay focused on the Lincoln Cent while disregarding the various other proposals, Leach pressed Brenner for a firm commitment:

If I understand you correctly, you offer to supply the government with one set of models to be used for the penny coin, embracing the bust of Lincoln for the obverse and the design sent here for the reverse, for the sum of one thousand dollars. If this is true your offer is accepted, with the understanding that these models will be altered so to suit the requirements of the statutes and the coinage operations. I would prefer that you come down here so that I can explain what is necessary to be done. It would be very difficult to do this through correspondence. The Government will pay your transportation and subsistence expenses while making this visit to Washington. I would like to have you be here next Monday forenoon.[17]

It was about this time that Leach learned the source of Brenner's branch design, though by what means is not known (a jealous Mint employee, perhaps). Leach informed Treasury Secretary Franklin MacVeagh of this and other developments on February 9:

In the matter of furnishing the designs for the proposed new one cent coinage, Mr. Victor Brenner is insistent upon introducing another design for the reverse side in place of the one first offered. It is necessary that we should have some other design than the one first submitted by him, for I have discovered that it is an exact copy of the design used by the Government of France on its two franc piece, the only difference being in the inscriptions. We should also refuse to adopt the second design offered, embracing a female figure, first, for the reason that there is a question as to its legality. This figure is supposed to symbolize Liberty, and to use it, it seems to me, would destroy our license to use the Lincoln head, so much desired, on the obverse side. The law does not provide for two impressions or figures emblematic of Liberty. Then, as this is the simplest coin we have, it seems to me it should call for the plainest and most distinct design.[18]

That same day Leach wrote also to Brenner informing him that both the female figure and the branch design were unacceptable. In his letter he makes reference to a memorandum furnished Brenner the previous day and setting forth the requirements for the design. Unfortunately, this memo has not survived, though its content may be inferred from the above letter.

Brenner replied on the 10th. After confirming the amount of his fee, he addressed the matter of the cent's design:

I beg also to acknowledge receipt of your letter dated Feb. 9th fixing the designs for the cent piece—for the Obverse to have the portrait of Mr. Lincoln with the word Liberty and the date of the coinage, for the Reverse to have "United States of America, One Cent, and E Pluribus

Unum."

I shall submit my arrangement of the design to you shortly.[19]

Brenner kept his word, and the new models were delivered to the Director's office on the 17th. The following day, Leach acknowledged their receipt, noting that President Roosevelt had taken exception to Brenner's use of the Latin letter V in place of the modern letter U, though it was then a common bid to neo-classicism:

I succeeded in having an interview with the President this morning for the purpose of showing him the models you left yesterday of the new penny. He was pleased with the general appearance of the new design for the reverse, but very emphatic in his objection to the use of the V in place of the letter U, consequently you will have to change your lettering in each and every instance where the V has been used for the U.[20]

The models submitted by Brenner were quite similar to the coin as ultimately adopted, with but a few exceptions. The bust of Lincoln was somewhat taller, extending from rim to rim, and the motto IN GOD WE TRUST had not been applied as it was not then required by law. At this stage in its development the obverse also carried the name "Brenner" in full. The reverse was virtually identical to the production coin, yet it was this side which bore the objectionable letters V.

In a touching gesture, Brenner presented a duplicate of his obverse model to Director Leach as a gift, one which Leach had to politely decline:

I do not remember whether or not in our conversation I informed you that all models and moulds used in the production of the finished design for the one cent piece must be surrendered to the government when the work is completed. This is a requirement that is exacted of all outside persons doing this kind of work.

For this reason I shall be unable to retain the plaster cast of Lincoln you so kindly gave me.[21]

Brenner persevered, replying to the Director on February 20, "With regards to the plaster model I presented to you, it seems to me, were you to cut away the lettering from around the head, you could keep same. In the finished model of the cent, many changes is [sic] to

Shown above are Brenner's rejected designs for the cent. (National Archives). Below is the 1915 2-Franc coin of similar design.

come in, so your keeping of the head would interfere little, but you know best." In a follow-up letter that same day, Brenner added "I shall surrender the moulds and models to [the government] for the finished cent piece."[22]

No simple matter

On February 26, Brenner again wrote to Leach:

I have the honor to inform you that I have to day Expressed to you the completed models of the Lincoln Penny, also three moulds of same. I trust you will find them satisfactory. I will appreciate the permission of examining the hubs before they are hardened, and should any retouching be necessary, to do so under the supervision of Mr. Barber.[23]

Director Leach wasted no time in seeking technical approval of the models, writing to Philadelphia Mint Superintendent John H. Landis the very next day:

I send you be express today the models adopted by the President of the design for the proposed new issue of the one cent piece. I notice that Mr. Brenner insists upon putting his name in full on the obverse side. I am sorry to have to disappoint him in this matter, but after consultation with the Secretary of the Treasury upon the subject it was decided that only his initials could be permitted, and that in an unobtrusive way.

Mr. Brenner writes me that he desires to see the hub in time to have touched up any imperfections that he might notice. I wish you would advise me whether or not his request is practicable.

As soon as the dies are ready and proof pieces struck I shall be pleased to be advised of the fact.[24]

On March 2, Leach wrote to Brenner to inform him that some minor changes would have to be made to his models and requesting that he go to the Philadelphia Mint and discuss these changes with Chief Engraver Barber. Brenner complied, writing back on the 4th:

I saw Mr. Barber to day, and have taken the plaster models with me for some alterations.

I fully agree with you that my name on the Obverse looks obtrusive and thanks for calling my attention to it. I shall take it out, and put it in small letters on the reverse near the rim.[25]

Brenner's encounters with Charles Barber had not

yet resulted in acrimony, despite the latter's track record of placing ceaseless obstacles in the paths of outside artists who dared to tread within his realm. In fact, Barber had been monitoring Brenner's work since the beginning. In a letter dated February 6, 1909, Barber reported to Director Leach that "I find upon coming to my office this morning that the one cent dies are both on radius 25 when soft. This may be of use to you when you see Mr. Brenner."[26]

Since no dies of Brenner's designs had yet been created, Barber was clearly referring to the Indian Head Cent dies then in use. His mention of radius 25 is a technical matter detailing the convexity of the die faces. It's doubtful that Brenner would have known how critical this information was in determining whether a coin design could be brought up in a single blow of the press as was required for mass production. Being a fine arts medallist, he enjoyed the luxury of using multiple impressions when preparing the finished product of his labors. It's quite possible that Barber tossed in this technical data simply to remind Leach that it was he and not Brenner who knew best how to make coins.

That there was some merit to this claim may be found in his February 13 letter to Brenner which addressed several technical matters. Again, given Barber's reputation for irascibility, it's not clear whether he was sincere in wanting to assist Brenner or merely attempting to intimidate him, yet he made some important points:

> Mr. Leach tells me that he has explained to you that he desired the field of [the] coin to be finished with a fixed radius or curve, therefore the model must be made with a fixed radius.
>
> I find in you[r] Lincoln medal that the field in front of the face is one place while the field at the back of the head is an entirely different plane, this you will see will never do as we have to finish the field of the dies mechanically in order to comply with the wish of the Director, namely to have the field finished smooth and one radius.
>
> The radius best suited for a coin must be determined by the disposition of the design and the area of the coin, in this connection I may say that the present cent dies are of 25 radius.
>
> In making your design you must avoid as much as possible one bold part of your design coming opposite another on the other side of the coin, as that would be fatal to the coining of the piece.
>
> In regard to what relief you had better adopt I am sorry to say that I cannot give you any fixed instructions as so much depends upon the design of both sides and the particular metal the design is for, also the area of the coin.
>
> You can look at the cent, judge from that, and that is the extent of the relief that can be successfully used for the one cent coin, and you will also see that from the point of utility, that the design is good, as it is so arranged that

no one point comes in opposition to another, and as these coins are struck by tons every year, not thousands, but millions and if the usual average per pair of dies was not produced, the Coiner would condemn the dies at once.

> In designing for a coin you must give due weight to the mechanical requirements of coinage and remember that great quantities of coin are demanded against time, and therefore, everything that can be done to simplify both the making of the dies and the production of the coin, must considered.
>
> You also know that the coins drop from the press at the rate of 120 per minute and that unlike a medal there is no bronzing or finishing of any description, no chance to bring out your design by coloring, it comes from the press one color and that [is] the color of the metal whatever that may be.[27]

The Chief Engraver was next heard from on March 1 when he wrote to Superintendent Landis complaining that Brenner's models were still of multiple radii and thus could not be basined. Barber somehow got the impression from Director Leach that this would be required of the new cent, even though the new gold eagles and double eagles coined since 1907 had lacked the single-radius feature and possessed deeply curved fields. Perhaps Barber longed for the conventional coin types used in earlier years, with their flat fields that allowed for the production of brilliant proofs. Though it contains some redundancies, Barber's letter is interesting enough to merit reproducing here:

> The plaster casts for the one cent coin have arrived this morning, also a letter from the Director, but I do not find any instructions or comment regarding the models, I therefore before proceeding to make reductions must ask for some instructions and also call attention to the condition of the models.
>
> In an interview with the Director I understood him to say that he desired the dies for the one cent to be finished with the field of one curve or as we term it, finished on a basin, the same as the coins for the Philippine Islands and all U. S. Coins formerly were finished.
>
> I therefore call your attention first to the obverse, which has evidently been modeled without regard to the Directors wish, as there is no one curve, the field being several different curves, and therefore, will not basin upon any fixed radius. The Director will at once understand the impossibility of using a basin as he will see before one part of the die came to the radius another part would be ground out, consequently we cannot use a basin at all, there not being one radius to the model.
>
> The field in front of the face is one radius, back of the head another, and the field above the head something entirely different from both.
>
> The next question before me is the reverse. While there appears to have been made an effort to establish a fixed radius to this side, it has the objection of being too round, as you will see. The model so far as I am able to ascertain has a radius of sixty and the reduction will be about ten or one tenth that of the model, this will bring the

first reduction to a radius of six, and by the time the dies are made and tempered they will be still rounder, or something less than six. Our one cent dies finish at twenty-five radius.

You will see from this explanation that the model for the reverse is entirely too round.

The next question is the borders, they are so narrow that by the time they are reduced ten times there will be nothing left, only a knife edge.

You will understand the difficulties before me and until I receive some instructions I do not know how to proceed.

I wish to explain, that there is no difficulty in making the reductions and if that is all that Mr. Brenner and the Director require, that can easily be accomplished, but if the dies are to basin and be made with any hope of them being suitable for coinage when made, then the models must be altered to meet the requirements of the coinage department, and the models must be made of such a radius that when reduced they will approach other coins the dies of which have proved to be adapted to coinage.

As stated before the one cent is of twenty-five radius, the twenty centavo Philippine coin of about the same diameter is twenty-five radius.

I beg to state that in response to a letter from Mr. Brenner making certain inquiry regarding the preparation of his models and in order to carry out the Directors wish in this matter, I wrote Mr. Brenner. I enclose a copy of my letter.

In conclusion, I beg to state that if the idea of having these dies to basin is abandoned, then the matter of die making is simplified and I will ask if when the reductions are made, are they to be sent to Mr. Brenner?[28]

Of course, this is exactly what did happen—the antiquated practice of basining the dies was cast aside for the Lincoln Cent. The one casualty in this decision, however, was the coining of brilliant proofs. It was not until more than a quarter century had passed that the Mint finally developed a satisfactory method for polishing dies of unequal radius.

That Barber's concerns may have been motivated by more than simple dedication to his duties is evident in a letter dated March 15 and addressed to Director Leach from an exasperated Brenner:

I saw Mr. Barber again to day, and had sent him the model last week, he thinks that now there is no hurry for the execution of the cent but I fail to see this reason except it be his personal reason.

It is my intention to avoid any friction, and I ask you therefore to kindly write to him not to delay the execution of the deed any longer.[29]

Leach must have driven this point home to Barber, as Acting Superintendent of the Philadelphia Mint Albert A. Norris was able to write back to Leach on the 23rd informing him that "Mr. Barber, the Engraver, informs me that he has the reductions from the models for the one cent Lincoln piece finished." Norris further inquired

whether he was authorized to ship the reductions to Brenner.[30]

(In speaking of "reductions," Norris was referring to the master hubs generated by mechanically reproducing the artist's sculpted model on the face of a steel cylinder through use of the Mint's Janvier reducing machine. If satisfactory, these are then driven into blank die steel to create the master dies from which all subsequent working hubs and dies are multiplied.)

In a seemingly gracious turn, yet one which betrays a certain defensiveness, Barber wrote to Acting Director Robert E. Preston on the 25th (Leach was then absent on an extended inspection tour of the western mints):

Mr. Landis has just shown me your letter regarding the request of Mr. Brenner to have the reductions from his models sent him for approval and any retouching that he may consider necessary for the proper representation of his work.

I hope that you will reconsider your refusal to comply with Brenners request as I think it only a reasonable one and most desirable and perfectly safe, as no doubt Brenner only wants to look the reductions over and sharpen up some points that he may think have lost distinctness in the process of reducing, this he ought to be allowed to do, and I know of no other way of his doing this, than sending him the reductions.

There can be no extra risk in this, as Mr. Brenner will have no advantage over the Mint that he does not already possess, as he has the model and also some medals having the Lincoln head and therefore, has all the opportunity to play crooked if he wanted to, which I do not think he has any disposition to do, his request being only natural, that before making this coin that he should be allowed to see that the reductions properly represent his work, and if not, that he should be allowed to touch up any parts that he may think ought to be improved.

I do not want to be in the position where Brenner can say that he was not allowed to do his best.

You know the St. Gaudens' people have appeared in print asserting that the Mint would not execute St. Gaudens work as he desired, and now Mr. [William Sturgis] Bigelow in his reply to [coin dealer Samuel H.] Chapman regarding the half and quarter eagle makes the statement, that the remark of Chapman "that the treatment of the head being hard and crude," refers to the retouching done at the Mint.

I want to be spared this humiliation and therefore ask that Brenner be allowed to do his own retouching as he requests, and I could not think of undertaking.

The reductions I have made from the Brenner models are good, but he may want to go over them in some points to satisfy himself and from the peculiar style of the modeling it would be impossible for any one else to retouch his work in a satisfactory manner to him.

I therefore can see no alternative but to let him have the reductions and return them as soon as he has passed upon them, which I am quite sure will be very soon, as he appears most anxious to have the coin brought out.[31]

As Don Taxay put it so eloquently, "Barber's appeal would come with better grace if he hadn't subsequently altered Brenner's design without the artist's knowledge."[32] It's just as well that Brenner did examine the hubs, as there had been changes from his models. In a rare *typed* letter, he responded to Barber on the 27th:

> I am sending back the hubs, having retouched the reverse, the obverse has been rubbed, and is too indistinct, so it will have to be recut. If it pleases you, you need not send me the die for the reverse for retouching, as there need only be a few lines rectified. Please suit yourself about that.
>
> It appears to me that something has happened to the model for the portrait side, as the whole neck looks rather fallen in.
>
> In the next reduction please use no brush over it, and send it on as it leaves the reducing machine.
>
> In case you shall finish up the die for the reverse of the cent, I would thank you to let me see an impression before its being hardened.[33]

Barber felt compelled to pass this letter on to Superintendent Landis, and in so doing he added his own assessment of the situation:

> In view of the fact that everything has been done to make this work entirely satisfactory to Mr. Brenner and we have failed, I beg to ask that Mr. Brenner be allowed to furnish a steel hub of his model, that is, that he be allowed to furnish the reduction, having it done in New York under his own supervision, the same as he is doing with his medals.
>
> I make this request as I am quite sure we cannot satisfy Mr. Brenner. He does not appear to understand that when he asks to have the relief of the model reduced mechanically, some detail must necessarily be sacrificed and, therefore, he must prepare his model accordingly, which he has not done.
>
> The model furnished is of soft impressionistic character and when reduced to one-tenth of the size of the model, and especially reduced in relief, the natural result is a want of detail, which Mr. Brenner complains of. It will facilitate the matter if Mr. Brenner be allowed to do as I suggest, but, if the Director positively objects, I can think of no way out of this difficulty, except to ask that we be furnished with a bronze casting of the model from which to make the reduction.
>
> I sincerely trust that the Director will grant this request to let Mr. Brenner furnish the reduction, as it will save much time and avoid friction of a most unpleasant character.[34]

Landis forwarded the letters of both Brenner and Barber to Director Leach, who was still in San Francisco inspecting the mint. Leach wrote back to Acting Director R. E. Preston on April 2, commenting first on the lack of appropriations from Congress which threatened a temporary shutdown of the Philadelphia and New Orleans Mints (no additional appropriation for New Orleans was forthcoming, and it ceased coining April 1, 1909).[35] He then continued with a report of the progress made on upgrading the San Francisco Mint before finally addressing the issue of Brenner's cent. From his reply, it seems that he had not yet read Landis' letter relating the latest complications:

> In the matter of the new pennies, I wish you would see to it that they do not undertake the regular coinage of the pieces until I have passed upon the proof or pattern pieces.
>
> I am willing, and think it is a good idea to try and have Mr. Brenner satisfied with the work before it is commenced, but it is not essential to the production of the pieces that we should depend upon Mr. Brenner, as I think it quite likely that we may finally have to do what was done finally with those of the Saint Gaudens design to make it a success.
>
> You are right in your idea about the issuing of the pennies. It should be impressed upon Mr. Landis that not a single coin should be allowed to go out of the institution until we have enough of them made to make a simultaneous distribution all over the country.[36]

From his above remarks it's clear that Leach believed the production of Lincoln Cents would begin shortly. He could not have imagined what obstacles still lay ahead. He got some inkling when Landis' package of letters finally caught up to him a day or two later. On April 5 he again wrote to Preston:

> I think you better communicate with Mr. Brenner and ask him if he is willing to make the hub as suggested by Mr. Barber, and get the cost of doing so beforehand. I suppose that would be required to get his claim for doing the work allowed.[37]

Preston duly requested of Brenner that the artist have the work of reducing his model to a hub done locally in New York and furnish a quote for its cost. Brenner acknowledged this letter on the 12th, adding that "I will be pleased to supervise the reducing of the obverse side of the Lincoln penny, and supply you with the finished hub for $100 One Hundred doll." The next day Brenner wrote Barber, stating "In a day or two I shall have a hard bronze casting and with such a model it seems to me you ought to get as good a reduction as Wile [Weil, in New York] can do. The matter rests entirely with you, I await orders."[38]

It's obvious that Barber was still reluctant to accept responsibility for the finished product, as revealed in his long-winded letter of April 14, 1909 addressed to Superintendent Landis. In it Barber raises the same objections as before:

The charge for making the reduction of the Lincoln model for the one Cent, is enough, but not exorbitant.

Regarding the reduction for the reverse I beg to state, that I have made that and Mr. Brenner has expressed himself as satisfied and returned the hub, which I now have ready for making coining dies.

I enclose a copy of a letter received this morning from Mr. Brenner.

In this connection I think it advisable to state that there is no difficulty in our making good reductions which we are doing constantly, provided, the model is made with a proper understanding of the effect that will be obtained when the work is reduced to one tenth of the size of the model, and the evidence that our reductions are correct, is shown in this particular case, the reverse model being chiefly a design consisting of letters has given a satisfactory result, but the Lincoln being very soft and undefined in character, when reduced to one tenth of the size of the model has lost all detail, which Mr. Brenner objects to, and therefore, it is not a question of our ability to make a reduction, which we can do equally as well as any one. The difficulty all rests with model, and therefore I can see no other way than to allow Mr. Brenner to provide the reduction and then if it is satisfactory to the Director pay him, and if not, insist on the model being made satisfactory. This I found Mr. Brenner not inclined to do, as when I called attention to the character of the model and pointed out that the detail would not carry and would be lost, when reduced so many times smaller than the model, Mr. Brenner did not agree with me.

As Mr. Brenner has had the model returned sometime and now writes that in a day or two he will have a casting, I infer that he has been making changes in the model which may prove advantageous. I hope it may so prove to be, and to facilitate this matter and bring it to a conclusion I certainly advocate Mr. Brenner furnishing the hub that the Director may have something to pass upon.[39]

On the 15th Brenner notified Acting Director Preston that his new model was completed and cast in bronze. He requested immediate instructions on whether to have the reduction made in New York or to send his casting to the Philadelphia Mint for Barber's attention. Preston replied the same day:

Your offer of the 12th instant to furnish a satisfactory reduction of the obverse of the Lincoln one-cent piece for the sum of $100 is accepted. I will thank you to proceed with the work and to forward a finished hub to the Mint at Philadelphia as early as practicable.

In accepting your offer it is understood that the reduction made by you will be one from which dies can be made that will produce a coin in every way satisfactory.[40]

The first strikings

Following a series of redundant messages to Brenner confirming that he was to prepare the master hub for the cent's obverse, his reduction was received by Barber, who then wrote to Preston with the results:

Regarding the one cent hub being prepared by Mr. Brenner I beg to say that he has made the reduction of the Lincoln bust and sent it to me to harden and make a die, and also asked to have the die sent him in the soft condition, that he might do some touching up.

As the word Liberty, also the date of the year were both very faint in hub and die I suggested that he should make both stronger before returning the die. The die was sent him yesterday and no doubt will be returned here this week, and in that case I will be able to send impressions for approval very shortly.[41]

(It should be noted that Barber in describing the obverse hub's features makes no reference to the motto IN GOD WE TRUST. That was simply because this element did not appear on the coin at this stage. The bust of Lincoln was then somewhat taller and actually occupied part of the space in which the motto would ultimately be placed.)

On May 12, Acting Superintendent of the Philadelphia Mint Albert A. Norris wrote to Superintendent Landis, who was then conferring with the Director in Washington. Norris stated succinctly, "I enclose three coins struck this day from the first pair of dies (proof) made for the one cent bronze coin, Brenner design." He followed this up two days later with an additional delivery of patterns:

As requested in your letter received today I beg to enclose herewith two specimens of the one-cent piece, Brenner design. There were but five of these struck by the Engraver, three of which were forwarded to Mr. Landis in your care, and the two enclosed. We have sent none to Mr. Brenner, as he has not requested any and we had no authority to do so even if he had.[42]

There was evidently something amiss with the patterns, as Landis transmitted additional pieces to Leach on the 20th, stating "I beg to enclose herewith four specimens of the new one cent piece, changed in accordance with your request, and two of those first submitted, for comparison."[43]

The nature of the problem is revealed is Director Leach's letter of May 22 to Brenner who, having already submitted his bill for $1100, had also learned of the pattern strikings and was requesting samples:

I have to inform you that I was not satisfied with the first proof of the Lincoln cent. I found that you had not dropped the Lincoln portrait down so that the head would come nearer the center of the coin, a matter I called your attention to when we were discussing the model. This is necessary to get the best result in bringing out the details of the features in striking the coin, therefore I had Mr. Barber make me a proof of this change, and as this left so much blank space over the top we concluded that it would be better to put on the motto "In God We Trust." This change has made a marked improvement in the appearance of the coin. I cannot send you a sample but if you feel enough interest in the matter it would be better for you to go down to Philadelphia where Mr. Barber can explain and show you what has been done.

There is such a demand from influential people for samples of this coin that we cannot comply without unjust discrimination, neither will we be able to make any distribution of the coins until enough has been struck to supply all demands.

I acknowledge receipt of your bill, and as soon as the design has been finally adopted I will file it for payment.[44]

Tradition has it that addition of the motto IN GOD WE TRUST was made at the urging of President William H. Taft, an account first published in *The Numismatist* for June of 1909, yet the above letter suggests otherwise. Indeed, there is no reason to believe that Taft had even seen an example of the new cent at the time this motto was fitted. It's more likely that its addition resulted from an attempt to balance the design elements, just as Leach claimed. Of course, the uproar which occurred in 1907 when this motto was deleted from the new issue of gold coins may have been on his mind as well, though no precedent existed for including it on the one-cent piece. The fact that it did not appear on the new type of five-cent piece adopted in 1913 suggests that its placement on minor coins was not then an issue. Coincidentally, however, the law authorizing the placement of this motto on United States coins was passed March 3, 1865, during the Presidency of Abraham Lincoln.

As for Leach's strict adherence to a policy of not making any advance distribution of Lincoln Cents, it seems that some exception could have been made in furnishing Brenner a few examples of his own work, especially when considering that the production coins were to be from models altered by Barber. The number of various patterns produced and their ultimate fate is revealed in a letter to the Director dated May 27, 1909 and signed by both Landis and Barber:

I beg to acknowledge receipt of your letter of the 26th instant in reference to the new one cent piece and enclosing the eleven samples which were sent to your office. I hereby certify that these eleven pieces, and two additional pieces - which include all specimen pieces of the new one cent Lincoln piece which were struck - have been totally destroyed this day in the presence of the Engraver and myself.[45]

Nothing more is heard of the Lincoln Cent in official correspondence until July 14, when Treasury Secretary Franklin MacVeagh formally approved the modified Brenner design in a letter to Director Leach:

The design of the one-cent piece bearing the head of President Lincoln, as prepared by Mr. Victor D. Brenner, and modified by the Director of the Mint by placing the head of President Lincoln nearer the center of the coin and adding the motto "In God We Trust", is approved, and the coinage of the one-cent piece of this design is hereby authorized.

The issue of these pieces will commence August 2, 1909.[46]

That this was a mere formality is evidenced by the fact that actual mass production of the new coins commenced at the Philadelphia Mint on June 10, 1909.[47] This work was interrupted by the annual closure of the various mint facilities on July 1 to make the traditional settling of accounts at the conclusion of the Mint's fiscal year. Some 22,313,575 pieces had been produced to that point.[48] Coining of Lincoln Cents resumed sometime in July, when the San Francisco Mint also began production of the new coins. Though the Denver Mint had been authorized since 1906 to issue minor coins, no dies for one-cent pieces were requested there until 1911.

The numismatic community reacts

Readers of *The Numismatist* first learned of the new Lincoln coin in the issue of February, 1909 through a Treasury Department release dated January 30:

President Roosevelt has given his consent to the placing of the head of Lincoln on one of the popular coins. He conferred to-day with Director Leach, of the mint, and the details are now under advisement.

Victor D. Brenner, the New York sculptor, has submitted to the director some models of Lincoln busts, and these have been shown to the President. The head of Lincoln will adorn one side of the coin and the customary coat of arms the other. It is probable that the half-dollar piece will be selected as the principal coin to bear the Lincoln head, but some legislation may be necessary to make the change."

An illustration of one of Brenner's Lincoln medals was included to furnish some indication of how the new coin might appear. In a letter to *The Numismatist* Director Leach responded with caution, warning that "Nothing has yet been decided upon in relation to the proposed issue of a coin bearing the head of Lincoln. The matter is only under discussion." Editor Farran Zerbe would not let the matter rest, however, and he urged the Mint to proceed with this proposal:

Let us have a Lincoln portrait coin for circulation and not be hampered by the time-worn objection to placing a citizen's portrait upon our coins.

The time to break all traditions or establish a precedent should be when endeavoring to honor such a man as Lincoln, and if our law makers are really sincere in their desire to show all honor to the "Saviour of His Country," they would take a long step in this direction by sanctioning the use of his reverenced portrait on a coin that had a tremendous circulation throughout the length and breadth of our country.

The March issue revealed that the new Lincoln portrait would appear on the cent. After describing the general arrangement of design elements Zerbe commented on the evolution of Brenner's portrait of the slain leader:

Sculptor Brenner has worked for more than a year on the Lincoln head design. At first, he thought that on his Lincoln medal was satisfying, but in comparison Mr. Brenner said, when interviewed for *The Numismatist*:

"The other yes, it is good, but this one is more intimate, deeper, more kind and personal. It is closer to the man; it makes you feel that you are sitting with him in his library. When it is finished I shall be nearly satisfied with it."

As to why he modeled for a cent, Mr. Brenner said: "You see the life of a coin is twenty-five years, according to law, and the time for the cent and the five-cent piece has expired. It seemed to me that the nickel already had a very practical design, and so I turned my attention to what would be most fitting the one-cent coin. Naturally, the portrait of Lincoln suggested itself, this being his centennial, and besides, I was going to make an anniversary medal for my friends and my mind was full of Lincoln."

The new cent debuts

As word spread of the impending change there were numerous accounts in the general press, many of them containing the usual quota of inaccuracies associated with the reporting of numismatic stories by unknowledgeable writers. A certain amount of editorializing was inevitable, as the propriety of depicting an actual person on the nation's coinage was debated. *The Rochester Post-Express* was in favor of the move on educational grounds:

If the Lincoln cent is a precedent, then American money may acquire an historical value. Why shouldn't other great Americans be nominated for similar distinction? Who knows but centuries and centuries hence, the archeologists will construct the fabric of this civilization on the coins found in the ruins of the nation.[49]

This optimism was not shared by *The Philadelphia Ledger*, which revealed a commonly held misunderstanding of the then-current cent with its portrait of the female goddess Liberty adorned in a feathered headdress:

The red Indian in his war bonnet, the sole survival of aboriginal North America, was of value as a culture memorial, if for nothing else. He should be replaced upon the cent and the foolish commemorative pennies should be permitted quickly to efface themselves, or find oblivion in the tills of coin collectors.[50]

A more common (and somewhat better informed) argument against discontinuing the Indian Head Cent was that offered by *The Richmond Times,* when it stated "No President, with the exception of Washington, occupies any such relation to the American people as justifies his being memorialized on their coins."[51]

Despite these varying assessments, the general consensus over the placing of Lincoln's portrait on the cent seems to have been that this action was a desirable one, and a nationwide mania for the new coins developed well before their issuance. Still, nothing more was seen in the pages of the *The Numismatist* until August of 1909, when the new cent's release was heralded by Editor Zerbe:

Anticipated for months and anxiously awaited, the one-cent coin bearing the head of Abraham Lincoln was issued from the Mint commencing August 2. Surrounded with much that makes it novel, the advance demand at the Mint for this piece was far greater than that accompanying any previous coin issue.

The new coin embodies simplicity with art and seems in every way qualified for utility, and being our coin of smallest denomination, it will bring to the low and wanting the features of the one who was the friend of their class.

Over 25,000,000 pieces were coined before any were issued for circulation. They will soon be widely scattered and the new coin will be known in every hamlet in the country; business houses, who have ordered them in quantity for distribution for advertising purposes and for use as change, will largely contribute to the early general circulation.

The dies were cut by Mr. Henry Weil, of New York [actually, the obverse only]. We append the Treasury Department's description of the new coin:

Obverse: Bust of Abraham Lincoln facing right; above the head the inscription, IN GOD WE TRUST; to the left of head the word LIBERTY and to the right the year of coinage. Reverse: Around the upper circle the inscription E PLURIBUS UNUM; across the centre the denomination, ONE CENT, and the inscription, UNITED STATES OF AMERICA; on either side of the coin and partially encircling the two last-mentioned inscriptions are ears of wheat treated in a very conventional manner.

On the reverse at rim, below centre, V. D. B., for Victor D. Brenner, the designer.

Notwithstanding the advance coinage, the demand for them in Philadelphia was so great that only a limited distribution was made to an individual. Banks were supplied with a portion of their order; at the Mint two specimens only to a customer, and at the Sub-Treasury one hundred was the most any one could purchase. Newsboys and others, taking advantage of the interest in the new coin, obtained them in hundred lots and found customers at from two for five cents to twenty-five cents each.

In the dual issue for September-October, Zerbe continued the tale:

No new coin type has ever commanded the interest of the public and editorial reference and news space in the general press as has the Lincoln cent. As soon as it became known that a new coin had been issued places of distribution were besieged, particularly in New York, Boston, Philadelphia, Chicago and Saint Louis, where long lines formed leading to Sub-Treasuries, and continued each day with increased interest until August 5th, when the sign was displayed "No More Lincoln Pennies."

Favorable comment on the design, the artist and the interest of the public appeared in the first day's papers, many illustrating the new type, with lines drawn across the cut or otherwise marked or divided, so as to keep within the law prohibiting coin illustrations in the general press. but the next day, and for several succeeding days the papers turned to adverse criticism, and about everything denunciatory that is possible to say in relation to a coin was published, even to stating that you could not spend them, which was the claim of some slot machine operators.

Among the many contemporary stories regarding the release of the Lincoln Cent is a report that Black Americans residing in Middletown, New York hailed the coin as their own, calling the new pennies "emancipation money." Quite a number of pieces were fashioned into good luck charms.[52]

Amid all this excitement over the new cents the American Numismatic Association held its annual convention in Montreal, August 9-14, where it was reported the attendees each "had a pocketful, which they liberally distributed."[53] These individuals appear to have been in the minority, as the frenzy to obtain one or more examples of the new cent quickly exhausted the advance supply, and this prompted cries of "foul" in letters and editorials published in the daily press. Mint officials were besieged with pleas for more pennies, yet a problem of even greater magnitude was then unfolding which would seriously jeopardize their ability to produce cents altogether.

Among the many positive reactions to the new cents were a few unfavorable remarks regarding the prominence of the artist's initials V.D.B. on the coins' reverse. A typical account from the general press, one which reveals a general ignorance of the nation's coinage, is the following story which appeared in *The Rochester Post-Express:*

Never before in all our coinage have the initials of the designers appeared on a coin. If one designer may put his initial on a coin, and the next one three initials, the next will want his whole name to appear, and if on coins, why not logically on postage stamps, greenbacks, and bonds."[54]

Contemporary cartoon by prominent numismatist Howland Wood (The Numismatist, September/October, 1909)

The New Orleans Picayune noted of the new cent "It may be said to mark the first visible and outward emblem of the transmogrification of the republic into an empire."[55] The paper further attributed this action to a deep-laid plot by Theodore Roosevelt, though to some degree it was quite correct. *The New York World* chose to defend the inclusion of Brenner's identity, noting "that except in the case of the painter and the sculptor the world is too little mindful of the artist's just claims to its recognition."[56]

While the removal of Brenner's initials has traditionally been blamed on the many denouncements of the artist's "vanity" and "commercialism," this is only partially true. The Treasury Department's own correspondence reveals that the decision was made too quickly after the coin's release for it to have been initiated by widespread public disfavor with the letters. Instead, it appears that the first questioning of their inclusion came from within the Department itself, specifically the office of Secretary MacVeagh. The following letter from Superintendent Landis to Assistant Secretary C. D. Norton written on August 4, just two days after the cent's release, confirms the Secretary's disfavor:

As requested in your communication over the telephone this morning I have investigated the matter of the designer's initials on the Lincoln cent and find they were authorized by the Director of the Mint in his letter of February 27, 1909, copy of which I enclose. The design, as completed, was approved by the Honorable Secretary of the Treasury and the Director of the Mint July 15, 1909, copy of which is also enclosed.

I would say that it was proposed that the initial of Mr. Brenner's last name only be used, but as this was the same as that on the present subsidiary silver coins designed by Mr. Barber, it was not distinctive enough and the three initials had to be used.

All the United States coins, with the exception of the eagle and the five-cent nickel piece, have the initials or monogram of the designer upon them.[57]

The following day MacVeagh fired off a memorandum to Norton detailing his instructions:

As to that cent, the policy will be to let those coins remain out which have been struck off; but I should like to have directions sent to the Mint to make no more of them and to rearrange the dies so as to omit those initials. At the same time, I do not see any reason for changing the rule— if it is a rule—that the designer should have, in some hidden way, his initial on the coin; but I should want to be very sure that this was not objectionable in form.

This plan of action can be made public. I spoke, indeed, to some newspaper men this morning, near the

White House, about it.[58]

On the 5th, Norton transmitted the Secretary's order to Acting Mint Director A. Piatt Andrew, whose Senate confirmation as the new Director (effective in November of 1909) was coincidentally made that same day:[59] "Please instruct the mints to coin no more of the Lincoln pennies until further notice. Request Engraver Charles E. Barber of Philadelphia to visit Washington in order to arrange with us a place to have the initial "B" placed upon the new one-cent pieces in an inconspicuous manner."[60]

MacVeagh's action only served to set off an even greater frenzy to obtain Lincoln Cents, as announcements in the press that the initials would be removed led to false reports that the existing coins would be recalled and destroyed. In the meantime, the plan to place a simple letter "B" on subsequent editions of the Lincoln Cent was proving unworkable, at least given the time permissible for making this change. Apparently facing criticism from above and below, Secretary MacVeagh required additional assurance that he had indeed approved Brenner's initials back in July. Both of these concerns were addressed in an August 6 letter to him from Assistant Secretary Norton:

> The first issue of the Lincoln coin was exactly similar to the present issue with the exception that the Lincoln head was placed near the top of the coin and more of the bust was showing and there was no motto "In God We Trust". In the second and final edition the only change was that the head was brought nearer to the center of the coin, part of the shoulders were cut off and the motto "In God We Trust" was set above. On the reverse side there has been no change. V. D. B.'s initials were in the samples which we showed to you and the President, — Mr. Barber states.
>
> The letter B could be engraved in the mother die easily but the letters V. D. B. cannot be erased from the mother die because it is intaglio. To make a new mother die with an inconspicuous B and without the V. D. B. would take at least fourteen days.
>
> This delay can be avoided by simply erasing the V. D. B. from the "hub" and having no B whatever on the coin. From this amended "hub" the coinage dies can be rapidly and promptly struck off within three days and the mint can continue the coinage of the pennies for which there is a great demand (and in which there is a great profit to the government).
>
> There are two reasons why Mr. Barber favors erasing the initials from the new penny; First, because it involves a delay of only three days in coining operations instead of a delay of about fourteen days. Second, because if the B is placed in an inconspicuous place, he fears that it may be confused with the B which now appears on the half-dollar which was engraved by himself. He is not willing to be held personally responsible for the Lincoln penny which he has always opposed and does not regard as a successful

coin.

> Mr. Barber states that it is very difficult to place [letter B] on the Lincoln shoulder inconspicuously because the bust comes to the edge of the coin. On the reverse side he thought that he had found the least conspicuous place for the initials which he regarded as very small, but the American newspaper reporters have made it very clear that the place was by no means inconspicuous and the initials were by no means small.[61]

Barber's resentment of outsiders is plainly evident from his testimony to Norton as revealed in Norton's letter. For this writer to explain how simple it would be to add a letter 'B' to Lincoln's shoulder on the master hub or die would require an explanation of the die-making process that goes beyond the scope of this book, so it must suffice to say that the contradiction of Barber's argument may be found on the cents coined 1918 and later. These feature the complete initials V.D.B. placed "inconspicuously" on the truncation of Lincoln's bust. The fact that this change was made successfully the year following Barber's death is a clear indictment of the late Engraver. His contention that placing the letters in that location was impossible due to the bust coming too close to the coin's border is pure balderdash, yet the claim was stated with a sufficient air of authority to persuade his superiors of its validity.

Given the pressure to resume coinage the Treasury Department had no choice but to direct that the initials be removed altogether and that new dies lacking the offending letters be produced immediately. On August 6 Assistant Secretary Norton transmitted these instructions to Acting Director Andrew, who was further ordered to obtain the approval of the Solicitor of the Treasury. The concurrence of Solicitor O'Connell was sought because Secretary MacVeagh feared that the removal of Brenner's initials might be a violation of the Act of September 26, 1890, which prohibited the changing of a coin's design more than once in 25 years. The Solicitor disagreed, however, determining that "The initials are no part of the devices of legends required on coins. It can not be claimed that such initials are a part of the design of the coin. I see no legal objection to omitting the initials."[62]

The way was now clear for complete removal of the letters V.D.B., and this was so ordered by Secretary MacVeagh on August 7, 1909. That same day Brenner wrote to MacVeagh seeking confirmation of his decision, as reporters were inquiring of him whether the rumors were true. Perhaps already knowing the answer, Brenner penned a second letter that day to Acting Director Andrew which clearly reveals his hurt:

> Much has been said for and against my initials on

the Lincoln Cent, and as the designer of same, it was natural for me to express indignation to their being taken off. In reality there is a feature in the new cent, which was brought in without my knowledge, and which concerned me most. Lincoln's bust in my design was to touch the edge of the coin—-in the minted cents, the bust is separated from the border. This feature makes my coin loose [sic] much of its artistic beauty.

I beg you Sir—-before more cents are minted, and before new dies are made, to kindly consider and advise.[63]

Brenner received a reply dated August 14 from Assistant Secretary Norton:

In the absence of the Secretary I am replying to your letter of the 7th instant. It was the intention of the Department to display your initials in an inconspicuous manner on the new Lincoln one-cent piece. When the first issue of the coin appeared, the initials were found to be more conspicuous than was intended and the mint officials were unable to make them less so, without changing the design and die.

In view of the urgent demand for the new coin it was deemed advisable to avoid delays and it was decided to erase the initials and proceed promptly with the coinage.[64]

That Brenner was even required to write his letter revealed all too clearly that he was out of the information loop and had been for some time. Such proved the fate of nearly all outside artists who dared to tread within the closed society of the U. S. Mint, and this was never more true than during the tenure of Chief Engraver Charles E. Barber. The Treasury Department's real attitude with respect to Brenner's subsequent public protestations against the altering of his work is found within an unsigned memorandum to the Secretary dated September 23, 1909: "Here is the best joke of the season: the silent Mr. Brenner wishes to wrap the cloak of modesty about him and retreat into a quiet zone."[65]

In defense of Barber and the Mint, however, it must be noted that to strike large numbers of any coin having a design which made its way to the very edge was a technical impossibility. Not only would this require multiple strikes to achieve, but it would further result in coins of uneven edge, a charge that was leveled at the Lincoln Cent even as revised by Barber.

As the controversy over his initials developed in the press, Brenner was pressed for a statement by the New York City papers. In an interview given shortly after his

The Panama Canal Service medal by Brenner depicting President Theodore Roosevelt. This commission led to Brenner's designing the new cent. (American Numismatic Association)

coin's debut, the artist responded:

When my design was first accepted, it had my full name in it. Secretary [George] Cortelyou, with whom I had most of my dealings, assured me that the name would be allowed to remain. Mr. Leach, of the government mint in Philadelphia, also understood this. Well, when I got the first die the name was there, just as I had engraved it, but after I sent it back, they returned it to me a second time, and it was then that I noticed that some one had substituted the initials 'V.D.B' in place of the name.

It struck me at the time as being a rather unusual thing to do. Nevertheless, I decided to let the matter drop, and not say anything about it. But now, if they propose to take even the initials off, I think it is time for me to say something. It seems only fair to demand that the original design, accepted when I got the commission, should be employed in the making of these coins.[66]

In defense of Brenner

The numismatic community reacted with dismay to the removal of Brenner's initials from his coin. Once again, Farran Zerbe editorialized on the subject:

Some day in the far distant future the numismatist may occasionally have to answer: "Say, Mister, how much will you give me for one of those rare Lincoln cents made away back in 1909 when the United States were in America—it's the rare kind with V. D. B. on it?" But to-day, and for untold days, so frequent will be the question that it seems advisable for the coin merchant to have in constant operation a phonograph that will grind out, "No premium on Lincoln cents with V. D. B. on them, or with anything else on or off them."[67]

After revealing some of the problems alleged for the new cents in the general press, Zerbe brought up a belief commonly held among numismatists of the day who were already quite wary of Barber and the Mint Establishment:

The origin of cause for these criticisms has been traced to Philadelphia and Washington, from sources where selfish motives are not unknown when a coin type has been issued other than that produced by a government employee. Sifting all the criticisms, there was but one on which a just claim could be made, the designer's mark (initials V. D. B.) appeared a little more prominent than on the coins now in use.

The new cent has produced many amusing quips. One now going the rounds of the press, is of where the vendor pointing out the prominence of the designer's name, said: "Can't you see it, E Pluribus Unum, that feller Mr. Unum certainly must be hot stuff to get his name up like that."[68]

Setting aside such humorous anecdotes in favor of a more serious role, Zerbe appealed to his fellow numismatists to join him in protesting Brenner's enforced anonymity on the cent:

Artists and Art—-the masters and the master product—-receive, at best, but little reward in their day. Years of study and application requiring great self-denial are given to the development of talent by those who gain a recognized place among the masters. It is not the dollars that may come—-they seldom do in commensurate form—-that leads talent to its best, it is in the product itself wherein is found the satisfaction.

Take from the artist the privilege of placing an identifying mark on his product and you rob him of his most prized reward. The brush, the chisel, the graver, the pen, are moved and inspired with the thought—-my works shall live and with them my name.

In the removal of the marks to identify the designer of the Lincoln cent a great injustice has been done sculptor-artist Victor D. Brenner. Not V. D. B., but Brenner was to appear on the new coin. When change was made from name to initials the artist was too modest to protest. Now that all identifying marks have been removed, it is not the particular instance, but it is for art—-that it may not be robbed of its reward—-that Mr. Brenner and all patrons of art should protest.[69]

The New York Numismatic Club, founded only the previous year but already quite prestigious, petitioned Treasury Secretary MacVeagh to restore to the cent the initials of its fellow member, Victor David Brenner. In its statement the club remarked that "Placing the initials of the designer upon a coin is a time-honored custom, and one that we, who are devoted to the coinage and medallic art of the world, feel to be no more than the just due of the artist who is fortunate enough to receive the commission to execute a design for a coin of the United States." In a biting reference the club added that "We petition you to restore the three initials of Mr. Brenner so that his work may be clearly distinguished from that of Mr. Charles E. Barber, the present chief engraver of the mint."[70]

Interest in the new cent had even led to its mentioning in *The Numismatic Circular,* published by Spink and Son in London. Included there was a letter dated August 17, 1909 from Dr. H. R. Storer of Newport, Rhode Island which further defended Brenner's right to recognition:

I enclose the new Lincoln cent, which, however, you have doubtless already seen. No coin was ever before so much discussed throughout this country. Probably through professional jealousy, the propriety of Mr. V. D.

Brenner's initials appearing upon it was challenged, although Mr. Bela Pratt, of Boston, of whom I wrote you, had previously done the same thing without objection. It is now reported that the U. S. Government has suspended further issue until the objectionable letters shall be removed.

The general question is of such importance to all numismatists that I would suggest you bring the matter up for discussion at the next meeting of the British Num. Association.

My own opinion is that for an artist to attach his initials or signature [to] coins or medals has the same advantages as for a painter to place his name upon his canvas. In both instances, the historical interest is increased, the pecuniary worth enhanced, and the standards of the ideal conception and mechanical execution materially advanced.[71]

At the request of Farran Zerbe, Brenner responded to the controversy August 23:

It is mighty hard for me to express my sentiments with reference to the initials on the cent. The name of the artist on a coin is essential for the student of history as it enables him to trace environments and conditions of the time said coin was produced. Much fume has been made about my initials as a means of advertisement; such is not the case. The very talk the initials has brought out has done more good for numismatics than it could do me personally.

The cent not alone represents in part my art, but it represents *the type of art of our period.*

The conventionalizing of the sheafs of wheat was done by me with much thought, and I feel that with the prescribed wording no better design could be obtained. The cent will wear out two of the last ones in time, due entirely to the hollow surface.

The original design had *Brenner* on it, and that was changed to the initials. Of course the issue rests with the numismatic bodies, and Europe will watch the outcome with interest.[72]

Further trouble with the cent

New dies lacking the initials "V.D.B." were in place by August 12 at the very latest, for on that date Philadelphia Mint Superintendent Landis sent to Mint Director Leach 100 newly struck cents without initials. Five days later the Treasury Department issued a press release announcing the removal and restating its official reasons for not relocating Brenner's initials to some other position or replacing the three letters with a single letter B.[73]

What was not revealed to the public is that this matter wasn't the only problem with the new cents. As soon as they appeared in circulation, reports began to appear that the coins were too thick and would not function in vending machines. Though such claims have been made against almost every new coin type debuting in the 20th

Century, in the case of the Lincoln Cent there seems to have been some truth to the rumors. There were many such contemporary newspaper accounts, but the following item from the August 17, 1909 edition of *The Courtland Standard* (New York) is representative and will suffice:

> The new Lincoln cents have caused all sorts of difficulties. The penny slot machine people don't like them because they are too large and won't go in. The users of coin cases for change object to them on the same grounds. And now the Bell Telephone pay stations find that people are working them instead of nickels and are getting five cents worth of talk for one cent's worth of coin and are having to change all their money boxes. Next time new coins are put out the treasury department will probably try to get a little advice before changing their size.[74]

These accounts still intrigued collectors nearly 50 years later, and a reader of *The Numismatic Scrapbook Magazine* wrote to the U. S. Mint in 1954 to inquire if the stories were true. Acting Director Leland Howard responded to her letter:

> It has been found that the Lincoln cent, when first issued, was somewhat thicker than the previous design. This was due to the fact that the Lincoln likeness was in high relief and the rim thickened proportionally to prevent wearing of the metal. When it was found that the coins did not work well in certain types of slot machines, the necessary steps were taken by the Mint to remedy the situation.[75]

It appears that Mr. Howard may have estimated the Mint's corrective action without doing any real research into the matter, for it was the coin's *reverse* which proved too thick. This is clearly evident to the trained eye of the numismatist through a simple comparison of 1909 V.D.B. cents with those of later issue. The author has verified this for himself, though there's no way to illustrate this peculiarity photographically.

That there was indeed a problem of depth with the new cents and that this problem was recognized by the Mint in 1909 is evident from contemporary correspondence. It was known at least as early as August 9, as revealed in the following letter from Landis to Leach:

> As requested in your letter of the 9th instant we have experimented with the reduction of the thickness of the Lincoln cent. We cut down the border of the reverse side on some of the old dies after removal of the initials, and also reduced the height of the border of the reverse side on the hub and made working dies from this. In neither case were the coins after being struck of any less thickness than those struck from the dies with the initials. The thickness is entirely due to the design, and to reduce it the dies will have to be modified.[76]

Chief Engraver Barber was the source of Landis'

information, and that alone renders it highly suspect. Barber's evident sense of vindication, as well as his simmering resentment of outsiders, can be interpreted from his letter of August 13 to Landis, written in Barber's typically rambling manner:

> In compliance with your request to make the new one cent the same thickness as the old I beg to state that I have made such changes as can be readily made without an entire reconstruction of the model.
>
> If it was desired that the new coin was to conform to all the conditions of the old coin it should have been so arranged and stipulated with the designer, as it is placing this department to great disadvantage to accept a model from an artist who never has modeled for coinage and knows absolutely nothing of the process of coinage and then insist that this department shall make dies that shall answer all Mint conditions, even to the thickness of the piece when struck.
>
> Independent of the fact that the model was made without any thought of this requirement, the change that takes place in hardening may be sufficient to create a difference in the convexity of the die which will show when the pieces are gauged in slot machines, or piled fifteen or twenty high, and are we to sacrifice the appearance of the coin or limit our production to satisfy the manufacturers and venders [sic] of slot machines, I think not, although of the change I have already made does not conform to these machines, the only possible thing to do is to remodel the design and alter it, that it will at least satisfy the slot machine manufacturers, although it may not be satisfactory to anyone else.
>
> The change I have made may interfere with the average number of pieces per pair of dies that the Coiner expects and is almost necessary when the demand for one cent pieces is great, but it is the only change that can be made without as I have already said an entire reconstruction of the model.
>
> The relief of the Lincoln head is so great that in order to protect it from abrasion the border must be higher than the highest point of the head and consequently to make both sides of the coin alike the reverse border must be high also and these two borders regulate the thickness of the coin. You will therefore see the difficulty is two fold, first if the borders are not the same height the two sides of the coin will differ, one from the other and the mechanical difficulty is, that the borders not being equal the strain on the lowest border is too great and the die cracks before a proper average of pieces is obtained. The change I have made does not reduce the thickness of the piece to the same thickness of the old coin which I do not hesitate to say cannot be done without new models and even then it will be only an experiment as the designes [sic] are so entirely different that it is impossible for any one to say how the metal will be swallowed up by the design, and the law regulates the diameter and weight of the piece we have no in that direction and therefore I earnestly advise that the change I have made be accepted as final unless, it proves to reduce our production in which case there is nothing to do but return to our present hub.[77]

That same day, Acting Philadelphia Mint Superintendent Albert A. Norris wrote to Director Leach, enclosing one sample each of the Indian Head Cent, the first issue of Lincoln Cent and a Lincoln of modified relief, as well as a gauge with which to measure them for himself! Norris brought Leach up to date regarding Barber's conclusions, further warning that if new [models] were made "It would only be a matter of experiment."[78] Though no further correspondence survives regarding the development of the Lincoln Cent, examination of the coins themselves proves that the reverse border was indeed lowered after the issue of 1909 V.D.B. cents.

Was Barber correct in stating that the side of the coin having a lower border would be more subject to early failure? For the cent coinage of 1912, produced from the modified dies with a lowered border, the following results were obtained. At the Philadelphia Mint, the average number of cents produced per obverse die was 345,136, as opposed to 355,886 for reverse dies. At the Denver Mint, this advantage was swapped, with each obverse die coining an average of 381,075 pieces versus 323,337 for the average reverse die. The San Francisco Mint provided a similar 5-4 ratio of 221,152 to 192,305.[79] These results are not conclusive, though the branch mint statistics suggest that reverse dies did fail a bit earlier.

Though the 1909 and 1909-S V.D.B. cents were all coined with the high reverse border, the Mint's correspondence suggests that some of the 1909 "plain" cents from either mint may have been coined with old style dies from which the letters were simply polished away. Thus far, however, no such coins have been observed by the author.

The Lincoln Cent in service

Once all of the controversy over the design of the Lincoln Cent and Brenner's initials in particular had settled down, the public accepted the coin as it had most previous new issues. This type appeared at a time when the demand for one-cent pieces was growing nationwide. Only a few years earlier the western states eschewed cents and nickels, accepting nothing less than silver or gold as money. By the turn of the 20th Century, however, the Philadelphia Mint began shipping minor coins west to supply an emerging market for them.

Why weren't these coins simply struck at the Denver or San Francisco Mints rather than sending them cross country? The answer is quite simple: The western mints were prohibited by law from striking anything other than silver and gold. Why their authorizing legislation specified these metals alone is not certain, but an act of Congress was required to permit the striking of minor coins in base metals at the two western mints. Such a law was passed April 24, 1906, the same year that the Denver Mint commenced coining operations. Even so, it was not until 1908 that minor coins were struck outside of the Philadelphia Mint. In that year San Francisco issued a modest number of cents, while Denver didn't produce coins of this denomination until 1911.

It developed that all three mints would be required to work three shifts a day to turn out enough cents to meet the demand which arose during World War I. A nationwide shortage of cents prompted by America's entry into the war had become so severe by the end of 1917 that one Kansas City theater was offering its patrons $1.05 for every 100 pieces brought in.[79a] *The Numismatist* was able to report the appearance of one-cent scrip notes from The Peoples Banking Company of Lewisburg, Ohio, of which numismatist Waldo C. Moore was Treasurer. Editor Frank G. Duffield went on to add:

> The new war revenue law has caused many odd-cent prices, making an extraordinary demand for one-cent pieces, the "movies," probably, making the greatest call. Away from centers of small-change supplies and the beaten paths of commerce many change inconveniences are reported, and other emergency scrip is to be expected . . .
>
> Regarding the scarcity of cents in Preble county [Ohio] and this issue of scrip, Mr. Moore writes: "Cents are so scarce out this way that one dry goods firm in Dayton has been advertising that they will pay $1 for every 95 cents brought in . . . We have been so hard pressed for cents that often we refuse change. At the close business on one occasion we had but seven cents on the tray."[80]

The U. S. Mint, working as it did from an annual appropriation, was caught short when the demand for cents rose so suddenly. In his *Annual Report* for 1917, Mint Director Raymond T. Baker made a plea for additional funds:

> It is further recommended that the necessary steps be taken to bring about legislation to increase the minor coinage metal fund from $200,000 to $400,000. We are now considerably embarrassed by lack of funds to pay for sufficient copper and nickel to operate the mints to full capacity on minor coins.

Although inconvenienced by the chronic shortage of cents during the war years, the public viewed this as just one more patriotic sacrifice. "The River of Liberty Pennies" was the title of an article published in *The Chicago Evening Post* in 1917:

> A new dignity is thrust upon the little bronze coin—useful chiefly hitherto as the means of furnishing us with the world's intelligence. Now the penny takes the front line as a fighter for freedom. The brown rivulets will

be rolling in from every corner of the country until they merge into a great stream that will take first a silver and then a golden tinge. Soldiers and sailors will be clothed and armed and fed by them; enemy trenches will be shattered by them; the flag will be carried forward on their current to speedier and greater victory. Who so mean as to grudge them or grouch at the inconvenience? Fit emblem of democracy, let there be reverence and gladness in their giving, whether from the hand of a little child or the coin pocket of a millionaire. Let us be a nation of cheerful taxpayers. All hail the Liberty pennies.[81]

Writing a few years later in 1921, Justin Fair of *The Washington Post* asked the question "What Becomes of the Cents?," providing something of a numismatic history lesson in the process:

Brenner's Lincoln Centennial medal was the direct precursor of the cent. Brenner would go on to create several variants of his Lincoln medals and plaques, and these proved quite lucrative to the artist. (ANA)

> The vogue of the cent is immense at this writing because it has to be employed in more than half the small cash transactions the average person undertakes.
>
> Of course, department stores have always created a large demand for cent coins because of the habit of marking a necktie for John at 69 cents, and those school umbrellas at $1.49, and guaranteed silk hosiery at $2.98. But these odd prices which called for cent coins for the change were not universal until Uncle Sam himself started the vogue with the war tax.
>
> Street car fares in 59 large American cities range from six to nine cents. In only 19 of these cities is there any plan for buying tickets or "tokens," as our own traction company blandly names the metal counters now issued.
>
> So in the traction game itself more than $5,000,000 [in] one cent coins are handled every day.
>
> The war tax on soda fountain beverages alone calls for the interchange of 15,000,000 one cent coins every day in the year, and in the shuffle probably 20,000 one cent coins are lost every day. This percentage of mysterious disappearance of the coins is based upon the steadily increasing demand for more cents.
>
> There are no counterfeiters of one-cent coins, because it wouldn't be worth the trouble. They could not be produced even in immense quantities so that the forger would reap a profit.
>
> Well-meant plans of congressmen who feel the urge to help the mint out of this predicament in authorizing a new coin—-a two-center or a three-center—-have not been encouraged, for the good reason that during the years when two-centers and three-centers were commonly current, they disappeared just as fast as they were made.
>
> There was a mountain of two-cent coins a quarter of a century ago.
>
> The mint decided to call them in, but relatively few were redeemed, and we made no more. The bulk of them just disappeared. So, too, with the three-cent pieces, which were not popular with shopkeepers, but which small boys thought to be a very fine institution, for many times one might pass one of them off for a dime.
>
> The half-dime, another silver coin, very thin and smaller in comparison with the dime, as the quarter-dollar is with the half, was a confounded nuisance, as all America agrees, and it lives today only as a reminiscence of the age when pretty high school girls wore a dozen of them strung on a silver wire, which performed all the functions of a bangle bracelet.
>
> So, reader, you will gather that the despised one-cent piece isn't so ornery as you fancied.
>
> Do not cast the cent aside as of no account. One cent will not help much when it's all alone, but if you are away out in Takoma Park, and plan to ride to the Post building, and find that you have only a nickel and two cents, oh! what will you do if you cannot find another cent hidden in your vest pocket!
>
> What will you do? You'll walk six miles, unless the street-car conductor is a good fellow.
>
> Five or ten millions of the one-cent coins disappear every year. A slightly smaller number of a certain large yellow-metal coin, one with an eagle rampant upon its face, also disappear from circulation.
>
> In this disappearance performance these two coins are similar.
>
> But there is a distinction. The wastrel who loses a cent never thinks about it, nor does he know where it goes.[82]

The end of the Lincoln Cent?

Interest in the cent as a topic within the general press faded after this time, and people simply took it for granted. There are a few amusing anecdotes from the 1920s and '30s regarding the Lincoln Cent and its many adventures, and these will be found in Chapter 7 placed under the year and mint most relevant to each respective news item.

Complacency with the Lincoln Cent came to an end in 1937, however, as a movement was launched to supplant it with another design. Under the law of September 26, 1890 this coin type was eligible for replacement after 25 years of production. Since the minimum figure was achieved in 1933, a new cent could be adopted any time after that year on orders from the Director of the Mint, subject to approval from the Treasury Secretary. The following story appeared in *The Numismatist* for March,

1937:

The alumni of the University of Pennsylvania wants some changes in our minor coins and don't hesitate to say so. For one thing, they want to "promote" Lincoln from the cent to the nickel.

"We are tired of Indians and Buffaloes on our nickels," several of them said, digging coins from their pockets as they held their annual meeting in Houston Hall, on Founders' Day. We want to put Abe Lincoln on the nickel, as has been suggested already, beginning in 1938," they declared. "If we move him up from one cent to five, that leaves the cent vacant. That's where we really come in. We want Ben Franklin put on the next American cent."

Inasmuch as Founders' Day is observed in honor of the University's patron saint, the same Dr. Franklin, a resolution to this effect was thunderously carried. The second half of the resolution urged that the United States Government erect a memorial to Franklin in the National Capital "commensurate with his patriotic, scientific and literary achievements."

So far as nickels and cents are concerned, it is time both of them are renovated, spokesmen for the resolution said.

Lincoln has dominated the penny since 1909, and it is about time he is promoted, they said. As for the buffalo nickel, it has been in circulation since 1913, but each year the buffalo gets more and more extinct, they added.

Though this movement achieved sponsorship from the International Benjamin Franklin Society and the Lincoln Fellowship of New York, nothing more was heard of it after 1938 when the new Jefferson Nickel debuted. It was then proposed that Franklin be placed on the dime instead, and this was seriously being considered by the Treasury Department when the onset of World War II and a resulting shortage of coins postponed further debate for the duration. Franklin finally received his due on the half dollar in 1948 when his portrait replaced the striding figure of Liberty in use since 1916.

The cent goes to war

Even before the United States entered World War II in December of 1941 there were indications that the cent as it then existed was threatened. Only the month before *The Numismatist* reported that copper was in short supply due to its growing use in defense industries. It was speculated that substitute metals might be introduced soon and the current coins withdrawn. These rumors only grew after the Pearl Harbor attack made America's commitment to war a reality:

It is reported that Treasury officials are giving serious considerations to a plan to gather in all the cents and nickels to help augment the supply of copper and other metals vital in many defense materials. Long-range plans envisaged by Treasury and Mint officials call for the use of some other metal than copper for coins for the duration.

The metal that would be used in place of copper and nickel has not been revealed. It is hard to think of any of the metal generally used for minor coinage throughout the world that is not on the critical list, copper, tin, zinc, brass, aluminum, et. Silver half dimes might be coined again—which would solve the 5-cent piece problem, although it might be hard on the juke box trade.[83]

Early in 1942, American Numismatic Association member and frequent correspondent Jack W. Ogilvie suggested to his fellow members that they remove from their collections coins of little or no premium value and use them to buy Defense Stamps and Bonds. This would serve the dual purpose of returning such coins to circulation and supporting the war effort. Regarding Lincoln Cents, Ogilvie considered the following coins not worth preserving:

From 1909 to 1915, all coins grading below very good.
From 1916 to 1926, all coins grading below fine.
From 1927 to 1934, all coins grading below very fine.
From 1935 to date, all coins that are not uncirculated.

He specifically excluded from this listing cents of recognized value in all grades; these included 1909-S V.D.B., 1909-S, 1914-D, 1922-D, 1923-S, 1924-D, 1926-S, 1931-S and possibly all S-Mint cents from 1910 through 1915. Ogilvie advised readers that "Uncle Sam would certainly welcome the use of these minor coins, and I'll wager the Defense Bonds will prove the better investment. What do you say, fellows?"[84]

The first step toward the reduction of critical metals occurred when the Treasury Department ordered the removal of all but a trace amount of tin from the cent's 5% alloy of tin and zinc, effectively rendering it brass rather than bronze. Though this action was put into effect January 23, 1942, there was no reason to not use up the existing supply of strip and planchets; 1942-dated cents from all three mints were probably coined from both alloys. Mint Director Nellie Tayloe Ross reported that this change was expected to save 100,000 pounds of tin annually, and she added that 40,000 pounds on hand at the mints had already been turned over to defense industries.[85]

Even with repeated patriotic appeals to the American people to turn in their accumulations of cents and nickels, the Mint came up short of the metals needed for full production. The minting of both coins was cut way back after the first six months of 1942 while experiments were made with various substitute metals, fibers, plastics and even glass.[86] Continuing her appeal to both collectors and the general public, Director Ross urged everyone to search high and low for overlooked cents:

Demand is greatest for one-cent pieces, and it is the penny that can be disgorged in greatest quantities from children's banks and sugar bowls, Mrs. Ross believes.

The Director cited a letter received from a former Mint employee now in the Navy. [He] told Mrs. Ross he had found enough pennies in bureau drawers and other caches about his home to buy a $25 War bond.

The increased use of smaller coins is due to such factors as increased popularity of vending machines and entertainment devices, application by many states of sales taxes, to the general increase in business activity, as well as to the accumulation of savings.[87]

Steel cents

Passed December 18, 1942, Public Law 77-815 was enacted "To further the war effort by authorizing the substitution of other materials for strategic metals used in minor coinage, to authorize the forming of worn and uncurrent standard silver dollars into bars for other purposes." In addition to condemning millions of silver dollars to the melting pot this legislation also provided for altering the composition of the one-cent and five-cent pieces, though such coinage could not be produced after December 31, 1946 without further action.[88] The Treasury Department wasted no time in implementing such changes, as the Mint had been experimenting with substitute alloys all that year and had settled upon its choices. The nickel was already being coined from a new alloy of copper, silver and manganese per a separate Congressional action. Now, however, it was the cent's turn.

On December 23, 1942, Treasury Secretary Henry Morgenthau, Jr. ordered that all cents struck after January 1 be comprised of a low-carbon steel plated with zinc. The zinc plating was to provide corrosion resistance, and it was to be no more than .001 inch thick. This resulted in a cent weighing 41.5 grains, as opposed to the conventional cent which weighed 48 grains. Zinc-coated steel planchets manufactured during 1943 had a slightly higher weight than those produced in advance during 1942, and they check in at 42.5 grains.[89]

It took some time to produce sufficient supplies of the new planchets, and the coining of steel cents commenced on February 23, 1943 at the Philadelphia Mint;

Steel was clearly not the best choice of materials for making cents, as this badly corroded example proves.

Denver and San Francisco began striking the new coins the following month. On February 27 the first delivery of these coins was made to the U. S. Treasury. At the same time, Mint Director Ross announced that while no more bronze cents would be coined, those in circulation would not be withdrawn.[90]

Within a few weeks the new coins had entered circulation to mixed reviews. Most people took note of their obvious resemblance to silver dimes, though the Treasury Department assured the public that the coins would quickly darken and become quite distinctive. This promise notwithstanding, the problem of mistaken identity was widespread and costly. Among the many contemporary accounts is one in which the Elevated Railway in Boston was warning its conductors and cashiers to be wary of the new coins, as so many had already been passed for dimes.[91]

As the complaints to the Mint and the Treasury Department swelled, Secretary Morgenthau was compelled to respond. He stated that it was impractical to change the size, color or shape of the new cents or to bore holes in them for identification. "Experts tell me," he reiterated, "that in time the coins will tarnish and no one will mistake them for dimes."[92] Assistant Mint Director Leland Howard verified that no holes would be punched into the cents, but he did allow for the possibility that the coins could be darkened at an accelerated pace if a suitable process for doing so could be found.[93]

Their appearance wasn't the only problem with the steel cents, however, as their magnetic property caused them to be rejected as slugs by all manner of mechanical devices. Since there were then quite a few uses for the cent, this was no small matter. The solution to this problem required manual inspection of each and every such coin, as in the following account from New York City:

Confusion, intention[al] or otherwise, of the new zinc-coated steel pennies has led the Third Avenue Railway Company to prepare tiny magnets to be installed in the coin boxes of its 800 trolley cars and 450 buses, it was learned recently.

The magnets, a square inch in size, will be inserted in the top of the coin boxes, near the slots. When they attract a steel penny or a slug the coin will stick halfway in the slot so that the conductor will be able to lift it out.[94]

The new cents were found so universally objectionable that the Treasury was moved to dispense them only when and where a shortage of bronze cents occurred. On September 28, 1943, Delaware Senator Douglass C. Buck introduced a bill requiring that all steel cents be withdrawn and that any cents struck henceforth be readily distinguishable from coins of other denominations.[95] Despite such antagonism toward the steel cents, the demand for one-cent pieces was so great that businesses and individuals had no choice but to work with them as best they could.

Still, the Mint was keenly aware that this measure had proved a miserable failure, and it could not go on producing steel cents very much longer. In the Fall of 1943, Director Ross announced that bronze cents of the pre-war alloy (but without tin) would be produced beginning January 1, 1944. No more steel cents would be struck after that date, though the ones already in circulation would not be withdrawn. These plans were formalized by order of Secretary Morgenthau on December 16, 1943.[96]

The Numismatic Scrapbook Magazine provided a fitting obituary for these despised coins:

> The steel cent's departure will still leave us guessing as to whether the piece would make a nice proof. About the only thing that can be said in favor of the "white Lincoln" is that it provided a slight break in the coin series that is becoming somewhat monotonous. From the general public's viewpoint the coin has been unsatisfactory; when in new condition it was often mistaken for a dime and at least here in Oklahoma where they represent about half the cent supply, they have been mistaken for nickels when at the proper stage of discoloration.[97]

Despite its projections that the steel cents would continue to circulate side-by-side with the bronze and brass pieces, the Treasury Department did begin recalling them once the war had ended. It continued to do so for the next 20 years and more. This operation was not publicized, the government preferring to quietly advise banks that such coins should be returned to the Treasury whenever they were received in the normal course of business. Those that found their way to the mints were also retrieved, along with any wartime silver "nickels." The mints operated mechanical devices which segregated such coins automatically, producing an estimated annual savings of $11,000 over the tedious visual inspection used previously.[98]

At least one account does survive to record the mass melting of steel cents. It dates from 1949 and ran in *The Pueblo Star Journal* (Colorado). This story was submitted by Al C. Overton (of half dollar fame) and summarized for readers of *The Numismatic Scrapbook Magazine*:

> The 20 tons of these cents were the first to be taken out of circulation by Federal Reserve banks for shipment to the Denver Mint. The coins were trucked from Denver, under guard, to the Minnequa plant of the Colorado Fuel & Iron Corp., at Pueblo. The guards stayed with the shipment until the last of the cents were in the melting furnace. With a face value of $68,446.36 they became worth about $1,000 as scrap.[99]

By 1950, steel cents were already becoming scarce, and by 1960 they had practically ceased to circulate altogether. This is perhaps just as well, since their condition deteriorated rapidly with only slight wear. In plating the steel strip *before* punching out planchets, the Mint had left these coins' edges vulnerable to rust and other forms of corrosion. This lesson was recalled in 1982 when the new zinc stock was copper plated only *after* being punched into blanks.

The Treasury's success in retrieving steel cents was far from complete, and this can be seen from the Department's own records, kept as late as

Summary of uncurrent zinc-coated steel one-cent coins withdrawn from circulation, by fiscal year.[100] (NOTE: The figures shown are for the number of cents *retrieved* by a particular mint, irrespective of where such pieces were coined)

Fiscal year	Philadelphia	San Francisco	Denver	Total
1945	690,218			690,281
1946	714,590			714,590
1947	1,379,510			1,379,510
1948	4,331,789	868,602		5,200,391
1949	8,070,590	861,333	6,844,636	15,776,559
1950	15,655,891	7,206,398	6,265,150	29,127,439
1951	12,751,379	4,498,554	7,942,640	25,192,573
1952	6,676,223	800,512	6,796,313	14,273,048
1953	5,292,415	1,161,890	4,137,565	10,591,870
1954	4,353,753	1,292,499		5,646,252
1955	6,874,524	1,006,574	5,834,013	13,715,111
1956	5,004,866		5,256,298	10,261,164
1957	2,975,238		3,568,479	6,543,717
1958	3,495,691		3,308,533	6,804,224
1959	2,891,221		3,434,440	6,334,661
1960	2,781,177		2,144,847	4,926,024
1961	905,469		1,599,362	2,504,831
1962	744,141		1,177,945	1,922,086
1963	376,903		553,913	930,816
1964	353,148			353,148
1965	144,033			144,033
1966	138,695			138,695
1967	81,400			81,400

1967. After that time steel cents were no longer considered to be circulating, even though some 930,586,247 were still officially outstanding. The table on page 22 shows the number of "steelies" withdrawn by the respective mints during each fiscal year from 1945 through 1967.

Shellcase cents

The demise of the steel cent meant that the Mint was once again faced with a shortage of copper. To augment the supply of newly-mined copper, a most unusual recycling program was initiated. Director Ross announced in the Fall of 1943 that spent artillery cartridges would be retrieved from the battlefront and rendered into new brass strip for coining cents. As the shellcases were only 70% copper with the balance being zinc, pure copper ingots would have to be added to augment the alloy and bring it up to 85-90% copper.[101] When actually coined, however, the new cents were of 95% copper and 5% zinc. This resulted in cents having essentially the same composition as those struck during 1942 but slightly different from ones dated 1941 and earlier.

All cents coined during 1944, 1945 and 1946 were of the brass alloy lacking tin. When the authority granted in 1942 to alter the legal composition of the cent ran out December 31, 1946, the Mint simply resumed adding a small amount of tin to the mix. Contemporary accounts relate that these cents were slightly lighter in color when new, but this is not apparent when examining them after 50 years.

How many of the 1944-46 cents were actually coined from metal retrieved from spent shellcases is unknown, though this source could not have accounted for the huge numbers produced in that three-year period. More likely is that the shellcase story was a morale-boosting maneuver to ease the public's frustration with the steel cents.

There is some firsthand evidence to support the shellcase story, however, and this was related in a 1982 article by David C. Moser titled "The Remarkable World War II Cents." In it Moser revealed that the original plan for dealing with the nation's shortage of copper called for spent cartridges cases to be retrieved intact and reloaded with powder and shells. As this proved unworkable it was then conceived that they could be melted down and made into coinage ingots and strip. Either operation called for a change in the normal procedure for handling spent cases, which hitherto had been caught by a "hot-shell-man" who then heaved them overboard. Serving aboard the aged destroyer *U.S.S. Greer* during 1943, Moser related how the crew's orders to save these expended

cases caused the shellman to instead pass them to an ungloved comrade whose instructions were to stack them for later recovery. Of course, in the heat of battle and with the limited space available on a destroyer it proved difficult to do this in an orderly manner. As the ship's Gunnery Officer cried out for more firing, the reply came back "Sir, we have to move the frozen potato sacks, gotta make a crib for these empties. They are smoking and rolling all over the place and we keep stumbling over them."[102]

Since the shellcase cents of 1944-46 were virtually indistinguishable from the pre-war cents there was never any need to withdraw them from circulation. Given their huge mintages they remained among the last Wheat cents to be found in circulation during the early 1970s. In fact, the successful employment of this alloy for three years only confirmed the uselessness of tin altogether, and Congress deleted this element from the cent on September 5, 1962. Public Law 87-643 made the official composition of the cent 95% copper and 5% zinc, which it remained until 1982.

A new reverse

Though collectors enjoyed assembling sets of Lincoln Cents, whether from circulation or through purchase and trading, there was a growing weariness with their continued appearance year after year. By the mid 1950s a movement arose to obtain new designs for the one-cent piece. Such a resolution was passed in 1955 at the annual convention of the American Numismatic Association in Omaha. When questioned about this action, Acting Mint Director Leland Howard revealed that there was then little sentiment in government circles for changing any of the current coin designs.[103]

Here the matter rested until 1958, when the approaching sesquicentennial of Lincoln's birth the following year prompted the formation of The Lincoln Sesquicentennial Commission. This was created by an act of Congress, and Senator John Sherman Cooper was its chairman. Since the image of Lincoln most familiar to the American people was that on the cent, it was only natural that the Commission's attention would be drawn to this coin. It originally proposed that the obverse portrait remain unchanged but that Lincoln's birthplace cabin in Hodgenville, Kentucky be depicted as a new reverse.[104]

Evidently the Commission carried some weight, as the reverse of the cent was changed for the coinage of 1959, though the grand Lincoln Memorial of 1922 was selected in place of his humble cabin. President Dwight D. Eisenhower gave his approval to the change December

20, though this step was not legally required under the Act of September 26, 1890. All cents struck though the end of 1958 were of the old type bearing Brenner's design, but one or more dispute examples exist dated 1959-D (see Chapter 7).

The new cents, displaying a reverse sculpted by Assistant Engraver Frank Gasparro, were first coined January 2, 1959. They were officially released on February 12, the 150th anniversary of Lincoln's birth, though a few banks misread their instructions and made the coins available sooner, much to the delight of lucky collectors and speculators. Just as in 1909 the demand for the new cents was insatiable, and banks were required to impose limits of from two to five coins per customer.[105]

Asked to comment on his design for the new reverse, Gasparro offered the following impressions:

My first inspiration for the Lincoln Memorial reverse of the one-cent goes back to a number of Greek coins I observed—-an ideal head on the obverse and a temple portal on the reverse with a diety in the portal. In fact, the Lincoln Memorial is Greek Classical in design, lending itself very well to a coin in linear design and detail.

The conception of this design for the Lincoln reverse was an accumulation of thumbnail sketches and ideas of a Lincoln coin going back ten years while I have been associated with the Mint. I have always been a great admirer of Lincoln, having made various sculptures of him in the past.

I remembered seeing several elevation plans for the Lincoln Memorial during its construction at the Philadelphia Public Library and I referred to these actual frontal elevation plans for correct proportions. In these plans the figure of Lincoln is an integral part of the Memorial; on the coin you can see this seated figure in the center of the portal as it is in the building at Washington, D.C. With the aid of a strong glass full details of the figure can be seen.

I feel that the design of the Lincoln Memorial on the reverse of the one-cent is a fitting token of esteem to this great president as it shows a national shrine.[105a]

Gasparro's original model for the reverse of the cent included an arc of stars around the memorial building, but this element was dropped at the advising of the Federal Commission of Fine Arts. The Commission also found other objections to the model, which of necessity had to be sculpted in very shallow relief. Knowing only too well the technical requirements of coinage, Gasparro

Dedication of the Lincoln Memorial on Memorial Day, May 30, 1922 (National Archives)

acquiesced to the mandated changes, though he still viewed the finished coin as something of a compromise between artistry and the goal of mass production. Unlike in 1909, the presence of his initials FG to the right of the memorial structure caused no uproar. Many people did take note, however, of the small letter "o" in the legend UNITED STATES oF AMERICA. The usual moronic rumors of a Mint error and imminent recall were quickly spread, but Gasparro clarified the situation immediately. "I did it to break up the pattern," he remarked, adding that a precedent existed with the Franklin Half Dollar, the Peace Dollar and several commemoratives.[106]

On the retirement after 50 years of Brenner's original cent, writer Walter Thompson reflected, "Whereas something new in the field of numismatics is always welcomed by collectors, the passing of the old Lincoln cent will leave all collectors with a sense of nostalgia."[107]

Stressed to the breaking point

It's just as well that collectors chose not to hoard the Wheat cents after 1959, as every available cent would soon be needed to meet a massive, nationwide coin shortage. The signs that something was amiss were evident to anyone who was paying attention: The combined mintages of cents at the Philadelphia and Denver Mints more than doubled from 1958 to 1960, only to rise again by nearly 50% during the following year. By the end of 1961, U. S. Mint Director Eva Adams was becoming aware of the problem, but it seemed that no amount of additional coinage could keep up with the swelling demand. At the beginning of 1963, banks and merchants were already cognizant of the chronic difficulty in keeping sufficient supplies of coins on hands, with cents being particularly troublesome in this respect. It was not until the end of that year, however, that the nation as a whole was alerted to the serious problem which then existed, and 1964 would only bring more headaches for both the Mint and the American economy.

Partly as a result of unprecedented prosperity, the United States was consuming coins at a hitherto unimagined rate. Much of this new demand emanated from the vending machine industry, and its slowness in making collections aggravated the shortage of coins still further. Banks and businesses began offering premiums for the return of coins, as it was becoming nearly impossible to secure enough pieces to make change. Confronted with an angry Congress demanding answers, Director Adams did not hesitate to remind it of the repeated pleas from herself and her predecessors for a new Philadelphia Mint of sufficient size and productivity to cope with the shortage which now existed. These requests dated as far back as the 1940s, but it was not until August 20, 1963 that Public Law 88-102 finally provided for the new mint. Still, it would be some five years before this plant was up and running, and solutions were needed immediately.

Among the unfortunate scapegoats in this little drama were coin collectors. Blamed for the popularity in recent years of hoarding entire bags of new coins as a speculative venture, legitimate collectors were lumped together with such mindless speculators as communal villains. Among the measures taken in 1964 which were both practical and punitive were the deletion of mintmarks after that year, the suspension of proof and mint sets, and the freezing of the date 1964. These actions resulted in the production of billions of cents and other coins carrying the 1964 date as late as 1966. Mintmarks, legally prohibited for a five-year period following passage of the Act of July 23, 1965, did not return until 1968, when the coin shortage had eased off sufficiently to reintroduce them somewhat ahead of schedule.

The San Francisco Assay Office, which had ceased coining operations in 1955, was reopened in 1964 to produce planchets for use at the Denver Mint. By the Fall of 1965 it was coining cents without mintmarks to supplement the production of the other two facilities. With record numbers of coins being struck, the coin shortage

Guard John McKindley stands watch over a truckload of 4,350,000 Denver Mint cents just delivered to the Federal Reserve Bank in St. Louis to meet the coin shortage. This photo was taken December 26, 1963. (Bowers & Merena Galleries Archive)

Treasury Department citation awarded to those turning in their cent hoards during the shortage of 1973-74. (Numismatic News)

finally abated in 1966, and normal dating returned the following year. When mintmarks reappeared in 1968, the popular 'S' was among them. This ultimately proved a mistake, as speculators retained huge numbers of S-Mint cents each year through 1974. It was finally decided that the future production of cents at San Francisco would include no mintmark, rendering such pieces indistinguishable from those struck at the Philadelphia Mint and the West Point Depository.

Aluminum cents?

The coin shortage of the early-mid 1960s was severe and far-reaching, yet both national and regional scarcities of cents have become a fact of life in recent decades. Most of the cents struck since the 1960s have merely been replacements for the many pieces which are discarded daily or thrown into ashtrays and jars. One-cent pieces have become simply too valueless to be worth recirculating, yet the totaling of sales to the exact cent requires that they be minted by the billions annually to make their one-way journey from the mint to the bank, from the bank to the store, from the store to the customer and from the customer to oblivion.

Usually taken for granted, the cent became the focus of national attention during one of the more severe cent shortages since the 1960s. This occurred throughout 1973, at a time when the price of copper was rising and there was some prospect of these coins being hoarded and even melted. By March 25 the combined metal value and production cost of a one-cent piece exceeded its face value. Though the expense of rendering cents into ingots still exceeded their value, just the threat of a total disappearance of cents prompted Congress to experiment with aluminum as a substitute metal.

On December 7, 1973, Treasury Secretary George P. Shultz submitted a draft bill to President Richard M. Nixon "To authorize the secretary of the Treasury to change the alloy and weight of the one cent piece." Shultz added, "It would be appreciated if you would lay the draft bill before the Senate. An identical bill has been transmitted to the Speaker of the House of Representatives." Shultz followed this action April 15, 1974 by placing a ban on the melting of cents, though history has shown such prohibitions completely unenforceable.[108]

Toward the end of 1973 some 1.57 million cents were coined in an alloy containing 96% aluminum and bearing the date 1974.[109] A number of aluminum cents were distributed to members of Congress for their inspection, and most of these were returned to the Philadelphia Mint and destroyed when the price of copper receded and the crisis passed. The balance of the cents retained by the Mint were likewise melted. Several pieces, however, remained outstanding, as their recipients were unable to produce the coins when requested to do so. Of the two Congressional committees involved in studying the aluminum cent, the Senate Banking, Housing and Urban Affairs Committee received five specimens, while nine additional pieces were loaned to the House Banking and Currency Committee.

In defense of the Mint and of the committee members, Acting Director Frank MacDonald replied to a letter from numismatic writer Ted Schwarz more than a year after the debate over the aluminum cent:

> You may be sure that appropriate steps are being taken to assure that these coins remain in the custody of the United States Government. Even while the proposed legislation was pending, all experimental aluminum pennies in Mint custody were ordered to be melted by the Director. The pieces provided to the Committee remain in their custody and will presumably be returned to the Bureau once the Committees no longer have any need for them.[110]

There seemed to be some confusion over whether the Congressmen were even required to return the cents, as some reported that the Mint had never asked for them back, while others related that "representatives" of the Mint had already retrieved them. Congressman John Conlan of Arizona, an opponent of the aluminum cent, remarked "I remember seeing the coins, handling them briefly and cursing them a bit. Beyond that, I don't have any idea what happened to them."[111]

At least one example has been preserved for the public benefit, as it was presented to the Smithsonian Institution's National Numismatic Collection by Charles B. Holstein, a staff member of the House Banking and Currency Subcommittee on Consumer Affairs. "For more than six months I kept the aluminum penny in my wallet," Holstein stated, "Mostly as a conversation piece, and as a reminder of the historical process that the subcommittee was deliberating on." After learning that the Mint wanted his cent returned so that it could be destroyed along with all the others, Holstein instead deposited it with the Smithsonian, not wanting to see it lost to posterity.[112]

Mock cents

The escalating price of copper in 1973 should have served as a warning bell to Congress that the cent was due for retirement, yet the seigniorage (profit) that it afforded proved too compelling in an era of continual deficit spending. When the inflation rate of the dollar briefly reached double digits in the early 1980s, this again signaled a dramatic increase in the price of copper and another threat to the cent. Since aluminum had already proved undesirable, an alternative alloy was sought. Public Law 93-441, passed October 11, 1974 following the last cent crisis, permitted a change in the composition of the cent on order of the Treasury Secretary without further Congressional action. This was implemented in 1981 and called for the issuing of cents consisting of a core of 99.2% zinc and 0.8% copper plated with pure copper. The overall ratio of zinc to copper would be 97.5% to 2.5%, the whole having a weight of 38.581 grains.[113]

The folly of making cents from zinc is apparent in this deeply corroded specimen removed from a coin album only a few years after its minting.

Contracts for the new blanks, which were to be fabricated entirely outside of the mints, were awarded July 22, 1981 to the Ball Corporation of Greenville, Tennessee. These blanks were to be delivered to the mints beginning in November, and the striking of zinc cents would be gradually phased into the Mint's production schedule beginning in December.[114]

Cents of both the old and new compositions were struck transitionally during 1981 and 1982, though all bore the latter date. By the end of 1982 the old alloy was discontinued, and all cents coined since 1983 have been of copper-plated zinc. The zinc cents dated 1982 and 1983 proved highly subject to corrosion, many revealing dark swirls on either side. Another problem common to the early zinc cents was bubbling. Occluded gases trapped beneath the copper plating were compressed during striking and formed tiny pimples of raised copper on the surfaces of many coins. While the dark swirling was largely eliminated by the end of 1983, the problem of bubbling remained evident in lessening degrees through 1986.

Epilogue?

The one-cent piece in the 1990s is a complete anachronism. It no longer has sufficient value to purchase any product or service except when presented in multiples, yet to do so is to invoke the disapproval of clerks and cashiers. Indeed, there are many businesses and vending machines which specifically prohibit cents. Still, with its ever-dwindling seignorage, this coin sol-diers on through a combination of greed, sentiment and bureaucratic inertia.

Recent opinion polls show that Americans favor retaining the cent. The percentage of persons supporting the cent tends to vary, however, with the way in which the questions are posed. When people are asked whether they would mind prices being rounded to the nearest five cents, objections are heard, as it is assumed that retailers would naturally round prices up rather than down. Yet these same individuals, when asked if they would stoop to pick up a cent from the street or sidewalk, will almost invariably answer "No." The sponsoring organization of a particular poll always knows how to word its questions so as to manipulate the results, and Congress has proved unable or unwilling to see around this ploy.

Whether or not the cent survives into the 21st Century, it seems likely that the Brenner/Gasparro design will be the last to grace this humblest of American coins. Only one thing is certain—-the end of the Lincoln Cent story has not yet been written.

Notes

[1]Lannon, Donald B., "A Living Coinage," *The Numismatist,* March, 1968.
[2]Ibid.
[3]Ibid.
[4]Ibid.
[5]Ibid.
[6]*The Numismatist,* March, 1909.
[7]Kunhardt, Philip B., Jr., Philip B. III & Peter W., *Lincoln: An Illustrated Biography.*
[8]Taxay, Don, *The U. S. Mint and Coinage.*
[9]National Archives, Bureau of the Mint, Records Group 104.
[10]Ibid.
[11]Ibid.
[12]Ibid.
[13]Ibid.
[14]Ibid.
[15]Ibid.
[16]Ibid.
[17]Ibid.
[18]Ibid.
[19]Ibid.
[20]Ibid.
[21]Letter dated 2-10-09, National Archives.
[22]National Archives, Bureau of the Mint, Records Group 104.
[23]Ibid.
[24]Ibid.
[25]Ibid.
[26]Ibid.
[27]Ibid.
[28]Ibid.
[29]Ibid.
[30]Ibid.
[31]Ibid.
[32]Taxay.

[33]National Archives, Bureau of the Mint, Records Group 104.
[34]Ibid.
[35]*Annual Report of the Director of the Mint for Fiscal Year Ended June 30, 1910.*
[36]National Archives, Bureau of the Mint, Records Group 104.
[37]Ibid.
[38]Ibid.
[39]Ibid.
[40]Ibid.
[41]Ibid.
[42]Ibid.
[43]Ibid.
[44]Ibid.
[45]Ibid.
[46]Ibid.
[47]*The Numismatist,* November, 1909.
[48]Ibid, July, 1909.
[49]Fink, Clarence M., "The Cent that Changed Its Face," *The Numismatic Scrapbook Magazine,* October, 1954.
[50]Ibid.
[51]Ibid.
[52]Ibid.
[53]*The Numismatist,* September-October, 1909.
[54]Fink.
[55]Ibid.
[56]Ibid.
[57]National Archives, Bureau of the Mint, Records Group 104.
[58]Ibid.
[59]Taxay.
[60]National Archives.
[61]Ibid.
[62]Ibid.
[63]Ibid.

[64]Ibid.
[65]Ibid.
[66]Perkins, John U., "The Story of a Penny," *The Philadelphia West and the Camera World,* September, 1909.
[67]*The Numismatist,* September-October, 1909.
[68]Ibid.
[69]Ibid.
[70]Ibid, November, 1909.
[71]Lindheim, Leon, T., "The Oldest Current U. S. Coin Design," *The Numismatist,* November, 1978.
[72]*The Numismatist,* September-October, 1909.
[73]National Archives, Bureau of the Mint, Records Group 104.
[74]*The Numismatic Scrapbook Magazine,* September, 1959.
[75]Ibid, February, 1960.
[76]National Archives.
[77]Ibid.
[78]Ibid.
[79]Annual Report, 1912.
[79a]*The Numismatist,* January, 1918.
[80]*The Numismatist,* November, 1917.
[81]Ibid, January, 1918.
[82]Ibid, March, 1921.
[83]*The Numismatic Scrapbook Magazine,* January, 1942.
[84]*The Numismatist,* February, 1942.
[85]*The Numismatic Scrapbook Magazine,* February, 1942.
[86]Annual Report, 1943.
[87]*The Numismatist,* November, 1942.
[88]Wallace, E. V., "A Numismatography of the Lincoln Head Cent," *The Numismatic Scrapbook Magazine,* October, 1952.

[89]Reed, P. Bradley, Editor, *Coin World Almanac.*
[90]*The Numismatic Scrapbook Magazine,* March, 1943.
[91]Ibid, April, 1943.
[92]Ibid, August, 1943.
[93]Ibid, September, 1943.
[94]Ibid, October, 1943.
[95]Ibid.
[96]Ibid, July, 1956.
[97]Ibid, December, 1943.
[98]*Annual Report,* 1953.
[99]*The Numismatic Scrapbook Magazine,* February, 1949.
[100]*Annual Report,* 1967.
[101]*The Numismatic Scrapbook Magazine,* November, 1943.
[102]*The Numismatist,* August, 1982.
[103]*The Numismatic Scrapbook Magazine,* October, 1955.
[104]Ibid, June, 1958.
[105]*The Numismatist,* March, 1959.
[105a]Talleyrand, Maxwell, "Artists and the Lincoln Cent," *The Numismatic Scrapbook Magazine,* December, 1964.
[106]Ibid.
[107]"The New Lincoln Cent," *The Numismatic Scrapbook Magazine,* January, 1959.
[108]*The Numismatic Scrapbook Magazine,* May, 1974.
[109]*Annual Report,* 1974.
[110]"The Case of the Missing 1973 Aluminum Cents," *The Numismatist,* August, 1976.
[111]Ibid.
[112]Ibid.
[113]Reed.
[114]*The Numismatist,* September, 1981.

Abraham Lincoln

Two Views of Abraham Lincoln
Photographed by Anthony Berger of Mathew Brady's Gallery on February 9, 1864. Brenner used the profile photo in designing his models.
(National Archives)

The first American to be portrayed on a circulating United States coin was born February 12, 1809 to Thomas Lincoln and the former Nancy Hanks. Named after his paternal grandfather, who'd been killed by an Indian when Thomas was just six years old, young Abraham was born in Hardin County, Kentucky. It was to this land that the elder Abraham and wife Bathsheba had relocated from Virginia with their five children in the early 1780s.

Tom Lincoln was self educated as a carpenter, yet he and Nancy chose to live out-of-town as farmers following the birth of their first child, Sarah, in 1807. They relocated to a patch of land with the unpromising name of Sinking Spring Farm, not quite three miles from Hogdenville, Kentucky. When baby Abraham arrived, his prospects for success in life were not many. The family owned a simple log cabin, with only packed earth for a floor and just a single window to the outside world.

Cousin Dennis Hanks recalled the youthful Abe Lincoln in a reminiscence recorded years later:

> Most o' the time he went bar'foot . . . Abe was right out in the woods about a soon's he was weaned, fishin' in the creek, settin' traps fur rabbits an' muskrats, goin' on coon-

hunts with Tom an' me an' the dogs, follerin' up bees to find bee-trees, an' drappin' corn fur his pappy. Mighty interestin' life fur a boy . . . [1]

Young Abe was quieter and more thoughtful than many of his rural peers, traits that he inherited from his mother, yet there were many acquaintances who recall him as having frequent bursts of exuberance. Like his father, Abe could spin a tall tale and perform the lion's share of the laughing. These contradictory aspects of his nature revealed a complex and sometimes troubled individual. Though his formal education amounted to just about a year, once he had learned to read and write he proved ready, willing and able to continue exploring on his own.

A signal event in his young life was the passing of his mother when he was just nine. The family was then living in Indiana, but Nancy's death prompted Tom Lincoln to return to Kentucky to seek a new wife. It didn't take long, as he already had in mind a friend of Nancy's, Sarah Bush Johnson, widow of the former county jailer.

As Abe entered his teenage years and was expected to work the land, he found his interests concentrated more and more on learning. He once said, "My best friend is the man who'll get me a book I ain't read."[2] Lincoln didn't read for mere pleasure, but rather he read with a conscious desire toward elevating his station in life. A certain distance inevitably grew between Abe and his father, who expected the boy to live the rough-hewn life he'd known and who had little use for fancy book learning.

But books gave Abe the vision of a larger world outside the backwoods, and he was driven to break away from his intellectual confinement. After helping his father to relocate to Illinois, the opportunity to build a flatboat and accompany it and its cargo downriver gave the young man his first taste of freedom. It also led to a job in the speculative town of New Salem, Illinois, overlooking the Sangamon River. At age 22, Lincoln accepted the offer of a job running Denton Offutt's general store, while also working at the town's principal industry, a saw- and gristmill.

The young politician

Impressed by his physical size and strength, as well as by his soft-spoken intelligence, the residents of New Salem recognized the young Abe as a promising individual. In 1832 this recognition prompted Lincoln to make a run for the Illinois state legislature. Though he had a winning way with the locals, his limited resources and even lesser attention to proper campaigning cost him the election. Not so two years later, however, and Lincoln was off to the state capital at Vandalia in 1834. Abraham was re-elected in 1836, and he opted to relocate to the future state capital of Springfield the following year. There he practiced law, which at that time doesn't seem to have required much formal education. After learning everything he could find on the subject, all that Abe Lincoln needed to be admitted to the Illinois bar was "a testament of good moral character and enrollment by the clerk of the State Supreme Court."[3]

Lincoln, though a rather private individual, was well liked by his neighbors in Springfield. Joshua Fry Speed recalled that "Mr. Lincoln was a social man, though he did not seek company; it sought him."[4] His peculiar nature manifested itself in his ill-fated engagement to Mary Owen, an episode which occurred in New Salem and may have contributed to his decision to leave that town. He agreed to marrying her in a promise to her sister, yet when Mary arrived in Illinois from Kentucky Lincoln found her rather unattractive and secretly desired to break the engagement. Too honorable to do so, he went ahead and proposed marriage to the young woman. To his utter shock and great relief she turned him down.

Another Kentucky belle, one from a family of some means and education, arrived in Springfield shortly afterward. Abe Lincoln was introduced to young Mary Todd in December of 1839, and the two hit it off instantly despite their widely divergent backgrounds. They were married November 4, 1842 and ultimately had four children. Only Robert, the eldest, and Thomas, the youngest survived into adulthood, though "Tad," as Thomas was called, succumbed at age 18. Edward died just shy of his fourth birthday, while William died at age 11, during the first year of Lincoln's Presidency. These multiple tragedies, combined with the death of her husband Abraham, ultimately led poor Mary Todd Lincoln to spend several of her remaining years in an insane asylum, largely at the insistence of estranged son Robert.

A very public life

Abraham Lincoln served in the Illinois state legislature from 1834 to 1841 before retiring to his family and law practice in Springfield. He was elected to the office of U. S. Representative from Illinois in 1846. He served only a single term when, as the lone Whig Party member from that state, Lincoln stood firm in his opposition to the Mexican War of 1846-48. Lincoln adopted this position after listening to the great Henry Clay of Kentucky, described by the young Congressman as "the man for whom I fought all my life."[5] This stand cost Lincoln re-election, as the Mexican War proved both a military and popular success for America.

Returning once again to Springfield in 1849, Lincoln resumed his practice there while performing also as a circuit lawyer. This involved traveling from town to town, following the progress of a state magistrate who brought the court to those outlying communities which possessed no formal judicial system. Highly regarded for his ability to win cases without resorting to slander and dirty tricks, Lincoln's reputation for honesty and integrity was gradually spread throughout the state of Illinois.

This ultimately prompted Abe to run for the office of U. S. Senator in 1858. Now a member of the newly-formed Republican Party, Lincoln engaged in a series of nationally-reported debates with his Democratic opponent (and former rival for the hand of Mary Todd), Stephen A. Douglas. Though Lincoln lost his Senate bid, he rose to national prominence as the result of his eloquent and memorable speeches. The greatest issue of the day was the increasingly emotional subject of slavery, on which the nation was polarized between North and South. Lincoln warned that "A house divided against itself cannot stand." He went on to assert that "I believe this government cannot endure, permanently half slave and half free. It will become all one thing or all the other."[6]

On the strength of such visionary leadership the Republican Party nominated Lincoln as its candidate for the presidency in 1860. His running mate was Hannibal Hamlin of Maine. Fortunately for Lincoln the Democratic Party was split asunder, officially nominating Lincoln's old rival Senator Douglas of Illinois as its candidate, while a splinter group backed John C. Breckenridge of Kentucky.

As predicted, Lincoln's election in the Fall prompted several southern states to secede from the Union, fiery South Carolina leading the way. Inaugurated in March of 1861, Lincoln made no secret of the fact that he intended to hold the rebellious states within the confines of the United States Constitution. Ignoring his warnings, the seceding states formed their own collective, calling it the Confederate States of America. War between the USA and the CSA seemed inevitable, and indeed it was not long in coming.

Wartime leader

An assault on the Union bastion of Fort Sumter in the harbor of Charleston, South Carolina came only a few weeks after Lincoln took office. At first it was believed that the small standing Federal Army, plus a few thousand volunteers recruited for 90 days, would quickly disable the CSA's troops and end the war. This notion was dispelled on July 21, 1861 when the North's ill-trained volunteers were routed in the first Battle of Manassas, just 20 miles southwest of Washington, D.C. Much of the war would be fought near the USA's capital and that of the CSA in Richmond, Virginia, though important engagements occurred in the West, as well.

Burdened with incompetent or overly cautious commanders who were no match for the brilliant and courageous Confederate leader, General Robert E. Lee, the Union's military campaigns achieved relatively little success despite the North's superior manpower and resources. As the war dragged on year after year Lincoln became deeply troubled, while his initial popularity declined and threatened his re-election in 1864. One of his former Commanding Generals, George B. McClellan, whom Lincoln relieved of duty in 1862, even had the temerity to run against Lincoln as the Democratic Party's presidential nominee. To his great vindication, Lincoln soundly defeated McClellan in the popular vote and was returned to office.

Seeking to restore moral support for the increasingly costly and painful war, Lincoln reminded the American people that his goal was not only to preserve the Union but also to bring an end to the abominable practice of slavery. Though it carried no power of enforcement in the South, Lincoln's Emancipation Proclamation of January 1, 1863 declared that all persons held in servitude within states presently in rebellion against the United States "shall be then, thenceforth and forever free."[7]

In his second great address of the Civil War and the one for which he is best remembered. Lincoln spoke only briefly during the dedication of a Union cemetery adjacent to the battlesite at Gettysburg, Pennsylvania. In closing his remarks on November 19, 1863, he spoke some of the most meaningful words in American history: ". . . that we here highly resolve that these dead shall not have died in vain; that this nation shall have a new birth of freedom; and that this government of the people, by the people, for the people, shall not perish from the earth."[8]

Martyr to the cause

Lincoln finally found a commander of both skill and fearlessness in one Ulysses S. Grant. Something of a failure in civilian life, Grant achieved several prominent victories in the West before capturing the attention of the Commander-in-Chief. Selected to lead the Union armies in March of 1864, Grant needed only 13 months to drive the South into submission. General Lee surrendered to Grant on April 9, 1865, bringing four years of slaughter to an end.

Lincoln had been inaugurated only the month before, and the war had aged him severely. Though he looked forward to a less demanding second term, this was never to be. While the armies may have put down their weapons, the passions which led to secession and war in the first place did not die a quiet death. Lincoln had been the target of every would-be assassin's anger since 1860, and his time finally ran out. Popular actor John Wilkes Booth, a bitter white-supremacist, forged an alliance with a handful of others who shared his view that the defeat of the Confederacy had left them no other means to vent their frustration short of murder.

In an ironic twist, Booth the actor chose Ford's Theater as the place to end his greatest enemy's life. No one questioned his presence in the theater the night of April 14, and he quietly crept into the Presiden't box and placed a small derringer pistol directly against Lincoln's head, firing just a single shot. Abraham Lincoln lingered on until early the following morning, never regaining consciousness. Fleeing the theater, Booth was pursued for almost two weeks before being cornered and killed on April 26. Previously, he had written in his diary, "I can never repent it, though we hated to kill. Our country owed all her troubles to him, and God simply made me the instrument of His Punishment."[9]

Booth's co-conspirators were all rounded up and ultimately hanged. One of them, Lewis Paine, had attempted to kill Secretary of State William H. Seward and his son on the same night that Lincoln was assassinated. Attacking them with a knife, he was driven away after causing the Secretary serious injury. Along with David Herold, George Atzerodt and Mary Surratt, Paine met his end on the gallows, July 7, 1865.

Legacy

There are very few who will dispute that Abraham Lincoln was among his nation's greatest Presidents. He resides in the exclusive pantheon with such figures as George Washington, Thomas Jefferson and Franklin D. Roosevelt. The long funeral procession from Washington to his burial site in Springfield was witnessed by countless Americans in mourning. That Lincoln's image of greatness has survived more than a century is

The Lincoln Memorial nears completion. Sculptor Daniel Chester French (left) and architect Henry Bacon. (National Archives)

testimony to the man and his selfless service to the country.

In 1922 a grand memorial to Abraham Lincoln in the Greek Revival style was completed in Washington, D.C. The work of architect Henry Bacon, within it is a superb seated figure of Lincoln by sculptor Daniel Chester French. This structure was chosen to grace the reverse of the Lincoln Cent on the sesquicentennial of his birth in 1959. 50 years earlier, however, it was a portrait of the great man which appeared on the humble cent for the first time. As soon as this coin was announced to the public, McLandburgh Wilson composed a sentimental poem for *The New York Sun* which was reproduced in numismatic journals for generations afterward, though its original source had been long forgotten:[10]

The Lincoln Cent

Not on the eagle golden
Will we behold his face,
Nor yet on gleaming silver
The honored features trace;
But to the common copper,
The lowly coin, instead,
Has fallen the distinction
Of bearing Lincoln's head

The millionaire may seldom
Those noble outlines grasp,
But childhood's chubby fingers
The image oft will clasp.
The poor man will esteem it,
And mothers hold it dear—
The plain and common people
He loved when he was here.

Notes

[1] Kunhardt, Philip B., Jr., Philip B. III & Peter W., *Lincoln: An Illustrated Biography.*
[2] Ibid.
[3] Ibid.
[4] Ibid.
[5] Ibid.
[6] Ibid.
[7] Ibid.
[8] Ibid.
[9] Ibid.
[10] *The Numismatist*, March 1909.

Victor D. Brenner

The creator of the Lincoln Cent was a prolific sculptor who worked almost entirely in the field of medallic art. As such pieces are seldom appreciated by those outside of numismatics, his name is not often encountered in museums or in reference to public artworks. One possible exception is his sculpture in the round titled *A Song of Nature,* found in Pittsburgh's Schenley Park.[1] Still, in his relatively short lifetime Brenner created a magnificent portfolio of medals and plaques, a number of which were produced in sufficient numbers to be collectable. His various medallic tributes to Abraham Lincoln form a handsome body of work in themselves.

Victor D. Brenner (Peter A. Juley & Son Collection, National Museum of American Art, Smithsonian Institution)

Born Viktoras Barnauskas, this native of Lithuania began life on June 12, 1871 in the town of Shavli.[2] At an early age he displayed a precocious talent for engraving, a skill no doubt encouraged by his father. The elder Barnauskas was well known as an accomplished stone cutter, seal cutter, die engraver and general artisan in metalwork. Young Viktoras became so proficient in the fine art of engraving that by the age of 13 he was employed by his father and would establish his own business just three years later.

His work so exceeded that of rival engravers that they resented both his youth and the increasing number of commissions that were coming his way. Conspiring to ruin the young man, they related to the Russian Imperial police that his prosperity resulted from counterfeiting. As the charges were patently untrue, the police were frustrated in their efforts to obtain evidence against Viktor. In what would now be condemned as a case of entrapment, undercover police came to his shop and commissioned him to create a duplicate of a particular seal belonging to a high official in the Russian Army. The creation of such a seal was limited to employees of the Imperial Government's engraving office, and to replicate it in any way was treasonous.

1897 one-peso coin of the Dominican Republic. Though not signed the models were sculpted by V. D. Brenner. The dies were prepared in Paris, France and bear its 'A' mintmark, but these coins were actually struck at the Philadelphia Mint. (American Numismatic Association)

Young Viktor, unaware of this fact, obligingly engraved a perfect copy and was immediately imprisoned. Awaiting his fate of exile to either Siberia or the Kamtchatka Peninsula, he was assisted by friends in his escape from prison and his subsequent clandestine emigration to the United States of America.[3] The year was 1890, and Viktor, now calling himself Victor David Brenner, was just 19 years old.

Like so many Jewish immigrants of the time he soon found himself eking a living on New York City's Lower East Side. The engraving work he undertook was unworthy of his talent and consisted mostly of applying simple sentiments to jewelry and watches. Though there's no evidence of it, the widespread popularity at that time of love tokens (coins planed off on one side and engraved with initials or some other personalization) suggests that he made have been engaged in this work as well. (Imagine being able to identify such a piece as having been engraved by the great V. D. Brenner!)

One story of how Brenner was discovered by 'society' and his formal studies launched was related by a friend of his some years later. In this tale, his talent was first recognized when he proved successful in repairing a watch which other jewelers had agreed would have to be returned to Switzerland. This watch belonged to Mrs. Felix Warburg of New York, and Brenner, motivated by her praise of his skill in repairing it, further volunteered to engrave its reverse for her. This proved to be a brilliant career move by the young man, for Mrs. Warburg displayed her engraved watch proudly at a subsequent family gathering. Her brother was moved to become Brenner's patron, sponsoring his studies in Paris under the great French sculptor Louis Oscar Roty.[4]

The above story of Brenner's entry into the art schools of Paris is probably apocryphal, as it just doesn't agree with other published accounts of his career and those of his contemporaries, many of whom found themselves in somewhat similar circumstances. A far more likely account has him employed in New York City as a die cutter and an engraver of badges. After long days at work in the shops of the Lower East Side, nighttime would find Brenner attending art classes and accepting whatever sculptural commissions came his way. He began his studies at the famed Cooper Union and then progressed to the National Academy of Design and the Art Students' League.[5] One particular work of his during this period, a bust of Ludwig von Beethoven prepared for a local musical society, was so well received that Professor Oettinger of New York City College introduced young Brenner at a meeting of the American Numismatic Society.[6]

Brenner created this medal for The Art Institute of Chicago in 1909. Seven years later, Hermon MacNeil designed a new quarter dollar which seems to have been influenced by Brenner's obverse. (ANA)

It's quite possible that this early entry into the realm of numismatics may have influenced his decision to concentrate on medallic work over more lucrative sculptural commissions. In addition, it was this acquaintance with the ANS that probably led to his participation in an 1895 design competition for a new silver dollar, a contest co-sponsored by the ANS and the National Sculpture Society. The entries submitted by numerous artists of merit were displayed in the Fine Arts Building on New York's 57th Street in May of that year, with prizes of $300 and $200 being awarded the winners.[7] Though the U. S. Mint totally disregarded this effort, the models which Brenner created may now be found in the collection of the ANS, to whom they were donated by him.

Brenner acquired several patrons during this period, and he was thus able to spend three years studying in Paris from 1898 to 1901. After some time in the studio of Louis Oscar Roty, he entered the Academmie Julian and was tutored by Peuch, Verlet and Dubois.[8] He perfected his skills there, learning also from Alexandre Charpentier and the great Auguste Rodin.[9] His final year in Europe was apparently spent just 'bum-

Brenner's plaque honoring Ambrose Swasey is doubly interesting to numismatists because Swasey is believed to have been the driving force behind the coining of the so-called "Chapman" proofs of the 1921 Morgan Silver Dollar. (ANA)

ming' around and taking in the world's beauty. His work earned awards at the Paris Exposition and Salon of 1900, best known to numismatists for Charles Barber's Lafayette Silver Dollar, which commemorated America's participation in the fair.

Returning to New York City in 1901, Brenner now possessed the confidence to open his own studio. The 1901 Pan-American Exposition in Buffalo, and St. Louis' Louisiana Purchase Exposition of 1904 provided further venues for the display and recognition of Brenner's talent.[10] He again relocated to Paris for about a year-and-a-half in 1904 but returned permanently to New York City early in 1906.[11] In addition to his commercial work, Brenner briefly served as an instructor in the design and crafting of jewelry for the American Numismatic Society and also taught at the National Academy of Design.[12]

Brenner's mastery of the medal made him a favorite with the rich and famous, and he never suffered for lack of work during the remaining 20 years of his life. In 1908 his address was given as 114 East 28th Street; two years later his studio was located at 105 East 17th Street.[13] Among the important commissions he received during the first decade of the 20th Century was Theodore Roosevelt's Panama Canal Service Medal. While sitting for his portrait the President first viewed Brenner's plaque of Abraham Lincoln, a work which the artist had evidently undertaken for his own gratification, though it proved a lucrative item with the public. It was this fateful meeting of like minds which led directly to Brenner's sculpting the Lincoln Cent, a story told in detail earlier in this book.

Victor D. Brenner married Anna Reeb in 1913, and she survived him by some years after his death at New York City's Montefiore Hospital on April 5, 1924.[14] He'd been ailing for quite awhile, and his career effectively ended in 1921. At the time of his death Brenner was a member of the

American Numismatic Society, the National Sculpture Society, the Architectural League and the National Arts Club of New York. He was also a member of the American Numismatic Association from 1906 to 1912. Relatively little is known of his personal life, aside from the facts presented above. In his short lifetime Brenner created an impressive body of work. This was cataloged by Glenn Smedley and published in *The Numismatist* for July and August of 1983.

Brenner penned a number of articles dealing with the subject of medallic art, mostly during the first decade of the 20th Century. The most popular of these was a pamphlet titled *The Art of the Medal*. It was published in 1910 by the DeVinne press on behalf of the American Numismatic Society.[15] In addition to his observations on the work of medallists, it features a photograph of Brenner at work in the engraving of a die.

Notes

[1] Glenn B. Smedley, "The Works of Victor David Brenner," *The Numismatist*, July & August, 1983.

[2] Dr. A. M. Rackus, "Twentieth Anniversary of Lincoln Cent," *The Numismatist*, December, 1929.

[3] Ibid.

[4] Maxwell Talleyrand, "Artists and the Lincoln Cent," *The Numismatic Scrapbook Magazine*, December, 1964.

[5] *The Numismatist*, March, 1909.

[6] Rackus.

[7] *The Numismatist*, April, 1895.

[8] Ibid, March, 1909.

[9] Rackus and Smedley.

[10] Rackus.

[11] *The Numismatist*, March, 1909.

[12] George C. West, letter to *The Numismatist*, November, 1982.

[13] Smedley.

[14] Obituary in *The Numismatist*, May, 1924.

[15] West.

Frank Gasparro

The future designer/sculptor of the new Lincoln Cent reverse of 1959 was seemingly pre-destined for this role. Frank Gasparro was born in Philadelphia on August 26, 1909, just three weeks after Brenner's original design debuted in circulation. Much like Brenner, he displayed a precocious talent for drawing and sculpting, and he was naturally inclined toward a career in art. His father, a professional violinist, knew only too well the financial uncertainty of earning a living in the arts and attempted to dissuade young Frank. The boy's interest was keen, however, and it ultimately won over his father. "After seeing that I wouldn't be dissuaded," Gasparro recalled decades later in an interview for *Numismatic News*, "I was allowed to take art classes at the Samuel Fleisher Art Memorial School."[1]

Gasparro was apprenticed to sculptor Giuseppe Donato, who had studied five years under Auguste Rodin, one of Brenner's mentors as well. Then only 12 years old, Gasparro later recalled, "I wasn't paid. Instead, I would spend a few hours helping in the studio and then for an hour at the end of the day he would give me materials to use and leave me to my artwork."[2] This activity continued throughout his years of high school, consuming weekdays and Saturdays during the Summertime. It was Donato who gave to Gasparro his passion for bas-

Informal portrait of Frank Gasparro taken in 1969.
(Frank Gasparro)

relief sculpture that would last a lifetime.

Graduating from South Philadelphia High School, young Frank entered the Pennsylvania Academy of Fine Arts, supporting his studies with jobs as a messenger and later clerk for Western Union.[3] His demonstrated skill earned him two scholarships for study abroad in Europe. "I did research in Italy, Germany and Belgium," Gasparro reminisced. "This was during the Depression and a lot of people told me to stay in Europe, but I came home and after graduating in 1932, I opened my own studio."[4]

Though he did accept the few rare commissions which became available during those leans years of the 1930s, his principal income was derived from the carving of stone figures for Philadelphia-area cemeteries. Opportunity arose with the Works Progress Administration's Federal Art Project, which employed Frank Gasparro in 1937. Among his lasting works from this period is a statue of the young Benjamin Franklin, a fellow native of Philadelphia. Gasparro related in 1994 that this statue was then in a salvage yard, having been removed from its long-time home in a condemned local high school. "During the Bicentennial [1976] the city tried to buy the statue from the yard owner for $10,000, but he wouldn't sell."[5]

A career with the Mint

As the economy picked up following America's entry into World War II, the WPA and other relief projects were considered unnecessary and were quickly discontinued. Never called for military service, the 33-year-old sculptor found himself with a wife and young daughter to support. Unable to gain entry to the requisite union, his efforts to secure a satisfactory living through the creation of ornamental and architectural art were frustrated. In 1942 he sought to put his knowledge of relief carving to work in the creation of coins by applying at the United States Mint, whose Engraving Department was located at the Philadelphia facility. After meeting with Superintendent Edwin H. Dressel, Chief Engraver John R. Sinnock and Assistant Engraver Adam Pietz, Gasparro came away without a job but with some encouragement for possible future employment, should any openings occur.

Gasparro at work in his office at the Philadelphia Mint..
(Coin World)

"Three months later I prepared some reliefs that I thought would fit as coinage," Gasparro recalled in 1994. "With the excuse of showing off this new work, I went back to the Mint building and asked to see Mr. Dressel." He again received well wishes from Dressel and Sinnock, but there simply wasn't a job for him at that time. Another four months passed before Gasparro returned with the mission of submitting a job application. This seemed to be a simple exercise at the time, and he again left without the hoped-for employment. A telegram arrived one month later informing him that he was to report at 9 a.m. on December 6, 1942, though it said nothing more. Believing that he was being summoned simply to fill out another application, Gasparro disregarded the notice. "Then I got another telegram two days later admonishing me for not reporting. It said there was a job opening and in fact they created an opening specifically for me. I was the Mint's first junior engraver and I made $2300 a year."[6]

After being put through all the mundane activities required of the Engraving Department, Gasparro finally received his first real opportunity to prove his skill. This was the reverse of the Guatemalan 25-centavos coin, modeled by the young junior engraver. It depicted an elevation view of Guatemala's National Palace, and 900,000 pieces were coined at the Philadelphia Mint in 1943-44.[7] Frank Gasparro remembered this challenge some 50 years later: "When my work was reduced on the reducing lathe, the die made from my design had to strike the coin properly. I didn't get any second chances. Luckily, it came out OK."[8]

When Chief Engraver Sinnock died in 1947 he was succeeded in that role by Gilroy Roberts. Gasparro served under Roberts until the latter retired in 1964. This was shortly after the two men had combined their talents in the creation of the new John F. Kennedy Half Dollar, Gasparro modeling its reverse. With Roberts off to accept a position with the newly-created Franklin Mint, Gasparro found himself shouldering the demands of Chief Engraver, a position to which he was named by President Lyndon B. Johnson in 1965. "I was a little upset that Roberts quit because the position had a lot of responsibility," Gasparro related to interviewer Christopher Batio in 1994. "If there's an error on a die, you're in trouble. The buck stops right at the engraver's door and it happened from time to time." So intense was the pressure to perform during this period of the great nationwide coin shortage that Gasparro drove himself to learn every aspect of the die-making process. While taking machine-shop classes at night, the Chief Engraver "spent so much time in [the die shop] that the die-maker's union had me barred . . ."[9]

Frank Gasparro weathered the storm of the great coin shortage and the usual hassles that civil service employees endure when attempting to do their best work. One coin of his which never saw the light of day was a proposed two-cent piece. This work was commissioned during the cent shortage of 1973-74 which resulted in part from speculation over the rising price of copper. His model for this coin was quite simple; it depicted a large numeral 2 superimposed over a laurel wreath with the word CENTS below and the legends UNITED STATES OF AMERICA and E PLURIBUS UNUM above.

His greatest career frustration, however, came with the new mini-dollar proposed in 1976 and first issued in 1979. When asked to begin work on this coin, he pre-

Three modern issues also designed by Frank Gasparro: the Kennedy Half Dollar, the Eisenhower Dollar and the Susan B. Anthony Dollar

pared models dated 1977 that featured a bust of the goddess Liberty with flowing hair for its obverse and a soaring eagle over the rising sun for its reverse. The Liberty portrait was adapted from his medal for the 1969 convention of the American Numismatic Association in Philadelphia and featured a liberty cap arrangement similar to the United States cents of 1793-96.

These attractive models were widely hailed by numismatists, but the coin design process ran afoul of Congressional politics. With the Equal Rights Amendment to the U. S. Constitution stalled in committee, advocates of women's rights were demanding action and recognition of their cause. In a poor attempt at compromise, the allegorical goddess of Liberty was replaced with a real woman, suffragist Susan B. Anthony (1820-1906). Gasparro's soaring eagle was replaced with a scaled-down version of his Apollo 11 logo from the Eisenhower Dollar.

Gasparro's unused models for the mini-dollar.
(Numismatic News)

Unfinished business

"I want that design revived," Gasparro asserted in 1994, referring to his beautiful Flowing Hair Liberty. "I must have it revived. I don't know how I'll do it at my late age, but I really think that's important."[10]

Aside from such frustrating episodes, Frank Gasparro enjoyed a long, satisfying and prolific career with the U. S. Mint, spanning nearly 40 years until his retirement as Chief Engraver in 1981. Retirement has been merely a relative term for him, however, as he's performed a number of private commissions since that time, including several for numismatic firms. His medals executed on behalf of Bowers & Merena Galleries form a particularly fine and collectable series.

During his many years with the Mint, Gasparro's work included the reverses of the Lincoln Cent (1959) and the Kennedy Half Dollar (1964), both sides of the Eisenhower (1971) and Anthony (1979) Dollars, several foreign coins struck by the U. S. Mint and countless Mint medals. Today (1996) he lives in a suburb of Philadelphia, the only surviving artist to have designed United States coins that are still in production (the Lincoln Memorial Cent and the Kennedy Half). Summing up his career, Gasparro noted "For many years I got to do one of the greatest jobs in the world."[11]

Notes

[1] Christopher Batio, "Gasparro is known for his persistence," *Numismatic News*, December 27, 1994.

[2] Ibid.

[3] *The Numismatic Scrapbook Magazine*, March, 1959.

[4] Batio.

[5] Ibid.

[6] Ibid.

[7] Charles G. Altz & E. H. Barton, *Foreign Coins Struck at United States Mints*.

[8] Batio.

[9] Ibid.

[10] Ibid.

[11] Ibid.

Chapter 2

Design Changes

•

Pattern & Experimental Coins

•

The Infamous General Motors Roller Press

Design Changes

Any series of coins produced over a span of more than 80 years will inevitably undergo some changes. As the longest running series in the history of United States coinage, Lincoln Cents have been revised and retouched quite a number of times. Some of these changes are quite evident and well known to most collectors, yet others are of a more subtle nature. Both categories will be described here in detail so that the reader may gain an appreciation of just how far this coin type has evolved from the original edition of 1909.

An inauspicious beginning

In that same year, of course, (in fact during the very week of its debut) the Lincoln Cent underwent the first of many noticeable changes when the designer's initials V.D.B. were removed from the its reverse. How this change was effected so quickly was the subject of speculation at the time and has remained so ever since. The most practical solution to providing working dies without the initials would have been to grind them off of the working hubs (on which the letters were raised) and sink new working dies from them. But could this have been done quickly enough to supply the dozens of new dies needed for both the Philadelphia and San Francisco Mints?

Officially, the answer was "yes." In replying to that very question posed by pioneer Lincoln Cent collector Commodore W. C. Eaton in 1911, E. D. Hawkins, Chief Clerk of the San Francisco Mint, stated "Entirely new dies were made for the coinage of the non-initialed one-cent pieces of the Lincoln-head design of 1909."[2] While that might seem to settle the matter, the fact remains that a very few Lincoln Cents dated 1910 have reportedly been found with vestigial traces of the initials, suggesting that their reverse die (or dies) had been created for the 1909 V.D.B. cents and altered to remain in use. Were existing dies polished to remove the initials, or were these letters not fully removed from the working hubs used to sink additional dies? This question will never be answered to anyone's satisfaction, as all those persons who knew what really went on are long deceased.

What is known from examining the cents of 1909 is that the early coins had noticeably deeper rims on the reverse, a feature which led to their not stacking to the same height as an equivalent number of Indian Head Cents. This was correctly fairly quickly, perhaps at the same time as a new master hub was prepared without the offending initials.

Improving on perfection

As handsome as the early Lincoln Cents were, it's a tribute to the U. S. Mint's engraving staff that they sought to enhance the sharpness of Lincoln's portrait still further. For the cent coinage of 1915, the obverse master die was skillfully retouched to sharpen the fine lines of his hair. This becomes readily apparent when studying several coins dated 1915 and comparing them with the issues that preceded.

This desire to improve upon an already splendid model was taken a step further in 1916 when both the Lincoln Cent and the Indian Head/Buffalo Nickel were furnished with new obverse master hubs. For both coins the editions struck in 1916, particularly the proof pieces, represent the highwater mark for their respective types. As for the Lincoln Cent, never before or since has it looked so elegant. Sadly, due to record mintages which began that very year, the finely-detailed additions to Lincoln's portrait started to disappear as early as 1917, when the demand for so many dies prompted the new master hub to wear ever-so-slowly. It continued to erode for generations until finally being replaced in 1969. For whatever reason there does not appear to have been similar erosion in the reverse master hub, and there is no visible evidence that it was ever replaced in the 50 years that the Heraldic Wheat Ear type was struck.

Brenner's return

When the initials V.D.B. were removed from the Lincoln Cent's reverse in 1909 it was suggested that substituting a simple letter B would find less criticism. This notion, of course, did not sit well with Chief Engraver Charles Barber, whose own work was distinguished in a similar fashion. On the pretense that adding a B to the new cent would create an intolerable delay in the production of new dies, Barber simply omitted any reference to Victor D. Brenner on the coins.

It was almost certainly no mere coincidence that the restoration of Brenner's initials to his coin occurred in the year following Barber's death. The Chief Engravership was then considered a lifetime appointment, and Barber was still serving the Mint in this capacity when he died at the age of 76 in 1917. The incused letters V.D.B. were added to the obverse of the cent beginning with the coinage of 1918, placed discreetly at the truncation of Lincoln's bust. No announcement was made of this addition, and it was not until 1922 that Farran Zerbe alerted readers of *The Numismatist* to their

Major Obverse Hub Types

| 1909-15 | 1916-68 | 1969-73 | 1974 |

| 1974-82 | 1982-83 | 1984-91 | 1992-95 |

Major Reverse Hub Types

| 1909 | 1909-58 | 1959-72 |

| 1973 | 1974-85 | 1986-95 |

presence, remarking that "While this may be generally known, it was news to me."[2] The truth is that it was not generally known, as very few persons were collecting Lincoln Cents at that time. In fact, in the absence of proper catalogs or guide books, hobbyists periodically rediscovered these initials for several years afterward.

Being such a shallow feature and one located in a recurring wearpoint, Brenner's initials were often visible only on coins struck from the earliest states of the die, and many cents dated 1918 and later are lacking the initials altogether. This problem only worsened with the general deterioration of the obverse master hub, and in later years even the earliest states of the working dies had diminished initials.

Amazingly, no further changes were made to the Lincoln Cent master hubs for another 40 years! In this time, the obverse master became so badly eroded that Lincoln was rendered scarcely recognizable. The fine lines of his beard disappeared during the 1920s, while the deeper lines wore away during the 1950s. Though the reverse master hub remained fairly distinct, its finest lines were also lost during the record mintages of World War I and its immediate aftermath (1916-20).

While there was little said in the numismatic press about this deterioration, an oblique reference to it may be found in an entirely different context. Writing to Congressman Vestal about the progress of the designs for the Huguenot-Walloon Half Dollar of 1924, Chairman of the Federal Commission of Fine Arts Charles Moore remarked "By dint of many struggles our silver coinage, the nickel, and the penny, have been brought up to a fair standard as compared with other leading nations. The only questions now in relation to those coins are questions of quality of work in producing the coins themselves."[3]

The Memorial Reverse

When President Dwight D. Eisenhower approved the adoption of the Lincoln Memorial reverse in December of 1958 it signaled the retirement of Brenner's Heraldic Wheat Ears design. Despite 50 years of continuous use it had held up quite well, though it was clearly not as sharp as in the early days. This transition was the proper time to replace the obverse master hub, as well. Instead, this veteran continued to soldier on through 1968, grossly distorted with its mottos working their way into the rim. In contrast, the new reverse by Assistant Engraver Frank Gasparro looked very sharp for the first year or two. The tremendous mintages of the 1960s, however, took their toll, and the finest features of its design were soon lost.

Lincoln gets a facelift

No advance announcement heralded the new obverse master hub of 1969, yet collectors spotted it immediately. Though not a complete return to the cent of 1909, the new Lincoln obverse was a distinct improvement over its immediate predecessor. It lacked the fine hairlines which so characterized the early issues, yet the features of Lincoln's face, hair and beard were again recognizable. The lettering was improved by spacing it more broadly, particularly in the motto IN GOD WE TRUST. In addition, a gradual spreading action as the result of decades of compression of the master hub had caused the entire design area of the obverse to become oversize and its depth to increase, and this was addressed by restoring the cent's design to its original proportions. Once again the Lincoln Cent had distinct borders, and its lettering was clear of the rim. The new obverse was also greatly reduced in overall relief to a level slightly below that of 1909 and vastly below that of 1968 and the few years preceding.

Though the reverse master hub had lost its finest detail by this time, its deficiencies were not as apparent, and the original hub continued in use through 1972. The following year saw a new master hub in which all features save for one were identical to those of 1959, their sharpness restored. The one obvious change was the enlarging of Frank Gasparro's initials FG. This must not have met with universal approval, as the initials were reduced slightly in size beginning in 1974, leaving the cents of 1973 a one-year subtype.

The year 1974 also saw further improvements to the cent's obverse, as not one but two hub changes occurred. While similarly proportioned to the cents of 1969-73, those coined from the first new hub of 1974 reveal much greater detail in Lincoln's hair and a more recognizable shape to his ear. A second hub, introduced during the production year, was used for some of the cents from all three mints (though not for proofs) and for those dated 1975-82. Unfortunately, it was a step backward aesthetically. The cents from this hub are fairly similar to those of 1969-73 and lack the bold detail of those generated from the hub used in 1974 alone.

It's been suggested that this abrupt change was prompted by the Mint's experiments late in 1973 with a coinage of aluminum cents dated 1974, though no documentation exists to support this theory.[4] A more likely reason for this reversion was to move the truncation of Lincoln's bust away from the coin's border, as there is a broader gap on the coins from the second hub. The date was also moved away from the border for the second hub, and this has led to it being called a small date variety. This may make it a marketable item, but it is somewhat misleading.

A time of change

The joint obverse and reverse changes of 1974 ushered in a period of frequent upgrading to both master hubs which is still ongoing as this is written (1996). Since 1974 the tremendous annual mintages of cents has demanded that multiple master dies be produced and has accelerated the deterioration of the master hubs. This had led to much more frequent replacement of these hubs which, in the 1990s, has become an annual event.

The changes since 1974, because they've occurred so frequently, are often not as noticeable, and only the more keen-eyed collectors will spot them. For the record, the changes known to the author are recorded in the paragraphs that follow.

OBVERSE

The second master hub of 1974 wore rapidly and already showed some loss of sharpness as early as 1975. It was not until 1982, however, that it was retired. The small date cents of 1982 are a manifestation of this replacement hub, which also features a sharpened portrait, sharpened mottos and a lower overall relief.

Though otherwise unchanged, the obverse of 1982 was modified in 1984 by noticeably depressing the relief of Lincoln's upper arm. This served to extend die life and also facilitated metal flow into the motto E PLURIBUS UNUM on the reverse, a feature which had been subject to flat spots ever since the Memorial type was adopted. Collectors will recall this same problem occurring with the letter O of ONE on the Wheat Ear cents.

The obverse of 1984 continued in use through 1989,

though the Mint Director's *Annual Report* indicates that some obverse changes, evidently indistinguishable, were made to the cent in 1986 and again in 1987.[5] The new obverse master hub introduced in 1990 featured slightly lowered relief, sharpened mottos and an almost imperceptible enlargement of the initials V.D.B.

The cents of 1992 through 1995 are from similar master hubs which feature what seems to be a flaw. Lincoln's portrait bears a long and irregular line which runs from his hairline to his temple, looking something like a vein. The Mint has been silent on this odd feature, though as the first cents of 1996 trickle in this peculiar element has been removed. Beginning in 1994, the relief of Lincoln's upper arm was lowered yet again to the point where it now looks completely unnatural.

REVERSE

The Director's *Annual Report* claims a greater sharpness to the cents of 1978 as the result of a new master hub, but this is not readily discernible from examining the coins.[6] Only slightly more obvious is the new hub of 1986, with its sharpened lettering and somewhat broader borders. An additional change, though not evident from the coins, may have been made in 1987; the Director's *Annual Report* is not clear as to whether the reverse was upgraded at the same time as the obverse.[7]

Both sides were revised in 1990, though again the difference in the reverse is not readily discernible. All of these minor changes were made to extend die life and to further address problems with the letters STA in STATES and parts of the Latin motto not striking up fully. These

Mintmark Styles for the Denver Mint

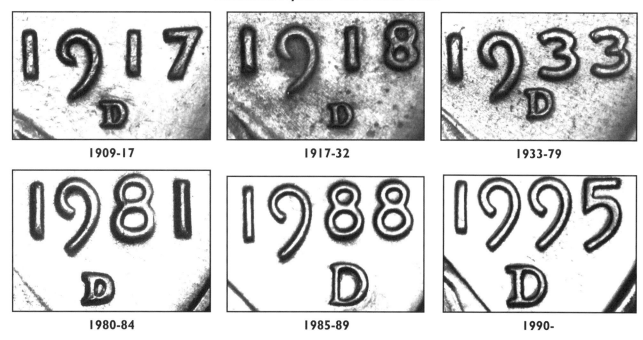

1909-17	1917-32	1933-79
1980-84	1985-89	1990-

steps seem to have been successful. Both elements are now routinely sharp, though at great sacrifice to the coin's sculptural qualities. The Lincoln Cent of the mid 1990s is so shallow and lacking in contour that it's virtually two-dimensional.

The most recent change to the Lincoln Cent's reverse has been the further lowering of relief in the Memorial's steps beginning in 1993. It may be presumed that this further extended the useful lifespan of working dies.

Mintmarks

Also undergoing many changes in the years since 1909 have been the mintmarks used to denote coins struck at the Denver and San Francisco Mints (cents struck at the Philadelphia Mint carry no mintmark). Mintmarks are actually applied at the Philadelphia Mint, where all dies are made (this will change beginning in 1996 when the Denver Mint opens its own die-making shop). Until quite recently, each working die intended for use at the Denver and San Francisco Mints received a tiny letter D or S which was punched into the die using

Mintmark Styles for the San Francisco Mint

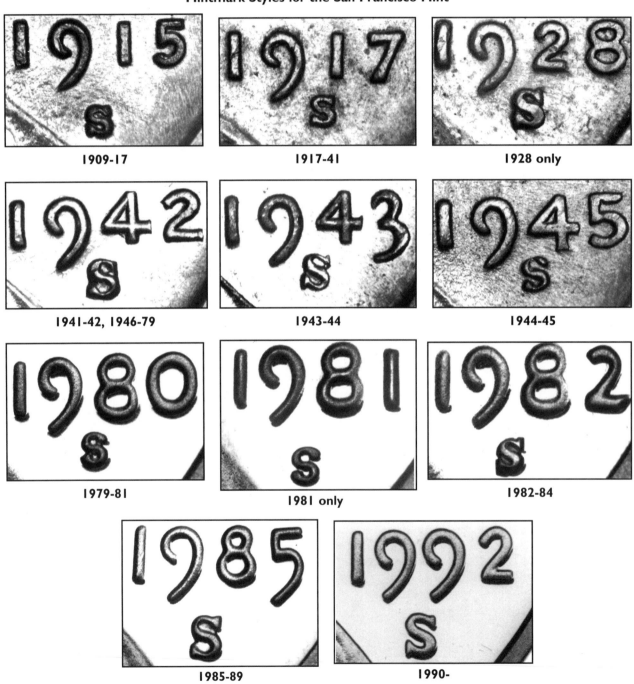

1909-17	1917-41	1928 only
1941-42, 1946-79	1943-44	1944-45
1979-81	1981 only	1982-84
1985-89	1990-	

small hand tools. The position and depth of punching varied from one working die to another, creating a multitude of minor varieties for each date, though these rarely carry any value.

More highly sought have been coins struck from dies in which the mintmark was punched repeatedly, these multiple impressions being slightly out of register. Known as repunched mintmarks (and abbreviated as "RPM"), such varieties are collectable, though the premium attached to them covers a broad range. Even more rare and desirable are repunchings which use the mintmarks of two different mints, such as a D punched over an S. These overmintmarks (abbreviated as "OMM") are few in number and do carry substantial premium values.

The styles of mintmarks used since the beginning of the Lincoln series have changed from time to time. Since these transitions are never mentioned in the Mint Director's *Annual Report*, it's not always known whether they occur as the result of an existing punch failing or merely as a cosmetic improvement. Sometimes, however, the reasons for replacing a mintmark punch are obvious, as in the years 1979-81. The S mintmark punch used in those years was replaced twice, and the deterioration of the old punches is evident from examining the coins.

Denver mintmarks

The first cents coined at the Denver Mint in 1911 bore a very small mintmark which was used through part of 1917. It was then replaced with one only slightly larger and of a different shape. This remained in use for cents through 1932 and for other coins as late as 1934. A new, much larger D mintmark appeared on the cents of 1933, and this punch (or duplicates of it) was used continually through 1979, becoming somewhat worn. A sharper mintmark of similar size was used for the cents of 1980-84, but it was replaced with a much larger one beginning in 1985. Commencing with the cent coinage of 1990 and continuing to this day, the D mintmark is engraved into each year's master die. Every D-Mint cent coined within a particular year will thus be identical as to the size and placement of its mintmark. This transition has eliminated the prospect of repunched mintmarks and overmintmarks, though it does provide for occasional die-doubling of the mintmark.

San Francisco mintmarks

Though the number of coins struck at this facility has almost always been smaller than the number issued from the Denver Mint, the shape of the S mintmark has caused it to wear out readily, necessitating more frequent replacement.

The first letter S of 1909, with its distinctive raised-dot flaw within the upper loop, lasted into 1917. It was then replaced with a slightly larger one of roughly similar configuration. Though this was used for every date from 1917 through 1941, a minority of the cents dated 1928 were struck from dies which featured a very large S with long serifs. 1941 was a transitional year, and while most of the S-Mint cents bearing that date have the mintmark introduced in 1917, a minority (perhaps 5-10%) are found with a new mintmark punch. This is much larger and has sharp serifs. It is found on all of the cents dated 1942-S, as well, though ones having the mintmark of 1943-44 may exist. The mintmark used in 1943 and 1944 has broader serifs and is more attractively proportioned. Why it was discontinued is not known. Also found on 1944-S cents is a new punch with rounded serifs or knobs, and this was used for the S-Mint cents of 1945, too.

The sharp-serif mintmark of 1941-42 returned with the cent coinage of 1946 and was used thereafter through 1955 (On coins from worn dies, this has been mistaken for the mintmark of 1944-45). When the S mintmark returned in 1968, it was of the same configuration, though it's not certain whether the very same punch was used. The original punch began to fill in around 1953, and it (or its successor of similar style) filled in almost completely during 1979. A new punch of similar size but with knobs in place of distinct serifs was used for a minority of the 1979 cents, those of 1980 and also the majority of 1981-S cents. This punch too began to fill, and it was replaced with another one lacking serifs, which was used on a minority of 1981 cents. The new mintmark used in 1982 had distinct serifs. It too began to deteriorate, yet it survived in use through 1984.

Beginning in 1985, the S mintmark was greatly enlarged and punched into a separate master die used exclusively for generating hubs and dies for proof coinage. Thus, there were no positional varieties within any given date, though the mintmark did vary slightly from one year to the next. Since 1990, however, the mintmarks for both the Denver and San Francisco Mints have been engraved into separate master dies, and there is now little or no variation from one date to the next.

Notes

[1] *The Numismatist*, April, 1911.

[2] Ibid, June, 1922.

[3] Don Taxay, *History of U. S. Commemorative Coinage.*

[4] Ken Potter, "Why did it happen?," *Coin World*, April 22, 1996.

[5] *Annual Report of the Director of the Mint*, 1986.

[6] Ibid, 1978.

[7] Ibid, 1986.

Pattern & Experimental Coins

The Lincoln Cent is one of a very few coin types from the years 1850-1916 which are not known in pattern form. Its contemporaries, the Indian Head/Buffalo five-cent piece and the three silver issues of 1916 are all known in pattern form, though extremely rare. There were at one time, however, 13 pattern cents dated 1909, but these were reportedly all destroyed at the Mint within weeks of their manufacture.

The first pattern strikings of Victor D. Brenner's cent design were made on May 12, 1909. The dies for them were sunk by Charles E. Barber from hub reductions furnished by Brenner. At this stage in its development the cent still lacked the motto IN GOD WE TRUST, but Brenner's name was already abbreviated with the letters V.D.B. The bust of Lincoln was larger than that seen on the final version, and it extended nearly rim to rim. Five specimens were struck as proofs from these dies, three of them being furnished to Philadelphia Mint Superintendent John H. Landis and the remaining two to U. S. Mint Director Frank A. Leach.[1]

Leach disapproved these patterns because the large bust of Lincoln would impair striking quality and die life. Barber then made a new obverse hub with the portrait reduced in size and the motto added above Lincoln's head. A total of eight specimens were struck as proofs from these dies, and there's no reason to believe that the resulting coins were any different from the 1909 V.D.B. proofs sold to collectors some months later. Even so, all 13 pattern strikings were destroyed by Barber and Landis on May 27, 1909 once this second edition was approved by Leach.[2]

Plastic cent trial dated 1942. The obverse die for this pattern was adapted from the Colombian minor coinage struck at various U.S. Mints from 1920 through 1947. (Auctions by Bowers & Merena)

Wartime predicament

Even before the United States entered World War II in December of 1941, there were reports of copper shortages as the result of accelerated use of that metal in defense industries. Early the following year, an item appeared in *The Numismatic Scrapbook Magazine* which summed up the situation:

It is reported that Treasury officials are giving serious considerations to a plan to gather in all the cents and nickels to help augment the supply of copper and other metals vital in many defense materials. Long-range plans envisaged by Treasury and Mint officials call for the use of some other metal than copper for coins for the duration.

The metal that would be used in place of copper and nickel has not been revealed. It is hard to think of any of the metal generally used for minor coinage throughout the world that is not on the critical list, copper, tin, zinc, brass, aluminum, et. Silver half dimes might be coined again— which would solve the 5-cent piece problem, although it might be hard on the juke box trade.[3]

Though there was never any general recall of the existing coins, plans were made to find suitable substitutes. Using a private contractor, the Mint had several tests made in the late Summer and Fall of 1942 in which various formulas of plastic and glass were employed as metal substitutes. These were stuck between specials dies prepared for that purpose. Adapting the obverse design of the Colombian minor pieces (which had been coined at the Philadelphia and Denver Mints at various times during the 1920s, '30s and '40s) the Mint retained the portrait bust of Liberty while replacing the existing legends with the words LIBERTY and JUSTICE. The date 1942 appeared below. For the reverse of these trial pieces the Mint created a simple heraldic wreath design enclosing the legend UNITED STATES MINT.

The tests were conducted by the Durez Chemical and Plastic Corporation of North Tonawanda, New York. The dies fabricated by the Philadelphia Mint arrived at Durez around September 16, 1942. A total of twelve synthetic compounds were tested, and these consisted of various combinations of powdered minerals, cotton flock and bonding resin. The sample tokens (for they can't really be called coins) were tested for hardness, weight and resilience. Being nonferrous, there was no point in testing their magnetic properties. The data from these tests does not appear to have survived, but numismatist Robert H. Lloyd prepared a table in 1967 giving the properties he'd observed for seven varieties:[4]

Specimen	Thickness	Weight	Color	Appearance
1	.069"	8 grains	light sand	shiny
2	.071"	25 grains	dark sand	dull
3	.092"	10 grains	dark red brown	high gloss
4	.104"	38 grains	gun metal [blue]	dull
5	.108"	41 grains	gun metal [blue]	granular face
6	.126"	43 grains	gun metal [blue]	smooth
7	.154"	57 grains	gun metal [blue]	shiny

Since the normal cent of 1942 weighs 48 grains, most of these proposed substitutes would have been noticeably lighter. This fact was of little consequence, since most of the plastic substitutes apparently failed the brittleness test. When found today they are usually in two pieces. Interviewed a quarter century after the tests were conducted, a chemist for Durez who was present during 1942 expanded on the results:

> Plastic coins were of little value because they were too brittle, too soft and would not meet bend specifications. Present day coin machine usage would eliminate our plastic from consideration because it would not have the required magnetic qualities.[5]

Robert H. Lloyd, one of the great chroniclers of numismatic developments during the 1920s and the next several decades and himself a resident of North Tonawanda, actually encountered one of the experimental plastic coins in 'circulation' during 1942:

> One Sunday in the late Fall of 1942 the author was observing the counting of a church-school offering on the desk of the secretary, when the latter made an exclamation about plastic coins, and promptly snapped the cent he held in his fingers in two pieces, flinging them into the waste basket.[6]

After tracing the synthetic cent to its place of origin, Lloyd wrote to Mint Director Nellie Tayloe Ross on March 24, 1943 seeking more information about the piece. He received the following reply dated April 20:

> During the latter part of 1942 the Mint experimented extensively in metals, plastic and glass, in an effort to substitute other than strategic materials in the one-cent piece. The experiments with plastics were discontinued after advice was received from the War Production Board that the supply of the only types of plastic materials found to be adaptable to coinage purposes would be required for other uses in the war effort.
>
> Sample one-cent coins were struck in plastic at only one plant, in the presence of two Mint representatives, and all sample coins were destroyed. I assure you, therefore, that any sample one-cent coins in existence are counterfeit.[7]

This second paragraph reveals the usual attempt by government officials to close the books on anything controversial or potentially embarrassing, and Lloyd knew at the time that there were indeed at least a few plastic cents to be found in the possession of Durez employees and their families. While most were of the nonsense design adapted from the Colombian coin, there appear to have been at least a few surviving specimens from actual cent dies dated 1942.

Employees of Durez also revealed to Lloyd that no Mint officials were present during the tests, though they may have met with the company's managers at various times. He also learned that a contingency plan called for the government to take over two additional plants in the region should the plastic cent go into full-scale production. These were the Waterbury Button Company in Connecticut and the Watertown Plastics Corporation in New York State, though there's no evidence that either company was actually engaged at any time.[8]

The experimental coins which still exist include mostly plastic examples of the Colombian type, these usually broken into two pieces, though a few are known in metal as well. It's believed that all of the metal specimens were struck within the Philadelphia Mint. Far more rare and somewhat controversial as regards their genuineness are the off-metal experiments made in the form of actual Lincoln Cents. These are very rarely offered, though three examples turned up in a Stack's auction of September 21-22, 1994. Lot 261 was described as "About Uncirculated. Aluminum or other white-metal alloy copper plate. 2.7mm thick, 19.2mm diameter planchet. 59.7 grains (3.87 grams). Regular Lincoln design, struck slightly off center with very high wire rims that show silver under-metal where contact has disturbed the plating. Edge shows dark coating like paint or India ink." Lot 262 was described as "About Uncirculated. Copper-aluminum alloy, 19mm diameter, 2.2mm thick, 56.7 grains (3.67 grams). Normal Lincoln design on thick planchet showing coated edge, broad borders. Silver-olive color suggesting a low-copper wartime experimental alloy." Finally, Lot 263 reads "Extremely Fine. Brass alloy, 19mm diameter, 2.6mm thick. 45.4 grains (2.94 grams as opposed to normal 3.11 for the Lincoln Cent). Believed to be experimental strike with greatly reduced Copper content."

Though it was clearly not intended that such trial coins and tokens find their way into the hands of collectors, the Treasury Department's Secret Service has looked the other way when these pieces trade hands. It therefore appears reasonably safe to buy and sell such rare items publicly, though the winds of Federal policy have been known to shift without warning.

As Mint Director Ross indicated in her letter above, the experiments with plastic were abandoned by the end of 1942, and another solution was sought. Among the metals tested within the Philadelphia Mint was a low-carbon steel with zinc plating, and this was its primary candidate for replacing the existing bronze alloy.

Legislation which permitted an alteration of the cent's composition (while not specifying how it was to be altered) was passed on December 18, 1942 as Public Law 77-518.[9]

There was some delay in securing enough planchets, and the new zinc-coated steel cents went into production at the Philadelphia Mint on February 23, 1943. The Denver and San Francisco Mints began striking the new cents the following month.[10] As detailed quite fully in this book's history of the Lincoln Cent, the steel cents proved a failure on a number of counts, including their appearance and magnetic qualities. Faced with the seeming impossibility of securing a replacement for the cent which both satisfied its users and did not interfere with wartime materials shortages, the Mint had no choice but to resume production of the conventional alloy in 1944, though the small amount of tin used previously was eliminated for the duration. This was replaced beginning in 1947, but the success of the 1944-46 tinless cents proved that its inclusion served no purpose, and tin was dropped from the cent by law in 1962.

Experimental cent struck in aluminum bronze (copper and aluminum). This coin was Lot 262 in Stack's 9-21/22-94 sale. (Stack's)

The aluminum cents and their kin

No serious consideration was given to changing the composition of the Lincoln Cent after 1944, aside from the perfunctory elimination of tin in 1962. The value and availability of copper ceased to be an issue until 1973 when the price of that metal rose to alarming heights. Though the expense of recovering copper from cents still exceeded the rewards, the mere fact that it would soon cost the mints more than one cent to coin these pieces required the immediate attention of Congress. On December 7, 1973 Treasury Secretary George P. Schultz submitted to President Richard M. Nixon a draft bill authorizing a change in the composition of the cent, though no specific changes were included.[11]

The Philadelphia Mint had already struck a quite a number of 1974-dated cents back on October 17, 1973 utilizing aluminum as the proposed substitute metal. On the day after this initial press run Deputy Treasury Secretary William Simon was furnished with two samples of the experimental cents so that he could be pre-

The famous aluminum cent of 1974
(Smithsonian Institution, National Numismatic Collection)

pared when discussing the situation with Secretary Schultz. Anticipating a changeover to aluminum, Schultz directed the Philadelphia Mint to strike a total of 1,441,039 cents in this metal between October 17, 1973 and March 29, 1974. To test whether mass production of the new coins could be sustained the Philadelphia Mint performed a 40-hour continuous press run commencing March 23. Just days later, on April 2, 1974, all but 59 of these cents were destroyed.[12]

Between April 12 and May 30, some 130,128 additional cents were coined in aluminum. By June 4, 1974, all but 67 had been destroyed. Dr. Alan Goldman of the Mint's Office of Technology retained two examples for reference, while the remaining pieces were locked within the Mint's safe. On May 28 the Philadelphia Mint struck 58 pieces in aluminum from dies dated 1975 and another eight pieces two days later. All were reportedly melted sometime during 1974.[13]

A U. S. Mint internal audit memo from August 18, 1976 reported that 14 examples of the 1974-dated aluminum cents were unaccounted for from among the ones distributed to parties concerned with the proposed change to aluminum. The missing coins included 11 pieces struck December 5, 1973, two coined February 7, 1974 and one from the April 18, 1974 press run. Also outstanding were two of the 1975-dated aluminum cents coined May 28, 1974. A total of 14 aluminum cents had been loaned to members of Congress serving on committees that dealt with coinage and banking issues,[14] but only a few of these were returned to the Mint for destruction when the crisis passed. Several of those that remained outstanding are still missing today. Estimates of the number still unaccounted for range from 13 (Walter Breen)[15] to perhaps eight to 25 (Q. David Bowers).[16] George E. Hunter, the Mint's Assistant Director for Process and Quality Control, asserted that just 11 pieces remained outstanding as of July 11, 1990.[17]

In a February 25, 1974 memo, the Mint's auditor J. A. Morgan addressed the difficulty of maintaining complete control over the coins in a production environment. Writing to William Humbert of the Mint's Internal Audit Staff, Morgan reported the following:

Accounting for coins struck in the Pressroom, even under optimum conditions, is impossible. Counters on the coin presses are inaccurate and there are too many areas where coins can be lost, either in the machinery itself or in the surrounding areas.

Experimental cent struck in bronze-clad steel (Coin World)

After examining the areas where the aluminum strip would be blanked and the coins struck, and discussing the situation with Mr. Frank Breen [the Pressroom Foreman], I concluded that production of a large number of aluminum pennies in the Pressroom would make it probable that some aluminum coins would leave the Mint either by accident or intent.[18]

A single example of the 1974-dated issue was donated to the Smithsonian Institution by a Congressional staff member, and this specimen is illustrated here. None of the outstanding examples have ever been offered for public sale, and it's anticipated that any such offering would be subject to confiscation by agents of the U. S. Secret Service.

One interesting speculation about the aluminum cents concerns the hubs employed to make their dies. The single example known (the Smithsonian coin) exhibits the obverse hub style adopted at the beginning of 1974 for circulating and proof cents. Is it possible that the 1975-dated cents coined in May of 1974 used the second obverse hub type of 1974, which appeared on circulating cents later in 1974 and continued in use as late as 1982? The timing for this transition is about right, given the ratio of old-style cents dated 1974 to those of the newer style, and it could account for the odd step of employing two distinctive obverse master hubs within a single calender year's production. Did the Mint anticipate that the revised master hub would work better with aluminum than the existing one?

Another by-product of the cent crisis of 1973 surfaced in 1994. It was a single specimen dated 1974 but struck on a magnetic planchet of bronze-clad steel. This was one of three compositions tested in 1973, the first being aluminum as described above. Also struck were trial pieces of .700 copper and .300 zinc, as well as ones having two outside layers of .900 copper and .100 zinc bonded to an inner core of low-carbon steel. The coin which surfaced some 20 years later was of the latter composition, and its anonymous owner claimed to have a total of five examples in his possession.[19]

There were already published accounts of the Mint's experiments with these various alloys, but what made this discovery so remarkable is that this new coin was of the regular Lincoln Cent design. The Treasury Department's accounts of its experiments state specifically that only the aluminum cents utilized actual coin dies, while the other metals were tested exclusively with "nonsense" dies having unintelligible legends. These were created merely to test the approximate size and relief of the Lincoln Cent. The publication *Alternative Materials for One-Cent Coinage,* issued in December of 1973, is quite clear on the matter:

The nonsense dies were designed to simulate the actual penny dies with regard to relief and location of images and lettering. In this way, coining characteristics of the alloys could be compared relative to one another without creating a large number of potentially valuable numismatic oddities . . . Finally, 1974 cent dies were used to strike a carefully controlled number of aluminum alloy coins."[20]

Of the three alloys tested as possible cent replacements all were rated by the Mint in a total of eight categories. Among these were "general public acceptability" and "coin-machine acceptability," the two in which the bronze-clad steel cent rated more highly than its aluminum competitor. What ultimately doomed the steel cent was its poor performance in the category of "ease of coin fabrication," as it proved costly both in the number of steps required and in reduced die-life. Since the goal in finding a substitute for the existing cent composition was to address a shortage of one-cent pieces, any delay in the fabrication of metal strip or increase in the frequency of die replacement was totally unacceptable. It was thus that the otherwise less desirable aluminum cent won out over bronze-clad steel.

The bronze-clad steel cent which surfaced in 1994 was submitted to *Coin World* for examination and publication. It proved to weigh 2.77 grams and possess a specific gravity of 7.9142. Both obverse and reverse were identical to that of a normal cent in appearance and feel, but the coin's edge was quite distinctive. As in 1943, the metal strip from which this steel cent's planchet was cut was evidently plated before going through the planchet cutter, exposing its steel core on the edge. The cent also proved to be magnetic, confirming its ferrous nature. Since there were no such planchets being used to strike foreign coins at the U. S. Mints during that time period, the possibility of a simple off-metal error was virtually eliminated.

The individual who furnished this specimen to *Coin*

World revealed that the Mint had indeed produced large numbers of the bronze-clad steel cents dated 1974 and had later brought them to the Alan Wood Steel Company in Pennsylvania for destruction when the experiment was concluded. Though not so stated, it's quite possible that this same company furnished the metal strip or even finished planchets. It was claimed that "at least 40 bags of the experimental pieces—200,000 pieces or more—were destroyed." The mystery informant continued his tale, as related by William T. Gibbs:

> According to the source, the bags of experimental cents were shoved down a chute from the third floor to a basic oxygen furnace on the second floor. The source said the cents were under heavy guard by five Mint guards.
>
> As the bags were being placed onto a lift to be transported to the chute, one bag fell to the floor and burst open, scattering the experimental pieces across the floor. The Mint guards made the employees move away from the spilled cents as they swept them up for melting.
>
> According to the source, as the cents from the burst bag poured down the chute, a gust of wind blowing through the plant picked up 10-12 pieces and blew them onto the floor of the furnace, which had not yet gone into operation. The five pieces possessed by the source came from those dozen or so survivors. Another three pieces may exist in burnt condition.[21]

Shortly after the *Coin World* story broke, the Mint's Michael White confirmed that such pieces were indeed struck, though he asserted that no records had been kept of their manufacture or subsequent destruction. In a statement issued August 15, 1994 he also revealed that two examples were then being retained by the Mint for future reference.[22] As for the status of those examples held by individuals, it's essentially the same as for the aluminum cents: Any coins which may be offered publicly are subject to seizure by the Secret Service. The Mint's chief legal counsel, Kenneth B. Gubin, confirmed this position in a letter to *Coin World* dated September 9, 1994:

> The Mint's policy regarding the 1973-dated [sic] aluminum one-cent pieces remains unchanged; since these pieces were experimental and never issued by the Mint, any still outstanding are considered property of the U. S. Government and may not be circulated, sold or held in collections. If they were to appear in the hands of the public, they are, and will continue to be, subject to confiscation by the U. S. Secret Service as no individual may acquire valid title to them. This policy also applies to other similar experimental pieces, including the experimental 1974 bronze-clad steel Lincoln cents.[23]

1982 cent trials

In anticipation that another crisis over the bronze cent could arise in the future, Congress passed Public Law 93-441 on October 11, 1974. This permitted the Treasury Secretary to authorize a change in the cent's composition without additional Congressional action. The need to implement this authority didn't appear again until 1981, when it was determined that the price of copper had risen to the level at which some threat to the coin supply existed. Accordingly, a new cent of the same Lincoln Memorial type was gradually phased in during 1981-82, though all of those coined from the new composition were dated 1982. An inner core of .992 zinc and .008 copper was plated with pure copper, resulting in a cent which was .975 zinc and .025 copper overall and weighed 39.581 grains.[24]

There was no suggestion that trial pieces may have been created at that time until an unusual piece surfaced in 1996. Appearing with a number of other coins and medals consigned to Auctions by Bowers and Merena by former Mint Director Donna Pope (1981-91), this piece was listed as Lot 2286 in that company's sale of June 24-25, 1996. The cataloger described it as "Apparently an experimental issue struck on a planchet that appears to have been nickel-plated prior to striking, although documentation of this does not survive." This coin weighed 39.5 grains, which is normal for a copper-plated zinc cent. The auction house cautioned prospective bidders that both the coin's apparent nature and right of title were uncertain, and before the sale took place this specimen was withdrawn. Submitted to the U. S. Mint for examination, it proved to be an ordinary zinc cent that was evidently stripped of its copper plating and then plated with nickel outside of the Mint.[25] There have been no genuine pattern strikings or test pieces discovered from the 1981-82 transitional period.

Notes

[1] National Archives, Bureau of the Mint, Records Group 104.
[2] Ibid.
[3] *The Numismatic Scrapbook Magazine*, January, 1942.
[4] Robert H. Lloyd, "Our War Time 'Plastic' Cent," *The Numismatic Scrapbook Magazine*, August, 1967.
[5] Ibid.
[6] Ibid.
[7] Ibid.
[8] Ibid.
[9] Ted Schwarz, "Steel Cent Wins over Plastic in 1943," *The Numismatic Scrapbook Magazine*, April, 1974.
[10] *The Numismatic Scrapbook Magazine*, March, 1943.
[11] Ibid., May, 1974.
[12] Paul Gilkes, "The Mint had a secret," *Coin World*, July 1, 1996.
[13] Ibid.
[14] Ibid.
[15] Walter Breen, *Walter Breen's Complete Encyclopedia of United States and Colonial Coins.*
[16] Q. David Bowers, "Question & Answer Forum," *Rare Coin Review*, No. 108.
[17] Gilkes.
[18] Ibid.
[19] William T. Gibbs, "1974 Lincoln cent experimental piece, bronze-clad steel, surfaces," *Coin World*, July 4, 1994.
[20] Ibid.
[21] Ibid.
[22] William T. Gibbs, "Mint confirms existence of 1974 bronze-clad steel cents," *Coin World*, September 5, 1994.
[23] Beth Deisher, "Experimental pieces at risk," *Coin World*, September 26, 1994.
[24] P. Bradley Reed, Editor, *Coin World Almanac.*
[25] *Numismatic News*, June 18, 1996.

The Infamous General Motors Roller Press

One of the more amusing tales in the long Lincoln Cent saga is the U. S. Mint's ill-fated experiment using a roller press to coin cents during the 1960s. A joint venture in cooperation with General Motors, the roller press was very clever in design and would have been tremendously productive in daily use were it not a monster to maintain.

The crippling coin shortage of 1963-65 was felt most heavily with respect to cents. Even working around the clock the Philadelphia and Denver Mints simply could not produce enough coins to replace those which were being withdrawn daily from banks. The idea which led to the development of the roller press was an outgrowth of this shortage, and it emerged from a most unlikely meeting of minds. The 1964 motion picture release *Goldfinger* centered around a plot to steal the United States gold reserve from its storage facility at Fort Knox, Kentucky. Alarmed by the mere suggestion that such a thing was possible, Treasury Department officials asked for and received a private viewing of the unreleased film in late 1963 to make certain that it included no security violations. A number of top executives from General Motors were invited to join in this viewing for no other reason than that they were business acquaintances of the Treasury officials. Following the showing of the film, conversation drifted toward the subject of the ongoing coin shortage which was causing the Treasury Department such fits. Louis C. Goad, GM's Executive Vice-President for manufacturing,[1] proposed that his company could devise a coin press having a capacity of 10,000 coins per minute. Intrigued by this prospect, the Mint and GM ultimately contracted to create a small-scale prototype of such a machine.[2]

From the outset it was intended that the roller press be designed to coin cents, as these were the coins needed in the greatest numbers. Though the Mint provided some funding, all of the engineering and construction work was undertaken by GM's Manufacturing Development Staff at the General Motors Technical Center in Warren, Michigan. The designer of both the

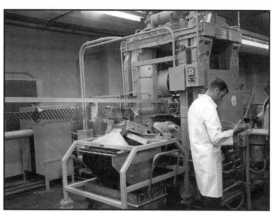

The General Motors roller press. (Numismatic News)

prototype and production presses was Chief Engineer Ronald A. Featherstone.[3]

The roller press worked in a simple but ingenious manner. Three cylinders or rollers were placed on a horizontal axis, stacked one atop the other. A sheet of coinage strip was fed between the top and middle rollers, these acting as a blanking press to produce planchets. The top roller had protruding from its surface a series of punch dies, and these pushed out metal planchets from the strip into matching receptacles on the middle roller. (The raised rim needed for a finished coin was formed during this same operation, rather than in a subsequent operation as is the case with conventional coining.) The punched out planchets were seated within the receptacles on the middle roller, each of which also contained an obverse coin die. As the middle roller continued to turn, it brought the planchets around to face a series of dies for the reverse of the coins, these being mounted on the lowermost roller. As each die pair met, a complete coin was formed. The middle roller, now holding in each die receptacle a struck coin, was linked with an eccentric cam which caused the obverse dies to thrust outward and eject the coins. These then fell into a waiting hopper.[4]

The results of these experiments with the small prototype press, conducted from June of 1964 through the Fall of 1965, were sufficiently promising that the Mint contracted with General Motors to build a full-scale, mass-production model. In a contract signed July 25, 1965, GM was to receive $500,000 for building the press.[5] A demonstration of its press in action at the Tech Center was performed for Mint officials on November 2, 1965. This confirmed each party's faith in the project's viability, and GM was directed to proceed with construction.[6]

The production model of the press actually consisted of two presses in tandem. This was done to maximize the usage of the metal strip, as a single press left too much unused metal between the punched holes. Completed sometime toward the end of 1966 or early 1967, the press was used for extensive tests at the GM

Tech Center. Early in 1968 it was relocated to the new Philadelphia Mint, then still under construction. (Some accounts give the date as December, 1968, but it's believed that this represents a final delivery date following trials). Subsequent to further onsite tests of the press, an actual demonstration was staged for the media during the Mint's dedication ceremony on August 14, 1969.[7]

Though strictly speaking the press did work as planned, producing cents at an unprecedented rate, the maintenance required to keep it operating proved its downfall. The chain was only as strong as its weakest link, and each time a die cracked or became worn the entire process had to be shut down. Of course, this idled all of the other dies while the replacement die was being fitted. The unusual motion of the roller-mounted dies apparently created a torque effect which accelerated their failure rate, and this led to a lesser number of strikes being achieved with each die than was the norm for a conventional coin press. Finally, both the press and its dies required frequent lubrication, and the squirting or leaking oil dripped onto the metal strip as it was fed into the press. In some cases the heat of the press caused the oil to vaporize and then condense as rain droplets. These conditions produced a certain percentage of coins having indistinct, slightly rippled surfaces which were considered unsatisfactory for circulation.[8]

A total of about 50 individuals worked on the development of the roller press between 1964 and 1968, when it left GM for installation at the Philadelphia Mint. Many of these employees were assigned during 1967-68 in an

This was the first version of the roller press cent, coined in June of 1964. The letters 'GM' stand for General Motors, 'MD' for Manufacturing Development. Two examples are known; this one weighs 64.2 grains and is .801 inch in diameter. Like all of the GM trials illustrated, its dies are in medal alignment, meaning that the coin is turned on its vertical axis. (Coin World)

The second trial occurred in August of 1964 and used a retired and partially mutilated cent die in combination with a die reading MANUFACTURING DEVELOPMENT STAFF. This piece weighs 61.6 grains and is .790 inch in diameter. (Coin World)

The third trial of the roller press occurred in January of 1965. It used another partially effaced Lincoln Cent obverse die and the same reverse die. Measuring 0.813 inch in diameter, this piece weighs 72.1 grains (a normal cent of the time weighed 48 grains). The additional weight resulted from extra thickness to prevent these pieces from being mistaken for actual cents. (Coin World)

attempt to salvage GM's investment in what was proving to be a big lemon. Among the figures brought in for damage control were Chief Designer Earl T. Barringer and Assistant Chief Designer Carl C. Christensen.[9] Despite their best efforts, no satisfactory solution appeared. Though the coin shortage had long since passed, the United States Mint continued to operate the roller press on a test basis for a year or more afterward, finally conceding defeat in a press release dated December 24, 1969. Millions of dollars had been spent by both GM and the Mint, and they cancelled further development in a mutual decision.

Assistant Treasury Secretary Eugene T. Rossides confessed: "The short die tool life and other mechanical problems make the coin roller uneconomical in comparison with the four-strike press which the Mint developed during the coin shortage and during the development of the coin roller."[10] The official decision to abandon the roller press came many months after several numismatic figures had already predicted its demise, raising the issue of why the Mint continued to spend good money after bad. It was suggested that its sole purpose was to avoid embarrassment at the new Philadelphia Mint's dedication ceremony by keeping up appearances until after that date.

A numismatic legacy

Though the roller press is no more, there survive a number of tangible reminders of this promising experiment. The Philadelphia Mint furnished all of the dies used by GM for both its small prototype and final production presses. To avoid the unwise (and illegal) use of actual coin dies outside of a U. S. Mint facility, experimental dies were prepared by Frank Gasparro, who was promoted to Chief Engraver during the course of these tests. The first trials of the small press were conducted in June of 1964 using very simple dies which simulated the approximate size of a cent but featured only the letters GM on the obverse and MD on the reverse. These stood for "General Motors" and "Manufacturing Development." An unknown quantity of these pieces were struck in a copper or bronze composition. Test coins of a second variety were struck in August of 1964 from a different pair of designs. Regular Lincoln Cent obverse dies were altered by removing all inscriptions and sandblasting their faces to blur the portrait of Lincoln. These were mated to dies reading MANUFAC-

The fourth trial of the roller press produced this variety weighing 3.52 grams and having a diameter of 0.807 inches. (Ken Potter)

The final trial of the roller press was the most sophisticated. This specimen and the other piece known are both struck on normal cent planchets weighing 3.11 grams and having a diameter of 0.748 inches. (Ken Potter)

TURING DEVELOPMENT STAFF. A third variety, produced in January of 1965, again featured partially defaced Lincoln Cent obverse dies mated to reverse dies similar to that used for the second variety but with the lettering placed further from the border. A final version features a similar obverse but has a more sophisticated reverse. The word STAFF appears within a rectangular cartouche. It's believed that this variety was the last one coined from the prototype press sometime in the Summer or Fall of 1965.[11] This variety is listed as Number 4055 in Andrew Pollock III's book *United States Patterns and Related Issues*. All of the above test pieces were slightly larger than actual cents. In the words of a GM Tech Center employee: "They were deliberately made larger than a Lincoln cent, and designed so they could never be mistaken for or used as circulating coins. We needed something to strike to see if the machine would work."[12]

When the production model of the tandem roller press was completed, further tests were made using additional dies supplied by the U. S. Mint and engraved by Frank Gasparro. The obverse dies feature a left-facing bust of a young woman surrounded by letters which approximate the positions of the legends found on the Lincoln Cent; seemingly non-sensical, these legends are coded to identify the individual dies. The reverse dies feature a wreath enclosing additional nonsense legends which similarly served to identify the particular die from which a test coin was struck. Unlike the earlier test pieces, the ones with the female head (Pollock-4060) were struck from planchets of the same size and weight as circulating cents. A former GM employee reported that "This coin was scientifically designed to produce the same amount of metal movement required to strike a Lincoln cent. It was an attempt to see if the roller press could strike a Lincoln cent."[13] It's believed that these pieces were produced in 1967 or early 1968 before the roller press was relocated to the Philadelphia Mint.

The Mint itself actually struck real cents with the roller press during 1969 and possibly as early as 1968. There's nothing to distinguish these cents from ones struck by conventional presses, though GM engineers reported that roller press coins have uniformly thick edges, while conventional cents have edges that vary in thickness with respect to the height of design elements near the borders.[14] This was one advantage of the roller press over conventional presses, but it may have also contributed to the problem of premature die failure which ultimately doomed this machine. The exact fate of the cents coined from the roller press is uncertain, and none were specifically identified as such by the Mint.

All of the experimental test coins described above are quite rare, though it's likely that more will turn up in the hands of former GM employees now retired or their descendants. Many of the administrative and engineering personnel who worked on the roller press project are now deceased, but their heirs may have such 'tokens' lying about the house without any knowledge of their potential value to numismatists.

Notes

[1] Eric M. Larson, letter to the author, September 23, 1995.

[2] Larson, "'Goldfinger' preview for Treasury officials gives birth to Mint, General Motors roller press testing," *Coin World,* May 29, 1995.

[3] Larson, September 23, 1995.

[4] Ibid.

[5] *Coin World,* April 22, 1970.

[6] Eric von Klinger, *Coins,* May, 1995.

[7] Eric M. Larson, "GM-Mint roller press experimental pieces unique bit of American numismatic history," *Coin World,* June 5, 1995.

[8] Ibid.

[9] Larson, September 23, 1995.

[10] "Treasury Shelves 'Greatest Development'," *The Numismatic Scrapbook Magazine,* February, 1970.

[11] Larson, *Coin World,* June 5, 1995.

[12] Larson, *Coin World,* May 29, 1995.

[13] Larson, *Coin World,* June 5, 1995.

[14] Ibid.

Chapter 3

COLLECTING LINCOLN CENTS

It almost seems as though the Lincoln Cent series was initiated for the sole purpose of giving Americans a reason to collect coins. Its debut nearly coincided with the first striking of cents by the Denver and San Francisco Mints, and this led quickly to a rich array of date-and-mint combinations that could be obtained at very little expense. The cent's low value meant also that its frequent use was universal, even a child being exposed to the Lincoln coins on a regular basis. The attention which this type received at its inception as the first circulating coin to bear a portrait of a real person prompted many people to look at coins in an entirely different light. The widespread hoarding of the new "pennies," which was aggravated by rumors of their imminent recall, led to the saving of many thousands of 1909-dated Lincolns in uncirculated condition. But when this initial excitement died down, just who was still interested in collecting additional specimens?

The early years

Apparently, there were very few who deemed the subsequent issues worthy of preservation in their coin cabinets. The collecting of any cents other than the large copper pieces of 1793-1857 was then still in its infancy. There were of course those who sought to complete a run of proof small cents from 1857 onward, but there was little interest in acquiring the currency strikes, and the few branch mint issues were similarly ignored. As the matte and satin proofs of the Lincoln type proved disappointing to collectors familiar with the brilliant proofs of the Indian Head type, the collecting of this series in general was not immediately popular.

There may have indeed been collectors saving uncirculated examples of each new issue during the early years of the Lincoln series, but the only individual to publicly acknowledge this activity was one Commodore W. C. Eaton. A frequent correspondent to *The Numismatist* on a variety of topics, Eaton stood out as one of the few collectors of his day to take notice of the different mints coining Lincoln Cents and of the variations in mintmark positions within given dates. He duly reported his findings to Editor Edgar H. Adams, who then published them in the American Numismatic Association's monthly journal.

Eaton obtained his cents at face value plus the cost of postage, 25 at a time, directly from the three mints. This was a necessity before the 1920s, as no dealers bothered to stock cents of recent dates. He occasionally ran into difficulty with various mint officers, depending on their disposition toward coin collectors. One instance in which his request was refused is contained in a letter to

him from the Superintendent of the San Francisco Mint:

Enclosed I return the money order No. 64660, for $0.35, in favor The Supt. of the Mint of the United States, received in your letter of January 19, 1912, with the information that one-cent pieces may be distributed only upon an order from the Treasurer of the United States or an Assistant Treasurer. A quantity of one-cent pieces has been made by this Institution during 1912. We have made no other minor coins to this date.[1]

Given such setbacks, and with no widespread interest in the collecting of current coins, hobbyists had little recourse but to seek out a sympathetic bank teller or store cashier. Oftentimes, the providing of small favors such as a bottle of liquor a couple times a year would prove effective in securing both old and new coins of interest that turned up in the normal course of business. Collectors of the time were a resourceful lot. Of course, both clerks and their employers were then of a more accommodating nature than they are today.

Little thought was given at the time to the collecting of Lincoln Cents from circulation, since most of the coins as yet had no premium value even in Uncirculated condition. A rare glimpse, though an incomplete one, survives from these early years and establishes that all dates and mints were then still collectable from circulation. In 1925, E. S. Thresher submitted an article to *The Numismatist* titled "Coins That Can Be Found in Circulation."

On June 1, 1919, I started an experiment to see how long it would take to find every date and mintmark of the coins of types now in circulation, that is, silver dollars since 1878, half dollars, quarter dollars and dimes since 1892, nickels since 1883 and cents since 1864. I put every date and mintmark on a card which I carried in my pocket, and whenever I found one I checked it off. Not being in a business where cash in handled, I had to depend on such coins as I would get for pocket money, except cents. For these I had access to the collections of about 200 "penny-in-the-slot" machines.[2]

Thresher went on to report that he had already found every cent with the exception of 1924-S, 1925-D and 1925-S. The absence of these last two he attributed to the newness of the year, but he grew quite animated in discussing 1924-S:

I am now frantically scanning the spoils from the above mentioned slot machines for a 1924-S cent. I have seen no mention of it in print, but it seems to me that this issue will become a rarity soon. Only 116,960 were coined, the smallest issue since 1823, and probably the second of third smallest since the beginning.[3]

His confusion over the number of 1924-S cents coined was the result of *The Numismatist*'s inconsistent reporting of mintage figures. These were alternately published as the number of pieces coined or their value in dollars. Thresher obviously mistook the figure of 116,960 dollars worth as the number of pieces struck! It's sincerely hoped that he ultimately came to understand this difference and that he did indeed find a 1924-S cent.

A market begins to emerge

As related above, dealers did not include Lincoln Cents in their advertising during the early years of this series, though they could perhaps be secured through a private inquiry accompanying the purchase of more valuable pieces. It was not until July of 1927 that the first advertisement offering Lincoln Cents appeared in the pages of *The Numismatist*. The submitter was H. A Brand of Cincinnati, and he offered a number of Indian and Lincoln Cents. The only dates of the Lincoln type available Uncirculated were 1909-S V.D.B. at 40 cents and 1909 plain, 1909-S plain and 1920-D at 10 cents apiece. Circulated examples of the Denver and San Francisco Mint coins of the 1910s were available at prices of five or 10 cents, though cents dated 1910, 1911 and 1914 were conspicuously absent. Reflecting the limited knowledge that both collectors and dealers had of recent issues, Brand additionally offered 1909-D cents, Uncirculated, at 10 cents each!

In some respect Brand knew what he was doing in advertising Lincoln Cents for sale, as he soon had several competitors. In 1928, George Patac of Smithtown Branch, New York offered both varieties of the 1909-P Lincoln Cents at six cents apiece, Uncirculated, but he wanted 50 cents for the 1909-S V.D.B., which he incorrectly identified as having a mintage of 300,000 pieces. It was known already that 1922-D was a scarce date, and he offered Uncirculated examples at 15 cents each.[4]

The 1909-S V.D.B. issue must have been a popular coin by the late 1920s, as F. J. Holthaus of Seneca, Kansas wanted 45 cents for an unused specimen.[5] About that same time, The Arcade Stamp and Coin Company of Cleveland offered to furnish several early-date Lincolns in Uncirculated condition. S-Mint cents dated 1910-17, excluding the rare 1914-S, could be purchased for 25 cents apiece. The same price was asked for Denver cents, though both the 1914-D and 1917-D issues were missing from his ad. P-Mint cents were naturally the least expensive, and 15 cents would secure any of the dates from 1910 through 1917, Brilliant Uncirculated.[6]

Comprehensive listings of Lincoln Cents were then still a few years away. It wasn't until February of 1931 that William Pukall of Union City, New Jersey ran his first advertisement offering a nearly complete inventory of Lincolns dated through 1929. Most were priced at 15

to 50 cents each in Uncirculated condition, yet there were already standout rarities. The 1914 issues were priced at $1.00 for the P-Mint, $1.25 for the Denver cent and $1.50 for the S-Mint variety. Why the 1914-P cent was considered so rare is not known, though it remains one of the scarcer P-Mint issues today. Other "big ticket" dates included 1910-S and 1923-S, both priced at 75 cents. Evidently Pukall was aware of how many 1909-S V.D.B. cents survived Uncirculated, as he wanted only 25 cents for one of his.[7]

William Pukall, along with A. C. Gies of Pittsburgh and Wayte Raymond of New York City, were often cited by scholar Walter Breen as the three most prominent hoarders of modern coins by the roll, though Raymond apparently acquired his stash by buying out the other two during the mid 1930s. In studying contemporary ads, however, it becomes apparent that the person to contact if one wanted to assemble an Uncirculated set of Lincoln Cents was F. C. C. Boyd of New York City. In the early 1930s, Boyd ran full-page advertisements in *The Numismatist* offering every date and mint of the Lincoln series in Uncirculated condition. In his ad from August of 1931, all coins were still priced below one dollar, with the exceptions of 1910-S ($1.00), 1914-P ($1.25), 1914-D ($1.50), 1914-S ($1.75) and 1923-S ($1.00).

Boyd was an executive with the Union News Company, which had newsstands set up in train stations and other lucrative venues. He was an avid and well-heeled collector, whose superb assemblage of United States coins was sold in a series of auctions during 1945-46. Billed as the "World's Greatest Collection," Boyd's holdings were sold by partners Abe Kosoff and Abner Kreisberg doing business as the Numismatic Gallery. It's likely that Boyd sold Lincolns through the mail more for the fun of it than from any financial need.

All the rage

By 1935 the collecting scene was changing, and Boyd's prices for Lincoln Cents had advanced remarkably in a period of just four years. Now there were very few coins obtainable at just 15-25 cents, and there were quite a number which approached the one dollar level. In addition, several more dates had broken that barrier. The cents now priced at a dollar or more included 1913-D ($1.15), 1913-S ($1.25), 1914-P ($1.15), 1914-D ($2.15), 1914-S ($1.65), 1923-S ($1.35) and 1926-S ($1.15). Proofs each cost one dollar or slightly over that amount, with the exception of the 1909 V.D.B. proof which then cost a whopping four dollars.[8]

What happened to cause such a rapid advance in the values of Lincoln Cents? In actual fact there is no single answer, as several significant developments occurred almost simultaneously to create a widespread market for Lincoln Cents where none had existed previously. First and foremost of these was the perceived rarity of several recent issues. The Great Depression which began in 1929 did not have an immediate effect on the number of coins being minted, though some of the coins dated 1929 and many of those dated 1930 went into storage for several years. It wasn't until 1931 that the lessened demand for fresh pieces led to a near halting of production and dramatic lay-offs at the three mints. The cents of 1931-33 were coined in small numbers, and collectors sought to hoard these coins from the very outset. 1931-S cents in particular were saved by the roll, and thus was born the speculative market for Uncirculated rolls which was to be such a factor in the collecting of Lincoln Cents for generations afterward.

This activity drew attention to earlier dates of proven scarcity, and the actual number of legitimate collectors grew at an accelerated pace between 1930 and 1935. Unlike previous generations of numismatists, these new hobbyists became fixated on modern coins, particularly small cents and copper-nickel five-cent pieces. The values of such coins rose dramatically at a time when the prices for older and more rare pieces were either static or in a temporary decline because of the overall economic state of the nation.

Seeking to take advantage of the growing market for Lincoln Cents, worn examples of which were still readily available from circulation, a new class of opportunist arose. Touting the rarity of "pennies" which might be found in anyone's pocket change, these individuals printed up cheap pamphlets which offered big cash rewards for certain issues, and these were widely distributed at prices ranging from 50 cents to one dollar. Also offered was an attribution service in which one's coins would be examined for a fee by "experts." The promoters were careful to obscure the fact that the coins which actually carried a premium were unlikely to be among the ones still circulating, yet thousands of hopeful treasure hunters were conned into buying premium lists. This scam, though not all that dissimilar from the promotions of legitimate dealers such as B. Max Mehl, was so widespread by 1935 that it gained the attention of Lee F. Hewitt, Editor of *Numismatic Scrapbook:*

The Post Office Department is finally "Catching Up" with the so-called numismatic firms who are operating the "Lincoln Penny Racket." Fraud orders have been issued against several Milwaukee and Chicago firms who were engaged in the business of offering fabulous prices for Lincoln cents and charging 25c to appraise the same.[9]

There's a certain irony in the fact that this trade developed in Milwaukee and Chicago, because in nearby Neenah, Wisconsin an idea was being hatched which would change forever the face of coin collecting in general and Lincoln Cent collecting in particular. Witnessing the new-found popularity of this series among an entirely new breed of coin collector, a man by the name of J. K. Post conceived a means of assembling and displaying one's set in a most economical manner, an aspect of numismatics which had been largely overlooked to that point. His new invention was soon to sweep over the very stodgy world of traditional collecting. Before continuing with his story, however, it's worth taking a look at some of the products which preceded Post's idea.

It's not known how pioneers of Lincoln Cent collecting such as W. C. Eaton stored their coins, but it's almost certain that they could not afford to place such lowly pieces in the fine wooden cabinets utilized by numismatists of the time. These were reserved for rarities, or at least pieces having a higher face value. Most coins were typically stored in small paper envelopes made exclusively for that purpose, and these were arranged back-to-back in boxes or drawers. Of course, the materials used for such envelopes were often high in sulfur and other corrosives, and this helps to explain the rarity of many Lincoln Cents in fully-red condition.

The first big development in coin storage since the advent of the wooden cabinet was the invention of Martin Luther Beistle of Shippensburg, Pennsylvania. Known also for his authorship of what was once the standard reference on United States half dollars, Beistle was the owner and manager of The Beistle Company, which produced paper novelties such as party favors. Beginning in 1928 he marketed cardboard pages containing holes into which coins could be inserted. These pages featured transparent, celluloid strips to permit viewing of both sides of the coins while simultaneously keeping them in place. His pages were hole-punched for inclusion in a ring binder, and this product was marketed as the Unique Coin Holder.

In the early 1930s the rights to Beistle's invention were bought by Wayte Raymond, who wanted a means to market the thousands of modern coins in his inventory. Raymond upgraded this product and renamed it the National Coin Album. In various forms and under different ownership, this pioneering coin album was offered through the early 1970s.

With the availability of albums the popularity of date-and-mint collecting grew steadily in the early 1930s. The problem with both Beistle's and Raymond's products, however, were their cost. At one dollar per page their use was limited to confirmed numismatists, who were willing to make some investment in a hobby they already knew and enjoyed.

It was into this void that J. K. Post stepped up and devised his solution. Contracting with Whitman Publishing Company, a producer of games, puzzles and children's books, Post designed a single-piece, cardstock holder for coins which housed an entire series in a product costing just 25 cents. A paper backing kept the coins from falling through the holes, though it also prevented the viewing of both sides. First offered in 1934 for Indian Head Cents and Lincoln Cents, Post's coin boards rode the crest of popular coin collecting that was just then becoming a national phenomenon. By 1935 thousands were being sold, and Post was quickly overwhelmed by the demand. He sold the rights to Whitman in the following year, and the list of titles was expanded to include any coin types which could then be found in circulation.

How successful were the coin boards in creating additional coin collectors? This account from 1938 tells just a part of the story:

Of course no one ever will know how many collectors were made by the arrival of the 25 cent coin boards—but we'll hazard a guess that they brought more bonafide numismatists into the fold than commemoratives have and will. One town with a population of less than 14,000 has 700 of these boards within its borders—at least retailers have sold that many. And the American Numismatic Association is averaging better than a member a month out of that town which before the end of May will have a coin collectors' club.

Officials of the company preferred not to publish the total amount of the boards actually made and sold. But

the figure will run into the millions, according to a stationer who should know what he's talking about. J. K. Post of Neenah, Wis., first submitted the idea of the boards to Whitman Publishing Co., Racine, Wis. The boards since that idea came in, however, have originated entirely within the Whitman organization, according to Lloyd E. Smith, speaking for that firm.

We say, orchids to the Whitman company for the job it did and the money it spent on promoting these boards—and consequently helping along the cause of numismatics.[10]

What made the boards so successful in attracting new collectors is that they were sold outside of the normal channels of numismatics. Coin collectors were something of a closed society before the 1930s. This was not necessarily by choice, but rather it was imposed by the somewhat scholarly and costly nature of numismatics at the time. The coin boards marketed by Post and Whitman, appearing at just the right time in American history, opened up the collecting of coins to an entirely new market and democratized the hobby. Sold in non-numismatic venues such as toy stores and novelty shops, the boards made even the most disinterested person aware of the fact that some coins were worth more than face value.

No longer just a gentlemen's club, numismatics (or more specifically coin collecting) became a family hobby in which people of ordinary means could search through their pocket change or rolls of coins obtained from banks and enjoy an evening's entertainment at little expense. Like so many fads of the 1930s, popular coin collecting was largely a product of the Great Depression, when people had to spend much of their leisure time in the home out of sheer economic necessity.

Reminiscing some 20 years later, veteran coin dealer Art Kagin recalled the arrival of the coin boards:

When I started working for the old Hollinbeck Stamp & Coin Co. in Minneapolis in March of 1933, coins were not looked upon as a particularly good investment. The nature of the hobby was entirely different at that time from that of today [1954]. Before the publication of Whitman coin cards in 1935, condition was not too important. If a collector did not obtain a coin that he wanted "today," he could wait and obtain it any time in the next year or so at the same price, or at a very nominal increase.

With the advent of Whitman coin cards, at the time

I left Minneapolis to take charge of the branch store in Omaha, the nature of coin collecting had already changed. The enthusiasm created by the new "collectors" trying to fill Whitman cards from circulation started the upward price rise for modern coins. I recall the 1909-S VDB selling for 15c in nice red uncirculated condition before the coming of Whitman cards, but it soon jumped to $1.00 when everyone wanted it to complete his card.

In 1936, when I took over management of the latest Hollinbeck store, coin collecting had really started to "catch on." I can still recall the youngsters we had "peddling" Whitman cards in offices and other places of business. I wholesaled them to barber shops, drug stores and anyone who would handle them throughout the state.[11]

While the greatest price increases were indeed for Uncirculated cents, the reluctance of some new collectors to pay premium prices for the dates needed to complete their sets prompted many previously valueless circulated coins to be offered for sale. In 1936, M. J. Carls of Racine, Wisconsin advertised all but the most common Lincoln Cents for sale at prices ranging from three cents upward. Most carried only a token service charge, since they could be obtained from circulation with diligent searching, but there were a few issues which already bore stiff premiums for the time. Among these were 1909-S V.D.B. ($1.00 in Very Good and $1.50 in Fine), 1914-D ($1.00 and $1.50, respectively), 1914-S (25c in G, 50c in VG, 75c in F) and 1922 "plain" ($1.00 in F). The latter was still misunderstood at that time, and it was listed with the Philadelphia Mint issues.[12]

Success breeds imitation, and there were soon competitors in the market for coin boards. Perhaps the most successful was Colonial Coin and Stamp Company of New York City. It marketed boards which featured attractive graphics and transparent celluloid in place of Whitman's paper backing, permitting the viewing of both sides of one's coins. Unlike most manufacturers of coin boards, who targeted the non-numismatic public, Colonial advertised its line of boards in *The Numismatist* as products worthy of a fine collection.

One off-shoot of the coin board phenomenon was a similar product known as a premium card. Assuming the same basic format as the boards for collectors, premium cards were marketed with a profit incentive as their primary appeal. Instructions appeared on the back of each board stating the range of prices paid for completed boards, provided that none of the coins were damaged or harshly cleaned. To obtain one's reward, these boards had to be returned to their distributor. It's not known how many collections were actually completed and redeemed, but it's likely that most purchasers of these boards became hooked on collecting coins and never claimed their reward.

Seizing on this notion of compensating people for finding coins with premium values, one town in Iowa even considered using it as an employment measure during the Great Depression, as related in this story from the October 7, 1938 *Muscatine Journal:*

A novel plan for putting a part of the local unemployed back to work was presented to the city council Thursday night.

L. J. Ashley, 1117 East Eighth street, in a communication directed the council's attention to the possibility of putting a crew of relief clients under bond, manning them with coin books and stationing one or two of them at each of the various stores in the city to check on coins that come in.

The belief was expressed that many coins pass by in the ordinary course of business that are worth more than their face value. As for remuneration, Ashley proposed, the checkers could work for a percentage of the extra values on the coins which they discovered.

A Mr. Houdek of Muscatine informed readers of *The Numismatic Scrapbook Magazine* that the city council shelved this proposal, deeming it impractical. Houdek added that "We have quite a few active collectors here. One store has sold from 500 to 700 penny boards alone, not counting nickel, dime, quarter and others. Muscatine is quite coin conscious. So you can see any scheme like that would fail."[13]

Table 1: Stack's June 1937 price listing for uncirculted Lincoln cents[14]

1909 V.D.B.	$.15	1918	.25	1928-S	1.25
1909 Plain	.25	1918-S	1.25	1928-D	1.00
1909-S V.D.B.	2.00	1918-D	1.25	1929	.25
1909-S Plain	1.00	1919	.35	1929-S	.25
1910	.25	1919-S	1.75	1929-D	.65
1910-S	.50	1919-D	1.25	1930	.25
1911	.50	1920	.20	1930-S	.35
1911-S	1.75	1920-S	1.00	1930-D	.50
1911-D	1.25	1920-D	.90	1931	.50
1912	.25	1921	.35	1931-S	.60
1912-S	.90	1921-S	2.00	1931-D	.75
1912-D	1.75	1922-D	1.00	1932	.40
1913	.35	1923	.35	1932-D	.50
1913-S	2.75	1923-S	3.00	1933	.50
1913-D	2.25	1924	.50	1933-D	.35
1914	1.50	1924-S	2.25	1934	.15
1914-S	2.75	1924-D	2.75	1934-D	.35
1914-D	8.00	1925	.25	1935	.10
1915	2.50	1925-S	1.25	1935-S	.15
1915-S	.85	1925-D	1.00	1935-D	.25
1915-D	.75	1926	.75	1936	.10
1916	.50	1926-S	2.75	1936-S	.15
1916-S	.85	1926-D	1.75	1936-D	.20
1916-D	.90	1927	.25	1937	.10
1917	.25	1927-S	1.75	1937-S	.15
1917-S	.90	1927-D	1.75	1937-D	.20
1917-D	.75	1928	.20		

The rapid development of coin collecting during the mid 1930s, though it paled in comparison to the hobby's growth during World War II, led to further dramatic price increases. Again this price pressure centered around Lincoln Cents and, to a lesser extent, Indian Head Cents and Buffalo Nickels. By June of 1937, the up-and-coming New York City firm of Stack's was able to advertise a complete listing of Uncirculated Lincoln's at the prices listed in Table 1.

In reviewing these prices it's evident that 1914-D really came into its own during the two years since 1935. It's also obvious that the rarity of 1912-S and 1915-S cents was not yet known. Surprisingly expensive at that time were 1914-P and 1915-P, while 1931-S was recognized as common in Uncirculated condition despite its very low mintage. (Another interesting feature of this advertisement, one which was true of all catalogs, price lists and coin albums until the 1950s, is that the coins were written sequentially as P, S and D. This is in contrast to the P-D-S sequence familiar to collectors in recent decades. This practice was picked up by early 20th Century catalogers from its usage in the *Annual Report* of the Director of the Mint, which listed all mints in the order of their authorization. As the only reliable source for mintage figures, writers reproduced their tables from these reports in the same order. During the 1950s this trend reversed itself to the P-D-S sequence used today, though coin albums continued with the old sequence until about 1960.)

That Stack's was able to present an accurate listing of date/mint combinations when earlier advertisers often overlooked certain issues or listed non-existing varieties was due in large part to the publication of Wayte Raymond's *Standard Catalogue of United States Coins*. This volume was the first comprehensive catalog of U. S. coinage in decades, and it improved steadily after its debut in 1934. Though ultimately extinguished by the popularity of R. S. Yeoman's less expensive *A Guide Book of United States Coins*, the *Standard Catalogue* was the sole guide for a generation of collectors. Raymond's book was also the final element in coin collecting's big breakthrough of the 1930s. The hobby as it would be known for decades developed between 1934 and 1940, and it was to enjoy even grander success in the years to follow.

Another publication which debuted in 1935 and quickly became the principal forum for the new breed of collectors was *Numismatic Scrapbook*, published by brothers Lee and Clifford Hewitt of Chicago and edited by Lee. Initially, it was just that—a scrapbook of reprints and news items culled from other sources and sent for

Table 2: Quinton Louthan's 1937 survey of 5,000 circulated Lincoln cents yielded the following quantities of each date[15]

1909	27	1917-S	28	1927-S	6
1909 V.D.B.	2	1918	141	1928	71
1909-S	1	1918-D	41	1928-D	145
1909-S V.D.B.	0	1918-S	31	1928-S	9
1910	82	1919	264	1929	68
1910-S	4	1919-D	89	1929-D	192
1911	28	1919-S	117	1929-S	35
1911-D	15	1920	186	1930	39
1911-S	1	1920-D	132	1930-D	136
1912	12	1920-S	42	1930-S	5
1912-D	9	1921	17	1931	4
1912-S	2	1921-S	14	1931-D	7
1913	25	1922-D	36	1931-S	0
1913-D	20	1923	28	1932	2
1913-S	5	1923-S	5	1932-D	183
1914	18	1924	43	1933	2
1914-D	3	1924-D	6	1933-D	113
1914-S	1	1924-S	10	1934	58
1915	9	1925	83	1934-D	147
1915-D	23	1925-D	79	1935	51
1915-S	5	1925-S	17	1935-D	700
1916	45	1926	94	1935-S	6
1916-D	34	1926-D	174	1936	12
1916-S	13	1926-S	1	1936-D	575
1917	88	1927	63	1936-S	0
1917-D	49	1927-D	120		

Table 3: H.B. Combest's survey of 5,000 circulated Lincoln cents a month after Louthan's yielded the following quantities of each date[16]

1909	29	1917-S	9	1927-S	4
1909 V.D.B.	10	1918	155	1928	166
1909-S	1	1918-D	33	1928-D	24
1909-S V.D.B.	0	1918-S	12	1928-S	5
1910	55	1919	229	1929	213
1910-S	2	1919-D	33	1929-D	31
1911	28	1919-S	99	1929-S	18
1911-D	13	1920	178	1930	176
1911-S	1	1920-D	40	1930-S	48
1912	26	1920-S	28	1930-S	10
1912-D	1	1921	32	1931	27
1912-S	3	1921-S	7	1931-D	24
1913	21	1922-D	7	1931-S	0
1913-D	2	1923	40	1932	12
1913-S	1	1923-S	4	1932-D	5
1914	39	1924	71	1933	8
1914-D	0	1924-D	3	1933-D	2
1914-S	0	1924-S	4	1934	382
1915	15	1925	103	1934-D	13
1915-D	10	1925-D	21	1935	496
1915-S	3	1925-S	8	1935-D	24
1916	54	1926	154	1935-S	12
1916-D	29	1926-D	24	1936	1,311
1916-S	3	1926-S	0	1936-D	9
1917	95	1927	163	1936-S	3
1917-D	28	1927-D	26		

free to any applicant. By 1937, however, it had emerged as a true hobby journal and was renamed *The Numismatic Scrapbook Magazine*. It now had paid subscribers and regular advertisers, and it led the rapid advance of popular coin collecting in a way that seemed to elude Frank G. Duffield, staid Editor of *The Numismatist*.

With the phenomenal success of coin boards during the 1930s, it became increasingly challenging for collectors to find the better-date Lincolns. This can be seen graphically in studies of circulation finds made just a few years apart. The pioneer of such studies was Quinton E. Louthan of San Benito, Texas. He published his first survey in *Numismatic Scrapbook* in 1937, after examining 5,000 cents with the results listed in Table 2.

Another reader, H. B. Combest of Chicago, responded to Mr. Louthan's survey just a month later with the results of his own search through 5,000 cents (see Table 3).

Combest also reported finding just three Indian Head Cents out of the 5,000 coins examined, as well as five Canadian cents. His survey provides an interesting contrast with that of Quinton Louthan, as it establishes that most of the cents circulating in Illinois were Philadelphia Mint issues while those found in Texas were

mostly products of the Denver Mint. For at look at the population of Lincoln Cents out West, a survey made in the Spring of 1938 by Harry Shipler of Salt Lake City will serve nicely. He examined a total of 10,000 coins, so his figures have been halved and rounded up to the nearest whole number for comparison purposes (see Table 4).

It seems that Salt Lake City was an ideal location when searching for Lincolns. Mr. Shipler was the only one of the three correspondents to actually complete the series from circulation, though he reported finding not a single 1922 plain. Two Indian Head Cents turned up in 10,000 coins, along with a couple of Canadian cents and 49 Lincolns having unreadable dates.

This survey clearly proves that living in the West did enable one to find the scarce S-Mint cents. Though P-Mint Lincolns were common there by virtue of the sheer numbers struck, the lower mintage San Francisco coins almost always outnumbered those struck in Denver. Even with Utah being a neighbor of Colorado it's obvious that the cents distributed in Utah came primarily from the San Francisco Mint.

Another survey of 5,000 cents, conducted by John W. Snyder of Robinson, Illinois in November of 1943, reveals how many of the early Lincolns had already been withdrawn in just a few years time. The bag which Snyder obtained from his bank had evidently been sealed early in 1942, as it contained only a single cent of that date and none dated 1943 (see Table 5).

In addition to confirming that the Illinois area received its cents primarily from the Philadelphia Mint, this survey also demonstrated that the completion of a Lincoln Cent collection was already quite difficult in the early 1940s. For the record Mr. Snyder also found in this $50 bag of cents two Indian Head pieces, 1893 and 1906, as well as 14 Lincolns with unreadable dates.

Quinton E. Louthan, who pioneered this form of survey, also performed another one 1943. He furnished only partial results, comparing the ratios of key and semi-key dates found in 1937 to those of cents found in 1943. It was his conclusion that the returns no longer justified the labor involved:

> As can be seen from the table below, the number of scarce date cents in circulation is rapidly declining. There are now not enough desirable Lincoln cents in circulation to justify spending time looking for them——a condition that did not exist until the past year or two.
>
> At any rate, the amount of money paid the "assistant" for looking through the 20,000 cents hardly justified the value of coins found, many of them not being in very good condition, so if anyone else has an idea of going through the local bank's supply of cents just forget it——and *buy* a few scarce dates instead.[19]

Table 4: Harry Shipler's survey in Salt Lake City yielded the following results (adjusted to 5,000 coins).[17]

1909	14	1917-S	64	1927-S	83
1909 V.D.B.	6	1918	74	1928	42
1909-S	1	1918-D	42	1928-D	61
1909-S V.D.B.	1	1918-S	49	1928-S	104
1910	41	1919	131	1929	47
1910-S	7	1919-D	76	1929-D	72
1911	26	1919-S	183	1929-S	488
1911-D	8	1920	93	1930	34
1911-S	7	1920-D	54	1930-D	88
1912	15	1920-S	104	1930-S	315
1912-D	5	1921	8	1931	4
1912-S	8	1921-S	56	1931-D	3
1913	17	1922-D	7	1931-S	36
1913-D	9	1923	19	1932	1
1913-S	13	1923-S	33	1932-D	29
1914	24	1924	21	1933	2
1914-D	2	1924-D	4	1933-D	5
1914-S	9	1924-S	45	1934	50
1915	5	1925	36	1934-D	79
1915-D	13	1925-D	45	1935	33
1915-S	10	1925-S	150	1935-D	79
1916	27	1926	44	1935-S	523
1916-D	27	1926-D	49	1936	49
1916-S	22	1926-S	31	1936-D	62
1917	53	1927	40	1936-S	571
1917-D	54	1927-D	49		

1909	17	1919-D	24	1931	16
1909 V.D.B.	6	1919-S	64	1931-D	9
1909-S	0	1920	115	1931-S	0
1909-S V.D.B.	0	1920-D	27	1932	3
1910	41	1920-S	9	1932-D	6
1910-S	0	1921	23	1933	7
1911	21	1921-S	5	1933-D	3
1911-D	1	1922-D	4	1934	198
1911-S	0	1923	28	1934-D	22
1912	23	1923-S	2	1935	199
1912-D	1	1924	43	1935-D	31
1912-S	1	1924-D	1	1935-S	7
1913	10	1924-S	1	1936	164
1913-D	9	1925	59	1936-D	31
1913-S	2	1925-D	10	1936-S	4
1914	19	1925-S	7	1937	278
1914-D	0	1926	86	1937-D	27
1914-S	1	1926-D	22	1937-S	9
1915	8	1926-S	1	1938	124
1915-D	10	1927	90	1938-D	7
1915-S	0	1927-D	11	1938-S	3
1916	28	1927-S	2	1939	260
1916-D	14	1928	104	1939-D	6
1916-S	9	1928-D	13	1939-S	3
1917	70	1928-S	9	1940	407
1917-D	25	1929	114	1940-D	99
1917-S	6	1929-D	28	1940-S	161
1918	94	1929-S	10	1941	951
1918-D	15	1930	108	1941-D	145
1918-S	13	1930-D	27	1941-S	145
1919	162	1930-S	7		

While his frustration is understandable, Louthan failed to recognize that for a new collector whose motivation was fun and not profit the hunt was still worthwhile.

Wartime popularity

The great drop-off in the number of collectable cents during the early 1940s was attributable to two causes. The first of these was simply the overwhelming number of new coins being minted each year. The supply of older pieces was spread so thinly after 1940 that a person would have to search through many thousands of cents to turn up even a few of the scarce ones. The second cause was the tremendous growth in the number of people saving Lincoln Cents and other coins dating from the early part of the century. While there had been a steady growth in the hobby since the mid 1930s, largely due to the popularity of coin boards, the greatest influx came during the war years.

What led so many individuals to become first-time coin collectors during the war years of 1941-45? The reason may be found in the restrictions placed on the way Americans could spend their money at that time. With virtually all industries converted to manufacturing military supplies of one sort or another there were very few consumer items that people could buy. Cars, radios, clothing—-all were in short supply. This shortage occurred at the same time as Americans were earning higher pay and working many hours of overtime to keep up with the needs of the war effort. With so much money in their pockets and few ways to spend it, people directed their discretionary income toward various forms of entertainment. Movie theaters, dance halls and amusement parks all posted record attendance figures during the war years.

Other outlets for this extra cash were hobbies of all sorts. Both coin and stamp collecting experienced unprecedented growth between 1941 and 1945, as these activities were less dependent on newly produced consumer goods. There was a shortage of paper, however, and this inhibited the manufacture of numismatic books and supplies. As an example, the first edition of R. S. Yeoman's *A Guide Book of United States Coins* (the Red Book) was planned for 1943 as a companion volume to his work *A Hand Book of United States Coins* (the Blue Book), introduced in 1942, but a shortage of paper postponed its debut until 1946. Also affected were *The Numismatist* and other hobby periodicals, which were printed on cheap paper during the war and for several years afterward.

One of the real breakthrough products which appeared just before the war and was seriously threatened by the rationing of paper was Whitman's coin folder. The invention of Richard Yeo (pen-name R. S. Yeoman), this was simply the old 11"x14" coin board of the 1930s broken down into smaller panels which folded over one another to form a book. More convenient than the one-piece boards, the new folders also afforded some element of protection for the coins, though not much. These folders debuted in 1940 and were an instant success, though the old-style boards by Whitman and competing companies remained in production at least as late as 1943 and possibly as late as 1945.

Whitman soon had competition for its new product. Though wartime rationing kept the number of brands below that of the pre-war coin boards, the Daniel Stamp Company (DANSCO) of Santa Monica, California. emerged as the leading rival to Whitman. Both produced quality folders from the early 1940s onward, and they remain competitors to the present day. The impact that these folders had on the popularity of coin collecting was

tremendous. As always, the primary focus of those searching their change for "keepers" was the Lincoln Cent series. It has led the popularity parade among collectors, both serious and casual, since the advent of the modern hobby in the mid 1930s.

A hobby for everyone

Servicemen returning from overseas usually brought back with them a few coins of the countries they'd visited, and in many cases this was the impetus to begin collecting coins on a casual basis. More common though was for these individuals to discover that their families had already begun saving Lincoln Cents and Buffalo Nickels in their absence. So many people were drawn into the hobby during and just after the war that this launched a golden age of coin clubs. Unlike the gentlemen's numismatic societies of the 1920s and earlier, the popular coin clubs which began to appear during the 1930s and at a much greater rate during the late 1940s and '50s were very much family affairs. Wives and kids were equally welcome, though women were typically more interested in the social and administrative aspects of the hobby than in actually collecting coins.

The hobby reached an early peak around 1947-48, only to see a drop-off in enthusiasm as the decade drew to a close. Still, quite a few people persevered in collecting coins, and there was a rapid resurgence beginning around 1952. That was the year that veterans *The Numismatist* and *The Numismatic Scrapbook Magazine* were joined by an upstart titled *Numismatic News*. Just like its predecessors, *Numismatic News* had very humble

beginnings under Editor and Publisher Chet Krause, a full-time carpenter and after-hours coin enthusiast. Within only a few years, however, Krause put down his hammer and rode his brainchild to tremendous success, ultimately forging a hobby publications empire.

Coin collecting enjoyed rapid and sustained growth throughout the 1950s. Just as before, Lincoln Cents continued to lead this increase in popularity, and a handful of new magazines and newspapers appeared catering to the many new hobbyists. Toward the end of that decade a rich array of new coin folders and albums began to appear, too many in fact to describe here. Novel among these products were several varieties of plastic holders for both single coins and complete collections. Though these had appeared in primitive form as early as 1945, it was during the 1950s that many advanced collectors made the switch to displaying their sets within acrylic or polystyrene holders.

Among the biggest boosts which the hobby received at this time was the discovery of doubled-die cents dated 1955. Though slow to acquire a following, by the end of the 1950s these had become big-ticket items. Other sure sellers were the proof sets issued since 1950. Their mintages grew rapidly during that decade, partly as the result of heedless speculation, but also as the consequence of many new coin collectors entering the hobby. One speciality which became quite popular during the 1950s and early '60s was the collecting of "BIE" varieties. The die steel used during those years was subject to numerous small breaks, and one which recurred on many different issues seemed to form a letter I between letters B and E of LIBERTY on Lincoln Cents. So common was this flaw that one or more books were devoted to listing its various manifestations, and a club for this specialty even existed during the 1960s.

How much of this enhanced activity was purely for fun as opposed to being profit motivated remains unclear, but one thing is certain—-many of those lured into numismatics by fantastic tales of modern rarities ultimately found themselves hooked on the sheer fun of filling holes in folders and albums. Hundreds of coin clubs were formed at this time, some towns of modest size having two or more. Most of the newcomers to the hobby were woefully ignorant of numismatics, and the counterfeiting and altering of coins flourished unchecked. Countless 1914-D Lincolns were devised by cutting away part of the first numeral 4 from 1944-D cents, as collectors of the time seldom knew that a 1944-D was easily distinguishable by its large mintmark and the presence of the initials V.D.B. at the truncation of Lincoln's bust, both features alien to a genuine 1914-D cent.

One aspect of coin collecting which had repeatedly defied codification in earlier generations was the subject of grading. While collectors and dealers have argued over grading finepoints since the hobby's inception in the 1850s, it wasn't until a century passed that a significant move was made to set the situation right. *A Guide to the Grading of United States Coins,* by Martin R. Brown and John W. Dunn, employed a combination of brief written descriptions and line drawings to present the various coin types in several circulated grades. Unappreciated today except by those old-timers who still use it, this work was one of the greatest breakthroughs in the successful maturing of the hobby. It thrived in several editions, though it has since been succeeded by the American Numismatic Association's own grading guide and other books (see Chapter 6).

In addition to the problems associated with grading and with counterfeit and altered coins there was another downside to the influx of so many new collectors. This was manifested in the rapid and in some cases unwarranted increase in values. As in every other aspect of the hobby, Lincoln Cents led the way in acquiring fairly high prices for even the most common coins. Just as in the 1930s, older coins of real rarity were sometimes pushed aside in the mania for hoarded issues such as 1931-S and 1954-P cents. This would come back to haunt many purchasers in the years ahead, though the very worst abuses were still around the corner.

The crazy years

The debut of the Lincoln Memorial Cent in 1959 coincided with and may have contributed to the wildly speculative market for rolls and bags of Uncirculated coins. Between 1959 and 1964 this activity spiraled completely out of control and nearly overwhelmed the conventional coin business. It ushered in the era of dealer-

to-dealer teletypes, and this system remains in effect today, though at a much more paced level of activity. When it all came to an end in the latter months of 1964, some dealers and speculators had become quite wealthy, while others were completely ruined or were burdened with enormous debts. In many respects the hobby would never again be the same.

Though the saving of coins by the roll had been popular ever since the low-mintage years of 1930-33, this activity remained somewhat limited in scale. A number of collectors acquired one or two rolls for long-term investment, but these were seldom traded on a daily basis, and their existence in the market didn't threaten established values. When the prices of coins began to rise more rapidly in the early 1950s, mostly as the result of genuine growth in the number of collectors, this prompted a number of individuals to begin saving multiple rolls of each and every issue. When the San Francisco Mint ceased coining operations in 1955, its final output of cents and dimes bearing that date instantly became the subject of massive hoarding. For the first time entire $50 bags of cents were being held back by speculators and traded intact. This trading of 5,000-coin bags was a hitherto unknown phenomenon, and it signaled the onset of the speculative mania for modern BU (Brilliant Uncirculated) coins.

From 1955 onward and lasting at least through 1964 every issue of the United States Mints was subject to widespread hoarding in bag quantities. The new Memorial Cents of 1959 were particularly prized despite their enormous mintages. With the discovery of the 1960 small date and large date varieties in April of that year, all rational restraints to the mindless hoarding of coins were let go, and established collectors and dealers were left to stare in wonder and with a certain contempt at those who staked their financial futures on coins minted by the millions and billions.

Soon, stories of collapsing floors became commonplace, as the hoards of BU coins accumulated. Those who lacked the capital to invest in bags of modern coins oftentimes took out loans, using these same coins as collateral. Though the speculative emphasis was on the more recent issues from 1934 onward, all Lincoln Cents rose substantially in value between 1955 and 1964. Some attained values that remain unequaled as recently as 1995. This is true mostly of later issues, though many of the older coins in lower grades were briefly overvalued by the sheer number of new collectors. Yes, there were still actual collectors entering the hobby in record numbers, though their influence was felt mostly in the amazing variety of folders, albums and other accessories offered at that time as well as in the creation of additional coin clubs. Exclusive of the established rarities, which still traded hands at auction, most of the cash entering the coin market was directed toward the speculative buying of modern issues.

As with all such speculations this frenzied roll and bag market came crashing down in the waning months of 1964. While many writers have blamed this sudden downturn on the suspension of mintmarks and proof sets and on the removal of silver from our coinage, both of these events actually followed the collapse of the roll market, though they were certainly present for its funeral. Quite a number of individuals were caught dancing when the music stopped, as they'd refinanced their homes or otherwise borrowed money to fund their imprudent purchases of rolls and bags. For the next several years, speculative issues such as 1954-S cents and 1951-S nickels became common in circulation in lightly worn condition from the many rolls dumped at face value.

There was one positive aspect to this period of frenzied activity in that the subject of coin collecting entered America's popular culture in a way unknown before or since. Coin collecting themes were frequently utilized in television shows, comic books and other non-traditional avenues. Quite a number of major department stores opened coin and stamp departments during the 1950s, and these lasted throughout the 1960s as well. Also frequently seen in hobby shops, discount stores and the like were coin collecting supplies such as folders, guide books

The joy of collecting Lincoln Cents, as recorded in May of 1967. The author (far right), father Walt (behind) and neighbors Bob and Robin Schneider are gathered around the Lange Family's kitchen table sorting Lincolns from plastic tubes. At nine years of age and after two years of searching through change, my collection was about as complete as it was ever likely to be, when Bob came to my rescue. A collector of many things, Bob had tubes nearly filled with most dates in the series, and he is seen here filling up all but the key dates in my Whitman folders. Mom and Dad helped with a couple more, though this childhood set is still lacking the toughest ones to be complete. I'm pleased to report that my memories of such evenings have outlasted by many years that tacky, stainless-steel furniture.

and other inexpensive items. Even actual coins were displayed for sale by a number of stores, a nostalgic twist now seemingly lost forever.

The author's earliest encounter with a coin department was at the F. W. Woolworth store in downtown San Francisco around 1965. Like most such non-traditional outlets it was stocked by a professional coin dealer who had a shop or office in some other part of the city and who was seldom present at this store. The coins for sale were typically overgraded and overpriced, and they were often sold by clerks having no knowledge of numismatics. Still, such displays fired the imagination of a child into visions of times and places long past.

Having cautious and skeptical parents, it was necessary for the author to engage in considerable pleading before his first purchase was made. As the world then revolved around his Lincoln Cent folders, this initial entry into the coin market consisted of a 1914-P cent in Good condition, price 75 cents. Not yet aware of Yeoman's *Red Book*, the author's purchase was made with a clear mind despite the coin's retail value of only 40 cents. As with so many other dates in the series, the value of this low-grade coin has since receded even further to just 20 cents. It was only after this inauspicious beginning that the author made the acquaintance of several coin professionals who provided a glimpse of the big picture.

There were other factors which also contributed mightily to the widespread popularity of coin collecting in the early 1960s. Debuting in 1960, just in time to benefit from the small date frenzy, a news weekly called *Coin World* became an overnight success under publisher J. Oliver Amos. Today it enjoys the largest circulation of any coin publication, though its competitor *Numismatic News* is likewise alive and well. Also appearing in the early 1960s were the slick-covered magazines *Coins* and its near-twin *Coinage*. Both were immensely valuable to the hobby, as they were distributed primarily through bookstores and newsstands. In such venues they brought news and information about coin collecting to the general public, fanning the fires of an already hot topic. These magazines remain popular to the present day, though a number of lesser imitators fell by the wayside decades ago.

The morning after

The tumble which the coin market took in 1964-65 lasted for just a few years, but in many respects its after-effects are still being felt today. Though countless coin collectors were added to the hobby during the late 1950s and early '60s, many lacked a real commitment and drifted away when the sense of excitement ran out after 1964. By that time veteran collectors had already pronounced the searching through pocket change for "keepers" a thing of the past, yet there were a great many people setting aside any silver coins, regardless of rarity. Ridiculed at the time, these individuals were ultimately proved correct in assuming that silver coins would soon be worth more than their face value. Sadly, however, this increase in value occurred for a reason entirely unrelated to the coins' numismatic appeal.

The suspension of mintmarks, the freezing of the date 1964 and the rapid withdrawal of silver coins after 1965 left the coin hobby in a state of malaise. Coins shops, though they still existed, were far fewer in number by the late 1960s. Many of the general merchandisers who operated coin departments discontinued this service after 1964, while others simply cut back their displays. The sales of coin folders and books, which had peaked around 1963-64, fell off dramatically in the years that followed. Many titles were dropped after 1965, and today Whitman's line of folders is limited to 20th Century coins, though deluxe albums from Whitman, Dansco and others are available for selected older issues.

The harvesting of Wheat Cents

Surprisingly, the replacement of Brenner's Wheat Ear reverse in 1959 did not result in large scale hoarding of this type. It was not until the last of the silver coins disappeared around 1968 that collectors and speculators began directing their attention to the humble cent. Though no longer common due to the sheer multitude of cents coined since 1959, "Wheaties" still comprised perhaps 5% of the Lincolns in circulation during the late 1960s. Most were dated in the 1950s, but a collector still had a reasonable chance of completing a set from 1940 onward, excluding the steel cents (these had largely disappeared by 1960). Even some high-mintage early dates such as 1917-P and 1919-P turned up from time to time, but P-Mint cents from the 1930s were about the best one could hope to find with any frequency.

By the early 1970s the population of Wheaties had dropped off dramatically, and those that remained were almost always dated 1956-58. Though this decline largely killed off the collecting of Lincolns from circulation, there was still the hope of turning up modern scarcities such as the 1960-P small date, the 1970-S small date and the 1972-P doubled-die. Even this prospect wasn't enough to excite collectors. Coin clubs began to see an alarming decline in membership, while those folks who remained were aging steadily. When Whitman introduced a new line of coin folders in 1972 designed specifically to house those coins which could still be found in circulation, sales were disappointing and the product was shortly discontinued.

Though the prospects for the coin hobby along traditional avenues seemed bleak during the 1970s, a subtle change was occurring which would transform the collecting of Lincoln Cents and other series and give the hobby a new lease on life. While not everyone has become accommodated to the more complicated coin market of the 1970s, '80s and '90s, it has offered the only hope for the continued popularity of date-and-mint collecting of coins such as Lincoln Cents.

The coin hobby comes of age

The general disappearance of pre-1959 cents after the early 1970s forced those still interested in collecting to seek their coins exclusively from dealers and other collectors. While there was nothing new in this, for many individuals the abandonment of collecting from circulation forced a re-evaluation of one's approach to the hobby. Previous generations since the 1930s had included many hobbyists who were content to buy the issues they needed to finish off their sets in grades similar to those of the coins obtained from circulation. Condition was often secondary to the more immediate goal of simply filling the holes in one's album or folder.

With the need for procuring coins exclusively through purchase came a growing awareness of condition as a factor of enjoyment and value. As long as collectors had to purchase all of their coins they were more inclined to pursue better-grade pieces. Within the space of just a few years the market for low-grade Lincoln Cents radically diminished, and this may be seen in the falling values for such coins between 1965 and 1980 as presented in Chapter 7. At the same time, the values of most early dates rose among the higher grades, particularly at the Uncirculated level. In addition, while there had been considerable price appreciation for Uncirculated cents of common dates during the 1950s and early '60s, these issues now remained stagnant or even fell as collectors developed a greater understanding of condition rarity among the pre-1934 cents.

Part of this emphasis came from the growing investment market of the 1970s. The successful track record of rare coins in keeping ahead of inflation between 1945 and 1970 became common knowledge during the 1970s, and there seemed no reason to believe that coins would not perform as well in the years to come. Of course, most of this growth had come as the result of legitimate demand from an expanding body of collectors, a condition which no longer existed in the 1970s. Still, the perception that coins were a superior investment was at least partly responsible for the trend which emphasized quality and boosted the values of choice and gem specimens.

As the coin market heated up toward the end of that decade use of the familiar *Red Book* as a determiner of retail values fell off, since prices in an investor-driven market were simply too volatile to afford only annual updating. The tool of choice became a weekly bulletin called *The Coin Dealer Newsletter*. It tracked the trading of BU rolls and reported this data in two columns, designated "Bid" and "Ask." The Bid price was theoretically the highest price being offered to purchase a roll or single coin, while Ask represented the lowest price at which such items were available for sale. In actual practice these figures became subject to manipulation by one or more dealers, but they still provided the majority of dealers with up-to-date teletype results.

In August of 1976 a supplemental newsletter appeared from the same publisher titled *The Coin Dealer Newsletter Monthly Summary*. It provided Bid and Ask prices for single coins over a number of grades, focusing on popular series such as Lincoln Cents. Though it too was intended for the use of professional coin traders, quick-witted collectors soon caught on to its value in estimating what dealers were actually paying for coins, and many of them began subscribing to the *Monthly Summary*. Over the years, the possession of such information has helped to reduce the profit margins that dealers enjoyed in the selling of coins and has blurred the lines of distinction between full-time professionals, "vest-pocket" dealers and advanced collectors. All now "talk the talk and walk the walk."

Other factors have also entered into play to further confuse the distinctions between collector and dealer and to accelerate the gulf in values between lower quality Lincoln Cents and those which qualify as choice and gem specimens. Easily the most influential development in recent years has been the advent of commercial grading services. Though the American Numismatic

Association and the International Numismatic Society both operated such services as early as the 1970s, it wasn't until grading certificates were sealed along with the coins inside plastic capsules that the modern coin market really came of age. The pioneer of this enterprise was the Professional Coin Grading Service (PCGS), which debuted in 1986. An immediate success, it was followed in 1987 by the Numismatic Guaranty Corporation of America (NGC). There have been others since that time, a few of which no longer exist, but these two remain the principal players in the grading industry.

Known colloquially as "slabs," certified and encapsulated coins dominate the market for high-grade Lincolns in the 1990s. While uncertified or "raw" Lincoln Cents still outnumber those in slabs, relatively few of the early-date, high-grade pieces are traded in this state except in auctions of old collections. The grading services have proved quite effective in screening out the counterfeit and altered coins which were so common in the 1960s and '70s. Officially, they also reject cents which have been cleaned or recolored, but a few of the more appealing ones have managed to slip through. By and large the domination of grading services has been beneficial to the coin market, as the widespread overgrading and "processing" of Lincoln Cents, so much of a hazard to previous generations of collectors, has been effectively eliminated. These coins still exist, but they are a pariah in the marketplace since they cannot be "slabbed."

The success of the commercial grading services is predicated largely on the use of an 11-point scale in grading Uncirculated coins. This is also the argument that so many veteran collectors have against certified grading, as they are not convinced that graders can consistently distinguish between all of the grades ranging from Mint State-60 through Mint State-70. While there are indeed occasional lapses in judgment, the marketplace has nevertheless determined that the grading services are accurate to a degree that enables the orderly trading of coins on both a sight-seen and sight-unseen basis, though the latter sales are usually made at a discount. For more information about the intricacies of modern grading practices, see Chapter 6.

One of the peripheral benefits of encapsulation has been in the preservation of coins. Whatever their appeal in the building of collections, the old folders and albums so popular in the past were often unkind to high-grade coins. Lacking the rich oxide layer of circulated pieces, bright red Lincolns were subject to spotting and staining, as well as simple tarnishing when stored in paper-based albums. As manufacturers became aware of these problems they made a conscious effort to reduce the sulfur content of their products, but tiny bits of paper dust could still become dislodged and settle onto the volatile bronze or brass surfaces of Lincoln Cents. Encapsulated coins are first blown free of such particles under a jet of compressed air and are then sealed within chemically inert plastic holders. Provided that the coins bear no contaminants before being submitted to a grading service and that they're not subjected to hostile environments, they should remain as they are for many years to come.

Other products now exist in the coin market which provide similar protection and can be purchased by any collector. These are made from one or both of two inert plastics, polystyrene and polyethylene. Marketed in several formats by a number of companies, a quick check of coin supply dealers will turn up most brands. If only such products had existed decades ago perhaps there would be fewer Lincolns that are rare in fully red condition.

The outlook for the future

As the 21st Century approaches, so too does the centennial of the Lincoln Cent. Will the one-cent piece actually survive until 2009? It seems doubtful, but then many numismatists and legislators were announcing the imminent demise of the cent as early as 1973. Clearly, this coin no longer serves any purpose for those outside of the coin collecting hobby, yet it has consistently proved politically impossible to eliminate.

As for collecting Lincoln Cents, what was said at the outset of this history remains as valid today as it was a generation ago: It almost seems as though the Lincoln Cent series was initiated for the sole purpose of giving Americans a reason to collect coins. While the focus of this collecting has largely shifted from circulation finds to selective purchases, the allure of collecting Lincolns by date and mint remains ageless. Excluding varieties, there are nearly 240 such date/mint combinations just through 1995, and it's as yet unknown when the series will terminate. One thing that's almost certain is that the Lincoln Cent will be the last coin of this denomination, bringing to an end a heritage that stretches all the way back to the first Chain Cents of 1793.

Unlike other coin type, for which many collectors have already abandoned the notion of completing a set, the Lincoln Cent series remains accessible in its entirety. Even in Uncirculated condition there are only a few very expensive issues. It seems that whatever increases in cost have occurred in recent decades have not dissuaded admirers of this series, as it presently enjoys a strong following across all grade levels. A club exists for the shar-

ing of information and experiences relating to this series; the Society of Lincoln Cent Collectors may be reached by writing to: SLCC, 13515 Magnolia Blvd., Sherman Oaks, CA, 91423.

The author is immensely proud of his two Lincoln Cent collections. There is the first one, mounted in a Whitman album and as yet incomplete. It was assembled from circulation and begun more than three decades ago at a time when knowledge remained subordinate to mere enthusiasm. Then there is the one neatly suspended in a series of plastic frames, containing mostly Uncirculated coins but with a few of the keys grading EF or AU. Assembled with a discriminating eye, it is the result of numerous friendly encounters with collectors and dealers alike. Both sets occupy a place of honor.

Both too can stir memories of discoveries big and small and of friends past and present, though their relative values in the marketplace may be widely disparate. Both are reflections of their owner's taste to varying degrees, one set acquired by simple chance, the other through careful selection. Finally, both sets will one day belong to others, and the coins once gathered together as a cohesive unit may ultimately be scattered among many individuals. It seems that coins, like people, must drift apart, only to form new bonds with the passage of time. Perhaps therein lies the human element that makes ours such a compelling pursuit.

Notes to Chapter 3

[1] *The Numismatist*, March, 1912.
[2] Ibid, July, 1925.
[3] Ibid.
[4] *The Numismatist*, February, 1928.
[5] Ibid, March, 1928.
[6] Ibid, April, 1928.
[7] Ibid, February, 1931.
[8] Ibid, October, 1935.
[9] *Numismatic Scrapbook*, March, 1935.
[10] *The Numismatic Scrapbook Magazine*, April, 1938.
[11] *The Numismatist*, February, 1954.
[12] Ibid, 1936.
[13] *The Numismatic Scrapbook Magazine*, November, 1938.
[14] *The Numismatist*, June, 1937.
[15] *Numismatic Scrapbook*, June, 1937.
[16] Ibid, July, 1937.
[17] *The Numismatic Scrapbook Magazine*, August, 1938.
[18] Ibid, December, 1943.
[19] *The Numismatist*, September, 1943.

Chapter 4

GALLERY
OF ERRORS

The Lincoln Cent series is fabulously rich in errors of all types, and it's fair to say that any calamity which can befall a coin in the United States Mints has occurred to the Lincoln Cent at one time or another. Most of these errors are fairly common and carry only modest premiums. A representative collection can be assembled at a reasonable cost, though some of the more exotic error coins illustrated in this chapter will cost a great deal more.

Included in this assembly are both common and rare items. Not surprisingly, most of are recent vintage, dating from the 1960s and later. Errors of earlier dates are more scarce, roughly in proportion to their age and the number of cents coined of a particularly date and mint. Since the 1950s the mints have used "riddle" machines to separate oversize and undersize planchets from the coining process, and this has cut down on the number and variety of errors occurring. Simpler types such as off-centered strikes and incomplete planchets remain fairly common.

Error coins are an excellent learning tool, as they afford insight into the way in which all coins are manufactured. The cents illustrated here, except where noted, are from the collection of Marian A. Sinton. The author extends his thanks to her for sharing these charming bloopers.

1921-S. This coin displays a very simple error, one common to many cents and nickels of this date and mint as the result of defective planchets. The irregular line projecting from the top of Lincoln's head to the word IN is a lamination or partial split which occurred when gas trapped within the planchet caused its metal to separate under the pressure of striking. (Tom Mulvaney)

1936-S. The obverse of this cent also shows a lamination split, but in this instance the metal actually flaked away prior to striking. Such errors are common and carry little premium value. (Author)

1942-P. Seemingly an ordinary cent, this Lincoln was coined on a blank intended for a foreign issue. The Philadelphia Mint was then coining five-centavos pieces in brass for Peru, and the composition of this cent is .8687 copper and .1313 zinc. (American Numismatic Association Authentication Bureau)

1943-P. Steel cents were not immune to errors, and this example was struck about 15% off-centered.

1943-D. Struck through grease-coated dies, a few design elements are shallow or missing from this cent. A curious yet unrelated feature is the crowded placement of its mintmark. (Tom Mulvaney)

1944-P. A severe form of lamination error, this cent has actually split along its edge, with its reverse warping outward.

Errors　　　　　　　　　　　　– 70 –　　　　　　　　　　　　*Lincoln Cents*

1964-P. Struck three times out-of-collar, this cent's reverse design became obscured by incoming planchets (Mulvaney)

1964-P. This cent was struck four times, while only the first impression was centered. The collecting of error coins grew in popularity around this time, and it was alleged that mint employees were creating pieces such as this one for sale to dealers. The careful placement of each strike, leaving the date and mintmark area untouched, suggests that this error may have been guided. Of course, since 1964 cents were struck at both the Philadelphia and San Francisco Mints without mintmarks, its origin is untraceable.

1973-D. The planchet for this cent was punched out from the end of the metal strip, leaving a ragged and incomplete portion.

1973-D. This cent appears to have been the victim of a damaged or mis-positioned collar. (Mulvaney)

1975-D. This coin was struck normally on its reverse but received a distorted obverse image from a brockage cent; it is known as a counter-brockage.

1977-P. A dime bearing this date became lodged inside the tote bin used to carry it and its brothers from the press. When this bin was later filled with cent planchets, the dime worked itself free and was struck within cent dies, which flattened portions of its design.

1981-P. Struck normally, this cent then adhered to the obverse die, which was in the upper or hammer position. It was beaten repeatedly against incoming blank planchets, one of which seems to be bonded to it. This coin may have been struck at Philadelphia, West Point or San Francisco, as none of these mints employed mintmarks for production cents.

1982-P. This large date cent suffered the same accident as the 1981-P at left, but with the additional error of two incoming planchets becoming bonded to it. This is a rare and valuable error type. Again, the mint of origin is unknown.

1982-P. Another large date cent, this one was struck off-centered and from a die broken below Lincoln's bust. Metal flowed into the missing portion of the die, as well as forming a flange around the neck of the die. (Mulvaney)

1990-P. Struck normally once, this cent then flipped over within the press as the dies separated and was struck a second time, off-centered. The blank projection at the left side of its obverse shows where it was compressed against the incoming planchet. (William Shamhart, Jr.)

1992-P. An example of a very minor and quite common error, this cent was struck normally but with a slightly misaligned obverse die. The die may have worked itself out of alignment, but it's more likely the result of simple carelessness on the part of the die-setter.

1993-P. Known as a centered broadstrike, the collar die was not in place when this cent was coined, and its planchet was permitted to flow outward without restraint. Though a relatively common type of error, this is a particularly nice example due to its excellent centering and clarity. (David F. Cieniewicz)

E19: Date and mint unknown. This cent's reverse die suffered a major break, popularly called a cud. Whenever the date and mint of such coins are known these are more properly classified as varieties, since every coin struck from that die state will be similar. Note how the rush of metal into the broken section left a depression in the corresponding area of the obverse, rendering the date and mint unreadable. Judging from the overall worn state of the dies it appears to be a Denver or San Francisco Mint cent from the late 1910s or the 1920s.

Date and mint unknown. This cent was struck at least three times, the later impressions against incoming planchets which distorted its reverse.

Date unknown, Denver Mint. Struck between the reverse die and a thin, bottle-cap cent, this coin received a faint impression of the obverse die through the other coin's metal.

Date and mint unknown. The planchet for this cent was punched from the side of the metal strip, leaving an incomplete portion having a straight edge. It was then struck off-centered. The obverse hub style dates this coin to 1974-82.

Date and mint unknown. The mechanism which feeds incoming planchets while simultaneously ejecting finished coins evidently jammed, and this piece was struck repeatedly. The distorted cent eventually folded over onto itself. The recessed relief of Lincoln's upper arm dates this coin to 1984 or later.

Date and mint unknown. A nicely centered saddle strike, this specimen appears to date from 1969-83. It has the sharpened LIBERTY introduced in 1969 but lacks the sunken relief within Lincoln's upper arm used beginning in 1984.

Date and mint unknown. This double-struck cent, circa 1984-89, was on-centered and in-collar for its first strike, off-centered and out-of-collar for its second. Between strikes, it landed atop an incoming planchet, and this caused its partially flattened reverse.

Date and mint unknown. Struck off-centered twice and bonded to a second planchet, these cents appear from the detail of Lincoln's portrait to date from 1982 or later.

Date and mint unknown. This amazing error occurred when the planchet entered the press on edge and was folded onto itself by the force of the dies coming together.

Date and mint unknown. The coin illustrated received a normal impression, though broadstruck. It was then partially obliterated by a brockage cent striking it a second time. It dates to 1974 or later, as revealed by the size of the initials FG.

Date and mint unknown. A bottlecap error, this one is quite unusual in that the coin adhered to the reverse die rather than the obverse die, which is more typical.

Date and mint unknown. This brockage was struck between the reverse die and the reverse of a previously struck coin which remained in the press. It dates from 1974 or later.

Date and mint unknown. A major die break, also known as a cud, is seen at the lower right of this cent's obverse and has caused the corresponding position on its reverse to suffer poor metal flow. The arcing line at the left of its obverse appears to be a second cud forming. Since it is still in place, it is properly called a retained cud. The sunken relief in Lincoln's upper arm dates this coin to 1984 or later.

ERROR COIN ROYALTY
THE OFF-METAL CENTS OF 1943-44

1943 Bronze

PHILADELPHIA
(mintage unknown)

RARITY: Only 10 examples have been confirmed and documented as struck in bronze. A few more may possibly exist, but the figure of 40 pieces published by Walter Breen in his *Encyclopedia* is without foundation.

POPULATION: MS TOTAL = 0

As of January, 1996 NGC had certified a single piece as XF45, while ANACS had certified one as AU50. PCGS does not certify off-metal strikes.

All of the ten examples certified by ANACS when it was managed by the American Numismatic Association (1972-90) have been examined by specialist Steve Benson, who provided the following grades assigned by ANACS for seven of them. There may be some duplication with the coins above: AU55 (1) AU50 (3) EF45 (2) EF40 (1)

There are also auction reports of single examples graded VG8 and F12 (damaged), but these specimens are not confirmed as genuine.

VALUES: Due to the infrequency with which these coins are traded there are no published retail figures for the 1943-P bronze cents, but sales in the $10,000-25,000 range are not unusual.

COMMENTS: These coins were almost certainly struck in error, though the temptation to create bronze novelties would have been great indeed. Errors of this type are not uncommon, as any planchet of equal size or smaller will fit within the collar surrounding cent dies and be struck as a cent. A number of silver dime planchets were also coined with 1943 cent dies by mistake.

This error occurs when a mobile tote bin containing planchets of one type is emptied into the press delivery system and then filled with planchets of another type. A few of the first batch may wedge themselves into the trap door at the bottom of the tote bin as it closes. These are then dislodged when the door is opened a second time to release the new batch of planchets. Thus, a few of the old ones are coined in a press run for some other coin type. What made this particular instance of a wrong-planchet error so compelling is simply the novelty of the regular steel cents themselves and the dramatic contrast between the steel and bronze alloys.

* * *

More falsehoods and fantastic lore have surrounded this coin than any other in the Lincoln series. Our story begins around the end of World War II when rumors were spread nationwide that automobile manufacturer Henry Ford would give a new car to anyone who could furnish him with a "copper" cent dated 1943. Since domestic goods of any sort were in short supply due to wartime rationing, this was a tempting offer indeed. Of course it proved false, but not before the Ford Motor Company was besieged with annoying inquiries. Stuart Mosher, Editor of *The Numismatist*, suggested that the author of this rumor "should be horse-whipped."[1] To which Groucho Marx might have added, "I'd have horse-whipped him——if I had a horse."

This was just the latest in a series of similar stories that were as old as the Lincoln Cent series and nearly as old as Ford cars. The first edition appeared around World War I at a time when the "flivver," as the Ford Model T was popularly known, was the butt of many a joke. It claimed that old Henry would trade one of his cars to anyone who could put together a set of four Lincoln "pennies" whose initials (mintmarks) spelled out F.O.R.D. While it showed that Americans were at least somewhat aware of the coins in their pockets, this tale also revealed a widespread ignorance of the various minting establishments!

During the mid 1930s a new edition of this popular tale appeared, but this time the ticket to motoring pleasure was to be found in any cent dated 1922. Apparently, only 200 were made, and Henry already owned 150 of them. In an effort to secure the remaining pieces, he was offering a new car in exchange. For more about this ludicrous tale see COMMENTS for 1922-D in Chapter 7.

Amid the silly rumors regarding 1943 "copper" cents, the first published reports of apparently genuine coins appeared almost simultaneously from Dr. Conrad Ottelin and Don Lutes, Jr. in 1947.[2] Nothing is known of what became of the Ottelin specimen, but Lutes, a 16-year-old boy, received his in change from the cafeteria in his Pittsfield, Massachusetts high school. He penned this letter to *The Numismatic Scrapbook Magazine*:

> It seems to me that the question of the possibility that any 1943 copper cents do exist, has been avoided entirely too much. Just because the mint record shows that none were struck doesn't necessarily mean that some copper blanks couldn't have slipped by.
> I have one of these cents which is not copper-plated steel nor does the date appear to have been changed.
> I would appreciate hearing from any fellow collector on this subject. Maybe this will prove to be another addition to the already long list of freak coins.[3]

Nothing more appeared in print regarding the Lutes and Otterlin coins. Most knowledgeable figures in the numismatic field doubted the validity of the few specimens which were found over the following ten years, as so many fake ones had been manufactured by altering other dates or by copper-plating ordinary 1943 cents. The first widespread acknowledgment of a 1943 bronze cent, one found in change in 1956 by 14-year-old Marvin Beyer, Jr. of Rivera, California, appeared the following year. In a story which ran in *The Huntington Park Signal,* it was claimed that the boy had turned down offers of a house and also a uranium mine in exchange for the cent. He exhibited the coin at several local coin clubs during the months following its discovery, and it was even displayed at the offices of Whitman Publishing Company, the source of many numismatic books and supplies. Whitman ultimately decided not to include it in R. S. Yeoman's *A Guide Book of United States Coins.*

Marvin and his two brothers all delivered newspapers and carefully monitored the change they received for "keepers." Their father, also a casual collector, instructed young Marvin to look through the family's jar of cents and joked that he should watch out for a 1943 copper one. "When Marv, Jr. showed me the penny he had discovered, I just glanced at it and went back to reading, but Marv got out the magnifying glass, and sure enough it was a 1943."[4]

The sale of this specimen was set for the 1958 ANA convention auction, conducted by veteran numismatist Abe Kosoff. Just minutes before the sale, with Kosoff holding several very high bids, Marvin Beyer, Sr. withdrew the coin for an unspecified reason. How the matter was ultimately settled was never publicized, but Kosoff was furious at the time and sued Beyer for "breach of contract, fraud, deceit and slander." He sought $60,750 in damages.[5]

A story that appeared in the February 1, 1959 issue of *The Los Angeles Examiner* claimed that Beyer's coin was sold privately to the Greer Company of that city for $40,000. Given that coins such as the 1804 silver dollar were then valued in the $10,000-15,000 range, this figure seems fanciful. While a sale may have indeed occurred, the sum reported was probably a publicity ploy by Greer or just the usual exaggeration built into every rare coin story written by non-numismatists. This episode only served to heighten the fame of 1943 bronze cents, and countless pieces were subsequently devised as either novelty items or outright scams.

Some credence is given to the notion that at least one was deliberately struck in bronze by the fact that such a coin turned up in the possession of a female acquaintance of the late John R. Sinnock, Chief Engraver of the U. S. Mint from 1925 until 1947. She informed the dealer purchasing the coin from her that Sinnock had given it to her as a Christmas present in 1943! This dealer, William Grichin, sold it and another piece obtained from the woman, a 1944-P steel cent, to prominent Philadelphia dealer Harry J. Forman. Both coins were subsequently sold by Forman in 1961 to numismatic dealer and researcher John J. Ford, and they remained unknown until appearing as sequential lots in an auction by Bowers & Ruddy Galleries. Held in conjunction with the 1981 convention of the American Numismatic Association, this sale was rich in exotica. The 1943 bronze cent appeared as Lot 414 and was graded Extremely Fine. It realized $10,000.

DENVER
(mintage unknown)

RARITY: Only a single specimen has been authenticated.

POPULATION: MS TOTAL = 1
    The only 1943-D bronze cent known was certified MS64 BN by NGC in May of 1996. NGC's PHOTO PROOF division supplied these photographs.

VALUES: The only sale of this single specimen realized $82,500 when it appeared as Lot 536 in Superior Stamp & Coin's auction of May 27-28, 1996.

COMMENTS: Though Walter Breen in his *Encyclopedia* reported that 24 examples were known of the 1943-D cent in bronze, this figure was entirely without foundation. Specialists were in agreement that no such coins existed, aside from a few spurious fabrications. It was thus a shock when this example surfaced, and its existence was highly publicized by Superior prior to its sale.
    This specimen was submitted to NGC for grading accompanied by certificate number E-8256-C from the American Numismatic Association Certification Service (now ANAAB). ANAAB records prior to 1981 were not available to researchers, and as this certificate had been issued in 1979 the existence of the coin was then a secret known only to its owners. This specimen had been in the possession of a former machinist at the Denver Mint, now deceased. His heirs inherited the coin and consigned it to Superior for sale. When it was submitted to NGC for certification, the author of this book was able to examine it in detail and concurred with the grading staff that it was genuine.
    The coin illustrated above is the only known 1943 bronze cent qualifying as Mint State. It is very sharply struck throughout, its obverse border being quite broad and squared. Only at its lower reverse is there any sign of incomplete striking. One peculiar feature is a series little flecks of what is presumably zinc adhering to the coin's surface and compressed against it. This reinforces the notion that this coin was struck following a run of zinc-plated steel cents and using the same dies. Some of the zinc plating must have worked it way off of one or more steel planchets and adhered to the dies, only to be driven into the bronze planchet at the moment of striking.

SAN FRANCISCO
(mintage unknown)

RARITY: Walter Breen's estimate of about six examples known seems to be accurate, though only four coins have been certified as genuine. None of these graded below EF. A seventh example, previosuly unknown to the hobby, was shown to the author as this book neared completion. Lightly worn, it had been authenticated by Smithsonian Institution curator Vladimir Clain-Stefanelli in 1957. The coin's owner stated that his father found it in circulation in 1948.

POPULATION: MS TOTAL = 0
    As of January, 1996 no 1943-S bronze cents had been certified by NGC, while ANACS had certified one each as XF40 and AU58. PCGS does not certify off-metal strikes.
    Steve Benson provided the above photographs and a table listing the three confirmed examples examined by ANACS when it was a division of the American Numismatic Association (1972-90). One of these was graded EF45, the remaining two as EF40. There may be duplication with the XF40 specimen certified more recently by ANACS.

VALUES: These coins are offered too infrequently to establish any retail value, yet they are more highly prized than comparable 1943-P bronze cents. Sales in the $10,000-25,000 range are typical, though there are reported figures as high as $35,000-50,000.

COMMENTS: The first reports of this issue appeared in 1959 and were probably prompted by the publicity given to Marvin Beyers, Jr.'s 1943-P bronze cent. One 1943-S was claimed to be in the possession of George Pearce of San Antonio, Texas, while another had been found by Lucille Steck of Belleville, Michigan. It's not known if either of these two discovery coins proved to be genuine.[6]
    There are several recorded sales of this issue dating back to 1973. Like the 1943-P bronze cents these were almost certainly coined in error when leftover bronze planchets adhered to the inside of tote bins which subsequently carried the new steel planchets. An error which is scarce but occurs periodically for other dates, wrong-planchet coins are normally not valued as highly as the 1943 bronze and 1944 steel cents. The appeal of these two years lies in their dramatic contrast between the intended alloy and the actual alloy, as well as the controversial role that steel cents played in America's coinage history.

Notes to Chapter 4
[1]*The Numismatist,* May, 1947.
[2]Ibid, June, 1947.
[3]Ibid.
[4]*The Numismatic Scrapbook Magazine,* November, 1957.
[5]*The Numismatist,* April, 1959.
[6]Ibid, October, 1959.
[7]Walter Breen, *Walter Breen's Complete Encyclopedia of U. S. and Colonial Coins.*
[8]*The Numismatist,* December, 1959.
[9]Charles G. Altz & E. H. Barton, *Foreign Coins Struck at United States Mints.*

1944 Steel

PHILADELPHIA
(mintage unknown)

RARITY: These are very rare, and only 27 examples are confirmed as genuine. Though none have appeared in grades below VF, a number of pieces are corroded. The finest known is a choice uncirculated specimen traced to John R. Sinnock, who was the U. S. Mint's Chief Engraver at the time (see COMMENTS below).

POPULATION: MS TOTAL = 0
      As of January, 1996 NGC had certified a single piece as AU58, while ANACS had certified one as XF40 and two for genuineness alone. When managed by the American Numismatic Association (1972-90), ANACS certified 27 examples for genuineness.
      Steve Benson provided the above photographs and a census for 13 of the 27 coins certified.
It reads as follows: MS63 (2)   AU50 (5)   EF40 (4)   VF30 (1)   VF20 (1)

NOTE: Readers should not be confused by the terms EF40 and XF40 which represent the same grade. The American Numismatic Association and many individuals use EF as the abbreviation for Extremely Fine, while the commercial grading services prefer XF. When XF appears in this book it denotes a coin certified by one of the commercial services.

VALUES: These rare cents are offered too infrequently to establish any firm retail value, yet they seem to have less appeal to collectors than the more famous 1943 bronze cents and typically trade in the mid four figures.

COMMENTS: Less well known than the bronze cents of 1943, the 1944 steel cents from the Philadelphia Mint are also not as scarce. The first piece discovered turned up in circulation around 1945 and was the lucky find of Richard Fenton. It was not publicized, however, until another ten years had passed.[7] Apparently, collectors were still not aware of this issue, as another "discovery" was reported in 1959 by W. H. Smith of Fayatteville, Ohio.[8]
      Two explanations for this error coin exist, and it's likely that both played a role. Leftover planchets from the previous year's coinage may have become wedged inside the tote bins used to transport unstruck planchets and finished coins. If these planchets worked their way loose during 1944, a steel cent of that date would result. In fact, the Philadelphia Mint's supply of remaining steel planchets was put to work during 1944 rather than being discarded. In an economy move, the 25,000,000 two-francs coins struck there for use in liberated Belgium were specifically designed to utilize these planchets. Their size and composition is unique for that denomination in Belgium's coinage history.[9] It's quite possible that some of the "Belgian" planchets made their way into a press set with U. S. cent dies.

*   *   *

      At least one 1944 steel cent seems to have been retrieved before entering circulation. Shortly after being coined it was presented by Chief Engraver John R. Sinnock (along with a 1943 bronze cent) to a female acquaintance, who later sold both pieces to coin dealer William Grichin. They were sold by him to Philadelphia dealer Harry J. Forman. These coins then passed to prominent professional numismatist John J. Ford, who consigned them to a Bowers & Ruddy Galleries auction held in conjunction with the 1981 convention of the American Numismatic Association. Offered as Lot 415 and graded MS-65, the 1944-P steel cent realized $3500.

DENVER
(mintage unknown)

RARITY: These are rare in all grades, though none have graded less than EF. It's likely that no more than 10 are known, as only seven have been certified by the American Numismatic Association.

POPULATION: MS TOTAL = 3

As of January, 1996 NGC had certified two as MS62 and one as MS63. ANACS had certified one as AU50, one as AU55 and three for authentication alone. PCGS does not certify off-metal coins.

When affiliated with the ANA (1972-90), ANACS certified for genuineness seven examples. Steve Benson has provided the above photographs and a table of the grades assigned to these seven coins:

MS62 (3)   AU55 (1)   AU50 (2)   EF40 (1)

VALUES: These coins are offered too infrequently to establish any firm retail value, but they seem to trade in the mid four figures.

COMMENTS: This is the second most available 1944 steel cent after 1944-P, by a ratio of approximately one to four. As is true of all the 1944 steel cents, examples are usually week around the rims. They were coined with the greater die-set distance adequate for bronze cents but insufficient to bring up all features on the harder steel planchets.

Since the Denver Mint did not strike any two-francs coins for Belgium, all of the 1944-D steel cents must have resulted from steel planchets adhering to the inside of tote bins during 1943 and being struck during 1944.

SAN FRANCISCO
(mintage unknown)

RARITY: This issue is of the greatest rarity and is probably unique.

POPULATION: MS TOTAL = 0

No examples have been certified by the commercial grading services, though the single confirmed specimen was authenticated by ANACS when this service was owned by the American Numismatic Association. It graded EF40 and is illustrated above courtesy of Steve Benson.

VALUES: The only known sale of a 1944-S steel cent realized $5,390 in 1983.

COMMENTS: The rarity of this issue is so great that it may be considered non-collectable in the practical sense.

The only known specimen appeared as Lot 787 in Bowers & Ruddy Galleries' auction of January 25-27, 1983. It was graded EF and had been cleaned. In fact, this great rarity was the last of three sequential lots comprising a complete set of 1944-dated steel cents from all mints, an opportunity for collectors that may never be repeated.

Since the San Francisco Mint did not participate in producing the two-francs coinage for Belgium, it must be assumed that this coin was the result of a planchet intended for 1943-S cent production finding its way accidentally between 1944-S dies.

Chapter 5

COUNTERFEIT &
ALTERED COINS

Given its low face value the Lincoln Cent has been spared the indignity of circulating counterfeits, but numismatic counterfeits are another story. Due to the popularity of this series and the inclusion in it of several key dates and varieties, bogus or altered Lincoln Cents have been a bane to collectors going as far back as the 1930s. It wasn't until the 1950s, however, that the counterfeiting and altering of American coins in general and Lincoln Cents in particular became a big business. The phenomenal growth that the hobby experienced in the years following World War II created an entire generation of neophyte collectors who had little or no knowledge of how coins were made and whose only goal was to fill the holes in their albums. The rapidly rising prices for key dates and varieties prompted the production of false coins, and these inexperienced hobbyists were easy prey.

This activity peaked during the late 1950s and '60s, but as the more casual collectors dropped out of the hobby after the mid '60s those who remained gradually became better educated. While many of the cruder fakes still make the rounds of flea markets and country auctions, only the more skillful examples are able to fool knowledgeable collectors and dealers. Passage of the Hobby Protection Act in 1973 tightened the definition of what constituted a fraudulent coin, but it has not stopped the flow of sophisticated, die-struck counterfeits.

More effective has been the quick detection and publicizing of counterfeit and altered coins by the American Numismatic Association Authentication Bureau (ANAAB). Currently headed by J. P. Martin, the ANAAB still provides the hobby with reliable counterfeit detection, and J. P. furnished information and photographs for this chapter. Another advance in the war against fake coins has been the growth of grading services. In order to protect their own integrity these services refuse to grade coins which are counterfeit or have been altered in some way. Since uncertified coins are less easily mar-

keted, this restriction has helped to drive the bad pieces underground. Collectors are urged to proceed with caution when buying recognized key dates that have not been certified.

The most experienced numismatists can perform their own counterfeit detection, though they will not have access to the extensive photographic files maintained by the ANAAB, some of whose photos are reproduced in this book. Most experienced coin dealers can spot a fake and will refuse to buy it in the first place. Sadly, not everyone who trades in old coins is an expert. Nor is being sold a coin that later turns out to be bogus proof that the seller is dishonest; it may simply be that he or she lacks sufficient knowledge to detect a bad coin. If one chooses to buy an uncertified, key-date Lincoln Cent there is an old saying in the hobby that still applies: "Know your coins or know your dealer."

Added and removed mintmarks

The simplest method of producing a rarity is to alter a genuine coin in some manner. Along with the 1916-D Mercury Dime, the 1909-S V.D.B. cent is probably the most widely altered coin. This is purely a matter of economics; the pay-off for faking these coins is greater than for most other popular issues and the demand for them more widespread. The most common way to create the key-date 1909-S V.D.B. cent is by adding an S mintmark to a genuine Philadelphia Mint cent of the same variety; a couple examples of this technique are illustrated. At one time such additions were soldered on, the coins then being cleaned and retoned to hide the resulting discoloration around the mintmark area. In more recent years, however, the fake S has been applied with sophisticated epoxies. No matter how skillfully the work is done, it can usually be detected by knowing how the real coin looks. The size and style of the mintmark used from 1909 through 1916 is quite distinctive, and a close-up of it is shown on page 98. There are only four known

1909-S V.D.B. with added mintmark. Note that the serifs aren't parallel as on genuine coins. (American Numismatic Association Authentication Bureau)

1909-S V.D.B. with added initials. Genuine coins have a sharply slanting center stroke to letter 'B'. (ANAAB)

1909-S V.D.B. with added mintmark. (Harry Miller)

obverse dies for this issue, each with a unique placement to the mintmark. Any coin not matching one of these placements is thus immediately suspect.[1]

The 1909-S Lincoln Cent without initials is typically faked in the same manner, though the financial incentive for doing so is somewhat lower. Again, detection lies in knowing the distinctive characteristics of the genuine mintmark used for both issues. It features parallel serifs and reveals a couple of flaws inherent in the mintmark punch itself. A tiny, raised dot is found within the upper loop, and a sunken notch or depression is evident on the face of the upper serif. This latter feature may disappear with wear, but the dot will remain visible on all but the most worn coins. Since eight or more obverse dies were used for the 1909-S cents, mintmark placement is not a practical tool for spotting fakes.[2]

A curious variant and one not often seen is the addition of letters V.D.B to the reverse of a genuine 1909-S cent without initials. Knowing what to look for can save a lot of regret. The center stroke of letter B on genuine coins slants upward from left to right, and the entire letter is tilted slightly to the left.[3] These are features which many counterfeiters fail to replicate.

After 1909-S V.D.B., the next most popular target for the faker has been 1914-D cents. These are easily simulated by cutting away part of the first numeral 4 from 1944-D cents. There are countless such alterations dating from the 1950s and '60s, and at one time these were even being publicly offered for sale as alterations at the price of one dollar apiece.[4] Compare the laughable fake shown here with the genuine article illustrated on page 115.

While cutting away part of the 4 leaves the date reading 19 14, there are other ways to spot this alteration. Genuine 1914-D cents do not have the initials V.D.B. at the truncation of Lincoln's bust, as these were not placed on it until 1918. Another simple way to spot an erstwhile 1944-D cent is by examining its mintmark. That of a 1914-D cent is much smaller and of a distinctive shape used only from 1911 through part of 1917. 1914-D cents were coined from at least six obverse dies, so the position of a particular coin's mintmark is not reliable in determining its genuineness.[5]

The 1922 "plain" cent is a very popular variety and one in which altered pieces clearly outnumber genuine coins. The former are produced by simply removing the mintmark from a genuine 1922-D cent. This is often followed by some buffing and recoloring to cover up tooling marks in the mintmark area. As if artificial coloring wasn't reason enough to pass up a coin, it should also serve as a warning of possible alteration. Once again, the solution lies in knowing how the real coin should look. Examples of genuine 1922 "plain" cents are shown on pages 138-139, while a couple of alterations are shown here.

The last regular issue in the Lincoln Cent series whose value merits faking is the 1931-S cent. This is typically done by altering another S-Mint cent, 1936-S being

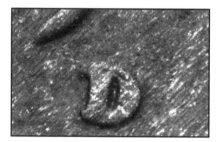

1914-D with sculpted mintmark formed by chasing away metal from genuine 1914-P cent. (ANAAB)

Crude attempt to create a 1914-D cent from a 1944-D example. Note the incorrect mintmark style.

1922-D cent with D removed and surfaces buffed to hide the tooling. (ANAAB)

Another example with removed mintmark. (Miller)

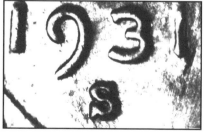

1936-S cents altered to read 1931-S. Compare these with the genuine date style shown on page 164. (ANAAB)

the most popular for this purpose. Fortunately, it's easy to spot such work, as all cents dated 1931 have a very distinctive date style that features a long lower stroke. Numeral 3 is different from any other year in the 1930s in which the San Francisco Mint struck cents. Though some good jobs have been done in reshaping the fourth numeral into a 1, it's the 3 which always gives these coins away. A couple of the more amateurish alterations are illustrated. Of course, it's possible to add a letter S to a genuine 1931-P cent, but this doesn't seem to have been done as often.

J. P. Martin reports that added mintmarks are usually fabricated outright rather than being lifted from genuine coins of other dates.[6] While it seems that it would be easier to start with an already formed mintmark and simply relocate it to another coin, those having firsthand knowledge of this procedure were unavailable for comment!

Other desirable issues frequently faked through the altering of genuine coins are the bronze cents of 1943. Though countless pieces have been produced by simply copper-plating genuine steel cents, it soon became common knowledge that these could be detected by their magnetism. Thus, counterfeiters advanced to reshaping the final numeral of the date on genuine cents of the 1940s to simulate a 3. A clumsy example of this technique is illustrated. Such work inevitably leaves tooling marks and discoloration, so this must be covered-up by buffing the coin and then recoloring it entirely.

Die-struck counterfeits

While experienced and educated collectors should be able to detect any altered coin, outright counterfeits pose a greater challenge. Some of those produced since the 1960s are of excellent quality and present a serious threat to the hobby. The ANAAB and the various grading services are alert to these coins and how to spot them, yet some coin dealers are still taken in and unknowingly pass the problem along to their customers.

Completely counterfeit coins are rarely cast in a mold; the quality of such work would not fool anyone but a beginner. Instead, most counterfeits are struck from steel dies, just as at the U. S. Mint. These dies are created by copying the contours of real coins in a mechanical transfer process. The ANAAB has prepared a study of such coins from which the following is excerpted:

> The most common method—as well as the most accurate and sophisticated—is the mechanical "one-to-one" transfer method, a procedure much like that used by the Mint to produce genuine dies.
>
> In this case, a genuine coin is mounted into an adaptation of the Janvier reduction engraving lathe. This device consists primarily of a rigid arm on a fulcrum. On one end of the arm is a point for tracing an image, while the other end carries a cutter for engraving. The host coin is rotated clockwise under the tracer; a blank die is set into motion at the same speed under the cutter. As the tracer moves from the center of the host coin outward in tight spirals, the cutter engraves a corresponding one-to-one negative image on the die. The process is repeated on a second die for the other side of the coin.
>
> The transfer dies, although very good copies, lack the fine detail of the host coin. The strength of strike and detail depend largely on the quality of the host coin and the efficiency of the transfer process. Details such as fine die cracks and die polish may show intermittently or not at all on the die. It is important to note that any defect on the host coin will be transferred to counterfeit dies.[7]

Since the transfer die may not be as sharp as the original coin, the counterfeiter will typically strike his product under great pressure to compensate by bringing out whatever detail is present. This produces a coin which has very broad and sharply squared edges, a quality typically found on genuine coins only for proof strikings. Genuine coins struck for circulation do not completely fill the dies at the point where they meet the collar, and they typically have some beveling near their rims. Thus, the unnaturally flat and broad edges of die-struck counterfeits often give them away. Such coins may also have wire rims where the excessive pressure used caused the planchet metal to flow into the tiny gap

1943-P bronze cent coined from counterfeit transfer dies. (ANAAB)

Altered date on genuine bronze cent. This coin has been buffed to cover tooling marks. (ANAAB)

1955-P doubled-die cent struck from counterfeit transfer dies. Note its rough surface and thin letters. (ANAAB)

between the collar and the two dies.

Popular subjects for counterfeiting with transfer dies include 1909-S V.D.B., 1914-D and 1931-S. There are lesser numbers of die-struck 1909-S counterfeits, but these frequently share the same obverse die used for counterfeit 1909-S V.D.B. cents. Some of the counterfeits of these coins are so good that to illustrate them here would only confuse the reader. One's best bet is to buy only certified examples of these key dates.

Also subject to die-struck counterfeiting are 1943 bronze cents from all three mints, as well as popular varieties such as the 1955-P and 1972-P doubled-die cents. Typically, not as much care was put into the counterfeits of these coins, as it was perhaps believed that they would come under less scrutiny or would be sold to less knowledgeable buyers. Examination of the photos presented here will reveal the crudeness of their workmanship.

Harmless forms of alteration

Many Lincoln Cents have been altered in some way for amusement or promotional purposes with no intent to deceive. One of the most popular uses for Uncle Sam's coinage debuted at the World's Columbian Exposition, held in Chicago in 1893. This was the rolled-out or elongated coin, and the earliest subjects of this gimmick were the Indian Head Cent and the Liberty Head Nickel. Passing an ordinary coin through a hand-cranked pair of rollers compressed it into an elliptical shape while raising a message or image of some sort on one side. The other side was left blank and usually revealed a distorted image of the host coin. Either sold or given away as souvenirs, these proved quite popular until being outlawed during the 1920s. When the Federal Government finally realized in the 1950s that no harm was being done with such rolled-out coins it stopped enforcing this prohibition. These novelties regained their former popularity with the several World's Fairs of the 1960s, and today they're a staple of gift shops and tourist attractions nationwide. The variety of Lincoln Cents found rolled-out is seemingly endless, and just a few of them are presented here.

Debuting at about the same time as the rolled-out cents were encasements. The first inexpensive process for extracting aluminum from its ore was developed in the 1880s, and this almost certainly accounts for the use of this metal in making encasements. Bearing a message or advertisement of some sort, the encasement was bonded to an otherwise ordinary cent by compressing the two between dies. The encasement became crimped over the coin's edge by this operation, and removing the subject coin will reveal some damage to it. Such removed coins have puzzled beginning collectors for generations. The early encasements fea-

On this cent both the message die and the host coin are dated 1995.

Rolled-out cents dated 1971-S and 1981-D (Ken Barr)

Abe Lincoln would roll over in his grave if he knew that he was sharing space with the State of South Carolina, the most aggressively rebellious of the Confederate States.

Elks Lodge Number 782 produced this commemorative by stamping the back of a 1976-P cent. (Barr)

The obverse rim of this 1973-D cent has been beveled inward so that when it's spun it will always land with the same side facing up. In a similar vein are the two-headed or two-tailed coins made by inserting a plug made from one cent into the cavity cut from another.

tured Indian Head Cents and are highly prized. Those created since 1909 have typically featured Lincoln Cents, sometimes entrapping key dates in the process. Though encasements can still be made at any time they seem to have been largely supplanted as souvenirs by rolled-out coins and wooden nickels.

Requiring more time and effort to produce are cents which have been engraved in some way. Sometimes the features of Abe Lincoln appear altered, much in the manner of the popular "hobo" nickels, yet such examples are rare for cents. More often seen are Lincolns which have had one side planed down and a message or image engraved. All hand-engraved pieces are unique, but punched or stamped examples can be cataloged as recurring items. It's typically the reverse which is removed in such operations, and a few specimens are illustrated.

Sometimes a cent may be left intact and some image simply punched into its field. The profile of President John F. Kennedy is a popular topic, as so many eerie comparisons may be made between his term and Lincoln's. States of the Union are also popular additions to the humble cent, and it's amazing how many collectors will write to coin publications seeking information about such "Mint" varieties. These popular novelties are still being produced in the 1990s, and they may often be found at the same locations where rolled-out cents are sold. Some amusing pieces from the author's collection are illustrated.

Notes to Chapter 5

[1] J. P. Martin, *"Authenticating the Lincoln Cent,"* American Numismatic Association Authentication Bureau.

[2] Ibid.

[3] Ibid.

[4] *The Numismatist,* December, 1957.

[5] Martin.

[6] Ibid.

[7] Ibid.

Novelty coins such as these are mass produced and sold nationwide in gift shops.

*The meaning of these symbols is unknown.
(Barr)*

Serving in the U.S. Navy during World War II, someone with the initials 'RWS' left us this commemorative. (Barr)

The slight deformation of this coin's obverse suggest that it rested atop a strip of leather when it was overstruck for a local landmark. (Barr)

This fascinating piece is a 1909-P Lincoln Cent overstruck on its reverse with the obverse die of a Hendrik Hudson Tercentenary medalet produced by New York coin dealer Thomas Elder. The obverse of the cent rested atop a copper plate which served as an anvil. This plate had already picked up the impression of a previously overstruck coin, a one-centavo piece of El Salvador dated 1889-H, and this impression transferred to the obverse of the Lincoln Cent. (David F. Cieniewicz)

Chapter 6

GRADING
LINCOLN CENTS

Aside from a few scarce varieties, Lincoln Cents dated 1934 and later are usually collected in Uncirculated grades. This situation has prevailed since the end of the 1960s, when the chance of finding cents dated 1958 and earlier in circulation dropped off so drastically. Until that time collectors had a reasonable hope of finding many earlier dates, and there existed an incentive to fill albums with coins obtained from bank rolls and loose change. Persons entering the hobby today may start with inexpensive, worn cents purchased from dealers' "junk boxes," but they are far more likely than were earlier generations of hobbyists to rapidly advance to purchasing Uncirculated coins. Lincoln Cents dated 1909-33, however, remain quite collectable in all grades, though the market for ones grading less than Fine is typically limited to the key dates.

Excluding coins which have been harshly cleaned or damaged in some way, the grading of circulated Lincoln Cents is a very straightforward exercise. The standards established by the American Numismatic Association in the 1970s have remained in place and are quite easy to follow, particularly when accompanied by high quality photographs as in the pages that follow. It is only when attempting to evaluate Uncirculated cents, whether currency strikes or proofs, that the going gets rough. Once it's been established that a particular coin is indeed Uncirculated the challenge that remains is to determine which of the single grade-point levels from Mint State-60 through Mint State-70 apply to that coin.

This is fairly recent phenomenon, as collectors active prior to the late 1970s typically utilized only two grades for unworn Lincoln Cents: Uncirculated (UNC) and Brilliant Uncirculated (BU). To these may have been added enhancements such as Choice and Gem, but there was no fixed method of comparing one cent against another. The adoption of the Sheldon System, which graded coins on a scale of one to 70, was simply a numerical supplement to this same system. UNC became MS-60; Choice BU became MS-63; and Gem BU became MS-65. When these numbers began to appear around the mid 1970s their inclusion created few problems for anyone who understood their equivalent adjectival grades. In addition there was also enough distinction between these grade levels that it wasn't too difficult to assign any particular coin its proper grade.

It wasn't until the 1980s when all of the various intermediate grades from MS-60 to MS-70 were first applied that collectors became confused and uncertain. The increasing values of many Lincoln Cents and other coins prompted such fine distinctions, but there remained little agreement as to what constituted the difference between single grade-points. The American Numismatic Association attempted to keep up with this expanded system of grading by publishing written descriptions of each grade level from MS-60 through MS-70. The appearance of commercial services offering to assign their grading opinion to a coin and then encapsulate it for a fee dates only to 1986. Such companies, however, are now collectively a dominant force in the market for United States coins, particularly the modern issues such as Lincoln Cents. Though the grading of Uncirculated coins is still challenging to most collectors, the widespread acceptance of the grades assigned by these services has helped to ease this transition to a modern grading environment.

The grading of Uncirculated copper and bronze coins is taken a step further by the grading services in assigning the suffixes BN (Brown), RB (Red & Brown) and RD (Red) to denote a coin's color. It's intended that this be applied only to coins which have never been cleaned and whose color is thus "original." While there are some exceptions among earlier issues, this practice is adhered to more strictly with modern coins such as Lincoln Cents.

A Brown cent is defined as one having no red color remaining or is less than about 15% red. A Red & Brown cent will show 15%-85% of its mint red color. Ones having 85% or more of their original color will typically be assigned the suffix RD for Red. While the degree of redness is a subjective matter, the experience of professional coin graders in handling so many copper and bronze coins has permitted a high degree of consistency in applying these designators.

Coins which have been damaged, harshly cleaned or artificially colored are rejected for certified grading by the two largest grading services, the Professional Coin Grading Service (PCGS) and Numismatic Guaranty Corporation of America (NGC). Other commercial grading services include ANACS, PCI (formerly Photo Certified Institute) and the International Numismatic Society (INS). These may certify a coin having one or more of the problems listed above, but these problems will be noted in their descriptions of it.

* * *

Rather than attempt to paraphrase the ANA's grading standards when that organization has already presented them so well, the author has elected to reprint these descriptions as published in the Fourth Edition of *The Official American Numismatic Association Grading Standards for United States Coins*. This book was co-authored by Ken Bressett and the late Abe Kosoff, and it was published by Western Publishing Company, Inc. It continues under Bressett's Editorship, and the following descriptions are reprinted here with the permission of Western and the ANA. The descriptions of grades MS-60 through MS-70 are generic in nature, as no detailed descriptions for those grades have been published exclusively for the Lincoln Cent.

Worn dies have weakened all peripheral elements, particularly the wheat ears. This is common for Denver and San Francisco Mint cents of the 1910s and '20s and makes such coins challenging to grade.

The accompanying photographs were selected by the author expressly for this book and accurately represent the ANA standards. Some exceptions have been made in that the circulated grades for Lincoln Memorial Cents are not included in the ANA's standards, yet photos depicting the grades of VF-20 through AU-50 have been included by the author. In addition, while written descriptions are provided for several intermediate grades of the Lincoln Cent, to attempt to portray these in photographs is challenging and potentially misleading to readers.

On a final note, it should be understood that the following descriptions were prepared for grading well struck coins from early to medium die-states. Cents which have been struck too softly or from badly worn dies will require a modification of these standards and should be graded on their overall surface quality. Certain issues were almost never well made, and some leniency is taken when grading uncirculated examples of these coins. Such issues will be noted in the date and mint analysis found in Chapter 7.

AG-2 (About Good)

Obverse: Head is outlined with nearly all details worn away. Legend and date readable but very weak and merging into rim.
Reverse: Entire design partially worn away. Parts of wheat and motto merged with the rim.

G-4 (Good)

Obverse: Entire design well worn with very little detail remaining. Legend and date are weak but visible.
Reverse: Wheat is worn nearly flat but is completely outlined. Some grains are visible.

VG-8 (Very Good)

Obverse: Outline of hair shows but most details are smooth. Cheek and jaw are smooth. More than half of bow tie is visible. Legend and date are clear.
Reverse: Wheat shows some details and about half of the lines at the top.

F-12 (Fine)

Obverse: Some details show in the hair. Cheek and jaw are worn nearly smooth. LIBERTY shows clearly with no letters missing. The ear and bow tie are visible.

Reverse: Most details are visible in the stalks. Top wheat lines are worn but separated.

VF-20 (Very Fine)

Obverse: Head shows considerable flatness. Nearly all the details still show in hair and on the face. Ear and bow tie worn but bold.

Reverse: Lines in wheat stalks are worn but plain and without weak spots.

VF-30 (Choice Very Fine)

Obverse: There are small flat spots of wear on cheek and jaw. Hair still shows details. Ear and bow tie slightly worn but show clearly.

Reverse: Lines in wheat stalks are lightly worn but fully detailed.

EF-40 (Extremely Fine)

Obverse: Wear shows on hair above ear, the cheek, and on the jaw. Traces of mint luster still show.

Reverse: High points of wheat stalks are worn, but each line is clearly defined. Traces of mint luster still show.

EF-45 (Choice Extremely Fine)

Obverse: Slight wear shows on hair above ear, the cheek, and on the jaw. Half of the mint luster still shows.

Reverse: High points of wheat stalks are lightly worn, but each line is clearly defined. Half of the mint luster still shows.

AU-50 (About Uncirculated)

Obverse: Traces of wear show on the cheek and jaw. Three-quarters of the mint luster is still present.
Reverse: Traces of wear show on the wheat stalks. Three-quarters of the mint luster is still present.

AU-55 (Choice About Uncirculated)

Obverse: Only a trace of wear shows on the highest point of the jaw. Almost all of the mint luster is still present.
Reverse: A trace of wear shows on the top of the wheat stalks. Almost all of the mint luster is still present.

AU-58 (Very Choice About Uncirculated)

Has some signs of abrasion: high points of cheek and jaw; tips of wheat stalks.

MS-60 (Uncirculated)

Unattractive, dull or washed out mint luster may mark this coin. There may be many large detracting contact marks, or damage spots, but absolutely no trace of wear. There could be a heavy concentration of hairlines, or unattractive large areas of scuff marks. Rim nicks may be present, and eye appeal is very poor. Copper coins may be dark, dull and spotted.

MS-61

Mint luster may be diminished or noticeably impaired, and the surface has clusters of large and small contact marks throughout. Hairlines could be very noticeable. Scuff marks may show as unattractive patches on large areas or major features. Small rim nicks, striking or planchet defects may show, and the quality may be noticeably poor. Eye appeal is somewhat unattractive. Copper pieces will be generally dull, dark and possibly spotted.

MS-62

An impaired or dull luster may be evident. Clusters of small marks may be present throughout with a few large marks or nicks in prime focal areas. hairlines may be very noticeable. Large unattractive scuff marks might be seen on major features. The strike, rim and planchet quality may be noticeably below average. Overall eye appeal is generally acceptable. Copper coins will show a diminished color and tone.

MS-63 (Select Uncirculated)

Note: the marketplace typically calls this grade "Choice Uncirculated"

Mint luster may be slightly impaired. Numerous small contact marks, and a few scattered heavy marks may be seen. Small hairlines are visible without magnification. Several detracting scuff marks or defects may be present throughout the design or in the fields. The general quality is about average, but overall the coin is rather attractive. Copper pieces may be darkened or dull. Color should be designated.

MS-64

Has at least average luster and strike for the type. Several small contact marks in groups, as well as one of two moderately heavy marks may be present. One or two small patches of hairlines may show under low magnification. Noticeable light scuff marks or defects might be seen within the design or in the field. Attractive overall quality with a pleasing eye appeal. Copper coins may be slightly dull. Color should be designated.

MS-65 (Choice Uncirculated)

Note: the marketplace typically calls this grade "Gem Uncirculated"

Shows an attractive high quality of luster and strike for the date and mint. A few small scattered contact marks, or two larger marks may be present, and one or two small patches of hairlines may show under magnification. Noticeable light scuff marks may show on the high points of the design. Overall quality is above average and overall eye appeal is very pleasing. Copper coins have full luster with original or darkened color as designated.

MS-66

Must have above average quality of strike and full original mint luster, with no more than two or three minor but noticeable contact marks. A few very light hairlines may show under magnification, or there may be one or two light scuff marks showing on frosted surfaces or in the field. The eye appeal must be above average and very pleasing for the date and mint. Copper coins display full original or lightly toned color as designated.

MS-67

Has full original luster and sharp strike for date and mint. May have three or four very small contact marks and one more noticeable but not detracting mark. On comparable coins, one or two small single hairlines may show under magnification, or one or two partially hidden scuff marks or flaws may be present. Eye appeal is exceptional. Copper coins have lustrous original color.

MS-68

Attractive sharp strike and full original luster for the date and mint, with no more than four light scattered contact marks or flaws. No hairlines or scuff marks show. Exceptional eye appeal. Copper coins must have lustrous original color.

MS-69

Must have very attractive sharp strike and full original luster for the date and mint, with no more than two small non-detracting contact marks or flaws. No hairlines or scuff marks can be seen. Has exceptional eye appeal. Copper coins must be bright with full original color and luster.

MS-70

The perfect coin. Has very attractive sharp strike and original luster of the highest quality for the date and mint. No contact marks are visible under magnification. There are absolutely no hairlines, scuff marks or defects. Attractive and outstanding eye appeal. Copper coins must be bright will full original color and luster.

Chapter 7

DATE & MINT ANALYSIS

How to Use the Information in Chapters 7 & 8

1. The figures which appear below the name of each mint are the total number of coins issued by that mint for the specified date.

2. **RARITY:** Readers familiar with previous books in *The Complete Guide* series will note the absence of specific rarity numbers, such as R1, R2, etc. Because this work deals with a coin series which is ongoing and for which recent issues have been coined in the billions, there is simply no way to make such comparisons. To express the relative rarities of, say, 1912-S cents and 1974-D cents, is completely impossible, as they exist in two different worlds. For this reason, the question of overall rarity versus condition rarity will be addressed in absolute terms, rather than relative ones.

3. **POPULATION TOTALS:** Unless otherwise specified, the figures given for each each grade category or level are the combined total of coins certified by Numismatic Guaranty Corporation (January, 1995) and Professional Coin Grading Service (February, 1995).

   MS BN is an abbreviation for Mint State Brown, and the figure which follows the equal (=) sign corresponds to the combined number of coins certified by both services for that category. MS RB stands for Mint State Red & Brown, while MS RD is shorthand for Mint State Red. The figure following TOTAL is just that—the total of the three previous categories. POPULATION TOTALS includes the total number of cents certified as MS65 RD for that particular date and mint. This is then followed by the highest grade yet assigned, as well as the number of cents achieving that grade. Starting with 1934, the MS65 RD classification is replaced by MS67 RD, as coins below this grade level are too common for their population figures to be meaningful. Starting with 1944, these data are replaced altogether with simply the total number of coins certified as Mint State. The value of coins dated 1944 and later, with only a few exceptions, is not high enough to prompt large numbers of submissions to the grading services, and the resulting figures by grade are not meaningful. Starting with 1959, all population data are omitted, with the exception of a few scarce and popular varieties for which meaningful figures are available.

4. **VALUES:** The retail figures used were taken from the 1st Edition of Wayte Raymond's *Standard Catalogue of United States Coins*, as well as the 4th, 18th, 33rd and 48th Editions of R. S. Yeoman's *A Guide Book of United States Coins*. These books were published at approximately 15-year intervals, providing retail values for 1935, 1950, 1965, 1980 and 1995. The MS65 values of 1995 for cents dated 1909-35 and PR65 values for cents dated 1936-42 were taken from the *Coin World Comprehensive Catalog & Encyclopedia of United States Coins*. Since that book doesn't identify these values as being for BN, RB or RD cents, it may be assumed that they are for average MS65 RB coins. Values are omitted for coins dated 1975 and later, aside from those major varieties which carry premiums.

5. **VARIETIES:** The abbreviations used include DDO (doubled-die obverse), DDR (doubled-die reverse), RPM (repunched mintmark) and OMM (overmintmark). These are followed by a dash (-) and a numeral which simply distinguishes the particular sequential variety of a given date and mint. Another term which appears often is "cud." This is an old and popular expression for a major die break in which a portion of the die has fallen away. A "retained cud" is one in which the broken piece remains in position though clearly separated from the die face. Cuds are usually identified as in the following example: LC-53S-1R. This stands for Lincoln Cent/1953/San Francisco Mint/Number One/Reverse. Sequential die states for single varieties of any type are identified by lower-case suffix letters, such as 1a, 1b, etc.

6. **COMMENTS:** This section is largely self-explanatory, as it includes the author's own observations and those of others as to how each issue was made and in what state it is found today. Notes of a more general nature, such as those describing activities at the mints during the year under study, are separated from the main text by three asterisks (* * *) and are intended for the reader's education and entertainment.

HERALDIC WHEAT
REVERSE

1909 to 1958

1909 V.D.B.

PHILADELPHIA
27,994,580

RARITY: As the first appearance of the widely heralded Lincoln "penny," this issue was hoarded in vast numbers by both established collectors and the general public. The removal of the controversial letters "V.D.B." only encouraged such speculative interest. Thus, the 1909 V.D.B. cent is very common in all grades. Even fully red gems are fairly plentiful.

POPULATION: MS BN = 35   MS RB = 468   MS RD = 3293   TOTAL = 3796
TOTALS   MS65 RD = 1741   HIGHEST = MS68 RD (1)

VALUES:

GRADE	1935	1950	1965	1980	1995
G	——	——	.75	1.75	2.00
F	——	.05	1.25	2.50	2.50
EF	——	——	2.50	3.50	3.00
MS60	.15	.25	6.00	12.50	10.00
MS63	——	——	——	——	23.00
MS65*	——	——	——	——	45.00

Because of hoarding, gems are not expensive for this issue. With most early dates, however, there is a wide disparity in value between MS65 BN and MS65 RB cents on the one hand and MS65 RD examples on the other.

VARIETIES: Two obverse doubled-die varieties are known; one of these is readily apparent within the word LIBERTY and the date (see photos), while the other is nearly undetectable. A single reverse doubled die is rather hard to discern. A retained-cud die break is known for the reverse of this issue at the 2 o'clock position. One or more of the periods following letters V.D.B. may be lacking due to a filled die.

COMMENTS: Coinage of the Lincoln Cent began on June 10, 1909. This first issue was produced at a frantic pace, with the Philadelphia Mint working both day and night on cents exclusively.[1]   This activity was halted August 5 by order of Treasury Secretary Franklin MacVeagh because of the controversy over Brenner's initials appearing on the coins.[2] No more of the V.D.B. variety were coined after that date.

1909 V.D.B. cents are typically very well struck and possess excellent luster. Uncirculated coins that are not toned usually display a pale coloration that is more akin to brass than bronze. These may also show light streaking from imperfect alloying, a condition which is also found on the Philippines one-centavo pieces coined at San

Francisco during this same period.

As noted above, this issue was widely hoarded in uncirculated condition at the time of its release in August of 1909, and original rolls may still exist. Adjusting for inflation, these coins have been losers during the thirty years between 1965 and 1995. The optimist may prefer to think of this situation as representing an excellent buying opportunity at current levels.

*　*　*

As the Lincoln Cent era dawned, the U. S. Mint realized a substantial seignorage on the coining of one-cent pieces, that is the profit between their unit cost and their face value. For every 1,000 cents coined, the Mint expended $1.12, which is just over 10% of face.[3] It seems that there was quite a bit of money to be made in the making of money!

1909 V.D.B.
DDO-1, Breen-2056
(Bill Fivaz & J.T. Stanton)

--- •◆ ◆ ◆• ---

SAN FRANCISCO
484,000

RARITY:　　Widely hoarded at the time of its release, uncirculated coins are actually quite common. Even fully red gems are generally available, though they sell very quickly to both complete-set collectors and those simply fascinated with this particular issue. Examples grading Very Fine through About Uncirculated are likewise plentiful. The most challenging coins to locate are problem-free specimens grading Good through Fine. These escaped the initial hoarding and were generally lost among the millions of ordinary cents in circulation. Many of the lower grade survivors have been cleaned or damaged in some way.

POPULATION:　MS BN = 218　　MS RB = 1306　　MS RD = 881　　TOTAL = 2405
TOTALS　　　MS65 RD = 360　　HIGHEST = MS67 RD (4)

VALUES:

GRADE	1935	1950	1965	1980	1995
G	——	——	125.00	140.00	300.00
F	——	8.50	165.00	165.00	400.00
EF	——	——	235.00	200.00	475.00
MS60	.25	12.50	335.00	340.00	600.00
MS63	——	——	——	——	700.00
MS65	——	——	——	——	1950.00

VARIETIES:　　With such a small mintage, it's not surprising that no significant varieties have turned up. A few have been found with various combinations of missing or incomplete periods following the designer's initials. Although collectable, these carry no premium. Breen noted that at least six obverse dies were furnished to the San Francisco Mint for Lincoln Cents, while the American Numismatic Association Authentication Bureau (ANAAB) has documented four of these. More about their use in counterfeit detection may be found below.

COMMENTS: The entire mintage of Indian Cents dated 1909-S, some 309,000 pieces, was executed in January.[4] Why no additional ones were coined is unknown, but the Lincoln dies were not ready until June.

Like its Philadelphia Mint cousin, 1909-S V.D.B. is usually well struck. Uncirculated coins cover a wide range from lustrous brown pieces to fully red gems. Many of the latter have just a touch of golden toning around their peripheries as the result of decades of storage in bank-wrapped paper rolls. Untoned or lightly toned pieces may display a streaky, wood-grained effect from imperfect alloying. This is quite common for cents produced during the first decade or so of cent coinage at San Francisco, and it is frequently seen on 1908-S and 1909-S Indian Cents, as well. This phenomenon gradually disappeared around the early-mid 1920s.

This coin is so widely counterfeited or assembled from the component parts of less valuable pieces that authentication by a reputable, third-party service is mandatory to avoid disappointment and financial loss. For those wishing to trust their own judgment, however, there are some characteristics of genuine coins that should weed out all but the most deceptive fakes. As noted above, four obverse dies have been documented by the ANAAB. The position of the S mintmark for each is thus known, and the same punch was used throughout. This letter S is very small and symmetrical and has squared-off serifs that are parallel to one another. A tiny, raised dot appears within the upper loop, tucked against its lower curve, and a diagonal groove is found on the surface of the upper serif. This mintmark punch is the same one used for all Lincoln Cents of 1909 through 1916 and for part of 1917. A little time spent studying Mint State examples of any of these dates will prepare one for inspecting a 1909-S V.D.B. that is being considered for purchase. The initials V.D.B. are also quite distinctive on genuine coins. They appear slightly to the left of center with respect to the stems of the wheat ears. The center bar of letter B slants upward from left to right, and the lower right curls of both D and B are slanted upward. The characteristics of known counterfeits of this issue vary so much that they are beyond the scope of this book. Readers are strongly urged to acquire Volumes I and II of *Counterfeit Detection*, published by the American Numismatic Association.

It was not until the coin collecting hobby's period of greatest growth from the late 1930s through early 1960s that the 1909-S V.D.B. cent became a particularly valuable coin. Earlier generations of collectors were well aware of the number hoarded and priced this issue accordingly. The highwater mark for small cent collecting is recorded in the values shown for 1965 (compiled in 1964). While these figures have risen since then, they have failed to keep pace with inflation. This fate has been shared by many Lincoln Cents, perhaps less so with this issue due to its legendary status.

An often repeated story attributed to numismatic researcher George Fuld recounts how coin dealer John Zug acquired some 25,000 uncirculated 1909-S V.D.B. cents directly from the San Francisco Mint at the time of their issue. Correctly surmising that these coins with the letters V.D.B. would grow in value, he held onto them for several

Genuine 1909-S V.D.B. cent.
Note the slanting middle stroke of letter 'B' which is characteristic of all genuine examples. Another thing to remember is that the initials are placed slightly to the left of center on genuine coins. (ANAAB)

Genuine 1909-S V.D.B. cent.
This style of mintmark was used exclusively through 1916. Diagnostic features include parallel serifs, raised dot inside upper loop and notch on surface of upper serif. (American Numismatic Association Authentication Bureau)

years. Around 1918, however, he decided to sell short, realizing 1.75 cents apiece for his hoard. Perhaps he was alarmed by the restoration of Brenners initials to the obverse of the cent beginning that year, fearing that this would lessen the value of his investment.

The Holy Grail for Lincoln Cent collectors, the acquisition of a 1909-S V.D.B. cent usually marks the completion of this series. While a number of other issues are more rare in Mint State, this coveted coin remains the rarest regular-issue entry in terms of the total number available in all grades. For many years it has also been the rare coin most widely known outside of the numismatic community, as it was used to publicize premium books and other introductory coin guides of the sort found at supermarket check-out lines. The general disappearance of Wheat Cents from circulation since about 1970 has largely stifled this form of promotion, as even the most mendacious of copywriters could scarcely claim that a 1909-S V.D.B. cent may be nestled in one's pocket awaiting discovery and instant riches!

In recent years, however, some boosters of the coin collecting hobby have attempted to do just that. Most notably Krause Publications, a leading issuer of numismatic newspapers and magazines, has surreptitiously placed a worn example of this and other rare Lincolns in circulation immediately preceding several recent conventions of the American Numismatic Association. This is accomplished by casually including it in a purchase made at a store somewhere within the city hosting that year's convention. Both the numismatic press and the local media are utilized to promote the search for its recovery, with a reward promised for its return. Since the reward will be made at Krause Publications' stall at the ANA Convention, this press release serves to generate publicity for both the convention and the hobby in general. To date, few persons have actually reported the discovery of these planted coins. Indeed, their fate largely remains unknown. The ANA itself has adopted a policy of returning rare dates to circulation in conjunction with the annual celebration of National Coin Week, the third full week in April. The story is usually the same; the coins are seldom recovered. Similar promotions by some local clubs have been more successful, with a number of the seeded coins being redeemed for their market value.

1909

PHILADELPHIA
72,700,420

RARITY: This issue is common in all grades including Choice BU, although not quite as common in Mint State as its immediate predecessor, 1909 V.D.B. The certified population figures below reinforce this notion, though the lower totals are due at least in part to a lesser demand for this variety from type collectors. Gems are available for a reasonable price, but they are noticeably scarcer than the 1909 V.D.B. cents. Circulated specimens are likewise less abundant, reflecting the difference in the quantities minted for each variety.

POPULATION:	MS BN = 15	MS RB = 163	MS RD = 899	TOTAL = 1077
TOTALS	MS65 RD = 492	HIGHEST = MS67 RD (14)		

VALUES:	GRADE	1935	1950	1965	1980	1995
	G	——	——	.35	.40	.50
	F	——	.05	.60	.60	.75
	EF	——	——	1.45	1.50	2.00
	MS60	.15	.30	8.00	10.00	16.00
	MS63	——	——	——	——	25.00
	MS65	——	——	——	——	65.00

VARIETIES: A single, quite minor doubled-die reverse is known. Three different obverse cud die breaks exist, all of these occurring at the 7 o'clock position. This location, where Lincoln's bust nearly touches the border, would prove throughout this series to be particularly vulnerable to die failure. Four reverse die cuds are known, these all occurring between the wheat ears and the border, again locations prone to die failure. A few pieces have reportedly been found from dies on which the letters V.D.B. were nearly but not fully effaced through filing or polishing. This bit of thrift on the part of the Philadelphia Mint reveals just how quickly the decision to remove the offending letters was made.

COMMENTS: Although lacking the glamour of the 1909 V.D.B. cents, these coins still represent the first year of issue. Mintage commenced within days of the release of the first 1909 V.D.B. cents, so quick was the public outcry over the artist's initials. Although most hoarders of anything new chose to focus on the first variety, enough rolls of the 1909 "plain" cents were set aside to meet the demand now and forever. The supply of choice and gem coins is more limited than for 1909 V.D.B., though the characteristics of color and strike are essentially the same. 1909 Lincoln Cents remained fairly commonplace in circulation until the coin collecting boom of the early 1960s caused the public to hoard nearly all cents dated before 1934.

SAN FRANCISCO
1,825,000

RARITY: As the population figures suggest, this coin is not too difficult to locate in Mint State. Fewer were saved than the 1909-S V.D.B. cents, as they lacked the popular appeal of that discontinued variety. This doesn't seem to have cut into the number of fully red gems, as these are usually available. Circulated pieces are slightly more common than 1909-S V.D.B. as a simple function of the number coined. Still, this is a scarce date within the Lincoln Cent series, and specimens grading Extremely Fine are especially difficult to find.

POPULATION: MS BN = 38   MS RB = 411   MS RD = 744   TOTAL = 1193
TOTALS   MS65 RD = 339   HIGHEST = MS67 RD (3)

VALUES:

GRADE	1935	1950	1965	1980	1995
G	——	——	27.50	26.00	35.00
F	——	1.00	40.00	33.00	45.00
EF	——	——	65.00	50.00	80.00
MS60	.25	4.00	110.00	90.00	150.00
MS63	——	——	——	——	175.00
MS65	——	——	——	——	310.00

VARIETIES: Among the most popular of Lincoln Cent varieties is the 1909-S over horizontal S (RPM-2), the first punching having occurred at 90 degrees from normal, followed by one or more in the correct position. Another, less spectacular repunched mintmark is also known (see photos).

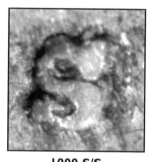

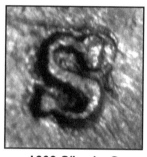

1909-S/S
RPM-1   (Tom Miller)

1909-S/horiz. S
RPM-2, Breen-2058
(Fivaz & Stanton)

COMMENTS: 1909-S cents are almost invariably well struck and have surfaces and coloration very similar to 1909-S V.D.B. That is to say, they are usually a pale, brassy color when untoned and will often display a wood-grain effect from imperfect alloying. Specimens toned a mixture of red and brown are not uncommon, and these usually retain excellent luster.

Like 1909-S V.D.B., this issue is often counterfeited by fabricating entirely false coins or simulated by adding an S mintmark (taken from a less valuable coin) to a genuine 1909 cent from the Philadelphia Mint. The mintmark characteristics of genuine 1909-S cents are the same as for 1909-S V.D.B., since they shared a common punch and, in some instances, the same obverse dies. Readers are again strongly urged to study the American Numismatic Association's two-volume book *Counterfeit Detection*.

Although overshadowed by the famous 1909-S V.D.B. cent, this issue is nevertheless a semi-key date within the series. With diligence and no small amount of luck, worn pieces could be found as late as 1960.

1910

PHILADELPHIA
146,798,813

RARITY: This issue is readily available in all grades including Choice BU. Although not truly common, enough red gems exist to meet the demand for this grade level. A number of slight tonal variations are found, but coppery red is the underlying color. Original rolls may yet exist.

POPULATION: MS BN = 25   MS RB = 150   MS RD = 443   TOTAL = 618
TOTALS   MS65 RD = 224   HIGHEST = MS67 RD (16)

VALUES:

GRADE	1935	1950	1965	1980	1995
G	——	——	.15	.20	.20
F	——	.05	.45	.45	.45
EF	——	——	1.50	1.60	2.00
MS60	.25	.65	10.00	11.00	14.00
MS63	——	——	——	——	20.00
MS65	——	——	——	——	70.00

VARIETIES: Two obverse cud die breaks are known, as well as three retained cuds for the reverse (see photo). Vestigial traces of the letters V.D.B. may yet turn up from leftover 1909 V.D.B. reverse dies that were only partly effaced.

The numeral 0 in the date is distinctly oversize in relation to the other numerals. This may have been an intentional action, as a smaller 0 would have increased the likelihood of its center (or "doughnut hole") breaking out of the die This phenomenon was behind the replacement of the 1960 small date hub with the large date hub.

This date was easily located in circulation as late as the 1960s, sometimes nearly worn slick. Inflation has eaten away at its value, particularly in the lower grades.

1910-P
Cud die break, LC-10-3
(Sam Thurman & Arnold Margolis)

* * *

In his *Annual Report* to Treasury Secretary Franklin MacVeagh, Mint Director George E. Roberts commented on what he considered the unsuitability of bronze coinage:

The composition of the 1-cent piece, 95 per cent copper and 5 per cent tin and zinc, is unsatisfactory. The coins soon become dull and dirty in appearance and when exposed to the salt air of the seacoast are rendered unfit for circulation.

This is particularly noticeable of coins which lie for a time in slot machines. They are offered for redemption in bad condition and must be remelted. When handled in the Treasury offices and mints an objectionable dust arises from them. The act adopting the present composition was passed in 1864, prior to which date the 1-cent piece was issued under the act of February 21, 1857, which provided for a composition of 88 per cent copper and 12 per cent nickel. The mint officials have always regarded the change as a backward step, and in the opinion of the bureau the percentage of nickel should have been increased instead of reduced.

As if to illustrate his point, as of Fiscal Year 1911 the U. S. Mints had destroyed a total of 41,205,127 bronze cents of earlier years which were deemed unfit for further circulation as the result of extreme wear or mutilation. This left a total of 1,944,304,861 pieces outstanding. Given such a high rate of attrition, it's amazing that so many early bronze cents still exist at all. In FY1911 alone, some 2,959,454 bronze cents were melted, along with $96.46 worth of obsolete half cents and large cents, 34,950 copper-nickel cents, 13,650 bronze two-cent pieces, 7225 copper-nickel three-cent pieces and an amazing 3,133,265 copper-nickel five-cent pieces! The Mint spent a grand total of $1.80 purchasing tin and zinc, which was added to the melted half cents and large cents to bring their metal to the proper alloy for coining new cents.[5]

SAN FRANCISCO
6,045,000

RARITY: Original rolls were known as late as the 1970s, and small hoards of red or red-brown coins were being marketed even in the 1980s, most notably by Bowers & Merena Galleries. The population report data verifies that this date is common in mint state, with many choice examples to be found. True gems are fairly easy to find, and they appear with more frequency than for other S-Mint Lincoln cents before 1929. In circulated grades, this issue has never been plentiful, and it qualifies as a semi-key date.

POPULATION TOTALS
MS BN = 29   MS RB = 332   MS RD = 523   TOTAL = 884
MS65 RD = 227   HIGHEST = MS67 RD (1)

VALUES:

GRADE	1935	1950	1965	1980	1995
G	——	——	3.50	5.75	6.00
F	——	.25	6.00	7.75	9.00
EF	——	——	12.00	12.00	20.00
MS60	.50	2.00	50.00	53.00	75.00
MS63	——	——	——	——	100.00
MS65	——	——	——	——	275.00

VARIETIES: Three repunched mintmark varieties are known, the first two being distinct even to the naked eye (see photo). Specimens have been reported having vestigial traces of the letters V.D.B. It's not clear whether these letters remained on the working die or the working hub, but the former is more likely.

COMMENTS: This date is generally quite well struck.

* * *

Among the improvements made to the coining process at this time was the adoption of automated feeding tubes for the coin presses at all three mints. This reduced the total number of employees required in the coining operation.[6]

The coinage of minor pieces (cents and nickels) did not call for the strictest security and standards. As a result, coin blanks were often purchased from outside contractors rather than being produced within the mints. During Fiscal Year 1911, which ran from July 1, 1910 through June 30, 1911, the mints used a combination of blanks from both sources. Contractors provided a little over 408,000 pounds in bronze cent blanks at a cost of $96,394.93. It isn't specified whether these blanks had already been milled, or upset, when received.[7]

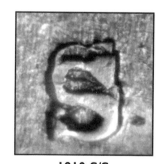

1910-S/S
RPM-2, Breen-2061
(Miller)

1911

PHILADELPHIA
101,176,054

RARITY: This issue is readily available in all grades, including Gem BU, yet uncirculated coins of this date are more likely than previous P-Mint cents to have unattractive toning or spotting. If original rolls exist, they may reflect this slightly lower quality. When gems are found, however, they more often than not have outstanding luster. 1911-P is fairly common in AU, the result of mishandling Mint State coins.

Like most early Lincoln Cents, this issue shows a great void in the availability of examples grading VF and EF. Circulated coins are common only in the grades of Fine and below, these specimens being saved from the mid 1930s onward by persons with coin boards and albums. Once the early Lincolns got into circulation, 20 years or more passed before worn examples were sought at all. By then, only lower grade coins remained to be found.

POPULATION: MS BN = 19   MS RB = 90   MS RD = 306   TOTAL = 415
TOTALS   MS65 RD = 136   HIGHEST = MS68 RD (1)

VALUES:

GRADE	1935	1950	1965	1980	1995
G	——	——	.20	.20	.20
F	——	.05	.50	.60	.60
EF	——	——	1.75	4.00	4.00
MS60	.25	.60	10.00	15.00	18.00
MS63	——	——	——	——	30.00
MS65	——	——	——	——	115.00

VARIETIES: None are reported.

COMMENTS: The quality of strike with this date varies somewhat, but most are fairly sharp. As is true of all early dates, a number of specimens have been seen that were chemically cleaned; these were offered for sale fully bright or artificially retoned.

* * *

As with the 1910-P cents, the value of lower grade examples has remained static for thirty years. Since this phenomenon recurs throughout the Lincoln Cent series, it's worthy of some explanation. The peak in the popularity of collecting Lincolns occurred during the early 1960s, about the same time that coin collecting itself most captured the public's imagination. A large number of casual collectors, including a great many children, were engaged in the simple act of filling the holes in their albums. Although alert to any opportunity to upgrade their specimens, most of these folks obtained their coins from circulation or from bank rolls. With thousands of coin clubs appearing nationwide during that period, there were also opportunities to trade and buy cents for finishing their sets or upgrading, but the primary goal remained merely to fill the holes. When coins were purchased to complete a set, the condition sought was usually comparable to that of the coins found in circulation, most of which were quite worn. A market for such low grade coins readily existed at that time, as evidenced by the fact that most advertisements in collecting publications consisted of long columns offering every date in low to mid grades, with little emphasis given to Mint State coins.

The number of persons engaged in coin collecting declined dramatically after the mid-1960s, as all older coins began to disappear from circulation. New recruits to the hobby were compelled to buy their coins from dealers or other collectors. Without circulation finds to provide an incentive for collecting in low grades, the newer generations of hobbyists were soon drawn to the more attractive specimens in higher grades. A growing emphasis on coins as an investment coincided with this trend, and the two philosophies fed on one another. The virtues of higher-grade coins were heralded by publishers of the new investment newsletters, which were another outgrowth of this changing market. As the expanding demand by collectors for high grade coins resulted in upward price pressure, this became a self-fulfilling prophecy. At the same time, however, the demand for low grade coins was either static or in decline. How many new collectors are seeking these hole fillers is uncertain, but it's likely that their number is greatly exceeded by the supply of coins.

When prices remain stationary for thirty years, as they have for many common Lincoln Cents in lower grades, this represents a loss of real value to inflation. Even with a growing emphasis on quality and condition, better grade Lincoln Cents have suffered the effects of inflation, though to a lesser extent. This may be interpreted as either a bad omen for the future or a wonderful opportunity now. It may depend on whether one considers these coins to have been overvalued during the 1960s or undervalued at the present time.

DENVER
12,672,000

RARITY: In Mint State, 1911-D is neither plentiful nor scarce. Enough brown or partly red examples survive to meet the demand for those seeking so-so quality. Truly choice and gem specimens, however, are quite difficult to find. This is aggravated by the tendency of this date to be softly struck and have a weakly-impressed mintmark.

POPULATION: MS BN = 42   MS RB = 165   MS RD = 193   TOTAL = 401
TOTALS   MS65 RD = 64   HIGHEST = MS66 RD (4)

VALUES:

GRADE	1935	1950	1965	1980	1995
G	——	——	1.35	2.50	4.00
F	——	.35	3.85	5.00	6.00
EF	——	——	11.50	17.00	30.00
MS60	.35	2.50	35.00	60.00	80.00
MS63	——	——	——	——	110.00
MS65	——	——	——	——	585.00

VARIETIES: None are reported.

COMMENTS: Although most examples are rather softly struck, a few very sharp specimens may be found. When found in Mint State, these shaper coins are almost always brown or with minimal red. It seems that most of the fully red pieces fall into the softly struck category. This is true of many early Lincoln Cents and can be quite frustrating to collectors. It appears that the smoother surfaces of softly struck cents actually imparted some preservative quality to them which is lacking in the more textured coins with fuller strikes. Cleaned and retoned coins are also very common for this date. Although nearly all of these are rejected by the major grading services, a few of the most professional jobs may slip past.

The first cents coined at the Denver Mint were released to circulation in May of 1911. Once scorned in the western states as being too valueless and containing no precious metal, cents were seldom seen there before the turn of the century. About that time, the inflated price structure of the Far West had settled to a point at which it was comparable to that of other regions. Grudgingly accepted at last, minor coins (cents and nickels) had to be shipped in from the Philadelphia Mint, since the Denver and San Francisco Mints did not have the authority to coin anything but silver and gold. This condition persisted until 1906, when Congress passed a law permitting the striking of minor coins at all mint facilities (a change prompted in large part by the U. S. Mint's desire to switch production of the Philippines territorial coinage from Philadelphia to San Francisco). The first mint to exercise this privilege was San Francisco, commencing the coinage of cents in 1908. These were still a novelty when the Lincoln design was adopted the following year. Apparently, no cent dies were requested by the Denver Mint until 1911. From this point onward, the nation's output of cents would be divided between three mints until 1955, when coining ceased at the San Francisco facility.

The Lincoln Cent debuted at a time when the mints were actually scaling back their activity and the number of persons they employed. In his *Annual Report*, Mint Director George E. Roberts remarked that "The new mint at Denver added to our coinage facilities at the very time when our requirements were being largely reduced." Indeed, the U. S. Mint's payroll was drastically reduced between 1909 and 1911, the Denver Mint suffering the loss of nearly half its work force. This same situation prompted the cessation of coining operations at the New Orleans Mint in 1909, Roberts reporting that "Altogether, it is quite impossible to operate four mints on an economical basis . . ."[8] Thus, there were to be no O-Mint Lincoln cents.

SAN FRANCISCO
4,026,000

RARITY: 1911-S has always been a scarce date in all grades, despite widespread hoarding of well-worn coins taken from circulation. While the population reports reveal a respectable number of red and red-brown specimens, these are quite dispersed and are difficult to locate at coin shows. Fully red gems may also be found with a bit of searching, but they sell very quickly. Desirable circulated examples are nearly as elusive.

POPULATION: MS BN = 53   MS RB = 196   MS RD = 137   TOTAL = 386
TOTALS   MS65 RD = 55   HIGHEST = MS66 RD (10)

VALUES:

GRADE	1935	1950	1965	1980	1995
G	——	——	9.50	9.00	16.00
F	——	.35	13.00	11.50	20.00
EF	——	——	25.00	20.00	32.00
MS60	.35	3.50	75.00	75.00	120.00
MS63	——	——	——	——	200.00
MS65	——	——	——	——	775.00

VARIETIES: A single repunched mintmark variety is known (see photo).

COMMENTS: Although 1911-S cents are usually well struck, they lack the crispness of the two preceding dates from the San Francisco Mint. The highpoints of Lincoln's head may be a bit soft, and the rims are usually shallower.

Cleaned and recolored examples are very common for this date, since the supply of original red and red-brown coins is not up to demand. Sol Taylor addressed this scarcity of desirable examples in *The Standard Guide to the Lincoln Cent*: " . . . the majority of Mint State specimens are average to late die state coins and far more red-brown than red . . . Many of the 'raw' [uncertified] 1911S cents appear to be MS64 quality or less and most seem to be red-brown versus full mint red."

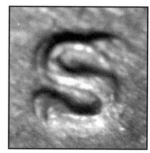

1911-S/S
RPM-1
(Miller)

* * *

The Engraving Department of the Philadelphia Mint created a total of 913 cent dies for the coinage of 1911 at all three mints. This figure was divided into 755 dies for Philadelphia, 48 for Denver and 110 for San Francisco. Compare this figure with the total of 545 dies for the Indian Head Cent coinage of 1907.[9]

* * *

One of the pioneers of Lincoln Cent collecting, and perhaps the only person to take this activity seriously within the numismatic community at the time, was Navy Commodore W. C. Eaton of Hamilton, New York. Eaton wrote frequently to *The Numismatist* during the early years of Lincoln Cent coinage, reporting his observations about mintmark positional varieties and his experiences in purchasing coins by mail directly from the three mints. New coins were obtainable at face value plus postage by writing to each mint individually. As there were then few persons with an interest in current coinage, a personal reply from the mints' superintendents frequently accompanied each request. Though the information he related to readers of *The Numismatist* is of little more than human interest value today, a few useful facts may be gleaned. In a letter dated February 14, 1911 from San Francisco Mint Chief Clerk E. D. Hawkins, which accompanied Eaton's order of 25 new cents, the commodore was informed that the expected life of a cent die at that facility was 150,000 strikes. He was also instructed that entirely new dies were utilized for the 1909 "plain" cents, rather than the existing dies being altered.[10]

1912

PHILADELPHIA
68,150,915

RARITY: The first slightly scarce date from this mint, 1912-P is generally available in grades up through Fine. In the higher circulated grades, it can be somewhat challenging to locate without damage or harsh cleaning, though by no means is it rare. Mint State coins are readily available in lower grades, but fully red pieces are slightly scarce without spotting or other blemishes. Still, there are enough true gems to meet the demand from advanced collectors.

POPULATION: MS BN = 13   MS RB = 108   MS RD = 245   TOTAL = 366
TOTALS MS65 RD = 127   HIGHEST = MS67 RD (2)

VALUES:

GRADE	1935	1950	1965	1980	1995
G	——	——	.15	.25	.35
F	——	.05	.50	1.25	1.50
EF	——	——	1.75	6.50	7.00
MS60	.25	.60	13.50	22.50	25.00
MS63	——	——	——	——	40.00
MS65	——	——	——	——	130.00

VARIETIES: None are reported.

COMMENTS: Nearly all examples are very well struck. Until the advent of grading services, this date survived in original rolls. While some rolls may still exist in collections assembled years ago and off the market ever since, each time such rolls are acquired by dealers the better pieces are sent out to be encapsulated and are usually sold shortly afterward to satisfy customer want lists. The lesser coins remain to make the rounds at coin shows.

* * *

A portrait of the three mints and their staffing may be found within the *Annual Report*. The Philadelphia Mint was the largest with 356 employees. Of this number, eight were employed in the Engraving Department, 13 in Assaying, 60 in Melting and Refining, 95 in Coining and the remaining 180 in various other capacities. Denver employed nine in Assaying, 16 in Coining, 22 in Melting and Refining and a balance of 53, for a total payroll of 100 persons. At the San Francisco Mint, there were 11 in Assaying, 30 in Coining, 35 in Melting and Refining and some 62 employees of a general nature, bringing its total to 138.[11]

DENVER
10,411,000

RARITY: 1912-D is a semi-key date coin. It is moderately scarce in all grades, and even worn specimens will find a buyer when problem-free. In the higher circulated grades and in Mint State, striking deficiencies become a problem (see Comments). Low-end Mint State coins are usually available, while choice and gem examples having original, fully red or even red/brown color are scarce and always in demand. The color of these cents tend toward a pinkish hue, while the more desirable red or tangerine shades are very rare.

POPULATION: MS BN = 26   MS RB = 105   MS RD = 127   TOTAL = 258
TOTALS   MS65 RD = 49   HIGHEST = MS66 RD (3)

VALUES:

GRADE	1935	1950	1965	1980	1995
G	——	——	1.50	2.50	4.50
F	——	.50	4.75	5.25	7.00
EF	——	——	15.00	20.00	38.00
MS60	.65	6.00	55.00	70.00	120.00
MS63	——	——	——	——	165.00
MS65	——	——	——	——	1250.00

VARIETIES: None are reported.

COMMENTS: While most 1912-D cents are well struck in their centers, they tend to have an "expanded" look to them, as in the illustrated specimen. Note that all of the lettering and numerals, including both date and mintmark, appear larger than normal. This is a form of die wear that seems to be peculiar to the Denver Mint issues. While not a serious problem, it does detract from the aesthetic quality of most 1912-D cents.

* * *

During 1912, the three mints recorded the following figures for the average number of cents coined per die:[12]

	Philadelphia	Denver	San Francisco
Obverse	345,136	381,075	221,152
Reverse	355,886	323,337	192,305

Why San Francisco produced lower figures was not explained, but it's interesting to compare these figures to the 1,000,000+ averages routinely achieved during the 1990s.

Another interesting fact which comes to light in the Director's *Annual Report* is that the Philadelphia Mint used a combination of in-house production and outside contractors for its supply of cent planchets, some 40,000 pounds being purchased ready-made from vendors this year. Philadelphia's machine shop also turned out the collars employed at all three mints.[13]

* * *

Commodore Eaton, who was introduced under COMMENTS for 1911-S, continued updating readers of *The Numismatist* on his observation of Lincoln Cents. In a letter to Editor Edgar H. Adams, Eaton announced that among the 25 cents he'd received from the Denver Mint in February were no less than three different mintmark positional varieties.[14] At a time when collectors understood very little about the way modern coin dies were prepared, this provided some mystery and adventure. Of course, so few persons were then interested in collecting current coins by date and mint that this information must have largely fallen on deaf ears. The collecting of small cents in particular, even Indian Cents, was then looked down upon by serious numismatists as an unworthy pursuit. Indeed, the very first advertisements for Lincoln Cents did not appear in *The Numismatist* until 1928.

SAN FRANCISCO
4,431,000

RARITY: 1912-S is another semi-key coin. In lower grades, specimens rarely turned up in circulation after the mid-1950s, and they remain difficult to locate at shows and shops without problems such as corrosion or harsh cleaning. Mid-grade specimens (F-EF) are particularly elusive. Most AU and Mint State coins have been dipped or otherwise cleaned, though many of these have since retoned to something approaching a natural appearance. Choice and gem specimens showing any degree of *original* red color are very scarce, while fully struck *and* fully red gems are nearly unknown. On the plus side, however, this issue is usually well struck overall.

POPULATION: MS BN = 54   MS RB = 173   MS RD = 104   TOTAL = 331
TOTALS   MS65 RD = 30   HIGHEST = MS66 RD (1)

VALUES:

GRADE	1935	1950	1965	1980	1995
G	——	——	5.50	8.00	11.00
F	——	.35	10.00	11.00	14.00
EF	——	——	20.00	23.00	35.00
MS60	.60	5.00	55.00	75.00	100.00
MS63	——	——	——	——	150.00
MS65	——	——	——	——	1000.00

VARIETIES: A single repunched mintmark variety is known.

COMMENTS: The 1912-S cent is usually found quite well struck, though a few pieces will fall short of the mark. The fact that most of the surviving high grade examples have been dipped at some point is not clearly reflected in the certified population data, as some leeway seems to have been given for this very scarce date.

* * *

Commodore Eaton, early chronicler of Lincolns, ran afoul of the bureaucracy in 1912 when attempting to place his usual order for 25 new cents, as this letter to him from the Superintendent of the San Francisco Mint reveals:

Enclosed I return the money order No. 64660, for $0.35, in favor the The Supt. of the Mint of the United States, received in your letter of January 19, 1912, with the information that one-cent pieces may be distributed only upon an order from the Treasurer of the United States or an Assistant Treasurer. A quantity of one-cent pieces has been made by this Institution during 1912. We have made no other minor coins to this date.[15]

This refusal to supply coins for collectors at face value plus postage was inconsistent with the informal practice of early years, and there would continue to be an on-again and off-again policy in furnishing new coins for the next 35 years. It wasn't until 1948 that the U. S. Mint began selling pre-packaged double sets of each year's coinage, commencing with issues dated 1947. This was a continuation of the policy in effect since the early 1930s of furnishing no more than two coins of each date and mint directly from the Treasury Department in Washington, D.C. A certain level of antagonism has existed between coin collectors and the Mint throughout much of the 20th Century, though it largely subsided after the 1960s. This is in stark contrast to the encouragement of stamp collecting by the U. S. Postal Service, an irony pointed out to no avail by successive generations of coin enthusiasts.

1913

PHILADELPHIA
76,529,504

RARITY: 1913-P is a common coin in most circulated grades, though EF specimens are very difficult to locate, as this date wasn't worth saving until most had worn beyond that level. Examples appearing nearly slick turned up in circulation as late as the mid 1960s. All of the middle grades are available, so there should be no difficulty in locating a specimen which is free of problems and displays its original surfaces. All grades of Mint State are available. Fully red gems are in more limited supply and when found, these are seldom fully struck. Whatever uncirculated rolls may have existed before the advent of certified grading have probably been broken up to cherrypick the "slabbable" coins.

POPULATION: MS BN = 9   MS RB = 111   MS RD = 198   TOTAL = 318
TOTALS   MS65 RD = 94   HIGHEST = MS67 RD (2)

VALUES:

GRADE	1935	1950	1965	1980	1995
G	——	——	.25	.20	.25
F	——	.10	.65	1.25	1.00
EF	——	——	2.50	7.00	8.00
MS60	.35	.60	13.50	21.00	22.00
MS63	——	——	——	——	38.00
MS65	——	——	——	——	190.00

VARIETIES: None are reported.

COMMENTS: Like most Philadelphia-Mint cents, 1913-P is almost always well struck. Like many of the more common Lincoln Cents, it has been a poor performer in low grades. Its 1995 value in grade Good is the same as it was in 1965, representing a real loss to inflation and reflecting a 30-year trend of condition-consciousness among coin buyers.

The small number of certified "brown" specimens does not mean that such coins are rare; they simply are worth too little to justify the cost of certification. This same scenario will replay for other dates which are not valued very highly in the MS BN classification.

Rather than displaying a long tail, a feature more in keeping with the text style employed by Brenner in 1909, numeral 3 in the date of 1913 cents is quite compact and symmetrical. This failure of the Mint's engraving staff to maintain a consistent style seems to have been limited to this series, as they were more careful with other types. This error would be repeated for years afterward, the early 1930s providing a particularly rich confusion of styles.

* * *

David W. Lange   *1913*

During his second term as Mint Director (1910-14), George E. Roberts repeatedly urged that the U. S. Mint's coin collection be augmented through the purchase of pieces which were missing. The publication in 1912 of a catalog of the collection's contents revealed its many deficiencies:

> The preparation of the catalogue has brought out very strikingly how fragmentary the collection is, a fact that has rendered the task of arranging the lists very difficult. It is exceedingly regrettable that this state of incompleteness pertains to the collection of the coins of our own country, which is limited, with but few exceptions, to the issues of the Philadelphia Mint. The only explanation of this state of affairs is, of course, the inadequacy of the purchase fund, which at present is small and in many years since the collection was formed was even less. In view of the importance of such a museum, as well as the special and general interest in it, this unfavorable situation should be speedily remedied, and the large economy introduced into the cost of maintaining the cabinet of coins and medals, resulting as it has in a reduction of about 50 per cent in the salary list, fairly warrants a greater liberality in the allowance for the purchase of coins.[16]

This sentiment was seconded by the members of the Annual Assay Commission, which met at the Philadelphia Mint early in each year to test the previous year's coinage. For several years running their reports included a call for the upgrading of the Mint's collection, but these pleas fell on deaf ears. The issue came to a head in 1923, when the entire collection was donated to the Smithsonian Institution. For many years afterward it was equally neglected there and the existing pieces permitted to deteriorate through poor storage. This sad trend was reversed somewhat during the late 1940s when numismatist Stuart Mosher became the collection's curator.

Its best years have come since 1957 under the guidance of Vladimir and Elvira Clain-Stefanelli. The former died in 1982, but his widow carries on as of this writing (1996). Though still underfunded, there is some hope for the nation's coin collection in that 15% of the surcharge revenue from the Smithsonian Institution Sesquicentennial commemorative coins dated 1996 is directed by law toward this cause. How this will be distributed, though, is subject to debate, as what was once the Numismatic Division has recently been absorbed into a larger bureaucratic entity.

DENVER
15,804,000

RARITY: This issue is relatively common in all grades through average Mint State. The only deterrent to finding an acceptable coin at most grade levels will be the quality of strike and the degree or originality (has it been cleaned or otherwise impaired?). Choice Mint State coins are available, but only fully struck, fully red gems can be considered scarce. Most of the certified gems (MS65 RD and MS66 RD) seem to be well struck coins.

POPULATION: MS BN = 24   MS RB = 114   MS RD = 186   TOTAL = 324
TOTALS   MS65 RD = 48   HIGHEST = MS66 RD (6)

VALUES:

GRADE	1935	1950	1965	1980	1995
G	——	——	1.10	1.35	1.75
F	——	.40	3.50	3.00	4.00
EF	——	——	11.00	16.00	20.00
MS60	1.00	6.50	50.00	67.50	80.00
MS63	——	——	——	——	150.00
MS65	——	——	——	——	700.00

VARIETIES: None are reported.

COMMENTS: The typical 1913-D appears poorly struck. More specifically, it was struck from worn dies. The piece illustrated is the exception, and it was coined from fresh dies which produced a complete impression throughout.

This single flaw was chronic with Lincoln Cents through the end of the Wheat Reverse series in 1958. The amount of metal displacement required to fill this die cavity was simply too great, given that the one of the deepest obverse die cavities (Lincoln's shoulder) was directly opposed. A similar flaw in the same location is evident in the Memorial Cents, again caused by the chronic problem of excessive metal displacement. This was not solved until 1984, when Lincoln's shoulder was lowered in relief.

SAN FRANCISCO
6,101,000

RARITY: Another semi-key coin, the 1913-S cent has always been scarce in the better circulated grades and in all uncirculated grades. Even in low grades, this date largely disappeared from circulation before 1960. Mediocre striking quality combined with the scarcity of fully red specimens has made this date quite rare in gem or even choice Mint State. A number of the coins offered as MS RD are suspect because of widespread dipping.

POPULATION: MS BN = 35   MS RB = 142   MS RD = 108   TOTAL = 285

TOTALS   MS65 RD = 34   HIGHEST = MS65 RD (34)

VALUES:

GRADE	1935	1950	1965	1980	1995
G	——	——	3.50	5.00	6.00
F	——	.30	6.75	7.25	8.00
EF	——	——	13.50	16.00	25.00
MS60	1.00	5.50	55.00	67.50	100.00
MS63	——	——	——	——	150.00
MS65	——	——	——	——	1325.00

VARIETIES: Two obverse cud breaks are known, both appearing between the truncation of the bust and the border. A single repunched mintmark may also be found.

COMMENTS: Although not as badly struck as branch mint coins from the 1920s, this issue is still found most often in a later die state, that is to say, coined from worn dies. The piece illustrated is well above average, although a slight softening of strike can be detected in the date and mintmark.

Like most key and semi-key Lincolns, the number of coins certified as MS RD includes many which just barely make the cut. Don't expect the typical red coin to blaze like a cent coined more recently. Instead, expect a subdued, mellow red.

* * *

More interesting facts may be found in the *Annual Report* for 1913. Cent dies produced that year include 645 for Philadelphia, 140 for Denver and just 70 for San Francisco, though it's not clear whether these figures refer to calendar year 1913 or the Mint's fiscal year, which then ran July 1 to June 30. Figures are available, however, for the average number of cents produced per die during calendar year 1913:[17]

	Philadelphia	Denver	San Francisco
Obverse	337,752	501,364	218,275
Reverse	323,621	391,309	160,835

1914

PHILADELPHIA
75,237,067

RARITY: Fairly common in all circulated grades, 1914-P is also readily available in the lower Mint State grades. Its higher uncirculated value in relation to earlier P-Mint cents is based solely on its scarcity in gem condition; average to choice quality Mint State coins are not difficult to locate.

POPULATION: MS BN = 33   MS RB = 166   MS RD = 249   TOTAL = 448
TOTALS   MS65 RD = 101   HIGHEST = MS67 RD (1)

VALUES:

GRADE	1935	1950	1965	1980	1995
G	——	——	.40	.25	.20
F	——	.15	2.30	1.70	1.25
EF	——	——	5.00	7.75	8.00
MS60	1.25	3.00	35.00	37.50	50.00
MS63	——	——	——	——	60.00
MS65	——	——	——	——	200.00

VARIETIES: None are reported.

COMMENTS: 1914-P cents are invariably well struck. The best of these even display the slightly textured fields which were readily apparent on 1909 V.D.B. cents and remained visible on subsequent matte proofs. The piece illustrated is particularly sharp, and it's the sort of coin which has been misidentified as a proof in the past. Note, however, that the borders are somewhat rounded in places, instead of fully squared as on a proof.

     Why was this date so highly valued in Mint State during the 1935-65 period? In the 1935 *Standard Catalogue* it was one of only 11 coins in the series to have broken the $1.00 barrier at a time when the 1909-S V.D.B. issue was worth only 25 cents! In the 1965 *Guide Book* (published in 1964), it carried an uncirculated value of more than twice that of the 1913-P cent. The author is not aware of any hoards breaking in the marketplace since that time, so the answer must lie elsewhere.

     Although the passage of years has largely corrected this anomaly, 1914-P cents are still more highly valued than comparable neighboring dates. In an analysis of the Lincoln Cent series (which is of interest primarily because it predates the advent of encapsulation and published population reports), *The Coin Dealer Newsletter* noted that "Of all the P-mints, the 14-P is the most under-valued in conditions above MS-63."[18] The subsequent reports of the third-party grading services, however, seem to belie this notion and indicate that 1914-P cents are comparable in high grade rarity to 1912-P and 1913-P, both of which are valued much lower. Still, reports from collectors indicate that this date remains difficult to locate in grades MS65 RD and higher.

     During Fiscal Year 1914, the Philadelphia Mint used a total of 655 cent dies, Denver utilized 54, while San Francisco required only 50 dies. The planchets used for cent coinage during FY1914 were all produced within the three mints, according to the *Annual Report*:[19]

1914-P cents were clearly common in circulation during 1938, based on this item from *The Numismatic Scrapbook* Magazine:

Goldblatt Bros., department stores, started in business in 1914. They recently offered a "soda" to anyone presenting a 1914 cent at their fountains.

Kenneth D. McQuigg inquired as to how many were presented and received a letter stating that 2463 were turned in. Of these, 29 were D mint and 40 S mint. McQuigg states that most of the coins were worn and over 95% were below good.[20]

DENVER
1,193,000

RARITY: A key date within the Lincoln series, 1914-D is scarce in all circulated grades, particularly in those most highly sought: Fine through About Uncirculated. Mint State coins of any quality are now and have always been in short supply. Gems of any color are very scarce; fully red gems are rare, as the figures below reveal. Like 1909-S V.D.B, this issue sells very quickly to both specialists and those simply intrigued by its aura. The high number of certified Mint State examples reflects a greater incentive to have this valuable issue certified and also to resubmit such coins one or more times in an attempt to obtain a higher grade.

POPULATION: MS BN = 53   MS RB = 176   MS RD = 100   TOTAL = 329
TOTALS MS65 RD = 29   HIGHEST = MS66 RD (2)

VALUES:

GRADE	1935	1950	1965	1980	1995
G	——	——	42.50	55.00	80.00
F	——	6.00	75.00	70.00	110.00
EF	——	——	200.00	210.00	400.00
MS60	2.00	20.00	700.00	750.00	750.00
MS63	——	——	——	——	1200.00
MS65	——	——	——	——	3800.00

VARIETIES: One variety is known in a late die state with a crack wandering up into Lincoln's coat from the border.

COMMENTS: 1914-D cents are generally better struck than the D-Mint cents of 1911 through 1913. Most show full details, with only slight softening of the numerals and lettering. For reasons unknown, the obverse dies were more likely to appear worn than the reverse dies. This contradicts the prevailing situation, in which reverse dies appear to have been used longer, as their anonymity permitted usage beyond the year of their manufacture.

Recognized as a rarity as early as the 1930s, this issue was tied at $2.00 with its San Francisco cousin for the most highly valued Lincoln Cents in the 1935 Standard Catalog. With the growing popularity of this series, its value really took off during the 1950s and early '60s. Like most Lincolns, however, its performance since that time has been relatively disappointing. The optimist will view this as an opportunity, the pessimist as a warning.

As one of the most valuable coins in this very popular series, the 1914-D cent has long provided an opportunity for those who would deceive collectors. The population of counterfeit and altered specimens probably exceeds the number of genuine coins. Purchasing only examples which have been certified by a grading or authentication service is the simplest way to avoid this trap, but there are still a great many 1914-D cents offered which have not been certified. The lack of a photo certificate or encapsulation doesn't mean that a "raw" coin is bad; the author acquired his own specimen uncertified because it passed his visual inspection and its seller was well known to be honest and knowledgable.

A thorough examination of counterfeit and altered 1914-D cents may be found in Chapter 5, but a brief review here is appropriate. Most of the bogus examples that exist were fabricated in the 1950s and '60s when a large number of inexperienced persons discovered coin collect-

Genuine 1914-D cent. Note the style of date and mintmark. The mintmark of this die sits within a slight depression caused by metal displacement during the punching process. (ANAAB)

ing; these fakes are fairly crude. The usual method was to either relocate a D mintmark from some common-date, D-Mint coin to a genuine 1914-P or to alter a genuine 1944-D by cutting away part of the first numeral 4. Both methods were practiced with varying degrees of skill, but a person armed with the knowledge of how a genuine 1914-D Lincoln should appear will be able to detect just about any alteration.

When a mintmark is added to a 1914-P cent, the size and style of the letter is often inappropriate. Only a letter D taken from a cent coined between 1911 and 1917 would match the size and style of punch used during 1914. Later mintmarks used from 1918 through 1932 are similar in size but are somewhat differently shaped. Those used 1933 and later are significantly larger and should not fool anyone who has seen a photo of a genuine 1914-D cent.

Cents dated 1944-D which have been altered to 1914-D are easy to spot. In addition to having an unnaturally large gap between the numerals 9 and 1, the initials V.D.B. will appear at the truncation of Lincoln's bust; since these initials were not added at that location until 1918, no authentic 1914-D cent would have them. Some fakers learned to remove these initials, but there are usually signs of tooling in that location. Also easy to spot on an erstwhile 1944-D cent is the distinctive, large D which was not used before 1933. Finally, to an experienced cent collector, the entire look or "fabric" of a 1944 cent from any mint is entirely different from that of any 1914 cent, due to the progressive erosion of the master hubs over thirty years.

SAN FRANCISCO
4,137,000

RARITY: Among the scarcest of the semi-key dates, 1914-S is tough in all grades. Problems with the planchet stock have caused many specimens across the entire grade spectrum to display signs of corrosion and other discoloration. Problem-free examples grading VF through AU are quite difficult to locate, and Mint State coins are in chronically short supply, as the following figures suggest. Note the extreme rarity of MS65 RD gems! When found, such coins are usually more orange than red.

POPULATION: MS BN = 42   MS RB = 118   MS RD = 46   TOTAL = 206
TOTALS   MS65 RD = 15   HIGHEST = MS66 RD (1)

VALUES:	GRADE	1935	1950	1965	1980	1995
	G	——	——	5.00	6.50	9.00
	F	——	.35	8.50	8.50	12.00
	EF	——	——	22.50	20.00	35.00
	MS60	2.00	8.50	100.00	92.50	165.00
	MS63	——	——	——	——	375.00
	MS65	——	——	——	——	3750.00

VARIETIES: A single obverse cud break variety may be found in the usual location, below Lincoln's shoulder.

COMMENTS: Many 1914-S cents are reasonably well struck, some remarkably so (a characteristic which would continue for S-Mint cents through 1916). The single great deterrent to locating an attractive example lies in the planchet stock used for this date.

Mint State coins which have not been cleaned at some point (and these are few in number) will be fairly dark, precluding the designation MS RD in all but a few instances. Despite their occasional leniency when it comes to grading the rarest dates, the commercial grading services have still certified very few 1914-S cents as MS RD.

A deterrent to finding a desirable coin is the conflict between strike and color. It seems that sharply struck coins are invariably dark, while the few bright examples tend to be mushy. This phenomenon was described under COMMENTS for 1911-D, and it is common to many dates during the 1910s. It's interesting to note also that this very same condition exists for the Philippines one-centavo pieces struck at the San Francisco Mint during 1914 and adjacent years.

The rarity of this date in uncirculated condition was known early on, and the 1935 *Standard Catalogue* valued it and 1914-D equally as the most expensive coins in the series. This book, however, was directed toward the serious collector who acquired his coins from dealers. As the collecting of coins from circulation became widespread in subsequent years, issues such as 1909-S V.D.B., common in Mint State but rarely seen in circulation, came to overshadow the importance of the condition rarities such as 1914-S and 1926-S.

1915

PHILADELPHIA
29,090,970

RARITY: While 1915-P may have been slightly scarcer than other P-Mint for those collecting from circulation in years past, it is readily available from dealers in grades below VG. In this and higher circulated grades, however, 1915-P can be challenging. Low end, Mint State coins are only slightly scarce, but choice and gem specimens are elusive. When found, however, gems tend to have very pleasing color and sharp details.

POPULATION: MS BN = 48   MS RB = 178   MS RD = 210   TOTAL = 436
TOTALS   MS65 RD = 91   HIGHEST = MS68 RD (1)

VALUES:

GRADE	1935	1950	1965	1980	1995
G	——	——	.50	.60	1.00
F	——	.15	4.00	4.25	3.50
EF	——	——	12.50	22.00	32.00
MS60	1.00	3.50	100.00	80.00	80.00
MS63	——	——	——	——	125.00
MS65	——	——	——	——	360.00

VARIETIES: None are reported.

COMMENTS: Due to its lower than usual mintage for a P-Mint cent, this issue has long enjoyed a premium. It was one of only 11 dates valued at $1.00 or more in the 1935 *Standard Catalogue*. It shares this distinction with 1914-P, another date which is only slightly scarce in Mint State. It may be that those prices reflected the value of fully red gems, as only in such condition are these two coins particularly hard to find.

Many 1915-P cents are reduced in grade and value by fingerprints and/or spotting. Attempts to remove these flaws have always met with only limited success, usually leaving the coins with an unnatural appearance.

The obverse master die for the cents of 1915 from all three mints appears to have been manually enhanced. The cents of this date are similar to those of earlier years yet, when coined from fresh working dies, they possess superior detail in Lincoln's hair and beard. This reworking proved so successful that for the cents of 1916 a new master hub was prepared incorporating these changes, but to an even finer state of detail.

The cents of this date display a short, compact numeral 5. This is inconsistent with the style set by Brenner in 1909 and maintained since that time for numeral 9 in the date. A correctly engraved 5 would possess a long tail following the curvature of the 9.

* * *

Numismatic author Q. David Bowers has often related the story of how two bidders once ran up the price of an uncirculated 1915 cent at auction, both thinking that they were bidding on a more valuable lot. He cites this as the reason for the 1915-P's unusually high value. While this incident undoubtedly did occur and is clearly reflected in the 1950 and 1965 valuations, there was already a precedent for this issue's high price.

DENVER
22,050,000

RARITY: Only slightly scarce in lower grades, the higher circulated grades and average Mint State coins are somewhat more challenging to locate. Only in gem, fully red condition, however, is 1915-D truly scarce.

POPULATION TOTALS

MS BN = 37   MS RB = 191   MS RD = 209   TOTAL = 437

MS65 RD = 99   HIGHEST = MS66 RD (10)

VALUES:

GRADE	1935	1950	1965	1980	1995
G	——	——	.70	.60	.60
F	——	.25	2.50	1.50	1.50
EF	——	——	8.00	11.00	10.00
MS60	.60	1.75	27.50	37.50	45.00
MS63	——	——	——	——	90.00
MS65	——	——	——	——	410.00

VARIETIES: A single repunched mintmark is known.

COMMENTS: While well struck examples may be found, most were clearly coined from lightly worn dies. The coin illustrated is exceptional in its sharpness.

    The mintage for 1915-D was 50% greater than for any previous issue from the Denver Mint, though it would be exceeded the following year. As the population figures suggest, it is readily available in all degrees of color, although few of the red or red/brown coins are true gems.

    During 1915, the Philadelphia Mint used 180 cent dies; Denver, 114 and San Francisco, 80. On January 2, 1915, some 159 dies from the previous year's coinage were destroyed as prescribed by law.[21]

SAN FRANCISCO
4,833,000

RARITY: Scarce to rare in all grades, 1915-S was among the several dates in this series which had virtually disappeared from circulation as early as the mid-1950s. Problem-free examples remain scarce in dealers' stocks, particularly in the most sought grades of VF-AU. Unattractive, Mint State coins may be found with diligence, but anything that could be described as choice or better is very rare. When found, however, gems are likely to have a very deep red color and outstanding detail.

POPULATION TOTALS

MS BN = 32   MS RB = 89   MS RD = 43   TOTAL = 164

MS65 RD = 17   HIGHEST = MS66 RD (1)

VALUES:

GRADE	1935	1950	1965	1980	1995
G	——	——	4.50	5.00	7.00
F	——	.30	6.75	7.00	9.00
EF	——	——	12.50	17.00	25.00
MS60	.60	4.00	50.00	65.00	100.00
MS63	——	——	——	——	185.00
MS65	——	——	——	——	1650.00

VARIETIES: None are reported.

COMMENTS: The certified population data says it all. This date, though still valued below 1914-S, is indeed as scarce or scarcer. Old perceptions tend to linger, otherwise the published value of this issue in MS63 would be higher.

    The typical 1915-S cent is well struck for a branch mint coin, and a few display needle-sharp impressions. Coined from planchet stock which was apparently similar in character to that used for 1914-S cents, most unaltered coins of this date are dark and unattractive when found in Mint State. So many have been cleaned and then artificially retoned that this may account in part for the small number of certified specimens (the grading services will not encapsulate coins which have obviously been "processed").

1916

PHILADELPHIA
131,832,627

RARITY: Quite common in Mint State, even gems are fairly plentiful. Sadly, some of the potentially finest coins are plagued by irremovable black spots. These serve as tangible reminders to never talk or eat over exposed coins. Original, uncirculated rolls of this issue may still exist.

Like so many early Lincolns, this issue is difficult to locate in grades EF and AU. By the time such coins were worth saving, nearly all had worn down to lower grades. Those that survived did so by pure chance. They may have resided in cookie jars, been lost in bureau drawers or suffered some other interruption in their normal destiny which preserved them for the benefit of collectors.

POPULATION: MS BN = 17   MS RB = 173   MS RD = 465   TOTAL = 655
TOTALS   MS65 RD = 227   HIGHEST = MS67 RD (8)

VALUES:

GRADE	1935	1950	1965	1980	1995
G	——	——	.15	.20	.20
F	——	.05	.50	.40	.35
EF	——	——	1.50	2.25	1.50
MS60	.45	.50	10.00	12.00	12.00
MS63	——	——	——	——	25.00
MS65	——	——	——	——	97.50

VARIETIES: One obverse cud die break is known in the familiar position below Lincoln's shoulder.

COMMENTS: The first issue to reflect wartime prosperity, the 1916-P cent is not only quite common in most grades, but it is superbly struck as well.

The small population of MS BN specimens simply reflects the low value of such coins and should not be misinterpreted as an indication of rarity. This statement is true of most P-Mint coins dated 1916 and later.

* * *

Walter Breen noted in his *Encyclopedia* that modified dies were introduced this year, and that certainly accounts for the extraordinary wealth of detail evident in Lincoln's beard. The master die for 1916 is indeed superior to all dates which preceded or followed, and these coins make ideal type specimens. It appears that the obverse master hub of 1909 was replaced altogether in 1916, as the relief of Lincoln's ear is noticeably higher than on earlier dates. Such a change is not likely to have been made in the master die alone, for it would then need to be repeated each year as a new master die was sunk from the master hub.

For 1916, the Philadelphia Mint used 505 cent dies; Denver, 164 and San Francisco, 60.[22]

DENVER
35,956,000

RARITY: 1916-D is fairly common in the lower circulated grades. Coins grading VF through AU are scarce, as collecting from circulation didn't become popular for another 20 years. In Mint State, choice brown or red/brown examples are scarce at the very least, while coins displaying full, *original* color are unquestionably rare. When found, these tend to have a pinkish hue and are usually less than fully struck. The sharper pieces are typically brown in color.

POPULATION: MS BN = 45   MS RB = 160   MS RD = 100   TOTAL = 305
TOTALS   MS65 RD = 27   HIGHEST = MS66 RD (2)

VALUES:

GRADE	1935	1950	1965	1980	1995
G	——	——	.35	.25	.20
F	——	.20	2.00	.85	.75
EF	——	——	5.50	6.75	7.00
MS60	.65	2.00	21.00	32.50	55.00
MS63	——	——	——	——	100.00
MS65	——	——	——	——	950.00

VARIETIES: A massive, obverse cud die break may be found at the 7 o'clock position, obliterating about 20% of the design (see photo).

1916-D
LC-16-D-1 (Thurman & Margolis)

COMMENTS: Well struck coins are scarce but may be found, a situation aided in part by the superior master die introduced this year. A few deficient coins struck from overused dies may be encountered, but this problem doesn't appear until the following year.

The rarity of this date in MS65 RD will come as a surprise to many who are new to collecting Lincolns in high grades but not to veteran specialists in the series. As with all branch mint Lincolns from the 1910s and 1920s (and to a lesser extent, P-Mint cents), beware of pieces which have been cleaned. These may be very deceptively recolored to an appealing red and brown. The fact that a specimen is certified and encapsulated will usually screen out such alterations. Cleaned and recolored coins are still collectable, but they should be purchased at a price which reflects their lessened desirability.

Most Lincoln Cents in lower grades have not performed well over the past thirty years, but 1916-D is a particularly shocking example. Compare its 1965 and 1995 values in grades Good and Fine! This is just another reminder of the increasing grade consciousness during this period and of the decline in the number of collectors who are simply "filling holes."

* * *

As mass production lowered the cost of small articles, there were increasing calls for some coin valued between one and five cents. In his *Annual Report* to Treasury Secretary William G. McAdoo, Mint Director F. J. H. von Engelken climbed onto the bandwagon:

> I beg to suggest the advisability of recommending to Congress the passage of an act authorizing the coinage of a copper and nickel 2-1/2-cent piece. Inquiry, prompted by requests contained in letters from many parts of the country, discloses a real demand for it. When you consider that we have no coin between the 1-cent piece and the 5-cent piece and that many an article worth more than a cent and less than 5 cents sells for the latter price because of the lack of an intermediate monetary unit of value, the economic importance of it will be readily seen. Articles which now sell for 15 cents each or two for a quarter would sell for 12-1/2 cents. Popular shops, such as the 5 and 10 cent stores, would undoubtedly place articles now selling two for 5 cents on sale at 2-1/2 cents each; and it is not at all unlikely that street car companies would carry children of school age for 2-1/2 cents. There is much interesting data available on this subject, and I respectfully request that you give it careful consideration.[23]

Like so many proposals for odd denomination coins that appeared during the first two decades of the 20th Century, this one ultimately faded away. Some, however, came quite close to fruition, passing one or both houses of Congress, only to be vetoed or simply allowed to expire.

SAN FRANCISCO
22,510,000

RARITY: Relatively plentiful in lower grades, only Mint State coins may be called scarce. Brown or red/brown uncirculated pieces are usually available, though they may not always be attractive. Fully red specimens are extremely rare, and their certified population in MS65 RD is among the lowest in the series.

POPULATION: MS BN = 57   MS RB = 144   MS RD = 64   TOTAL = 265
TOTALS   MS65 RD = 10   HIGHEST = MS66 RD (1)

VALUES:

GRADE	1935	1950	1965	1980	1995
G	——	——	.60	.55	.75
F	——	.20	2.50	1.25	1.75
EF	——	——	7.50	6.90	8.00
MS60	.65	3.50	35.00	35.00	60.00
MS63	——	——	——	——	125.00
MS65	——	——	——	——	3250.00

VARIETIES: A single doubled-die obverse is known, with doubling visible on LIBERTY (see photo).

COMMENTS: Like the 1916-D cents, only a few are poorly struck. Most are fairly sharp, while a select few will display a fantastic degree of sharpness. These are equal to any proof in their central details, although they will lack the squared inner and outer borders which typify proof coins.

1916-S
DDO-1 (Fivaz & Stanton)

As with most S-Mint cents of the years 1908-23, the planchet stock utilized for 1916-S was seldom alloyed properly. Uncleaned, Mint State coins with original color will frequently display a wood-grain pattern of faint, elongated stains, such as those seen on the example illustrated. The effect of elongation occurs when the strip is processed through a succession of rollers to obtain its proper thickness before punching out the blanks. This coloration is desirable to some and distracting to others, but it only affects a coin's grade and subsequent value when truly severe. Beware of cleaned and retoned examples in grades EF and higher; these probably outnumber coins having their original surface by a sizable margin.

* * *

The coinage of cents at the San Francisco Mint was still considered something of a novelty to collectors as late as 1916, as indicated by this item from *The Numismatist*:

California is rapidly learning to use the 1-cent piece. Mr. and Mrs. San Francisco accept it in change. Attesting to the popularity of the humblest American coin are the figures from the local mint for April. During the month no less than three hundred thousand cents were minted.[24]

1917

PHILADELPHIA
196,429,785

RARITY: 1917-P is common in all circulated grades, and Mint State coins grading up through MS64 are readily available in any shade from brown to red. Fully red gems are also obtainable without too much difficulty, their certified population being almost comparable to that of 1916-P. Virtually all 1917-P cents are sharply struck. Original, uncirculated rolls may still exist.

POPULATION: MS BN = 9   MS RB = 80   MS RD = 329   TOTAL = 418
TOTALS MS65 RD = 150   HIGHEST = MS68 RD (2)

VALUES:

GRADE	1935	1950	1965	1980	1995
G	——	——	.15	.15	.20
F	——	.05	.50	.35	.30
EF	——	——	1.50	2.00	1.50
MS60	.25	.50	9.50	11.00	12.00
MS63	——	——	——	——	25.00
MS65	——	——	——	——	110.00

VARIETIES: Two reverse cud break varieties exist for 1917-P. The first obliterates a portion of the letters UM in UNUM, while the second appears at the 5-6 o'clock position.

COMMENTS: A distinct, doubled-die obverse is known for this date and has become extremely popular with specialists (see photos). Uncirculated examples remain quite rare. This variety is illustrated in *A Guide Book of United States Coins* (the Red Book), also in *Walter Breen's Complete Encyclopedia of U. S. and Colonial Coins* and *The Lincoln Cent doubled-die,* by John A. Wexler. This assures that it will always be in demand and will command a premium price when properly attributed. The adventurous may wish to attempt cherrypicking this variety from unattributed 1917-P cents in dealers' stocks, a task made easier with *The Cherrypickers' Guide to Rare Die Varieties,* by Bill Fivaz and J. T. Stanton. All of these books are essential for any serious collector of Lincoln Cents.

1917-P
DDO-1, Breen-2081 (Fivaz & Stanton)

The finely detailed obverse master hub introduced in 1916 was used again this year to produce the 1917 master die. The sharpness of 1917-dated cents is not quite equal to that of 1916 Lincolns, but the P-Mint coins struck this year are superior to all that came afterward.

1917-P cents remained obtainable from circulation through the 1960s, and the author discovered his final, well-worn example as late as 1977, by which time all "Wheaties" were becoming rare.

* * *

The onset of America's involvement in World War I led to a nationwide shortage of cents. Because the U. S. Mint worked within the constraint of an annual appropriation, it was initially unable to meet the demand for more coins. Director Raymond T. Baker bemoaned this fact in his *Annual Report* to Treasury Secretary William G. McAdoo:

> It is further recommended that the necessary steps be taken to bring about legislation to increase the minor coinage metal fund from $200,000 to $400,000. We are now considerably embarrassed by lack of funds to pay for sufficient copper and nickel to operate the mints to full capacity on minor coins.[25]

One by-product of the America's entry into the war was the closing of the three mints to tourists for security reasons on February 3, 1917. Until that time, the Philadelphia Mint had been receiving about 75,000-85,000 visitors per year, Denver around 65,000 and San Francisco some 75,000.

For Fiscal Year 1917 (July 1, 1916 to June 30, 1917), there were 860 cent dies made for the Philadelphia Mint, 425 for Denver and 320 for San Francisco. The Philadelphia Mint's machine shop turned out a variety of parts for the other mints, including 18 collars for use in Denver and 6 for the San Francisco Mint.[26]

The *Annual Report* of the Director of the Mint provided a wealth of information for the years up to about 1920. After that time, it became increasingly brief and non-specific in describing the Mint's operations. This is truly sad, because the original documents recording the day-to-day activities of the various mint facilities were irretrievably lost during the administration of Mint Director Stella Hackel. In a misguided bid toward President Carter's cost-cutting program, Director Hackel's office ordered that the original records be destroyed, rather than forwarding them to the National Archives.

The Grand Old Man of the United States Mint, Chief Engraver Charles E. Barber, died on February 18, 1917.[27] He was succeeded by his assistant and frequent rival, George T. Morgan.

DENVER
55,120,000

RARITY: This issue is common in the lower circulated grades. Examples grading EF-AU are usually available, but a great many have been cleaned and retoned. Striking sharpness will also be a deterrent to finding nice specimens in both the higher circulated grades and in all grades of Mint State. As is so often the case with early Lincolns, the sharpest ones are brown, while the brightest ones are a tad mushy. As the numbers below suggest, there are quite a few certified coins available, but very few of these exceed MS64, whether brown, red/brown or fully red. Spotting is also a serious problem with this issue.

POPULATION: MS BN = 38   MS RB = 158   MS RD = 156   TOTAL = 352
TOTALS   MS65 RD = 43   HIGHEST = MS66 RD (4)

VALUES:

GRADE	1935	1950	1965	1980	1995
G	——	——	.35	.25	.25
F	——	.20	1.40	.75	.65
EF	——	——	7.25	6.75	7.00
MS60	.50	2.75	30.00	37.50	55.00
MS63	——	——	——	——	110.00
MS65	——	——	——	——	700.00

VARIETIES: A single obverse cud variety is known. It partially obliterates letters D and W of the motto IN GOD WE TRUST. Cud breaks affecting this portion of the motto have been humorously dubbed "atheist" cents by past generations of collectors.

COMMENTS: Despite the asset of a sharp master hub die for 1917, most D-Mint cents of this date were coined from overused working dies which ranged in condition from obviously tired to absolutely terminal. In short, 1917-D cents are mushy, with blurred date, mintmark and mottos being the rule. The wheat stems are frequently merged with the reverse border.

In its 1980 study of this series, *The Coin Dealer Newsletter* remarked of this coin and its brethren: "Finding a 17-D that looks like a top quality 1912-15 D-mint presents a major problem. In fact, from 1917 thru 1928 or 1929, practically none of the mintmarked issues will be of the quality of the pre-1916 coins."[28] Expanding on this issue, Sol Taylor wrote in *The Standard Guide to the Lincoln Cent*: "The details in the obverse tend to be soft with considerable metal flow evident. Even early die state pieces lack the sharpness seen in the 1917 Philadelphia pieces."[29]

SAN FRANCISCO
32,620,000

RARITY: Relatively plentiful in lower grades, only Mint State coins may be called scarce. Brown or red/brown uncirculated pieces are usually available, though not always attractive. Fully red specimens are very scarce, and their certified population in MS65 RD is among the lowest in the series.

POPULATION:	MS BN = 39	MS RB = 154	MS RD = 45	TOTAL = 238
TOTALS	MS65 RD = 10	HIGHEST = MS66 RD (1)		

VALUES:	GRADE	1935	1950	1965	1980	1995
	G	——	——	.35	.25	.25
	F	——	.20	1.40	.75	.65
	EF	——	——	7.25	6.75	7.00
	MS60	.65	3.50	30.00	37.50	60.00
	MS63	——	——	——	——	125.00
	MS65	——	——	——	——	2250.00

VARIETIES: This date is a fertile hunting ground for cud die breaks. Three obverse varieties are known, all at the usual 7 o'clock position. No less than six reverse cuds are recorded, most of these at 9-10 o'clock. One cud is known in a progressive pair of die states.

A new mintmark punch was introduced this year, and all of the 1917-S cents examined have displayed this new letter S.

COMMENTS: The population data for 1917-S is remarkably similar to that for its older brother of the previous year. This date is more challenging than 1916-S in most grades, as fewer were sharply struck. Only a small portion of this mint's output will display sharp detailing in Lincoln's hair and beard. Like the 1917-D cents, many will be poorly struck as a consequence of overextended die usage during the critical wartime period. The mints were working three shifts around the clock during 1917-18, and it shows in the quality of their product. This is less true, however, of the P-Mint cents, perhaps because they were made at the same facility which produced the dies for all three mints, and replacement dies could be had as soon as needed.

Like most S-Mint cents from the years 1908-23, 1917-S is subject to the woodgrain toning which resulted from improper mixture of the alloy in strip preparation. Unless severe, this coloration shouldn't have much effect on a coin's value.

1917-S has been another abysmal performer in low grades over the past thirty years. Perhaps it may be time to just spend those rolls of worn-out, early Lincolns, rather than saving them in a hopeless effort to recoup one's 1965 investment! The creation of a new coin collector or the revitalization of a veteran hobbyist is probably more valuable than these coins will ever be.

1918

PHILADELPHIA
288,104,634

RARITY: 1918-P is common in all circulated grades, and Mint State coins grading up through MS64 are readily available. Fully red, MS65 gems are not rare, but the certified population for 1918-P is not quite equal to those of 1916-P and 1917-P, and it's way below those of 1919-P and 1920-P. Original rolls may still exist, but most have been broken up to retrieve the better pieces.

POPULATION: MS BN = 3   MS RB = 84   MS RD = 268   TOTAL = 355
TOTALS MS65 RD = 139   HIGHEST = MS68 RD (1)

VALUES:

GRADE	1935	1950	1965	1980	1995
G	——	——	.20	.20	.20
F	——	.05	.50	.40	.40
EF	——	——	1.50	2.25	1.50
MS60	.25	.50	10.00	13.00	13.00
MS63	——	——	——	——	25.00
MS65	——	——	——	——	115.00

VARIETIES: Only a single obverse cud variety is reported for 1918-P; it appears in the usual place between shoulder and border.

COMMENTS: 1918-P cents are typically very well struck, though a few will show some signs of die wear. Fully red coins turn up with some frequency, but this date seems more susceptible than most to unpleasant spotting on otherwise choice and gem coins. The low certified population of MS BN coins does not reflect rarity; it merely denotes the lack of economic incentive for submitting such pieces to grading services.

Another obverse appeared this year bearing Brenner's initials V.D.B. on the truncation of Lincoln's bust. Since this modification could easily have been made to the existing obverse master hub in use since 1916, it may be assumed that this was indeed done. In any case, there's nothing to suggest that 1918 and later cents through 1968 were from a different hub than the one used 1916-17. This master hub, however, became noticeably worn during 1919, and its progressive deterioration may be seen for each subsequent date until it was finally scrapped at the beginning of 1969's coinage.

* * *

Collectors of this time were not particularly observant when it came to current coinage, and the presence of Brenner's initials on the obverse remained a secret until 1922, when it was published in *The Numismatist* in a letter from prominent figure Farran Zerbe:

A Lima (Ohio) collector has brought to may attention "V. D. B." in minute letters, incused, at the base of Lincoln's bust on cents of different mints dated 1918, 1919 and 1920, and cents of the same mints and dates on which the "V. D. B." does not appear. It may be that those without letters had become obliterated. I am not interested in cent varieties and do not know of these marks as to other dates.[30]

In his *Annual Report*, Mint Director Raymond T. Baker acknowledged the extraordinary production of coins during the preceding 12 months:

The fiscal year 1918 was for the Mint Service the most active in its history, the three coinage mints at Philadelphia, San Francisco, and Denver working 16 to 24 hours per day for the greater part of the year to keep up with the demand for coin of denominations below the dollar.

The unprecedented demand for fractional coin is doubtless due to war activities—general acceleration of business transactions requiring more frequent settlements; larger earnings of the people, resulting in more expenditures; demands of camp activities, etc. Internal revenue taxes on amusement entrance fees and on numerous other services, as well as increased street car fares and additions to other prices, required many 1-cent pieces.[31]

The number of cent dies utilized during Fiscal Year 1918 reflected this increased output. Philadelphia required 1,715, Denver 467 and San Francisco 400. Some 25 dies were produced but never issued from the Engraving Department.

The number of Mint employees was also up because of the war. Philadelphia now had 499, Denver 92 and San Francisco 178.[32]

DENVER
47,830,000

RARITY: 1918-D cents are common in all of the lower circulated grades through Fine. VF and EF coins are usually available, if one is not too particular about strike and surface quality. Despite the enormous number coined, Mint State pieces do not survive in abundance. Very few of the ones seen will even qualify as choice, let alone gem. Top-notch pieces in either red/brown or fully red are rare, as the figures below suggest. Many of the more sharply struck examples are plagued by spots.

POPULATION: MS BN = 19   MS RB = 111   MS RD = 100   TOTAL = 230
TOTALS   MS65 RD = 26   HIGHEST = MS67 RD (1)

VALUES:	GRADE	1935	1950	1965	1980	1995
	G	——	——	.30	.25	.25
	F	——	.20	2.00	.70	.65
	EF	——	——	8.00	6.00	5.00
	MS60	.60	4.50	37.50	37.50	50.00
	MS63	——	——	——	——	105.00
	MS65	——	——	——	——	800.00

VARIETIES: None are reported.

COMMENTS: The vast majority of 1918-D cents were coined from severely overused dies displaying advanced wear. Although it gives some hint of this condition, the coin illustrated is actually one of the finer specimens to be found.

Most uncirculated 1918-D cents fall into the categories of brown or red/brown. Fully red examples are virtually unknown, and many of the pieces certified as such in reality possess a somewhat subdued red color, nothing like that of a fiery 1918-P. The poor condition of most 1918-D cents as struck precludes their ever grading higher than MS64. This accounts in part for the fairly small number of MS BN and MS RB entries; while such coins constitute the majority of Mint State survivors, they're simply not appealing enough to encourage submissions for grading.

Far from being an isolated occurrence, this quality control catastrophe fits into a pattern for all denominations coined at Denver in 1918 and for most branch mint Lincolns issued from 1917 through the late 1920s. Addressing this fact, *The Coin Dealer Newsletter* remarked: "Frankly, even many of the 'fussiest' collectors almost invariably settle for slightly lower quality Denver and San Francisco coins between 1917 and 1928 since the finest details (whiskers, etc.) are nearly always lacking."[33]

1918-D performed very poorly in circulated grades during the period from 1965 to 1995. Although the low 1995 value in grades Good and Fine is understandable, given the changing nature of the hobby, its value of only $5 in EF condition seems absurdly low in light of how few coins possess enough detail to qualify as EF.

* * *

At the close of the fiscal year (June 30, 1918), the U. S. Mint in all its divisions had a total of 961 employees. Of these, 499 were engaged in Philadelphia, 92 in Denver, 178 in San Francisco and the remainder in the eight Federal Assay Offices spread around the country.[34]

SAN FRANCISCO
34,680,000

RARITY: 1918-S cents were widely hoarded in low grades during the 1940s and 1950s, and such coins are plentiful. Grades F and VF and likewise available, though not in such numbers. The higher circulated grades are slightly scarce, due mostly to deficiencies in quality, as made. This same problem afflicts most Mint State coins, the typical pieces being brown or red/brown with poorly rendered details. Any fully red coin is a rarity, while fully red *and* fully struck gems are extremely rare.

POPULATION: MS BN = 30   MS RB = 111   MS RD = 44   TOTAL = 185
TOTALS   MS65 RD = 10   HIGHEST = MS65 RD (10)

VALUES:

GRADE	1935	1950	1965	1980	1995
G	——	——	.30	.25	.25
F	——	.20	2.00	.70	.65
EF	——	——	8.00	6.00	5.00
MS60	.65	6.00	40.00	37.50	55.00
MS63	——	——	——	——	125.00
MS65	——	——	——	——	5000.00

VARIETIES: Four retained cud die break varieties are recorded, all affecting the reverse wheat ears.

COMMENTS: Mushy coins struck from worn dies are the rule for this issue, although not quite to the extent of the 1918-D cents. A few well struck 1918-S Lincolns are around, though these seldom show their complete red color. Most collectors will have to seek well struck, red/brown coins as the best pieces available. Be particularly watchful for cents which have been cleaned (or "dipped"). These are often deceptively retoned to a charming red/brown appearance. While still collectable, they should not command high prices.

Like the 1918-D cent, this issue has suffered mightily in circulated grades since the highwater mark of 1965. The value of just $5 for a 1918-S cent in EF is deceptively low and does not reflect the difficulty of locating an original, well-struck, problem-free example.

* * *

When American troops arrived in France in the Spring of 1918 they carried with them some familiar coins, as reported in the following item from a soldier's magazine, *The Spiker:*

Coins of American mintage are fast gaining favor in France, and in many small shops they are accepted in lieu of French money. Newspaper vendors, boat ticket sellers and others who deal largely in pennies would much rather accept an American nickel or a couple of cents than change a 5-franc note. They are readily taken where there will be a later opportunity to pass it back in change to an American customer.

The French like the American 5-cent piece. "Elle est jolie," they say, comparing it with the French coin of the same denomination with a square hole in the center. They don't think so much of the American coppers. Being hardly half as large as the sou they have been accustomed to, they can't see why it has the same value.[35]

Among the doughboys who went off to war in 1917-18 were a number of U. S. Mint employees. The Philadelphia Mint furnished 17 men, San Francisco gave up 16, and the New York Assay Office was short six men. No figures were furnished for the Denver Mint.[36]

The ban on visitors to the mints was lifted shortly after an armistice was declared on November 11, 1918.[37]

1919

PHILADELPHIA
392,021,000

RARITY: 1919-P is common in all circulated grades. Mint State coins are likewise quite plentiful, with choice and even fully red gem pieces appearing with some frequency. This is entirely supported by the population data, though the low value of brown specimens has limited their certified total. Original rolls may exist, but most have been picked over to isolate the gems.

POPULATION: MS BN = 4   MS RB = 73   MS RD = 669   TOTAL = 746
TOTALS   MS65 RD = 307   HIGHEST = MS69 RD (1)

VALUES:

GRADE	1935	1950	1965	1980	1995
G	——	——	.15	.20	.15
F	——	.05	.40	.40	.40
EF	——	——	1.50	2.00	1.50
MS60	.25	.50	9.00	10.00	11.00
MS63	——	——	——	——	20.00
MS65	——	——	——	——	77.50

VARIETIES: Two obverse cud break varieties are noted at the truncation of Lincoln's bust, and a single, very dramatic cud occurred at the lower reverse, an uncommon position (see photo).

COMMENTS: The shortage of cents which developed in the Fall of 1917 went on unabated. As a consequence, this issue set a record for the largest mintage of a single denomination at a single mint. 1919-P cents remained common in circulation through the 1960s and into the early years of the '70s, though coins found that late were almost unidentifiable.

1919-P
LC-19-3-R (Thurman & Margolis)

1919-P cents are invariably well struck, and Mint State pieces may be found with a vibrant, brassy color. As befits its high mintage, there are a great many gems. Note that a single example has been certified MS69 RD!

* * *

Those who don't collect coins invariably overestimate the rarity of early Lincoln Cents, believing that because they're relatively old they must be rare. This assumption has been the downfall of countless merchants seeking what they thought would be a novel promotion for their businesses. A case in point, this item from 1955:

A Utica, N.Y., appliance dealer decided to mark the anniversary of his 36th year in business with a special offer — anyone who brought a 1919 cent into his store would received 36 cents in trade. Of the older date Lincoln cents, 1919 was one of the largest coinages. A local collector turned in 878 pieces and walked out with a new refrigerator.[38]

Mint Director Raymond T. Baker remarked on the astonishing production of the U. S. Mints during the preceding 12 months:

> During the fiscal year 1919 the demand for coin of denominations below the dollar continued to be very large, as compared with the period before the war. The demand for one-cent pieces was the largest ever known and our presses were run 24 hours a day on this coin for months. Over 1,600 tons (of 2,000 pounds), or 466,839,600 one-cent pieces, were issued by the mints during the year. Of this number approximately 158 millions were issued in May and June, and the unusually large demand was still unsatisfied. This demand was doubtless due principally to putting into effect, April 1, 1919, of certain internal revenue taxes.[39]

After producing its own cent blanks exclusively since FY 1914, the Philadelphia Mint was again compelled to seek assistance from outside suppliers to meet the demand for cents. Some 2,539,410.42 troy ounces of blanks were obtained at a cost of $75,060.67.

Aggravating the Mint's situation further was the demand from various branches of the armed services for award medals, insignia bars and collar ornaments. Being die-struck, most of these items had to be furnished by the three mints. In subsequent years, the War Department (later the Defense Department) acquired its own presses to produce some of these items, though medals were still struck exclusively by the U. S. Mint. When a massive coin shortage gripped the nation during the 1960s, these Defense Department presses were loaned to the Mint and refitted to strike coins!

DENVER
57,154,000

RARITY: Given its high mintage, 1919-D has never been scarce in lower grades. VF through AU examples are slightly scarce, especially with their original color and surfaces. Mediocre Mint State coins are the rule, most lacking a decent strike and appealing color. Choice examples are still fairly plentiful, while true gems may also be found with some searching.

POPULATION TOTALS: MS BN = 21   MS RB = 144   MS RD = 151   TOTAL = 316
MS65 RD = 35   HIGHEST = MS67 RD (1)

VALUES:

GRADE	1935	1950	1965	1980	1995
G	——	——	.30	.25	.25
F	——	.20	1.25	.70	.45
EF	——	——	5.00	5.25	4.00
MS60	.60	1.50	22.50	26.00	45.00
MS63	——	——	——	——	80.00
MS65	——	——	——	——	500.00

VARIETIES: A single repunched mintmark variety exists.

COMMENTS: Most cents of this issue show moderate to heavy die wear. Indistinct lettering and distorted peripheral elements (such as the wheat ears) are the rule. Sharply struck coins (like that illustrated) may be found with diligent searching, but they often fall short of gem in other respects. Pieces which retain their original surfaces tend to be dark and are often spotted or splotchy. Beware of cents that have been cleaned and retoned.

As with most early Lincoln Cents, this date has performed poorly in the circulated grades. The most consistent loser has been the Fine category, with nearly all dates posting moderate to heavy losses, particularly when adjusted for inflation. This phenomenon, which reflects a changing coin market since the 1960s, has affected several of the popular series. Lincolns, however, seem to have been hit the hardest, perhaps because they were the most popular coins during the "hole-filling" heyday of the 1950s and '60s.

* * *

The shortage of cents which contributed to record mintages in 1916-20 was periodically documented in the pages of *The Numismatist*:

> It is reported that since May 1, when the new luxury tax went into effect, there has been an extraordinary demand for cents for the purpose of making change, although not so great as the demand several months ago. Not withstanding the

immense quantities of this coin that have been minted for months past, the supply does not seem to equal the demand. A dispatch from Washington says that the U. S. mints and subtreasuries have been flooded with orders for millions of one-cent pieces, and these coins have been shipped to banks by the bushels. To meet the continued demand the Philadelphia and Denver mints are working almost exclusively on one-cent pieces, and an extra shift of workers has been ordered for the Philadelphia mint. Beginning May 7, 2,000,000 one-cent pieces were expected to be turned out daily.[40]

SAN FRANCISCO
139,760,000

RARITY: 1919-S is common in all grades short of choice and gem, though quality of strike is a factor for both circulated and uncirculated coins. Despite the very high mintage of this issue, desirable Mint State coins are in short supply. Most are from heavily worn dies, while the planchet stock used (as with most S-Mint cents from this decade) precluded the survival of many pieces with bright, mint red. So many have been dipped or otherwise cleaned in an attempt to compensate for their natural dullness that coins displaying any amount of original red color are very rare.

POPULATION: MS BN = 38   MS RB = 126   MS RD = 78   TOTAL = 242
TOTALS   MS65 RD = 17   HIGHEST = MS66 RD (1)

VALUES:

GRADE	1935	1950	1965	1980	1995
G	——	——	.30	.25	.15
F	——	.10	1.25	.50	.40
EF	——	——	5.00	3.00	2.50
MS60	1.00	1.50	22.50	22.00	30.00
MS63	——	——	——	——	70.00
MS65	——	——	——	——	2600.00

VARIETIES: Single cud varieties are known for both obverse and reverse, each appearing in the usual locations (below Lincoln's shoulder and between a wheat ear and the rim). A single repunched mintmark is also noted (see photo).

COMMENTS: Although not as poorly struck as the typical 1918-S cent, most pieces dated 1919-S will still be noticeably deficient. Patience will procure a well struck coin, but precious few of these will be of choice or gem quality overall.

1919-S Lincolns were widely hoarded in low grades during the 1940s and '50s and are among the early dates most often seen in unsorted hoards. Their mintage was such that they still turned up in the western states as late as the 1970s.

1919-S/S
RPM-1 (Miller)

* * *

San Francisco recorded a phenomenal mintage this year, being far greater than anything attempted previously. In response to a severe shortage of cents prompted by temporary, wartime taxes, the West Coast mint was called on to coin for the East and Midwest, in addition to supplying its usual customers. The shortage of cents had a profound effect on all three mints, as indicated in this story which appeared in *The Chicago Herald-Examiner* in the Summer of 1919:

Uncle Sam has placed his money factories on a 24-hour basis to make money enough for people to pay the war tax. All resources are to be used in turning out copper cents at the rate of 100,000,000 a month to meet the demand of the post-war revenue placed on small commodities.

Ray Baker, Director of the Mint, in Oakland with his wife on a ten-day tour of investigation, gave the order. During his stay he will handle the annual settlement of the finances of the San Francisco mint, investigate silver production and tour the new mining region of Southern Nevada.

The demand is in excess of 150,000,000 cents a month, and with the new production San Francisco for the first time, will be shipping pennies to fill the coin demand in Chicago and the Middle West. Heretofore the Philadelphia mint has coined all the copper. Since the introduction of coppers the mints have coined 3,300,000,000, most of which has passed into the small boys' banks.[41]

All of these coins required a great many dies during Fiscal Year 1919: 1552 for the Philadelphia Mint, 240 for Denver and 220 for San Francisco.[42]

1920

PHILADELPHIA
310,165,000

RARITY: 1920-P is common in all grades, including choice and gem uncirculated. Not all cents of this issue appear well struck, though enough exist to make desirable coins readily available. Original rolls may yet exist, but reassembled rolls (with the best coins removed for certification) are more likely to be encountered.

POPULATION: MS BN = 5   MS RB = 76   MS RD = 516   TOTAL = 597
TOTALS   MS65 RD = 214   HIGHEST = MS67 RD (2)

VALUES:

GRADE	1935	1950	1965	1980	1995
G	——	——	.15	.20	.15
F	——	.05	.50	.35	.35
EF	——	——	1.35	2.00	1.50
MS60	.25	.50	9.00	10.00	10.00
MS63	——	——	——	——	20.00
MS65	——	——	——	——	80.00

VARIETIES: A minor, obverse doubled-die is discernible in the motto LIBERTY. Four obverse cud varieties may be found. All but one of these has the die break in the usual 7 o'clock position; the fourth is broken at 5 o'clock.

COMMENTS: Fully red coins with outstanding luster are usually available, though it's interesting that no coins have been certified higher than MS67 RD (and only two at that level).

Like the 1918-P and 1919-P cents, those dated 1920-P, even when quite well struck, lack the sharpness seen on the best 1909-15 Lincolns and particularly the ones dated 1916-17. The years 1918-20 are about equal in their finest details, but progressive deterioration of the obverse hub had already begun and would continue unabated through the 1920s and later years.

* * *

As the fiscal year drew to a close (June 30, 1920), Mint Director Baker remarked on the ceaseless demand for coins, improvements at the mints to meet this demand and the need for pay increases for mint personnel (severe wartime inflation had left the dollar worth only half of its pre-war value):

> In order to meet the enormous demand for coin made upon the Mint Service during recent years, which demand has not yet shown signs of diminishing, the director has given much time during the past fiscal year to personally devising and supervising installation of improved methods and appliances for increasing the capacity of the coinage mints. These improvements include the use of large capacity electric melting furnaces in lieu of small gas and oil burning furnaces; mechanical conveyors in lieu of hand-propelled, heavily loaded trucks; rearrangement of floor space and of machinery so as to facilitate and expedite operations; and addition of new machinery.

Partial results of these improvements are evidenced by the materially increased output of the Philadelphia Mint, where the coin manufactured exceeded the prior year's product by 46 per cent . . .

It has been possible and necessary to make material increases in the pay of per diem employees, but the salaried employees, who were supervising and directing the work of those on a per diem basis, could not be increased beyond the small bonus of $240 per annum also paid to per diem workers. This situation should be adequately remedied at the earliest practical date to avoid further embarrassment to the service.[43]

Baker went on to note that 117 fewer persons were employed in the mints and assay offices than at the end of the previous fiscal year and that reductions were continuing. It's likely that some of these employees left voluntarily because they could obtain greater pay outside of government service, a subject touched upon by the Assay Commission in its report:

Your committee beg to suggest that the peculiar kind of service rendered by the employees of the mint commands a greater return for the skill demanded, and we recommend that the schedule of wages and salary, which in some instances has remained the same for a period of more than 37 years, be submitted to the proper authorities with a view of providing a basis of pay commensurate with the service rendered.[44]

* * *

Quite a few of the 1920-P cents found they way out of the country, as reported in this clipping reprinted in *The Numismatist*:

The scorn of the Cuban during war prosperity times for such low grade cash as pennies, drove the bronze coins out of circulation on the island. A few days ago, however, the penny, or rather 150,000 pennies, started back triumphantly on the Ward liner Morro Castle.

The pennies, newly turned out by the Philadelphia mint, were in kegs, which were carefully locked up in the ship's strongroom with all the attendant ceremony of gold shipments. With the price of sugar down to its present rate, there are lots of things which may be purchased for a few cents in Cuba.[45]

These cents may have borne a curse, as a later Morro Castle caught fire and burned with great loss of life in 1934.

DENVER
49,280,000

RARITY: This issue is common in all circulated grades through Fine, but the higher grades are less often encountered, due mostly to the use of worn dies. Mint State examples of mediocre quality are not hard to find, but choice and gem specimens are quite elusive. The culprit again is the late state of the dies employed in their coining, though irregularities in color are also a factor. When found, fully red cents are actually more of a pinkish color and are usually deficient in strike. The perfect combination of color and strike is very elusive for 1920-D.

POPULATION: MS BN = 14   MS RB = 134   MS RD = 187   TOTAL = 335
TOTALS   MS65 RD = 54   HIGHEST = MS66 RD (2)

VALUES:	GRADE	1935	1950	1965	1980	1995
	G	——	——	.30	.25	.25
	F	——	.20	1.50	.60	.60
	EF	——	——	6.50	4.50	4.00
	MS60	.60	3.00	42.50	37.50	50.00
	MS63	——	——	——	——	100.00
	MS65	——	——	——	——	525.00

VARIETIES: None are reported.

COMMENTS: The typical 1920-D cent was coined from dies which were already in a terminal die state or were well on their way to it. An indistinct portrait of Lincoln and blurred, distended lettering are common, as are wheat ears merging with the reverse border.

Aside from pieces which have been cleaned and recolored (and there are many of these), Mint State 1920-D cents will usually display an even brown to blotchy or streaked red/brown coloration. Most of the coins certified MS RD are really a subdued red bordering on red/brown or a peculiar pink color. Coins with the "flash" of a gem 1920-P are essentially non-existent. For those who place more emphasis on the certified grade than on the coin itself, this may not matter, but experienced collectors will recognize the difference.

      This was the last coinage of cents at the Denver Mint until 1922.

*   *   *

      During Fiscal Year 1920, the Philadelphia Mint's Engraving Department turned out 1580 dies for use there, as well as 310 for Denver and 520 for San Francisco.[46]

SAN FRANCISCO
46,220,000

RARITY: Widely hoarded in low grades, 1920-S cents are thus deceptively common below VF. The slipshod manner in which they were coined, however, makes for a very elusive issue in full VF and higher grades. Mint State coins of any grade level are scarce, and anything even approaching the choice category (MS63) is very scarce. True gems of any color are genuine rarities, while fully red gems are nearly unknown. The figures below present this quite clearly. Note in particular the low number of MS65 RD specimens and the absence of anything in higher grades. Specialists in the Lincoln Cent series consider this to be one of the rarest, if not *the* rarest issue in fully struck, fully red gem condition.

POPULATION: MS BN = 24   MS RB = 102   MS RD = 42   TOTAL = 168
TOTALS   MS65 RD = 7   HIGHEST = MS65 RD (7)

VALUES:

GRADE	1935	1950	1965	1980	1995
G	——	——	.30	.25	.25
F	——	.20	1.50	.60	.60
EF	——	——	6.50	4.50	4.00
MS60	.60	4.50	42.50	36.00	65.00
MS63	——	——	——	——	140.00
MS65	——	——	——	——	2900.00

VARIETIES: A single reverse cud variety exists at the 9 o'clock position.

COMMENTS: The problem of heavily worn dies, hitherto only a nuisance for collectors, became with this issue a nearly insurmountable problem. By far the majority of 1920-S cents never possessed full details from the outset, and the worst were scarcely recognizable as portraits of Lincoln. The reverse dies were even worse for this issue than the obverse ones; the wheat ears are often merged with the border to form a single contour. It's quite possible that the reverse dies, being undated, were used in more than a single year until they broke (see VARIETIES, above).

      Another characteristic of many 1920-S Lincolns and one often seen for other S-Mint cents of the 1917-29 period is a peculiar, inward curvature to the rims. Instead of forming a distinct border, the edges of such coins wrap around to form a very narrow, saucer-shaped rim which the author has dubbed "the San Francisco Roll." It occurs with other denominations coined at the San Francisco Mint during the same period and is perhaps most obvious on silver dollars of the 1920s.

      As noted above, very few red examples are known for this date (aside from those which have been chemically or mechanically assisted). The few red pieces known are of a slightly subdued tone, and their overall grade may be hampered by the technical deficiencies already described. Many collectors, the author included, have opted to go with a choice AU example as being more desirable than the usual Mint State coins. This topic was touched on by Sol Taylor in his book, wherein he noted that "nicely struck AU coins sell for more than MS60 coins."[47] This observation has become increasingly true for many key and semi-key coins in popular series.

1921

PHILADELPHIA
39,157,000

RARITY: Although not rare in circulated grades, 1921-P cents are clearly more elusive across the board than the high-mintage cents coined at Philadelphia from 1916 through 1920. Mint State coins remain plentiful, as the certified population suggests. Fully red coins, including some quite spectacular examples, may readily be found, but these frequently fall short of the gem category because of spotting or indifferent striking quality. The survival or original rolls is possible but not likely after several years of "slabbing."

POPULATION: MS BN = 7   MS RB = 103   MS RD = 312   TOTAL = 422
TOTALS   MS65 RD = 138   HIGHEST = MS68 RD (2)

VALUES:

GRADE	1935	1950	1965	1980	1995
G	——	——	.30	.25	.20
F	——	.15	1.50	.60	.60
EF	——	——	5.00	4.50	3.00
MS60	.25	2.00	21.00	31.00	40.00
MS63	——	——	——	——	70.00
MS65	——	——	——	——	140.00

VARIETIES: None are reported.

COMMENTS: Like the silver coins of this date, most 1921-P cents are not of the same sharpness that one would expect from the Philadelphia Mint; quality control was clearly down from previous years. Moderate to heavy die wear resulted in blurred peripheral elements such as the mottos IN GOD WE TRUST and E PLURIBUS UNUM.

The preference of many collectors for choice AU coins over so-so Mint State pieces is again noted for this date by Sol Taylor: "Choice AU 1921 cents can bring as much or more per coin than the Mint State red-brown coins under MS64."[48] Dr. Taylor added another interesting note to the effect that circulated rolls of 1921-P cents may often contain one or more examples dated 1921-S, as the latter is often found with a weakly defined mintmark.

* * *

The minting of all coins save for the newly-mandated silver dollars was way down in 1921, due to a short but severe recession which set in following the end of the World War. Nearly all 1921 cents from both mints were struck in the months of January through March. Another 1,153,000 were coined in July, followed by just 868,000 in November.[49] After that, the demand for additional cents ended; the massive quantities issued 1916-20 were more than sufficient to meet the reduced requirements of the post-war economy. This was the last coinage of cents at the

Philadelphia Mint until March of 1923.

The Philadelphia Mint was still purchasing cent blanks from outside contractors at this time. For Fiscal Year 1921, it paid $17,450 for 598,416.67 troy ounces of cent blanks. According to the Mint's owns statistics, the percentage of good cents per total number struck was as follows: Philadelphia, 99.51%; Denver, 98.71 %, San Francisco, 97.16%. In judging the quality of D-Mint and S-Mint coins of this period, it seems that the government's own standards for a "good cent" were somewhat lower than those of present-day collectors![50]

SAN FRANCISCO
15,274,000

RARITY: A semi-key date in the Lincoln series from its very inception, the 1921-S cent has long commanded a premium. Examples were rarely found in circulation after the mid 1950s. Today, it is only slightly scarce in lower grades, but VF and higher grade pieces are still challenging to locate well struck and with original (uncleaned) surfaces. The certified population totals suggest that average to slightly above average Mint State coins are not rare, but fully red gems are few in number. Note that none have been certified above MS65 RD. The peculiar "woodgrain" toning described for earlier S-Mint cents is again a problem with this issue as the result of poor alloy mixture.

POPULATION: MS BN = 46   MS RB = 253   MS RD = 69   TOTAL = 368
TOTALS   MS65 RD = 12   HIGHEST = MS65 RD (12)

VALUES:

GRADE	1935	1950	1965	1980	1995
G	——	——	.75	.60	.75
F	——	.25	3.50	1.25	1.50
EF	——	——	22.50	10.00	13.00
MS60	.75	16.00	165.00	195.00	110.00
MS63	——	——	——	——	250.00
MS65	——	——	——	——	2450.00

VARIETIES: None are reported.

COMMENTS: Although generally better struck than 1920-S cents, the 1921-S coins are likewise most often found in mid to late die states, with an overall softening or expanding of the design elements and lettering. Uncleaned, Mint State coins are typically a subdued, brassy color and may display irregular streaks from improper mixing of the alloy. For that reason, many have been cleaned, most of these subsequently retoned.

Collectors may want to seek this date with a distinctly impressed mintmark, since this is the exception for 1921-S.

All 1921-S cents were coined early in the year, before a nationwide recession slowed business activity. Due to a lack of demand from banks, the San Francisco Mint still had in its vaults on June 30, 1922 some 15,493,230 cents awaiting distribution. Thus, no more were coined until the latter part of 1923.[51]

1922

DENVER
7,160,000

RARITY: Due to its low mintage, 1922-D is a scarce date in all grades. Attractive, circulated examples in grades VF and higher are scarce to rare; most have been cleaned and retoned. Low end Mint State coins are usually available, but anything approaching the choice level is decidedly difficult to locate. What usually passes for gem is often of lower quality than earlier D-Mint Lincolns, being more akin to the troublesome dates of the mid-to-late 1920s. Fully red, fully struck examples are in constant demand and sell quickly.

POPULATION: MS BN = 35   MS RB = 197   MS RD = 225   TOTAL = 457
TOTALS   MS65 RD = 52   HIGHEST = MS66 RD (6)

VALUES:

GRADE	1935	1950	1965	1980	1995
G	——	——	3.40	4.75	5.00
F	——	.35	6.50	6.75	7.00
EF	——	——	15.50	16.00	19.00
MS60	.50	3.00	45.00	65.00	80.00
MS63	——	——	——	——	125.00
MS65	——	——	——	——	450.00

VARIETIES: A massive, cud die break may be found on the obverse above and to the right of Lincoln's head, taking out the words WE TRUST (see photo).

One of the most famous and costly varieties in the Lincoln Cent series is the 1922-D cent without a mintmark. This had more than one cause, and intermediate stages exist in which a partial D may be seen. These different variations are treated fully in the pages which follow.

1922-D
LC-22D-1 (Thurman & Margolis)

COMMENTS: Most 1922-D cents were coined from dies exhibiting moderate to heavy wear. This phenomenon in its most extreme stage is responsible for one of the "no-D" varieties. Of course, these dies were presumably fresh and sharp when initially placed into the press, so there are a few cents of this issue which may be found quite well struck; these are rare and worthy of patient searching. Finding any of these sharp coins possessed of attractive, original surfaces is the ultimate goal of the serious collector. Very few 1922-D cents display full, original red, and those which have been certified as MS RD are mostly a slightly subdued shade of red, many displaying unattractive spotting.

With the exception of these few million pieces hastily struck during January and February of 1922, the Denver Mint coined no other cents from the end of 1920 through most of 1924. A short but severe nationwide recession following the end of World War I, combined with the repeal of various temporary, wartime taxes, negated the demand for additional cents, while the massive mintages of 1916-20 were more than enough to meet the immediate post-war demand. The exact reason for this anomalous coinage is not known; the Mint Director's Report does nothing more than acknowledge it, although the Denver Mint was shown to have on hand at the end of the fiscal year (June 30, 1922) some 20,250,700 cents![52]

Commenting informally on the limited coinage of cents for 1922, Mint Director F. E. Scobey remarked: "There have been approximately $46,000,000 worth of pennies coined since the mint began in 1792, so what's the use of making more, when about the only things you can still buy with a penny nowadays are lollypops?"[53]

Collectors took notice of this issue fairly early on. Prolific commentator Robert H. Lloyd was among the small number of hobbyists actually examining their pocket change during the 1920s, a practice which didn't take hold in a big way until the mid 1930s. In 1927 he remarked: "The 1922 cent from the Denver mint is in demand, and although the coinage of 7,160,000 pieces would indicate that there are plenty to go round, they are much sought after and are difficult to find in circulation."[54]

Some 10 years later, Maurice D. Scharlack added: "This [1922-D] is a comparatively small issue, and the writer feels confident that these pennies will increase in value as time goes on and collectors begin to take notice of their absence from circulation. I have 25,000 of them packed away in a little wooden chest, and in all due modesty I honestly believe this is the largest collection of this one cent."[55]

The ultimate tribute to this issue, however, came in the way of an absurd hoax, as reported by *The Numismatist* in 1935:

> Rumors regarding coins are always going the rounds. The latest one is that Henry Ford has 150 of the 200 1922 Cents and in [an] effort to accumulate all of them he is offering a new Ford car for each one presented. The letters regarding the truth of this story became so numerous that the Director of the mint was forced to make a newspaper statement that over 7,000,000 cents were coined that year and she didn't believe Mr. Ford cared to give a new auto for one.[56]

One wonders what Mr. Ford would say to Mr. Scharlack with his hoard of 25,000 pieces! This silly rumor was revived in the late 1940s, but the subject coin that time was the 1943 bronze cent.

* * *

After briefly reopening to tourists following World War I, the Philadelphia Mint was again closed for some unknown reason, only to reopen yet again on April 1, 1922. A robbery of the Denver Mint eight months later caused Director Scobey to order that all three mints be closed to visitors indefinitely. In 1923, partly as a result of this incident, the U. S. Mint's coin collection was donated to the Smithsonian Institution in Washington, D.C.[57]

1922 No D

DENVER
Mintage Unknown

RARITY: The several varieties of "no-D" and "partial D" cents of this date range from scarce to rare in all grades, though their relative values vary with their perceived desirability. Most coins of these varieties were pulled from circulation between the mid 1930s and the early 1950s; as a consequence, nearly all are quite worn, a condition exacerbated by their poor quality as made. Examples grading VF and higher are rare and in constant demand.

Since the normal 1922-D cents are already scarce in Mint State, the no-D and partial-D varieties, forming a minority of the total mintage, are that much more so. Choice uncirculated examples are very rare, while true gems are probably non-existent; nevertheless, one specimen has been certified MS65 RD. Given the fact that the varieties themselves reflect inherent deficiencies in the coins, one should not become obsessed with quality when seeking this issue.

POPULATION: MS BN = 12   MS RB = 30   MS RD = 5   TOTAL = 47

TOTALS   MS65 RD = 1   HIGHEST = MS65 RD (1)

VALUES:

GRADE	1935	1950	1965	1980	1995
G	——	2.50	25.00	90.00	165.00
F	——	——	50.00	140.00	300.00
EF	——	——	125.00	325.00	1900.00
MS60	——	——	600.00	2250.00	4500.00
MS63	——	——	——	——	10000.00
MS65	——	——	——	——	——

VARIETIES: There are three recognized die pairings for the no-D and partial-D varieties, and the absence of the D mintmark has been attributed to either a worn die or a filled die, depending on which of the three die parings is being described. The second die pairing bears a sharp reverse and is considered far more desirable than the other two. It's the only one which commands the prices listed, and it's illustrated above.

Attribution of 1922 no-D cents is handled differently by the major grading services. PCGS will certify all varieties, but it distinguishes them on its labels with the qualifiers WEAK D, WEAK REVERSE or STRONG REVERSE. NGC and ANACS will certify only the second die pairing as "No-D", the one having a sharp reverse.

COMMENTS: The significance and great value attached to the 1922 cent without mintmark D is based entirely on the curious coincidence of no cents being coined at the Philadelphia Mint during 1922. There's no telling how many other times that cents were issued from the branch mints without a visible mintmark; such pieces are automatically branded as P-Mint coins, though the generally poor state of the dies would be a clue to their real status.

Since this variety has been faked by removal of the mintmark from normal 1922-D cents, authentication by a reputable service should be included as a provision in any purchase. For examples of altered no-D cents, see Chapter 5.

The most popular variety of no-D cent is the one coined from Die Pair 2. This is the one which commands the high prices listed above, while the less desirable Die Pairs 1 and 3 are valued lower in proportion. The no-D variety of Die Pair 2 resulted when normal dies clashed (came together with no planchet between them), leaving both dies with shallow and inverted impressions of one another. The obverse die was then abrasively polished to remove these clash marks, leaving it without a mintmark and with several low-relief elements (including the date) noticeably weakened. The reverse die, however, was removed altogether and replaced with a fresh one. Thus, Die Pair 2 is the mating of a damaged and partly obscured obverse with highly-detailed reverse; this is the variety most sought by collectors for its overall attractiveness.

Heavy die cracks found on some normal 1922-D cents. (ANAAB)

Die Pairs 1 and 3 are similar in that both feature severely worn obverse and reverse dies. The condition of these dies accounts in part for the absence of a mintmark, but the real culprit is believed to have been grease and other contaminants filling the mintmark cavity in the obverse dies. As coins were struck from these die pairs, the grease gradually lifted from the mintmark cavity, restoring a partial or "ghost" mintmark which was very shallow and indistinct. Unlike Die Pair 2, from which no partial-D variety is known, Die Pairs 1 and 3 have provided collectors with both no-D and partial-D varieties. The generally poor condition of these dies resulted in coins which, while qualifying as no-D cents, are of lesser aesthetic and market value than those coined from Die Pair 2.

Some additional diagnostic features exist for the no-D and partial-D varieties. On the reverse of Die Pair 1, a crack runs from letter L in PLURIBUS through letter O in ONE, terminating at the base of letter O. This crack does not follow a straight course, but rather it shifts to the left after passing downward through the upper part of letter O. This crack is diagnostic for the reverse of Die Pair 1, but as it exists for both the no-D and partial-D varieties, it cannot be used as proof of the more valuable no-D variety. A similar crack is found on some normal 1922-D cents, but this crack follows a straight course through the top of letter O and continues onward after passing through the bottom of the letter. The presence of this straight crack may be used to detect the alteration of a normal coin to simulate the no-D variety.

Most collectors of the 1920s took little notice of current coins of the regular types, a fact made quite obvious when no mention of this variety appeared until late in the decade. Ten years later, readers of *The Numismatist* were still writing in to announce their "discovery" of 1922 cents seemingly made at the Philadelphia Mint. Little was known about the coining process, leading to all manner of imaginative explanations for such irregularities. It wasn't until the 1960s that errors and varieties in general were studied with a more scientific approach and the real explanation of this popular oddity became known.

The obverse and reverse of Die Pair 1. (ANAAB)

The obverse and reverse of Die Pair 3. (ANAAB)

1923

PHILADELPHIA
74,723,000

RARITY: 1923-P is very common in all grades, a fact reflected in its pricing structure. Gems are generally available, though not to the extent that one might imagine from this fairly large mintage. Original rolls may still exist, but most have been broken up to retrieve the better pieces for "slabbing."

POPULATION: MS BN = 2   MS RB = 42   MS RD = 236   TOTAL = 280
TOTALS   MS65 RD = 99   HIGHEST = MS68 RD (1)

VALUES:	GRADE	1935	1950	1965	1980	1995
	G	——	——	.15	.15	.15
	F	——	.05	.40	.35	.35
	EF	——	——	1.50	2.00	2.00
	MS60	.35	.50	9.50	9.50	12.00
	MS63	——	——	——	——	20.00
	MS65	——	——	——	——	165.00

VARIETIES: Only a single obverse cud variety is reported for 1923; it appears in the usual place between shoulder and border.

COMMENTS: This issue may be found in all grades through fully red gem. Some pieces may exhibit slightly worn dies, but there are enough examples from fresh dies that the lesser coins may be passed over. Blazing gems that seem to have been made only yesterday may be located.

   The mintage of cents for 1923 was performed almost entirely during the final quarter of the year. The figure of 1,431,000 pieces for March is believed to have included only P-Mint cents, while the balance of the coinage for both mints occurred entirely during the months of September (2,549,000), October (15,600,000), November (33,500,000) and December (30,343,000).[58]

   The performance of this date has been typically lackluster in lower grades, but the loss incurred has been due primarily to inflation. Perhaps this issue was spared from the overpricing which characterized the height of the market in 1960-64, because there was never any pretense of it being rare.

   The Mint's engraving staff once again failed to conform to Brenner's choice of text style, and numeral 3 in the date of all cents coined during 1923 is symmetrical. A correct interpretation would have given in a long, sweeping tail.

   This is the first issue of cents at the Philadelphia Mint since 1921.

SAN FRANCISCO
8,700,000

RARITY: 1923-S cents are fairly common in lower grades, but pieces grading VF and EF are somewhat scarce. AU and Mint State coins are very elusive, particularly with sharp detailing. As the population data indicate, fully red gems are quite rare. When found, such coins are usually a deep red in color and may possesses a decent strike, but softly struck cents with a brassy color are by far more often seen. Beware of the many cleaned and retoned examples.

POPULATION: MS BN = 21   MS RB = 139   MS RD = 57   TOTAL = 167
TOTALS   MS65 RD = 15   HIGHEST = MS65 RD (15)

VALUES:

GRADE	1935	1950	1965	1980	1995
G	——	——	1.25	1.40	1.50
F	——	.20	5.00	2.50	3.00
EF	——	——	27.50	12.00	18.00
MS60	1.50	15.00	250.00	260.00	180.00
MS63	——	——	——	——	365.00
MS65	——	——	——	——	3250.00

VARIETIES: None are reported.

COMMENTS: Mushy coins struck from worn dies are the rule for 1923-S. One or both sides will usually exhibit extreme erosion of the dies, visible as a bulged or expanded effect around all lettering, also as the filling-in of the lines on the wheat ears and a migration of all peripheral elements toward the borders. Like the 1921-S cents, some have shallow mintmarks, though this is not nearly the problem that it is for the earlier date.

So many 1923-S cents have been cleaned that determining the correct appearance of an uncleaned, Mint State coin is challenging. These will typically be a deep red or an even darker, reddish brown. A few may be found with lighter, original coloration, but these often display the streaked, woodgrain effect of poor alloying seen on so many S-Mint cents from 1908 until well into the 1920s. Finding a problem-free, well-struck and appealing 1923-S cent is all but impossible, as the certified population data reveal.

1923-S cents were widely hoarded in low grades during the 1940s and '50s. As a consequence, their value has fallen during the past 30 years. In higher grades, however, their performance has been mixed. In the 1935 *Standard Catalogue*, this date was tied with 1924-D, 1924-S and 1926-S as the second-highest priced coins in uncirculated condition, only 1914-D and 1914-S being valued higher. While the order of values has shifted a bit in 60 years, 1923-S cents are still among the most expensive coins in Mint State. In contrast, however, the 1995 figure for EF specimens, taken from *A Guide Book of United States Coins*, seems far too low given the scarcity of such coins. Perhaps this reflects the poor aesthetic quality of the typical EF 1923-S Lincoln, which is usually a poorly struck, AU coin that is too mushy to bring an AU price. A well struck, problem-free example of this date in grades EF or AU is quite rare and may exceed the desirability of a typical, Mint State coin. The best AU specimens will typically exceed the value of an MS60 cent.

All 1923-S cents were seemingly coined during the final four months of that year.

1924

PHILADELPHIA
75,178,000

RARITY: This issue is common in all grades up through VF. Those grading EF and AU are scarcer than the mintage figure would imply. Average to choice quality Mint State coins are abundant, while fully red gems are usually available as well. Original rolls may conceivably still survive, but since the advent of encapsulation in 1986 most have been broken up to retrieve the better pieces.

POPULATION: MS BN = 1   MS RB = 80   MS RD = 281   TOTAL = 362
TOTALS   MS65 RD = 139   HIGHEST = MS67 RD (1)

VALUES:

GRADE	1935	1950	1965	1980	1995
G	——	——	.15	.15	.15
F	——	.05	.50	.35	.35
EF	——	——	2.00	3.50	3.00
MS60	.25	1.75	18.00	22.00	22.00
MS63	——	——	——	——	40.00
MS65	——	——	——	——	125.00

VARIETIES: One obverse cud is known at the usual shoulder position, as well as one which takes out the letters ST of TRUST.

COMMENTS: 1924-P cents are often not equal in quality to other P-Mint issues from the 1920s, yet gems should not be considered rare; the population data confirms this. A 1980 analysis of Lincoln Cents by *The Coin Dealer Newsletter* exaggerated their slight scarcity enough to prompt higher prices, which in turn coaxed more pieces into the marketplace.[59] It's interesting to note, however, that in grade EF this was one of the very few Lincolns to actually rise in catalog value since 1965 (although still losing to inflation).

The Philadelphia Mint cents of 1924 were coined both from blanks made in-house and those purchased from contractors, the ratio being about 3-to-1.[60]

* * *

1924 marked the first year since 1920 that cents were coined at all three mints. The recession of 1921-22 began to lift during 1923, as noted by Mint Director Robert J. Grant in his *Annual Report* to Treasury Secretary Andrew W. Mellon:

> During the first half of the fiscal year the demand for small coins—quarters, dimes, nickels, cents—in the territory served by the Philadelphia Mint was such that the stocks of those coins were exhausted and it was necessary to operate the Philadelphia Mint on a 24 hours per day basis. It is thus evident that notwithstanding the enormous issues of small coins during the five-year period 1917-21 there is no redundancy of coins below the dollar.[61]

An interesting footnote to any study of this series is that the February 1924 issue of *The Numismatist* was devoted almost entirely to a catalog of numismatic items depicting Abraham Lincoln. Although the Lincoln Cent was included in this listing, it didn't seem to have any influence in creating new collectors of this coin series. Widespread interest in collecting Lincolns by date and mint didn't develop until the early-mid 1930s, when a series of low-mintage issues and the introduction of inexpensive, punched-hole coin boards combined to prompt the urge for completeness among many novice and veteran collectors.

DENVER
2,520,000

RARITY: A semi-key date in all grades, 1924-D is scarce and always in demand. There are no grades in which this date is common, but examples grading EF and higher are particularly scarce. Fully red, choice and gem pieces are very rare. Collectors should be on the alert for cleaned and retoned examples, which are quite often seen for this issue.

POPULATION: MS BN = 35   MS RB = 144   MS RD = 56   TOTAL = 185
TOTALS   MS65 RD = 11   HIGHEST = MS65 RD (11)

VALUES:

GRADE	1935	1950	1965	1980	1995
G	——	——	15.00	8.00	10.00
F	——	.60	27.50	11.00	13.00
EF	——	——	47.50	28.50	50.00
MS60	1.50	9.50	200.00	300.00	225.00
MS63	——	——	——	——	350.00
MS65	——	——	——	——	3000.00

VARIETIES: A single cud variety is known in the usual shoulder location. In addition, some 1924-D cents may be seen from a damaged reverse die. This is visible as a long, vertical line piercing the second letter U in PLURIBUS and passing through letter N in ONE and touching letter N in CENT. This variety was known at least as early as 1939, since a coin board (published that year) in the author's collection lists it and assigns a small premium value. Probably the result of some machinery piece or other foreign object being impressed into the die, this mark is not especially rare and carries no added value today.

COMMENTS: 1924-D Lincolns almost always show signs of being struck from dies with varying degrees of wear. This problem is pervasive, but it's not as extreme as with other dates from this mint such as 1918-D and 1925-D. A number of 1924-D cents will show particular weakness at the right side of both obverse and reverse, probably the result of dies which were not quite parallel. Another characteristic feature is weakness in letter O of ONE. In addition to striking deficiencies, coloration is another problem for this date, conditions summed-up quite nicely in *The Coin Dealer Newsletter*:

"The 1924-D is a tough coin above VF — and another one of the real "stoppers" when a collector is looking for an outstanding example. Even lower quality uncirculated 24-D's are very few and far between and these usually have defects of one sort or another. The strike is generally weak to moderate — but seldom really sharp; the color is generally splotchy and/or deeply toned to a reddish brown — with accompanying spots. Fully brilliant and spot-free examples are very scarce."[62]

Although there exists some incentive to create 1924-D cents by the addition of a D mintmark to a 1924-P or by altering dates such as 1944-D to simulate the scarcer piece, bogus examples of this issue are not nearly so prevalent as for more often targeted dates such as 1909-S (with or without V.D.B.), 1914-D and 1931-S.

All 1924-D cents were coined during the final months of that year and represent the first issue of that denomination from the Denver Mint since February of 1922.[63]

SAN FRANCISCO
11,696,000

RARITY: 1924-S cents were widely hoarded in low grades during the 1940s and 1950s, and such pieces remains plentiful today. In the better circulated grades of VF through AU, quality examples are fairly scarce. Mint State coins of mediocre quality are usually available, but choice specimens, whether brown, red, or anything in between are rarely seen. Fully red gems are of the highest rarity, and it's not unusual for well struck MS64 RB coins to be more highly desired than indistinct examples certified MS64 RD.

POPULATION: MS BN = 28   MS RB = 141   MS RD = 36   TOTAL = 205
TOTALS   MS65 RD = 5   HIGHEST = MS65 RD (5)

VALUES:

GRADE	1935	1950	1965	1980	1995
G	——	——	1.25	.60	.75
F	——	.35	3.25	1.40	1.50
EF	——	——	17.50	7.00	12.00
MS60	1.50	9.50	95.00	125.00	110.00
MS63	——	——	——	——	185.00
MS65	——	——	——	——	3850.00

VARIETIES: A single repunched mintmark may be found, this variety having a very broad separation between punchings.

COMMENTS: The only other variety known for this issue is the so-called "goiter" variety. This consists of a raised, bar-shaped lump at Lincoln's neck. Believed to have the same cause as the 1924-D variety with a raised, vertical line on its reverse, this probably resulted from a loose part of the press or some foreign object being impressed into the obverse die. Attaining some popularity during the 1930s (when it appeared on some of the premium cards marketed for this series), this variety reappeared in print sporadically through the mid 1960s, when interest in coin collecting in general began to wane. Today, it carries no premium value and is considered fairly common.

In 1963, Jack H. Tod published his theory on how this variety may have occurred. Noting that the raised deformation on the obverse of some 1924-S cents lined up quite closely with another raised lump on the reverse of certain 1925-S cents, he suggested that the two dies in question were once mated and that the same accident damaged both simultaneously. As for why the two varieties were not seen in a single coin, he added that the press operator may have removed the reverse die while failing to notice the less obvious damage to the obverse die. If the reverse die had been returned to the die locker rather than being tagged for destruction, it could have been retrieved the following year and mated to a normal 1925-S obverse die. While this theory provides food for thought, it's the author's opinion that the damaged reverse die would never have been re-used. Of course, given the generally poor quality control at the San Francisco Mint during the mid 1920s, such flaws may have provided little concern to mint workers.[64]

The population data is quite revealing for 1924-S: Very few fully red coins are known, and fewer still qualify as gems. This date has the second lowest combined total of MS65 RD examples, with only 1926-S having fewer. Uncleaned coins never show more than a subdued red, with no really bright pieces known. Some may show the woodgrain pattern so common on earlier S-Mint cents, but 1923 was really the last year in which this peculiarity was prevalent.

As with so many of the branch mint coins from the 1920s, poorly-struck and ill-defined coins were the norm for this issue. Only a few will show the sharpness of a fresh die; the reverse dies were particularly subject to overuse, as they may have been carried into the following year's coinage.

* * *

Collectors of the time were curiously silent regarding the poor quality of branch-mint coinage during the 1920s, though there's ample evidence that a few people were collecting these issues as they were released. Proof that at least someone was aware of the appalling product emanating from the Denver and San Francisco Mints circa 1924 may be found in an off-hand remark by Charles Moore, Chairman of the Federal Commission of Fine Arts. In a letter that year to Congressman Vestal of the House Committee on Coinage discussing a proposed commemorative half dollar design, Moore noted that "By dint of many struggles our silver coinage, the nickel, and the penny, have been brought up to a fair standard as compared with other leading nations. The only questions now in relation to those coins are questions of quality of work in producing the coins themselves."[65]

1925

PHILADELPHIA
139,949,000

RARITY: There is little to say about this date other than that it's common in any and all grades through MS65 RD. In fact, MS66 RD examples are fairly plentiful as well. Original rolls may still exist for this and most later dates from the Philadelphia Mint, despite the tremendous temptation to break these up for "slabbing."

 (This may be a good opportunity to remind readers that a low certified population of MS BN 1925 cents does not imply rarity, only that this and other common dates are not worth the cost of encapsulation in such grades.)

POPULATION: MS BN = 1 MS RB = 65 MS RD = 509 TOTAL = 575
TOTALS   MS65 RD = 276 HIGHEST = MS67 RD (9)

VALUES:

GRADE	1935	1950	1965	1980	1995
G	——	——	.20	.15	.15
F	——	.05	.35	.35	.35
EF	——	——	1.25	2.00	1.50
MS60	.20	.50	7.50	9.00	10.00
MS63	——	——	——	——	22.50
MS65	——	——	——	——	65.00

VARIETIES: None are reported.

COMMENTS: 1925-P cents are typically very well struck, though a few will show some signs of die wear. Collectors may simply ignore those coined from late die states; sharp, MS65 RD examples are fairly plentiful, and even fully red gems of the very highest quality may be found with some diligence. Bear in mind, however, that even the sharpest 1925-P will never have the wealth of fine detail evident on cents coined before 1918; the obverse master hub was simply wearing away with each successive year.

 Cents dated 1925 display a numeral 5 which is quite compact and does not conform to the long-tailed 9. Why no one at the Mint took note of this inconsistency remains a mystery.

* * *

 The three mints produced all of their own cent blanks during 1925.[66]
 After nearly 50 years employment with the United States Mint, Chief Engraver George T. Morgan died on January 4, 1925. He was succeeded in this position by John Ray Sinnock, who had been with the Mint since 1917.

DENVER
22,580,000

RARITY: 1925-D cents are plentiful in low grades, thanks to the widespread hoarding which developed in the 1940s and accelerated dramatically between 1955 and 1960. Because of their poor quality as made, very few examples grading VF and better have survived relative to their fairly substantial mintage. Mint State examples of mediocre quality are readily available, but they are seldom pleasing. Coins having a substantial amount of original red color are not unusual, but these are generally soft strikes. Though a number of coins have been certified MS65 RD, these are not in any sense equal to the typical MS65 RD 1925-P. Choice pieces are very scarce, while true gems (in the strictest sense) are probably non-existent.

POPULATION: MS BN = 17   MS RB = 176   MS RD = 164   TOTAL = 357
TOTALS   MS65 RD = 19   HIGHEST = MS66 RD (1)

VALUES:

GRADE	1935	1950	1965	1980	1995
G	——	——	.30	.30	.20
F	——	.10	1.25	.60	.40
EF	——	——	4.00	4.50	5.00
MS60	.40	2.50	28.00	40.00	50.00
MS63	——	——	——	——	85.00
MS65	——	——	——	——	1500.00

VARIETIES: One obverse and four reverse cud varieties are known, all in the expected positions (under Lincoln's shoulder or alongside the wheat ears).

COMMENTS: 1925-D vies with 1925-S for the title of most poorly made issue in the entire Lincoln series. It's difficult to believe that the dies for the 1925-D cents were ever new, as sharply-rendered specimens are essentially unknown. Gross distortion of the design elements (particularly toward the peripheries) is the norm for these coins. It's quite possible that the Philadelphia Mint was not properly hardening the dies that it produced during this period. This would have led to premature erosion.

While red or reddish coins do exist for 1925-D in fairly large numbers, they are usually quite dull and/or spotted.

* * *

In a classic bit of irony, Frank G. Duffield, editor of *The Numismatist* during the 1920s, made a point of emphasizing to his readers as each year's coinage totals became available that there would be no rarities resulting from such large mintages. Of course, almost no one was collecting Lincoln Cents at the time, and those who were paid little notice to the poor quality of these coins. It wasn't until the collecting of modern coins by date and mint achieved widespread popularity during the 1930s that collectors learned of the rarity of many issues in choice and gem condition. It was later still, during the 1970s and '80s, that the rarity of such coins was finally reflected in their prices. The best specimens rose in value, while average quality coins either remained static or actually declined in value.

SAN FRANCISCO
26,380,000

RARITY: This issue is quite common in lower grades, being among the most widely hoarded dates during the heyday of collecting coins from circulation, circa 1935-64. Better-grade circulated examples are somewhat scarce, due to the poor quality of most pieces as made. Choice AU and better coins are scarce, despite a generous mintage. Mint State specimens, while not rare, are usually of mediocre quality. Quite a number survive with a moderate amount of original red color, yet these are almost invariably poor strikes. Choice 1925-S cents are very scarce, while anything even approaching the gem category is of the highest rarity. Some specialists consider this issue to be the rarest in true gem condition after 1926-S and 1920-S.

POPULATION:	MS BN = 18	MS RB = 92	MS RD = 40	TOTAL = 150
TOTALS	MS65 RD = 7	HIGHEST = MS65 RD (7)		

VALUES:	GRADE	1935	1950	1965	1980	1995
	G	——	——	.50	.25	.20
	F	——	.20	2.50	.55	.35
	EF	——	——	6.00	4.25	5.00
	MS60	.40	6.50	40.00	40.00	60.00
	MS63	——	——	——	——	135.00
	MS65	——	——	——	——	4250.00

VARIETIES: Five repunched mintmark varieties exist for this date (see photo), one of them actually triple-punched. The repunched mintmark varieties known for this and other dates as of the early 1980s were compiled into an excellent work called *The RPM Book* by John A. Wexler and Tom Miller. Though in need of updating, this work is still very useful and entertaining.

Another variety which turns up occasionally, though it's far from being common, is the damaged reverse cent. A large, raised lump appears between letters CE of CENT on a small number of 1925-S cents. For a possible explanation, see VARIETIES for 1924-S.

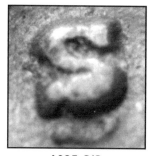

1925-S/S
RPM-1a (Miller)

COMMENTS: Along with 1925-D, this issue is a contender for the most poorly made in the entire series. Indifferent quality is the rule for 1925-S, and the specimen illustrated is quite exceptional. The reverse dies in particular were clearly used beyond their desirable lifespan and may have included some leftover from previous years. The obverse dies for 1925 are also in poor condition, though not quite to the same extreme. It seems that overextended die usage was combined with exaggerated die set (the distance between the dies when the press was at rest) in an attempt to economize. Why this was the case at Denver and San Francisco, while not true of the Philadelphia Mint, remains unknown. All of the U. S. Mint records and correspondence were destroyed in 1978 in a subsequent and equally misguided effort at practicing thrift.

Fully red 1925-S cents, in any grade, are very rare. In gem condition, they are extremely so, and those certified as MS65 RD are graded by a standard which takes into account their peculiarities of strike and color; that is, a 1925-S grading MS65 RD will not be as satisfying to the eye as the typical 1925-P grading MS65 RD. The latter's blazing luster is simply unknown for 1925-S cents, which display a more subdued, "burnt" red. Because of the rarity of red specimens, cleaned and retoned coins are very common for this date.

1926

PHILADELPHIA
157,088,000

RARITY: This issue is the most common issue in gem, fully red condition since the 1909 V.D.B. cent. All circulated and Mint State grades are readily available. Original rolls may still exist, but most have been broken up to retrieve the better pieces.

POPULATION: MS BN = 2   MS RB = 34   MS RD = 1065   TOTAL = 1101
TOTALS   MS65 RD = 569   HIGHEST = MS67 RD (27)

VALUES:

GRADE	1935	1950	1965	1980	1995
G	——	——	.20	.15	.15
F	——	.05	.35	.35	.30
EF	——	——	1.50	2.00	1.25
MS60	.30	.60	6.50	9.00	8.00
MS63	——	——	——	——	16.00
MS65	——	——	——	——	32.50

VARIETIES: The only report is of a doubled obverse die, listed by Walter Breen in his *Encyclopedia*.[67]

COMMENTS: 1926-P cents are usually well struck, though some coined from later die states may be found. Of course, this date is so common that collectors can afford to be picky. Brilliant, blazing gems ranging in color from brassy yellow to coppery red are readily available.

———◆•◆•◆———

DENVER
28,020,000

RARITY: 1926-D cents are common in the grades of Good and VG. Those grading Fine through AU are usually available, if one is not too particular about strike and surface quality. Mint State pieces are not rare in overall numbers, but their consistently poor quality is a major obstacle to locating an attractive example and prevents most from achieving the MS65 level. Fully red gems are very rare and tend to have the pinkish color so characteristic of early D-Mint cents. Many of the potentially high grade 1926-D cents have been spoiled by irremovable black spots.

POPULATION: MS BN = 23   MS RB = 115   MS RD = 99   TOTAL = 237
TOTALS   MS65 RD = 21   HIGHEST = MS66 RD (1)

GRADE	1935	1950	1965	1980	1995
G	——	——	.25	.25	.25
F	——	.20	1.10	.60	.60
EF	——	——	3.50	3.25	5.00
MS60	.35	2.50	27.50	37.50	50.00
MS63	——	——	——	——	85.00
MS65	——	——	——	——	1300.00

VARIETIES: A single cud die break is known, this appearing opposite Lincoln's face in the 3 o'clock position.

COMMENTS: The vast majority of 1926-D cents were coined from dies displaying advanced wear. Among the possible causes for this lack of quality control that of economy has already been mentioned. Another possible cause, however, is poor die steel. Improperly hardened tool steel will succumb rapidly to the erosive effect of continued use. If the incoming planchets are not adequately annealed (softened through heating and slow cooling), this situation is then further aggravated. Any one of these abuses or a combination of one or more may have led to the mediocre quality of coins struck by the Denver and San Francisco Mints throughout most of the 1920s.

In addition to being poorly struck the typical uncirculated 1926-D will display irregularities of color, including spotty or blotchy surfaces. As described by Sol Taylor, "The Mint State red coins seen both raw and slabbed tend to be dark or dull red."[68] Those coins graded MS65 RD by the grading services will not be equal in their aesthetic qualities to a 1926-P in the same certified grade.

SAN FRANCISCO
4,550,000

RARITY: 1926-S cents were widely hoarded in low grades during the 1940s and 1950s, and these are fairly plentiful. Examples in grades F and VF are more challenging. EF, AU and Mint State coins are quite scarce, though low quality pieces are usually available. It's only in the choice and gem categories that this date emerges as a key rarity, if not the most challenging coin in the entire series. The few examples displaying full red are invariably soft and indistinct, while the few well struck cents are invariably brown or red/brown at best. The specimen illustrated above is quite exceptional.

POPULATION: MS BN = 40   MS RB = 145   MS RD = 26   TOTAL = 211
TOTALS MS65 RD = 1   HIGHEST = MS65 RD (1)

VALUES:

GRADE	1935	1950	1965	1980	1995
G	——	——	3.00	3.00	2.00
F	——	.25	6.50	5.00	4.00
EF	——	——	22.50	12.50	11.00
MS60	1.50	7.50	140.00	165.00	100.00
MS63	——	——	——	——	200.00
MS65	——	——	——	——	——

VARIETIES: None are reported, though Sol Taylor remarked in his book that this date features two obverse dies with mintmarks which are quite distant from their anticipated position, appearing very low and to the right of the date.[69] The position of the mintmark varies from one obverse die to another on all mintmarked cents through 1989, and this was a normal facet of the die-making process. These different mintmark positions do not qualify as varieties, despite the careful documentation made of them by past generations of enthusiastic collectors.

COMMENTS: Mushy coins are the rule for this issue. Most seen are from worn dies revealing distorted details, particularly toward the peripheries.

1926-S is another issue which seldom comes in fully red condition (unless cleaned, as are many seen). Dull red or reddish brown is about the most to which one may aspire, and many of these bear distracting streaks and stains. A well struck example, regardless of color, is usually preferable to an indistinct red coin. This date has the lowest certified population of MS65 RD coins, only a single example appearing in the listings. This, by the way, is also the highest certified grade for 1926-S. Although obviously an extreme rarity in the topmost grades, this date is usually considered more available at the choice (MS63) level than 1924-S.

1927

PHILADELPHIA
144,440,000

RARITY: Like 1926-P, this issue is fairly common in all grades, including fully red gem. Most examples seen are well struck. Original rolls still exist and have recently turned up in auctions.

POPULATION: MS BN = 1   MS RB = 32   MS RD = 324   TOTAL = 357
TOTALS   MS65 RD = 171   HIGHEST = MS67 RD (9)

VALUES:

GRADE	1935	1950	1965	1980	1995
G	——	——	.20	.15	.15
F	——	.05	.45	.30	.30
EF	——	——	1.35	2.00	1.25
MS60	.20	.50	6.00	8.50	8.00
MS63	——	——	——	——	16.00
MS65	——	——	——	——	67.50

VARIETIES: Only one variety is known, but it's a good one: A distinct doubled obverse die is most apparent within the mottos LIBERTY and IN GOD WE TRUST (see photos) and to a lesser degree in the date.

COMMENTS: There's little to say about 1927-P, being that it's generally well struck and quite common in all grades. This date, along with other P-Mint cents from the years 1917 onward, would occasionally be found in circulation during the mid 1960s, when the author began his search for old coins.

    As in 1917, the Mint again failed to fashion a long tail to numeral 7 which would have been more stylistically attuned to numeral 9.

1927-P
DDO-1 (Fivaz & Stanton)

DENVER
27,170,000

RARITY: Common in most circulated grades, only AU and better coins can be considered scarce. Mint State coins of mediocre quality are fairly common, while choice and gem examples are scarce, due primarily to the twin plagues of bad strike and bad color. Fully struck coins of any color are quite scarce.

POPULATION: MS BN = 25   MS RB = 183   MS RD = 124   TOTAL = 332
TOTALS   MS65 RD = 33   HIGHEST = MS66 RD (2)

VALUES:

GRADE	1935	1950	1965	1980	1995
G	——	——	.30	.25	.25
F	——	.20	1.10	.50	.50
EF	——	——	4.00	2.75	2.75
MS60	.40	2.50	25.00	25.00	25.00
MS63	——	——	——	——	65.00
MS65	——	——	——	——	775.00

VARIETIES: A single repunched mintmark is known (see photo), though this is another date (like 1926-S) which is notable for its wildly placed mintmarks. Evidently, whoever was punching in the mintmarks on each die (a task usually undertaken by an apprentice engraver) was either bored or simply careless.

1927-D/D
RPM-1 (Miller)

COMMENTS: This is the first D-Mint cent since 1917 in which coins of acceptable quality are available with a bit of patience. Although few examples are well struck, enough are of average quality (moderately worn dies) that a nice brown or red/brown example can be secured. Even the certified gems, however, tend to fall short of the quality found in 1927-P cents of the same certified grade. This conclusion takes into consideration the off-color of many such coins, but it's based primarily on the softness of strike exhibited by most of the higher grade specimens.

SAN FRANCISCO
14,276,000

RARITY: Another issue which was widely hoarded in low grades during the 1940s and 1950s, 1927-S cents were subsequently found to be fairly common, with the inevitable price collapse resulting (see table below). In grades VF and higher, however, 1927-S remains respectably scarce. All Mint State examples are likewise scarce, regardless of quality, while choice and gem examples are very scarce to rare. Well struck specimens of any color are very rare, and the specimen illustrated may be the finest known.

POPULATION: MS BN = 14   MS RB = 98   MS RD = 149   TOTAL = 261
TOTALS   MS65 RD = 12   HIGHEST = MS65 RD (12)

VALUES:

GRADE	1935	1950	1965	1980	1995
G	——	——	.40	.40	.40
F	——	.25	2.50	.90	.90
EF	——	——	7.50	4.25	6.00
MS60	.40	6.00	45.00	50.00	65.00
MS63	——	——	——	——	125.00
MS65	——	——	——	——	1750.00

VARIETIES: None are reported, aside from some oddly situated mintmarks. Readers interested in this aspect of collecting should locate a monograph published by author W. B. Doughty in 1957 titled *Mint Mark Positions of Lincoln Cents*. It lists more than 1100 positions known to him for each date through 1953. A similar listing may also be found published serially in *The Numismatic Scrapbook Magazine* during 1957-58.

COMMENTS: Nearly all cents of this issue were poorly made. Worn, eroded dies were the rule, and early die state examples are exceedingly rare. In its 1980 study of the Lincoln Cent series, *The Coin Dealer Newsletter* observed that "Finding a 1927-S to fit a top quality set will not be a simple matter. The strike is often horrible and the color is often dreary. In fact, the 27-S is as bad as either the 24-S or the 25-S; it is difficult to find agreement among even the specialists as to rarity order for these three dates."[70]

To illustrate this point further, the 1927-S cent in the author's own collection is an attractive and original red/brown example which grades only AU-58, yet it possesses an absolutely needle-sharp strike. So rare is such sharpness that he opted to retain this coin and dispose of the Mint State, almost fully red coin which had previously represented this issue, since it was from the typical later state of the dies. Despite being flawed by an old scratch on Lincoln's nose, the well-struck AU coin was aesthetically superior. It's not unusual for well made yet lightly circulated coins to be valued more highly by collectors than mediocre Mint State examples. This is an important axiom to remember when assembling a collection.

* * *

To illustrate the Mint's view of its quality control procedures, it's instructive to note what percentages of each mint's coinage Director Grant considered "good" in 1927. For Philadelphia, this figure was 99.48%, Denver 99.50% and San Francisco 99.67%![71]

1928

PHILADELPHIA
134,116,000

RARITY: Common in all grades, even fully red gems are usually available, though perhaps not to the extent of surrounding dates from the Philadelphia Mint. Original rolls, once commonplace, have now largely succumbed to the siren call of certified grading. Rolls which may be offered nowadays (and this rarely happens) are likely to have been assembled from the remnants, after the gems were certified.

POPULATION: MS BN = 1   MS RB = 36   MS RD = 389   TOTAL = 426
TOTALS   MS65 RD = 221   HIGHEST = MS67 RD (6)

VALUES:

GRADE	1935	1950	1965	1980	1995
G	——	——	.15	.15	.15
F	——	.05	.40	.30	.30
EF	——	——	1.00	1.70	1.25
MS60	.20	.50	4.50	8.00	8.00
MS63	——	——	——	——	16.00
MS65	——	——	——	——	67.50

VARIETIES: None are reported.

COMMENTS: 1928-P cents are almost always well struck, with very little evidence of die erosion. Bear in mind, however, that the obverse master hub continued to wear throughout the 1920s, and cents of this date will never equal the wealth of fine detail seen on those from the first decade of coinage.

The color of Mint State coins ranges all the way up to a dazzlingly brilliant, light red to brassy yellow. Note that six examples have been certified MS67 RD.

* * *

Collectors have long acknowledged a general improvement in the sharpness of cents and other coins (particularly those of the branch mints) which began around 1928. The extreme deformities seen in the dies used at the Denver and San Francisco Mints from the late 1910s through the mid 1920s were no longer in evidence. One explanation for this greater durability may be found in the 1928 *Annual Report* of Mint Director Robert J. Grant to Treasury Secretary Andrew W. Mellon:

> At the Philadelphia Mint a chromium plating plant has been installed and is being used for greatly improving the wearing qualities of dies, coin collars, machinery parts, and models. A new type of reducing machine has greatly facilitated the preparation of more perfect coin and medal dies.[72]

DENVER
31,170,000

RARITY: This issue is quite common in low grades. Even VF and EF coins are quite often seen at coin shows. AU and Mint State pieces are nearly as common, and their quality is generally superior to that of D-Mint cents of earlier years. Choice and gem examples, while not really common, are indeed obtainable.

POPULATION TOTALS

MS BN = 14   MS RB = 85   MS RD = 172   TOTAL = 271
MS65 RD = 54   HIGHEST = MS66 RD (8)

VALUES:

GRADE	1935	1950	1965	1980	1995
G	——	——	.30	.20	.20
F	——	.10	.85	.40	.40
EF	——	——	3.50	1.75	2.00
MS60	.40	2.50	16.00	22.50	22.00
MS63	——	——	——	——	50.00
MS65	——	——	——	——	450.00

VARIETIES: None are reported.

COMMENTS: Although some 1928-D cents are victims of worn and indistinct dies, this problem is not nearly as severe as for D-Mint cents of the years 1917-27. In any case, enough well made specimens survive that collectors can afford to shop around.

Quite a large number of 1928-D cents survive in the lower levels of Mint State, as quantities of unissued coins were still available from banks during the early 1930s. Finding one with bright, mint-red color is more challenging. Most are a subdued or dullish red to red/brown. Contemporary reports and advertisements in *The Numismatist* suggest that Lincoln Cents were just beginning to become popular with collectors around this time. While this should have resulted in the preservation of many gems, the storage materials available to hobbyists in 1928 (most of them paper products having a high sulfur content) were not conducive to long-term preservation.

SAN FRANCISCO
17,266,000

RARITY: 1928-S cents were, like all S-Mint cents dated 1917-30, widely hoarded during the 1940s and 1950s. As a result, low grade examples remain quite common. Problem-free coins grading VF-AU are surprisingly difficult to locate and are almost certainly undervalued in guide books. Mint State coins are quite scarce, irrespective of quality. Choice and gem examples of any color are very scarce to rare. Fully struck, fully red gems are essentially unknown, the ones certified as MS65 RD and MS66 RD being so graded on the basis of color and surface condition alone, without the requirement of a full strike. When a small hoard of high quality coins emerged from Mid-American Rare Coin Galleries in the early 1990s prices temporarily fell, but these cents were quickly absorbed.

POPULATION TOTALS

MS BN = 6   MS RB = 71   MS RD = 116   TOTAL = 193
MS65 RD = 28   HIGHEST = MS66 RD (2)

GRADE	1935	1950	1965	1980	1995
G	——	——	.30	.25	.25
F	——	.15	1.10	.60	.60
EF	——	——	4.50	2.50	3.50
MS60	.40	3.50	28.50	37.50	45.00
MS63	——	——	——	——	100.00
MS65	——	——	——	——	400.00

VARIETIES: In addition to the regular S mintmark punch, a larger and very distinctive one was employed in this year alone for cents, dimes, quarters and halves. Large S cents are quite a bit scarcer than the normal, small S cents. A study of their relative rarity by Jack H. Tod, published in *The Numismatic Scrapbook Magazine*, revealed that only one out of every 25 1928-S cents examined was of the large S variety.[73] This matches quite closely the author's initial impression that the ratio was about one in 30.

Why this distinctive punch was used in 1928 alone is not known; why such an interesting, naked-eye variety is not more widely publicized and sought by collectors also remains a mystery. The two sizes of mintmark were first reported by readers of *The Numismatic Scrapbook Magazine* in 1938 and initially denied by Mint officials, an approach which remained their standard practice as late as the 1960s.[74] The specimen illustrated above is of the small S variety, though it appears a bit larger than usual because it was so deeply punched into the die. A close-up of the large S variety is included for comparison (see photo).

Four repunched mintmark varieties are known for this issue, and all of them feature the large S (see photo). Two of these (RPM-1 and RPM-2) are actually triple-punched.

1928-S
Large S, Breen-2113

1928-S/S
Large S, RPM-3 (Miller)

COMMENTS: Mushy coins struck from worn dies are the rule for 1928-S. This problem is particularly severe for the reverse dies, as these were almost certainly retained from previous years.

Like many of the coins in this series, the 1928-S cent has suffered dramatic reversals in value since the peak years of popular coin collecting during the early 1960s. This is warranted for the lowest grades, as these coins were indeed overpriced relative to their rarity. EF examples are another matter, however, and their current value does not reflect the difficulty of locating such coins. Given these depressed values, it's almost certain that many owners of such cents are reluctant to sell. Perhaps, a more realistic pricing structure will bring some coins out of hiding and provide a better view of their overall availability.

* * *

A table prepared by the Director's office at the end of Fiscal Year 1928 (June 30) revealed that 4,266,712,683 bronze cents had been coined at the Philadelphia Mint since 1864. Of these, some 100,523,534 had been redeemed and destroyed to date, leaving more than four billion outstanding. Denver had coined 406,290,000, all of the Lincoln type. Of these, 1,778,850 had since been destroyed. The San Francisco had produced 396,008,000 cents, nearly all of the Lincoln type, and some 2,320,519 had already been melted.[75]

1929

PHILADELPHIA
185,262,000

RARITY: This issue is common in all circulated grades. As the figures below reveal, Mint State coins of choice and gem quality are also readily available. Original rolls likely exist.

POPULATION: MS BN = 2   MS RB = 39   MS RD = 533   TOTAL = 574
TOTALS   MS65 RD = 256   HIGHEST = MS67 RD (19)

VALUES:

GRADE	1935	1950	1965	1980	1995
G	——	——	.10	.15	.15
F	——	.05	.20	.30	.30
EF	——	——	.65	1.35	1.35
MS60	.10	.40	4.50	7.00	7.50
MS63	——	——	——	——	13.00
MS65	——	——	——	——	62.50

VARIETIES: A very slight doubled reverse die is known, just barely detectable in the legend E PLURIBUS UNUM.[76]

COMMENTS: The typical 1929-P cent was coined from dies which were in an early die state or only moderately worn. Well struck examples are the rule.

Sol Taylor reported that many of the untoned, Mint State survivors are "tomato red," perhaps a slight exaggeration but not too far from the truth.[77] This coppery red color is commonly seen on Philadelphia cents of this and the next several years.

* * *

In his *Annual Report* for 1929, Mint Director Robert J. Grant commented on the notable increase in production:

The coinage feature of the fiscal year ended June 30, 1929, was a greater output of pieces than for any fiscal year since 1921. This was incident to . . . the increased demand for 1-cent pieces."[78]

An amusing story appeared in *The Chicago Herald and Examiner* for December 19, 1930:

Pennies were worth $1 apiece in Evanston last night. One particular kind of pennies, of course, but 100 of them were in the hands of police and there was every reason to suppose that there might be many more of them in circulation. So Evanstonians will probably be examining their change today at the corner news stands and on the street cars.

A sorrowful drug store clerk, who thought he had been swindled by a counterfeiter, discovered the rare coins. The clerk, W. S. Woods, had just exchanged a $1 bill for 100 pennies in a drug store at 2538 W. Railroad St., when he noticed that the Lincoln heads were too small. He summoned Detectives William Johnson and Edward Busseau, who took into custody Fred Moore, of 2539 Prairie Avenue. Moore admitted he had given Woods the pennies, but said he got them from a bank.

Federal authorities were called in. They telegraphed the Government mints and found that the pennies, instead of being counterfeit, were of imperfect coinage, and that they should never have been put into circulation.

Mint officials asked that the imperfect coins be withdrawn from circulation at once. But Evanston coin collectors, learning of the situation, began bidding $1 each for the pennies, on the theory that the strange circumstances surrounding them make them of high value. Moore, Brown and the police are trying to decide who owns them.

The pennies bear the date 1929. The Lincoln head is considerably smaller than on other pennies, and the edges are rough.[79]

Accounts of rare coins as published in the non-numismatic press are usually rich in misinformation and gross errors. Assuming, however, that there was some truth to this story, then what exactly were these coins? A smaller than usual head could occur only with a severely polished die, in which the outline of Lincoln's features were reduced through the application of an abrasive. This is done to remove clash marks after the dies strike one another without a planchet between them, leaving faint impressions of their features. Lapping or polishing the dies will then remove these marks, yet it also diminishes or eliminates any shallow features This still doesn't account for the rough edges that were reported, a phenomenon which would occur only if the coins were struck out of collar. Is it possible that they were broadstrikes, oversize cents on which the heads only appeared smaller in relation to their diameter? As with so many vintage reports, we'll probably never know.

DENVER
41,730,000

RARITY: Circulated coins are quite common, though pieces grading EF-AU are challenging to locate due to the late die state for many 1929-D cents. Uncirculated coins are also quite common, but they are equally disappointing in overall quality. Choice examples are available, but fully red gems are more elusive than the population data indicates. Most of the examples certified in high grades have achieved these numbers on the basis of color and overall eye appeal, while striking quality was, of sheer necessity, discounted. Original rolls may still exist.

POPULATION TOTALS

MS BN = 1   MS RB = 33   MS RD = 171   TOTAL = 205
MS65 RD = 75   HIGHEST = MS66 RD (7)

VALUES:

GRADE	1935	1950	1965	1980	1995
G	——	——	.15	.15	.15
F	——	.05	.30	.35	.35
EF	——	——	.85	1.35	1.35
MS60	.25	.90	9.00	11.00	17.00
MS63	——	——	——	——	32.00
MS65	——	——	——	——	125.00

VARIETIES: Nothing important is reported, though at least one die featured a mintmark placement to extreme right, centered below the second 9.

COMMENTS: Most cents of this issue show moderate to heavy die wear. Indistinct lettering and distorted peripheral elements (such as the wheat ears) are the rule. Sharply struck coins may be found with diligent searching, but they often fall short of gem in other respects. Uncleaned cents of this date are typically dark and/or spotted. The specimen illustrated above is sharper than average, but there is clearly some softening of highpoint and peripheral details.

With the possible exception of the half dollars, all denominations of 1929-D coinage were saved by the roll in large numbers. These coins were evidently on hand in banks for some years afterward, as they were being offered for sale by dealers and collectors throughout the 1930s, primarily from addresses in the central states. The economic slowdown which became the Great Depression affected the Midwest before spreading to the rest of the nation, and it's likely that many of the coins dated 1929-D were not needed for commerce at the time they were produced.

SAN FRANCISCO
50,148,000

RARITY: 1929-S is one of the most common S-Mint cents before 1935 in circulated grades. Striking quality is the only deterrent to owning an attractive specimen. Mint State coins are also fairly plentiful. Choice examples are not difficult to locate, but fully red and *fully struck* gems are scarcer than the certified population implies. A small hoard of such desirable cents surfaced in 1995 and was quickly absorbed by collectors. Original rolls may still exist.

POPULATION: MS BN = 1   MS RB = 44   MS RD = 344   TOTAL = 389
TOTALS   MS65 RD = 157   HIGHEST = MS66 RD (12)

VALUES:

GRADE	1935	1950	1965	1980	1995
G	——	——	.15	.15	.15
F	——	.05	.30	.35	.35
EF	——	——	.90	1.35	1.25
MS60	.25	.45	5.50	8.50	9.00
MS63	——	——	——	——	18.00
MS65	——	——	——	——	115.00

VARIETIES: Two repunched mintmarks are known (see photo).

COMMENTS: Although well struck 1929-S cents can be located from the large number of Mint State survivors, most were coined from moderately to heavily worn dies having blurred lettering and indistinct highpoints. This is true of many of the certified gem coins, as these were graded primarily on the basis of color and surface quality. When strike is factored into the equation, the number of truly gem coins is greatly diminished.

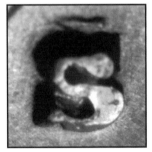

1929-S/S
RPM-1 (Miller)

Like the 1929-D cents, these were widely hoarded by the roll. The reason is probably the same: This was the first date affected by the onset of the Great Depression, and the demand for new coinage dropped off dramatically. When these coins finally emerged from banks and Treasury vaults around 1934-35 they were scooped up by eager collectors and dealers. This window of opportunity largely created the tradition of saving uncirculated rolls which became so prevalent during the 1930s and later decades.

1930

PHILADELPHIA
157,415,000

RARITY: 1930-P is common in any and all grades through superb gem MS67 RD. The certified population data is indisputable. Original rolls almost certainly exist in old collections and estates, but these will be broken up for "slabbing" as soon as they enter the market.

POPULATION: MS BN = 1   MS RB = 16   MS RD = 1404   TOTAL = 1421
TOTALS   MS65 RD = 705   HIGHEST = MS67 RD (119)

VALUES:

GRADE	1935	1950	1965	1980	1995
G	——	——	.15	.10	.10
F	——	.05	.30	.25	.25
EF	——	——	.50	1.00	.90
MS60	.10	.15	3.00	5.00	5.00
MS63	——	——	——	——	11.00
MS65	——	——	——	——	25.00

VARIETIES: Two reverse cud break varieties are known, one each between either wheat ear and the border. (Note: These and other cud varieties are thoroughly documented in a series of articles by Sam Thurman and Arnold Margolis appearing in *Error Trends Coin Magazine* from July 1994 through June 1996.

An example of the sort of minor variety which is obtainable at little or no premium is the 1930-P cent with a scratch in its reverse die (see photo).

COMMENTS: Fully red coins with outstanding luster are readily available. Early to mid die states are the rule, very few of this date appearing from heavily worn dies. Of course, the sharpness of even fully struck coins was affected by the gradual wearing down of the Lincoln Cent master hubs. Even the best 1930-P cent will pale in comparison to the detail evident on cents coined in 1917 and earlier.

1930-P
Scratch in die

* * *

Once again, the Mint's engraving staff failed to cut a numeral 3 that was in keeping with the style adopted by Brenner in 1909. The stubby, symmetrical 3 of 1930 cents instead recalled those of 1913 and 1923.

It's interesting that the coinage of cents remained fairly substantial throughout this depression year, even when other denominations were all but discontinued. There were interruptions, however, as no coins of any denomination were struck at any of the mints during July.[80] This is quite telling, as that month was the beginning of the U. S. Mint's fiscal year, and its annual appropriation became available. Coinage during July was normally quite heavy each year, as presses were often shut down during June while the three mints conducted their annual settlement of accounts.

An explanation for the large mintage of cents at a time when most other denominations were in redundancy is found in Director Grant's *Annual Report*:

> Continued large demand for 1-cent and 5-cent coins . . . featured the fiscal year ended June 30, 1930. Overtime operation was required at the Philadelphia mint to meet this demand, but of shorter duration than during the prior fiscal year because of improvements made in operating processes."[81]

* * *

Some sort of cottage industry developed in the plating of 1930 cents at the time of their issue. A reader of *The Numismatist* reported receiving a flyer which advertised for sale 1930 cents in white metal, these priced at 10 cents apiece.[82] A few years later, another reader responded with a possible explanation:

> I enclose a Lincoln cent which has been treated, I believe, as the one mentioned in this item. The enclosed cent has been tin plated in a machine which plates pistons for automobile engines. This plating is about .00025 inch thick and requires about 25 minutes to apply the tin.[83]

Needless to say, a coin such as the one described has no collector value, though it may serve as a curiosity. This is just one of the countless abuses to which the lowly cent has been subjected.

DENVER
40,100,000

RARITY: Although relatively scarcer than the 1930-P and 1930-S cents, those of 1930-D cannot be considered scarce in an absolute sense. Fully struck, fully red gems are usually available, though at a higher cost than the more commonly seen examples of indistinct strike. Original rolls may still exist, as many of these cents were retained by banks during the Great Depression and discovered years later.

POPULATION: MS BN = 2   MS RB = 38   MS RD = 581   TOTAL = 621
TOTALS   MS65 RD = 321   HIGHEST = MS67 RD (4)

VALUES:

GRADE	1935	1950	1965	1980	1995
G	——	——	.25	.15	.15
F	——	.05	.40	.30	.30
EF	——	——	1.10	1.00	1.50
MS60	.25	.75	9.00	9.00	12.00
MS63	——	——	——	——	25.00
MS65	——	——	——	——	57.50

VARIETIES: Four repunched mintmarks are reported (see photo). As is the case for most such varieties, the premium attached in circulated grades is slight. In addition, Walter Breen listed a variety with the numeral 0 filled from a chipped die. Its value is likewise minimal.[84]

COMMENTS: Generally well struck for a Denver Mint cent, some will show moderate die wear, but there are enough sharp pieces to meet the demand.

The color of most 1930-D cents is a bit off, probably due to prolonged storage in paper wrappers. Widely hoarded (as were most cents from the depression years), these coins were largely withheld from circulation by banks and the U. S. Treasury until the demand for additional coins picked up around 1934.

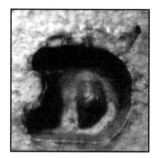

1930-D/D
RPM-2 (Miller)

SAN FRANCISCO
24,286,000

RARITY: Widely hoarded in all grades, 1930-S cents have taken a well-deserved beating in value since 1965. Countless pieces were pulled from circulation during the 1940s, '50s and even the early '60s. Mint State coins survive in large numbers from the many rolls hoarded during the mid-1930s. Both the color and strike of these coins is usually superior to that of most 1930-D cents, and fully red gems are plentiful. Original rolls probably exist.

POPULATION: MS BN = 0   MS RB = 39   MS RD = 759   TOTAL = 798
TOTALS   MS65 RD = 441   HIGHEST = MS67 RD (23)

VALUES:

GRADE	1935	1950	1965	1980	1995
G	——	——	.25	.15	.15
F	——	.05	.40	.30	.30
EF	——	——	.85	1.00	1.00
MS60	.25	.35	9.00	7.00	8.00
MS63	——	——	——	——	13.00
MS65	——	——	——	——	50.00

VARIETIES: Three repunched mintmarks are noted (see photo), while a minor obverse doubled-die affecting the letters IN GOD is accompanied by a die crack through the date. One die features its mintmark placed extremely low.

COMMENTS: The last large scale coinage of cents at the San Francisco Mint until 1935, this issue was probably not needed at the time of coining, and many were placed into storage.

The overall quality of strike for this issue is superior to all previous S-Mint cents since 1916. For reasons not documented (the fear of unemployment, perhaps?), the employees of all three U. S. Mints produced a superior product throughout the worst years of the Great Depression (1930-33). It's quite possible that production was slowed deliberately, sustaining the employee roster for awhile longer. If that was the case, it worked only temporarily. As demand for new coinage slackened, the total number of employees on the Mint's payroll fell from 652 at the end of Fiscal Year 1927 to just 538 at the end of FY1933.[85]

1930-S/S
RPM-1 (Miller)

1931

PHILADELPHIA
19,396,000

RARITY: This date was slightly scarce in circulation from its inception. Survivors in all grades up through Fine are not difficult to locate, but those grading VF through AU are challenging. Enough rolls were preserved to make Mint State coins of average to choice condition fairly plentiful. Gems are another matter, these being fairly scarce. This changed for the better with the release in the early 1990s of several rolls, distributed by Mid-American Rare Coin Galleries. The certified population seems to be large enough to meet the demand, but few of the ones graded MS65 RD will be as appealing as the those dated 1930-P. Original rolls may still exist.

POPULATION: MS BN = 1   MS RB = 32   MS RD = 421   TOTAL = 454
TOTALS   MS65 RD = 240   HIGHEST = MS67 RD (1)

VALUES:

GRADE	1935	1950	1965	1980	1995
G	——	——	.25	.25	.25
F	——	.05	.75	.45	.45
EF	——	——	1.75	1.80	1.80
MS60	.10	1.50	17.50	16.00	17.00
MS63	——	——	——	——	38.00
MS65	——	——	——	——	80.00

VARIETIES: A very minor doubled-die reverse variety is evident in the letters E PLURIBUS, accompanied by a shallow die scratch through several of the letters.

COMMENTS: Most 1931-P cents were coined from fresh dies or those showing only moderate wear. Their color can be either coppery red or a more brassy shade, and many of the survivors are plagued by spotting and other signs of poor storage.

   The style of numeral 3 in the cents of 1931 is similar to that used the previous year, though it is less symmetrical and a bit more flamboyant.

∗ ∗ ∗

   The coinage of cents was way down this year, and the monthly reports from the Mint Director's office reveal an interesting deception. In an apparent effort to maintain uninterrupted production, the mints turned out relatively small numbers of cents every month but November, even though any of the mint facilities could easily have turned out the entire year's production in a single month. For the month of February, cents were indeed the only denomination coined, though the available data does not reveal which mint produced these pieces.[86]

As production wound down, vacancies at the mints due to retirement were not filled. At the close of Fiscal Year 1931, there were 272 employees at the Philadelphia Mint, 79 in Denver and 101 in San Francisco.[87]

DENVER
4,480,000

RARITY: Given its low mintage, it's not surprising that this date was always scarce in circulation. These coins remain fairly elusive today. Average quality Mint State coins are only slightly scarce, but anything grading choice or better is decidedly difficult to locate. Fully red gems are rare, as the population data reveals. At that, many of the certified gems are not very sharply struck, and a few will have tiny spots. Though original rolls may yet exist, this becomes increasingly unlikely with each passing year.

POPULATION: MS BN = 16   MS RB = 142   MS RD = 155   TOTAL = 313
TOTALS   MS65 RD = 54   HIGHEST = MS66 RD (4)

VALUES:	GRADE	1935	1950	1965	1980	1995
	G	——	——	3.50	3.00	2.25
	F	——	.15	6.25	4.00	3.50
	EF	——	——	15.00	7.00	7.50
	MS60	.25	3.50	85.00	55.00	50.00
	MS63	——	——	——	——	80.00
	MS65	——	——	——	——	385.00

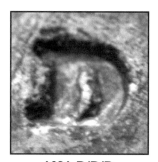

1931-D/D/D
RPM-1 (Miller)

VARIETIES: One triple-punched mintmark is known (see photo). This and other repunched mintmark varieties have been carefully photo-documented in *Errorscope* in a series of articles by James Wiles beginning in January 1996.

COMMENTS: Although generally well struck, most uncirculated cents of this issue are spotted or possess dull and unattractive toning.

As with all of the depression-era cents, this issue was largely unneeded when coined, and most of the finished product remained idle in vaults for the next several years. So difficult was it for Lincoln Cent collectors to acquire recent coinage during this period that a campaign was begun to have the Treasury Department supply the needed dates through mail orders. This effort was successful, and many collectors thus secured their first 1931-D cents through this source. As the economy slowly began to recover around 1934-35, a great many of these cents were subsequently released to circulation. Their low mintages, however, attracted the attention of speculators, and a market for trading coins by the roll was created for the first time.

The poor price performance of this date is reflective of many semi-key Lincolns during the 30+ years which have passed since the hobby's peak in popularity during the early 1960s. It's conceivable that many more of these coins will return to the marketplace if and when their value recovers.

SAN FRANCISCO
866,000

RARITY: In circulated grades, 1931-S cents have always been very scarce and in continual demand. They are more available at the higher grade levels, for reasons given below under COMMENTS. Mint State coins of average to choice quality are readily available due to widespread hoarding during the early 1930s. Gems are more elusive, since these hoarded coins were subject to poor storage methods and environmental hazards. In addition, most have less than perfect strikes. Original rolls may exist, but these will eventually be broken to retrieve the best singles.

POPULATION: MS BN = 17 MS RB = 228 MS RD = 826 TOTAL = 1071
TOTALS MS65 RD = 348 HIGHEST = MS66 RD (23)

VALUES:

GRADE	1935	1950	1965	1980	1995
G	——	——	27.50	25.00	32.00
F	——	.75	42.50	30.00	37.00
EF	——	——	57.50	35.00	45.00
MS60	.25	1.60	85.00	52.50	65.00
MS63	——	——	——	——	85.00
MS65	——	——	——	——	235.00

VARIETIES: Nothing significant is known, though one old report is found of a crescent-shaped raised area extending from letter P in PLURIBUS to the top of letter C in CENT.[88]

COMMENTS: 1931-S cents are usually well struck but not quite fully struck. Most survivors have toned or become spotted over the years, since they were stored in paper rolls or canvas bags, neither of which is conducive to long-term preservation. Cleaned or dipped coins are more prevalent for this date than for many adjacent ones, perhaps due to a greater economic incentive. The price spread for this coin across all grades is slight, since Mint State examples are at least as common as worn ones, if not more so. Only at the gem level do Mint State 1931-S cents command a strong price.

* * *

All but 66,000 of the 1931-S cents were coined during the early months of that year.[89] Very few were issued during 1931 or for several years afterward, as there was simply no demand for additional cents in the states serviced by the San Francisco Mint. As a matter of course, however, *The Numismatist* dutifully reported the coinage totals for each mint at the beginning of the following year. When the mintage figure for this issue became known, it was immediately targeted by speculators. Bank tellers could usually be recruited in an effort to secure these desirable cents in exchange for some other favor which, during those years of prohibition against alcohol (1920-33), might have included a bottle of the illicit nectar.

The result of all this mad scrambling was to make 1931-S cents plentiful by the uncirculated roll or bag but almost impossible to locate in circulation. The finds of collectors reported to periodicals such as *The Numismatic Scrapbook Magazine* during the 1940s, '50s and into the early '60s include countless 1909-S V.D.B. and 1914-D cents but almost never the find of a 1931-S Lincoln. Walter Breen reported a hoard of 200,000 Mint State cents of this date once held by Maurice Scharlack (introduced earlier as a hoarder of 1922-D cents). That's nearly one-quarter of the entire mintage![90] Sol Taylor recounts a tale told by famed dealer Abe Kosoff in which Kosoff acquired two Mint State rolls from a dealer who allegedly owned hundreds more rolls.[91] If true, this may have been the same hoard described by Breen. In any case, there were many collectors and dealers in the western states who acquired large quantities of this issue. These included Richard A. Webb of San Francisco and Norman Shultz of Salt Lake City.

1931-S cents have often been faked by altering some other genuine cent. The simplest method was to reshape the final digit of some date such as 1936-S or 1937-S. Of course, the distinctive shape of the numeral 3 on genuine 1931-dated cents should make these alterations easily detectable. Another trick was to add an S mintmark taken from some common date to a genuine cent dated 1931-P though this form of alteration is not often seen for 1931-S. For more on counterfeit and altered 1931-S cents, see Chapter 5.

Date style of genuine 1931-S cents (ANAAB)

1932

PHILADELPHIA
9,062,000

RARITY: Due to their low mintage, 1932-P cents have always been among the scarcer dates in circulation. The supply in all grades, however, is more than adequate. Mint State examples are plentiful due to hoarding, and quite a few blazing gems survive. Original rolls probably exist.

POPULATION: MS BN = 0   MS RB = 15   MS RD = 588   TOTAL = 603
TOTALS MS65 RD = 317   HIGHEST = MS67 RD (15)

VALUES:

GRADE	1935	1950	1965	1980	1995
G	——	——	.60	.90	1.50
F	——	.05	1.60	1.50	2.00
EF	——	——	3.50	3.00	3.00
MS60	.10	.75	17.50	16.00	18.00
MS63	——	——	——	——	30.00
MS65	——	——	——	——	57.50

VARIETIES: None are reported.

COMMENTS: Most 1932-P cents display slight to moderate die wear, though early die state examples may be found. Their color is generally good, being a bright coppery red in most instances.

The style of numeral 3 in the date was a carry over from 1931 but was making its final appearance.

The total output of cents from the Philadelphia Mint was the lowest for any year in the series. Only about 20 million cents were produced at the Philadelphia and Denver Mints combined, with San Francisco refraining altogether. Had the U. S. Mint intended merely to coin this quantity of cents for 1932, it could certainly have done so in just one or two months time, yet exactly one million cents were coined during each of six of the twelve months of 1932. Larger totals were reported only for April, June, October and November. None were coined during July, a not uncommon occurrence as the various mints made their annual settlements at the end of the fiscal year (June 30).[92] It seems that the entire cent coinage of 1932 may have been just a "phantom", performed primarily to keep mint employees from becoming idle and thus subject to termination.

Most of the 1932-P cents were bagged and stored, awaiting better times. Due to their attractive low mintages, many of these were scooped up by speculators when released circa 1934-35.

* * *

From the pages of *The Numismatist* comes another amusing anecdote, this one dated 1947:

The lowly cent has not been swinging much weight of recent years but down in Cumberland, Maryland, it recently had a brief moment of glory.

Alfred Hutter reports that a grocery store of that city celebrated its 15th anniversary by accepting cents of 1932 for practically any item in the store.

The little cent would get you a can of kippered herring, two cans of beer, [a] jar of dill pickles, a corn straw broom, and other useful items, including a fifth gallon of apple wine.

Alfred got rid of 140 cents of 1932 during the sale, but he didn't say what he bought.[93]

DENVER
10,500,000

RARITY: Always a bit scarce in circulated grades, the current supply of this issue seems adequate to the demand. Mint State coins were widely hoarded, so that average to choice quality pieces are common. Fully-struck, fully red gems are not common, but they too are available in sufficient numbers to supply collectors willing to pay for them. For generations, the four issues dated 1932-33 have been lumped together in high grade rarity, but 1932-D has emerged with a slight edge in this respect. Original rolls probably exist, as a few have turned up at auction during recent years.

POPULATION: MS BN = 1   MS RB = 26   MS RD = 389   TOTAL = 415
TOTALS   MS65 RD = 218   HIGHEST = MS67 RD (9)

VALUES:

GRADE	1935	1950	1965	1980	1995
G	——	——	.60	.60	.70
F	——	.05	1.60	1.20	1.20
EF	——	——	3.50	3.00	2.50
MS60	.25	1.00	17.50	16.00	15.00
MS63	——	——	——	——	30.00
MS65	——	——	——	——	60.00

VARIETIES: A barely discernible doubled obverse die is evident in numerals 32.

COMMENTS: Slightly worn dies are the rule for this date, though in all other respects the quality for Mint State coins is usually excellent. Sharply struck examples can be located, and when combined with the blazing red color often found for this date provide a good value for the collector.

Like the 1932-P cents, these coins were largely unneeded at the time of their striking and appear to have been a make-work project. One interesting facet of this story is that the one million cents coined for August's allotment were all struck at the Denver Mint, as though the work was being distributed in an equitable manner to maintain activity where it was needed.

Most 1932-D cents were bagged and stored for several years after manufacture. Collectors had to buy them by mail from the Treasury Department in Washington, D.C., though a few dealers managed to acquire small quantities through some means. The low mintage of this issue attracted speculators to these cents when they were finally released in quantity during the period 1934-35. This accounts for their rarity in circulation from the outset, as a great many were hoarded in Mint State.

1933

PHILADELPHIA
14,360,000

RARITY: This issue was always scarce in circulation, and specimens grading VF through AU are challenging to locate. The generous quantity of Mint State survivors tends to depress the value of worn coins. Uncirculated examples in all degrees of preservation through fully red gem are readily available, despite the relatively low mintage for this date. Original rolls probably exist.

POPULATION: MS BN = 0   MS RB = 26   MS RD = 430   TOTAL = 456
TOTALS MS65 RD = 214   HIGHEST = MS67 RD (10)

VALUES:

GRADE	1935	1950	1965	1980	1995
G	——	——	.70	.50	.75
F	——	.15	2.00	.70	1.25
EF	——	——	4.50	2.00	2.75
MS60	——	1.00	25.00	17.50	16.00
MS63	——	——	——	——	30.00
MS65	——	——	——	——	45.00

VARIETIES: None are reported.

COMMENTS: Well struck, fully red gems are available for a price and make for very attractive coins. Many rolls of this issue and its Denver-Mint counterpart were preserved intact for decades, until the advent of certified grading exposed the best singles to the marketplace.

     Cents dated 1933 bear matching numerals 3 that are modeled after the 3 employed in 1930. These fail to conform to the style set by Brenner in 1909, a mistake repeated often in preparing the obverse master dies for the Lincoln Cent. Why is this of interest to numismatists, you ask? It reveals something of how the master die was prepared, for one thing. The original master hub of 1909 bore all four date digits, as these had been sculpted by Brenner into his plaster model and then transferred to a galvano by the Mint. The master hub was reduced from this galvano, and the master die for 1909, as well as all working hubs and working dies taken from it, then included these numerals. For the coinage of 1910, however, the last two numerals 09 had to be ground off of the master hub. When a new master die was sunk from this hub it lacked the numerals 10, and these were then engraved by hand into it to prepare the matrices for 1910 cent coinage. Each subsequent master die was similarly lacking the final two digits, and this accounts for the slight stylistic variations seen from year to year.

Like the cents of 1932, the 1933 issue was coined in small batches spread out over many months. Slightly over two million cents were struck by the Philadelphia and Denver Mints combined during each of the months January, February, March and May. More than four million were coined during April and then no more until September and October, each of which witnessed the coining of 500,000 cents.[94] The remaining six million or so cents appear to have been coined during the final two months of the year, though the records for that period were not published. Clearly, though, this was a coinage of convenience rather than necessity.

The employee payroll of the United States Mint reached its lowest point of the 20th Century during Fiscal Year 1933. As of June 30, there were just 231 persons employed at the Philadelphia Mint, 71 in Denver and another 90 in San Francisco, for a total of only 392.[95] Under these solemn conditions, most 1933-P cents were simply bagged and stored, only to be swept up by speculators at a later date.

DENVER
6,200,000

RARITY: 1933-D cents were always scarce in circulation, and they still carry a respectable premium despite some setbacks since 1965. Mint State coins are fairly common at the choice (MS63-64) level, their value being based more on perception than fact. Enough are poorly struck, however, that fully struck gems are scarce. Original rolls may exist.

POPULATION: MS BN = 1   MS RB = 24   MS RD = 641   TOTAL = 666
TOTALS   MS65 RD = 355   HIGHEST = MS67 RD (11)

VALUES:	GRADE	1935	1950	1965	1980	1995
	G	——	——	2.50	1.60	1.75
	F	——	.15	3.50	2.25	2.25
	EF	——	——	7.50	4.00	4.00
	MS60	——	.60	32.50	20.00	20.00
	MS63	——	——	——	——	32.00
	MS65	——	——	——	——	47.50

VARIETIES: A new mintmark punch was introduced this year for the Denver Mint. It was larger and better proportioned and appeared on all cents dated 1933-D through 1979-D.

COMMENTS: Like its close counterparts, 1932-P, 1932-D and 1933-P, the cents dated 1933-D were generally made with greater care than preceding issues from the 1920s. Sharp or only slightly worn dies were the rule, and fussy collectors should have no difficulty in securing a gem example.

In his book *The Standard Guide to the Lincoln Cent*, specialist Sol Taylor recounts a couple of anecdotes that are worth including here. The first concerns the use of this date in souvenir encasements created for Chicago's Century of Progress Exposition in 1933-34. Obtaining these coins probably involved a special request, as very few were released to circulation at the time of coining. Another point relates to the arrival of "penny boards," 11" x 14" pieces of cardboard which included labeled holes for collecting each coin in a particular series. These first appeared in 1934 and quickly gained enormous popularity, as it was about this time that the collecting of Lincoln Cents and other circulating coins from pocket change became popular.

The early boards included notations for particular dates indicating that these were rarely found in circulation. 1933-P and 1933-D cents were among such issues, since nearly their entire mintage remained in storage at the time. In fact, with just a few exceptions, most of the dates after 1925 identified as rare on these early boards subsequently proved to be common in uncirculated condition, appearing only as the Great Depression came to an end and the vaults were emptied. These included coins such as the 1931-S nickel, the 1931-D dime and the 1926-D quarter.

1934

PHILADELPHIA
219,080,000

RARITY: 1934-P is common in all grades, as the values and population data suggest. Original rolls almost certainly exist of this and all subsequent dates.

POPULATION: MS BN = 0   MS RB = 3   MS RD = 362   TOTAL = 365
TOTALS   MS67 RD = 143   HIGHEST = MS67 RD (143)

VALUES:

GRADE	1935	1950	1965	1980	1995
EF	——	——	——	.60	.60
MS60	——	.15	4.00	3.00	4.00
MS63	——	——	——	——	6.00
MS65	——	——	——	——	12.50

VARIETIES: Two minor obverse doubled-die varieties are known. The first is evident only within the motto IN GOD WE TRUST, while the second is only apparent by the extra thickness of the numerals in the date. The same thickening effect is seen on the wheat stems in a single doubled-die reverse variety. All three are illustrated in *The Lincoln Cent Doubled Die* by John A. Wexler.

     Finally, there are no less than four obverse and three reverse cud varieties, all in the familiar positions below Lincoln's shoulder (see photo) or along the outside of the wheat ears.

1934-P
LC-34-4 (Thurman & Margolis)

COMMENTS: This issue is typically well struck, as the dies used were replaced when only moderately worn. Fully red gems are fairly common, though not nearly so available as the dates to follow. From this point onward, the number of coins certified MS67 RD is far more meaningful than the MS65 RD data appropriate for earlier dates, and this figure is presented hereafter through the year 1943.

     Cents dated 1934 at last conform to the correct date style. The numeral 3 bears a long, sweeping tail, as it rightly should. What happened to awaken this knowledge in Chief Engraver John R. Sinnock is not known, but it failed to prevent a return to the incorrect style in 1935 and subsequent years through 1939!

* * *

Cents of this date were made in very large numbers relative to those of years just past, a reflection of the modest economic upswing which accompanied the innovative public works programs of the Roosevelt Administration and a general regaining of optimism. This fact, in combination with the growing popularity of coin collecting and the newly-discovered phenomenon of roll hoarding, led to vast numbers of freshly minted coins being set aside for all dates, mints and denominations. Excluding certain varieties and those issues which were poorly made, there are truly no rare U. S. coins from 1934 onward, even in high grades.

DENVER
28,446,000

RARITY: Slightly scarce in the higher circulated grades, this may be due to the poor quality of many coins. Their late die state often resulted in cents which grade VF or less with just the slightest wear. While one of the scarcer issues from 1934 onward, choice and gem examples of 1934-D are usually available, either red or red/brown. Specialists are a bit skeptical of the pieces certified MS67 RD, as these are not all fully struck. Original rolls likely exist.

POPULATION: MS BN = 2   MS RB = 129   MS RD = 1245   TOTAL = 1376
TOTALS   MS67 RD = 11   HIGHEST = MS67 RD (11)

VALUES:

GRADE	1935	1950	1965	1980	1995
EF	——	——	——	1.25	1.00
MS60	——	.25	12.00	18.50	16.00
MS63	——	——	——	——	25.00
MS65	——	——	——	——	37.50

VARIETIES: A minor obverse doubled-die is identifiable by extra thickness in the numerals of the date. Four cud varieties are known: one obverse, one reverse and two more on the reverse having retained cuds. Finally, no less than five repunched mint-mark varieties exist (see photo).

COMMENTS: Often plagued by moderately to heavily worn dies, sharply struck examples of this date are in the minority. When found, however, they may possess excellent definition and fully red color.

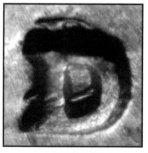

1934-D/D
RPM-4 (Miller)

1935

PHILADELPHIA
245,388,000

RARITY: Common in all grades through fully red gem, original rolls likely exist.

POPULATION: MS BN = 0   MS RB = 2   MS RD = 392   TOTAL = 394
TOTALS   MS67 RD = 178   HIGHEST = MS67 RD (178)

VALUES:

GRADE	1935	1950	1965	1980	1995
EF	——	——	——	.40	.40
MS60	——	.10	1.75	1.50	2.00
MS63	——	——	——	——	3.50
MS65	——	——	——	——	6.00

VARIETIES: Two minor doubled-dies are known, the first an obverse variety visible in the motto IN GOD WE TRUST and the date, while the second is a reverse variety evident only as extra thickness in E PLURIBUS UNUM. This date is rich in cud varieties, including two obverse breaks at the familiar shoulder position and no less than eight reverse cuds along the wheat ears, four of them retained. In addition to those already described, there are two distinct varieties which combine obverse and reverse cuds in the same die pairings.

COMMENTS: 1935-P cents are frequently found in extraordinary condition, with full, original color and very sharp details.

Why the Mint regressed to an incorrect style of numerals 35 for the date 1935 and continued this shortsighted policy in following years remains a mystery.

* * *

After several years of economic depression and greatly reduced coinages, activity picked up at the mints in 1934-35. Director Nellie Tayloe Ross confirmed this heightened activity in her 1935 *Annual Report* to Treasury Secretary Henry Morgenthau, Jr.:

> The coinage mints operated for long periods on the basis of two shifts or three shifts daily. The great demand for domestic coin during the fiscal year 1935 was evidently occasioned principally by increased business activity incident to progress toward economic recovery.[96]

This renewed activity prompted all three mints to resume purchases of ready-made blanks for cent coinage, apparently for the first time since 1924.[97]

DENVER
47,000,000

RARITY: Common in nearly all grades, only in fully struck, superb gem condition can this date be considered scarce. Original rolls likely exist.

POPULATION:	MS BN = 0		MS RB = 3		MS RD = 339	TOTAL = 342
TOTALS	MS67 RD = 53		HIGHEST = MS68 RD (1)			

VALUES:	GRADE	1935	1950	1965	1980	1995
	EF	——	——	——	.40	.40
	MS60	——	.20	3.75	2.25	4.00
	MS63	——	——	——	——	7.00
	MS65	——	——	——	——	11.00

VARIETIES: A single doubled-die reverse variety is visible only as extra thickness to the letters in E PLURIBUS UNUM. Two obverse and two reverse cud varieties exist, one of the latter being a retained cud. In a curious departure from the norm, the obverse cuds appear in the 3 o'clock and 10 o'clock positions, respectively, rather than the more typical shoulder location. Three repunched mintmarks are known.

COMMENTS: This date is troubled by moderate to heavy die wear, yet many such pieces appear within the population of certified gems. Collectors will want to sift through these late die-state cents and find the ones which qualify as gems on all counts, including sharpness.

SAN FRANCISCO
38,702,000

RARITY: Circulated examples are quite common, as are Mint State coins through the choice level (MS63 RD). Better quality examples become elusive, due to the deficiencies described below under COMMENTS. True gems are fairly rare. Despite the scarcity of gem singles, original rolls likely exist.

POPULATION:	MS BN = 0		MS RB = 13		MS RD = 322	TOTAL = 335
TOTALS	MS67 RD = 30		HIGHEST = MS67 RD (30)			

VALUES:	GRADE	1935	1950	1965	1980	1995
	EF	——	——	——	.60	.60
	MS60	——	.20	5.00	5.00	8.00
	MS63	——	——	——	——	12.00
	MS65	——	——	——	——	57.50

VARIETIES: Two repunched mintmark varieties exist for this date (see photo).

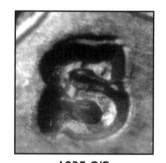

1935-S/S
RPM-1 (Miller)

COMMENTS: 1935-S cents often have a most peculiar look to their fields. This could be described as glassy or liquid in appearance. Sadly, this effect is usually indicative of worn dies of a sort not seen since the 1920s. While not as bad as the worst dates of that decade, cents of this issue are typically blurred around their peripheries. As is often the case, the grading services tend to overlook these technical considerations when certifying gems on the basis of eye appeal and marketability; collectors may want to be more particular.

Sol Taylor also reports that this date tends to come toned to a brownish shade rather than the blazing red sought by collectors. Other observers of the Lincoln Cent scene are in agreement with his finding. This may be the last issue in the Lincoln series which is a challenge to find in gem condition, though some of the cents from the 1950s and 1960s are contenders.

Some 29,010,000 1935-S cents were coined during the first half of that year, the balance during later months.[98]

* * *

In 1935, ground was broken for a new San Francisco Mint. In an account published the previous year, *The Wall Street Journal* revealed the reasons behind this move:

Officials of the U. S. Mint in San Francisco now are considering 45 sites as possible new locations of a proposed new mint, for the construction of which the Public Works Administration has set aside $1,225,000. The present mint provides cramped quarters for the unusual activities brought about by the Government's silver and gold buying programs, and the 60-year old building is in need of a complete modernization and expansion of facilities. Present-day conditions have necessitated the employment of about twice as many workers as before and the 145 employees, now working in the various departments, make expansion of facilities necessary, mint officials say.[99]

PHILADELPHIA
309,632,000

RARITY: Extremely common in all grades, even the finest gems exist in sufficient number to satisfy most collectors. Original rolls almost certainly survive.

POPULATION: MS BN = 0   MS RB = 4   MS RD = 342   TOTAL = 346
TOTALS   MS67 RD = 207   HIGHEST = MS67 RD (207)

VALUES:

GRADE	1950	1965	1980	1995
EF	——	——	.30	.30
MS60	.10	1.50	1.40	——
MS65	——	——	——	5.00

VARIETIES: An amazing total of 13 obverse cud die breaks are reported for this date, all looking remarkably similar, with the break occurring at Lincoln's shoulder. Two reverse cuds are also known, these occurring at the usual locations, one of them a retained cud.

This date offers one of the most popular doubled-die obverses in the Lincoln series, second only to those of 1955, 1958 and 1972 in clarity (see photos). As is frequently the case with major varieties, there are actually several doubled-dies of varying significance for this date. John A. Wexler lists and illustrates no less than five in his book, plus a couple of very minor reverse doubled-dies visible only as extra thickness in the letters of E PLURIBUS UNUM.[100] The most appealing varieties are the three obverses illustrated by Bill Fivaz and J. T. Stanton in *The Cherrypicker's Guide to Rare Die Varieties.* The authors further specify that the first and second varieties are the most desirable. These are readily identified by strong doubling in the date and LIBERTY.

COMMENTS: Like the other denominations coined during 1936, a near record number of cents was produced at the Philadelphia Mint. Most examples are well struck from early-mid die states, and superb gems with blazing luster can be found.

* * *

For the second year in a row, activity at the mints was greatly increased, as noted by Director Ross:

1936-P
DDO-1 (Fivaz & Stanton)

1936-P
DDO-2, Breen-2135 (Fivaz & Stanton)

Domestic coinage demand continued very large during the fiscal year 1936, it being necessary at times to use an extra daily shift of employees in addition to working the regular force overtime for the purpose of keeping abreast of shipping orders.[101]

Despite this increased demand for coins, the U. S. Mint was able to keep up its production with blanks made entirely in-house, no contractors being used during Fiscal Year 1936. The number of employees was up dramatically from 1933, as there were now some 783 persons engaged at the three mints.[102]

DENVER
40,620,000

RARITY: These are common in all circulated grades. Mint State coins were hoarded by the roll, and some rolls may survive intact. Choice and gem coins are not difficult to find, though most specimens are a bit indistinct, such as the piece illustrated above.

POPULATION: MS BN = 0   MS RB = 2   MS RD = 477   TOTAL = 479
TOTALS   MS67 RD = 216   HIGHEST = MS68 RD (2)

VALUES:	GRADE	1950	1965	1980	1995
	EF	——	——	.45	.45
	MS60	.15	2.25	1.50	——
	MS65	——	——	——	8.00

VARIETIES: One obverse cud variety occurred between Lincoln's lapel and the date, a position not often seen. Another cud may be found on the reverse, between the right wheat ear and the rim. In addition, two repunched mintmarks are known.

COMMENTS: Unlike the nickels of this date and mint, the cents were generally well struck from dies showing little or only moderate wear. Some may be found from later die states, but better pieces are common enough that the undesirable ones may be ignored.

SAN FRANCISCO
29,130,000

RARITY: 1936-S cents were widely hoarded by the roll and remain common in all grades. Choice and gem specimens may be easily located.

POPULATION: MS BN = 0   MS RB = 1   MS RD = 230   TOTAL = 231
TOTALS   MS67 RD = 63   HIGHEST = MS67 RD (63)

VALUES:	GRADE	1950	1965	1980	1995
	EF	——	——	.55	.55
	MS60	.20	3.00	2.25	——
	MS65	——	——	——	12.00

VARIETIES: A single repunched mintmark variety is known.

COMMENTS: Die states range all across the board, but well struck gems are readily available.

It should be noted that the peculiarities which defined the San Francisco Mint cents during the period from 1908 through the mid 1920s were not seen at all during the 1930s. These include the "woodgrain" effect of improper alloying and the odd, inward curvature to the rims. The overall quality of workmanship was vastly superior during this decade and would remain so until about 1944, when the combination of tremendous mintages and many inexperienced employees led to an erosion of quality control. An enviable product was not achieved again until this mint reopened during the mid 1960s, following a ten-year hiatus in coining.

1937

PHILADELPHIA
309,179,320

RARITY: Common in all grades through superb gem, many rolls likely remain. Some of these, however, may have been picked over for the best pieces and then reassembled with lesser coins.

POPULATION: MS BN = 0   MS RB = 2   MS RD = 635   TOTAL = 637
TOTALS MS67 RD = 471   HIGHEST = MS67 RD (471)

VALUES:

GRADE	1950	1965	1980	1995
EF	——	——	.30	.30
MS60	.10	1.50	1.50	——
MS65	——	——	——	5.00

VARIETIES: One obverse cud is known in the familiar position below Lincoln's shoulder, while some four reverse cuds exist, all of them with the broken portion retained. Three obverse doubled-dies and one reverse doubled-die are also known, all of them quite minor.

COMMENTS: There's little to say about this date, since it's generally well struck and quite common in all grades. Cents of this and most dates after 1934 were still to be found in circulation when the author began collecting coins in 1965. Within three years, however, only those dated in the 1940s and later were seen with any regularity. By the mid 1970s, all "Wheaties" had become scarce, and the appearance of one in circulation has been noteworthy ever since.

Cents dated 1937 should have displayed a long tail to numeral 7, but the Mint turned a blind eye to this obvious oversight.

* * *

For the 1941 convention of the American Numismatic Association in Philadelphia, local coin dealer Ira S. Reed made up sets of 1937-P cents and nickels which had their edges reeded by a machinist. These "Reeded" coins were, of course, a play on his name. According to contemporary accounts, some 104 sets were prepared and offered for sale at the show at a price of $4 for the pair.[103] For several years thereafter, these coins would reappear singly or in sets, and the real story of their origin was typically supplanted by some fanciful tale of a mischievous mint employee. They are clearly genuine coins, yet their reeding was applied commercially outside of the mint. Such reeding could be replicated at any time, so the value of original pieces should never exceed the cost of having this work done.

DENVER
50,430,000

RARITY: This issue is common in all grades through superb gem (MS67 RD). Original rolls likely exist.

| POPULATION: | MS BN = 0 | | MS RB = 3 | | MS RD = 709 | | TOTAL = 712 |
| TOTALS | MS67 RD = 548 | | HIGHEST = MS67 RD (548) | | | | |

VALUES:	GRADE	1950	1965	1980	1995
	EF	——	——	.35	.35
	MS60	.15	1.75	1.50	——
	MS65	——	——	——	6.50

1937-D/D
RPM-2 (Miller)

VARIETIES: One obverse cud is known, and it's a large one, encompassing the entire truncation of Lincoln's bust. A minor obverse doubled-die exists, affecting the motto IN GOD WE TRUST. Finally, two repunched mintmark varieties may be found (see photo).

COMMENTS: It seems that all denominations made at Denver in 1937 are generally of very high quality, and the cents are no exception. These are typically sharp and quite lustrous.

* * *

Production was up again in Fiscal Year 1937, as noted in the *Annual Report* of Director Ross:

Domestic coinage manufactured during the fiscal year ended June 30, 1937, amounting to 760,915,737 pieces, exceeded the production of any previous fiscal year in the history of the Government . . . the greater part was in the 1-cent and 5-cent denominations.[104]

One consequence of this increased demand for coins was the addition of a two-story with basement, 6,000 square-foot wing to the Denver Mint structure of 1904.

SAN FRANCISCO
34,500,000

RARITY: Very common in all grades through gem, it's likely that original rolls will still turn up when estates are sold. For the time being, there are plenty of reassembled rolls to be had, some of dubious quality.

| POPULATION: | MS BN = 0 | | MS RB = 0 | | MS RD = 303 | | TOTAL = 303 |
| TOTALS | MS67 RD = 189 | | HIGHEST = MS67 RD (189) | | | | |

VALUES:	GRADE	1950	1965	1980	1995
	EF	——	——	.40	.40
	MS60	.15	2.50	2.00	——
	MS65	——	——	——	9.00

1937-S/S
RPM-1 (Miller)

VARIETIES: Two repunched mintmarks are known (see photo), along with a very minor obverse doubled-die.

COMMENTS: Cents of this issue will turn up from moderately worn dies, but superior coins are common enough that the less desirable ones may be passed over.

The San Francisco Mint was transferred to its new facility in stages beginning in May of 1937; a dedication ceremony was held there on May 15, complete with an invocation, the requisite speeches and even several musical numbers.[105] This transitory situation resulted in no coinage of any kind from this mint during the months of June through August. In fact, no more cents were coined until after operations resumed in the new structure on October 22, 1937.[106]

By the late 1930s, collectors were receiving monthly mintage reports through the pages of *The Numismatist* and *The Numismatic Scrapbook Magazine*. Whenever coinage was delayed until late in the year (as it was frequently during the 1930s and 1940s), speculators seized on this opportunity to stock up on newly released issues and hoard them by the roll. This sort of activity was unknown to the hobby until the low mintage coins of the years 1931-33 created an entirely new market for modern issues. It may come as a surprise to collectors today to read that coin publications routinely carried dealer ads selling the current year's coinage as singles or by the roll. In an era before government issued sets of annual coinage, this was the only means for most collectors to obtain uncirculated specimens.

1938

PHILADELPHIA
156,696,734

RARITY: Common in all grades, even superb gems are usually available without too much looking. Original rolls probably exist, but these are reportedly quite difficult to find.

POPULATION:	MS BN = 0		MS RB = 2		MS RD = 258		TOTAL = 260
TOTALS	MS67 RD = 167		HIGHEST = MS67 RD (167)				

VALUES:	GRADE	1950	1965	1980	1995
	EF	——	——	.30	.30
	MS60	.10	2.25	1.60	——
	MS65	——	——	——	6.00

VARIETIES: Two minor reverse doubled-dies exist, as does a small obverse cud variety at Lincoln's shoulder.

COMMENTS: 1938-P cents are generally well struck from early to medium die states.

DENVER
20,010,000

RARITY: This date proved to be very elusive in circulation as early as the 1960s, probably as the direct result of a smaller than usual mintage. The typical number of uncirculated rolls were saved, however, so gems are no scarcer than for other dates of the period.

POPULATION:	MS BN = 0		MS RB = 0		MS RD = 475		TOTAL = 475
TOTALS	MS67 RD = 376		HIGHEST = MS67 RD (376)				

VALUES:	GRADE	1950	1965	1980	1995
	EF	——	——	.65	.65
	MS60	.15	3.00	2.50	——
	MS65	——	——	——	8.00

VARIETIES: A minor doubled-die reverse variety is known, and one of the obverses paired with this die bears a repunched mintmark. Five other repunched mintmark varieties are also known (see photo), as is an obverse cud below the date.

1938-D/D
RPM-1 (Miller)

COMMENTS: Typically well struck from fresh or only slightly worn dies, this is another date which was made with care.

After several years of hesitant economic recovery, the nation relapsed into recession during the years 1937-38. This is reflected in the lower mintages recorded for 1938.

SAN FRANCISCO
15,180,000

RARITY: Circulated examples are slightly scarcer than surrounding dates, due to their low mintage. The usual number of uncirculated rolls was set aside, and even top-notch gems are fairly abundant.

POPULATION: MS BN = 0   MS RB = 1   MS RD = 479   TOTAL = 480
TOTALS   MS67 RD = 304   HIGHEST = MS67 RD (304)

1938-S/S/S
RPM-2 (Fivaz & Stanton)

VALUES:	GRADE	1950	1965	1980	1995
	EF	——	——	.75	.75
	MS60	.15	5.00	——	——
	MS65	——	——	3.50	10.00

VARIETIES: A single retained cud variety is known for the reverse. In the "also-ran" category is a very minor obverse doubled-die which is visible only at numeral 8 in the date.

By far the most popular varieties for 1938-S are two readily distinguished repunched mintmarks. One exhibits two S mintmarks, while the second and most desired is actually tripled (see photo). Fortunately, this triple S variety is not particularly rare, and the author has been shown examples that were "cherry picked" by novice collectors. Sol Taylor notes that these "are medium die state and show some minor die breaks, stress lines, and nice mint gold color."[107] A third RPM is also known.

COMMENTS: Most rolls on the market have been picked over, so the best bet is to look for early die state, gem singles.

As in 1937, the coinage of cents at San Francisco was erratic. Just over ten million were struck in January and February, after which no more were coined until the 200,000 of November, followed by 4.8 million in December. In fact, the San Francisco Mint produced no domestic coinage from March through June. This came about as the result of several unrelated developments. The first was the recession which dominated that entire year. Also, during those months the mint was largely occupied with filling an order of coins for China. Finally, though this is merely speculation, a third cause is possible, one which while amusing on the surface carried very serious implications.

The new mint facility was formally dedicated on May 15, 1937, though the relocation process occupied the better part of 1937, '38 and into 1939. In the Winter of 1938, less than a year after the mint's opening, two teenagers named Paul Francis and William Gallagher managed to slip through a ground floor window and were surprised inside by a security guard. Their intent was not theft but mere adventure, but the Bureau of the Mint was not amused. The incident was quite embarrassing, and bars were subsequently installed over those windows which were previously thought to be too small for entry. Apparently, no one ever imagined children breaking into a United States Mint facility! The sum of $9,490 was expended on further improvements, including a five-foot high rock wall, three sets of iron gates and a series of floodlights surrounding the entire building.[108] This could account, at least in part, for the near total shutdown of the San Francisco Mint during the Spring of 1938.

1939

PHILADELPHIA
316,479,520

RARITY: This issue is quite common in circulated grades, and even fully red, superb gems are obtainable without too much searching. Original rolls almost certainly exist, but assembled ones are more prevalent.

POPULATION: MS BN = 0   MS RB = 1   MS RD = 383   TOTAL = 384
MS67 RD = 293   HIGHEST = MS67 RD (293)

VALUES:

GRADE	1950	1965	1980	1995
EF	——	——	.25	.25
MS60	.10	1.35	——	——
MS65	——	——	1.10	3.00

VARIETIES: Of two doubled-die obverse varieties known, only one is significant. While the doubling on this variety is limited to the date and LIBERTY, it's quite distinct (see photos). A very minor doubled-die reverse is also known. No less than seven obverse cuds may be found, all but one in the usual location. This last is a spectacular break, obliterating everything from 12 o'clock to 2 o'clock (see photo). Finally, two retained cuds are known for the reverse.

COMMENTS: 1939-P cents are typically well struck from early to medium die states. Sol Taylor noted that their color is more of a reddish shade than the brassy color of P-Mint cents from 1935 though 1938. This may be true, although the presence of even light toning tends to mitigate its effect.

* * *

1939-P
LC-40D-1 (Thurman & Margolis)

It was reported in 1939 that Leland Howard, acting Director of the Mint, had gone on record as saying that the Treasury Department was not contemplating any change in the design of the Lincoln Cent that year.[109] Well, there was still hope for 1940!

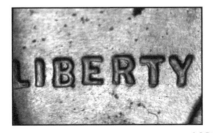

1939-P
DDO-1 (Fivaz & Stanton)

DENVER
15,160,000

RARITY: This issue was already rare in circulation by 1965 when the author began collecting Lincolns. In fact, 1939-D never was found in any grade, and an example was eventually obtained from a friend who had access to more coins. Today, however, it's available from dealers in any grade desired.

POPULATION: MS BN = 1   MS RB = 2   MS RD = 401   TOTAL = 4404
    MS67 RD = 274   HIGHEST = MS67 RD (274)

VALUES:	GRADE	1950	1965	1980	1995
	EF	——	1.75	.85	.85
	MS60	.20	6.00	——	——
	MS65	——	——	4.50	11.00

1939-D/D
RPM-1 (Miller)

VARIETIES: A single cud die break is known, this appearing opposite Lincoln's face in the 3 o'clock position. Two repunched mintmark varieties may be found (see photo).

COMMENTS: Well made and widely hoarded due to its low mintage, this date will present no problems when selecting a gem.

SAN FRANCISCO
52,070,000

RARITY: 1939-S cents were common in circulation (at least in the West) through the 1960s, and they remain abundant in dealers' stocks. Widely hoarded in Mint State rolls, even gems are fairly plentiful.

POPULATION: MS BN = 0   MS RB = 18   MS RD = 574   TOTAL = 592
    MS67 RD = 408   HIGHEST = MS67 RD (408)

VALUES:	GRADE	1950	1965	1980	1995
	EF	——	——	.40	.40
	MS60	.12	2.50	——	——
	MS65	——	——	1.75	8.00

1939-S/S
RPM-2 (Miller)

VARIETIES: A single retained cud is known for the reverse. Two repunched mintmarks are also reported (see photo).

COMMENTS: Although there are many superb gems certified, Lincoln Cent specialist Sol Taylor indicated in his book some problems with this date: "The 1939S does not compare to the other mints. Most are lackluster, medium to late die state, and reddish hues. True MS65 Red coins do not hold up to the 1939P or even the 1939D MS65 Reds."[110]

The San Francisco Mint was up to its tricks again, producing no coins at all during the months of March through June, yet putting out great numbers of cents from July through the end of the year. The recent recession was partly responsible for this period of idleness both directly and indirectly. Not only did the demand for new coins drop-off after 1936, but the lower projected need led to a reduction in the various mints' appropriations from Congress. Thus, a recession in 1937-38 led to a lower budget for Fiscal Year 1939, which ran from July 1, 1938 through June 30, 1939. When the demand for additional coins picked up in the calendar year 1939, there were no funds left for the purchasing of prepared planchets (used for cents and nickels). It's no coincidence that coinage resumed in July, as this was budgeted within the more generous Fiscal Year 1940. The U. S. Mint would be burdened with this inefficient system for decades to come, and the problem wasn't really solved until the 1990s.

Another reason for the suspension of coining during the Spring of 1939 may be found in *The Numismatic Scrapbook Magazine*. In his column for March, West Coast correspondent Roy Hill noted that the last remaining bullion housed in the old mint structure was still being relocated to the new facility and that this had led to an interruption in coining.

1940

PHILADELPHIA
586,810,000

RARITY: 1940-P is very common in all grades. There would almost certainly be a greater number of certified MS67 RD coins if the value of such pieces was higher.

POPULATION: MS BN = 0   MS RB = 3   MS RD = 238   TOTAL = 241
MS67 RD = 175   HIGHEST = MS67 RD (175)

VALUES:

GRADE	1950	1965	1980	1995
EF	——	——	.20	.20
MS60	.15	.95	——	——
MS65	——	——	1.00	3.00

VARIETIES: Numeral 4 in the date bears horizontal and vertical serifs, or "crosslets" as Walter Breen called them in his *Encyclopedia*.[111] This was a feature of the master die for 1940 and is unique to this date. Four minor doubled-die varieties exist, one obverse and three reverse. Three obverse cuds and one reverse cud are known, the latter a retained break.

COMMENTS: A tremendous mintage (the highest thus far), combined with the usual squirreling away of rolls, has made this issue quite common. Although many of these rolls may contain spotted or otherwise spoiled coins, there seems to be no shortage of gems in relation to the number of serious collectors desiring them.

* * *

After a slump in coinage activity during the latter part of 1937 and through early 1939, the result of a slowdown in the economic recovery, things picked up toward the end of 1939, and new records were set:

Domestic coin manufactured during the fiscal year ending June 30, 1940, amounting to 768,090,830 pieces, exceeded the production of any previous fiscal year in the history of the Government. As in previous years, the coin most largely produced was the 1-cent piece.[112]

* * *

The suddenness with which a shortage of cents can take hold is revealed in this account from 1940:

According to a press dispatch of July 1, the Philadelphia mint was out of cents on that date. A stock of 384,130,000 was reported to be on hand June 24 but the new tax laws effective July 1 created a demand for cents all over the country.

It is said that the mint has a production capacity of 1,400,000 cents on an 8-hour shift or a total of 4,200,000 a day when three shifts are working.

It is not likely that 1940 Philadelphia cents will ever be scarce if the mint goes on a 24-hour cent schedule.[113]

This may have been exactly what the mint did, as shortly later it was reported that finished planchets were again being ordered from outside contractors, something not generally done after the heavy coinages of 1916-20. These blanks were furnished by the Riverside Metal Company of Riverside, New Jersey, which provided some 60,000,000 cent planchets.[114] The use of commercially prepared strip and/or planchets became increasingly common after this time, and modern cent coinage is struck entirely on planchets purchased from contractors.

DENVER
81,390,000

RARITY: 1940-D is common in all grades through superb gem MS67 RD.

POPULATION: MS BN = 0 MS RB = 1 MS RD = 270 TOTAL = 271
MS67 RD = 239 HIGHEST = MS67 RD (239)

VALUES:

GRADE	1950	1965	1980	1995
EF	——	——	.25	.25
MS60	.10	1.25	——	——
MS65	——	——	1.00	4.00

VARIETIES: Three obverse cuds are known. One is in the usual position below Lincoln's shoulder, while the others are at 2 o'clock and 10-11 o'clock, respectively. The latter obscures most of IN GOD, and such varieties have been labeled "atheist cents" (see photo). One very minor doubled-die may be found for the reverse, as well as five repunched mintmarks (see photo).

Walter Breen's listing in his *Encyclopedia* of "Plain 4" and "Crosslet 4" varieties is misleading. The cents of this date did have tiny horizontal and vertical serifs on numeral 4, but the plain variety appears to be simply a later die-state in which the serifs have been polished away.

COMMENTS: Nearly all uncirculated cents of this date are well struck from early to medium state dies.

* * *

A shortage of coins developed at the beginning of 1940, as prosperity returned to the United States after a decade of severe economic depression:

1940-D/D
RPM-2 (Miller)

1940-D
LC-40D-1 (Thurman & Margolis)

Mrs. Nellie Tayloe Ross, Director of the Mint, said that an increased demand for coins has forced operation of the Philadelphia and Denver Mints on twenty-four hour schedules, and the one at San Francisco on sixteen hours daily. She said that it had been necessary to draw on the Denver Mint for coin shipments to the Philadelphia region. Better business conditions are attributed as the cause.[115]

SAN FRANCISCO
112,940,000

RARITY: Common in all grades through superb gem, original rolls likely exist.

POPULATION: MS BN = 0   MS RB = 0   MS RD = 385   TOTAL = 385
             MS67 RD = 288   HIGHEST = MS67 RD (288)

VALUES:

GRADE	1950	1965	1980	1995
EF	——	——	.25	.25
MS60	.10	1.50	——	——
MS65	——	——	1.00	5.00

VARIETIES: A single reverse doubled-die is known, this one fairly minor. In addition, no less than seven repunched mintmark varieties exist (see photos).

The dies used at San Francisco must have been improperly hardened or somehow mis-set in the press, as this date has an extraordinarily large number of cud varieties. Nine obverses are known, two of them retained breaks, along with some 39 reverse cuds, all but two of them retained breaks One of these is even a dual cud, both wheat ears showing breaks. The many cud breaks of this and all other years of the series are thoroughly documented in a series of articles which began in the August 1994 issue of *Error Trends Coin Magazine* and at press time was expected to run through the Summer of 1996.

In his *Encyclopedia,* the late Walter Breen listed several varieties for this date, among these a large S mintmark of the sort employed in 1941 and subsequent years.[116] The author of this book has never seen a large S for 1940 and doubts that it actually exists. This newer size of mintmark was not introduced until 1941, and more will be found about it under the listing for 1941-S. Also a bit misleading is Breen's listing of "Plain 4" and "Crosslet 4" varieties. All the cents of this date were coined with short horizontal and vertical serifs on numeral 4, but the plain variety appears to be simply a later die-state in which the serifs have been polished away.

 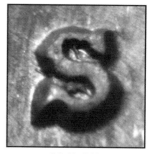

1940-S/S   **1940-S/S**
RPM-2 (Miller)   *RPM-4b (Miller)*

COMMENTS: Worn dies are more common for this date than for those S-Mint cents of the several preceding years. The large coinage for this issue may have caused overusage of the dies in an economy measure. Certainly, the number of cud varieties for this date seems to suggest this.

After coining cents in the months of January through April, the San Francisco Mint suspended this denomination until September. They were thereafter struck regularly through the end of the year.[117] Peculiar lapses such as this were typical of the San Francisco Mint throughout much of the 1940s and early 1950s and contributed to the Treasury Department's decision to cease coining there altogether in 1955.

Toward the end of the year, however, the demand for new S-Mint coins rose sharply:

The Philadelphia mint, which normally supplies the entire area east of the Mississippi, has been unable to keep up with the demand for minor coins in the east, and it was necessary for Chicago to draw on the Denver mint during September and October, however, this source of supply ran low, too, and 163 tons of San Francisco mint coins were delivered to the Federal Reserve Bank during November. A sizable fleet of express trucks was required to deliver the coins. It is believed that this is the first time that "S" mint coins have been brought as far east as Chicago for distribution.[118]

1941

PHILADELPHIA
887,039,100

RARITY: Common in all grades through fully red gem.

POPULATION:

MS BN = 0	MS RB = 1	MS RD = 336	TOTAL = 337
MS67 RD = 268	HIGHEST = MS67 RD (268)		

VALUES:

GRADE	1950	1965	1980	1995
EF	——	——	.20	.20
MS60	.10	1.00	——	——
MS65	——	——	.75	3.00

VARIETIES: Four obverse cuds are known, one of them retained. For the reverse, three are known, all retained breaks. This issue is rich in obverse doubled-die varieties (see photos). There are five in all, including one rotated clockwise and two rotated counterclockwise. The remaining two are less spectacular, and one of these is visible merely as a thickening of LIBERTY and the date. A minor reverse doubled-die variety is also known, slightly visible as a thickening of E PLURIBUS UNUM.

1941-P
DDO-1, Breen-2155 (Fivaz & Stanton)

COMMENTS: Countless rolls were saved of this and all subsequent dates for the next 25 years, until the craze for rolls subsided during the mid 1960s. Consequently, this issue is readily available by the roll, though the quality of these coins may be variable due to spotting and unattractive toning. Sharply struck, gem singles are nevertheless always available.

1941-P
DDO-2 (Fivaz & Stanton)

For years, collectors have puzzled over the "thick" cents of this date. First discovered that same year, they caused quite a stir in Chicago, as reported by Lee F. Hewitt, editor of *The Numismatic Scrapbook Magazine*:

Well, inflation is here! The cents (at least a few of them) are now almost a third larger. It seems that one of the downtown Chicago banks was busy rolling four million bright new 1941 cents and the counting machine was "stuck" several times by coins that were too thick And working in that said bank is a chap who keeps his eyes open for numismatic items and he charged the inflated cents to his account. Next a tour of the dealers was made; of course, the pieces were easily sold.

The dealer who brought one to us for examination expressed the belief that an even dozen of the coins were found and he had purchased all of them. It seems that a few more turned up as other dealers now have them too.

The piece we had for examination weighed 63 grains which is 15 more than the standard 48 grains. Its thickness is slightly more than that of a five-cent nickel; otherwise it has the appearance of any ordinary 1941 Philadelphia mint cent.

These "thick" cents were probably caused by one of the rolling machines not doing its work properly. How many strips were rolled too thick before the error was discovered is problematical, however, it does seem to us that about 400 blanks are cut out of each strip, so if only one strip went thru thick, then the 1941 inflated cents can be classified as a rarity.[119]

Hewitt's inquiry addressed to Philadelphia Mint Superintendent Edwin H. Dressel drew a similar explanation, though Dressel added that each strip produced 390 blanks and that there were six strips formed from each ingot.[120]

It was later determined by numismatists that these coins were probably the result of planchets intended for one of the Philadelphia Mint's foreign contract coinages being struck by Lincoln Cent dies. Possible candidates include the Panamanian 1-1/4 centesimos coin, of which 1,600,000 were coined with the date 1940, or the Dominican Republic one-centavo piece, of which some 2,000,000 were struck and dated 1941.[121] Such planchets may have become lodged inside one of the large tote bins, only to work free when the bin was again loaded with U. S. one-cent planchets.

DENVER
128,700,000

RARITY: 1941-D is common in all grades. Original rolls still exist.

POPULATION:

MS BN = 0	MS RB = 3	MS RD = 703	TOTAL = 706
MS67 RD = 617	HIGHEST = MS67 RD (617)		

VALUES:

GRADE	1950	1965	1980	1995
EF	——	——	.25	.25
MS60	.10	1.50	——	——
MS65	——	——	2.75	7.50

VARIETIES: Two obverse cud varieties are known. One of these obliterates the word GOD, a variety popularly called the "atheist" cent (see photo). Single doubled-die varieties are known for either obverse or reverse, but these are quite minor. Eight repunched mintmarks are also documented (see photo).

COMMENTS: This issue is slightly more subject to worn dies than many surrounding issues. Enough sharp ones survive, however, that a suitable coin may be found.

1941-D proved to be strangely scarce in circulation as early as 1965, when the author began his collecting. In fact, this issue and 1954-P were the only cents after 1939 that ultimately had to be purchased to complete his collection.

1941-D/D
RPM-1 (Miller)

1941-D
LC-41D-2 (Thurman & Margolis)

SAN FRANCISCO
92,360,000

RARITY: Superb gem MS67 RD singles exist in plentiful supply, as the figures below suggest. Original rolls still exist, although they may contain mediocre coins.

POPULATION: MS BN = 0   MS RB = 0   MS RD = 429   TOTAL = 429
MS67 RD = 368   HIGHEST = MS67 RD (368)

VALUES:

GRADE	1950	1965	1980	1995
EF	——	——	.30	.30
MS60	.10	1.70	——	——
MS65	——	——	4.00	9.00

VARIETIES: The most noteworthy variety for this issue features the new large S mintmark punch introduced this year for the cent through quarter dollar and in 1942 for the half dollar. Although not rare in an absolute sense, large S coins are outnumbered by those bearing the small S of 1917-40 by about 15 to one.

This variety is routinely ignored by most collectors and dealers, despite being of more potential interest than the many repunched mintmarks. The coin illustrated above is of the small S variety, while that shown in close-up is of the large S variety. The close-ups also reveal mechanical or strike doubling. This is due to looseness in the die or the press and is not the same as die doubling. Note the flat and shallow quality of the secondary image; this is a clue to its nature. Coins with this form of doubling carry little or no premium and must not be confused with doubled-die varieties.

There are no less than 10 repunched mintmark varieties known for this issue (see photo); all but two are of the large S. 1941-S is a fertile date for cuds, as well. One obverse variety is known, along with nine for the reverse; all but two of these are retained breaks.

The different mintmark sizes were spotted by collectors at that time and generated several letters of inquiry, prompting Lee F. Hewitt, Editor of *The Numismatic Scrapbook Magazine*, to pursue the matter further:

> While touring the Mint last month we asked Mr. Sinnock, the chief engraver, about "large and small mint marks." He stated that only ONE punch for each mint was used so the mint marks had to be the same size — at least during his thirty years at the mint the same punches have been used. When a die wears the mint mark may appear to be thicker.[122]

While it's remotely possible that Sinnock didn't know that his assistants were using more than one style of punch, his response is far too typical of the U. S. Mint's attitude toward numismatists during the period of approximately 1920-70. Having since learned that knowledgeable collectors can't be fooled, the Mint now has a less defensive posture.

COMMENTS: 1941-S cents are difficult to locate in problem-free condition. Many were coined from overused dies which were moderately worn, and the certified population of gem coins may include some of these on the basis of overall eye appeal. For reasons unknown, this date also comes more often toned or spotted than many surrounding issues.

After coining 2,870,000 cents in January, the San Francisco Mint did not strike this denomination again until August. From then through the end of the year, many millions were turned out. Actually, none of the three mints produced domestic coinage during the months of February through April, as they were entirely engaged in filling foreign orders.[123]

1941-S/S
Small S, RPM-1, Breen 256 (Miller)

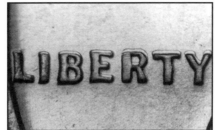 

1941-S
Large S, Breen 2157, with strike doubling

1942

PHILADELPHIA
657,828,600

RARITY: 1942-P is very common in all grades. The low certified population reflects a lack of value and should not suggest rarity. Original rolls still exist.

POPULATION: MS BN = 0   MS RB = 0   MS RD = 150   TOTAL = 150

MS67 RD = 98   HIGHEST = MS67 RD (98)

VALUES:

GRADE	1950	1965	1980	1995
EF	——	——	.20	.20
MS60	.10	.60	——	——
MS65	——	——	.45	2.00

VARIETIES: Two obverse and one reverse doubled-die varieties are known, all of them fairly minor. A single reverse cud may be found in the familiar position between the right wheat ear and the rim.

COMMENTS: Both early and medium die-state cents are common for this issue, so collectors will want to hold out for a sharp one.

* * *

These cents were coined in the normal alloy of 95% copper, 4% zinc and 1% tin, as well as with virtually all tin removed. This action was prompted by the lack of adequate supplies in the United States. Tin was obtained primarily from Bolivia, and the waters off of South America were heavily patrolled by German submarines and surface raiders. The U. S. Treasury Department ordered that tin be deleted effective January 23, 1942, though any existing stock of the old alloy could be used up. There are conflicting accounts from this period as to whether tin was deleted altogether or its percentage in each coin merely reduced. The Mint Director's Report curiously says nothing on the matter. Whatever the exact action taken, the resulting coins are indistinguishable from previous issues by appearance alone.

Copper too was soon in short supply, as America's domestic production was normally supplemented by Chile's output. This situation ultimately led to the ill-advised adoption of zinc-plated steel for cent coinage in 1943. The circumstances which prompted such a drastic measure are summed up in this following account from *The Numismatist*:

> The United States Mint, seeking to conserve vital war metal, has curtailed production of one-cent pieces by 50 percent in recent months, according to a report made to Secretary Morgenthau.

However, demand for coins, arising from the high level of business, continues at an unprecedented rate, seriously threatening this conservation program.

Production of pennies in September was 59 million pieces, a moderate rise over August, but only about half the production level of the early summer.

Mrs. Nellie Tayloe Ross, Director of the Mint, asked that all coins, and especially one-cent pieces now "hiding" in children's banks and other receptacles, be returned to circulation. She pointed out that if each of an estimated 33,000,000 American families should discover and return to use just ten one-cent pieces, and these should stay in circulation, the Nation's supply would be increased by an amount equal to one-third of the record 1941 production of the coin. More than 1,000 tons of copper might thus be saved for war manufacture, she said.[124]

During much of 1942 the U. S. Mint experimented with various substitutes for the conventional copper-zinc-tin alloy. Not all of these were metallic, as several plastic compounds were also tested. For more about these interesting trial pieces see Chapter 2.

DENVER
206,698,000

RARITY: This issue is common in all grades, and original rolls still exist.

POPULATION: MS BN = 0   MS RB = 1   MS RD = 236   TOTAL = 237
MS67 RD = 125   HIGHEST = MS68 RD (1)

VALUES:

GRADE	1950	1965	1980	1995
EF	——	——	.20	.20
MS60	.10	.65	——	——
MS65	——	——	.65	3.00

VARIETIES: Two minor obverse doubled-dies exist, along with 10 repunched mint-mark varieties (see photo).

COMMENTS: Like 1941-D, many were coined from medium die state, softly worn dies. Collectors will want to hold out for one which combines excellent color with a decent strike.

The order of January 23 eliminating or reducing tin from the cent's alloy presumably led to the coining of both varieties at the Denver Mint, though there's no practical way to distinguish one from the other.

1942-D/D
RPM-2 (Miller)

* * *

As America's first year of involvement in World War II drew to a close, cents were in increasingly short supply, as this contemporary account reveals:

Agitation continues for restoring to circulation the hundreds of millions of cents that have been issued in recent years. The shortage of copper is critical, and no doubt some more or less drastic change will need to be made in the metallic content of the smallest of our coins.

Word comes from Washington that the Treasury is urging 30 million school children to enlist in a pre-Christmas drive to put these idle coins to work.[125]

SAN FRANCISCO
85,590,000

RARITY: 1942-S cents are slightly scarce in fully struck, fully red gem, though perhaps not as much as the listed value suggests. Original rolls still exist.

POPULATION: MS BN = 0   MS RB = 0   MS RD = 552   TOTAL = 552

MS67 RD = 199   HIGHEST = MS67 RD (199)

VALUES:

GRADE	1950	1965	1980	1995
EF	——	——	.45	.45
MS60	.20	4.75	——	——
MS65	——	——	6.00	18.00

VARIETIES: A couple of obverse doubled-dies may be found. These are minor, though one is of greater interest because it also features a repunched mintmark, one of 13 known for this date (see photo). Three obverse cuds are reported, along with five for the reverse, all of them retained breaks.

All 1942-S cents seen by the author have borne the large S mintmark which debuted in 1941. It's possible, however, that some may turn up with the style of mint-mark used for 1943.

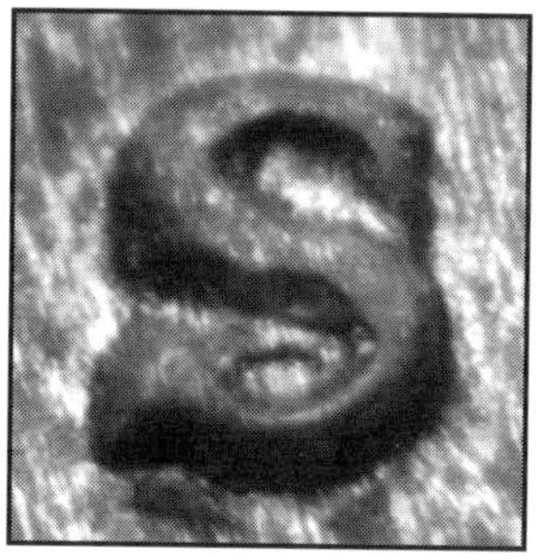

COMMENTS: Many of this date are from slightly to moderately worn dies. Their color tends to be a bit subdued, as well. It's not certain whether this had anything to do with the change of alloy ordered early in the year.

From January through March, the San Francisco Mint coined cents alone, per-haps to make up for getting a late start in 1941. Cents were produced there in lesser numbers for most of the year as well, but virtually halted by December.[126] During the Christmas season, merchants in the San Francisco region were reportedly rounding all change to the nearest five cents.[127]

1942-S/S
RPM-2 (Miller)

1943

PHILADELPHIA
684,628,670

RARITY: This issue is pretty much unknown below the grade of Very Good, as all steel cents had virtually disappeared from circulation by 1960. Gems are very common, but their preservation should be a primary concern for anyone owning such coins.

POPULATION: MS TOTAL = 571
MS67 = 532   HIGHEST = MS68 (1)

VALUES:

GRADE	1950	1965	1980	1995
EF	——	——	.30	.30
MS60	.10	1.00	——	——
MS65	——	——	.70	4.00

VARIETIES: The steel planchets were very hard on dies, and many cud breaks are found. No less than 30 obverse cuds have been documented, five of them retained breaks. There are 13 for the reverse, all but three retained (see photo). In the realm of doubled-dies, collectors may find two for the obverse and two for the reverse, all of them minor.

1943-P
LC-43-7R (Thurman & Margolis)

COMMENTS: 1943-P cents are usually well struck, and many survive with their brilliant, pristine surfaces intact. Since these surfaces are zinc, a quite reactive metal, preserving their beauty requires that the coins be kept away from air and moisture, the two principal components of oxidation. Zinc readily corrodes to a whitish, powdery texture, while the underlying steel is subject to plain old rusting. A worse combination of metals for coinage could not have been devised by a madman, and their use during 1943 reveals the critical situation in which the United States of America found itself.

Cents dated 1943 are noteworthy for the fact that a correctly styled numeral 3 was employed for only the second time since the series' inception; the other occasion was in 1934.

No cents of any kind were coined during the month of January, while only the Philadelphia Mint struck them during February. It's possible that the requisite planchets were not yet ready. The steel used for this issue was known to be harder than the bronze and brass alloys used previously, so the mints were required to reduce the set distance between dies when coining cents. This compensated in part for the harder metal and resulted in coins which are generally quite well struck. When deficiencies are present, they tend to manifest themselves in the peripheral mottos, which may be indistinct at the borders.

The coining of several examples in the bronze alloy was probably unintentional. Although wrong-planchet errors exist for many dates within the Lincoln series, their occurrence during 1943-44 was so obvious that they've held the fascination of collectors ever since the first piece surfaced in 1947. See Chapter 4 for additional information.

By the middle of 1943 it was already evident that this experiment was an unqualified failure. So many complaints were received from persons who mistook these cents for dimes that the Mint was already preparing to return to the copper and zinc alloy used for most of 1942. It waited until the first of the year, however, as every precaution was taken to prevent further confusion and the creation of unintentional rarities. In the meantime, steel cents were distributed only when existing supplies of the earlier cents had been exhausted. This happened all too quickly, as the demand for cents during 1941-43 was seemingly insatiable. The immediate goal of saving copper for the war effort was effective, Mint Director Ross estimating that during Fiscal Year 1944 (July 1, 1943 to June 30, 1944), some 3,194 tons of copper, 350 tons of nickel and 120 tons of zinc had been spared through the coinage of steel cents and copper-silver-manganese five-cent pieces.[128]

* * *

One interesting tale of cents, the sort of story that could only come from World War II, puts an amusing spin on the situation. In his column "News and Views," numismatic writer Joseph Coffin revealed what happened:

> The cent was featured in another way in the daily press through the unprecedented demand for the insignificant coin, which led to a real shortage in many sections of the country. Shortage or not, the papers recently carried pictures of a bomber with $1,000 in cents and other coins pasted on its sides, when a workman started the idea by pasting a cent he had found on the side of the plane "for luck." The money was given to the Army's War Orphans fund.[129]

DENVER
217,660,000

RARITY: There is no reason to think that this issue is anything but common in superb gem, as the figures indicate. Circulated coins are usually quite dark and/or corroded.

POPULATION: MS TOTAL = 2212
MS67 = 1777   HIGHEST = MS68 (34)

VALUES:

GRADE	1950	1965	1980	1995
EF	——	——	.30	.30
MS60	.10	1.10	——	——
MS65	——	——	1.00	4.50

VARIETIES: Some 17 repunched mintmarks are known, of which RPM-1 is the most appealing (see photo). Despite the destructive potential of steel planchets, only a single obverse cud variety is documented.

COMMENTS: Popular only with coin collectors, many rolls of this issue were saved. If left in their original paper wrappers or stored improperly, these will have become spotted and corroded by now. Enough gems survive, however, that there should be a coin for every collector. The popularity of encapsulation will almost certainly assist in their preservation.

1943-D/D
RPM-1, Breen-2169 (Miller)

A newspaper for its employees, *The Denver Mint Reporter*, acknowledged the difficulty in producing steel cents. Describing them as "terribly hard on dies," it added that die life had been severely reduced and that dies were being replaced with much greater frequency.[130]

A cottage industry has long existed in stripping and replating steel cents, both worn and unworn examples. In a less enlightened time, mercury was often used. More common now is to plate these stripped cents with chromium. While quite attractive to the inexperienced eye, these "processed" coins are of no numismatic value whatsoever, yet they can still be an inexpensive entry to the hobby for someone who had previously never thought of coins as anything but money.

Only a single authentic 1943-D cent in bronze alloy has been confirmed (see Chapter 4).

* * *

The introduction of steel cents was cause for concern within businesses handling large quantities of them. These included banks, as related in the following account from *The Kansas City Star*:

Gloversville, N. Y. bank patrons saw a pile of bright, silvery coins on a counter and a sign reading, "The new pennies—take one." The bank was giving away 3,000 of the steel pennies prior to their general circulation in the city.[131]

Despite efforts by the government and businesses to promote acceptance of the new coins, they were almost universally disliked. *The Minneapolis Star Journal* reported how one disgruntled merchant took action:

He doesn't like steel pennies, so Gerald Martin, Joliet, Ill., news vendor, is waging a one-man campaign to take them out of circulation. He recently turned 7,775 steel pennies over to the internal revenue office as his income tax payment. He had 1,875 pennies left over for a bond.[132]

SAN FRANCISCO
191,550,000

RARITY: Of the three steel cent issues, this is the scarcest in gem, though the population data suggests that they're anything but extinct. Rolls of mediocre quality still exist.

POPULATION: MS TOTAL = 1753
MS67 = 938   HIGHEST = MS68 (4)

VALUES:

GRADE	1950	1965	1980	1995
EF	——	——	.55	.55
MS60	.15	2.25	——	——
MS65	——	——	1.75	10.00

VARIETIES: Five repunched mintmarks are recorded, along with two minor doubled-dies, one obverse and one reverse.

A new 'S' mintmark punch having distinct serifs of equal size was used for all 1943-S cents. Its use continued into 1944.

As in the past several years, the San Francisco Mint produced a great many cud varieties. Some 16 are known for the obverse, four of them retained breaks. There are ten reported for the reverse, all but two of them retained. Of the varieties enumerated, one features a mating of one obverse cud and one reverse cud!

COMMENTS: 1943-S cents are a bit sharper than in several of the preceding years, probably because the mint compensated for the hardness of their metal by diminishing the set distance between obverse and reverse dies.

Although saved in vast numbers, the majority of Mint State coins have deteriorated to some degree over the intervening decades. White spotting and even a slight encrustation are not unusual. In *The Standard Guide to the*

Lincoln Cent Sol Taylor notes that "The true BU coins have a bluish haze over a steel silvery surface. These are the gems which have been submitted for encapsulation."

A few 1943-S cents were unintentionally produced on bronze planchets leftover from 1942. For more about these popular errors, see Chapter 4.

* * *

While steel cents were a nuisance at best, they posed a serious health threat to any small child inclined to swallow them. Reacting with stomach acids, the zinc could prove deadly. Fortunately, there appear to have been no fatalities among the little folk, though a hapless seal succumbed in 1945. A follow up account was published in *The San Francisco Chronicle* for October 7, 1946:

> It looks as if Oscar, Golden Gate Park's late great collector of coins, has left estate litigation in her wake.
>
> Oscar, who was a lady, swallowed coins thrown by a generous public for three years at the park's Academy of Sciences.
>
> Zinc chloride poisoning from wartime coins killed Oscar. In her stomach were found 514 pennies, 27 nickels, 8 dimes, 1 quarter, 1 Canadian penny, 1 street car token and 1 amusement token.
>
> This adds up roughly to $7.83 1/3, which is a lot of dough for a three-year-old seal, but Oscar should've known she couldn't take it with her.
>
> Latest reports from the Academy indicate that the scramble is on for Oscar's life savings. Dr. Robert C. Miller, Academy director, says he has received requests for the coins from coin collectors all over the country.
>
> Some of the letters express great sympathy for Oscar's demise. One comes from fourth graders at the Germantown Friends School in Philadelphia who condemn a "Publick" who would feed zinc coins to seals. They want one of the pennies.
>
> Another is from a young street-car token collector in Fort Worth, Tex., who wants the lone token found in Oscar and sent a Fort Worth token in exchange.

1944

PHILADELPHIA
1,435,400,000

RARITY: Common in all grades Very Good and higher, many rolls still exist. The number of certified specimens is reduced because of this coin's value, even when in high grades.

POPULATION: MS TOTAL = 189   HIGHEST = MS67 RD (88)

VALUES:

GRADE	1950	1965	1980	1995
MS60	.05	.60	——	——
MS65	——	——	.30	1.10

VARIETIES: Two obverse and one reverse doubled-die varieties are illustrated in *The Lincoln Cent Doubled Die* by John A. Wexler, all of them very minor.

This issue is very rich in cud varieties. Curiously, all 25 of them are on the obverse, most in the familiar position below Lincoln's bust. A few "atheist" cuds are included which obscure the motto IN GOD WE TRUST (see photo).

Although not actually varieties as such, zinc-coated steel cents were coined by error from dies dated 1944. More about these rare coins will be found in Chapter 4.

1944-P
LC-44-5c (Thurman & Margolis)

COMMENTS: The steel cents of 1943 proved a miserable failure, one that rightly should have been anticipated by Congress and the Mint. No one wished to continue them into 1944, and they probably would have been aborted during 1943 had not the fear of creating rarities prevented it. Inadvertently, however, such prizes were coined by accident when leftover steel planchets found their way between 1944 dies.

Much publicity was given to the recycling of spent shellcases from the battlefront in providing the metal for the cents of 1944 and following years. This was indeed done, the 70% copper content of the shellcases being augmented with pure copper stock to bring the ingots up to the proper content of 95% copper and 5% zinc. The amount of metal coming from this source, however, was entirely insufficient to provide for the tremendous coinages of these years, and it's likely that the main value of this program was in propaganda and morale building.

The color of these coins was reportedly a bit yellower than for pre-war issues, but this has proved difficult to confirm from modern observation. Most survivors show at least some toning, and those that don't appear only slightly more pale. Although gems may be readily found, most uncirculated cents have some discoloration in the form of streaks and/or spotting. Dr. Sol Taylor attributed this problem to chemical residue from explosives in the shellcases, but since this source of metal made up only a portion of that required, another cause seems likely. Given the generally poor quality of coins made during World War II, it may have just been that the usual care extended in the preparation of ingots and strip was simply bypassed for the sake of expediency.

The absence of the 1% tin usually employed seems to have had no effect whatsoever. It's surprising that this trace element was restored in 1947 only to be deleted once and for all in 1962. Commenting on the new cents, numismatic columnist Joseph Coffin remarked: "While there is no change in design, the cents do look a little lighter in color than the old copper cents, although the change is hardly noticeable, due, no doubt, to the fact that new copper is used along with reclaimed shell copper."[133]

A few cents of this date and mint were coined on zinc-coated steel planchets by error. More about these will be found in Chapter 4.

* * *

The huge mintage of cents this year and their ready acceptance by the public brought to an end the cent scarcity of 1941-43, as noted in *The Numismatic Scrapbook Magazine*:

> The shortage of cents which had the Philadelphia Mint working on a 24-hour basis has been relieved. No reason for the slackening of demand is given. However, in spite of all the pleading of Treasury officials, we read of a man in West Hartford, Conn., who carted three boxes containing 7,500 cents to the bank for a $100 war bond. Maybe getting those 7,500 back in circulation helped to relieve the shortage.[134]

The record mintage for this issue was noted by numismatists of the time. It was observed that during Fiscal Year 1944 the three mints combined produced an average of 62 cents per second, as opposed to 10 per second in 1939. It was also believed that this manic coining accounted for the greater number of errors being found by collectors.[135]

DENVER
430,578,000

RARITY: Cents of this mint are common in all grades Very Good and higher, and original rolls still exist.

POPULATION: MS TOTAL = 160 HIGHEST = MS67 RD (81)

VALUES:

GRADE	1950	1965	1980	1995
MS60	.05	.60	———	———
MS65	———	———	.30	1.50

VARIETIES: Given the large mintage of this issue, it's surprising that so few cud breaks occurred. Only three are known for the obverse and just a single one on the reverse. A minor obverse doubled-die exists, as well.

The most highly sought variety of this issue is the overmintmarked 1944-D/S. There are actually two varieties with this repunching; the more desirable has a fairly distinct letter S above and partly covered by letter D. On the lesser variety, letter D covers much more of letter S, which is most visible to the left of the D. Both varieties are very scarce in gem condition (see photos).

The large number of dies required for this extensive coinage produced no less than 12 repunched D mintmarks (see photo).

A few cents of this date and mint were coined on zinc-coated steel planchets by error. More about these will be found in Chapter 4.

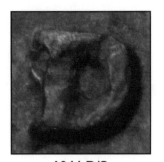

1944-D/D
RPM-2a (Miller)

1944-D/S
OMM-1, Breen-2177
(Fivaz & Stanton)

1944-D/S
OMM-2, Breen-2177
(Fivaz & Stanton)

COMMENTS: 1944-D cents are perhaps the best made of the six issues from the years 1944-45. They are more consistently well struck and bright, though a certain amount of die wear is usually evident from overextended use. For years these coins were carelessly handled because of their low value, and many of those now seen will evidence unattractive toning, spotting, etc.

SAN FRANCISCO
282,760,000

RARITY: 1944-S cents are common in all grades Very Good and higher. These were widely hoarded, and many rolls of mediocre quality survive.

POPULATION: MS TOTAL = 142   HIGHEST = MS67 RD (61)

VALUES:	GRADE	1950	1965	1980	1995
	MS60	.05	.75	——	——
	MS65	——	——	.35	1.50

VARIETIES: Only two obverse cuds are known, both below Lincoln's bust. Two obverse doubled-dies, both trivial, are also confirmed along with nine repunched mintmark varieties.

     The mintmark punch used in 1943 was continued this year, though it never appeared afterward. Some 1944-S cents bear the mintmark used for the 1945-S issue. This is readily distinguished by its rounded knobs in place of sharp serifs. It's not certain which is scarcer, but collectors presently don't seem to care.

COMMENTS: The typical 1944-S cent reveals the haste with which it was made. Many are from very shallow and worn dies and may show streaky or hazy toning. With so many uncirculated coins saved, however, gems may still be found amidst the countless thousands of poorer quality examples.

     The coinage of cents was suspended at the San Francisco Mint after July. This action was prompted by the impending recapture of The Philippines by Allied forces. San Francisco's supply of brass planchet strip was diverted to producing and coining one-centavo pieces of the pre-war Philippine type. These were shipped overseas in the Fall and were on hand not long after the first landings in October.[136]

* * *

     An important tool in achieving the tremendous domestic and foreign mintages recorded during 1944-45 was the adoption of the dual-die collar. This device, the invention of San Francisco Mint employees Joseph Steel and William P. Kruse, permitted the placement of two die pairs in a single press, fitted with a single collar having two openings. Steel, Superintendent of Coining, and Kruse, the mint's machinist, devised this clever tool late in 1943, and it increased a coin press' output by 90%.[137] In 1952, these individuals were awarded cash bonuses of $10,000 each for their invention, which the Mint estimated had already saved some two million dollars![138] This device was later adapted to all other denominations. In the 1960s, the U. S. Mint expanded on this concept with the quad-die collar, which provided for four die pairs and thus produced four coins in a single stroke.

* * *

Another story which could only have been told during the war years is this amusing item from *The Numismatist*:

"This cent has been to war! Mined in Utah, fabricated into a shell case by the Ordnance Department, shipped to the South Pacific, fired at the Japs, returned to Tooele Ordnance Depot as a fired cartridge case, reclaimed and shipped to U. S. Mints, returned to Tooele Ordnance Depot as a United States coin and presented to you as a souvenir of the T. O. D."

We are indebted to Norman Shultz of Salt Lake City for sending along one of these interesting 1944-S souvenir cents. It's attached to a neatly printed card and is rather a novel idea.[139]

Perhaps the most revolutionary social change of World War II was the entry into the workplace of large numbers of women. The U. S. Mints were not immune to such a development, as their workload had increased dramatically at a time when labor was in short supply. *The Numismatist* reported on this situation as it affected the San Francisco Mint:

For the first time in history, women are making money in San Francisco. Literally, that is.

By the sackful, the ladies are turning it out in the heavily-guarded United States Mint which supplies federal reserve banks in Salt Lake City, Seattle, Portland, Los Angeles and San Francisco.

Although this is not the first time women have been employed at the San Francisco mint, it is the first time they've had a hand at actually manufacturing the money, says Supt. P. J. Haggerty.

Years ago women employees were hired to weigh the coins, but retired when modern weighing machinery replaced the slow, tedious, by-hand method. Women also have been used in clerical posts and at one time were employed as machine "feeders." It was not until masculine money makers marched off to war, however, that many women came to work in the mint.

Today, the mint employs 72 women as punching machine operators; on the reviewing table where they pounce upon odd-sized or badly-stamped coins; at the automatic weighing machine, where coins are rejected if so much as a hair's weight above or below tolerance; on the counting and stacking machines and as press operators.

A. R. Hodgson, chief clerk, says the women are good workers, although they need help in heaving money bags around. Each is under civil service, investigated carefully by the Secret Service and hired for her "good character and honesty."[140]

The total number of employees (both men and women) was then at an inflated figure of 2687, due to the tremendous demand for both domestic and foreign coinage.[141]

1945

PHILADELPHIA
1,040,515,000

RARITY: Common in all grades Very Good and higher through fully red gem, original rolls still exist.

POPULATION: MS TOTAL = 61   HIGHEST = MS67 RD (24)

VALUES:

GRADE	1950	1965	1980	1995
MS60	.05	.70	——	——
MS65	——	——	.35	1.25

VARIETIES: Two trivial doubled-die varieties are known, one each on obverse and reverse. This issue is rich in cud varieties, some 23 in all. Nine are on the obverse, the remainder on the reverse. Ten of the reverse cuds are retained breaks, including one which exists in two die states with only the first one retained.

COMMENTS: Cents of this date are subject to streaking and other forms of discoloration, but their sheer numbers allow for a bit of shopping. Fully bright, early die state gems may be found, yet their certified population is low due to a lack of incentive for submitting such inexpensive coins.

      After its promising show in fashioning the date numerals for 1943, the Mint once again regressed during 1945 by utilizing a squat numeral 5 which lacked the requisite tail. This was to be nearly the last time, however, as recognition of the appropriate styling in date numerals became universal for the Lincoln Cent series, with the exceptions of 1957 and 1970.

DENVER
266,268,000

RARITY: Common in all grades Very Good and higher, original rolls still exist.

POPULATION: MS TOTAL = 109   HIGHEST = MS67 RD (59)

VALUES:

GRADE	1950	1965	1980	1995
MS60	.05	.65	——	——
MS65	——	——	.70	1.50

VARIETIES: Only one minor obverse doubled-die is known, but there are no less than 14 repunched mintmark varieties (see photo). What's most surprising is that only one obverse cud break is known.

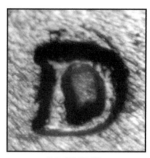

1945-D/D
RPM-3 (Miller)

COMMENTS: Most uncirculated cents of this date are of so-so quality, with a fair amount of spotting and streaking. Careful shopping, however, will reveal a number of well struck, fully red gems.

No cents were coined at the Denver Mint during the months of May through August.[142] Throughout the war years, the various U. S. mints were engaged in producing large numbers of foreign coins, and this probably accounts for such breaks in the domestic coinage.

SAN FRANCISCO
181,770,000

RARITY: 1945-S cents are quite common in all grades Very Good and higher. Both original and reassembled rolls of uncirculated coins may be found, though the former are becoming scarce for this and all dates of the Lincoln series. The quest for certifiable gems has largely prompted the breaking up of the original, bank-wrapped rolls.

POPULATION: MS TOTAL = 215   HIGHEST = MS67 RD (105)

VALUES:

GRADE	1950	1965	1980	1995
MS60	.05	.70	——	——
MS65	——	——	.50	1.50

VARIETIES: An amazing 23 repunched mintmark varieties are known (see photo). Only one trivial obverse doubled-die has been found, along with three obverse cud break varieties.

1945-S cents seem to all bear the knobby 'S' punch introduced in 1944. It's likely that continued searching will turn up the sharply serifed 'S' seen on some other denominations of this date and used for many years afterward. This punch is similar to the Large S of 1941, but it's a bit more symmetrical.

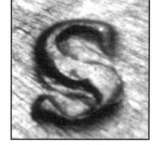

1945-S/S
RPM-4 (Miller)

COMMENTS: Cents of this issue often have the same indistinct quality seen on many 1944-S Lincolns, but the percentage of well struck pieces is noticeably higher for this date. Streaks and other signs of poor alloy mixing are not uncommon.

The suspension of cent coinage at the San Francisco Mint which began in August of 1944 continued through March. The reason was the same: This facility was preoccupied with foreign coinage as well as resupplying our own overseas possession, The Philippines.[143]

1946

PHILADELPHIA
991,655,000

RARITY: Common in all grades Very Good and higher, original rolls still exist.

POPULATION: MS TOTAL = 50   HIGHEST = MS67 RD (7)

VALUES:

GRADE	1950	1965	1980	1995
MS60	.05	.60	——	——
MS65	——	——	.25	1.25

VARIETIES: Three doubled-die varieties are known for the reverse, all of them quite minor. Three obverse cuds may be found. Some 12 are known for the reverse, and all but three of them are retained breaks.

COMMENTS: Well struck, fully red gems are common and have little value. This accounts for the small number certified.

The cents of 1946 from all three mints sport a broad and rakish numeral 4 in their dates, the only time that this style was employed during that decade.

The color of these cents varies from the fiery red of the pre-war issues to the lighter, brassy color of the so-called shellcase cents.

* * *

A profile of U. S. Mint personnel may be gained from a table prepared for the 1946 *Annual Report* of Mint Director Nellie Tayloe Ross to Treasury Secretary John W. Snyder. Of the Mint's total of 2,547 employees on June 30, 1946, 50 were employed at the Bureau's offices in Washington, D.C. and 1,652 were employees of the Philadelphia Mint. This figure included 32 members of the Engraving Department, a function unique to the Philadelphia Mint. Another 819 were assigned to the Coining Department, 354 to Melting and Refining, 10 to Assaying, 116 to Mechanical, and the balance was composed of guards, clerks and administrators. The Denver Mint employed 334 persons, of whom 114 were in coining, 81 in Melting and Refining, 8 in Assaying, and the balance were of a general nature. San Francisco had only 263 employees, due to the smaller size of its facility. 76 were assigned to the Coining Department, 72 to Melting and Refining, 12 to Assaying, and the remainder were in non-coining functions.

It's interesting to note also that the total of 2,547 employees in Mint service at the end of Fiscal Year 1946 was down from the figure of 3,736 at the end of FY1945, when the mints were at their wartime peak of production. The wage and price ceilings imposed by the war were eventually lifted, with the result of rapid inflation. The Mint was unable to meet workers' demands for higher pay until April 19, 1946, when a joint resolution of Congress provided for wage increases.[144]

DENVER
315,690,000

RARITY: Rolls were widely hoarded as the hobby of coin collecting grew rapidly after the war. Examples are common in all grades VG and higher.

POPULATION: MS TOTAL = 97   HIGHEST = MS67 RD (39)

VALUES:

GRADE	1950	1965	1980	1995
MS60	.05	.60	——	——
MS65	——	——	.30	1.25

1946-D/D
RPM-4 (Miller)

VARIETIES: Only a single cud variety is reported, the break appearing over letter L of LIBERTY. No less than 17 repunched mintmark varieties have been documented (see photo).

COMMENTS: Worn dies are a bit of a problem for this issue, and most specimens will be lacking in sharpness toward their peripheries.

SAN FRANCISCO
198,100,000

RARITY: Common in all grades Very Good and higher, many rolls were saved by speculators and remain in the marketplace.

POPULATION: MS TOTAL = 66   HIGHEST = MS67 RD (33)

VALUES:

GRADE	1950	1965	1980	1995
MS60	.05	.70	——	——
MS65	——	——	.70	1.50

1946-S/D
OMM-1 (Fivaz & Stanton)

VARIETIES: One obverse and three reverse cud varieties exist.

There are 29 repunched mintmark varieties to attract collectors, but by far the most interesting and valuable is the overmintmark S/D. Coins of this variety have proved to be quite rare, particularly uncirculated (see photo).

In his *Encyclopedia*, Walter Breen listed two different styles of mintmark, one with sharp serifs and one with blunt ends. The author believes that only the serif-style was employed beginning in 1945 or 1946 and used until 1979. Breen's dual listings of 1946-48 seem to represent die states in which the mintmark's features have become worn or were distorted through die polishing. The severe overuse to which most S-Mint dies were put during the mid-late 1940s is entirely consistent with such observations.

COMMENTS: Although sharp coins may be found with a bit of searching, the vast majority were coined from worn dies. These show signs of having been polished numerous times in an attempt to prolong their usefulness, and the resulting coins have a shallow and incomplete look to them.

1947

PHILADELPHIA
190,555,000

RARITY: Common in all grades Very Good and higher, original rolls survive.

POPULATION: MS TOTAL = 26   HIGHEST = MS67 RD (1)

VALUES:

GRADE	1950	1965	1980	1995
MS60	.05	1.10	——	——
MS65	——	——	.30	3.00

VARIETIES: Just a single cud break may be found in the familiar position below Lincoln's bust. In addition, a slight doubled-die variety is evident for the obverse, affecting the mottos and the date.

COMMENTS: For reasons not known, gems of this issue are a bit elusive. They seem more susceptible than usual to spotting and other discoloration.

The post-war recession brought a lessened demand for new cents, and this was reflected in an article which appeared in *The Philadelphia Inquirer* for November 16, 1947:

> Approximately 200 employees of the Philadelphia Mint, 16th and Spring Garden streets, were laid off at the close of the work week yesterday. Edwin H. Dressel, superintendent, said the employees furloughed will be recalled "as soon as new orders for coins are received." He attributed the reduction in force to a decrease in requests or orders for coins and to limited appropriations.
>
> The Mint, which reached an all-time peak of about 2,600 employees during the war, has now about 600 employees, a normal figure, he said.
>
> William Fehlinger, president of the American Federation of Government Employees (AFL), said "This reduction in force is a normal procedure at this time of the year." There was no labor trouble at the Mint, he declared.
>
> On Nov. 3, employees at the large coin-making plant received an increase of three to 10 cents an hour according to classification.[145]

DENVER
194,750,000

RARITY: Common in all grades Very Good and higher through fully red gem, original rolls still exist.

POPULATION: MS TOTAL = 73   HIGHEST = MS67 RD (24)

VALUES:	GRADE	1950	1965	1980	1995
	MS60	.05	.65	—	—
	MS65	—	—	.30	1.25

VARIETIES: Seven repunched mintmarks may be found (see photo).

COMMENTS: Better made than than its P and S counterparts, most 1947-D cents will show greater detail.

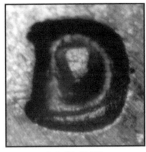

1947-D/D
RPM-2a (Miller)

SAN FRANCISCO
99,000,000

RARITY: 1947-S cents are common in all grades Very Good and higher. While original rolls of this and most surrounding issues still exist, they typically appear only when old collections are offered. The rolls more commonly traded may have been raided for gems and lesser coins substituted.

POPULATION: MS TOTAL = 78   HIGHEST = MS67 RD (12)

VALUES:	GRADE	1950	1965	1980	1995
	MS60	.05	1.25	—	—
	MS65	—	—	.80	1.75

VARIETIES: A single obverse cud is reported, and a minor obverse doubled-die is also noted. Finally, six repunched mintmark varieties may be found (see photo).

1947-S/S
RPM-2 (Miller)

COMMENTS: Overusage of the dies was the rule for this issue, and only a few examples will appear sharp and fully formed. Most, however, fall somewhere between the extremes.

This abuse of coin dies was noted by collectors of the time. In 1949, a reader of *The Numismatic Scrapbook Magazine* sent Editor Lee F. Hewitt a 1947-S cent which was one of several dates he had found on which an inverted impression of Lincoln's bust could be seen on the reverse. Forwarding the coin to the U. S. Mint in Philadelphia, Hewitt received the following reply from Chief Engraver Gilroy Roberts:

> The impression of Lincoln's bust has been caused by the use of worn dies. After a long run (800,000 to 1,000,000 pieces) the reverse die will begin to show wear, caused by the flow of metal into the deeper parts of the design on the obverse die."[146]

Assuming that the coin didn't simply exhibit clash marks from dies which struck one another without a planchet between them, Roberts' explanation is plausible. The effect he described is known as "ghosting," and it occurs when the displacement of metal is unequal between one side of a coin and the other.

Roberts became Chief Engraver in 1947, following the death that year of John Ray Sinnock, who had served in this role since 1925.

* * *

In the years following World War II, large numbers of American soldiers were stationed in the occupied nations formerly at war with the United States. These troops were discouraged from engaging in trade with the local populace, and to restrict their purchases to the post exchanges they were paid in Allied Military Currency and its successor, Military Payment Certificates. These were valued from five cents to twenty dollars, but the lowly cent was evidently used for lesser amounts and for making exact change, as suggested by this report from 1947:

> A large quantity of U. S. cents were recently shipped to Japan for use in Army Post Exchanges. Now 8th Army HQ has issued an appeal to American personnel to conserve the coins as they have practically disappeared in a few short weeks after issue. It seems that after the coins are passed out of the PX as change they don't return due to the soldiers giving them away to Japanese children.[147]

1948

PHILADELPHIA
317,570,000

RARITY: Common in all grades Very Good and higher, original rolls still exist.

POPULATION: MS TOTAL = 49   HIGHEST = MS67 RD (25)

VALUES:

GRADE	1950	1965	1980	1995
MS60	.05	.80	——	——
MS65	——	——	.60	1.50

VARIETIES: Two obverse cuds and two reverse cuds are known, the latter both retained breaks.

COMMENTS: Most cents of this issue were well made from sharp or only moderately worn dies. Fully struck, fully red gems are thus fairly plentiful.

DENVER
172,637,500

RARITY: Common in all grades Very Good and higher, original rolls still exist.

POPULATION: MS TOTAL = 19   HIGHEST = MS67 RD (1)

VALUES:

GRADE	1950	1965	1980	1995
MS60	.05	.85	——	——
MS65	——	——	.30	1.50

VARIETIES: Six repunched mintmark varieties are reported (see photo). One cud variety each is known for both obverse and reverse, the latter a retained break.

1948-D/D
RPM-2 (Miller)

COMMENTS: Unlike most denominations of this date and mint, the cents were not as well made as the those of the Philadelphia Mint. Still, given the tremendous number of uncirculated coins from which to chose, it shouldn't be much of a challenge to find a gem.

———— •◆•◆◆•◆•• ————

SAN FRANCISCO
81,735,000

RARITY: Common in all grades Very Good and higher, original rolls still exist but may be of poor quality.

POPULATION: MS TOTAL = 56   HIGHEST = MS67 RD (28)

VALUES:

GRADE	1950	1965	1980	1995
MS60	.05	1.25	——	——
MS65	——	——	.90	1.90

1948-S/S
RPM-1 (Miller)

VARIETIES: Six repunched mintmarks are recorded (see photo). Given the current growth in the specialized area of variety hunting, or "cherrypicking," the number of repunched mintmark varieties is likely to increase. Any figure given in this book is subject to becoming obsolete within a year or two.

COMMENTS: The San Francisco Mint continued producing coins of poor quality, a trend which developed in 1944 and would last through the suspension of production there in 1955. The cents of this issue were largely coined from worn and overly polished dies. Many shallow features of the design will be weak or missing.

A recession which began during 1947 and lasted into 1950 hit the West Coast more heavily than the rest of the nation, partly because of the post-war slump in the aircraft industry, a major component of the California economy. This slowing of business activity is reflected in the reduced demand for new coinage. From January through June, the San Francisco Mint coined nothing but cents. The sole exception was the requisite production of non-circulating Booker T. Washington Half Dollars in May. After that, no cents were coined during September, October and November, and only 135,000 were struck off in December.[148]

* * *

In his December 20, 1948 column for *The San Francisco Chronicle*, Herb Caen related an amusing situation at the local mint:

> Deflation has set in at the U. S. Mint here—on account every time a bunch of school kiddies takes a tour around the place, some of the wiser moppets kiddingly ask Supt. George Gillin for a "sample." For a while, George was handing 'em a shiny, new dime until he discovered that this going-along-with-a-gag was costing him about $40 a month . . . So now he's presenting the kids with neatly printed cards containing a brand new penny, inserted in a slot over the word: "Sample." Sighs George: "Hadda do it. After all, I'm no Rockefeller!"[149]

1949

PHILADELPHIA
217,775,000

RARITY: Common in all grades Very Good and higher, original rolls still exist.

POPULATION: MS TOTAL = 17   HIGHEST = MS66 RD (3)

VALUES:

GRADE	1950	1965	1980	1995
MS60	.05	1.10	——	——
MS65	——	——	.75	1.75

VARIETIES: None are reported.

COMMENTS: Fully struck gems are plentiful, though it's interesting to note that none have been certified MS67 RD. More common, however, are pieces having a pattern of shallow stains which has been described as "cobwebbing." An unappealing feature which often affects every coin in a roll, it's common for many Philadelphia Mint cents dated 1949-52. It was almost certainly caused by some chemical treatment of the planchets prior to coining, but why it appears particularly for these years is not known.

DENVER
153,132,500

RARITY: Common in all grades Very Good and higher, original rolls still exist.

POPULATION: MS TOTAL = 17   HIGHEST = MS66 RD (7)

VALUES:

GRADE	1950	1965	1980	1995
MS60	.05	1.10	——	——
MS65	——	——	.60	2.00

VARIETIES: A single obverse cud is known in the usual position. Some 10 repunched mintmark varieties may be found, including one which is triple-punched (see photo).

COMMENTS: Although some will exhibit slightly worn dies, most coins of this date were well made, and fully struck gems are plentiful. Note, however, that none have been certified MS67 RD.

1949-D/D/D
RPM-1 (Miller)

SAN FRANCISCO
64,290,000

RARITY: 1949-S cents are fairly common in all grades Very Good and higher, despite their lower than usual mintage.

POPULATION: MS TOTAL = 63   HIGHEST = MS67 RD (24)

VALUES:

GRADE	1950	1965	1980	1995
MS60	.05	2.25	——	——
MS65	——	——	1.40	4.25

VARIETIES: A very trivial obverse doubled-die is known, along with 10 repunched mintmarks.
More interesting is one obverse die with a stray S mintmark peering out from underneath numeral 4 in the date. The upper loop of the S is visible above the diagonal of the 4. It's not known whether this die was used at the Philadelphia or San Francisco Mint.

COMMENTS: Choice examples are readily available, though most fall short of the fully red gem classification. Spots and irregular toning are a problem with this issue.
Domestic coinage at the San Francisco Mint was suspended from May through September while foreign orders were filled. Several denominations were coined only at the end of the year, though the cent was not among these.[150]

1950

PHILADELPHIA
272,635,000

RARITY: Common in all grades shy of fully red gem, original rolls survive.

POPULATION: MS TOTAL = 47   HIGHEST = MS67 RD (22)

VALUES:	GRADE	1950	1965	1980	1995
	MS60	.05	.75	——	——
	MS65	——	——	.50	1.50

VARIETIES: One obverse cud and two reverse cuds have been reported, the reverse varieties being retained breaks.

COMMENTS: Although quite plentiful in Mint State, fully red gems are slightly scarce. Sol Taylor reported that this issue "tends to be dull red, average die state, and average luster. True gems are seen, but many fewer than other P-Mint dates of the same era."[151]

* * *

As post-war productivity increased at the mints, the number of employees fell. By the end of Fiscal Year 1950, there were only 1,272 individuals on the Mint's payroll, as opposed to 3,736 just five years earlier.[152]

DENVER
334,950,000

RARITY: Common in all grades Very Good and higher, original rolls still exist.

POPULATION: MS TOTAL = 92   HIGHEST = MS67 RD (67)

VALUES:	GRADE	1950	1965	1980	1995
	MS60	.05	.55	——	——
	MS65	——	——	.30	1.00

VARIETIES: This issue is rich in cud varieties (see photo). Four are known for the obverse and seven for the reverse. Two of the latter are retained breaks. Seven repunched mintmarks exist for 1950-D (see photo).

COMMENTS: Although this issue often lacks full luster, 1950-D cents are still available in fully struck, fully red condition. Finding such coins, however, may take a bit of patience.

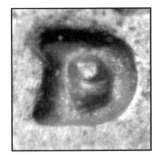

1950-D/D
RPM-2 (Miller)

1950-D
LC-50D-3 (Thurman & Margolis)

SAN FRANCISCO
118,505,000

RARITY: Common in all grades Very Good and higher, original rolls still exist.

POPULATION: MS TOTAL = 19   HIGHEST = MS67 RD (3)

VALUES:

GRADE	1950	1965	1980	1995
MS60	.05	1.10	——	——
MS65	——	——	.55	1.25

VARIETIES: A total of 12 repunched mintmark varieties may be found for 1950-S (see photo). A trivial obverse doubled-die is also known.

COMMENTS: Most 1950-S cents are superior in their quality of strike to those produced at the San Francisco Mint in the years immediately preceding. Fully struck, fully red gems may be found, though many examples of this date and 1951-S display a peculiar dark streaking of unknown cause. If one were to have interrogated San Francisco Mint employees at the time, it's quite possible that the solution may have been found in some otherwise innocuous practice whose effect was discovered only later by collectors.

1950-S/S
RPM-5 (Miller)

* * *

The years immediately following World War II were a time of increasing automation at the three mints. Much of this consisted of simplifying the number of steps involved in rolling the metal coinage strip and punching out the blanks. The use of long, continuous operations to perform these tasks required that existing machinery be relocated to provide an uninterrupted flow of metal from one operation to the next. Through this means, much larger ingots could be processed. The physically cramped facility in San Francisco made such arrangements difficult and, as costs dropped at the other two mints during the early 1950s, the San Francisco operation began to be viewed as a liability.

1951

PHILADELPHIA
294,576,000

RARITY: Every grade Very Good and higher through fully red gem is readily available, and original rolls still exist.

POPULATION: MS TOTAL = 10   HIGHEST = MS66 RD (4)

VALUES:

GRADE	1965	1980	1995
MS60	.70	——	——
MS65	——	1.70	1.50

VARIETIES: A minor obverse doubled-die affects the motto IN GOD WE TRUST.

COMMENTS: The cents of this issue were well made, and fully struck gems are common.

* * *

As it had following World War I, inflation ravaged the value of the dollar after World War II. Wartime rationing and price controls had held matters in check for the duration, but when these were lifted the cost of every product and service shot upward. This was reflected in the Government's payroll, as well. In her 1951 *Annual Report* to Treasury Secretary Snyder, Mint Director Ross noted that average salaries in the Mint Service had gone up 73% since Fiscal Year 1946. Conversely, coinage costs had actually diminished as the result of cost-saving automation. The expense of producing 1,000 cents had fallen from $1.59 in FY1946 to $1.21 in FY1951. She further added that had the cost of coinage kept pace with the rise in salaries it would then cost some $2.75 to produce 1,000 cents.[153] What she failed to note, however, is that the quality of cents had been diminishing for some time. Sadly, this trend would only intensify over the next few years.

DENVER
625,355,000

RARITY: Common in all grades Very Good and higher, original rolls are available.

POPULATION: MS TOTAL = 59   HIGHEST = MS67 RD (17)

VALUES:
GRADE	1965	1980	1995
MS60	.55	——	——
MS65	——	.25	.60

VARIETIES: Two obverse cuds are known, while no less than 32 repunched mintmark varieties are recorded for this date, including one which has been identified as an overmintmark D/S variety (see photos). In addition, a minor obverse doubled-die may be found, similar to that for 1951-P.

COMMENTS: Well struck, fully red gems are readily available, as the low value for this issue suggests.

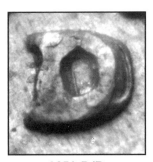

1951-D/D
RPM-10b (Miller)

1951-D/S
*OMM-1, Breen-2202
(Fivaz & Stanton)*

SAN FRANCISCO
136,010,000

RARITY: All grades Very Good and higher are common, though fully struck gems form a minority of the Mint State survivors.

POPULATION: MS TOTAL = 61   HIGHEST = MS67 RD (43)

VALUES:
GRADE	1965	1980	1995
MS60	1.50	——	——
MS65	——	1.00	2.00

VARIETIES: Two retained cuds are reported for the reverse. At least 12 repunched mintmarks may be found as well (see photo).

COMMENTS: Although fully red gem coins are readily found, the discriminating buyer will note that many of these display the same worn and shallow look seen for dates such as 1944-S and 1946-S.

1951-S/S
RPM-5b (Miller)

1952

PHILADELPHIA
186,765,000

RARITY:　　　Common in all grades Very Good and higher, original rolls still exist.

POPULATION:　MS TOTAL = 13　　HIGHEST = MS66 RD (3)

VALUES:

GRADE	1965	1980	1995
MS60	.70	——	——
MS65	——	.60	.75

VARIETIES:　　A minor obverse doubled-die is noted. There are at least four cud breaks for the reverse, all but one of them retained.

COMMENTS:　　Fully struck, fully red gems are readily located.

　　　　1952 was the only date during the 1950s in which the numeral 5 sported a short and clearly attenuated tail. Was this intentional or simply an oversight?

* * *

　　　　The Mint Director's *Annual Report* for 1952 records a further drop in the cost of producing 1,000 cents to $1.10. Cutting costs in all operations seems to have been the highest priority during this period, as frequent mention is made of improved equipment and handling. One novel method by which employees were encouraged to become more efficient was through the viewing of educational films shot at the various mints. The improvements at one facility were thus demonstrated to employees at another, and even outside industries were studied for their advanced methods of manufacturing. Wouldn't it be fun to see these films now, if in fact they still exist?[154]

DENVER
746,130,000

RARITY: Common in all grades Very Good and higher, original rolls exist.

POPULATION: MS TOTAL = 46   HIGHEST = MS67 RD (22)

VALUES:

GRADE	1965	1980	1995
MS60	.50	——	——
MS65	——	.25	1.00

VARIETIES: Two dies have been identified as D/S varieties. In addition, there are at least 21 repunched mint-mark varieties (see photos). Cud die breaks include nine for the obverse and one retained break for the reverse. Note that retained breaks are almost always on the reverse. This is because the reverse die is in the anvil position, and the broken portion of the die is permitted to remain in place. The obverse die is mounted in the hammer position, and the broken portions will typically fall away.

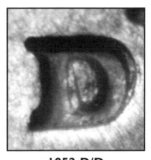

1952-D/D
RPM-5 (Miller)

1952-D/S
OMM-1, Breen-2206
(Fivaz & Stanton)

COMMENTS: In his book *The Standard Guide to the Lincoln Cent*, Sol Taylor notes that 1952-D cents are more often found in a red/brown state than fully red. While this is true for collectors seeking these coins by the roll, there is no shortage of fully red, gem singles.

SAN FRANCISCO
137,800,004

RARITY: Common in all grades Very Good and higher, original rolls still exist.

POPULATION: MS TOTAL = 15   HIGHEST = MS67 RD (28)

VALUES:

GRADE	1965	1980	1995
MS60	1.25	——	——
MS65	——	.65	1.25

VARIETIES: One obverse and two reverse cud breaks may be found. In addition, 17 repunched mintmarks are noted (see photo).

COMMENTS: Like 1951-S cents, those dated 1952-S often feature worn, shallow dies as the result of overly extended use and aggressive polishing. Still, their sheer numbers preclude the possibility of rarity even in fully struck, fully red gem condition.

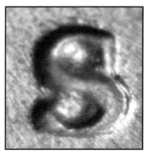

1952-S/S
RPM-3 (Miller)

1953

PHILADELPHIA
256,755,000

RARITY: Common in all grades Very Good and higher, original rolls still exist.

POPULATION: MS TOTAL = 27   HIGHEST = MS67 RD (6)

VALUES:

GRADE	1965	1980	1995
MS60	.45	——	——
MS65	——	.25	.50

1953-P
LC-53-1R Retained (Thurman & Margolis)

VARIETIES: One obverse and two reverse cud varieties exist, and both of the latter are retained breaks (see photo). With a retained break, the broken portion of the die remains in place. As the force of gravity precludes the upper, obverse die from remaining in place, retained breaks are generally seen for the lower, reverse die.

COMMENTS: 1953-P cents are readily available in fully struck, fully red gem condition.

* * *

It was noted by Mint Director William H. Brett in his *Annual Report* to Treasury Secretary George M. Humphrey that during Fiscal Year 1953 the one-cent piece comprised 71% of all coin shipments from the mints. The cost of producing these cents fell again to only $1.03 per 1000 pieces.[155]

——•◆•——

DENVER
700,515,000

RARITY: Another very common issue, all grades Very Good and higher through gem are available, and original rolls still exist.

POPULATION: MS TOTAL = 21   HIGHEST = MS66 RD (6)

VALUES:

GRADE	1965	1980	1995
MS60	.45	——	——
MS65	——	.25	.70

1953-D/D
RPM-1a (Miller)

VARIETIES: A single obverse cud is noted in the usual position below Lincoln's bust. A trivial doubled-die is reported for the obverse. Some 23 repunched mintmark varieties are known (see photo).

COMMENTS: A very generous mintage, combined with widespread hoarding, has assured that this issue will never be anything but common. Curiously, however, no example has been certified MS67 RD.

1953-D cents are known measuring only 18.7mm in diameter. These are of normal weight, and the reason for their small size is a mystery.

* * *

The Mint Director's *Annual Report* for 1953 reveals two interesting anachronisms which were then being addressed. It seems that both the weighing of coin blanks and the inspection of finished coins were still being performed manually, though it's doubtful that each individual coin was examined. Machines were in development for the electronic weighing of blanks and sorting out of defective coins. In the meantime, however, it was reported that "Coin blanks are visually inspected for imperfections by passing over a moving belt, and defective or discolored pieces are picked out manually, a tedious and costly procedure." Both of these operations were automated by the end of the decade, but the quality of coins produced showed little improvement.

One procedure had been successfully transferred to machines, as noted in the report:

Coins unfit for further circulation are returned to the mints in large quantities each year for recoinage. Costly procedures were formerly employed in counting and reviewing uncurrent coins, and sorting out counterfeit pieces, foreign coins, slugs, etc. New streamlined procedures have been effected eliminating much of the tedious labor formerly expended, and spot checking and test counting verification methods have been substituted. Wartime steel pennies and silver nickels are picked out mechanically by unique mechanisms constructed for that purpose. (Estimated annual savings, $11,000).[156]

SAN FRANCISCO
181,835,000

RARITY: Common in all grades Very Good and higher, original rolls still exist.

POPULATION: MS TOTAL = 19   HIGHEST = MS67 RD (2)

VALUES:

GRADE	1965	1980	1995
MS60	.85	——	——
MS65	——	.45	1.00

VARIETIES: There are 25 repunched mintmark varieties, and more will almost certainly be found (see photo). A single obverse cud break and five reverse cuds are recorded, all of the latter retained.

COMMENTS: The technical problems noted for 1951-S and 1952-S are present with this issue as well, and 1953-S cents are further subject to spotting, streaking and other discoloration problems.

* * *

In the course of describing cost-cutting improvements made at the various mints, Director Brett sounded an ominous note regarding San Francisco:

An intensive study has been made of conditions and production facilities at the San Francisco Mint to determine what steps can be taken there, at justifiable cost, to provide such modernization of equipment as will reduce coinage costs. Specialists from outside industry and engineers from the Public Buildings Administration have collaborated with Mint technicians on this study.[157]

1953-S/S
RPM-2 (Miller)

1954

PHILADELPHIA
71,640,050

RARITY: Slightly scarce in circulated grades, Mint State coins of mediocre quality are abundant, while fully struck, fully red gems are quite elusive.

POPULATION: MS TOTAL = 35   HIGHEST = MS66 RD (7)

VALUES:

GRADE	1965	1980	1995
MS60	1.00	——	——
MS65	——	.50	1.25

VARIETIES: Two cuds are known for this issue, one on the obverse and a retained break on the reverse.

COMMENTS: 1954-P cents are notable for their generally poor quality. Most are dark and were coined from severely overused dies. None have been certified MS67 RD, and the 1995 retail value of $1.25 given for MS65 is unlikely to secure a coin in that grade. The reasons for both the low mintage and the drastically inferior quality of this issue remain unknown.

DENVER
251,552,500

RARITY: Common in all grades Fine and higher, original rolls still exist.

POPULATION: MS TOTAL = 59   HIGHEST = MS67 RD (28)

VALUES:

GRADE	1965	1980	1995
MS60	.40	——	——
MS65	——	.25	.40

VARIETIES: Five repunched mintmark varieties are known, including one which is triple-punched (see photo).

COMMENTS: Most are well struck, though some die wear is evident on many examples. Given the sheer number of Mint State survivors, there should be no obstacle to locating a fully struck, fully red gem.

1954-D/D/D
RPM-1a (Miller)

SAN FRANCISCO
96,190,000

RARITY: 1954-S cents are common in all grades Fine and higher, and original rolls still exist.

POPULATION: MS TOTAL = 47   HIGHEST = MS67 RD (2)

VALUES:

GRADE	1965	1980	1995
MS60	.70	——	——
MS65	——	.35	.75

VARIETIES: One popular variety is the so-called "San Jose" cent. This name is derived from a curved die break just to the right of the mintmark which creates the appearance of the letters SJ. This issue is also rich in repunched mintmarks, at least 16 being known (see photo). In addition, five reverse cuds have been documented, three of them retained breaks. Finally, a minor doubled-die is known for the obverse.

COMMENTS: Quality control declined a little further at the San Francisco Mint from previous years, and the cents of this date were poorly made. Assorted die breaks are common, as are worn and severely polished dies.

No cents were coined at the San Francisco Mint from March through June. In fact, no coins of any kind were struck there or at the Denver Mint during June.[158] Activity usually slowed during that month as the mints prepared to conduct their annual settlement of accounts (the U. S. Mint's fiscal year ended June 30), but it was rare for coining to cease altogether.

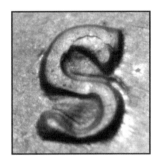

1954-S/S
RPM-4a (Miller)

1955

PHILADELPHIA
330,580,000

RARITY: Common in all grades Fine and higher, original rolls still exist. Quality singles are fairly scarce, due to the late state of the dies employed.

POPULATION: MS TOTAL = 28   HIGHEST = MS68 RD (1)

VALUES:

GRADE	1965	1980	1995
MS60	.35	———	———
MS65	———	.20	.25

VARIETIES: Certainly the most highly sought Lincoln Cent variety is the dramatically doubled obverse die for this issue. More on this important rarity will be found on the following pages.

All of the work in preparing 1955-P cents seems to been have hasty and careless, including the die making process. This accounts at least in part for the major doubled-die of this date and for several lesser ones. These include four additional obverse doubled-dies, all minor, including two for proofs. There are also four reverse doubled-die varieties, all minor and all but one of which are for proofs.

Four cud varieties are recorded; one is a retained break on the obverse, while the others are retained breaks on the reverse. In addition, there are a number of lesser die breaks affecting the lettering. Among the more common are the "BIE" varieties in which the die has broken between letters B and E of LIBERTY, creating the appearance of a letter I. This flaw was so prevalent during the 1950s that collectors at one time formed a club specializing exclusively in this phenomenon. It was called the BIE Mint Oddities Collectors Guild, and in 1972 it published a 109-page catalog of known varieties, edited by Howard O. Hardy. "BIE" cents exist for virtually every date during the 1950s and to a lesser extent through 1968, the final year of the old obverse master hub.

COMMENTS: The generally poor quality of cents during the mid-late 1950s was particularly severe for this issue. Poor quality die steel and extended usage of these dies in an effort to address a shortage of cents were the likely culprits.

Commenting on the deficiencies of 1955-P cents, one writer for *The Numismatic Scrapbook Magazine* was quite impassioned:

Attention speculators! Save your perfect 1955-P cents and you too can own future rarities!
The reader needn't take this confidential money-making tip too seriously of course, but just look through a few 1955 cents and see what I mean. Foosh! The penny-makers should hide in shame.[159]

Full, blazing red examples are quite common, though their status as choice or gem is conditional to some degree on the state of the dies. Commercial grading services don't place much emphasis on this quality, however, and this probably accounts for the single specimen certified MS68 RD.

* * *

One factor affecting the poor quality of 1955-P cents is the haste with which many were made. The severe shortage of cents which developed in the Fall of 1955 came after a year in which the Mint had voluntarily requested a budget cut as part of its cost-saving programs.[160] This left it in a bind when several unrelated circumstances conspired to increase the demand for cents, particularly in the East. It also had many persons wondering why the San Francisco Mint had been shut down the previous Spring.

The Philadelphia Mint went on a 12-hour shift, seven days a week that Fall to meet the demand for millions of additional cents. One cause was the one-cent tax on cigarettes imposed by Pennsylvania as a temporary measure to pay for damage caused by Hurricane Diane August 17-19, 1955. In the waning months of 1955, the Philadelphia Mint turned out well over 100 million cents per month. The shortage ultimately extended to Alliance, Ohio, hometown of U. S. Mint Director William H. Brett. Quoted in a local paper, Mr. Brett remarked "It won't last long. In perhaps 30 days, there'll be so many pennies and other coins, there will be a shortage of storage space." He further added that the overall demand for coins had increased 742% from the previous year.[161]

———◆———

DOUBLED-DIE OBVERSE

PHILADELPHIA
(mintage unknown)

RARITY: This popular variety is essentially unknown below the Extremely Fine level, since it became valuable within a few years of its discovery. Most survivors are EF-AU, many of them cleaned and/or recolored. Virgin, Mint State examples are fairly scarce and choice and gem pieces quite rare, as the population data reveals.

POPULATION: MS BN = 184   MS RB = 235   MS RD = 92   MS TOTAL = 511
            MS65 RD = 8   HIGHEST = MS65 RD (8)

VALUES:
GRADE	1965	1980	1995
EF	——	250.00	500.00
MS60	250.00	550.00	725.00
MS65	——	——	4000.00

VARIETIES: There are a few less distinctive doubled-dies than the ones illustrated, and these are listed under VARIETIES for the regular 1955-P cent. In addition, there is the so-called "Poor Man's doubled-die," which is actually a heavily worn die on which the second numeral 5 displays a shadow image caused by metal flow erosion. It carries very little premium.

COMMENTS: Most authentic examples are well struck, but few have been preserved in pristine condition. This variety was the first of its kind generally recognized in the coin hobby, and no one was quite sure whether it should be valuable or not. Several years passed before these coins acquired much of

1955-P Doubled-Die
DDO-1, Breen-2214 (Fivaz & Stanton)

a premium, but they were firmly established as a popular addition to the Lincoln series by 1960.

Like all doubled-die coins, this one resulted when a working die was improperly aligned with the working hub between impressions. The result was two distinct impressions rotated around one another with respect to the die's center. Coined during the late Summer of 1955, the cents produced from this defective working die and its normal mate were the product of a sudden and severe shortage of cents resulting from the recent imposition of new taxes. The increased demand for cents led to production around the clock and more casual inspection of newly-made dies. The fact that this obverse die was used at all suggests that it was never inspected until after the peculiar cents were coined. Under normal circumstances, some seven persons were charged with inspecting each die. According to Sydney C. Engel, newly appointed as Chief Coiner of the Philadelphia Mint when this variety was struck, these included the hubbing-press operator, the heat treator, the foreman of the die shop, the engraver or a representative, the foreman of the coining room, the die-setter and the press operator.

On genuine coins, two nearly vertical die-polishing lines form a compressed letter X just left of the T in CENT. (ANAAB)

Struck off during the midnight-8 a.m. shift, the doubled-die cents were discovered by Engel's assistant on duty. When Engel arrived in the morning and was presented with a few examples, he faced a difficult decision. Since these coins had already been mixed with cents from other die pairs and awaited loading onto trucks, Engel decided to let them through rather than condemn an entire night's production. It was his estimate that between 20,000 and 24,000 pieces were coined before the error was discovered and the faulty die removed. To prevent their release would mean the destruction of some 10 million cents in all.[162]

The first specimens turned up in Massachusetts, late in 1955. Contemporary accounts place their discovery in the town of Greenfield, though the lack of importance placed on this variety at the time suggests that a number of persons may have noticed these coins before reporting them to the numismatic press. Additional coins were found in adjacent towns, but the greater number were discovered in and around Boston. Other "hot spots" were western Massachusetts and upstate New York. Quite a few were found sealed within packages of cigarettes dispensed from vending machines. With these packs then priced at 23 cents each, change of a quarter was already provided by the cigarette manufacturer along with the cigarettes to avoid the nuisance of loading cents separately into their machines.

Counterfeits of this popular and quite valuable variety have been made. For more information about these, see Chapter 5. Recognizing a genuine coin is not difficult. For starters, it should look like the one illustrated here. If it doesn't, that's a sure sign of trouble! A more thorough examination will reveal two important diagnostic markers on the reverse. All genuine pieces were struck from a reverse die which bore criss-crossing polishing lines just to the left of letter T in CENT. These lines may be difficult to see on worn or cleaned coins, while one die state does not show them at all. Some but not all 1955 doubled-die cents show additional diagnostics including a raised lump beneath the left wheat ear, just below the left side of letter O in OF. The earliest state of this die also revealed several filing lines which appear raised on the coins. These are found just below the left wheat ear, but these lines disappeared from the die with subsequent repolishing.

* * *

Clyde D. Mervis, a popular numismatic writer of the 1960s, revealed the humorous side of this variety:

I saw in a dealer's case, a 1955 double die cent, possessing the distinctive mashed edge of an encased cent. Just imagine some outfit ordering about ten thousand "lucky cents" and receiving them made up with the expensive double-die cents. That of course is pure conjecture, but of one instance I known to be positively true is the case of a manufacturer of cheap dollar charm bracelets. This manufacturer would press Lincoln cents into a coin loop, then string ten of them on a cheap bracelet, and chrome plate the entire finished bracelet. He made these by the thousands, and evidently had no trouble getting new coins in 1955, because many of his bracelets contained 1955 double die cents, encased and beautifully chrome plated!

My first encounter with these chrome plated 1955 double die cents was a few years ago, when a dealer asked me if I could remove the chrome plating from his coin. After recovering from the initial shock, I explained that since chrome is so hard, removal might damage—but that a good coat of copper plate would make the coin appear normal. He agreed, and when the first coin came out so nice, he produced some thirty more 1955 double die cents—all chrome plated![163]

DENVER
563,257,500

RARITY: Common in all grades Fine and higher, original rolls still exist.

POPULATION: MS TOTAL = 21   HIGHEST = MS67 RD (1)

VALUES:

GRADE	1965	1980	1995
MS60	.30	——	——
MS65	——	.25	.25

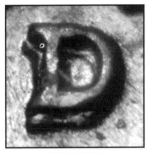

1955-D/D
RPM-2a (Miller)

VARIETIES: Surprisingly, there are only two cud breaks recorded, one a rare, retained obverse break and the other a reverse break, not retained. Given the poor condition of the dies during these years, more discoveries may be expected.

A single doubled-die is known for the obverse, but it's quite minor. More interesting is the horizontal D variety, one of the 13 repunched mintmark dies reported. The first punching placed the mintmark on its side with the straight part at top. This was corrected by placing a properly oriented D directly over it.

Finally, a minor doubled-die variety is known for the obverse.

COMMENTS: Fully red coins are readily available, but they are often seen from worn and distorted dies. The problem is not as severe as it is for 1955-P, but collectors will find it a challenging task to distinguish the best specimens from among the many Mint State survivors.

Variety collectors may wish to include the many defective cents of this date from all three mints, including Denver. The dies employed were of poor quality, as were many of the planchets struck from them. Too numerous to list, these minor varieties include filled dies (such as the once-popular BIE cents), distorted letters and numerals and a wide assortment of cracks and chips in the dies.

SAN FRANCISCO
44,610,000

RARITY: Along with the 1950-D nickel and the 1955-S dime, this issue was among the most widely hoarded of United States coins. Worn examples are far more challenging to find than Mint State pieces.

POPULATION: MS TOTAL = 73   HIGHEST = MS68 RD (1)

VALUES:

GRADE	1965	1980	1995
MS60	1.00	——	——
MS65	——	.50	.70

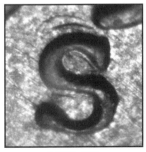

1955-S/S
RPM-1 (Miller)

VARIETIES: Only four repunched mintmark varieties are reported (see photo), but there are some six cud breaks known. All of these are on the reverse in the usual positions between wheat ear and border, and all but one are retained breaks.

COMMENTS: Perhaps the best made of the three issues for this date, 1955-S cents are still of generally poor quality. Although fully red coins are plentiful from widespread hoarding, most exhibit mid-late die states with severe wear, particularly on the reverse. Some of the reverse dies were undoubtedly leftover from the previous year.

In a letter to Editor Elston Bradfield, one reader of *The Numismatist* felt compelled to comment on this poor quality:

> Am enclosing a 55-S cent I received from the mint in my treasury mint set today. I would not feel bad about it except that about 65% of a $50.00 mint sealed bag I purchased were in the same condition. The reverses were the sorriest sight I ever saw! I wonder if the two remaining mints will, in their efforts to turn out coins, make botches on coins that any private enterprise would throw out as poor "seconds." Wonder how many collectors getting sets from the mint to bring their collections up to date will get junk like this to represent our mints' excellent workmanship and fine inspection system.[164]

It was this coin more than any other which prompted the saving of entire mint-sewn bags of coins containing $50 or 5000 cents. Previously, collectors and speculators had been content to satisfy themselves with a roll or two, a practice popular since the mid 1930s. Commencing with this issue and continuing at least through 1964, when the market finally broke, the hoarding of entire bags of each and every date, mint and denomination became the driving force behind the rapid growth of the coin market. Years later, Lee F. Hewitt credited Barney O'Hea with the dubious honor of creating the bag market in coins: "In 1955 he started advertising San Francisco cents and dimes by the bag lot. Prior to that no one had thought of offering coins in original bags."[165]

The popularity of Lincoln Cents peaked during the early 1960s, and many of the more common issues have never regained their 1965 value. The 1955-S cent is a good example, as its listed value of $1 in 1965 reflected the speculative mania over uncirculated rolls and bags which had recently crested and was about to collapse.

The entire mintage of 1955-S cents was completed by March 24, 1955. That was the last day of coining at the San Francisco Mint, and the only other denomination struck there in 1955 was the dime.[166] Both coins were deliberately produced in large enough numbers to discourage speculation, but this proved a futile effort. Bank tellers conspired with coin dealers in the West to acquire millions of these coins in unused condition. One individual reportedly held a stash of 30 mint bags (150,000 cents), and he was holding out for $3 per roll.[167]

* * *

The San Francisco Mint was closed as part of a budget reduction plan devised by Mint Director William H. Brett who correctly pointed out that providing the western states with coinage could be achieved more economically by the Denver Mint, even when the cost of transportation was factored into the equation. The restrictive size of San Francisco's mint structure was largely to blame. Increased automation after World War II had proved cost effective, yet such machinery worked well only when situated in a long, uninterrupted sequence. The San Francisco Mint simply didn't allow for the continuous processing of metal strip and blanks. While the Denver Mint could process a 400-pound ingot, San Francisco could accept nothing larger than 14 pounds.[168]

Despite the sound logic behind it, Brett's decision to close the San Francisco Mint as a cost-cutting measure came back to bite him in the Fall of 1955, a fact referred to only obliquely in his *Annual Report*:

> Since the demand for coins increased greatly during [Fiscal Year] 1956, it was necessary for the Mint to attain maximum possible production with available funds. A second shift was employed at the Denver Mint, and one-cent coin blanks which Denver produced in excess of its press capacity were shipped to Philadelphia to be finished into coins for use in the Philadelphia area.[169]

Though no longer producing coins after March 24, 1955, the mint continued to function as a United States Assay Office, bringing it full circle to its 1851 origin. Of the 148 workers then employed, only 84 were to be retained after April 1, 1955.[170] By 1958, this figure had dropped to just 35. Arthur C. Carmichael, Superintendent, actually resigned at that time claiming "There is nothing for me to do."[171]

Nearly ten years after coining ceased, the San Francisco Assay Office (so-named since July 11, 1962) was enlisted to prepare planchets for use at the Denver Mint, as the nation was then experiencing a severe shortage of coins. In 1965, the presses rolled again. Cents and quarters dated 1964 (but carrying no mintmark) were struck there to supplement the general pool of coinage. The S mintmark was restored in 1968, and the SFAO regained full mint status in the 1980s.

1956

PHILADELPHIA
420,745,000

RARITY: Common in all grades Fine and higher, original rolls and probably bags still exist.

POPULATION: MS TOTAL = 11   HIGHEST = MS66 RD (4)

VALUES:

GRADE	1965	1980	1995
MS60	.20	——	——
MS65	——	.25	.35

VARIETIES: Two obverse cud breaks are reported, one of them retained. A single reverse cud is also known, and this too is a retained break. Two doubled-die obverse varieties exist, one of these for proofs, and a single reverse variety may be found, all three quite minor.

COMMENTS: Readily available in fully red gem condition, there's little else to say about this issue. Some were coined from worn dies, and all of the obverse dies were prepared from a worn master hub. The poor quality of this issue was noted by contemporary collectors, one of whom reported his dissatisfaction to *The Numismatist*:

> I have just received my mint set and to say the least I am disappointed. The silver coins are o.k. But the 5c pieces from both mints are tarnished and the cents from both mints look like they had been put on the top of a stove and allowed to get very hot. The coins of the Philadelphia mint are the worst. I wonder if they are all that way or if I was just unlucky?[172]

DENVER
1,098,201,100

RARITY: The first issue since 1945-P to exceed one billion, 1956-D is common in all grades Fine and higher. Original rolls and probably bags still exist.

POPULATION: MS TOTAL = 13   HIGHEST = MS66 RD (7)

VALUES:

GRADE	1965	1980	1995
MS60	.15	——	——
MS65	——	.20	.20

VARIETIES: Three obverse cud varieties are known, along with 15 repunched mint-marks. The most dramatic and popular of these is RPM-8, in which the first D, though shallow, is visible beneath the final D and is entirely free of it (see photo).

One variety has what appears to be the horizontal and vertical segments of an additional numeral 5 titled at a 30 degree clockwise angle to the date. Since dates are engraved rather than punched, the cause of this condition is uncertain.

1956-D/D
RPM-8, Breen 2219
(Fivaz & Stanton)

COMMENTS: Fully struck, fully red gems are readily available in almost any quantity. The insanity of hoarding entire bags of BU (Brilliant Uncirculated) cents should be apparent when given such an enormous mintage.

So large was this coin's mintage that worn specimens still turn up in circulation from time to time, even though the Wheat Ear type has generally ceased to be current.

1957

PHILADELPHIA
282,540,000

RARITY: Common in all grades Fine and higher, original rolls and probably bags still exist.

POPULATION: MS TOTAL = 9   HIGHEST = MS67 RD (2)

VALUES:

GRADE	1965	1980	1995
MS60	.15	——	——
MS65	——	.20	.20

VARIETIES: Two obverse cud varieties exist, along with a single, retained break for the reverse. Doubled dies include three obverse and one reverse, all of them minor.

COMMENTS: Fully struck, fully red gems are available in quantity, as are Mint State coins of any lesser quality. It must be noted, however, that the term "fully struck" is used with respect to the condition of the master hubs. Although the reverse master held up fairly well through the end of the Wheat Ear series, by 1957 the obverse master had suffered extreme wear and noticeable distortion.

When it seemed that incorrect date styling was a thing of the past, the Mint slipped up in 1957 with a short-tailed 7.

DENVER
1,051,342,000

RARITY: Common in all grades Fine and higher, original rolls and probably bags still exist.

POPULATION: MS TOTAL = 16   HIGHEST = MS66 RD (5)

VALUES:

GRADE	1965	1980	1995
MS60	.15	——	——
MS65	——	.20	.15

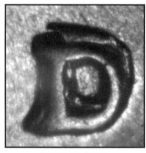

1957-D/D/D
RPM-2a (Miller)

VARIETIES: Cud varieties include six for the obverse and seven for the reverse. Four of the reverse cuds are retained, a common feature. More curious is that most of the obverse cuds do not appear in the usual position below Lincoln's bust but rather are seen within the motto IN GOD WE TRUST, resulting in the so-called "atheist" varieties (see photo).

Three minor doubled-dies are known, all of them on the obverse. There are at least 17 repunched mintmark varieties, including one which is triple-punched (see photo).

COMMENTS: Widely hoarded (as were all cents 1955-64), this issue is available in any and all grades. Fully struck, fully red gems are plentiful. With its huge mintage, specimens occasionally turn up in circulation.

1957-D
LC-57D-11
(Thurman & Margolis)

1958

PHILADELPHIA
252,525,000

RARITY: Common in all grades Fine and higher, original rolls and probably bags still exist.

POPULATION: MS TOTAL = 14   HIGHEST = MS66 RD (5)

VALUES:

GRADE	1965	1980	1995
MS60	.25	——	——
MS65	——	.25	.15

VARIETIES: Three obverse cud varieties are known, and more may turn up.

What was once widely heralded as a 1958/7 overdate has been largely discredited. A flaw in the die beneath numeral 8 gives the presentable illusion of a numeral 7.

A major obverse doubled-die is known (see photos). A single specimen has been certified by ANACS, and authenticator Michael Fahey of that company described it as "an early strike off a pair of normally polished dies."[172a] Graded MS64 RD, it is one of only three believed to exist.

COMMENTS: 1958-P cents are readily available in any and all grades through fully red gem. Most uncirculated coins, however, are of simply average quality.

The Philadelphia Mint was largely occupied with coinage for other countries during 1958. This fact, combined with a nationwide recession that year, accounts for the lower than usual mintages for all denominations. In fact, this mint coined only cents during the months of June, July, August and October. Nickels alone were added to the cent coinage during September and halves during November.[173]

1958 DDO-1
(Fivaz)

DENVER
800,953,300

RARITY: Quite common in all grades Fine and higher, original rolls and probably bags still exist.

POPULATION: MS TOTAL = 15   HIGHEST = MS66 RD (2)

VALUES:

GRADE	1965	1980	1995
MS60	.15	——	——
MS65	——	.20	.15

VARIETIES: Like 1958-P, an overdate made headlines during the 1970s, but this has since been discounted as a simple die flaw.

    Legitimate varieties do exist in some 19 repunched mintmarks (see photo) and seven cuds. All of the latter are on the obverse. As with 1957-D, the majority of the cuds are positioned within the motto IN GOD WE TRUST rather than the more familiar location beneath Lincoln's bust. This points to a recurring flaw in die steel and preparation, one which may also account for the prevalence of BIE breaks within LIBERTY. So common is the BIE phenomenon during the 1950s that it doesn't warrant specific mention here. Readers may assume that it is found for all dates and mints beginning around 1952 and lasting through 1968.

1958-D/D
RPM-1a (Miller)

COMMENTS: Fully struck, fully red gems are abundant, and there are no specific problems associated with coins of this date and mint.

    Although the recession of 1958 prevented this issue's mintage from equaling that of 1956-D and 1957-D, enough were coined to make 1958-D cents common in circulation until Wheat Ear cents disappeared almost entirely during the early-mid 1970s. A stray example can still be found from time to time in the 1990s. Why collectors, speculators and the non-numismatic public continue to hoard all of the worn coins of this and other common issues is anyone's guess.

Possible Transitional Piece

1959-D Wheat Reverse

PROLOGUE: A bit of unfinished business is the debate over the genuineness of this apparent muling of a normal 1959-D obverse with the obsolete Brenner reverse of 1909-58. Some have declared it an authentic product of the Denver Mint, albeit a clandestine one, while others have argued strongly that it is a clever counterfeit. The author has not examined the single known specimen and cannot say with certainty which side is right. The available facts are presented here, and readers may decide for themselves.

EVIDENCE: The early history of this cent is shrouded in mystery, as is often the case with coins of an unauthorized nature. Though this tends to arouse suspicion, it is not automatically proof of fraudulent activity. As an example, the 1913 Liberty Head Nickels have a similarly murky background, yet no one has seriously disputed their U. S. Mint origin.

Rumors of a muling between the old and new type Lincoln Cents are as old as the changeover to the Memorial reverse. A few clumsy fabrications made by hollowing out one side of a cent and inserting a plug cent of the other type have only muddied the waters further.

The first public appearance of the specimen illustrated above was in 1986. The coin's owner, Mr. Leon Baller of California, submitted it to the United States Secret Service in the hope of having it authenticated. This was a risky move, as any coin of a suspicious nature is subject to immediate seizure without compensation. To his delight, Baller received the following letter dated February 7, 1986, signed by Richard M. McDrew, Special Agent, United States Secret Service, Department of the Treasury:

> Enclosed is your United States 1c coin, dated 1959-D, with wheat reverse.
> This coin was microscopically examined by our Forensic Services Division in Washington, D.C., and it is their opinion the coin is genuine.

While to the layman this letter should settle the matter once and for all, anyone who has read this far in the present book will have learned that the Federal Government has a less than stellar record when it comes to either confirming or denying the legitimacy of numismatic objects. Still, on the basis of this authentication, the coin was sold shortly thereafter to Lincoln Cent specialist Steve Benson for an undisclosed sum in the five-figures.

It was also believed that this coin had been authenticated previously by the American Numismatic Association Certification Service, though there was no way to be certain that it was the very same piece. Though ANACS had indeed certified a cent of this description around 1976, it later reversed this decision on the premise that the coin proved to be a "cup and saucer" fabrication of the type described above.[174] How ANACS could have failed to notice this fact initially, given the great importance of such a specimen, was not clearly explained.

The real trouble arose when new owner Benson attempted to have the coin certified and graded by the Professional Coin Grading Service in 1993. In a letter dated April 20 of that year, PCGS President David Hall gave Benson the bad news:

> In our opinion the 1959-D Wheat Reverse cent is not a U. S. Mint product. We feel that it was made from fabricated dies, probably spark erosion. Our opinion is based on a visual examination. Our opinion was so strong that we felt more elaborate tests were unnecessary.

In a follow-up interview with *Coin World*, however, Hall conceded that "there is some chance that the coin could be genuine."[175]

One expert who disputed the finding of PCGS that this cent was a counterfeit was Sol Taylor, President of the Society of Lincoln Cent Collectors. His response to Coin World Editor Beth Deisher reads in part:

> I had examined the coin shortly before Mr. Hall got to look at it. I believe the coin is a U. S. Mint product.
>
> The fact that one such piece surfaced in the numismatic press does not make it a fake—in fact why would a counterfeiter go to the effort and expense of making a set of fake dies to make a single coin? The history of counterfeiting shows that many pieces are produced when the counterfeiter has made counterfeit dies.
>
> In time, I feel the 1959D mule (wheat back) cent will be certified as genuine and wind up in the standard numismatic guides.[176]

Taylor's argument regarding the pointlessness of coining a single example from counterfeit dies is a compelling one. Whatever the counterfeiter's own logic may be, at some point in his scheme greed will overcome him, and additional specimens will be struck. In fact, this is typically the undoing of most numismatic counterfeiters, as authenticators are able to match peculiarities in several coins that are ordinarily of a random nature and do not repeat.

In the same *Coin World* story which reported the PCGS declaration, Charles Hoskins, who was an authenticator with ANACS at the time it examined a 1959 muled cent, expressed his doubt that this single piece could be genuine. His argument was that a press run of mis-matched dies would result in 50,000 cents or more before the error could be spotted and the presses stopped. This supposes, of course, that this coin was the result of an error, but what if it was made intentionally as a piece de caprice?

Frank Gasparro, designer of the new Memorial reverse and at that time an assistant engraver at the Philadelphia Mint, denied this possibility in an interview with *Coin World*. He stated that no test specimens were made utilizing the 1959 obverse with the 1958 reverse. He also assured readers that access to the die vault was so restricted that no one could produce such a coin under these conditions. "Nobody gets to see that, absolutely nobody," Gasparro reported. "The only thing that could happen is [if a similar situation were to develop as] when they created an investigation into the gold deposit at Fort Knox."[177]

Despite Gasparro's protestations, when taking a tour of the San Francisco Mint during 1987 the author was permitted to visit its die locker and examine the as-yet unused dies for the Constitution Bicentennial Dollar, albeit under the supervision of a foreman. Taking this a step further, it's not difficult to imagine a trusted employee of the Philadelphia Mint gaining access to coinage dies as an ordinary function of his duties and placing them in a press during a quiet shift, though there's certainly no evidence that this actually occurred. Gasparro, who was himself Chief Engraver 1965-81 reported that opening the die vault requires two keys, one held by the Chief Engraver and one in the possession of his assistant.

Gasparro further asserted that no 1959-dated cents were coined before January 2, 1959, though the mints have in recent years begun producing the next year's coins at the onset of its fiscal year, October 1. It's not known whether this practice was in fashion during 1958-59, but there certainly could have been some overlap in production. If both types had been in production simultaneously, that would have facilitated the temporary muling of mis-matched dies. Defending the Mint, Gasparro stated that cents dated 1958 were coined right through December 31 of that year:

> They made it a point to see that everything was under eagle eye observation. When you start a new date, it has to occur on the first working day in January, which is the second.

They're pretty tight though with the security all the way around on those dies, so there's no chance of a mistake of, for instance, a 1958-dated coin still being struck into 1959.[178]

Diagonal die-polishing lines (ANAAB)

Close-up of date (ANAAB)

LINCOLN MEMORIAL REVERSE

1959 to DATE

1959

PHILADELPHIA
609,715,000

RARITY: Common in all grades Fine and higher, original rolls and bags still exist. For those collecting from circulation, this issue is now scarce.

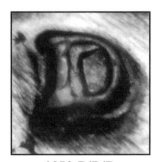

VALUES:	GRADE	1965	1980	1995
	MS60	.15	——	——
	MS65	——	.10	.10

VARIETIES: A single cud variety is known, the break appearing beneath Lincoln's bust (see photo). The only other variety, aside from the commonplace BIE breaks, is a minor obverse doubled-die.

1959-P
LC-59-1 (Thurman & Margolis)

COMMENTS: The design change led to this issue being even more widely hoarded than normal for Lincoln Cents of the period. Fully red gems are abundant.

Shortly after these coins entered circulation, reports began circulating that the 1959 cents were slightly thinner than previous issues and were a bit greater in diameter. Collectors claimed that 51 cents fit easily into a tube designed to stack 50, while the holes in plastic holders for cents had to be reamed to allow for the new coins. Mint Director William H. Brett denied that any changes had occurred in the physical dimensions of the cent, and nothing more seems to have been heard about this interesting possibility.[179]

* * *

In Fiscal Year 1959, a total of 16,115,529 cents were withdrawn from circulation as either mutilated or worn beyond further usefulness. These were taken in by the Treasury and the Federal Reserve Banks and then shipped to the various mints for melting and recoining.[180]

DENVER
1,279,760,000

RARITY: Common in all grades Fine and higher, original rolls and bags still exist.

VALUES:	GRADE	1965	1980	1995
	MS60	.10	——	——
	MS65	——	.10	.10

VARIETIES: At least 20 repunched mintmarks are known, the best of which (RPM-1) is tripled-punched (see photo). On one variety a stray D is obscured by the second numeral 9. This comes in several die states, of which the one illustrated is 1c. This date is also rich in cud varieties. All 12 are on the obverse, and all are in the usual position between Lincoln's bust and the rim.

1959-D/D/D
RPM-1c (Miller)

COMMENTS: Like 1959-P, this issue was widely hoarded in bag quantities and will never be rare in Mint State. Ironically, in the 1990s examples of both mints have become difficult to find in circulation. Still not rare, their elusiveness is almost certainly due to the general public tossing its "pennies" into jars and bowls rather than recirculating them.

Small Date

1960

Large Date

PHILADELPHIA
586,405,000

RARITY: Common in all grades Fine and higher, original rolls and bags still exist. This statement is true of the small date cents in greater proportion than their small mintage implies, yet both varieties were widely hoarded.

VALUES:	GRADE	1965	1980	1995
SMALL DATE:	MS60	9.00	——	——
	MS65	——	3.00	3.00
LARGE DATE:	MS60	.10	——	——
	MS65	——	.10	.10

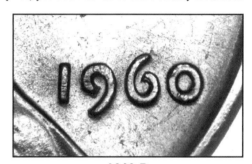

1960-P
Small Date, Breen-2228

VARIETIES: Surprisingly, no cuds are reported for either variety. Three obverse doubled-dies are noted for proofs only, also one which is common to both proofs and currency strikes. One is small date over large date, the other two large date over small date. This type of doubling is the consequence of using mismatched hubs during the die-sinking process. The first impression was made from a working hub of one size date, while the second and deeper impression was taken from a hub with the other date style. Also noted are two minor doubled-dies for the reverse, these on non-proofs.

1960-P
Large Date, Breen-2230

COMMENTS: The two varieties utilized this year represent distinct master dies derived from the common master hub. Since the final two numerals of the date were engraved into the new master die each year, their configuration will vary somewhat from one year to the next. Changes in midyear are very rare, as the Mint attempts to maintain uniformity. In fact, the only other known instance for Lincoln cents occurred in 1982 and created similar varieties for that date.

Early in 1960, it was determined that numeral 0 in the date 1960 was too small and was susceptible to breakage and filling in of the die. The master die for the cents of 1960 was quickly discarded and replaced with a new one into which a larger and more rounded numeral 0 was engraved. Numerals 6 and 9 were also lengthened and enlarged to better balance the larger size of the 0 and to reduce their own vulnerability to failure.

This change was not announced by the U. S. Mint, and that institution's personnel probably anticipated that no one would notice the difference. How wrong they were, as the discovery of this variety in the early Spring of 1960 energized the hobby and set off a nationwide treasure hunt for the scarcer small date varieties which ultimately involved the general public. Countless individuals received their first notice of the coin collecting hobby from news stories generated by this find.

The first inquiries about this obvious revision to the cent prompted official denial from Washington. Mint Director William H. Brett was quoted as saying "All U. S. one cent production stamping dies were forged from the same master hub containing the 1960 date element. No change was made."[181] Confronted with the hard evidence, the Mint later relented and admitted that a change had indeed been made.

Some 2,075,000 cents were coined at the Philadelphia Mint in January before production was halted. None were struck in February, and then cents alone were coined in March and April as the mint attempted to make up for lost production.[182] It's a reasonable assumption that the two million cents of January represent the total production of small date 1960-P cents for circulation. The fact that the large date coins were found so early in the year tends to reinforce this theory. The balance of the 1960-P cents seem to have been of the large date variety.

Because of massive hoarding, fully struck, fully red gems may be found of either variety. The small date coins are proportionally more scarce and have been nearly unobtainable from circulation. Note how dramatically the value of small date cents has fallen since 1965, after the initial excitement and speculative mania died down.

<hr />

DENVER
1,580,884,000

RARITY: Common in all grades Fine and higher, original rolls and bags still exist. Like 1960-P, the small date cents survive in smaller numbers overall yet in greater proportion with respect to the number minted.

VALUES:	GRADE	1965	1980	1995
SMALL DATE:	MS60	.60	——	——
	MS65	——	.30	.25
LARGE DATE:	MS60	.10	——	——
	MS65	——	.10	.10

1960-D/D
Small date over large date, RPM-1, Breen-2232 (Fivaz & Stanton)

VARIETIES: There are so many repunched mintmark varieties for this issue that they almost defy counting. There are 11 for the small date variety and at least 90 for the large date (see photo). RPM-1 is the most interesting, for it combines very widely separated mintmarks (the first of which touches numeral 9) with a small date over large date hubbing (see photo). RPM-9 features D over horizontal D. One other obverse doubled-die is also known, this one less interesting. Only a single obverse cud variety is known, though more may be expected from such a large mintage. Finally, this issue is rich in minor die breaks and cracks of all sort.

COMMENTS: There are no reliable projections on the number of 1960-D small date cents coined. Although forming a minority of the total mintage, small date coins are common enough that they carry only a modest premium. Both major varieties are readily available in fully red gem condition, yet quality cents of this issue are more scarce than for 1960-P. Denver Mint cents of this date and those that follow through 1964 have a rougher look to their surfaces than corresponding coins from the Philadelphia Mint, a trait that was common for other denominations as well.

1960-D/D
Large date, RPM-1a (Miller)

1961

PHILADELPHIA
753,345,000

RARITY: Common in all grades Fine and higher, original rolls and bags still exist.

VALUES:

GRADE	1965	1980	1995
MS60	.05	——	——
MS65	——	.10	.10

VARIETIES: One obverse and one reverse doubled-die is known for proofs only, both quite minor. There are no cud varieties reported for this date, as the Mint's die steel seems to have improved beginning around 1959-60.

COMMENTS: Fully red gems are quite common for this issue. As noted under 1960-D, the Philadelphia Mint coins dated 1960 through 1964 are generally superior in surface quality to their Denver Mint counterparts. Fuller strikes seem to have smoothed out the irregularities typically found on the planchets prior to striking.

*   *   *

As the speculative market in rolls and bags heated up following the discovery of small date and large date cents in 1960, collectors began to focus on monthly mintage reports with renewed intensity. This caused a peculiar excitement during the early months of each calendar year, as production figures were consistently quite small during the first quarter. This related to a budgetary factor, as the mints tended to use up their annual fiscal year appropriations right about the time that the new calendar year began. To justify the minting of proof coins, however, relatively small numbers of each denomination were struck off for circulation before production slowed, pending the new annual appropriation on July 1. Speculators, failing to understand this reasoning, repeatedly bid up the value of rolls early in each new year on the basis of the low production figures, only to have their plans foiled after the onset of the new fiscal year in July. Again and again Lee F. Hewitt, Editor of *The Numismatic Scrapbook Magazine*, reminded his readers of this fact, but just as regularly the farce was repeated each new year through the mid 1960s.

DENVER
1,753,266,700

RARITY: Common in all grades Fine and higher, original rolls and bags still exist.

VALUES:

GRADE	1965	1980	1995
MS60	.05	——	——
MS65	——	.10	.10

VARIETIES: At least 65 mintmarks are known, with more being found from time to time. The best of these is RPM-1, D over horizontal D (see photos).

COMMENTS: Fully red coins are common, yet many will display incomplete strikes and slightly rough surfaces. Still, enough coins survive in Mint State that a suitable example may be found with a bit of searching.

*   *   *

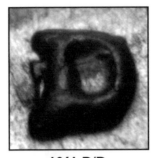 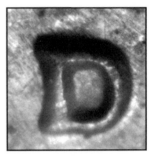

1961-D/D
RPM-1b, Breen-2237 (Miller)

1961-D/D
RPM-7a (Miller)

1961 was the first year in which a growing nationwide coin shortage became apparent. There were a number of causes, but the most persistent were the continual expansion of the vending machine industry and the slow collection of coins from such machines. Though it's hard to imagine today, in 1961 there were still uses for the one-cent piece in connection with the vending industry. Products which were dispensed for a "penny" typically included gumballs and hard candy, but most municipal parking meters still accepted these coins as well.

In her *Annual Report* to Treasury Secretary C. Douglas Dillon, Mint Director Eva Adams reported on the Mint's efforts to combat the great coin shortage, which was then still in its infancy:

> A sustained demand for domestic coins resulted in an extremely heavy manufacturing workload, and efforts were made to attain the maximum production possible with available funds. Coinage operations at the Denver Mint were started on an overtime basis and by September, 1961, three 8-hour shifts operated six days per week. The Philadelphia Mint, also on overtime, operated much of the year with two 12-hour shifts five days a week for all divisions except the proof coin production section which operated three shifts seven days a week, and the melting room which operated two additional 8-hour shifts on Saturdays.[83]

1962

PHILADELPHIA
606,045,000

RARITY: Common in all grades Fine and higher, original rolls and bags exist.

VALUES:

GRADE	1965	1980	1995
MS60	.05	——	——
MS65	——	.10	.10

VARIETIES: Five obverse doubled-dies are known, all minor and two of them for proofs. Seven doubled-dies are known for the reverse, three of them for proofs. Surprisingly, there are no cuds or other significant die breaks reported.

COMMENTS: 1962-P cents are usually well struck and fully lustrous, and countless gems may be found from among the hundreds of thousands saved by speculators.

The demand for cents was such in 1962 that the Philadelphia Mint coined this denomination alone from February through March and again from August through October. In April, only cents and halves were coined, in July only cents and nickels.[184]

* * *

Public Law 87-643, approved September 5, 1962, eliminated tin from the composition of the one-cent piece. It may be assumed that cents dated 1962 were coined of both the old and new compositions. These are indistinguishable by color or weight, as the amount of tin used in the alloy since that metal was restored in 1947 was evidently only one-tenth of one percent![185] Before World War II, tin had comprised as much as one percent of the alloy, the balance of each coin being 95% copper and 4% zinc.

DENVER
1,793,148,400

RARITY: Common in all grades Fine and higher, original rolls and bags still exist.

VALUES:

GRADE	1965	1980	1995
MS60	.05	——	——
MS65	——	.10	.10

VARIETIES: Three obverse cud varieties are reported, all in the familiar location below Lincoln's bust. At least 15 repunched mintmarks have been found, with more likely as collectors begin to break open all of the rolls and bags put away during the height of the 1959-64 boom in modern coins (see photo).

COMMENTS: Despite the large number of available specimens, true gems are difficult to find. The surface texture of D-Mint cents dated 1960-64 is often rough, revealing the irregularities which were present on the planchet prior to striking.

1962-D/D
RPM-7 (Miller)

1963

PHILADELPHIA
754,110,000

RARITY: Common in all grades Fine and higher, original rolls and bags still exist.

VALUES:

GRADE	1965	1980	1995
MS60	.05	——	——
MS65	——	.10	.10

VARIETIES: No cud varieties are reported, but one or more may yet turn up as the many unopened bags are finally searched. Four reverse doubled-dies are known, two of them for proofs, all of them minor.

COMMENTS: As with 1962-P, gems are not too difficult to find among the countless Mint State examples saved. The quality of P-Mint cents from this period is markedly superior to that of D-Mint coins.

———◆◆●◆◆———

DENVER
1,774,020,400

RARITY: Common in all grades Fine and higher, original rolls and bags still exist.

VALUES:

GRADE	1965	1980	1995
MS60	.05	——	——
MS65	——	.10	.10

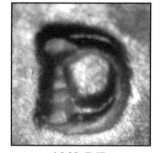

1963-D/D
RPM-4 (Miller)

VARIETIES: No cud breaks are recorded, but it seems likely that some will turn up from such an enormous mintage. At least 15 repunched mintmarks are known, with more being found from time to time (see photo).

   Of the four obverse doubled-dies reported, the most interesting is distinguished by the first impression having a much lower numeral 3 in the date. In *The Lincoln Cent Doubled Die,* author John A. Wexler speculated that this may have been the product of two different hubs, the first with numeral 3 placed lower than on the second. While this is quite possible in theory, it may also be that the entire obverse was doubled until this error was spotted by the engraver or the coiner. A vigorous polishing of the die would have eliminated most signs of the first impression, but an oversight may have left only the 3 remaining. Wexler added that this feature is diminished in later states of the die, leaving only part of the 3 visible.

COMMENTS: As with other Denver Mint cents of the early 1960s, gems form a very small percentage of the many coins saved. This issue was coined rather carelessly from inadequately prepared planchets, leaving many irregularities and rough spots visible. This problem is aggravated by the fact that coins produced after World War II seem to have spent more time being jostled about by the mints and the banking system. Contact marks from other coins are almost always a problem with cents of the late 1940s through 1968. This phenomenon eases a bit with the lower-relief cents coined since 1969, as they are better protected by their rims.

1964

PHILADELPHIA
2,451,945,000
SAN FRANCISCO
196,630,000
TOTAL
2,648,575,000

RARITY: Common in all grades Fine and higher, original rolls and bags exist.

VALUES:

GRADE	1965	1980	1995
MS60	.05	——	——
MS65	——	.10	.10

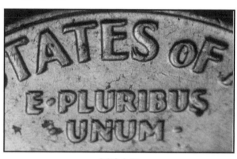

1964-P
DDR-1 (Fivaz & Stanton)

VARIETIES: Two obverse cud varieties are reported, with more likely to be found. Six reverse doubled-dies are known, with four of them for proofs. Only one is significant, as it shows good separation in the lettering (see photo).

COMMENTS: The enormous mintage for this issue has resulted in a broad variance in quality. Many reveal worn and overly polished dies, but gems are available with a bit of searching.

* * *

The severe coin shortage which developed in the early 1960s reached a peak in 1964. Despite requests as far back as the 1940s that a new Philadelphia Mint be built, this appropriation was not forthcoming until 1963, and the new, modern facility desired was not operational until 1969. In testimony before a Congressional committee, Mint Director Eva Adams revealed that the delay in authorizing a new mint structure had been caused by various factions within the city of Philadelphia arguing over where it would be located.[186]

With only its two aging facilities built during the very early years of the 20th Century, the U. S. Mint was ill-prepared to cope with the tremendous increase in demand for additional coins. The post-war spread of sales taxes was largely responsible for the increased demand, as was too the ever-growing application of vending machines and parking meters. More frequent collections of the coins held captive by these machines would have largely relieved the slow return of coins to the banking system, but this fact was not revealed until a few years later when it came out during Congressional hearings on the coin shortage.

In 1963-64, the shortage of coins was mistakenly linked to the growing popularity of coin collecting. Citing the trend toward hoarding rolls and bags of newly issued coins, a defensive Mint Bureau recommended that measures be taken to discourage the hoarding of coins by collectors and speculators. Of course, the hundreds of thousands of coins then being squirreled away as potential investments were just a tiny fraction of the billions being minted, yet this explanation was readily swallowed by a baffled Congress. As a result, legislation was passed September 3, 1964 authorizing the Mint to freeze the 1964 date on all coins produced until such time that the crisis was declared over. Cents dated 1964 were thus coined through 1965, accounting for their record mintage. On December 29, 1965, the mints were ordered to switch to 1965-dated dies, and no more cents bearing the 1964 date were coined.[187]

Once again, one had to wonder why the San Francisco Mint had been closed at a time when the United States economy was growing. Mint Director Adams was among those who questioned the wisdom of that decision, and she so indicated on July 2, 1964 in her testimony before Congress' Subcommittee on Legal and Monetary Affairs, Committee on Government Operations:

Please bear in mind that there have been no new mints built in this country for many, many years. Everybody avoids and never mentions the subject of the closing of the San Francisco Mint in 1955. Since it has been brought up I must say very frankly that we wish it had never been closed, however, it was closed, and that, so far as we are concerned, takes care of it, because it was very thoroughly closed.[188]

Strictly speaking, while the mint was closed and its presses removed, the structure still housed a Federal assay office. In fact, Public Law 87-534, passed July 11, 1962, had officially renamed this mint as the San Francisco Assay Office. In addition to housing this operation, the old mint building was occupied by offices of the National Park Service, the Bureau of Commercial Fisheries of the Department of the Interior, and the General Services Administration. The coin shortage would simply not go away, however, and on September 1, 1965 the San Francisco Assay Office, recently equipped with four refurbished presses, began striking 1964-dated cents for circulation without mintmarks. These are indistinguishable from those coined at Philadelphia.

The mid 1960s was probably the most stressful period in the history of the United States Mint since it was threatened with abolition in the early 1800s. Everyone wanted to know what was being done to relieve the coin shortage, and Director Adams was called before Congressional committees on several occasions. At the same time that it was achieving record-setting production figures, the Mint was adopting numerous improved methods for further enhancing its output. These are described in the *Annual Report* for Fiscal Year 1964:

> To achieve this unprecedented rate of production in fiscal year 1964, the Bureau of the Mint adopted a number of innovations. Rolled nickel strip, ready for blanking, was purchased from private industry for use in the five-cent cupro-nickel coinage. This procedure then permitted all of the melting and rolling capacity of the two Mints to be utilized in the production of the bronze cents and the subsidiary silver denominations. One-cent coinage at Philadelphia was further implemented by the purchase of zinc in weight-controlled slabs, cast in a size appropriate for adding directly to a bronze melt, thus eliminating the shearing of the zinc. Late in the year contracts for bronze strip were awarded to private industry. This, in turn, eliminates melting and rolling of the bronze alloy at the Mints, a measure of particular significance since the one-cent denomination is required in greatest volume for circulation.

Even these measures proved inadequate, as the coin shortage intensified throughout 1964. Desperate measures were called for, and these even included the return from museums of two antique coin presses, which were then slightly modified and put into actual production! These two historic presses may now be seen, respectively, at the Nevada State Museum in Carson City and the American Numismatic Association Museum in Colorado Springs, Colorado. Machines then being used by the General Services Administration and the Department of Defense were borrowed and hastily converted into blanking presses for the manufacture of planchets.[189]

<img_1>

DENVER
3,799,071,500

RARITY: Common in all grades Fine and higher, original rolls and bags still exist.

VALUES:

GRADE	1965	1980	1995
MS60	.05	—	—
MS65	—	.10	.10

1964-D/D
RPM-9a (Miller)

VARIETIES: Three minor doubled-dies are known, two for the obverse and one for the reverse. Some 17 repunched mintmarks are known, with more being found from time to time (see photo).

Six obverse cud varieties are reported. All of these are fairly small breaks and are confined to the space below Lincoln's bust. This suggests greatly improved die stock over that which was employed during the 1950s.

COMMENTS: 1964-D cents, though extremely abundant in uncirculated condition, are usually of poor quality. They may possess excellent luster and be generally well struck, but more often they display some roughness of surface and light to moderate striations from crude polishing of the dies.

To discourage speculators from saving them, cents dated 1964-D were struck for a full two years, their production continuing until December 29, 1965.[190]

1965

PHILADELPHIA
301,470,000
DENVER
973,364,900
SAN FRANCISCO
220,030,000
TOTAL
1,494,864,900

RARITY: Common in all grades Fine and higher, original rolls and possibly bags still exist.

VALUES:

GRADE	1980	1995
MS65	.10	.20

VARIETIES: Four cud varieties are known, all but one on the obverse.

COMMENTS: The quality of this issue varies widely, with fully struck, early die-state gems being somewhat elusive.

Mintmarks were omitted from 1965 through 1967 in a misguided effort to foil coin speculators. The Mint needn't have bothered, as the speculative market in rolls and bags of common, late-date coins broke toward the end of 1964, leaving thousands of so-called numismatists quite literally holding the bag. With no further economic incentive to hoard cents, it's doubtful that as many examples were saved of this and later issues as were saved 1955-64.

All three mints coined 1965-dated cents, with production not commencing until December 29, 1965; cents coined in 1965 up to that time had all been dated 1964. In fact, only 1,085,000 cents dated 1965 were actually coined in that year! The 1965 date was then utilized exclusively through July of 1966, the Mint switching to production of 1966-dated cents on August 1, 1966.[191] This situation was confusing to all concerned, but it did preserve date continuity. Doing so was not particularly important in the case of cents and nickels, but Washington wanted to maintain an illusion of normality with respect to the new silverless dimes, quarters and halves. Had that not been the case, it's likely that 1965-dated cents would not exist today.

* * *

With the one-cent piece serving as the primary focus of the Mint's efforts to eradicate the coin shortage, this denomination was ultimately declared the first to become available in adequate supply. Testifying before Congress in the Spring of 1965, Mint Director Eva Adams remarked "At this moment, gentlemen, we can tell you with pride and conviction that the coin situation is definitely improved. In fact, the serious shortage of the one-cent piece is practically over, from all available information."[192]

Chief Engraver since 1947, Gilroy Roberts resigned his employment with the United States Mint in 1965 to join a commercial coining operation in Pennsylvania which would shortly thereafter adopt the name Franklin Mint. He was succeeded in this role by veteran employee Frank Gasparro.

The Numismatist for August, 1968 carried an interesting story regarding a 1965 Lincoln Cent that won't fit into one's album and is already a "slab" in its own right:

A tribute to the memory and ideals of Abraham Lincoln, the Lincoln Coin Memorial is now under construction in Sudbury, Ontario, Canada. Designed by Edward Reid, this monument, will stand in Sudbury's Canadian Centennial Numismatic Park.

Construction of the Lincoln Coin Memorial is now being completed by Bruno Cavallo, artist-designer of all the coin monuments presently erected in the Park, of which the 42 foot Big Nickel is the centerpiece.

Because 1965 marks the 100th Anniversary of the assassination of President Lincoln, a 1965 one cent piece was chosen for the Lincoln Coin Memorial, and an exact copper replica of the coin, 10 feet in diameter and one foot thick, will be erected. The base of the 18 foot monument will be a replica of the Lincoln Memorial in Washington, D.C.

Atop the Lincoln Memorial, a symbolic yoke will be suspended by stainless steel bars which will also hold the giant penny aloft.

As is the custom with each coin monument, the owners and developers of the numismatic park will provide a medallion souvenir of this latest addition to the park. Proceeds from the sales of these medallions help to finance the construction of the coin monuments.

1966

PHILADELPHIA
811,100,000
DENVER
991,431,200
SAN FRANCISCO
383,355,000
TOTAL
2,185,886,200

RARITY: Common in all grades Fine and higher, original rolls and possibly bags still exist.

VALUES:

GRADE	1980	1995
MS65	.10	.20

VARIETIES: A single obverse doubled-die is noted, this one quite minor.

Amazingly, no less than 23 obverse cud varieties are known, along with two for the reverse. It's quite possible that the hurried production schedule for this issue cut into the quality of die steel. Note, however, that nearly all cud breaks since the adoption of the Memorial reverse have been confined to the obverse. With their much greater relief and more demanding metal displacement, the obverse dies are far more subject to stress and failure (see photo).

1966-P
LC-66-10   (Thurman & Margolis)

COMMENTS: The cents of 1966 seem to be especially bright and lustrous, with gems fairly easy to find. It's likely, however, that fewer were saved of this issue than of those struck 1955-64.

Coined entirely during the final five months of 1966, these cents were struck at all three mints without distinguishing marks. Although attractive coins may be found, they all suffer from the withered condition of the obverse master hub used since 1916. Already grossly worn and distorted when the Memorial reverse was introduced in 1959, by 1966 this hub was ghastly. The tremendous mintages of the 1960s only accelerated its deterioration. Had it not been for the coin shortage of 1961-65, remedial action might have been taken sooner. Instead, relief was not forthcoming until 1969.

1967

PHILADELPHIA
907,575,000
DENVER
1,327,377,100
SAN FRANCISCO
813,715,000
TOTAL
3,048,667,100

RARITY: Common in all grades Fine and higher, original rolls still exist. Sol Taylor reported in his book that bags have yet to turn up.[193] It's quite possible that no bag quantities were saved. This fact reflects the withered condition of the speculative market in 1967 after collapsing in 1964-65.

VALUES:

GRADE	1980	1995
MS65	.10	.20

VARIETIES: Among cud varieties, 11 are found for the obverse and only one for the reverse. As is typical for reverse cuds on the Memorial cents, this one is quite small. Given the enormous coinage, it's surprising that there aren't any doubled-dies known.

COMMENTS: Aside from the deficiencies imposed by the worn obverse master hub, 1967 cents are relatively easy to find in gem condition.

Contemporary reports indicate that the great coin shortage was history by the end of 1965, but the Treasury Department wasn't taking any chances. The authority to both freeze the 1964 date and suspend the use of mintmarks remained in effect, though only the latter was employed in 1967. All cents of this date were actually coined in 1967, and no other dates were coined that year.

1968

PHILADELPHIA
1,707,880,970

RARITY: Common in all grades Fine and higher, original rolls still exist.

VALUES: | GRADE | 1980 | 1995 |
            |-------|------|------|
            | MS65 | .15 | .25 |

VARIETIES: Two minor obverse doubled-dies are noted.

COMMENTS: In all respects save for sharpness, gems are readily available. Most dies were used far too long, and the worn condition of both the obverse master hub and the working dies of either side combined to produce cents with very poor strikes.

In the rush to hoard 1968-S cents, this issue was somewhat overlooked, perhaps accounting for its premium value in the 1995 listing.

* * *

1968 marked the final date for which the obverse hub of 1916 was employed. The years had taken their toll, and there were few recognizable features left to Lincoln's portrait. His face and beard had long ago blended into a single shapeless mass, and his bow tie was similarly obscure. Repeated impressions from this hub had not only worn the design but caused it to spread outwardly toward the borders. Lincoln's bust had actually become larger than it was in 1909 or 1916, and all of the peripheral lettering was touching the rim on cents dated 1968. As for a border, there really wasn't any by this time, only the rim raised up by the upsetting mill during planchet preparation.

DENVER
2,886,269,600

RARITY: Common in all grades Fine and higher, original rolls still exist.

VALUES: | GRADE | 1980 | 1995 |
            |-------|------|------|
            | MS65 | .10 | .10 |

VARIETIES: Five obverse cud breaks are reported, along with four repunched mint-marks (see photo) and one obverse doubled-die.

1968-D/D
RPM-1b (Miller)

COMMENTS: Fully red gems are readily available, but most show moderate to heavy die wear in addition to the flaws inherent in the obverse master hub.

Although the Denver Mint had coined cents steadily throughout the years 1965-67, this was the first issue since 1964 to bear a mintmark. The D mintmark was restored on all coins struck there at the beginning of the year, as noted in a Treasury Department release dated January 4:

The 1968 United States coins, which carry mint marks for the first time since the 1964 dated coins, were shown today at the Denver Mint, Miss Eva Adams, Director of the Mint, and Mrs. Marian Rossmiller, Superintendent of the Denver Mint, presided at ceremonies which included the inspection of a specimen proof coin set bearing the San Francisco mint mark.[194]

Since the Coinage Act of 1965 had suspended the use of mintmarks for a period of five years following its enactment, special legislation was required to restore them prematurely. This was achieved through Public Law 90-29, passed June 24, 1967.[195]

* * *

The great coin shortage over, the three minting facilities were now staffed at normal levels. Their personnel figures are quite revealing. At the end of Fiscal Year 1968 (June 30), the Bureau of the Mint had a total of 1,700 employees, down from the 2,070 persons one year earlier. Of this number, 71 were located in the Office of the Director in Washington, D.C. The largest number, 562, were employed at the Philadelphia Mint, which was soon to relocate to a new and much greater structure. The Denver Mint had 388 employees, the San Francisco Assay Office 414. Other facilities within the Bureau of the Mint included the New York Assay Office (202, The West Point Depository (31), and the Fort Knox Depository (32). For the three locations which struck coins, the greatest number of employees were naturally in their Coining Departments. Building and Mechanical workers made up the next largest figures, with the exception of the Philadelphia Mint, which alone had 74 persons engaged in the Engraving Department. Cash and deposit handlers were next in descending order, followed by administrators, guards, Melting and Refining employees, custodians, and those engaged in assaying. San Francisco alone had 34 persons assigned to numismatic products, including the assembly and distribution of proof sets, uncirculated sets and medals.

SAN FRANCISCO
258,270,001

1968-S/S
RPM-1   (Miller)

RARITY: Though common in all grades Fine and higher, 1968-S is one of the few scarcities among Lincoln Memorial Cents in circulation. Original rolls and possibly bags still exist.

VALUES:

GRADE	1980	1995
MS65	.10	.10

VARIETIES: Three minor obverse doubled-dies may be found, one of these for proofs. Two repunched mintmark varieties are known, with others likely (see photo).

COMMENTS: Gems may be found with little difficulty, although few cents of this issue were coined from sharp dies. It's likely that the worn condition of the obverse master hub made even newly sunk dies appear old.

The San Francisco Assay Office (so-named after 1962) had been coining cents since 1965 without mintmarks, and it was a daring move to restore the romantic letter S to these coins beginning in 1968. The Mint's action proved a mistake, as the relatively low mintage of this issue combined with the special aura that all S-Mint coins held for collectors led to widespread hoarding. 1968-S is perhaps among the few post-1964 cents for which bag quantities were saved by speculators.

The decision to include mintmarks on cents coined for circulation at the San Francisco Mint was a critical one for another reason, as well. It had already been announced by the Mint in the Fall of 1967 that proof coinage would resume in 1968, with all such coins to be made in San Francisco and carrying the S mintmark. As the Mint began taking orders, it drew an inquiry from *The Numismatic Scrapbook Magazine* as to whether San Francisco's circulating coins would also be mintmarked. The desirability of proof sets was the ultimate issue, since their value to collectors would be greatly enhanced if they were the only source of S mintmarks.[196] The Mint's response that only cents and nickels would be coined for circulation at the San Francisco Mint and that they would indeed carry mintmarks came too late to prevent a large oversubscription of proof sets, and the only persons dissatisfied with the results were those who failed to obtain all the sets they wanted.

1969

PHILADELPHIA
1,136,910,000

RARITY: Common in all grades Very Fine and higher, original rolls still exist.

VALUES: | GRADE | 1980 | 1995 |
|---|---|---|
| MS65 | .15 | .35 |

VARIETIES: A single obverse doubled-die is known; it is quite minor.

COMMENTS: Fully struck, fully red gems are readily available. In the rush to hoard 1969-S cents, this issue was somewhat overlooked, perhaps accounting for its premium value in the 1995 listing.

    A new obverse master hub was employed beginning with the cent coinage of 1969 and was used through 1973. This restored the scale of Lincoln's portrait to what it had been in 1909, although the original galvano may not have been used. While similar to the cent of 1909, the fine details are treated differently, and the mottos have broader letters which are less subject to breaking and filling in the die.

*   *   *

    One of the great scandals in recent numismatic history was the creation of the 1969-P "doubled-die" cents. These were outright fabrications and are not to be confused with the legitimate 1969-S doubled-die cents. The spread of the doubling on the 1969-P cents was so extreme that no engraver or coiner could have missed it, and it's nearly inconceivable that such a die would have been placed in the press.

1969-D/D
RPM-1 (Miller)

DENVER
4,002,832,200

RARITY: Common in all grades Very Fine and higher, original rolls still exist.

VALUES: | GRADE | 1980 | 1995 |
|---|---|---|
| MS65 | .10 | .15 |

VARIETIES: Seven obverse cud varieties are known, along with 10 repunched mint-marks (see photos).

COMMENTS: Fully struck, fully red gems are readily available.

1969-D
LC-69D-5 (Thurman & Margolis)

SAN FRANCISCO
544,375,000

RARITY: Common in all grades Very Fine and higher, original rolls and possibly bags still exist. 1969-S cents are somewhat elusive in circulation.

VALUES: | GRADE | 1980 | 1995 |
|---|---|---|
| MS65 | .10 | .15 |

VARIETIES: Six obverse cuds and one reverse cud are known. Amazingly, one of the obverse varieties is for proof cents! At least two repunched mintmark varieties are also known.

Easily the most highly sought variety for 1969-S is an obverse doubled-die, the only one for this issue but a very dramatic doubling that is comparable to the more widely heralded 1972-P doubled-die. More about this may be found below.

COMMENTS: 1969-S cents were generally quite well made, and fully struck, fully red gems are common. Hoarding of this issue was widespread, and it's one of the few issues after 1964 saved in bag quantities. These bags may have already been searched for the doubled-die variety.

DOUBLED-DIE OBVERSE

SAN FRANCISCO
(mintage unknown)

1969-S
DDO-1, Breen-2252 (Fivaz & Stanton)

1969-S
DDO-1, Breen-2252 (Fivaz & Stanton)

RARITY: This variety is rare in all grades. The figures below date from January 1996 and do not include the number of coins certified by NGC, as this information was not available at press time.

POPULATION: MS BN = 0   MS RB = 1   MS RD = 3   MS TOTAL = 4
               MS65 RD = 2   HIGHEST = MS65 RD (2)

VALUES:

GRADE	1980	1995
MS65	——	——

COMMENTS: In addition to the data above, several circulated examples have been certified. The complete breakdown looks like this: XF45 (1), AU50 (1), AU53 (1), AU55 (2), AU58 (6), MS62 RB (1), MS65 RD (2)

This variety is as distinct and impressive as the more widely heralded 1972 doubled-die. Dual impressions are clearly visible in the date and the motto IN GOD WE TRUST (see photos). Quite rare, no more than 15-20 examples have turned up, this despite the thorough searching of all variety enthusiasts. Given such a small survival rate, it's doubtful that more 100 could have been released, if even that many.

Mechanical or strike doubling of the mintmark is common on 1969-S cents and should not be confused with the doubled-die variety. The doubled-die will show no doubling in the mintmark, as this was applied to the die after it was hubbed.

When the counterfeit 1969-P doubled-die cents were exposed, it led to an unfortunate situation in which the legitimate 1969-S doubled-die cents were viewed with the same suspicion. In its zeal to stamp them out, the U. S. Secret Service seized several specimens of the 1969-S doubled-die coins from their owners and had them destroyed by the Mint. It even went so far as to provide photographs of the supposed counterfeits to *The Numismatic Scrapbook Magazine*, which ran them in its October 1970 issue. There's no indication that the Secret Service or the Mint ever admitted its error, though no effort has been made since the 1970s to seize the few known specimens.

1970

PHILADELPHIA
1,898,315,000

RARITY: Common in all grades Very Fine and higher, original rolls still exist.

VALUES:

GRADE	1980	1995
MS65	.15	.25

VARIETIES: There are no less than six obverse doubled-dies listed by John A. Wexler in *The Lincoln Cent Doubled Die*. All are of little significance, with the exception of two which combine hubbings from both the small date and large date hubs. Since these hubs were used to produce a number of working dies, these varieties exist for all three mints. For a description of the small date and large date hubs, see VARIETIES for 1970-S.

COMMENTS: Fully struck, fully red gems are readily available, and there doesn't seem to be any logic to the premium that this issue carries. Whatever perceived scarcity may exist is understandable only to those who collect by rolls and bags.

In preparing the obverse master die for 1970, the Mint was caught napping. A correct styling of numeral 7 would have given it a long tail to match numeral 9, but this wasn't addressed until 1971. To date, this has been the last such mistake, and one hopes that no more will occur. Of course, should the Lincoln Cent still be in production as late as the year 2000, the absence of a numeral 9 as the second digit may permit a rethinking of the whole matter of conformity.

DENVER
2,891,438,900

RARITY: Common in all grades Very Fine and higher, original rolls still exist.

VALUES:

GRADE	1980	1995
MS65	.10	.10

VARIETIES: Five obverse and two reverse cuds may be found, along with six repunched mintmarks (see photo).

Three minor obverse doubled-dies are known, along with the two mismatched hub doubled-dies described for 1970-P, these appearing on working dies of all three mints.

COMMENTS: Fully struck, fully red gems are readily available.

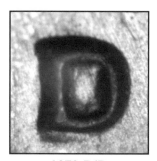

1970-D/D
RPM-1 (Miller)

RARITY: Common in all grades Very Fine and higher, original rolls and possibly bags still exist.

VALUES:

GRADE		1980	1995
SMALL DATE:	MS65	2.00	40.00
LARGE DATE:	MS65	.10	.15

1970-S/S
RPM-1 (Miller)

VARIETIES: Five obverse cuds and one reverse cud exist, in addition to four repunched mintmarks (see photo).

Six obverse doubled-die varieties may be found. DDO-1 is quite pronounced and extremely rare, perhaps too rare to be considered collectable (see photos). In addition, there are the mismatched hub varieties described for 1970-P and found with this issue as well.

The small date and large date varieties are also known as high 7 and low 7, respectively. They represent two different working hubs, although they appear to have been generated from the single master die of 1970. On the scarcer small date variety, the top of numeral 7 is aligned with the top of numerals 9 and 0. The more common large date variety features this numeral 7 noticeably lower at its top than the adjacent numerals. The word LIBERTY is also smaller on the small date variety, a result of the same flawed hub. These varieties exist for both proof and currency strikes. No records were kept by the Mint for the individual mintages of these varieties, if indeed the Mint was even aware of them until alerted by collectors.

1970-S
Small date, Breen-2256 (Mike Sulak)

1970-S
DDO-1 (Fivaz & Stanton)

1970-S
Large date, Breen-2255

COMMENTS: Like all S-Mint cents coined 1968-74, these were widely hoarded by the roll and the bag. Fully red, fully struck gems are readily available, though the small date variety exists in proportionally smaller numbers.

The small date and large date varieties were reported early in the year, the first finds coming from Pennsylvania, New York, Virginia, Tennessee and Texas.[197] It's interesting to note that none of these states are close to the coins' place of manufacture, suggesting that the Mint was already combating the hoarding of S-Mint cents by distributing them far afield. Doubt of the small date cent's validity quickly turned to scorn on the part of numismatic authorities. The fact that the distinctions were not as clear as in 1960 prompted many to describe the small date variety as the product of simple die polishing, and specialists in the error/variety field warned collectors away from it.[198] Though still not as celebrated nor as eagerly sought as the 1960 small date cent, the 1970-S edition appears to have gained general acceptance since that time.

1971

PHILADELPHIA
1,919,490,000

RARITY: Common in all grades Very Fine and higher, original rolls still exist.

VALUES:

GRADE	1980	1995
MS65	.10	.40

VARIETIES: Of the four obverse doubled-die varieties known, only one shows clearly enough to interest the non-specialist.

COMMENTS: 1971-P cents are readily available in gem condition. Like the P-Mint cents of the preceding three year, there is some premium attached to this issue due to its slight scarcity in roll quantities.

* * *

Mint Director Mary Brooks was present for the unveiling June 10, 1971 of a statue of Benjamin Franklin in Philadelphia, honoring the 100th anniversary of Philadelphia's Paid Fire Department. This figure was formed by sculptor Reginald E. Beauchamp from 80,000 cents that had been raised by Philadelphia's school children.

"The nation's most popular coin is the penny," Mrs. Brooks remarked. "The Mint makes over 5 billion pennies a year and 76 percent of its coin production is devoted to making pennies."[199]

One hopes that before her term was over in 1977, Mrs. Brooks learned that these coins are properly called *cents.*

DENVER
2,911,045,600

RARITY: Common in all grades Very Fine and higher, original rolls still exist.

VALUES:

GRADE	1980	1995
MS65	.10	.40

VARIETIES: Six obverse cuds are known, including two which obliterate at least one third of the design. In addition, a single reverse cud may be found. Finally, there are four repunched mintmark varieties (see photo).

COMMENTS: There's little to say about these coins; they're readily available in gem condition.

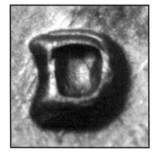

1971-D/D
RPM-2 (Miller)

SAN FRANCISCO
525,133,459

RARITY: Common in all grades Very Fine and higher, original rolls and possibly bags still exist. Specimens are rarely encountered in circulation due to mindless hoarding of anything that carries the S mintmark.

VALUES:

GRADE	1980	1995
MS65	.10	.40

1971-S/S
RPM-1   (Miller)

VARIETIES: Of the five obverse cud varieties two are quite prominent. The only doubled-dies are two proof varieties, both distinctive enough to be collectable. Exclusive of the proof dies, there are four repunched mintmark varieties (see photo).

COMMENTS: Fully struck, fully red gems are common, and the premium attached to this issue is purely speculative.

1972

PHILADELPHIA
2,933,255,000

RARITY: Common in all grades Very Fine and higher, original rolls still exist.

VALUES:

GRADE	1980	1995
MS65	.10	.10

VARIETIES: The two known obverse cud varieties are both "atheist" coins on which part of the motto IN GOD WE TRUST has been obliterated.

There are some nine obverse doubled-dies for this date and mint, suggesting a fundamental flaw in the die making process. Hubs and dies are supposed to be keyed and grooved to prevent such misalignments, but this practice was allowed to lapse from time to time, particularly when a large number of working dies were needed quickly.

Of the nine doubled-die varieties, only one warrants the large premiums listed in retail catalogs, though two others are distinctive enough to be collectable. A detailed study of the most popular variety may be found on the following page. In his book *The Lincoln Cent Doubled Die*, John A. Wexler provides a more comprehensive treatment of the other doubled-die varieties than is possible in this volume. It's worth noting, however, that one of the minor doubled-dies was apparently due to a defective master die for 1972. Doubling is thus evident on as many as half of all the cents coined that year from all three mints, including the S-Mint proofs. Presumably, the defective master die was replaced by another sometime during the year.

COMMENTS: 1972-P cents are readily available in gem condition. Although rolls are still common, a number have been broken up by those searching for doubled-die cents.

*   *   *

An amusing tradition centers around cents dated 1972 from any of the three mints. The crew of the aircraft carrier *U.S.S. Abraham Lincoln* each wear a single cent of this date affixed to plastic nametags. Why? Its hull number is CVA-72. Sailors, being traditionally superstitious, affix some importance to this number, and acquiring one's '72 penny is a rite of passage.

In her *Annual Report* to Treasury Secretary George P. Shultz, Mint Director Mary Brooks announced an apparent innovation in coin manufacture:

> A new system of scheduling production in the two principal mints (Philadelphia and Denver) was introduced whereby each is assigned to work exclusively on given denominations, on a 4-month cycle, except for cents, which are continuously in production at both places. A reversal of denominations is made at the end of each cycle. A goal of this system is to reach and maintain a 4-month inventory of each denomination (except cents) at the end of each cycle at each Mint, in order that each Mint can effectively serve its geographic area.[200]

What Mrs. Brooks evidently didn't realize was that a system virtually identical to the one she describes had been in place during the early 1960s until it was swept away under the pressure of a nationwide coin shortage.

DOUBLED-DIE OBVERSE

PHILADELPHIA
(mintage unknown)

RARITY:
Though lightly circulated examples may be found, most of the known specimens have been preserved uncirculated. Choice and gem coins exist in sufficient numbers to meet the demand.

1972-P
DDO-1, Breen-2265 (Fivaz & Stanton)

POPULATION: MS BN = 12   MS RB = 122   MS RD = 1488
MS TOTAL = 1622
MS65 RD = 837   HIGHEST = MS67 RD (4)

VALUES:	GRADE	1980	1995
	MS65	225.00	275.00

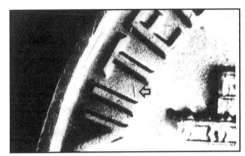

Die scratch between I and T, found on genuine examples (ANAAB)

COMMENTS: The only 1972 doubled-die variety which commands the listed premiums is DDO-1, illustrated here. Other than the famous 1955 doubled-die, which started this entire area of collecting, the 1972 variety is the most widely known and collected doubled-die in the Lincoln series.

Walter Breen reported that cents of this variety were released the week of August 2-9, 1972, but their appearance clearly predates this time.[201] In fact, Philadelphia coin dealer Harry Forman displayed several examples at a coin club meeting as early as July 5. Though a few early reports came from as far away as California, most of the larger finds occurred in Indiana and Pennsylvania. By August 2, 1972 doubled-die cents were already trading on dealer teletypes at prices ranging from $60-125 for singles and $4000 per roll of 50 coins.[202]

John Wexler's estimate of 75,000 coins issued seems a bit high with respect to the number seen in the marketplace and the total certified population.[203] Unlike the 1955 doubled-die, which was slow to be publicized and gain a collector following, this variety was front-page news from the outset, and it's doubtful that more than a few escaped detection. Sol Taylor's estimate of 20,000 coins released is more in keeping with this cent's availability.[204]

Despite its fiasco with the 1969-S doubled-die cents, the U. S. Mint acknowledged the genuineness of this variety. On July 21, 1972, Dr. Alan J. Goldman, Assistant Mint Director for Technology, confirmed that these cents were legitimate products of the Philadelphia Mint, thus signaling a boon for the hobby, as well as a new era of cooperation between numismatists and the Mint.[205]

Counterfeits are known of this variety, and more about these will be found in Chapter 5. One useful diagnostic of genuine examples is a raised line from the base of letter I in UNITED extending to a point about one-third of the height of letter T. This line was caused by a scratch in the individual working die.

DENVER
2,665,071,400

RARITY: Common in all grades Very Fine and higher, original rolls still exist.

VALUES:	GRADE	1980	1995
	MS65	.10	.15

1972-D/D
RPM-1 (Miller)

VARIETIES: This issue is rich in cud varieties; 14 are documented for the obverse and eight for the reverse, two of these being retained breaks (see photo).

Doubled dies include one inherited from the defective master die described for 1972-P. The other four unique to this mint are all quite minor. There are eight repunched mintmark varieties (see photo).

A few examples lack the initials V.D.B. on the truncation of Lincoln's bust. There were probably all from a single obverse working die and are almost certainly the result of clumsy polishing of that die. This phenomenon reappears for a number of other issues as well, and no large premium is attached to it.

1972-D
LC-72D-14R (Thurman)

COMMENTS: 1972-D cents are readily available in gem condition.

* * *

Invited to speak at the Educational Forum of South Florida Coin Club's Mid-Winter Convention on January 8, 1972, Director Brooks remarked on one of the Mint's more interesting products for coin collectors and souvenir hunters:

> To date, all our projects have been successful—too successful I'm embarrassed to admit. Because of recent Government budget and personnel ceilings, we are forced to curtail one of our newest projects. I'm speaking about the Penny Bags. The over-the-counter requests at Philadelphia, Denver, and San Francisco for pennies bearing these different mintmarks have been phenomenal and we've been hard pressed to sort, count, and bag the pennies in sufficient quantities for adequate inventories required at these mint facilities as well as the Department of the Treasury.
>
> When we offered them through our Philadelphia mail order service, the flood of requests hampered our ability to bag the pennies and package and mail the orders with our present personnel ceiling.
>
> In December, I had to issue a press release cutting off the mail orders for 1971 Penny Bags at the end of the year. I would like to make them available over the counter and by mail order in 1972. If circumstances permit later in the year, we will announce a date when it will be feasible to start selling these over the counter and accepting mail orders again.[206]

The "Penny Bags" to which she referred were indeed offered in 1972 and again in 1973. These consisted of a canvas sack with drawstring that measured approximately three inches by four inches. Labeled "CENTS/15c/U.S. MINTS/P-D-S, these souvenir bags contained five cents each from the three mints, all of them uncirculated. A single bag cost 50 cents, or they could be obtained at quantity discounts ranging from $2 for five bags up to $8 for 25 bags.[207] These remained very popular with both collectors and the general public until another cent shortage in 1973-74 led to their discontinuance.

SAN FRANCISCO
377,019,108

RARITY: Common in all grades Very Fine and higher, original rolls and possibly bags still exist. Examples are scarce in circulation due to hoarding.

VALUES:

GRADE	1980	1995
MS65	.10	.15

VARIETIES: The only cud break reported is on the obverse of a 1972-S proof die! The two known doubled-dies are also proofs but are difficult to discern. A single repunched mintmark variety is known (see photo).

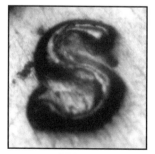

1972-S/S
RPM-1 (Miller)

COMMENTS: Fully struck gems are readily available.

1973

PHILADELPHIA
3,728,245,000

RARITY: Common in all grades Very Fine and higher, original rolls still exist.

VALUES:

GRADE	1980	1995
MS65	.10	.10

VARIETIES: The only noteworthy varieties are two obverse doubled-dies and one for the reverse.

COMMENTS: Cents of this issue are readily available in gem condition.

A new reverse hub was introduced for the cents of 1973 and featured enlarged initials FG. It was used in this year only.

* * *

The *Annual Report* reveals that during Fiscal Year 1973 the Philadelphia Mint coined 1,700,000,000 cents from metal strip and planchets fabricated entirely within the mint. The balance of its cent coinage was the product of strip obtained from commercial contractors.[208] In previous decades, the U. S. Mint alternated between producing its own product entirely and purchasing pre-formed strip or press-ready planchets. Different administrations took differing views of each option's cost-effectiveness. It seemed that every time an innovation was introduced at the mints which lowered the cost of internally produced strip and planchets, an even greater advance would be made within private industry which shifted the balance back in its favor. The matter was decided once and for all, at least for cents, when the mints switched from coining bronze to coining copper-plated zinc. Since that time, all cent planchets have been purchased from contractors.

DENVER
3,549,576,588

RARITY: Common in all grades Very Fine and higher, original rolls still exist.

VALUES:

GRADE	1980	1995
MS65	.10	.10

VARIETIES: This date is rich in cud varieties. There are at least eight for the obverse, including two which obliterated half of the design (see photos). Of the seven reverse cuds, one is retained. Five repunched mintmark varieties are also known (see photo).

1973-D/D

RPM-1 (Miller)

1973-D

LC-73D-14 (Thurman)

1973-D

LC-73D-13a (Thurman)

COMMENTS: Gems are readily available.

All 1973-D cents feature the new reverse hub with enlarged letters FG. Of the cents coined at Denver during Fiscal Year 1973, some 503,000,000 were the products of metal strip formed within the mint, while the balance were coined from metal strip fabricated by contractors.[209]

SAN FRANCISCO
317,177,295

RARITY: Common in all grades Very Fine and higher, original rolls and possibly bags still exist. This issue is scarce in circulation, as there are many persons who hoard any coins bearing the S mintmark.

VALUES:

GRADE	1980	1995
MS65	.10	.15

VARIETIES: A single reverse cud break has been documented.

COMMENTS: Gems are readily available.

All 1973-S cents were coined with the modified reverse used only in this year.

*   *   *

The *Annual Report* for 1973 contains some interesting information about the production of cents:

We must recognize that in total piece count, 75 percent of our production is in cents, and these coins are the easiest to manufacture. For example, we derive a much greater die life from cent production, thus the coin presses can operate with fewer shutdowns and at a greater speed. Also, we can strike four coins simultaneously on a press producing cents, nickels, and dimes, but we can only strike two quarters, half-dollars, and dollars at a time. We must also recognize that other production equipment such as blanking presses, blank annealing furnaces, and upset mills have a far less capacity in terms of number of dollars than for pennies.

1974

Large Date

Small Date

PHILADELPHIA
4,103,183,000
WEST POINT
128,957,523
TOTAL
4,232,140,523

RARITY: Common in all grades Extremely Fine and higher, original rolls still exist.

VALUES:

GRADE	1980	1995
MS65	.10	.10

VARIETIES: Two obverse hub types exist. Five cuds are known, all of them on the obverse.

COMMENTS: Gems are readily available.

   Both the obverse hub of 1969 and the reverse hub of 1973 were replaced this year. The new obverse (large date) was quite attractive and more skillfully sculpted than the its predecessor, though it still lacked the wealth of fine-line detail seen on the hubs of 1909 and 1916. A second and less detailed obverse master (small date) was introduced in 1974, and both types were struck at all three mints. The designations "small date" and "large date" are used for convenience; in actuality, the small date hub simply has its date placed further from the border. The most important distinction is really in the treatment of Lincoln's hair (see photos). For all three mints the small date cents are scarcer. The new reverse was virtually identical to that used since 1959, yet the initials FG, greatly enlarged in 1973, were now reduced to something in-between their 1959 and 1973 sizes.

The cent shortage which erupted toward the end of 1973 and lasted through most of 1974 prompted tremendous mintages of these coins. On June 13, 1974, the Philadelphia Mint established a new one-day record for cent production of 27,420,000 pieces. During that same month, the three mints combined set a new record for total coin production of 1,138,196,000 pieces, breaking the previous record established in October of 1966.

The extension of coining operations to the West Point Depository was noted in Mint Director Brooks' *Annual Report*. This action was permitted under Public Law 93-127, and production was scheduled to begin on August 1, 1974. It was estimated that West Point could produce between 1 billion and 1.5 billion coins per year, depending on the denominations issued.[210] These coins were to carry no mintmark, and they would be indistinguishable from those minted at Philadelphia.

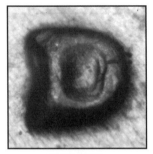

1974-D/D
RPM-1 (Miller)

1974-D
LC-74D-4b (Thurman)

1974-D
LC-74D-11b (Thurman)

DENVER
4,235,098,000

RARITY: Common in all grades Extremely Fine and higher, original rolls still exist.

VALUES:

GRADE	1980	1995
MS65	.10	.10

VARIETIES: Two obverse hub types exist. This issue provided a bonanza for cud hunters. There are 23 for the obverse alone, including several which have differing die states (see photos). Only a single cud is known for the reverse, its lower relief being less stressful to dies. In addition, there is a single obverse doubled-die variety and one repunched mintmark (see photo).

COMMENTS: Gems are readily available.

1974-D cents were coined with dies taken from both the large date and small date obverse hubs. Small date coins are scarcer, particularly in Mint State.

* * *

By the end of 1973 it was apparent that a shortage of cents had developed. This problem was attributed to the rising price of copper, which had reached $1.39 per pound. At this level there was speculative interest in hoarding cents, as it seemed likely that the price would soon achieve a figure at which cents became worth more than their face value. The cost of rendering them into copper for industry and other uses should have discouraged such speculation, but it didn't.

Once the price of copper reached $1.20 per pound, the cost of producing each cent exceeded its face value, though they were still not profitable to melt. One solution to the rising price of copper and its effect on the one-cent piece was to substitute a less valuable metal. Director Brooks announced on December 7, 1973 that the Mint was requesting Congress to grant it standby authority to change the composition of the cent to an aluminum alloy at the Treasury Secretary's discretion. The Mint had already begun testing seven different alloys in an effort to determine which components worked best in a cent containing 96% aluminum.[211] For more information about these 1974-dated cents in aluminum and other experimental alloys, see Chapter 2.

The severity of the cent shortage which lasted through much of 1974 prompted Mint Director Brooks to issue a statement on May 21 beseeching the public to return its cents. When read today, it has the flavor and spirit of a religious sermon:

> I'm calling on every American to get the penny back in circulation and keep it there. I'm calling on the banking industry to welcome the return of pennies during the month of June. I'm urging schools, churches and charities to examine ways and means to involve their members in collecting pennies for deposit.
>
> The price of copper has retreated, closing at $1.15 per pound on May 20. There will be no aluminum penny. The 62 billion pennies produced during the past 15 years have no numismatic value and because of the huge mintage they will never attain great value.
>
> Nevertheless, speculators and hoarders of pennies have caused what seems to be a shortage of pennies in certain areas of the country.
>
> But there is no shortage of a supply of pennies.
>
> Creating a shortage where it does not exist can adversely affect every public spirited citizen, taxpayers and conservator of the earth's resources. It is inflationary should merchants start to round off sales to the next nickel due to lack of pennies to make change.
>
> Again I'd like to emphasize: There are plenty of pennies. But they are in the wrong places.
>
> It is estimated that over 30 billion pennies are in circulation—doing the job for which they were intended. Somewhere in this vast country of ours, however, in excess of 30 billion pennies are in hiding. These are the pennies I'm looking for. They are in dresser drawers, shoe boxes, pickle jars; most anyplace you can think of that will get them out of pocket and out of sight. They are unwanted, unused and unappreciated.
>
> For the Mint to be forced to continue increasing its penny production to meet the current extraordinary demand is wasteful. Wasteful of a natural resource, copper, that cannot be replenished by man. And wasteful of the taxpayers' hard earned money. One billion pennies returned to circulation will save the taxpayers $10,000,000.
>
> . . . Fifteen years ago, the reverse design of the Lincoln cent was changed from wheat to a view of the Lincoln Memorial. The Mint produced 25.7 billion Lincoln wheat pennies during a 50-year period.
>
> The Lincoln wheat pennies do enjoy collector interest—some years commanding more numismatic value than others. Rarity is one of the determinants in establishing value of almost any collectible item. Especially this holds true for coins. A general rule of thumb is the lower the mintage of a given coin, the higher the numismatic value. Coin collecting is a very wholesome hobby. I'm happy to have young people looking at their coins.
>
> Sixty-two billion pennies of identical design, however, can never qualify as numismatic rarities and so cannot ever reach great numismatic value. The true collector knows this and collects only those pennies needed to complete his coin collection sets. The true collector likes bright, uncirculated coins also. Not the dull and discolored ones, unless they are rare.
>
> For every $25 worth of pennies cashed in at a bank, the Treasury and the Mint are prepared to issue a Treasury Department certificate to the individual or group responsible.
>
> Obviously, this campaign to get the penny back in circulation will require the cooperation of the banks in forwarding the names to be cited for an award to Mary Brooks, Director of the Mint, 55 Mint St., San Francisco, Ca. 94175.
>
> Truly this is a challenging project for anyone who participates. It will give every American family a chance to help control inflation, protect the environment and cut Government expense.[212]

The certificates mentioned by Director Brooks were later offered as rewards for cashing as little as $5 in cents.

SAN FRANCISCO
409,426,660

RARITY: Common in all grades Extremely Fine and higher, original rolls still exist. 1974-S cents are scarce in circulation due to hoarding. The small date type is the scarcer of the two.

VALUES:

GRADE	1980	1995
MS65	.10	.15

VARIETIES: Cents dated 1974-S were coined from dies of both the large date and small date obverse master hubs.

COMMENTS: Gems are readily available. In *The Standard Guide to the Lincoln Cent*, Sol Taylor notes that: "Circulated rolls bring almost as much as BU rolls—a phenomenon seen in other hoarded issues."

*   *   *

During 1974, the Mint was once again pressed for an answer as to why banks couldn't obtain enough cents to meet their customers' needs. While the real reason lay in the cent's obsolescence (it simply wasn't worth enough to bother carrying and recirculating), Mint Director Mary Brooks revived that old argument from the 1960s that coin collectors were to blame. In a gracious turn, she did distinguish between legitimate collectors and mindless speculators, blaming the latter for hoarding cents in general but S-Mint cents in particular:

> I think that the offering of a $50 bag of 1974-S cents by coin dealers for $475 is highway robbery. There will be no further release of 1974-S cents, although we are going to produce, and will continue to produce, a quota of 400,000,000 1974-S cents. These cents will be placed in inventory and will not be issued for immediate circulation.[213]

To foil speculators, Director Brooks ordered that cents from the San Francisco Mint be mixed with those of the other mints in unlabeled bags before being shipped to the Federal Reserve Banks. This action, plus her announcement that no more cents would be coined in San Francisco, only intensified the hunt for 1974-S cents, and huge quantities were indeed captured by speculators who simply separated them when found in mixed bags of cents and assembled their own rolls. Mrs. Brooks addressed the American Numismatic Association Convention on August 17, 1974, commenting on the status of S-Mint cents:

> I, of course, cannot continue to argue for production of a circulating coin that, in fact, does not widely circulate. Add to this the tactics of a few selfish coin dealers and you can see why I may not, in good conscience, be able to support the production of "S" cents next year."[214]

The production of circulating coins at the San Francisco Mint was halted altogether in May of 1975, and only dimes were produced for circulation that year.

1975

PHILADELPHIA
3,874,182,000
WEST POINT
1,577,294,142
TOTAL
5,451,476,142

RARITY: Common in all grades Extremely Fine and higher, original rolls still exist.

VARIETIES: Two obverse doubled-dies are known, both of them quite minor. There are ten obverse cud varieties including one retained break. Most of them are not in the familiar position below the bust.

COMMENTS: Well struck and lustrous coins are the norm for this issue.
The cents of 1975-82 were coined from dies taken from the second obverse master of 1974.

*   *   *

Experimental cents dated 1975 were coined in aluminum. For more about this experiment, see Chapter 2.

DENVER
4,505,275,300

RARITY: Common in all grades Extremely Fine and higher, original rolls still exist.

VARIETIES: Nine obverse cuds may be found, only a few of them in the usual position below Lincoln's bust (see photo). It seems that the new hubs beginning in 1969 relocated the principal obverse stress point to the motto above Lincoln's head. Such stress was diverted from the reverse almost entirely.

COMMENTS: High quality choice and gem coins are always available.

1975-D
LC-75D-2b (Thurman)

1976

PHILADELPHIA
3,133,580,000
WEST POINT
1,540,695,000
TOTAL
4,674,275,000

RARITY: Common in all grades Extremely Fine and higher, original rolls still exist.

VARIETIES: Two minor obverse doubled-dies are noted, while some nine obverse cud breaks may be found (see photo).

COMMENTS: Well struck, fully lustrous coins are readily available.

* * *

1976-P
LC-76-3 (Thurman)

The United States Mint's payroll grew dramatically during the 1970s. While only 1,700 persons were employed by it in 1968, that number had swelled to 3,112 in 1976.[215]

For generations the Mint's fiscal year ran from July 1 through June 30. Beginning with Fiscal Year 1976, however, the Mint operated its accounting calendar from October 1 through September 30.

DENVER
4,221,592,455

RARITY: Common in all grades Extremely Fine and higher, original rolls still exist.

VARIETIES: None are reported.

COMMENTS: Gems are common from both Mint packaged sets and original rolls.

* * *

It was during Fiscal Year 1976 that the Denver Mint discontinued the fabrication of coinage strip for cents; future supplies were furnished by contractors.[216]

In a 1976 column for *The Numismatist*, Glenn B. Smedley reported an interesting proposal which history has shown never came to pass:

> It's too early to predict but not to speculate that the familiar 70-year old D mint mark may be replaced with an L in a few years. With estimates of the cost of a new Denver mint being revised higher and higher, there is speculation in that area that the Gates Rubber plant in nearby Littleton, Colorado, may be converted to a mint. Gates plans to discontinue making auto tires in Littleton and is offering the plant for sale, according to a U. S. Representative from Colorado. Based on present estimates, it is said that buying and revamping the Gates plant would result in a saving of $29 million to us taxpayers.[217]

The struggle to build a new Denver Mint had actually been ongoing since 1972, when $1,500,000 was appropriated for a new site within the city. The following year another $2,000,000 was appropriated for architectural and engineering studies. These plans were stalled, however, when a railroad easement prevented Denver from transferring the desired site to the Federal Government![218]

1977

PHILADELPHIA
3,074,575,000
WEST POINT
1,395,355,000
TOTAL
4,469,930,000

RARITY: Common in all grades Extremely Fine and higher, original rolls still exist.

VARIETIES: Of 13 recorded cud varieties, most occur within or near IN GOD WE TRUST (see photo). Four are known in progressive die states.

The 1977/6 overdate cents which caused such a stir in 1977 proved to be clever fabrications. Though one specimen reportedly of much more convincing character was authenticated by the U. S. Mint's Laboratory, this coin was subsequently condemned with the more obvious fakes.[219]

1977-P
LC-77-5   (Thurman)

COMMENTS: Like most issues of this and later years, well made gems are common.

* * *

During Fiscal Year 1977, the Mint began shipping used reverse dies of the cent and nickel from San Francisco to the other mints. These dies had been chromium plated before being used to strike proofs, and this plating enhanced their durability to the extent that they remained suitable for mass production.[220] The practice of chrome plating was ultimately extended to all dies, including those intended for currency strikes from the outset.

With so many incidents of cent shortages since the 1960s, it's interesting to note that during 1977 the U. S. Mint actually had to lay-off workers because of a cent surplus![221]

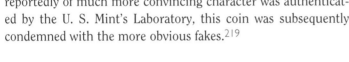

DENVER
4,194,062,300

RARITY: Common in all grades Extremely Fine and higher, original rolls still exist.

VARIETIES: Only a single, massive cud break is known for this issue.

COMMENTS: Abundant in Mint State, gems may be secured easily.

* * *

In a report commissioned the previous year from the Research Triangle Institute, it was revealed that the cent was becoming or had already become obsolete. The Treasury Department's summation repeated what was in that report:

> An increasing fraction of the Mint's cent coin production represents replacement of coins which have been voluntarily withdrawn from circulation by the public. This withdrawal is related to the lack of purchasing power of the cent and indicates that the public apparently perceives the coin as having very little utility.
>
> Compounding the situation, estimated cost increases for coinage metal and increases in manufacturing and distribution costs will cause the cost of producing the cent to exceed its face value by about 1980.[222]

1978

PHILADELPHIA
3,735,655,000
WEST POINT
1,531,250,000
SAN FRANCISCO
291,700,000
TOTAL
5,558,605,000

RARITY: Common in all grades Extremely Fine and higher, original rolls still exist.

VARIETIES: The eight recorded cud breaks are all on the obverse.

COMMENTS: Sharply struck gems are readily available.

*   *   *

The *Annual Report* for 1978 indicates that a new reverse hub was introduced for the cent that year. Sharper details were claimed as the result of its use, though this is not clearly discernible from observation of the actual coins.

The San Francisco Assay Office resumed the minting of cents for general circulation in July after having produced none since 1974. The new issues bore no mintmarks and, like those coined at the West Point Depository, are indistinguishable from cents of the Philadelphia Mint.

While the Philadelphia Mint produced a portion of the bronze coinage strip it used in 1978 to punch out blanks, Denver and San Francisco employed only strip fabricated outside by contractors. West Point received its planchets press-ready from the Philadelphia Mint.[223]

DENVER
4,280,233,400

RARITY: Common in all grades Extremely Fine and higher, original rolls still exist.

VARIETIES: Seven cud varieties are known for the obverse, most with the break above Lincoln's head. A single repunched mintmark may also be found.

COMMENTS: Though the new obverse hub of 1974 was showing wear by this time, well struck gems are available. Reverse dies were from a new master hub introduced this year.

*   *   *

The past several years had witnessed endless wrangling over the issue of a new Denver Mint. This project was finally abandoned in 1978 and a study begun to determine the feasibility of installing a satellite mint within the Rocky Mountain Arsenal.

The tradition of shipping finished coins in canvas bags was challenged by a new method employed on an experimental basis beginning in 1978. Large bulk containers with space for hundreds of thousands of cents were tested and found quite satisfactory. Since that time, this method of shipment has become the standard, and the old canvas bags are being retired.

Another cost-cutting measure introduced in 1978 was the shipment of completed coins directly to commercial banks, rather than delivering them exclusively to Federal Reserve banks.[224]

1979

PHILADELPHIA
3,560,940,000
WEST POINT
1,705,850,000
SAN FRANCISCO
751,725,000
TOTAL
6,018,515,000

RARITY: Common in all grades Extremely Fine and higher, original rolls still exist.

VARIETIES: Five obverse cud varieties are known.

COMMENTS: Choice and gem examples are easily found, and their retail price reflects a minimum service charge rather than any real numismatic value. This is true of nearly all Lincolns after 1955.

DENVER
4,139,357,254

RARITY: Common in all grades Extremely Fine and higher, original rolls still exist.

VARIETIES: A single obverse cud variety is known.

In his *Encyclopedia*, Walter Breen reports a variety lacking the designer's initials FG. This almost certainly resulted from a vigorous polishing of the reverse die in an attempt to remove clash marks or some other flaw. While it's unusual for the reverse initials to be missing, the letters V.D.B. on the obverse are far more susceptible to this kind of overpolishing, and such varieties may appear for any date. The value of die-polishing errors on Lincoln Cents is quite minimal, with the exception of the 1922 no-D cents.

COMMENTS: High grade examples are readily available.

1980

PHILADELPHIA
4,653,915,000
WEST POINT
1,576,200,000
SAN FRANCISCO
1,184,590,000
TOTAL
7,414,705,000*

RARITY: Common in all grades Extremely Fine and higher, original rolls still exist.

VARIETIES: A distinct doubled-die may be found for the obverse (see photos).

1980-P
DDO-1   (Fivaz & Stanton)

COMMENTS: The type 2 or "small date" obverse hub of 1974 was by this point showing its age, and cents dated 1980 through 1982 large date will not be as sharp as the dates immediately preceding. In all respects, however, gems are easy to locate.

* * *

*Beginning with 1980, the *Annual Report of the Director of the Mint* began providing coinage figures only by the Mint's fiscal year, which runs from October 1 through September 30. This has created a nightmare for catalogers and researchers attempting to establish the number of coins produced during the calendar year. This situation remains in effect as of this writing (1996), and many of the published figures for 1980 and later years which appear in other references are inaccurate and inconsistent from one title to another.

The figures in this book were carefully reconstructed from all of the available data. They may nevertheless contain some errors, as the Mint is often negligent and tardy in providing this information. In addition, calendar year figures do not necessarily represent the number of coins bearing that date, as mintages overlap during the final quarter of each calendar year. Of course, with figures in the billions, it will never matter if the numbers provided are off by a few million, but every attempt has been made to provide the correct totals by date and mint.

RARITY: Common in all grades Extremely Fine and higher, original rolls still exist.

VARIETIES: There is a single repunched mintmark variety for this issue.

COMMENTS: A new D mintmark punch was used beginning with the cents of 1980, though the Director's *Annual Report* dated its introduction to 1981.

High grade coins are easily obtained from the billions coined and the many thousands preserved. Though complete bags of 5000 coins have been saved for some dates beginning in the late 1950s, the trading of such quantities seems to have peaked during the early 1960s, and collectors are usually content with rolls these days.

* * *

On July 5, 1979 Mint Director Stella B. Hackel announced that commencing with the coinage of 1980, all nickels, dimes, quarters and halves struck at the Philadelphia Mint would henceforth bear a 'P' mintmark. At the same time, she stunned the numismatic community with another announcement:

In 1980, 1-cent coins produced for circulation in Philadelphia, Denver, San Francisco, and the West Point bullion Depository will bear no mint marks. At present there is considerable withdrawal from circulation by collectors of "D" marked 1-cent coins. Elimination of any distinction among coins struck at the four Mint locations should increase the circulating 1-cent pool.

Only two months later, however, the Director reversed this policy, much to the relief of collectors:

In response to comments received from the general public and in deference to the judgment of numismatic collectors, the Director of the U. S. Mint, Stella B. Hackel, today announced that 1-cent coins produced at the Denver Mint will continue to bear the "D" Mint mark. "The Bureau of the Mint had planned to eliminate the 'D' Mint mark from 1-cent coins minted at Denver to reduce attrition of 1-cent coins in the market place. After thorough reconsideration, however, we found that such action was not essential at this time," Mrs. Hackel said.[225]

1981

PHILADELPHIA
4,728,905,000
WEST POINT
1,882,400,000
SAN FRANCISCO
880,445,000
TOTAL
7,491,750,000

RARITY: Common in all grades Extremely Fine and higher, original rolls still exist.

VARIETIES: None are reported.

COMMENTS: 1981-P cents are readily available in choice condition, though gems seem to be a bit elusive.

The Philadelphia Mint produced only a portion of its cent mintage from strip rolled within its own walls. The majority of cents coined there in 1981 came from planchets punched from commercially prepared strip. The days when cents were fashioned entirely in-house were nearing an end.[226]

The difficulty in finding nice singles dated 1981 is due in no small part to the odd surfaces found on specimens taken from the Mint's packaged sets. It's obvious that these coins, along with the other denominations from the Philadelphia Mint, were put through some sort of washing process before being assembled into sets. It's likely that delays in getting the sets assembled and the resultant toning that set it prompted the chemical wash, and this problem may even have been a contributing factor in the Mint's decision to discontinue selling such sets after 1981.

* * *

Frank Gasparro retired in 1981 after nearly 40 years with the United States Mint. He was succeeded in the office of Chief Engraver by Elizabeth Jones, who served until 1990. After she resigned there was no immediate interest in replacing her, as the position is viewed within the Treasury Department as obsolete. It is now doubtful that there will ever again be a Chief Engraver. This nearly 200 year-old tradition passed away without fanfare.

DENVER
5,373,235,677

RARITY: Common in all grades Extremely Fine and higher, original rolls still exist.

VARIETIES: None are reported.

COMMENTS: Choice and gem coins are readily available.

* * *

All of the cents coined at the Denver Mint and the San Francisco Assay Office were struck from strip purchased from commercial vendors, these two facilities having abandoned their in-house strip rolling. West Point coined its cents from blanks furnished by both the Philadelphia Mint and commercial sources.

The Mint forestalled a threatened shortage of cents by rationing shipments of these coins to 1.1 billion pieces per month. The Federal Reserve banks followed suit with similar rationing. An increasing number of these shipments were in bulk containers, the Mint noting that each container eliminated the cost of 70 canvas bags.[227]

Large Date

1982

PHILADELPHIA
7,135,275,000
WEST POINT
1,990,005,000
SAN FRANCISCO
1,587,245
TOTAL
10,712,525,000

Small Date

RARITY: None of the four major varieties is really common in gem condition, though fairly choice examples may be found for the brass coins. Circulated examples from 1982 to date rarely grade below About Uncirculated (AU).

VARIETIES: Two obverse doubled-dies may be found for the brass, large date cents. Only one of these is distinctive enough to interest the non-specialist; its doubling is strongest on the motto IN GOD WE TRUST.

     1982 cents are very rich in cud varieties. These are all on the obverse and are about evenly mixed between large date and small date, but nearly all are found only with brass cents (see photos).

COMMENTS: While the brass composition in use since 1962 produced fairly decent coins of both large date and small date varieties, the same cannot be said for the zinc cents. These are usually discolored to some degree, and those that are not already will probably become so in time.

     It took the mints a couple of years to master the process of bonding a copper coating to the zinc planchets, and the zinc cents of 1982 and many of those of 1983 show serious flaws. The most common is black spotting or streaking, caused by the naturally corrosive tendency of zinc penetrating the protective and aesthetic layer of copper. Another common condition is the appearance of raised dots or pimples on the surface of zinc cents. This is caused by trapped or occluded gas underneath the copper coating being compressed at the moment of striking. All of these flaws were worked out over time, but salvation came too late for the zinc cents of 1982. It may be that gems will simply not exist for future generations of collectors.

* * *

     The need for a replacement composition for the cent was recognized as early as 1973, when the Mint struck off 1974-dated cents in various metals. Though the crisis at that time subsided with a drop in copper prices, the specter of the cent's demise was never far away. The 1976 study by the Research Triangle Institute revealed that the traditional bronze cent (technically brass since 1962) was indeed doomed at some time in the not-too-distant future. Though this study recommended the elimination of this denomination altogether as being too valueless for any utility, the Mint's mindset was directed toward a replacement metal. It guessed correctly that Congress lacked the nerve to discontinue the nation's lowest-value coin, as this would be seen as a concession to inflation.

     The Mint began re-studying alternatives as early as 1979. Director Stella Hackel noted that "The savings resulting from a change to a zinc alloy or a coated steel would be substantial, but not as great as if an aluminum alloy were used."[228] By 1981 the details had been worked out, as her successor, Donna Pope, revealed in her 1981 *Annual Report* to Treasury Secretary Donald T. Regan:

> The final specifications for the new copper plated zinc cents were determined and two contracts totaling $8,743,119.00 were awarded in July 1981 for the fabrication of 20.8 million pounds of blanks with deliveries commencing by the end of the first quarter of fiscal year 1982. The new alloy contains 97.5% zinc and 2.5% copper.

     The conversion to a predominately zinc cent was a major blow to the domestic copper industry, and it fought back with litigation. The Mint ultimately prevailed, as recorded by Director Pope:

> The Mint received a favorable decision from U. S. District Court, District of Columbia, in the case of Copper & Brass Fabricators Council v. Department of the Treasury. The lawsuit, filed in October 1981, alleged that the Treasury Department was not authorized under 31 U.S.C. 317(b) to alter the copper content of the penny. The case was dismissed on the grounds that the Council lacked legal authority to sue. In June 1982, the U. S. Court of Appeals, for the District of

Columbia Circuit, affirmed the District Court decision.[229]

The first zinc cents coined were struck at the West Point Depository on January 6, 1982; these were of the large date variety. The first small date cents were coined beginning September 3. Brass cents bearing the new master hub turned up in October, while the first zinc examples weren't seen until December.[230]

1982-P
LC-82SD-13 Cu (Thurman)

1982-P
LC-82SD-4 Cu (Thurman)

✳ ✳ ✳

Why the Mint's Engraving Department chose to introduce a new obverse master hub during midyear while at the same time changing the cent's composition is a complete mystery. Generally cautious about creating anything collectable, the Mint should have waited until 1983 before employing a modified obverse to replace the aging master of 1974. Instead, both actions seem to have occurred independently, thus accounting for the mixture of two hubs with two compositions for a total of four major varieties from the Philadelphia Mint alone. The large date type of 1982 cent is actually the small date type of 1974.

The new obverse hub was in lower relief and bore smaller, sharper lettering (small date type). These are both attributes which were to become standard goals for all of the numerous upgrades made to each denomination during the 1980s and 1990s. The trend since the mid 1980s has been toward lower relief and more sharply incised details. While the coins of recent years bear little resemblance to their original editions, they have extended the useful life of coining dies from the 100,000-150,000 strikes typical of 1909 cents to the 1,000,000+ strikes often achieved during the mid 1990s.

DENVER
6,012,979,368

RARITY: Common in all grades AU and higher, original rolls still exist. Both varieties of zinc cents are challenging to find in gem condition and even more difficult to preserve as such.

VARIETIES: A single repunched mintmark may be found.

COMMENTS: The same problems which plague the 1982-P zinc cents are common to this issue as well. Because quality control at the Denver Mint has been consistently higher than at the Philadelphia Mint since the mid 1960s, 1982-D cents are slightly easier to find choice. Preserving the zinc issues will remain a problem, and the volatility of this metal may condemn many such coins to eventual spoilage.

The Denver Mint made a smooth transition from brass to copper-plated zinc. The last brass issues were struck on October 21, 1982, and it began striking zinc cents on October 27.[231]

Though there's no report of 1982-D small date cents being coined in brass, some may indeed exist. The Mint denied that any were produced, but it's likely that a few were made in error from leftover planchets in much the same way as the 1943 bronze cents. Until every specimen is examined carefully, such coins will remain a possibility.

✳ ✳ ✳

Though many collectors questioned the need for abandoning the alloy of 95% copper and 5% zinc in favor of a primarily zinc cent, the Mint's figures for producing the old coins give a clear indication of trouble ahead had they not been retired. Back in Fiscal Year 1952, the cost of producing 1000 cents had been reduced to a record low of only $1.10, or just over 10% of their face value. By FY1982, the last time in which the old alloy was employed to a great extent, this cost had risen to $8.61, some 86% of face value. Switching to zinc then reduced this cost to $6.35 per 1000 coins in FY1983, buying the cent a bit of time though still revealing its inevitable obsolescence.[232]

The Mint did not issue any uncirculated sets for collectors in 1982. Though it would seem that the availability of coins minted in the billions would be unaffected by the two or three million sets issued by the Mint each year, these do indeed play a role. While none of the seven varieties issued for circulation by the Philadelphia and Denver Mints will ever be rare, singles are not easily located. Holders of rolls are disinclined to break these for such low value coins, while many of the broken rolls have been assembled into seven-piece sets which can be mass marketed. Attempting to buy an attractive, single example of any of these coins proved a somewhat frustrating task during the preparation of this book. Available singles tended to be scuffed and tarnished.

1983

PHILADELPHIA
7,569,585,600
WEST POINT
2,004,400
SAN FRANCISCO
180,765,000
TOTAL
7,752,355,000

RARITY: Common in all Mint State grades, original rolls still exist.

VARIETIES: One minor variety, caused by vigorous polishing of the reverse die in an apparent effort to remove clash marks, shows letter E in CENT reduced to a letter F. Three minor obverse doubled-dies are known, along with a more distinct reverse doubled-die. It alone has become widely known and collected, due primarily to effective promotion. More about this popular variety may be found below.

1983-P
LC-83-46R   (Thurman)

This date is rich in cud varieties, perhaps due to the Mint's difficulty in working with zinc planchets. An amazing 43 cuds may be found for the obverse, nearly all of these above or below Lincoln's bust. Four reverse cuds are known (see photo), including one retained break.

COMMENTS: All 1983 cents were coined of copper-plated zinc. The quality of these coins is only marginally better than for the 1982 zinc cents, and most reveal myriad tiny pimples where gases trapped by inadequate bonding between the metals were compressed into cells. The troublesome discoloration, so prevalent in the 1982 zinc cents, is less of a problem for those dated 1983.

* * *

Rather than attempt to fabricate its own zinc strip, the Philadelphia Mint terminated its melting and rolling operations entirely and began relying on commercially produced strip for all of its needs. The other coinage denominations were equally affected by this conversion. None of the United States Mint facilities now produce their own coinage strip, Philly having been the last.

This was also the last year in which the San Francisco Assay Office coined cents for circulation.

The Mint did not issue any uncirculated sets for collectors in 1983. Though cents of this date are not in danger of becoming rare, dealers must rely on bags and rolls to supply their customers.

DOUBLED-DIE REVERSE

PHILADELPHIA or WEST POINT
(mintage unknown)

RARITY: The problems common to all 1983 cents are a factor with this variety as well. Choice examples have survived, though as the population data reveals, gems are elusive in relation to the number of cent collectors.

POPULATION: MS BN = 3   MS RB = 31   MS RD = 436   MS TOTAL = 470
MS65 RD = 253   HIGHEST = MS67 RD (1)

VALUE: GRADE   1995
               MS65   200.00

COMMENTS: There is evidently only a single die pairing for this variety. The doubling shows quite plainly on ONE CENT, UNITED STATES oF AMERICA and E PLURIBUS UNUM (see photos). Walter Breen reported that most of the few thousand known specimens turned up in and around Lewiston, in northwest Pennsylvania.[233] Sol Taylor added that this variety was also obtained in quantity from northern Florida.[234] Given that the certified population had not exceeded 470 coins by 1995, the actual number of coins in existence may be less than 2,000 pieces.

1983-P
DDR-1, Breen-2310 (Fivaz & Stanton)

1983-P
DDR-1, Breen-2310 (Fivaz & Stanton)

1983-P
DDR-1, Breen-2310 (Fivaz & Stanton)

DENVER
6,467,199,428

RARITY: Common in all Mint State grades, original rolls still exist.

VARIETIES: Two repunched mintmarks.

COMMENTS: Poorly made from the outset, 1983-D cents are highly subject to bubbled surfaces and discoloration. Preserving choice and gem examples will be a challenge for future generations of collectors.
There is evidently The Mint did not issue any uncirculated sets for collectors in 1983.

1984

PHILADELPHIA
6,114,864,000
WEST POINT
2,036,215,000
TOTAL
8,151,079,000

RARITY: Common in all Mint State grades, original rolls still exist.

VARIETIES: Two obverse doubled-dies are known. One is fairly minor, but the more popular variety is covered on the following page. No less than 43 cud breaks may be found, all of them on the obverse (see photo).

Also reported by Walter Breen is a variety lacking the initials FG as the result of overpolishing of the die. As noted for this same variety under 1979-D, such minor flaws are fairly commonplace among low-relief elements of the dies. Another area subject to eradication by overpolishing is the lapel of Lincoln's coat. These minor irregularities are of little value to the knowledgeable numismatist, though they do spice up a search through uncirculated rolls.

1984-P
LC-84-21R (Thurman)

COMMENTS: The problems of the early zinc cents had largely been solved by 1984, but this issue is still somewhat subject to spotting and minor bubbling. Even so, gems are not too difficult to find.

A new obverse master hub was used for the cents of 1984 through 1989. The only significant distinction between the cents of 1983 and those of 1984 is the latter's lowered relief at Lincoln's upper arm. This facilitated metal flow into the reverse die and reduced the flatness often seen in E PLURIBUS UNUM.

The sale by the Mint of packaged sets of uncirculated coins resumed in 1984.

DOUBLED-DIE OBVERSE

PHILADELPHIA or WEST POINT
(mintage unknown)

RARITY: Though rare, this variety seems to be slightly more common than the 1983 doubled-die reverse variety both in absolute numbers certified and in condition rarity.

POPULATION: MS BN = 0   MS RB = 7   MS RD = 683
                 MS TOTAL = 690
                 MS65 RD = 277   HIGHEST = MS68 RD (1)

1984-P

DDO-1, Breen-2314 (Fivaz & Stanton)

VALUE: GRADE   1995
            MS65   120.00

COMMENTS: The doubling is quite distinct at Lincoln's ear, a little less so at his chin and beard (see photo). Both Breen and Taylor cite dealer Robert Brock as the source for an estimated population of 2,000 examples. This seems quite plausible, given the number certified.

DENVER
5,569,238,906

RARITY: Common in all Mint State grades, original rolls still exist.

VARIETIES: A minor obverse doubled-die is known, the doubling most evident in the date. Three repunched mintmarks have been found.

COMMENTS: Though still subject to quality-control problems resulting from the difficult copper-zinc bonding, this issue is readily available in choice and gem condition. This is the last year that bubbling was a noticeable occurrence.

    The sale by the Mint of packaged sets of uncirculated coins resumed in 1984.

1985

PHILADELPHIA
4,951,904,887
WEST POINT
696,585,000
TOTAL
5,648,489,887

RARITY: Common in all Mint State grades, original rolls still exist.

VARIETIES: Some 19 cud varieties are known, all but two of them on the reverse (see photo).

COMMENTS: Choice and gem examples are readily available. The problems associated with the early zinc cents were overcome by 1985, and such flaws are the exception rather than the rule for this and later dates. If stored in a dry, temperate atmosphere, these coins should hold up reasonably well despite their volatile composition.

1985-P
LC-85-3 (Thurman)

*   *   *

The use of chromium plated dies, a common practice for proof coins since the early 1970s, seems to have been extended to circulating coinage around this time. The smooth, uniform surface that such plating imparts to the coins made from these dies is evident on the earlier strikes, though later coins will have the usual frosty luster historically associated with mass-produced coins. This results from metal flow on the die face as the product of wear.

Coining operations at the West Point Depository fell victim to the budget cutting mandate of the Gramm-Rudman Deficit Reduction Act. There have been no additional coins struck there for general circulation, though this facility continues to produce commemorative and bullion coins, both of which are classified as reimbursable products.[235]

DENVER
5,287,399,926

RARITY: Common in all Mint State grades, original rolls still exist.

VARIETIES: A single cud variety is known for the obverse, along with nine repunched mintmarks.

COMMENTS: Choice and gem examples are readily available.

Though several other denominations of the 1985 coinage from both mints were plagued with striking problems and improperly prepared planchets, the cents seem to have been executed with sufficient care. This may have been the result of using commercially manufactured planchets rather than in-house productions for the cents.

A new, much larger mintmark punch was employed for all denominations beginning this year. It is the only size to appear on 1985-D coinage and was used for several years thereafter. Still punched into the working dies at this time, the mintmark would eventually become an integral part of the master die, ending forever the collectable varieties of repunched and overpunched mintmarks.

1986

PHILADELPHIA
4,491,395,493

RARITY: Common in all Mint State grades, original rolls still exist.

VARIETIES: There are 13 obverse cud varieties known (see photo).

COMMENTS: Choice and gem examples are readily available.

* * *

An advance was made this year in the production of master dies and working hubs. Where previously each such operation required that two or more impressions be taken, with annealing (softening) in-between, new technology permitted the completion of such hubs and dies in a single impression. It was expected at the time that this technique would soon be extended to working dies.

1986-P
LC-86-3 (Thurman)

The Mint began experimenting with computerized models of the various United States coins, studying their contours to determine their patterns of metal flow and to seek improvements in them. The results of this work are discernible in the lowered relief of the Lincoln Cent (particularly in Lincoln's upper arm, which has gradually "caved-in" since 1984). The coins obtained from such studies may extend die life and produce sharper strikes, but they're exceedingly poor from a sculptural standpoint.

A new reverse hub was introduced with the 1986 coinage. It is distinguishable only by its sharpened design elements and slightly broader borders. In her *Annual Report* to Treasury Secretary James A. Baker III, Mint Director Donna Pope indicated that both sides were upgraded in some respect, but whatever change was made to the obverse master hub is not readily discernible.[236]

Hub changes for both sides became a frequent occurrence during the 1980s and '90s. The distinctions are typically not as dramatic as with past hub changes for the simple reason that the Mint didn't let existing hubs suffer so much erosion before replacing them.

DENVER
4,442,866,698

RARITY: Common in all Mint State grades, original rolls still exist.

VARIETIES: Some 10 repunched mintmarks are reported.

COMMENTS: Choice and gem examples are readily available.
All are from dies which were sunk from the new master hubs of 1986.

1987

PHILADELPHIA
4,682,466,931

RARITY: Common in all Mint State grades, original rolls still exist.

VARIETIES: A total of five cud breaks may be found, all but one on the obverse.

COMMENTS: Choice and gem examples are readily available.

*   *   *

    The Mint Director's *Annual Report* indicates that the obverse and possibly the reverse were slightly modified, however these changes are so subtle as to be entirely indistinguishable. Perhaps the Mint's experiments with computer-generated models resulted in microscopic adjustments in contour to facilitate metal flow and extend die life.[237]

    Beginning around 1987-88, the Mint began a conscious effort to place into its uncirculated sets coins produced from fresh dies. These often reveal the smooth, metallic sheen associated with chromium plating of such dies. While this resulted in superior cents when purchased, it has been observed by the author that these coins seem to tarnish more rapidly than ordinary cents obtained from rolls. It's not known whether the smooth surface is inherently more susceptible to discoloration than a roughened, frosty surface or if the cents obtained from Mint-packaged sets are subjected to some cleaning process which activates their surfaces and promotes toning.

DENVER
4,879,389,514

RARITY: Common in all Mint State grades, original rolls still exist.

VARIETIES: At least 11 repunched mintmarks are known.

COMMENTS: Choice and gem examples are readily available.

1988

PHILADELPHIA
6,092,810,000

RARITY: Common in all Mint State grades, original rolls still exist.

VARIETIES: The only items of interest are seven cud varieties, all on the obverse and all but one quite minor.

COMMENTS: Choice and gem examples are readily available.

* * *

The progress made in extending die life since the Lincoln Cent was first introduced is evident in the production figures furnished by the Mint for 1988. While the dies used in 1909 and shortly thereafter typically produced around 100,000 to 150,000 impressions before they either failed or became too worn, by 1988 the number had grown several-fold. The average for obverse dies was now 1,100,000 strikes, while the average reverse die produced 900,000 impressions before being retired.[238] It's interesting that the obverse dies have proved more durable, as virtually all of the major die breaks or cuds have occurred on the obverse in recent years.

DENVER
5,253,740,443

RARITY: Common in all Mint State grades, original rolls still exist.

VARIETIES: Five repunched mintmarks are known.

COMMENTS: Choice and gem examples are readily available.

1989

PHILADELPHIA
7,261,535,000

RARITY: Common in all Mint State grades, original rolls still exist.

VARIETIES: An amazing 17 cud breaks may be found, all but three on the obverse.

COMMENTS: Choice and gem examples are readily available.

*   *   *

    The collecting of Lincoln Cents dated after the mid 1980s presents two divergent paths to the buyer. Cents coined for general circulation, though showing smooth, metallic surfaces when coined from fresh dies, are more often seen with slightly worn and more textured dies. This is the conventional mint luster so characteristic of Lincoln Cents until this time. It is readily apparent in the 1989-P and 1989-D cents illustrated, both of which were obtained from rolls.

    Compare these, however to the cents dated 1988 and 1990 illustrated in this book, and you will detect quite a difference. These cents were obtained from the U. S. Mint's uncirculated sets sold to collectors each year. Since the mid-late 1980s, the Mint has followed a deliberate policy of using only fresh dies to produce these coins, ones with the chromium plating still quite smooth. Study the very different qualities of these cents with the ones shown above.

DENVER
5,345,467,111

RARITY: Common in all Mint State grades, original rolls still exist.

VARIETIES: Nine repunched mintmarks are known. 1989 is the last date for which this variety may occur, as the mintmark has been included in the cent's master die since 1990.

COMMENTS: Choice and gem examples are readily available.

1990

PHILADELPHIA
6,851,765,000

RARITY: Common in all Mint State grades, original rolls still exist.

VARIETIES: All that have turned up are two obverse cud varieties and one on the reverse.

COMMENTS: Choice and gem examples are readily available.

* * *

New obverse and reverse master hubs were introduced for this year's coinage. The distinctions are very subtle, consisting of a slight lowering of the relief on either side, sharpening of all lettering and a nearly imperceptible enlargement of the initials V.D.B. In addition to extending die life, the Mint was determined to eliminate the recurring flatness often evident in letters STA of STATES and in the first few letters of the Latin motto. Being directly opposite a point of great metal displacement, these elements were often incomplete.

The cost of producing cents, dramatically lowered with the introduction of the copper-plated zinc edition, was creeping up at an alarming rate. While the cost of minting $1000 worth of cents in Fiscal Year 1983 had been only $635, by FY1990 it was up to $772. The Mint attributed this higher cost to an increase in the price of prefabricated metal.

To combat these rising costs, the mints began a conversion process to dial-feeding presses. These fed planchets and knocked out finished coins at a rate so great the human eye cannot follow them. One peculiarity of these presses is that they strike coins in a horizontal stroke, rather than the vertical motion associated with coining from ancient times.

Collectors mourned another Mint tradition which fell victim to increased standardization—that of punching mintmarks by hand into each working die. Since 1985 the mintmarks for proof coins had all been applied to the obverse and reverse master dies, eliminating any variance in position and virtually eliminating the possibility of repunched and overpunched mintmarks. Beginning with the cents dated 1990, this procedure was extended to the master dies for circulating coinage. The other denominations followed in 1991.[239]

DENVER
4,922,894,533

RARITY: Common in all Mint State grades, original rolls still exist.

VARIETIES: None are reported.

COMMENTS: Choice and gem examples are readily available. All are from the new obverse and reverse hubs introduced this year.

* * *

Beginning in 1990, the D mintmark was applied directly to a separate master die from that used for Philadelphia Mint cent coinage. This is in contrast to having it punched into individual working dies, the conventional practice since this series' inception. Although new to circulating coinage, this technique had been standard for all proof coinage since 1985. What it means to collectors is that there will never again be a repunched or overpunched mintmark variety unless all of the coins for that mint are so affected, an unlikely occurrence indeed.

As early as 1973 Congress had raised the issue of abolishing the one-cent coin, recognizing that it had ceased to be of much use in commerce. One answer to why such action hasn't yet been taken may be found in the *Annual Report* of Mint Director Donna Pope to Treasury Secretary Nicholas Brady. In reviewing the results of a study undertaken by the General Accounting Office regarding the adoption of a dollar coin, Pope revealed that "The study also recommended the continued minting of both the penny and half dollar **because both coins cost less to manufacture than their face values**.[240] There it its—these two unwanted coins are still being issued because the government's seigniorage, or profit, is too valuable to surrender. How long this remains true for the cent is anyone's guess. The time will soon come when it costs more than one cent to produce each coin, regardless of the value of its material.

1991

PHILADELPHIA
5,165,940,000

RARITY: Common in all Mint State grades, original rolls still exist.

VARIETIES: Two large reverse cuds may be found (see photo).

COMMENTS: Choice and gem examples are readily available.

* * *

The 1991 *Annual Report* confirms that the mints had by that time totally abandoned the in-house punching of cent blanks, though it still performed this operation for the other denominations using strip purchased in huge coils from commercial suppliers. Cents were produced from blanks already punched out and copper plated when received from the contractors.

1991-P
LC-91-1R (Thurman)

The cost of producing cents rose dramatically once again. In Fiscal Year 1990, the cost of manufacturing $1000 worth of cents was $772, but in FY1991 this amounted to some $923![24]

DENVER
4,158,442,076

RARITY: Common in all Mint State grades, original rolls still exist.

VARIETIES: None are reported.

COMMENTS: Choice and gem examples are readily available.

1992

PHILADELPHIA
4,648,905,000

RARITY: Common in all Mint State grades, original rolls still exist.

VARIETIES: None are reported.

COMMENTS: Choice and gem examples are readily available.

A new obverse hub was introduced for this year's cent coinage. Lincoln's upper arm, just above the truncation, was drastically lowered in relief to solve the metal displacement problem with letters STA and the Latin motto on the coin's reverse. A curious feature of this new hub, seemingly a flaw, is a long, raised and irregular line running from Lincoln's hairline to his temple. It clearly does not belong in the design, yet it has remained evident through several hub changes and is still visible on the cent coinage as late as 1995. Subtle hub changes have occurred since 1992 on a nearly annual basis, but these are virtually indistinguishable.

DENVER
4,448,673,300

RARITY: Common in all Mint State grades, original rolls still exist.

VARIETIES: None are reported.

COMMENTS: Choice and gem examples are readily available.
All are from the new obverse hub introduced this year.

1993

PHILADELPHIA
5,684,705,000

RARITY: Common in all Mint State grades, original rolls still exist.

VARIETIES: A single obverse cud variety is known.

COMMENTS: Choice and gem examples are readily available.

Beginning with 1993 the replacement of existing obverse and reverse master hubs appears to have become a routine, annual occurrence. While the obverse hub of 1993 is quite similar to that of 1992, the reverse is noticeably lower in relief on the Memorial's steps.

DENVER
6,426,650,571

RARITY: Common in all Mint State grades, original rolls still exist.

VARIETIES: None are reported.

COMMENTS: Choice and gem examples are readily available.

1994

PHILADELPHIA
6,500,850,000

RARITY: Common in all Mint State grades, original rolls still exist.

VARIETIES: Two obverse cud breaks may be found.

COMMENTS: Choice and gem examples are readily available.

  The new obverse hub of 1994 revealed a further drastic lowering of the relief on Lincoln's upper arm to the extent that it looks entirely unnatural. That artistry has become subordinate to economy is all too obvious when examining recent cents. Though the Mint boasts of the superior detail evident on recent coins, it fails to acknowledge that these coins are totally lacking in any sculptural or dimensional quality.

DENVER
7,131,765,000

RARITY: Common in all Mint State grades, original rolls still exist.

VARIETIES: None are reported.

COMMENTS: Choice and gem examples are readily available.

*   *   *

  The latest in a series of periodic cent shortages dating as far back as 1917 took hold during the Summer of 1994:

  "The level of retail economic activity, which is one of the big drivers of coin demand, has been a heck of a lot stronger than anyone expected," remarked Mint Director Phillip N. Diehl. "We went into fiscal year 1994 expecting to produce 15 billion coins. Now we're thinking demand will be around the 19 to 20 billion coin level. That is an unprecedented increase." Nearly repeating the words of embattled Mint Director Eva Adams, some 30 years earlier, Diehl continued to say that "we don't have a national cent shortage, what we have is a circulation problem. Whatever shortages there are can be described as local and short-lived."

  This *Numismatic News* report included an interview with James Benfield of The Coin Coalition, a lobbying group which advocated replacing the paper dollar with a dollar coin. In calling for abolition of the one-cent piece, he echoed the sentiments of many a weary Mint Director:

  "There is very strong anecdotal evidence to suggest that most of these coins are lying in people's dresser drawers and will eventually end up in a landfill. It is estimated $8,000 per day ends up in the trash for every 1 million people in the United States. That means that about $2 million each day is disappearing into the trash, and I'll bet most of it is pennies."

  It was noted, however, that not only was Congress disinclined to do away with the cent, but it had just recently approved a plan whereby the Mint would reallocate some of its appropriation to hire more people for the sole purpose of coining even greater numbers of cents. As long as the Federal Government continues to turn a profit on the coinage of the humble cent, this situation is unlikely to change.[242]

1995

PHILADELPHIA
6,411,440,000

RARITY: Common in all Mint State grades, original rolls still exist.

VARIETIES: Three obverse doubled-dies are known. The most obvious and popular variety (DDO-1) has proved very common and is covered in detail below. Five cud varieties are also known, all for the obverse.

COMMENTS: Choice and gem examples are readily available.

DOUBLED-DIE OBVERSE

PHILADELPHIA
(mintage unknown)

RARITY: Virtually all examples have been preserved uncirculated, and these are quite numerous. Though the Mint has no data on this issue, it has been estimated from the numbers seen in the marketplace that several hundred thousand may have been coined.

   The population data below represents the combined number of coins certified by PCGS and ANACS for DDO-1. At press time, the NGC figures for this issue had not been published.

POPULATION: MS BN = 0   MS RB = 0   MS RD = 6525   MS TOTAL = 6525
                MS67 RD = 902   HIGHEST = MS68 RD (5)

VALUE: GRADE   1995
           MS65   30.00*

Note: This value was taken from the 50th Edition of A Guide Book of United States Coins.

VARIETIES: The doubling is quite apparent in LIBERTY and IN GOD (see photos). This obverse die survived long enough to clash with it reverse mate. Vigorous polishing to remove the resulting clash marks resulted in two or more known die states for this same variety. On the latest of these, a fine crack runs through the motto LIBERTY.

COMMENTS: The doubling is most evident within LIBERTY and IN GOD, although it's difficult to see without some magnification. Not as prominent as the 1955 and 1972 doubled-die varieties, this one nevertheless received massive publicity, even appearing on the front page of the popular nationwide newspaper *USA Today*.[243] Its popularity has been sustained by the fact that so many have surfaced that every collector of Lincoln Cents can obtain a specimen. The fact that multiple die states exist suggests a long press run, and as many as a million or more may have been produced!

1995-P

DDO-1

Discovered early in the year, most examples have survived in choice and gem condition. Though the first coin was reported in Connecticut, the greatest number seems to have been centered in and around Virginia.

DENVER
7,128,560,000

RARITY: Common in all Mint State grades, original rolls still exist.

VARIETIES: Of the four obverse doubled-dies, only one (DDO-3) is equal in clarity to 1995-P DDO-1. Some are discernible by what appears to be a repunched mintmark, but since the mintmarks from 1990 to date are integral to the working hubs and dies their doubling is now a part of the hubbing process.

COMMENTS: Choice and gem examples are readily available.

Notes to Chapter 7

[1] *The Numismatist*, November 1909.

[2] Memorandum from MacVeagh to Assistant Secretary Norton, August 5, 1909, National Archives, Records Group 104.

[3] *Annual Report of the Director of the Mint for Fiscal Year Ended June 30, 1908*.

[4] *The Numismatist*, February 1909.

[5] *Annual Report*, 1911.

[6] Ibid, 1910.

[7] Ibid, 1911.

[8] Ibid.

[9] *Annual Report*, 1908 and 1911.

[10] *The Numismatist*, April 1911.

[11] *Annual Report*, 1911.

[12] Ibid, 1912.

[13] Ibid.

[14] *The Numismatist*, March 1912.

[15] Ibid.

[16] *Annual Report*, 1911.

[17] Ibid, 1913.

[18] *The Coin Dealer Newsletter Monthly Summary*, October 1980.

[19] *Annual Report*, 1914.

[20] *The Numismatic Scrapbook Magazine*, November, 1938.

[21] *Annual Report*, 1915.

[22] Ibid, 1916.

[23] Ibid.

[24] *The Numismatist*, June, 1916.

[25] *Annual Report*, 1917.

[26] Ibid.

[27] The *Annual Report* for 1917 gives the month as January.

[28] *The Coin Dealer Newsletter Monthly Summary*, October, 1980.

[29] Sol Taylor, *The Standard Guide to the Lincoln Cent*.

[30] *The Numismatist*, June, 1922.

[31] *Annual Report*, 1918.

[32] Ibid.

[33] *The Coin Dealer Newsletter Monthly Summary*, October, 1980.

[34] *Annual Report*, 1918.

[35] *The Numismatist*, October, 1918.

[36] *Annual Report*, 1918.

[37] Ibid, 1919.

[38] *The Numismatic Scrapbook Magazine*, June, 1955.

[39] *Annual Report*, 1919.

[40] *The Numismatist*, June, 1919.

[41] Ibid, August, 1919.

[42] *Annual Report*, 1919.

[43] Ibid, 1920.

[44] Ibid.

[45] *The Numismatist*, January, 1921.

[46] *Annual Report*, 1920.

[47] Taylor.

[48] Ibid.

[49] *The Numismatist*, September, 1921 and January, 1922.

[50] *Annual Report*, 1921.

[51] Ibid, 1922 and 1923.

[52] Ibid, 1922.

[53] *The Numismatist*, August, 1922.

[54] Ibid, June, 1927.

[55] Ibid, July, 1937.

[56] Ibid, May, 1935.

[57]*Annual Report,* 1922 and 1923.

[58]*The Numismatist,* May, September, October and December, 1923; January and February, 1924.

[59]*The Coin Dealer Newsletter Monthly Summary,* November, 1980.

[60]*Annual Report,* 1924.

[61]Ibid.

[62]*The Coin Dealer Newsletter Monthly Summary,* November, 1980.

[63]*Annual Report,* 1924.

[64]*The Numismatic Scrapbook Magazine,* March, 1963.

[65]Don Taxay, *Illustrated History of United States Commemorative Coinage.*

[66]*Annual Report,* 1925.

[67]Walter Breen, *Walter Breen's Complete Encyclopedia of United States and Colonial Coins.*

[68]Taylor.

[69]Ibid.

[70]*The Coin Dealer Newsletter Monthly Summary,* November, 1980.

[71]*Annual Report,* 1927.

[72]Ibid, 1928.

[73]*The Numismatic Scrapbook Magazine,* August, 1961.

[74]Ibid, March and October, 1938.

[75]*Annual Report,* 1928.

[76]John A. Wexler, *The Lincoln Cent Doubled Die.*

[77]Taylor.

[78]*Annual Report,* 1929.

[79]*The Numismatist,* January, 1930.

[80]Ibid, September, 1930.

[81]*Annual Report,* 1930.

[82]*The Numismatist,* March, 1931.

[83]Ibid, July, 1935.

[84]Breen.

[85]*Annual Report,* 1927 and 1933.

[86]*The Numismatist,* April, 1931.

[87]*Annual Report,* 1931.

[88]*The Numismatic Scrapbook Magazine,* August, 1938.

[89]*Annual Report,* 1932.

[90]Breen.

[91]Taylor.

[92]*The Numismatist,* various issues of 1932.

[93]Ibid, December, 1947.

[94]Ibid, various issues of 1933.

[95]*Annual Report,* 1933.

[96]Ibid, 1935.

[97]Ibid.

[98]Ibid.

[99]*The Numismatist,* August, 1934.

[100]Wexler.

[101]*Annual Report,* 1936.

[102]Ibid.

[103]*The Numismatic Scrapbook Magazine,* November, 1941.

[104]*Annual Report,* 1937.

[105]Ibid.

[106]*The Numismatic Scrapbook Magazine,* October, 1937.

[107]Taylor.

[108]*The Numismatic Scrapbook Magazine,* April, 1939.

[109]Ibid, July, 1939.

[110]Taylor.

[111]Breen.

[112]*Annual Report,* 1940.

[113]*The Numismatic Scrapbook Magazine,* July, 1940.

[114]Ibid, August, 1940.

[115]*The Numismatist,* March, 1940.

[116]Breen.

[117]*The Numismatist,* various issues of 1940.

[118]*The Numismatic Scrapbook Magazine,* January, 1941.

[119]Ibid, November, 1941.

[120]Ibid.

[121]Charles G. Altz & E. H. Barton, *Foreign Coins Struck at United States Mints.*

[122]*The Numismatic Scrapbook Magazine,* September, 1941.

[123]*The Numismatist,* various issues from March, 1941 through February, 1942.

[124]Ibid, November, 1942.

[125]Ibid, January, 1943.

[126]Ibid, various issues from March, 1942 through February, 1943.

[127]*The Numismatic Scrapbook Magazine,* December, 1942.

[128]*Annual Report,* 1944.

[129]*The Numismatic Scrapbook Magazine,* February, 1944.

[130]Ibid, December, 1943.

[131]Ibid, October, 1943.

[132]Ibid, June, 1944.

[133]Ibid, February, 1944.

[134]Ibid, March, 1944.

[135]*The Numismatist,* February, 1945.

[136]Ibid, October, 1944 through February, 1945.

[137]*Annual Report,* 1945.

[138]*The Numismatic Scrapbook Magazine,* July, 1952.

[139]*The Numismatist,* August, 1945.

[140]Ibid, April, 1944.

[141]*Annual Report,* 1944.

[142]*The Numismatist,* various issues of 1945.

[143]Ibid, March through May, 1945.

[144]*Annual Report,* 1946.

[145]*The Numismatist,* January, 1948.

[146]*The Numismatic Scrapbook Magazine,* May, 1949.

[147]Ibid, April, 1947.

[148]*The Numismatist,* March, 1948 through February, 1949.

[149]Ibid, February, 1949.

[150]Ibid, July, 1949 through January, 1950.

[151]Taylor.

[152]*Annual Report,* 1950.

[153]Ibid, 1951.

[154]Ibid, 1952.

[155]Ibid, 1953.

[156]Ibid.

[157]Ibid.

[158]*The Numismatist,* May through August, 1954.

[159]*The Numismatic Scrapbook Magazine,* April, 1957.

[160]Ibid, October, 1955.

[161]Ibid, January, 1956.

[162]*Coin World,* June 26, 1995.

[163]*The Numismatic Scrapbook Magazine,* February, 1966.

[164]*The Numismatist,* May, 1956.

[165]*The Numismatic Scrapbook Magazine,* December, 1964.

[166]*The Numismatist,* May, 1955.

[167]*The Numismatic Scrapbook Magazine,* February, 1956.

[168]*Annual Report,* 1964.

[169]Ibid, 1956.

[170]*The Numismatic Scrapbook Magazine,* February, 1955.

[171]Ibid, August, 1958.

[172]*The Numismatist,* March, 1957.

[172a]*Numismatic News,* June 25, 1996.

[173]Ibid, August, 1958 through January, 1959.

[174]*Coin World,* May 10, 1993.

[175]Ibid.

[176]Letter from Taylor to Deisher, December 28, 1993.

[177]*Coin World,* May 10, 1993.

[178]Ibid.

[179]*The Numismatic Scrapbook Magazine,* November, 1959.

[180]*Annual Report,* 1959.

[181]*The Numismatic Scrapbook Magazine,* May, 1960.

[182]*The Numismatist,* March through May, 1960.

[183]*Annual Report,* 1962.

[184]*The Numismatist,* April through December, 1962.

[185]*Annual Report,* 1962.

[186]Ibid, 1964.

[187]Ibid, 1966

[188]Ibid, 1964.

[189]Ibid.

[190]*The Numismatist,* February, 1966.

[191]*Annual Report,* 1967.

[192]Ibid, 1965.

[193]Taylor.

[194]*Annual Report,* 1968.

[195]Ibid.

[196]*The Numismatic Scrapbook Magazine,* December, 1967.

[197]Ibid, April, 1970.

[198]Ibid, June, 1970.

[199]*Annual Report,* 1971.

[200]Ibid, 1972.

[201]Breen.

[202]*The Numismatic Scrapbook Magazine,* August, 1972.

[203]Wexler.

[204]Taylor.

[205]*The Numismatic Scrapbook Magazine,* August, 1972.

[206]*Annual Report,* 1972.

[207]Ibid, 1973.

[208]Ibid.

[209]Ibid.

[210]*Annual Report,* 1974.

[211]Ibid.

[212]Ibid.

[213]*The Numismatic Scrapbook Magazine,* July, 1974.

[214]*Annual Report,* 1975.

[215]Ibid, 1976.

[216]Ibid.

[217]*The Numismatist,* April, 1976.

[218]*Annual Report,* 1974.

[219]*Coin World,* July 13 & August 3, 1977.

[220]*Annual Report,* 1977.

[221]Numismatic News, March 12, 1996.

[222]*Annual Report,* 1977.

[223]Ibid, 1978.

[224]Ibid.

[225]Ibid, 1979.

[226]Ibid, 1981.

[227]Ibid.

[228]Ibid, 1979.

[229]Ibid, 1982.

[230]Breen.

[231]Ibid.

[232]*Annual Report,* 1983.

[233]Breen.

[234]Taylor.

[235]*Coin World,* February 5, 1986.

[236]*Annual Report,* 1986.

[237]Ibid.

[238]*Coin World,* April 12, 1995.

[239]*Annual Report,* 1990.

[240]Ibid.

[241]Ibid, 1991.

[242]*Numismatic News,* August 2, 1994.

[243]*USA Today,* March 6, 1995.

Chapter 8

COINS FOR COLLECTORS:
PROOF &
MINT SETS

Proof Coinage

HISTORY

A proof coin is a special edition of the regular coinage struck as a representative of each coin at its finest. Special care is taken in selecting both the dies and planchets used, and both are typically polished to a high brilliance. Proof coins are struck two or more times to fully bring up their design and then handled with great care so that they don't come into contact with other coins.

Scholars disagree as to when the first actual proof coins were issued by the United States Mint, though specimens made with particular care and then carefully preserved are known from the late 18th and early 19th Centuries. Created for presentation purposes, these coins were distributed in small numbers to government officials, foreign dignitaries and educational institutions. A few were also preserved within the Philadelphia Mint as the foundation of its own coin collection, now held by the Smithsonian Institution in Washington, D.C. The coinage of proofs was sporadic and selective, so not all dates and denominations are represented.

As a handful of Americans developed an interest in collecting coins and other numismatic objects during the early decades of the 19th Century, these individuals naturally sought out the Philadelphia Mint as a possible source for desired items. In addition to providing these pioneers proof coins of the current year at face value, the Mint often obliged in restriking coins of earlier dates, as it stored a number of old hubs and dies. This informal relationship existed until the 1850s when the growing popularity of numismatics in the United States prompted the adoption of a more structured program. Beginning in 1858 the Mint offered proof coins of all denominations to the public on an annual basis. A small premium was charged to cover the cost of striking the proof coins, while those ordering by mail were also required to include the cost of postage.

From 1858 through 1915, proofs were offered for each denomination and for every date. All of the coins sold publicly were struck at the Philadelphia Mint and carried no mintmark, though a very small number of proofs were coined sporadically at the branch mints for special occasions. These were distributed to VIPs and not offered to the public, a source of consternation among the few collectors who knew of them.

Proofs were occasionally offered as single pieces during this period, but for the most part they came in sets. Coins not struck in the precious metals of silver and gold were called minor coins, and they were offered as minor proof sets. The exact makeup of these sets varied from one decade to another (the two-cent piece, for example, was dropped after 1873), but they generally included all coins from the copper-nickel five-cent piece on down through the cent. The silver proof set included all silver denominations, as well as the minor coins. The gold proof set, for those few dozen collectors who could afford it, included all of the gold coinage up through the double eagle, or 20-dollar piece.

ENTER THE LINCOLN CENT

By 1909, when the Lincoln Cent made its debut, the minor proof set consisted of only two coins, the bronze one-cent piece and the copper-nickel five-cent piece. At that time it was the Mint's policy to offer these coins only in sets of two, and the mintage figures for proofs of these denominations are identical during the years leading up to 1909.

Proofs were generally coined from the very outset of each year, so collectors could and usually did purchase their sets as early as January. When each calendar year came to a close, the proofs of that year would no longer be offered, and it was directed that the unsold coins be destroyed. This, at least, was the official policy. In actual practice, however, coin dealers in the Philadelphia area usually bought up all of the remaining proofs early in the following year, sometimes paying only face value. This activity was not widely known within the numismatic community at the time, though it was revealed later in the recollections of veteran dealers.

Knowledge of the impending Lincoln Cent was only spotty during the early months of 1909, so most collectors blissfully sent away for their 1909 proof sets, receiving a cent of the Indian Head Liberty type. Some 2,175 minor proof sets were sold before the Indian Head was discontinued in May. When the Lincoln Cent became available in August, collectors again ordered minor proof sets to obtain the new coin, and 420 sets were sold before the designer's initials V.D.B. were dropped from the cent's reverse. Whether collectors truly wished to obtain both varieties of the Lincoln Cent is not certain, yet some 2,198 more proofs dated 1909 were coined without the initials. As the coins were not available individually, each new order was for the complete minor proof set, and this resulted in the highest mintage of proof Liberty Head Nickels since that type was introduced in 1883! The figures do not add up perfectly, as the Mint's records list some 30 more cents than nickels coined as proofs during

1909, but it's still evident that quite a few collectors must have had duplicate nickels for sale that year. [1]

YOU CALL THAT A PROOF?

Collectors receiving their new Lincoln Cent proofs in the Summer and Fall of 1909 were quite disappointed with these coins. They had come to expect proof coins having a particular look, one that was quite distinctive from the ordinary currency strikings. Historically, proofs of the Indian Head Cent and other U. S. coins possessed very brilliant fields and frosted devices or relief elements. The spectacular contrast between these two finishes provided what collectors call the "cameo" effect, and it was highly prized.

This treatment worked quite well with coin models sculpted by the U. S. Mint's own engraving staff (whose work was typified by very flat fields), but outside artists such as Victor D. Brenner modeled in a more contemporary style, their coins having contoured fields which rose up to meet the borders. Confronted with this new development, the Mint in 1909 found itself unable to produce the brilliant, cameo proofs of earlier years, and it was compelled to adopt a different manner of proofing for the Lincoln Cents.

The Mint's experience with the new gold coinage of 1907-08 suggested that a uniformly matte or satin finish would be more suitable to the contoured cent. While not exactly dull, the surfaces of such coins are definitely subdued and carry less punch than those of ordinary currency strikes. It was only natural that purchasers of matte proofs would object to paying a premium for coins which seemed in some respects inferior to ordinary pieces obtainable at face value. The superior sharpness of the proofs was little consolation, since the Philadelphia Mint cents of 1909 struck for circulation are generally quite distinct as well.

Though collectors continued to purchase minor proof sets in succeeding years, their disenchantment grew. It's quite possible that they placed their orders primarily to obtain the five-cent piece, which retained the old style of proofing through 1912. (Interestingly, that was the last year in which the mintages of one-cent pieces and five-cent pieces were uniform; subsequent years saw these denominations coined in dissimilar numbers.) The introduction in 1913 of James Earle Fraser's new Indian Head Nickel, however, prompted the coining of matte proofs for this denomination too. Disappointment with these coins led to declining mintages for both denominations during the next few years.

By 1916 there was consideration within the Mint of discontinuing proofs altogether. The new designs planned for the silver coinage held up the production of silver proof sets, as these coins weren't ready for minting until very late in the year, and the Mint didn't anticipate striking any silver coins of the old type dated 1916. The Philadelphia Mint had already determined that it would not coin gold for circulation in 1916, so proofs of these coins were also on hold. That left only the minor coins as the sole proofs offered bearing the date 1916, though a few silver pieces of the new types were ultimately coined with the dates 1916 and 1917 and distributed privately. These too were of the matte or satin finish, and the disappointing results suggested that there was no point in offering them publicly.

Collectors and dealers beseeched the Mint throughout 1916 for silver and gold proofs to complete their sets for that year, but officials continued to point to the delay in adopting new designs as the cause for inaction. As the year drew to a close without such coins being struck, the Mint was compelled to issue a circular dated January 1, 1917 which announced the end of proof coinage:

> Owing to the designs of gold, silver and minor coins not being adapted to the striking of proof coins readily distinguishable from the regular issue, the manufacture of proof coins has been discontinued. [2]

THE REVIVAL OF PROOFS

Collectors learned to live without proof coins for the next 20 years. There were periodic inquiries to the editor of *The Numismatist* and other coin publications as to why proofs were not then available, and it seemed that most in the hobby had forgotten the Mint's reasoning behind its decision to discontinue proof coinage. Since the typical collector of the 1920s and early 1930s had little interest in coins of the current types by date, there was surprisingly little agitation for a resumption of proof coinage.

It was not until a general shift in the hobby's focus occurred during the mid 1930s that serious demands for the revival of proof sets were heard. The extremely low mintages recorded for several coins during the early part of that decade had prompted a renewed interest in current coins and sparked a mad scramble to obtain rolls of these scarce issues. With this speculative activity came a general desire among collectors to start assembling sets of the current coin types by date and mint. Previously, the focus had been on more traditional areas of coin collecting such as large cents, early gold and silver pieces and vintage medals and tokens.

The dawn of the date-and-mint collecting era coincided with the introduction of inexpensive cardboard sheets, punched and printed to accommodate complete sets of popular series such as Indian Head and Lincoln Cents. The distribution of these coin boards was widespread after 1935, and it introduced an entire new element of the population to coin collecting. What had once been the nearly exclusive realm of the wealthy gentleman and the prosperous professional class suddenly became a family hobby for the masses. As these new collectors filled their boards with coins obtained from circulation they soon desired to upgrade these collections with uncirculated and proof coins of earlier years. It was inevitable that these new hobbyists would inquire why proof coins of the current year were not available.

Editor Lee F. Hewitt posed this very question in the May 1935 issue of *Numismatic Scrapbook,* a publication launched the previous January for this new class of hobbyist. The agitation for proof coins grew during 1935-36 and culminated in the following announcement, made exactly one year later:

[Treasury] Secretary Henry Morgenthau, Jr. on April 28th authorized the mint to resume the practice of striking proof coins for the benefit of coin collectors.

According to press reports the suggestion to renew this practice was made by the late Louis McHenry Howe, secretary to President Roosevelt. Howe was said to have been interested in numismatics.

No proofs of silver dollars will be made unless a substantial coinage is authorized later.[3]

The resumption of proof coinage was undoubtedly aided by the contemporary markets for commemorative coins and stamps, both of which were then enjoying widespread popularity. The administration of President Franklin D. Roosevelt proved unusually receptive to both programs, perhaps because FDR was himself a well known stamp collector.

The Mint was correct in 1916 when it doubted its ability to create satisfactory proofs of the new coin types. When coinage resumed in the Spring of 1936 there was no prospect of offering matte proofs, but nor was the Mint sufficiently skilled to produce brilliant proofs of the type so prized by collectors. The first few thousand proofs were already struck when they began to be received by collectors, who quickly voiced their disappointment with the coins' quality. Though clearly superior to ordinary coins in both sharpness and brilliance, they fell far short of the superb appearance offered by brilliant proofs dated 1915 and earlier. Singled out for criticism was their lack of contrast between frosted devices and brilliant fields, as the new proofs were of a uniform, satiny finish throughout.

Frank G. Duffield, Editor of *The Numismatist,* inquired of the Mint why the proofs of 1936 weren't equal to those of earlier years, requesting a description of the process used in their production. He received this reply from Director Nellie Tayloe Ross:

Your letter of June 13th, relative to proof coins, has been referred to this Bureau for attention. The Superintendent submits the following explanation in regard to the method of preparing proof coins:

Proof coins being struck at the mint at the present time are made in every detail exactly as they have been made in the past, namely, the planchets are carefully selected and each one struck individually on a hydraulic press, and handled so that one coin cannot mar another. The dies are polished to a mirror finish at frequent intervals.

The difference between the recent proofs and those struck in the past is due to the difference in the design and the method used in preparing the master dies. All the present coins are made from sculptured models without retouching with a graver in any way in order to preserve the exact quality and texture of the original sculptor's work. This gives a more or less uneven background with less sharpness in the details. In other words, they are produced the same as small medals might be struck.

The master dies for the gold coins struck previous to 1907, and the silver coins struck prior to 1916, were prepared in the older and entirely different method, being lower in relief and much greater sharpness in detail by re-engraving, even though the original design was reduced from a sculptured model. The inscriptions were usually put in the master dies by means of punches. In addition, they were prepared with a "basined" background or field, that is, the field was polished to a perfect radius on a revolving disc, which again produced a much clearer definition between motif and field, and this gave an entirely different appearance to the coin.

With the present coins, the models were never prepared with the intention of "basining" and it could not be done without many radical alterations in the relief of the present designs.[4]

This account is unusually frank and accurate, coming at a time when the Mint typically dodged most technical discussions or provided spurious explanations, albeit ones which the writer may have believed to be correct. Director Ross did make one mistake in claiming that the Mint's engravers perform no retouching of the models submitted to it "to preserve the exact quality and texture of the original sculptor's work." The smooth fields seen on the Type 2 Buffalo Nickels and on the modified silver coins struck 1917 and later are proof enough that additional work was performed to make the sculptors' original textured models more suited to Mint conventions.

THE PRE-WAR POPULARITY OF PROOFS

It's possible that by the time collectors began complaining about the quality of their proof coins the Mint had already solved the problem to some degree. While very few proofs of the 1936-42 period display frosted relief elements, those coined in the latter part of 1936 and in succeeding years are fully brilliant in their fields. A great number of the early style, satiny proofs were produced in 1936, yet their survival rate is somewhat lower, as many collectors may have spent them either mistakenly or intentionally.

In his column "Capital Comment," Harry X Boosel addressed this situation in 1937:

When the mint at Philadelphia resumed striking proofs last year, after a lapse of 20 years, the first efforts weren't acceptable to numismatists. Consequently not many sets were sold. During the latter part of the year the mint improved the process, but not many knew it. Those proofs that were coined late in 1936 were, in our opinion, every bit as good as those of the early years.[5]

Collectors today recognize these two different finishes as either "satin" proofs versus "brilliant" proofs or with the designations Type 1 and Type 2. From 1937 through 1942, all proofs are of the fully brilliant style.

The proofing process continued to gradually improve during this period, and the proof cents struck in 1942 are generally superior to those of the 1930s in one critical aspect. While they are all available with outstanding brilliance and sharp details, the earlier dates were often coined from dies which were overly polished. They tend to lack certain low-relief design elements which were diminished or totally eradicated through aggressive polishing of the dies. These include the lapel of Lincoln's coat, the initials V.D.B., the stems of the wheat ears and much of the lettering. With experience, the Philadelphia Mint's employees learned to polish the dies only as much as needed and to retire them before excessive polishing became necessary to maintain their brilliance.

Unlike in earlier years, proofs were offered to the public as single pieces during this period, and that accounts for the varying mintage figures between different denominations. In actual practice, however, most collectors purchased all five coins, though there was a definite market for additional cents and nickels. Because of its dreary design, the quarter dollar proved the least popular coin, and its lower mintage usually provided the cap for the number of complete sets which may exist for each date. The total number of proof sets minted grew steadily from their humble beginning in 1936, when only 3,837 sets were issued, to 1942, when some 21,120 sets were produced.

With the growth in mintage figures came a growth too in the value of earlier sets. All of the emphasis seemed to be placed on the sets issued since 1936, and that year's set was actually valued more highly than some of those dated before 1916! Much of this interest was purely speculative, but there's no doubt that the hobby experienced genuine growth during the years leading up to the war.

WARTIME HIATUS

America's entry into World War II created a shortage of labor and materials at the same time as the demand for circulating coinage grew. With its resources stretched to the limit, the Philadelphia Mint had no option but to discontinue the coining of proofs. Those dated 1942 would be the last proofs until 1950, as both the war and its aftermath conspired to deprive collectors of their treasures.

This was not readily apparent to hobbyists of the time. In 1943, collectors were still hoping that they would be able to obtain proofs of the current year, including a proof steel cent. Their hopes were dashed, however, by a press release issued by the Superintendent's Office of the Philadelphia Mint:

In view of the extremely heavy demand for coinage and service medals, the facilities of the Mint are taxed almost beyond capacity. Due to this fact, the striking of proof coins will necessarily be delayed for an indefinite period.[6]

This was followed a short time later by a brief statement from H. C. Moore, Acting Superintendent, revealing that "no proof coins have been struck in 1943, and none will be struck for the duration of the war at least."[7]

The interest in proof coins only intensified as the result of tremendous growth in the hobby's popularity during the war. Americans, earning high wages and working overtime, found themselves unable to spend their money on consumer goods because wartime rationing and redirected production made them unobtainable. Americans instead channeled their income toward entertainment such as motion pictures and toward hobbies like coin and stamp collecting. Both of these collectibles experienced rapid price increases beginning around 1943, and the value of pre-war proofs led this growth.

WAITING AND WATCHING

Collectors seemed to accept the suspension of proof coinage during the war, but there was agitation for their return as soon as the war ended. Stuart Mosher, Editor of *The Numismatist*, inquired about proof coins for 1946 and received this reply from Leland Howard, Acting Director of the Mint:

Reference is made to your inquiry of May 9th. In response thereto you are informed that resumption of the practice of striking proof coins depends upon the pressure of work at the Philadelphia Mint.

May we ask that you tell your readers not to write to the Treasury for the information? Both this office and the Philadelphia Mint (where proofs are made) have been swamped with inquiries from interested persons. Your letter will be placed on file in order that you may be notified when plans for striking proofs again are decided upon. In all probability nothing will be done until next year.[8]

For the first few years after the war's conclusion the standard reason for not resuming proof coinage was that the Mint was overwhelmed in producing circulating coinage, as well as the many service medals owed to veterans. Since both medals and proof coins utilized the few hydraulic presses available, the production of one suspended the other. Frustrated collectors inquired how the Mint could find the time and resources needed to strike coins for foreign countries yet was unable to supply proofs of the domestic coinage. In replying to Editor Mosher, Leland Howard revealed his willingness to comply with collectors' demands but also his inability to do so:

The fact is we have coining presses that are not operating full time in the western Mints. San Francisco, for example, is operating on a one shift basis and Denver on only two. If it were possible to strike a proof coin on coinage presses we should be glad to strike them at the western Mints with our idle coinage capacity.

We have orders for over 10 million medals for the armed forces and I believe that you and all the coin collectors will agree with the Mint's policy that medals for the boys who did the fighting should come before proof coins.

I hope that you will see your way clear to correct the erroneous impression that the Mint is producing foreign coins which, in turn, precludes the making of proof coins. It would be a physical impossibility to satisfactorily produce a proof coin on a regular coinage press. I known that on second thought you will realize the impracticability of producing proof coins on regular coining presses.[9]

With each passing year, however, collectors began to suspect that there was more to this delay than the Mint was letting on. They were correct as it turned out, and the greater truth was revealed to Stuart Mosher in further conversation with Leland Howard.

Mosher discovered that the real reason for continuing the suspension of proof coinage year after year was budgetary. As America took stock after several years of war and had a good look at its new Federal deficit, the impact was staggering. Between the many social programs of the 1930s and the tremendous military build-up that followed, the nation had mortgaged its future in a manner which was to become the norm for succeeding generations to the present day. The newly-elected Republican majority Congress of 1946 slashed the budgets of many departments, including the Bureau of the Mint. Cost-cutting measures were in order for the next decade or so, as the Mint sought new ways to increase productivity.

One of the victims of the new austerity was the proof coin program. Because the profits from the sale of proof coins accrued to the Treasury's General Fund and not to the Mint itself, the production of proofs was simply another expense which came directly out of the Mint's annual operating budget. With this being slashed during the late 1940s, the Mint could not afford to produce proof coins at the risk of not having enough funds to meet the nation's needs for circulating coinage. This would mean going to Congress with hat in hand and begging for an additional appropriation, something that no government administrator anticipates with pleasure.

Mosher revealed to readers of *The Numismatist* the Mint's estimated cost of $50,000 for producing one year's proof coinage. He added that a bill was pending in Congress which would enable the Mint to retain the profits from proof sales to apply against the additional operating expense that their production entailed, the remaining balance to be turned over to the Treasury.[10]

PROOF COINAGE RESUMES

The draft bill of 1948 to which Howard referred died in committee, and another bill, S.1069, was introduced by Senator Maybank on February 25, 1949. This second bill passed in the Senate the following July and was referred to the House of Representatives for action. Editor Lee F. Hewitt of *The Numismatic Scrapbook Magazine* urged collector to write to their Congressman with an appeal for prompt reading of the bill.[11] Instead, the bill moved slowly through the House, not being passed until May 2, 1950. Again showing his good intentions toward the numismatic hobby, Howard personally telephoned American Numismatic Association President M. Vernon Sheldon with the news.[12] The bill was signed into law eight days later by President Harry S Truman, and the way was paved for the resumption of proof coin sales.[13]

Collectors were asked by Lee Hewitt to refrain from calling or writing the Mint seeking ordering instructions; the necessary information would be published as soon as it was made available. Acting Director Howard indicated that proof coins for 1950 would not be issued until the new fiscal year, which began July 1; he anticipated an actual start-up date of July 15 or later. The timing of this action was serendipitous, as regular coinage at the Philadelphia Mint was shut down for a two-month inventory beginning June 13, 1950.[14]

The sale of proof coins began July 17, and some

10,000 sets had already been produced as of that date. Unlike the years 1936-42, proofs were no longer available individually but only in complete, five-piece sets from cent through half dollar. Though it was anticipated that collectors would eventually be able to order as many sets as they desired, a temporary limit of five sets per customer was in effect to insure fair distribution.

In a replay of 1936, the quality of 1950 proof coins was mixed. While a number of fully brilliant proofs were issued, most were of less than full brilliance and some were simply satin proofs like the early issues of 1936. Some collectors distinguish between the satin and brilliant proofs as Type 1 versus Type 2, but the lines are usually not so clearly drawn. A certain percentage of the 1951 proofs were also of less than full brilliance, but most were satisfactory. From 1952 through the suspension of proof coinage in 1964 nearly all proofs were fully brilliant. The quality of those from the early 1950s, even when brilliant, is sometimes mediocre due to overly polished dies. Like many of those produced in the 1930s, these coins are lacking in some low-relief design elements and may have an overall blurry appearance from a lack of sharp edges between the fields and the relief elements.

A total of 51,386 sets were produced and sold during 1950, nearly two and a half times as many as in 1942 and more than 13 times as many as in 1936! This reflected the extent to which the hobby had grown during that 15 year period. Speculation in the proof sets of 1936-42 and the early 1950s developed around 1953, and that year witnessed the first mintage to exceed 100,000. By 1957, the feverish buying and selling of proof sets in quantity had become so widespread that the Mint seemingly retaliated by overproducing the 1957 sets. It did this by simply neglecting to cut off orders at its anticipated capacity and producing the sets in any quantity desired. At 1,247,952 sets, the mintage for 1957 was nearly double that of 1956, and the speculative bubble burst. Sales retreated below one million in 1958, but they bounced back again in 1959 as the coin market in general grew at an accelerated pace.

The early 1960s witnessed the highwater mark in the popularity of coin collecting. It's safe to say that there were more persons interested in United States coins at that time than at any period before or since. While much of this activity was purely profit-motivated and centered around the trading of rolls and bags of modern coins, there were enough legitimate collectors of all ages to push proof set mintages consistently into the low millions. The discovery of the small date and large date cents in 1960 played a big role in promoting the hobby of coin collecting and in boosting the sales of proof sets.

PROOF COINAGE SUSPENDED AGAIN

The introduction of the John F. Kennedy Half Dollar in 1964 pushed the mintage of proof sets to nearly four million. This was the last year of proof coins until 1968, as a crushing nationwide coin shortage taxed the Mint's resources to their absolute limit. Among the emergency measures adopted to cope with this crisis was the suspension of proof coins until further notice.

This action came just as the speculative fever in recent coinage was cresting, and collectors were extremely disappointed that there would be no proofs for 1965. The Mint stood firm, however, and there were no actual proofs coined with the date 1965. There were sets of ersatz proofs struck at the San Francisco Assay Office early in 1966 bearing the date 1965. These were marketed as "special mint sets." The assembling of regular uncirculated sets (consisting of one each of the various coins produced at each mint) had likewise been suppressed after 1964, and the special mint sets were a compromise between uncirculated coins and proof coins. Of course, they were neither fish nor fowl, and they found little favor with collectors. The announcement of the new sets came in a Treasury Department press release dated March 8, 1966:

> Coins in the new sets will be struck one at a time from specially prepared blanks, on high tonnage presses, and handled individually after striking. They will have a higher relief than regular coins and be better in appearance than any of the regular uncirculated sets heretofore issued. All coins in the new sets will be dated 1965. They will not carry mint marks.
>
> The Special Mint Sets will be sold in lots of one, two, five, or ten sets, only, to a customer. They will be made at the San Francisco Assay Office.[15]

The SMS coins varied in finish from satiny to semi-brilliant. Despite the Treasury Department's reassurances to the contrary these coins bore minor nicks and scratches, and their sharpness of strike was only slightly superior to that of ordinary coins. The 1966 edition (coined later that year) was more fully brilliant, but it too had assorted flaws and was a mediocre substitute for real proofs. The 1967 special mint sets came fairly close to the quality of proof coinage, but even this couldn't prevent their sales from sliding. The coin market was itself in decline during these years and this may account in part for the poor showing of these sets. Aggravating the situation still further was the Mint's rather ill-timed decision to price these pseudo proofs at $4 per set when the real proof sets had cost only $2.10!

One interesting development to come from the proofless interlude was the creation of coins from cent through half dollar dated 1964 bearing an experimental finish somewhat similar to that of the satiny 1965 issues. It is assumed that these were prototypes for the special mint sets of following years. They were unknown to the hobby until the early 1990s, and even then they were largely ignored until properly diagnosed and publicized by this writer in 1995. For more about these very rare coins, see the date 1964 in the analysis which follows.

PROOF COINS GO WEST

By 1967 Mint Director Eva Adams was able to declare the great coin shortage over. Prompted by her testimony before Congress May 2, a bill was passed June 24 which repealed 1965's five-year ban on mintmarks effective January 1, 1968. The return of proof coins was announced shortly afterward. In a new twist, proofs would henceforth be produced by the San Francisco Assay Office. It was there that the special mint sets had been coined, and this arrangement proved quite satisfactory to the Bureau.

Though proofs had been coined on rare occasion at the San Francisco Mint, these were limited-issue pieces struck for presentation purposes, and none had been offered for sale by the government. With the transfer of proof production to the San Francisco Assay Office, the sale of these coins was also handled from that address. When the Old San Francisco Mint of 1874-1937 was reopened as a museum in 1973 the administration and distribution of proof coin sales was relocated there to a floor not open to the public. The use of simple computers to process orders had been introduced as early as 1961,[16] and persons who purchased proof sets by mail from 1968 through the 1970s were required to fill out punch cards and detach tabs from their order forms indicating the number of sets desired. Despite this primitive attempt at automation, purchasers waited for many months for their proof sets to arrive, ordering them after November 1 of the previous year and typically not receiving them until Spring!

PROOF COINAGE IN RECENT YEARS

As more powerful computers were developed in the late 1970s and early '80s, the clumsy system of punch cards and tear-off strips was reduced to the simple filling in of an order blank. By the end of the 1980s, proof sets were being received in a more timely fashion, and orders were not taken until the year of coinage. As the 1990s dawned, the turnaround time between ordering and receiving one's sets was down to as little as three or four weeks.

Though the prices of proof sets rose frequently during the 1970s and '80s, their quality grew apace, and collectors have been generally satisfied in that respect. With the introduction of new commemorative coins and the "Prestige" proof sets which include them, collectors have had an alternative to the simple five-coin proof sets which typified most of the years from 1936 to date.

To mark the U. S. Mint's Bicentennial in 1992, silver proof sets were offered that year and each subsequent year to date. This means that the dime, quarter and half are available in both the conventional copper-nickel-clad alloy used since 1965 and the traditional "coin silver" alloy of .900 silver and .100 copper employed employed 1837-1964. While some collectors have approved of this option, those collecting cents and nickels have decried it, as the offering of both versions results in redundant strikes of these two coins. The mintage of cents and nickels is thus increased beyond any realistic demand.

Given the confusing jumble or ordering options that the Mint now offers annually, it should come as no surprise that such redundancy develops. Despite a general decline in the number of active coin collectors since the mid 1960s, the mintage of proof coins annually remains in the three million range when all of the various packaging options are totaled. Even after years of watching the values of most proof sets fall in the secondary market there are still many individuals who persist in buying multiple sets each year. These ultimately get dumped into the marketplace at bargain prices, depressing the prospects for future price appreciation still further. The final straw is the Mint's policy of offering discounts to bulk purchasers of proof sets, with the result that as many as 100,000 sets may be ordered by a single distributor to supply some promotional campaign targeted at inexperienced collectors or investors.

While the U. S. Mint's proof coins have achieved a state of technical perfection, its marketing of them as so many widgets has served to destroy their perceived value. At one time the Mint limited the number of sets it would produce annually, this limitation being imposed by an operating budget which in turn was limited by annual appropriations. With the Mint now having an "enterprise fund," there are no longer any limitations to the number of sets produced nor in the packaging options that may result. The entire concept of the proof set as being something rare and desirable has been negated by such short-sighted profit-taking. It seems that while the proof coins of earlier generations will continue to advance in value, those produced in more recent decades will wallow in a saturated market.

Also as a consequence of the many packaging options and an ordering period which typically extends into the early months of the following calendar year, the Mint is often unable to account for the total number of proof coins issued for each denomination. The numbers will not match from one denomination to the next, as several are offered in a variety of packaging options. For these reasons, the final mintage data for proof cents and other denominations is not only tardy and inconsistent, it is also somewhat suspect. While it really doesn't matter in terms of rarity whether the San Francisco Mint struck 2,700,000 proof cents in a particular year or 2,800,000, the published figures since the mid 1980s must not be taken too literally.

* * *

METHODS OF MANUFACTURE

No one knows exactly how early United States coins were minted. Beyond a basic understanding of the tools available at the time, one has only the coins to provide some circumstantial evidence of the techniques employed. This is especially true of early specimen and proof strikings, as these go beyond the normal methods of manufacture. We can make some assumptions, however. It's likely that both dies and planchets were selected for the absence of flaws, though this was not true in every case. Proofs are indeed known from cracked or mis-punched dies and on planchets showing minor adjustments marks where their weight was reduced to the legal standard by working them with a file.

When the production of regular coinage was transferred from human-powered screw presses to steam-driven knuckle-action presses after 1836, medals and proofs continued to be coined with an old screw press. This produced a slower and more effective squeezing action which more completely filled the die cavities. Beginning in 1893, the screw press was succeeded by a hydraulic press which simulated the qualities of the old press but in an accelerated and more powerful manner. Modern proofs minted since the 1950s are still struck two or three times, but they use the same electrically-driven presses as ordinary coins. The difference lies in the number and speed of the strokes. Even after 200 years, a slow squeeze remains more effective in bringing up relief than a quick slam.

MATTE PROOFS

Despite attempts by numismatic researchers to reconstruct the method by which the proof Lincoln Cents of 1909-16 were made, much of this still remains a mystery. When the persons who witnessed their manufacture were still living, no one thought to record their memoirs. Later scholars have had to rely on the accounts from other mints of the world that were using similar techniques, as well as on the circumstantial evidence of the coins themselves.

What is known from published contemporary accounts, such as that of James Rankin Young in the book *The United States Mint at Philadelphia* (1903), is that the production of proof coins was then in a separate office from the regular production floor. Proofs were struck in the Medal Room which, as its name implies, was also the location of medal production. This room contained two electrically-activated hydraulic presses as well as the retired screw press, perhaps kept for sentimental purposes. In the basement beneath this room was found a huge hydraulic press which was used for the coining of large medals up to four inches in diameter.

The dies for conventional, brilliant proofs such as those coined in 1903 were polished to a fine, mirror-like finish. There was, however, a sandblasting chamber which was used to dull the finish of medals so that their design might be more easily studied without glare. This technique, pioneered at the Paris Mint only a few years before, was gaining a growing acceptance among coiners and medallists. It had been used in preparing the proof set of 1902 marking the coronation of England's King Edward VII.

The practice of sandblasting had yet to be extended to actual coins at the Philadelphia Mint, but the necessary device was already in place. Young described it as "a small wooden box with glass sides. A pipe on the inside blows down a fine shower of sand. The operator, wearing a big pair of mits to protect his hands, holds the coin [medal] under this stream of sand until the operation is finished, when it has a delicate frosted appearance."[17]

Dies too were sandblasted to give them a textured surface, followed by a vigorous polishing of just their flat fields. This resulted in a contrast between brilliant fields and frosted cavities which was imparted to the finished coins. These were the frosted proofs so popular with collectors of the late 19th and early 20th Centuries.

Also a common practice at the U. S. Mint was the cleansing in acid of coin and medal planchets. This removed any residual grease or oxidation which may have accrued from the casting, rolling and planchet-punching processes. These planchets were then dried by tumbling them within sawdust and polished by additional tumbling against one another, sometimes with the assistance of metallic beads.

The combined application of sandblasting and acid baths is believed to have been behind the matte proofs coined 1908-16, as the new designs introduced beginning in 1907, with their sculpted surfaces and irregular fields, did not lend themselves to the traditional method of proofing. The French matte process was thus applied in 1908 and subsequent years, though both the methods and the results varied somewhat from year to year. There appear to be only two variant finishes on early proof Lincoln Cents, the true matte finish and the softer satin finish. It's not known for certain whether these two variants were the product of intent or a simple evolution. The author believes that the satin proofs were simply coined from the same dies as the matte proofs, but after these dies had lost their rough texture from very slight wear and additional polishing.

If sandblasting was used in the manufacture of proof Lincolns, it was probably in the die finishing process and not with the struck coins themselves. Even at that, the sand must have been extremely fine so as to not diminish any of the subtle details found on these coins. There is also no real evidence that acid was used on the struck coins, though it was undoubtedly a step in the normal cleansing of the unstruck planchets.

In short, we simply don't know exactly how the proof cents of 1909-16 were made. Some subtle distinctions appear within particular dates and from one date to the next. These are described in detail within the date analysis that follows.

BRILLIANT PROOFS

When proof coinage resumed in 1936, an attempt was made to create the style of brilliant proof used for cents of the Indian Head type. At first, this met with only limited success, as recounted by Lee F. Hewitt:

> The coins struck during the first month of two in that year were very little better than those issued for general circulation—they were improved in the fall but it is felt that the poor quality of the early sets held down sales. In fact the Philadelphia Mint had a quantity of 1936 sets left on hand at the end of the year; a Chicago collector visiting Philadelphia in February of 1937 was able to buy ten sets at the Mint office.[18]

Though very sharply struck, the first proofs displayed more of a satiny glow than the full brilliance which collectors had anticipated. Even when the Mint overcame this obstacle with more effective polishing methods, the resulting coins usually lacked the frosted relief elements which had made proofs of past generations so visually stunning. This feature was reserved for only the first few strikes from new dies, as whatever texture the die cavities may have had when new was quickly worked off through repeated contact with planchets.

Another flaw in the proofs of 1936-42, though one which was gradually corrected toward the end of that period, is that the dies were often overly polished. This stemmed from economy, as the Mint did not want to replace the dies when they became slightly worn. The result, however, was that subsequent repolishings caused a loss of fine detail in the dies, particularly among low-relief elements such as the lapel of Lincoln's coat and the initials AW on the reverse of the half dollar.

There are no specific accounts available which detail the proof making process during the years 1936-42, and once again no one thought to obtain this information while those who knew it were still living. By comparing the proof coins of 1936-42 with those of 1950-64 it may be assumed that many of the same steps were undertaken, as the finished coins are quite similar. We do have some information dating from the 1950s and '60s, and this reveals what was probably a common technology.

After being selected for an absence of flaws, hardened proof dies were cleansed of grease and other contaminants with a solvent. The dies were then dipped or "pickled" in a bath consisting of 5% nitric acid and 95% alcohol. This provided them with an overall frosting of minimal depth. Any portion of the die cavities which was lacking in sufficient frostiness was then touched up by hand with a cotton swab that had been dipped in the same solution. Polishing of the die fields came next, using a compound containing diamond dust. Applied at first with a wooden mandrill, the finishing of the die was completed with a felt mandrill for finer work. This left the die with contrasting surfaces which were brilliant in the fields and lightly frosted in the cavities. Coins struck from these dies displayed similar contrast between fields and devices and are known as "cameo" proofs, since the portraits stand out from the background as in an engraver's cameo. Because this frosting in the die was so delicate and unprotected from wear, it quickly rubbed away after the first few dozen impressions.[19]

One fact which is quite obvious even to the beginning collector of proof Lincoln Cents is that those coined since the early 1970s are more often found with frosted devices than are previous issues, while those struck beginning in the late 1970s are almost always cameo coins. This is due to two major advances in the production of proof dies. The first of these is sandblasting, which replaced the acid baths of the 1960s and earlier. It was known by the Mint that collectors desired cameo coins, and the application of fine sand at high pressure gave the dies of 1971 and later a greater depth of frosting. Still, this quality wore off after the first few hundred impressions, and many proofs of the early 1970s are uniformly brilliant in fields and devices.

The solution to this problem lay in plating the dies with chromium for superb durability. The Mint had experimented with the chromium plating of dies, collars and other press parts as early as 1927-28,[20] but it's doubtful that this practice was employed to any great extent before the 1970s. When chromium plating became routine during that decade, the result was entire runs of proof coins with deep cameo contrast. To ensure this quality, worn dies were re-sandblasted and repolished only once or twice before being retired. This is in contrast to earlier years when dies were either never repolished and lost their brilliance (as in 1950) or were polished too many times, losing much of their detail.[21]

When the practice of sandblasting dies was re-introduced in the early 1970s, the polishing of their fields followed in a subsequent step. As made today, however, proof dies are first polished to a high degree of brilliance and their fields then masked off with tape. The sandblasting is applied afterward, the brilliant fields of the die being protected by heavy masking tape. This is applied to the die face and then carefully trimmed away to expose only the die cavities. While this seems an extraordinarily tedious process, it does produce the very finest results. Proof coins made from such dies have a much finer delineation between brilliant fields and frosted devices than can be achieved with the former method.

Dies are shipped in a hardened but unfinished state from the Philadelphia Mint to the mint where they'll actually be used. In the case of proof Lincoln Cents, this has been San Francisco exclusively since 1965, if one includes the special mint set coins.

The preparation of planchets for proof coins is initially the same as for regular coins and will not be described here. When a batch of planchets has been designated for proof coinage, it then undergoes an additional step. The planchets are tumbled within a horizontal barrel for up to 24 hours while in contact with small metal beads. This burnishes their surfaces and enhances the brilliant finish already possessed by the dies.[22]

The subtleties of proof coin manufacture since 1950 are many, and persons interested in learning more about this specialized area of American numismatics are encouraged to read the book *Cameo and Brilliant Proof Coinage of the 1950 to 1970 Era* by Rick Jerry Tomaska. It covers this subject in greater depth than is possible here.

* * *

THE PACKAGING AND PRICING OF PROOFS

MATTE PROOFS

When the Lincoln Cent was introduced in 1909, coins of this denomination could not be purchased singly. Instead, they were obtainable only in two-coins sets consisting of the cent and the five-cent piece. As incredible as it seems today, the cost for both was a mere eight cents, with postage and insurance being additional. The Mint must have realized that this sum was too small, since it raised the price to 15 cents beginning in 1912.[23]

With proof coins priced so low, not much consideration could be given to their housing. In fact, persons ordering proofs by mail in the years 1909-16 received their coins wrapped individually in tissue paper. This had a high sulphur content, and cents left in such paper for many years acquired deep toning. The predominate color was typically purple, as this was a combination of the coins' natural redness and the blue tint produced by sulphur. If a collector was lucky, his cents toned in an even and concentric pattern, with their centers perhaps retaining some redness. More common, however, were cents showing blotchy and irregular toning, perhaps with the unwanted additions of tiny black spots and some Mint employee's fingerprint.

While such deeply toned proofs were once a common sight on the bourse floor and in auctions, most have since been cleaned in some manner and then retoned to varying degrees. When done properly, the result is a very attractive coin which will qualify for certification by the grading services. If cleaned using harsh chemicals or abrasives, as were many during the 1950s, '60s and '70s, the result is an unnatural appearance which leaves these coins difficult to grade and impossible to have certified. With the restorative processes for coins becoming ever more sophisticated, however, there may yet be hope for these orphans.

EARLY BRILLIANT PROOFS

When proofs were again offered to the public beginning in 1936, both their pricing and packaging had advanced with the times. While most collectors typically purchased complete proof sets for $1.89 per set (which included eight cents for postage) each denomination was also available singly. Proof cents cost 16 cents apiece, with an additional eight cents for postage. Delivery was typically made in a celluloid envelope, though the old tissues were reportedly seen as well. It may be that buyers who purchased their coins in person at the Philadelphia Mint were given the tissues, while celluloid was reserved for mail orders.

After the first few years the Mint appears to have switched from celluloid to the more sophisticated and versatile cellophane. If the circumstantial evidence of the coins themselves may be believed, this conversion occurred around 1940. The proof coins of that year through 1942 are typically found less toned than the earlier pieces.

The toning of proof cents dated 1936-42 can be quite deep, though it tends to be more creamy and cloudy than colorful. So many cents of these years have been dipped or otherwise cleaned that it has become difficult to find many dates, particularly the earliest ones, in their natural state. The popularity of third-party grading and encapsulation has largely segregated the natural coins from those which have been cleaned and recolored.

LATER BRILLIANT PROOFS

When proofs were again offered in 1950 it was in complete sets only. The packaging of each piece was similar to that of the pre-war years, but the individual cellophane envelopes were stapled together one atop the other and mailed in a small cardboard box rather than in the regular mailing envelopes used previously. The box was stuffed with tissue paper to limit the coins' movement. Both the material used and the placement of the coins in stacked fashion encouraged abrasion of their delicate surfaces, and many proofs were impaired by their initial delivery and subsequent transportation from one coin show to another. Still, when priced at only $2.10 for coins having a collective face value of 91 cents, these sets were a bargain.

The most serious problem with the plastic was its chemical make-up. Chemist and inventor of "Kointains," Dr. F. Stevens Epps, diagnosed this problem as early as the 1950s. In a 1960 letter to Elston Bradfield, Editor of *The Numismatist*, Dr. Epps noted that the cellophane used by the Mint during the early 1950s included as much as 5% nitrate and sulphur, which acted upon both the coins themselves and the staple used to hold the cellophane envelopes together. In emphasizing his point, Dr. Epps remarked that "Anyone who buys a proof set through 1954 without looking at it should be subjected to a psychiatric examination."[24] The passage of nearly 40 additional years has only proved him right, as sets left in their original packaging are now often quite deeply toned.

The plastic used from mid-1954 through mid-1955 was of a different quality than that used in earlier years. Softer to the touch, it was less abrasive to the coins, but it also accelerated the pace of unattractive toning. Midway through the 1955 deliveries the Mint switched to

a configuration which laid out the five coins flat within a single "pliofilm" envelope. This consisted of two outside layers of inert polyethylene bonded to a structural base of cellophane. The assembled and sealed set was then placed between two cardboard inserts and enclosed within an outer mailing envelope. In this fashion proof sets were delivered through 1964, though the Mint briefly reverted to the old packaging toward the end of 1956 when its existing stock of pliofilm ran short.[25] While the proof cents of these years may show some orange or brown toning, these are far less subject to the hairline scratching found on cents dated 1950-54. The success of pliofilm and its very similar successors prompted the Mint to switch to this medium for its uncirculated sets beginning in 1959.

The special mint sets dated 1965 were housed in a similar manner. Given that the price was raised from $2.10 for the 1964 proof set to $4 for this pseudo proof set, there was much resentment among collectors. In an attempt to address this issue (without lowering the price of the set), the Mint introduced a hardshell plastic holder for the 1966 edition. This consisted of two outer halves of clear polystyrene shaped to hold the coins securely, with a flexible plastic insert used as a mat to provide some color and a place for printing the title. This sealed plastic holder was then placed inside a tight-fitting box of heavy blue paper. The same packaging was used again for the 1967 special mint sets. These holders have protected their contents quite well from both chemical action and physical contact.

With the return of actual proof coins in 1968, the price was raised again to $5, this sum now including the cost of registered mail. Clear polystyrene was used to produce a picture frame type of holder with a frosted border. Inside were the coins, held in place by a black mounting template. Outside was a blue or black box of heavy paper, the whole then shipped in an ordinary cardstock mailer. This form of packaging proved quite safe and was used in various configurations through 1982. Beginning in 1983, the plastic insert was replaced by one of fiberboard. These same materials are used to the present day. While there have been some problems of corrosion associated with the fiberboard inserts (the 1984 sets were particularly susceptible), they've been generally satisfactory provided that one's sets are not stored in a moist environment or where they may experience extremes of temperature.

The price of the U. S. Mint's proof sets has been raised several times beginning in 1973. Priced at $7 that year due to the inclusion of the Eisenhower Dollar for the first time, the figure was raised again to $9 in 1977.

In 1980 it advanced to $10 for one year only before being increased to $11 in 1981. Though that was the last year in which these sets contained a dollar coin their price remained at this figure for many years afterward. To hold the line on price increases the Mint quietly stopped paying for registered delivery during the 1980s. The price for the basic five-coin proof set was not raised again until 1993, when it advanced to $12.50. It remains at this figure as of this writing (1996).

THOSE OTHER PROOF SETS

With the return of commemorative coinage in the early 1980s, the Mint devised new ways of packaging its basic proof set to include these additions. Often priced above the combined individual prices for the various coins these sets were marvels of packaging design. The "Prestige" proof sets were joined in 1992 by the silver proof sets, which contained regular proof cents and nickels but also included proof dimes, quarters and halves struck in the historic composition of .900 silver and .100 copper. These have been priced annually at $21, though they typically fare just as poorly in the secondary market as their less noble brethren. The "Silver Premier Set" is this same mix of five coins, three of them silver, in a deluxe presentation box. Debuting in 1992 at $37.50, it has retained this issue price to date (1996), though its value on the bourse floor has witnessed the same abysmal returns as most of the U. S. Mint's products of recent years.

Mint Sets

HISTORY

Though the coins they contain are ordinary production strikes, the Mint's sets of uncirculated coins issued since 1948 are nonetheless collectable and provide a convenient source for modern coins of all dates and mints.

This program grew out of the sustained demand for each year's coinage from collectors. In the 19th and early 20th Centuries, collectors simply wrote to each individual mint to obtain newly-struck coins, paying their face value plus the cost of postage and, if desired, insurance. In addition, a handful of individuals visited one or more mints in person seeking coins. These were obligingly provided at face value alone. Such an informal system was satisfactory during the hobby's infancy, but by the 1910s Mint personnel were becoming increasingly irritated at such disruptions in their regular duties. It was in the early years of Lincoln Cent coinage that persons applying for new coins from the respective mints were first told to go to their bank instead.

One such pioneering collector of this series was Commodore W. C. Eaton, a frequent correspondent to *The Numismatist* during this period. In placing his annual order for 25 new cents from the San Francisco Mint in 1912 he received the following reply from its Superintendent:

Enclosed I return the money order No. 64660, for $0.35, in favor The Supt. of the Mint of the United States, received in your letter of January 19, 1912, with the information that one-cent pieces may be distributed only upon an order from the Treasurer of the United States or an Assistant Treasurer.[26]

This matter remained unresolved for the next several years, and those few collectors saving current issues were really at a loss to secure new coins. Dealers did not waste their advertising dollars on Lincoln Cents until the late 1920s and early '30s, but in actual practice they would provide any such coins as a courtesy at a slight advance over face value.

For 20 years after Commodore Eaton forwarded his reply letter to *The Numismatist* nothing more was published on the matter of obtaining current coins. This silence wasn't broken until the early 1930s when record low mintages piqued the interest of a new class of coin enthusiast—the speculator. The Great Depression not only reduced the production of new cents, it also eliminated the demand for them. As a consequence, most of the coins dated 1930-33 were not issued until 1934 and later. Seeing opportunity in these modern rarities, both legitimate collectors and the emerging speculators sought to obtain examples.

The U. S. Mint was of little help, as it then had no structured policy of providing coins for collectors. Pointing with dismay to the ease by which stamp collectors could obtain new issues, coin hobbyists protested this neglect by the Mint's administration. Leading the call to arms was the American Numismatic Association:

A special effort has been made during recent weeks by Nelson T. Thorson, chairman of the Board of Governors of the ANA, through influential men in Washington, to have the Treasury Department furnish, upon request, Uncirculated United States coins to collectors, dealers or others. This action was taken by Mr. Thorson, it is said, by the refusal of the Treasury Department to furnish a dealer with such coins.

In the correspondence it was pointed out that the government philatelic agency in Washington employs a number of clerks regularly in the selection of the finest specimens of postage stamps for sale to collectors or dealers, by mail or over the counter, and a similar arrangement was sought for collectors of coins.

So far results have not been very favorable. The Treasury Department says it does, however, undertake to provide specimens of coins for collectors when it is possible to do so in order to aid them in completing collections, but it is not intended to lend aid to dealers in coins for profit.[27]

While it was thus possible to obtain coins from the Treasury Department, the mechanism for doing this was not publicized. It's evident that few collectors knew of this service, and the A.N.A. pressed for further information. In August of 1932, *The Numismatist* included an announcement regarding the ordering of uncirculated coins:

These applications must state definitely the coins desired, the mint by which manufactured, the amount and denomination, as well as the purpose for which desired, and they must be accompanied by a remittance in cash or money order payable to the Treasurer of the United States for the full face value of the coins, plus an amount sufficient to cover the postage thereon by first-class mail and the registration fee, if it is decided the shipment must be registered.

In case coins are desired from all three mints it is necessary to include postage, etc., for three different shipments.[28]

This clumsy arrangement remained in effect through 1947, though it seemed to satisfy most coin collectors at the time. One interesting by-product of this policy was that the Treasury published a listing, updated several times during the 1930s, of older coins from its vaults available at face value. While no cents dated earlier than 1930 were included in these listings, some very desirable coins were. Among them were a number of silver dollars from the 1920s, including the low-mintage 1928-P issue. Several branch mint nickels, dimes and quarters from the late 1920s and early '30s were also available. Halves, however, seemed to have all been distributed at or near their time of minting, which may account for their greater rarity today. By far the greatest missed opportunity was found in the first edition of this listing from 1932, for it included gold pieces which were then still legally obtainable. Among the coins available for face value plus postage was the 1927-D double eagle, an issue now valued in six figures!

THE ADVENT OF MINT SETS

During and immediately after World War II the growth of the coin collecting hobby was rapid and widespread. Much of this new interest centered around modern coins of recent vintage, which were often acquired by the roll as a speculative venture. Less ambitious collectors were typically satisfied with a single specimen of each date and mint, though some favored two so that both sides could be displayed in an exhibit case.

Since the 1930s, the Treasury Department had used this same reasoning in supplying just two specimens of each date, mint and denomination. It did not want to encourage speculation by delivering larger numbers outside of the normal banking channels. Despite such measures the request for uncirculated coins grew along with the unprecedented growth of the hobby, and the Treasury found itself burdened with a very labor-intensive system of delivering coins to collectors in individual tissues.

This was remedied early in 1948 when the Department announced that henceforth uncirculated coins would be furnished only in complete sets of all three mints. These consisted of two coins each, mounted in cardboard holders and placed alternately heads and tails so that both sides could be viewed simultaneously. Covered with a paper flap glued down to the cardboard in hinge fashion, each holder was then inserted in a mailing envelope for shipment or over-the-counter sales at the Treasury Department in Washington. Sales of the sets were later extended to the individual mints, as well.

Both the cardboard mounting and the paper flap which covered it were highly sulfurous, and coins left in these holders for more than a few years are typically quite deeply toned. In the case of the silver pieces this often resulted in quite attractive coloration popularly known as "mint set" toning. For the more reactive cents and nickels, however, the result was usually an unsightly mess of blotches, streaks and fingerprints.

The first sets issued in 1948 were of coins dated 1947, and this policy of not selling a particular year's coinage until the following year remained in place for more than a decade. Only a small premium was charged for these sets, and their price varied from year to year with the number of denominations issued from the three mints. For example, the 1947-dated set was priced at $4.87, as it included only four half dollars (two each from the Philadelphia and Denver Mints). In contrast, the 1949 set included two half dollars from each of *three* mints, and it was priced at $5.45. This irregular pricing structure was probably behind the Treasury Department's policy of waiting for year's end to see which coins had been struck at each of the three mints.

MODERN UNCIRCULATED SETS

The cardboard and paper holders lasted through 1958, when the Mint discontinued sales of double sets. The uncirculated coins offered in 1959 included only a single piece of each denomination from the two mints then active. Each mint's coins were packaged in a transparent pliofilm envelope of the same style used for proofs since 1955. The two envelopes were then inserted into a paper mailing envelope, accompanied by two sheets of cardstock to provide some protection for the coins. This same basic format remains in place to the present day (1996).

Priced at a fixed figure of $2.40 for the first time, the new sets remained at this price level through 1964. Discontinued during 1965-67, the sets returned at $2.50 in 1968. This increase was partly justified by the inclusion of two additional coins, the cent and the nickel from the San Francisco Assay Office. Nevertheless, critics pointed out that the new sets included only a single half dollar, as Philadelphia did not coin this denomination

again until 1971. This was just the first of many increases in price during the following decades, the most recent coming in 1993 when the price of a complete set advanced from $7 to $8.

A complete history of issue prices and the number of sets sold may be found in the following table. This information has been taken from the 1995 Edition of R. S. Yeoman's *A Guide Book of United States Coins,* published by Western Publishing Company, Inc.

(NOTES: No uncirculated sets were issued for 1950, as it was thought that the return of proof sets would eliminate the demand for these. Sets were also not issued in 1965-67 during the special mint set interlude and in 1982-83 when their production was simply not included in the Mint's annual budget. Collector demand forced a return in 1984, and these sets have remained a staple of the Mint's product line ever since. Though called "mint sets" by the hobby, they are known to the Treasury Department as "uncirculated sets." The retail values given are for sets still in their original packaging.)

MINT SETS: NUMBERS SOLD AND PRICE HISTORY

Date/Mints	Quantity	Face Value	Issue Price	1995 Value	Date/Mints	Quantity	Face Value	Issue Price	1995 Value
1947-P,D,S	?	$ 4.46	$ 4.87	$ 650.00	1972-P,D,S	2,750,000	1.83	3.50	3.00
1948-P,D,S	?	4.46	4.92	200.00	1973-P,D,S	1,767,691	3.83	6.00	7.25
1949-P,D,S	?	4.96	5.45	525.00	1974-P,D,S	1,975,981	3.83	6.00	5.50
1951-P,D,S	8,654	5.46	6.75	400.00	1975-P,D	1,921,488	3.82	6.00	6.00
1952-P,D,S	11,499	5.46	6.14	285.00	1976-P,D	1,892,513	3.82	6.00	6.00
1953-P,D,S	15,538	5.46	6.14	225.00	1977-P,D	2,006,869	3.82	7.00	5.50
1954-P,D,S	25,599	5.46	6.19	100.00	1978-P,D	2,162,609	3.82	7.00	5.50
1955-P,D,S	49,656	2.86	3.57	75.00	1979-P,D	2,526,000	3.82	8.00	5.50
1956-P,D	45,475	2.64	3.34	60.00	1980-P,D,S	2,815,066	4.82	9.00	6.50
1957-P,D	34,324	3.64	4.40	100.00	1981-P,D,S	2,908,145	4.82	11.00	7.00
1958-P,D	50,314	3.64	4.43	90.00	1984-P,D	1,832,857	1.82	7.00	4.25
1959-P,D	187,000	1.82	2.40	15.00	1985-P,D	1,710,571	1.82	7.00	5.00
1960-P,D	260,485	1.82	2.40	14.00	1986-P,D	1,153,536	1.82	7.00	18.50
1961-P,D	223,704	1.82	2.40	12.50	1987-P,D	2,890,758	1.82	7.00	5.00
1962-P,D	385,285	1.82	2.40	10.00	1988-P,D	1,646,204	1.82	7.00	4.00
1963-P,D	606,612	1.82	2.40	8.00	1989-P,D	1,987,915	1.82	7.00	4.00
1964-P,D	1,008,108	1.82	2.40	7.00	1990-P,D	1,809,184	1.82	7.00	5.00
1968-P,D,S	2,105,128	1.33	2.50	3.00	1991-P,D	1,352,101	1.82	7.00	6.50
1969-P,D,S	1,817,392	1.33	2.50	4.00	1992-P,D	1,500,143	1.82	7.00	9.00
1970-P,D,S	2,038,134	1.33	2.50	10.00	1993-P,D	1,297,094	1.82	8.00	10.00
1971-P,D,S	2,193,396	1.83	3.50	3.00	1994-P,D	1,234,813	1.82	8.00	9.00

PROOF LINCOLN CENTS
DATE ANALYSIS

1909 V.D.B.

PHILADELPHIA
420

RARITY: The Mint's decision to abort coinage of this type affected the number of proof cents minted as well. Proofs of this issue have the lowest total of certified specimens, the third lowest number of pieces certified PR RD and also the third lowest total of ones certified PR65 RD. Only 1912 and 1916 are greater condition rarities.

POPULATION: PR BN = 9   PR RB = 46   PR RD = 25   TOTAL = 80
TOTALS   PR65 RD = 9   HIGHEST = PR67 RD (1)

VALUES:	GRADE	1935	1950	1965	1980	1995
	PROOF	——	7.00	275.00	550.00	——
	PR63	——	——	——	——	1500.00

VARIETIES: None are reported, aside from the individual dies described below.

COMMENTS: As made, this issue typically bore deep, matte surfaces, an attribute which found little favor with collectors of the time. Walter Breen noted, however, that the specimen held by the American Numismatic Society bears satiny surfaces which are similar to those of 1909 proofs without the initials.[29]

Proofs of this date and type are often difficult to distinguish from currency strikes; this is particularly true for examples which have been cleaned at some point, and that applies to the majority. The high quality of most ordinary 1909 V.D.B. cents make detection of proofs by sharpness alone a risky game. Collectors are urged to acquire examples which have already been certified as proofs.

Like all genuine proofs, however, there are several features of a general nature common to this and other dates. In addition to their extraordinary sharpness of strike and complete filling of the dies, proofs are distinguished by their unusually broad borders, thick edges showing no beveling at the rims and sharply raised and squared-off inner borders.

The American Numismatic Association Authentication Bureau (ANAAB) has identified several distinguishing characteristics of known 1909 V.D.B. proofs, though not all genuine coins may show these.[30] Useful die markers include diagonal polishing lines on and in front of Lincoln's nose, running NW to SE. Also found is a diagonal die scratch running the same direction behind Lincoln's coat and below letters TY. Finally, on the reverse, a crescent-shaped die chip appears to the right of letter M in UNUM.

Its status as a one-year type, combined with its indisputable rarity, have made proofs of the 1909 V.D.B. cent highly sought and quite expensive with respect to other proof cents 1909-16. Still, its current value seems a bargain given the small number available. The general unpopularity of matte proofs is likely to blame.

1909

PHILADELPHIA
2,198

RARITY: Most collectors seeking a proof of the new cent had to satisfy themselves with this variety lacking the initials V.D.B. Though its mintage is not particularly high with respect to later proofs of this period, more seem to have survived in overall numbers and particularly in higher grades. This issue has the largest total of certified coins and the largest total of PR65 RD examples. Finally, it includes one of only two examples among the early proofs (1914 is the other) certified PR68 RD.

POPULATION: PR BN = 23   PR RB = 174   PR RD = 117   TOTAL = 314
TOTALS PR65 RD = 46   HIGHEST = PR68 RD (1)

VALUES:

GRADE	1935	1950	1965	1980	1995
PROOF	——	3.00	70.00	110.00	——
PR63	——	——	——	——	300.00

VARIETIES: None are reported, aside from the individual dies described below.

COMMENTS: Though initially coined with the same matte surfaces as the 1909 V.D.B. cent, this issue is more often found with satiny surfaces. This feature was probably the result of the dies becoming slightly worn when coining the later impressions.

The obverse die used to coin V.D.B. cents was continued with this issue, and the same diagnostics may be found. A second obverse die was also used, and it's distinguished by a fine crack running from the truncation of Lincoln's bust to the rim. A couple of short die gouges run vertically from the top of letter L in LIBERTY, while letters TY reveal some fine, vertical polishing lines. A third obverse features heavy die polish to the right of Lincoln's nose.

Two reverse dies were used, one with tiny chips appearing between each wheat ear and the border and the other with numerous, vertical die polishing lines around letters O and E of ONE and letter T of CENT. A few more such lines appear between letters CA of AMERICA and the wheat stem. It's not known which combinations of these dies may have been used.

1910

PHILADELPHIA
2,405

RARITY: 1910 is one of the most available of the early proofs, both in the overall numbers certified and in the population of coins graded PR65 RD.

POPULATION: PR BN = 43   PR RB = 139   PR RD = 82   TOTAL = 264
TOTALS   PR65 RD = 37   HIGHEST = PR67 RD (1)

VALUES:	GRADE	1935	1950	1965	1980	1995
	PROOF	——	3.00	70.00	110.00	——
	PR63	——	——	——	——	250.00

VARIETIES: None are reported, aside from the individual dies described below.

COMMENTS: The coarse matte finish of 1909 was replaced by one having a somewhat brighter and more eye-appealing look. As the dies wore with repeated strikings, this finish evolved into satiny surfaces with a bit more brilliance.

Two obverse dies were used for this date. The first exists in both early and late die states. In the early state, the only diagnostics are a number of criss-crossing, diagonal polishing lines within the word WE and extending toward letter T of TRUST. In its later state, this die includes heavy gouges around letters US of TRUST. The second obverse die is identifiable by polishing lines and gouges above letter N and to the left of letter G in the words IN GOD.

A single reverse die was used to coin 1910 proofs. The American Numismatic Association's study of this date indicates that the die scratches running NE to SW from the right and left legs of letter M in UNUM are a flaw in the master die for 1910 and may be seen on currency strikes as well as proofs. Exclusive to the latter, however, is a similar flaw running from the center section of letter M.

1911

PHILADELPHIA
1,733

RARITY: In keeping with its low mintage, the 1911 proof is among the scarcer issues within the 1909-16 period. While the total number certified is comparable to other dates, the number of certified PR RD and PR65 RD coins is relatively low.

POPULATION: PR BN = 58   PR RB = 147   PR RD = 33   TOTAL = 238
TOTALS   PR65 RD = 16   HIGHEST = PR66 RD (3)

VALUES:

GRADE	1935	1950	1965	1980	1995
PROOF	——	3.00	70.00	110.00	——
PR63	——	——	——	——	275.00

VARIETIES: None are reported, aside from the individual dies described below.

COMMENTS: 1911 proofs are similar in appearance to those of 1910, the satiny strikes coming as the dies wore and lost their roughened texture. In his general *Encyclopedia*, Walter Breen reported that true matte proofs are in the minority, a contradiction of his earlier statement in his proof *Encyclopedia*. It's evident that the Mint did not consciously maintain one finish or the other. Instead, the satiny finish was an evolutionary progression of the matte finish. Breen noted also that the specimen held by the American Numismatic Society displays a satin finish on its obverse and a matte finish on its reverse![3]

It's not certain if two different dies were used for both sides or whether these differences represent successive states of the same dies. The first obverse die combines fine polishing lines at the date and below letter L in LIBERTY with a build-up of metal within the branches of letter Y. On the second die or die state, slim file marks are visible above the first numeral 1 in the date.

Fine die polishing lines through letter AME of AMERICA distinguish the first reverse die. A later die or die state reveals a very slight crack running atop letter O on ONE and continuing to the top of letter N. Another die state, possibly of the same die, bears a small crack running from the right wheat ear to the border.

1912

PHILADELPHIA
2,145

RARITY: Despite their generous mintage, 1912 proofs are scarce. It's quite possible that the published figure is for the quantity of coins struck, while a number may have remained unsold at the end of the year and were destroyed. This issue is also a major condition rarity. Only five examples have been certified PR65 RD, a figure lower than for 1909 V.D.B. and 1916, coins which are far more rare overall. 1912 and 1916 are the only dates among early proofs not certified higher than PR65.

POPULATION:	PR BN = 80	PR RB = 119	PR RD = 16	TOTAL = 215
TOTALS	PR65 RD = 4	HIGHEST = PR65 RD (4)		

VALUES:	GRADE	1935	1950	1965	1980	1995
	PROOF	——	3.00	60.00	110.00	——
	PR63	——	——	——	——	275.00

VARIETIES: None are reported, aside from the individual dies described below.

COMMENTS: Most examples of this issue have a deeper or coarser matte finish than the 1910 and 1911 proofs, and this unattractive quality may account for the small number of specimens receiving high certified grades. Walter Breen noted that uncleaned examples are usually stained.[32] As is usual with all of these early proofs, the dies for 1912 acquired a slightly satin finish as successive impressions wore down their original texture.

The ANAAB reports only a single pair of dies used for this date. The obverse, however, existed in two recognizable die states. In the early state, fine die polishing lines run diagonally through numerals 91 of the date from NW to SE. Additional fine lines appear horizontally through letters ERTY of LIBERTY. In the later state, a couple of raised lines are seen to the left of letter Y in LIBERTY, while deeper lines appear at the top of letter T in TRUST. More die polishing lines are above GOD, and long arcs or swirls of polishing lines may be seen just inside the obverse border from 2 o'clock to 4 o'clock.

1913

PHILADELPHIA
2,848

RARITY: Although 1909 "plain" and 1910 have higher certified populations graded PR65 RD, 1913 is generally the most available of the early proofs in choice and gem condition. It also holds the highest number of examples certified, irrespective of grade. These figures are merely relative, of course, and all early proofs must be considered scarce to rare when compared against circulating coins.

POPULATION: PR BN = 44   PR RB = 188   PR RD = 95   TOTAL = 327
TOTALS   PR65 RD = 33   HIGHEST = PR67 RD (2)

VALUES:

GRADE	1935	1950	1965	1980	1995
PROOF	——	3.00	67.50	110.00	——
PR63	——	——	——	——	275.00

VARIETIES: None are reported, aside from the individual dies described below.

COMMENTS: 1913 proofs are primarily of the matte finish as used in 1912. Later strikes will show some softening to a near-satin state.

The fact that so many have been cleaned over the intervening decades has made it difficult to determine how each specimen appeared when new. Uncleaned specimens are often deeply toned from the tissue paper in which the coins were originally delivered. The predominate color is purple, and this may be accompanied by random spotting and staining.

The ANAAB has identified two obverse and two reverse dies. Obverse die 1 reveals a line of die polish projecting NW from the top of the first numeral 1 in the date. Irregular polishing lines and a die gouge may be seen at the word IN, while additional polishing projects SE from the top of letter G in GOD. Obverse Die 2 was used in two states. The early state is distinguished by shallow polishing lines above the date, at letters T and Y of LIBERTY, below LIBERTY and at IN and GOD. The late state shows rough polishing at the base of the first numeral 1 in the date. A long, curving line projects upward from a point just to the right of numeral 3, while scratches appear within letter G and above letters OD of GOD. Reverse die A is essentially perfect, with no distinguishing characteristics. In its early state, Reverse B shows myriad, irregular lines through UNUM and a long, arcing line to the right of letter N in CENT. In its late state, additional lines appeared between letter T of CENT and the wheat ear.

It seems that these dies were paired as follows: 1/A, 2 (early)/B (early), 2 (late)/B (late). It's conceivable, however, that there may be some overlap.

*   *   *

Walter Breen recounts in his proof coin *Encyclopedia* how in the 1940s and '50s he used to "make lunch money" cherrypicking proof cents of the 1909-16 period from dealers who failed to recognize them for what they were!

1914

PHILADELPHIA
1,365

RARITY: With their low mintage, 1914 proofs are understandably scarce. This date has the fourth lowest total of certified specimens after 1909 V.D.B., 1916 and 1915, in that order. These coins are also important condition rarities, only 18 having been certified PR65 RD.

POPULATION: PR BN = 25   PR RB = 121   PR RD = 49   TOTAL = 195
TOTALS PR65 RD = 18   HIGHEST = PR68 RD (1)

VALUES:

GRADE	1935	1950	1965	1980	1995
PROOF	——	6.00	150.00	200.00	——
PR63	——	——	——	——	325.00

VARIETIES: None are reported, aside from the individual die states described below.

COMMENTS: 1914 proofs are of the deep matte style employed for 1911-13, though the latest strikes will have some satin quality. Walter Breen described proofs of this date as having a slightly finer grain than for 1913 proofs, "Often strangely and wonderfully iridescent or toned to rainbow shades."[33]

Only a single pair of dies was used to produce proofs for 1914. The reverse die bore no distinguishing features, but the obverse die was employed in both early and late states. The former displays a die chip projecting upward from the first numeral 1 in the date. Nearly horizontal polishing lines may be found in letters WE and within LIBERTY. The later die state is readily identified by heavy, vertical lines extending from Lincoln's chin to his coat.

*   *   *

After several years of experimenting with different finishes for proof coins the Mint saw sales of these pieces declining. The numismatic community never warmed to the textured surfaces of matte or sandblast proofs, and collectors yearned for the brilliant style proofs produced in earlier years. Ironically, Lot 1542 in Rarcoa's session of "Auction '80" was a proof cent dated 1914 and featuring this brilliant finish. Authenticated by Walter Breen in 1978, he noted in a long letter accompanying the lot that it was one of two he'd examined and that two more reportedly existed. The dies for this coin were heavily polished, and the lapel of Lincoln's coat was nearly eradicated. In his extensive analysis, Breen speculated that these proofs were produced clandestinely by the same parties responsible for the 1913 Liberty Head Nickels. Much to Breen's chagrin, he later revealed in his 1988 *Encyclopedia* that these coins had proved to be counterfeits. What became of these four coins is uncertain, but collectors should beware of any such offering.

1915

PHILADELPHIA
1,150

RARITY: Proofs of this date are very scarce. Only 1909 V.D.B. and 1916 have lower certified totals, and just 11 pieces have been certified PR65 RD.

POPULATION: PR BN = 41   PR RB = 92   PR RD = 22   TOTAL = 155
TOTALS   PR65 RD = 11   HIGHEST = PR67 RD (1)

VALUES:

GRADE	1935	1950	1965	1980	1995
PROOF	——	7.00	220.00	250.00	——
PR63	——	——	——	——	500.00

VARIETIES: None are reported.

COMMENTS: 1915 proof cents are of the matte style, though they have a more delicate surface quality than those dated 1911-13 and are most similar to 1914 cents. Proofs which have been cleaned are extremely difficult to distinguish from ordinary cents, since the latter are so often sharply struck.

The enhancement performed this year to the existing obverse master hub greatly improved the fine detailing of Lincoln's hair and beard, qualities which are fully evident on both proofs and currency strikes. Unfortunately, there are no die markers to separate one from the other, and any attempt to verify proof status must be based on the general characteristics of proofs. These include sharp inner and outer borders and broad, unbeveled edges.

1916

PHILADELPHIA
1,050

RARITY: The rarity of this date in proof suggests that not all of the pieces reportedly coined were actually distributed. It's comparable in rarity to 1909 V.D.B., though more than twice as many 1916 proofs were produced. This issue follows a close second in the total number of examples certified, while it leads the pack in condition rarity; only five specimens have been graded PR65 RD, and this is the highest grade level recorded for 1916.

POPULATION:	PR BN = 13	PR RB = 62	PR RD = 11	TOTAL = 86
TOTALS	PR65 RD = 5	HIGHEST = PR65 RD (5)		

VALUES:	GRADE	1935	1950	1965	1980	1995
	PROOF	——	8.00	220.00	275.00	——
	PR63	——	——	——	——	700.00

VARIETIES: None are reported.

COMMENTS: Though of matte finish, 1916 proofs have finer surfaces than the proofs of 1911-15. Uncleaned examples are very rare, somewhat hampering authentication. The dies for this issue were very skillfully prepared, the only evidence of polishing lines being between numerals 1 and 9 of the date, between letters US of TRUST and just a few fine lines at WE. The single reverse die bears some polishing lines above PLURIBUS which follow the curve of the border.

The new obverse master hub introduced this year greatly enhanced the already rich detailing of Lincoln's hair and beard, making proofs of this date perhaps the most desirable from a technical and aesthetic standpoint.

* * *

Cents and nickels were the only proofs coined for sale to collectors in 1916. The gold matte and satin proofs proved unpopular, and their sales thus far did not encourage further coinage. Silver proofs continued through 1915 with the popular brilliant style of earlier years, as their uncontoured fields permitted such bright finishing. Proofs of the dime, quarter dollar and half dollar were not struck for 1916 only because the Mint expected the new designs to be ready by midyear and did not anticipate coining any silver of the old designs. When delays with the new issues mandated a resumption of the old types, this coinage was hurried and did not allow for the inclusion of proofs. Though the new designs did appear at year's end, their sculpted fields vexed the Mint's engraving and coining departments. Brilliant proofs were judged impossible with the new coins, while matte proofs had become a sore subject by 1916. Thus the whole system of coining proofs was rendered a shambles, and the lackluster sales of recent years caused the Mint to discontinue proof coinage altogether.

1917

PHILADELPHIA
(mintage unknown)

RARITY: Though a few examples dated 1917 have traded hands as proof or specimen strikings, these coins remain in a shadowy netherworld. Walter Breen asserted that matte proofs of the style employed in 1916 do indeed exist for this date. The grading services have declined to certify any 1917 cents as proofs, just as they have for all alleged 1917 proofs of various denominations. The author has not personally examined a cent of this date bearing any characteristics of proof coins, though he has seen a 1917 quarter dollar which he believed to be a proof.

POPULATION: PR BN = 0   PR RB = 0   PR RD = 0   TOTAL = 0

VARIETIES: No information is available.

COMMENTS: Very little information exists regarding the diagnostics of this controversial issue. In his proof *Encyclopedia* Walter Breen reported having examined one specimen from a complete, five-coin proof set dated 1917. This specimen, though cleaned, bore a matte surface on its obverse similar to that of 1916 proofs. Its reverse, however, was not prepared as a proof.[35]

   Of the few 1917 coins offered as proofs, the cent and the dime seem to be the rarest, while the quarter dollar is most frequently encountered. Yet, unlike the new silver coin types introduced in 1916, the cent has several dates of matte proof coinage against which to compare any specimen offered as a proof. Thus, except for coins so harshly cleaned as to make an evaluation impossible, there exists no reason why a 1917 proof cent would look substantially different from one dated 1916.

   The coin illustrated has sold as a proof, though it remains uncertified. Judging from the photographs alone it does not appear equal in sharpness to the proofs of 1909-16.

1936

PHILADELPHIA
5,569

RARITY: Though not rare in an absolute sense, proof cents of 1936 are quite scarce relative to the demand for them and to the numbers available for later dates. Most have suffered from poor storage, and gems are very elusive. Though satin finish proofs are clearly scarcer than brilliant proofs, circumstantial evidence suggests that a greater number were made. The Mint's own estimate was that two-thirds of the total number coined were of the satin finish.[36] It's quite possible that their owners' disappointment with them caused these coins to be spent or otherwise mishandled.

    The Professional Coin Grading Service (PCGS) and ANACS distinguish between satin and brilliant proofs, while Numismatic Guaranty Corporation (NGC) does not. This muddies the waters a bit regarding relative rarity, but the totals furnished below seem consistent with market availability. Gems of this date exist in much smaller numbers than for any subsequent issue.

SATIN FINISH OR "TYPE 1"

POPULATION:	PR BN = 4	PR RB = 48	PR RD = 72	TOTAL = 124
TOTALS	PR65 RD = 24	HIGHEST = PR66 RD (5)		

BRILLIANT FINISH OR "TYPE 2"

POPULATION:	PR BN = 2	PR RB = 71	PR RD = 294	TOTAL = 367
TOTALS	PR65 RD = 41	HIGHEST = PR67 RD (1)		

NOT IDENTIFIED AS TO TYPE

POPULATION:	PR BN = 6	PR RB = 34	PR RD = 73	TOTAL = 113
TOTALS	PR65 RD = 14	HIGHEST = PR65 RD (14)		

VALUES:	GRADE	1950	1965	1980	1995
	PROOF	8.50	80.00	225.00	——
	PR63	——	——	——	135.00
	PR65	——	——	——	600.00

VARIETIES: None are reported.

COMMENTS: As one would expect, proofs are as sharply struck as the condition of the master hubs permitted. While the reverse hub used since 1909 was still quite distinct, the obverse of 1916 had already suffered extensive erosion within the fine details of Lincoln's hair and beard. In addition to these flaws, the proofs of 1936-42 were typically coined from overpolished dies, leaving a number of low-relief elements such as the lapel of Lincoln's coat diminished or even detached from other features. While brilliant and flashy, such proofs are not necessarily the best representation of this coin type.

    Most 1936 proof cents are impaired to some degree, usually from unwise cleaning. Such cleaning may have been prompted by the tendency of these coins to acquire unsightly toning, spotting and fingerprinting. Sol Taylor has pointed out that some of these flaws may have originated with careless handling by Mint employees not yet attuned to the quality demanded in proof coins by collectors.[37]

A matter of some debate concerns the materials used to distribute the proof coins of 1936-42. The few published sources are in conflict; while one will assert that celluloid or cellophane envelopes were employed, another will claim that tissue paper of the sort used 1909-16 was standard. Sol Taylor reports that tissues were used and cites his experience in obtaining a 1938 proof cent from the Mint in 1940.[38] If this is correct, it would help to explain the unappealing streaks and blotches seen on uncleaned specimens, a characteristic they share with the proofs of 1909-16. Countering this is the fact that the proofs of 1950-55, still obtainable from dealers in their original, individual plastic bags, will show similar effects, though to a lesser degree.

Collectors are advised to beware of "processed" cents. These are ordinary, well-struck 1936 cents buffed or plated to simulate proofs. While they will not fool anyone who knows what a real proof looks like, such coins were often sold by unscrupulous persons during the 1950s and '60s. Taking advantage of the great number of new, inexperienced collectors during those years, these cheats particularly targeted those living in rural areas who had no access to coin shows and shops and thus did all of their buying through the mail. Though such coins were already being driven from the market by the 1970s, the advent of certified grading has virtually eliminated them altogether. They may yet, however, turn up in country auctions, estate sales, etc.

1937

PHILADELPHIA
9,320

RARITY: Proofs of 1937 are all of the fully brilliant style as perfected in the waning months of 1936. With greater regard from collectors has come a much higher survival rate in gem condition.

POPULATION: PR BN = 2   PR RB = 93   PR RD = 687   TOTAL = 782
TOTALS   PR65 RD = 211   HIGHEST = PR67 RD (1)

VALUES:

GRADE	1950	1965	1980	1995
PROOF	4.00	35.00	110.00	——
PR63	——	——	——	60.00
PR65	——	——	——	175.00

VARIETIES: None are reported.

COMMENTS: Though quite a number of certified gems are available for this date, the total falls far short of the number needed to satisfy the demand for such coins. Prices for gems are thus quite high, while lesser quality coins have performed poorly in the marketplace. These mediocre examples comprise the majority of 1937 proofs cents. Many are spotted, stained or hairlined, while others reveal the unpleasant results of chemical cleaning.

From 1936 through 1942, collectors could order proof coins individually. In 1937, only about 5500 pieces were ordered for the silver types while a few more were purchased of the nickels, which enjoyed some popularity among series collectors. The much higher mintage of 1937 proof cents is reflective of their great popularity with collectors of that time. The 5500 figure provides a guideline as to how many complete sets were desired.

The same cautions regarding "processed" 1936 cents are valid for 1937 as well, though later dates are less often targeted due to their lower values.

1938

PHILADELPHIA
14,734

RARITY: Though gems comprise a minority of the surviving coins, there are a greater number of such coins than for any previous date. This is partly a result of the greater number coined with each succeeding date since 1936. Several thousand examples of average or poor quality are available for those simply wishing to fill a hole in their collections.

POPULATION: PR BN = 1   PR RB = 99   PR RD = 851   TOTAL = 951
TOTALS   PR65 RD = 329   HIGHEST = PR67 RD (7)

VALUES:

GRADE	1950	1965	1980	1995
PROOF	1.75	15.00	50.00	——
PR63	——	——	——	40.00
PR65	——	——	——	90.00

VARIETIES: None are reported.

COMMENTS: 1938 proofs are all of the fully brilliant style, though it's possible that a few may exist from fresh dies having lightly frosted devices. The commercial grading services do not label proof coins dated 1936-42 as "cameo," so any such designation is a matter of opinion on the part of a coin's owner.

1939

PHILADELPHIA
13,520

RARITY: Enough gems (MS65 RD) survive to meet the needs of the more determined collectors, though most will have to get by with choice examples (MS63-MS64). Coins of mediocre quality are abundant.

POPULATION: PR BN = 0   PR RB = 53   PR RD = 892   TOTAL = 945
TOTALS   PR65 RD = 378   HIGHEST = PR67 RD (1)

VALUES:

GRADE	1950	1965	1980	1995
PROOF	1.25	12.00	25.00	——
PR63	——	——	——	35.00
PR65	——	——	——	85.00

VARIETIES: Some proofs have a thin second numeral 9 in their date as a consequence of vigorous die polishing.

COMMENTS: Proofs of this date are fully brilliant. This brilliance was frequently achieved by polishing the dies to the point where low relief elements were diminished or eliminated altogether. The Mint was reluctant to create multiple dies for such low coinages, and the same die pair was usually polished repeatedly for a single year's proof production, each successive die state showing less detail than the previous one. This problem lasted through the 1960s and wasn't solved until the Mint began chromium plating its proof dies around 1971. This enabled a greater number of strikes with fewer polishings, since the plating made the dies more resistant to wear.

The slightly lower mintage for this year as compared with 1938 suggests that a bit of speculation occurred with the earlier date. This was undoubtedly prompted by the rapid rise in value of the 1936 proofs during 1938. The disappointing quality of the satin proofs discouraged sales in 1936, and many collectors had to buy the more brilliant proofs of that year on the secondary market, initiating a price rise. When similar gains failed to materialize for the 1938 cents, sales slowed during 1939. The introduction of the Jefferson Nickel in 1938 may also have prompted greater sales of proof sets, even though the nickel was available separately.

1940

PHILADELPHIA
15,872

RARITY: Though subject to the same flaws which have reduced the number of gems for earlier dates, proofs of 1940 are generally available in nice condition. If they carried a higher value in PR65 RD there would no doubt be a greater number certified; as it is, an economic incentive for submitting gems of this date to a grading service simply doesn't exist for most collectors.

POPULATION: PR BN = 1   PR RB = 67   PR RD = 780   TOTAL = 848
TOTALS   PR65 RD = 321   HIGHEST = PR67 RD (3)

VALUES:

GRADE	1950	1965	1980	1995
PROOF	1.25	11.00	23.00	——
PR63	——	——	——	30.00
PR65	——	——	——	90.00

VARIETIES: None are reported.

COMMENTS: 1940 proofs are of the fully brilliant style initiated in 1936. Early strikes from fresh dies may show some light frosting on the raised devices. This quality was quickly lost from the dies as repeated impressions created a self-polishing action that soon equalized all surfaces to a uniformly brilliant finish.

*   *   *

The mintage of proof cents stayed consistently ahead of the figures recorded for the other denominations throughout the 1936-42 period, always being larger by several thousand pieces annually. Their greater popularity continues to this day and has actually increased since 1975, when proofs became the only cents available from the San Francisco Mint. It's interesting to speculate on what the mintages of the other denominations have been since 1950 if the separate-purchase option had not been discontinued at that time.

1941

PHILADELPHIA
21,100

RARITY: Though gems comprise a minority of surviving examples, there are sufficient high quality coins to meet the demand, and lower grade pieces are often difficult to sell for this very reason. It's worth noting, however, that no proof cents of this date have yet been certified higher than PR66 RD, an aspect of condition rarity that they share with the 1942 proof cents.

POPULATION:	PR BN = 0	PR RB = 90	PR RD = 775	TOTAL = 865
TOTALS	PR65 RD = 271	HIGHEST = PR66 RD (36)		

VALUES:	GRADE	1950	1965	1980	1995
	PROOF	1.00	8.00	23.00	——
	PR63	——	——	——	27.50
	PR65	——	——	——	92.50

VARIETIES: None are reported.

COMMENTS: These proofs were fully-red and brilliant as made, though many will have toned to varying degrees. If this toning is consistent throughout and not too deep it can be an asset, though most collectors prefer pieces which are entirely untoned. Definitely weighing against any specimen are irregular streaks and blotches, black or green spots, hairline scratches and the other blemishes so prevalent on proof cents of this era.

Considered a common date, even in fairly high grades, it's still worth taking a reflective moment to compare the mintage of the 1941 proof cent with those of cents from the late 1950s and subsequent years. A total of 21,200 pieces is amazingly small when measured against the millions produced annually in recent decades. The concept of rarity is indeed a relative one, and collectors should always ask themselves where real value lies when making their purchases.

1942

PHILADELPHIA
32,600

RARITY: Fully red gems are available for this date, though perhaps not in the same quantity as for the year or two preceding. Perhaps the change in alloy eliminating or reducing tin had some impact on this issue's survival rate in gem condition. As with the proof cents of 1941, none of this date have been certified above PR66 RD. This is true of no other dates during the 1936-42 period nor for any proofs since then.

POPULATION: PR BN = 1   PR RB = 138   PR RD = 1169   TOTAL = 1308
TOTALS   PR65 RD = 272   HIGHEST = PR66 RD (39)

VALUES:

GRADE	1950	1965	1980	1995
PROOF	1.00	7.50	22.00	——
PR63	——	——	——	27.50
PR65	——	——	——	95.00

VARIETIES: None are reported.

COMMENTS: As noted above, fully-red gems are somewhat elusive. Because more than a single die pairing was required for its relatively higher mintage, the chance of finding examples having light frosting on their relief elements is increased with 1942 cents.

* * *

The onset of World War II, with its accompanying shortage of labor and increased demand for production coins, brought a halt to proof coinage for the duration. It's unfortunate that no proofs were ever coined of the 1943 steel cents, though collectors anticpated a resumption of proof coinage throughout that year.

1950

PHILADELPHIA
51,386

RARITY: Despite their much higher mintage, the proofs of 1950 are as scarce in gem condition as those of the early 1940s, perhaps more so. The individual plastic envelopes used for proof coins 1950-55 were only slightly better at preserving these coins than the plastic or tissues used earlier. Coins of average or below average quality are readily available, though there don't seem to be any large accumulations.

Those certified as "cameo" have only light frosting, while deeply frosted coins (designated by the grading services as either "Deep Cameo" or "Ultra Cameo" are of the greatest rarity. In either case, both sides must show at least some frosting on their relief elements to be certified. Cameo proof authority Rick Jerry Tomaska noted in his book *Cameo and Brilliant Proof Coinage of the 1950 to 1970 Era* that while cameo proofs of the 1950 cent are scarce they are more readily available than several other dates in the 1950s.

POPULATION: PR RD = 644   PR RD CA = 77   PR RD DC = 4   TOTAL = 725
TOTALS   PR65 RD = 322   PR67 RD = 30   HIGHEST = PR68 RD (2)

VALUES:

GRADE	1965	1980	1995
PROOF	42.50	37.50	——
PR65	——	——	45.00

VARIETIES: None are reported.

COMMENTS: The proof cents of 1950 come with the fully brilliant finish perfected during 1936-42 and also with subdued, satiny surfaces, even more so than on the first proofs of 1936. Just as before, customer complaints led to a more satisfying product.

* * *

Most numismatic writers have claimed that the satin pieces were the ones made first, before the Philadelphia Mint's employees learned how to fully polish the dies. The author disagrees, as the coins themselves prove otherwise. The fact that satin pieces also exist for 1951 is evidence that the conditions which caused the satin proofs of 1950 had not been overcome, despite the fact that brilliant proofs were coined in 1950. Satin proofs are the natural evolution of dies which have gone too long between polishings. This same condition resulted with the matte proofs of 1909-16, these becoming more satiny with successive impressions.

When new, proof dies are fully brilliant in their fields and moderately to heavily frosted in their cavities, these same qualities being transferred to the coins struck from them. After the first few dozen impressions, their frosty elements becoming fully brilliant, as are any coins struck from this die state. After a few hundred more coins are struck, a general erosion of the die fields and cavities sets in from continued metal flow across the dies. They gradually lose their brilliance, which evolves into a more satiny texture. When the dies are once again polished, their brilliance returns, though many low-relief elements in the dies and some of their lettering may be reduced through such polishing. This is clearly evident on the proofs of 1950-53 in particular, the Mint being quite careless in overpolishing existing proof dies rather than installing fresh ones.

1951

PHILADELPHIA
57,500

RARITY: Gems of this and all subsequent dates are available to interested collectors. Their certified population represents only a fraction of the number of high grade coins extant, a situation which will no doubt change should prices rise substantially. Note, however, that cameo cents dated 1951 are very rare, while none have yet been certified as deep cameo pieces. In fact, Rick Jerry Tomaska noted that "of all the cameo proofs minted since 1950, this is the rarest coin in the series in the higher levels of contrast."[39]

POPULATION: PR RD = 419   PR RD CA = 20   PR RD DC = 0   TOTAL = 439
TOTALS   PR65 RD = 153   PR67 RD = 41   HIGHEST = PR68 RD (1)

VALUES:

GRADE	1965	1980	1995
PROOF	25.00	18.00	——
PR65	——	——	40.00

VARIETIES: A very minor doubled-die obverse is discernible in the motto IN GOD WE TRUST. Though a rare variety, the market for such coins is limited with respect to the overall number of Lincoln Cent collectors.

COMMENTS: Some cents of this date are satiny, though fully brilliant examples predominate. Many are from harshly polished dies with greatly diminished details and lettering.

1952

PHILADELPHIA
81,980

RARITY: Gems are readily available, though of course not in the same numbers as for cents dated 1956 and later. Both cameo and deep cameo examples are very scarce to extremely rare. Rick Jerry Tomaska asserted that no deep cameos of this date are known, though a single specimen appears in the population data below.[40]

POPULATION:	PR RD = 465	PR RD CA = 24	PR RD DC = 1	TOTAL = 490
TOTALS	PR65 RD = 158	PR67 RD = 60	HIGHEST = PR68 RD (12)	

VALUES:	GRADE	1965	1980	1995
	PROOF	14.00	14.00	——
	PR65	——	——	38.00

VARIETIES: None are reported.

COMMENTS: All examples are of the fully brilliant style, the Mint having reacted to complaints from customers who received satin coins in 1950-51.

This was perhaps the last date issued in proof before the coin collecting hobby began to grow in leaps and bounds. Its mintage seems amazingly small by present day standards, yet collectors of the time remarked at how much the annual proof mintages had grown! As old estates are broken up, more 1952 proof sets are continually being found in their original boxes of issue. Most have acquired some toning, not always of the attractive variety. Still, unless these sets have been kept in harsh environments, they tend to hold up better than coins which have been in albums, 2x2 holders and other popular storage media of that time.

1953

PHILADELPHIA
128,800

RARITY: 1953 proof cents are common in all grades through gem. With this year's increased mintage came a greater number of new dies and thus a greater number of cameo coins. Deep cameo pieces remain quite rare and may have originated from a single obverse die.[41]

POPULATION: PR RD = 423   PR RD CA = 78   PR RD DC = 6   TOTAL = 507
TOTALS   PR65 RD = 125   PR67 RD = 84   HIGHEST = PR68 RD (14)

VALUES:

GRADE	1965	1980	1995
PROOF	6.00	11.50	——
PR65	——	——	27.00

VARIETIES: A single obverse doubled-die is known, the doubling being only slightly evident within the date.

COMMENTS: By 1953 the Mint had mastered the technique for coining proofs that it would employ for the next dozen years. The only obstacle still to overcome was its reluctance to use a sufficient number of dies. The dies for 1953 and adjacent years are often overpolished, resulting in a loss of low-relief detail and diminished legends and mottos.

* * *

The first signs that collectors were buying proof sets as an investment appeared this year. The proofs of 1950 had caught collectors sleeping, just as happened with those dated 1936. Within a year or two of issue they were bringing notable premiums, and the rush was on to acquire new proofs as they were released. This speculative fever, combined with legitimate growth in the number of coin collectors at this time, led to rapidly advancing mintages.

1954

PHILADELPHIA
233,300

RARITY: With nearly twice the mintage of 1953 cents, gems are readily available, while anything less is often a tough sell. Cameos and deep cameos comprise just a small number of the total population, yet they are far more likely to be submitted for certification. The same poor quality metal strip was seemingly used to punch out blanks for proofs as well as currency strikes, and many of these cents are deeply toned.

POPULATION: PR RD = 323   PR RD CA = 64   PR RD DC = 9   TOTAL = 396
TOTALS   PR65 RD = 60   PR67 RD = 95   HIGHEST = PR68 RD (33)

VALUES:	GRADE	1965	1980	1995
	PROOF	6.00	6.50	——
	PR65	——	——	13.00

VARIETIES: Two obverse doubled-dies are known, both minor.

COMMENTS: 1954 proofs were made a little more skillfully than those of 1950-53 and are less subject to abusive polishing of their dies. The plastic employed for the individual envelopes of 1954-55 was of a slightly different quality than that used since 1950. This factor, combined with poor alloying of the metal strip, has caused 1954 proof cents to tone more readily. Still, enough were removed from their original packaging at or near the time of issue to spare them from serious harm.

* * *

The growing popularity of commercially produced, hard plastic holders accounts at least in part for the higher survival rate of gem proofs from the 1950s and later years. These first appeared on the market in 1945, but they really caught on during the mid 1950s. Ironically, the arrival of soft plastic, single coin holders later in the '50s threatened to reverse this trend toward higher survival rates, as the harmful qualities of these "flips" were not understood for another 20 years.

1955

PHILADELPHIA
378,200

RARITY: Fully red gems are readily available. Were their value higher, many more would have been certified by now. The greater number of new dies used also resulted in an increased population of cameos, though deep cameo examples are still quite rare.

POPULATION:	PR RD = 328	PR RD CA = 112	PR RD DC = 4	TOTAL = 444
TOTALS	PR65 RD = 52	PR67 RD = 129	HIGHEST = PR68 RD (176)	

VALUES:	GRADE	1965	1980	1995
	PROOF	6.00	3.00	——
	PR65	——	——	10.00

VARIETIES: Two obverse and three reverse doubled-dies are documented by John A. Wexler.[42] Though all are discernible with close study, none can rival the whopping doubled-die found on some non-proofs of this date.

COMMENTS: Commencing this year and lasting through 1964 the Mint's output of proof coins was of consistently high quality. Properly polished dies and planchets resulted in coins that represented outstanding technical and aesthetic achievements.

Mintages rose dramatically again, as a more than 50% increase in sales was recorded over 1954. The acquiring of multiple proof sets for investment purposes was clearly becoming a hobby within the hobby.

* * *

The packaging of proof sets shifted this year from the boxed collection of individual envelopes used 1950-54 to the multi-coin, pliofilm "flat-packs" which became standard through 1965. Both types were used to assemble 1955 proof sets, the changeover having occurred sometime around April or May.[43] Some years ago the flat-packs carried a premium over the boxed sets, but increased concerns about long-term storage have prompted a move away from saving proof sets in their original packaging altogether and have largely ended this silly practice.

The reason for this change was not merely one of aesthetics or marketing. It was a reaction to a peculiar fraud which had appeared since the resumption of proof set production in 1950. A speculative market developed in the trading of "mint-sealed" proof sets, those still enclosed in their little cardboard boxes and sealed with brown paper tape, as delivered by the Mint. At some point owners of these sets who elected inclined to open them discovered to their horror that they contained foreign coins, washers, rocks or even coal. Obviously, their previous owners had devised a method of opening the boxes, replacing their contents and then resealing them!

The conversion to flat-packs should have solved the fraud problem were it not for the determination of speculators to place additional value on some feature of no consequence. This time the emphasis was on flat-packs still sealed within their original mailing envelope. Though collectors usually slit the tops of these envelopes with a letter opener to examine their sets, at some point in the late 1950s buyers began insisting that the outer mailing envelopes be left unopened. Sets were traded back and forth without their contents ever being viewed. This vast opportunity for fraud was finally exposed when the lucrative market for the small date cents of 1960 prompted owners of 1960 proof sets to examine their coins. After it was discovered that many sets had been carefully steamed opened and their original contents filched the silly market in mint-sealed sets collapsed, seemingly forever.

1956

PHILADELPHIA
669,384

RARITY: The mintage of proof sets in 1956 nearly double the previous year's total, as the speculative market intensified. In consequence, proof cents in all grades are readily available and carry only small premiums.

While cameo proofs of the dime, quarter and half are fairly common for this date, those of the cent and nickel are somewhat elusive. Still, based on the certified population data, deep cameo cents seem to be more common for 1956 than for any other date in the 1950s, with the single exception of 1959. These figures, however, contradict the assertion by specialist Rick Jerry Tomaska that deep cameo proofs dated 1956 are "quite rare."[44]

POPULATION: PR RD = 68   PR RD CA = 40   PR RD DC = 15   TOTAL = 123
TOTALS   PR67 RD = 22   HIGHEST = PR68 RD (3)

VALUES:	GRADE	1965	1980	1995
	PROOF	2.50	2.00	——
	PR65	——	——	3.00

VARIETIES: A single doubled-die obverse may be found, but it's quite minor. More pronounced is the lone doubled-die reverse variety.

COMMENTS: It's hard to believe that this date commanded a retail price of $2.50 in the mid 1960s, yet it demonstrates how very popular Lincoln Cents were at that time and how wildly speculative the market for them had become.

1957

PHILADELPHIA
1,247,952

RARITY: Gems are readily available, as are problem coins with spotting and unsightly toning. The fairly large number of cameo pieces reflects the use of many dies in producing this year's large mintage. Not all of these cameos, however, are frosted on both sides, since obverse and reverse dies were not necessarily replaced simultaneously. Deeply frosted cameos are quite rare.

POPULATION: PR RD = 99   PR RD CA = 61   PR RD DC = 4   TOTAL = 164
TOTALS   PR67 RD = 30   HIGHEST = PR68 RD (2)

VALUES:

GRADE	1965	1980	1995
PROOF	1.50	1.00	——
PR65	——	——	2.25

VARIETIES: None are reported.

COMMENTS: Nearly twice as many proofs were coined in 1957 as in the previous year, and this number may have been reflective of a deliberate policy aimed at discouraging coin speculators.

* * *

The frenzied market for proof sets since 1953 did not sit well with the Mint, which had just entered into a period of icy relations with the coin collecting community that would last through the 1960s. While the mintage of proof coins had usually been limited to the Philadelphia Mint's capacity to process orders, it has been alleged that for 1957 the Mint authorities attempted to crush the speculative market by overproducing sets and thus destroying their allure. There's no documentary evidence to support this contention, but whatever the reason, the large mintage of 1957 proof sets did indeed break the speculative fever, and these sets have been a drug on the market ever since.

1958

PHILADELPHIA
875,652

RARITY: These proofs are common in any and all grades. Cameos, though forming a minority of the pieces extant, are not as rare as once believed. As interest in them increases so too does the number of certified coins. Deep cameos, however, remain very rare.

POPULATION: PR RD = 101   PR RD CA = 94   PR RD DC = 7   TOTAL = 202
TOTALS   PR67 RD = 36   HIGHEST = PR68 RD (7)

VALUES:	GRADE	1965	1980	1995
	PROOF	4.00	2.00	——
	PR65	——	——	2.50

VARIETIES: None are reported.

COMMENTS: The mintage of 1958 proofs was below what it would have likely been had the progressive growth of 1950-56 continued. The excessive number of proof sets produced in 1957 discouraged sales in 1958, though they rebounded the following year.

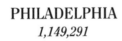

1959

PHILADELPHIA
1,149,291

RARITY: The huge mintage of this issue has guaranteed that gems will always be common. The number of certified cameos and deep cameos is up from previous years in direct proportion to the increased mintage. They still, however, represent a tiny percentage of the total coinage and must be considered quite rare in a relative sense.

POPULATION: PR RD = 99   PR RD CA = 64   PR RD DC = 19   TOTAL = 182
TOTALS   PR67 RD = 49   HIGHEST = PR68 RD (8)

VALUES:	GRADE	1965	1980	1995
	PROOF	2.75	1.00	——
	PR65	——	——	1.50

VARIETIES: None are reported.

COMMENTS: How the mighty have fallen! Though representing a small loss in actual dollars, the collapse of the 1959 proof cent's value between 1965 and 1995 is substantial when multiplied by more than a million coins. The hazard of speculative buying has seldom been more obvious.

1960

PHILADELPHIA
1,691,602

RARITY: Large Date proofs, forming the majority of the pieces coined, are very common in high grades. It's likely that fewer than one in ten were of the Small Date variety, so these are fairly scarce. Rick Jerry Tomaska noted that, despite their differing availability overall, proofs of the Small Date and Large Date were of nearly similar rarity as cameos.[45] This assertion doesn't agree completely with the certified population data.

SMALL DATE	POPULATION:	PR RD = 253		PR RD CA = 44	PR RD DC = 11		TOTAL = 308
	TOTALS	PR67 RD = 120		HIGHEST = PR68 RD (46)			
	VALUES:	GRADE	1965	1980	1995		
		PROOF	45.00	19.50	——		
		PR65	——	——	12.00		

LARGE DATE	POPULATION:	PR RD = 75		PR RD CA = 65	PR RD DC = 39		TOTAL = 179
	TOTALS	PR67 RD = 22		HIGHEST = PR69 RD (4)			
	VALUES:	GRADE	1965	1980	1995		
		PROOF	2.75	1.00	——		
		PR65	——	——	1.10		

VARIETIES: The employment of both small date and large date working hubs early in the year produced three working dies that were clearly hubbed from both of these hub varieties. The result was three doubled obverse dies, two that are large date over small date and one which is small date over large date. Fivaz and Stanton rate all three varieties as having a "high interest factor."[46] The small date over large date variety is probably the rarest of the three (see photos).

In addition to these popular varieties, another doubled obverse die may be found, though it's of the large date variety only.

COMMENTS: Starting this year the number of cameo and deep cameo specimens available to collectors shows a marked increase. This availability continues to increase in proportion to the growing mintages through 1964. In addition, for every date 1960-64 with the exception of 1961, there are one or more coins certified PR69 RD.

Walter Breen estimated the mintage of small date proofs at 100,000 to 200,000. The lower figure is more likely given their present availability. The coinage of small date cents for circulation seems to have been terminated by the end of January, 1960, so it's probable also that no more proofs of the small date were coined after that time.

* * *

The excitement over the small date and large date cents of 1960 resulted in some wildly speculative buying with both proofs and currency strikes. The inevitable collapse of such a market is clearly evident in the figures shown above. In a sort of backlash against such activity the values of many modern coins, including scarce ones such as the 1960 small date proof, have been held in check. At just $12 this variety does seem a bargain.

1960-P
Large date over small date, DDO-1, Breen-2229 (Fivaz & Stanton)

1960-P
Small date over large date, DDO-2, Breen-2229 (Fivaz & Stanton)

1960-P
Large over large over small Date, DDO-6, Breen-2229 (Fivaz & Stanton)

1961

PHILADELPHIA
3,028,244

RARITY: The publicity generated by the 1960 small date cents created many thousands of new coin collectors and an even greater number of speculators. This translated into huge proof set mintages, as everyone wanted to obtain multiple sets as an "investment." 1961 proof cents are thus extremely common in all grades through superb gem.

    Though they are more available with each successive date after 1960, cameo and deep cameo proofs are still scarce enough and popular enough to command substantial premiums.

POPULATION: PR RD = 94   PR RD CA = 51   PR RD DC = 41   TOTAL = 235
TOTALS   PR67 RD = 38   HIGHEST = PR68 RD (16)

VALUES:

GRADE	1965	1980	1995
PROOF	1.00	.75	——
PR65	——	——	1.00

VARIETIES: Minor doubled-dies, one each, are known for both obverse and reverse.

COMMENTS: This is the only proof cent from the years 1960-64 not yet certified as PR69 RD. While this will matter to only a few collectors, it's likely that one or more specimens will ultimately achieve this status.

*   *   *

    Though collectors of the time were aware of cameo coins with their frosted relief elements and considered them desirable, the term "cameo" did not appear until decades later. A few persons sought them out by cherrypicking proof sets, but there was no established market for these coins until the 1980s. Books by Val Webb in 1984 and Rick Jerry Tomaska in 1991 did much to publicize the desirability of modern cameo coins and to have them differentiated by the various grading services.

*   *   *

    The growing popularity of proof coins kept the Philadelphia Mint jumping, as in this item from Eva Adams' *Annual Report* to Treasury Secretary C. Douglas Dillon:

> Because of the tremendous demand for proof coins, additional presses and other equipment were purchased for that operation. Late in the year the proof coin manufacturing operation was moved from a basement location to larger quarters, with better lighting. The room was air-conditioned to reduce dust and dirt, and thus will improve the quality of proof coins. It is expected that there will be fewer rejects, and productive capacity will be substantially increased. The processing of proof coins orders was facilitated greatly by the use of automatic data processing equipment.[47]

1962

PHILADELPHIA
3,218,019

RARITY: Gems are very common and will probably never carry much of a premium. Cameo and deep cameo cents command more respect and bring hefty prices, their value being highly influenced by the depth of frosting and whether it appears on one side of the coin or both. Dual cameos for this and most preceding dates are fairly rare, as proof die pairs were not necessarily replaced simultaneously.

POPULATION: PR RD = 127   PR RD CA = 106   PR RD DC = 60   TOTAL = 293
TOTALS   PR67 RD = 49   HIGHEST = PR69 RD (2)

VALUES:	GRADE	1965	1980	1995
	PROOF	1.00	.75	——
	PR65	——	——	1.00

VARIETIES: Five doubled-dies are known, all minor, two obverse and three reverse. These are described and illustrated in *The Lincoln Cent Doubled Die* by John A. Wexler.

COMMENTS: Although proofs are supposed to represent a coin design at its best, the extreme erosion evident in the Lincoln Cent's obverse master hub renders even the finest proof of this period an eyesore. The U. S. Mint's failure to correct this when adopting the new Memorial reverse in 1959 stands out as nothing less than gross negligence.

Proofs of this date may have been coined in both the French Bronze alloy adopted in 1864 and the tinless brass alloy used during World War II and again from 1962 to 1982. There is no way to distinguish one from the other, nor is their any economic incentive to try. Collectors simply don't care which is which.

1963

PHILADELPHIA
3,075,645

RARITY: Gems are very common, and their present value represents more of a handling charge than a real numismatic premium. Cameo and deep cameo coins are more available for this date than for preceding ones. Still more of them turn up each year as old hoards of proof sets come onto the market.

POPULATION: PR RD = 135   PR RD CA = 117   PR RD DC = 86   TOTAL = 338
TOTALS   PR67 RD = 57   HIGHEST = PR69 RD (1)

VALUES:

GRADE	1965	1980	1995
PROOF	1.50	.75	——
PR65	——	——	1.00

VARIETIES: Two minor doubled-dies may be found for the reverse.

COMMENTS: Why this coin was valued higher than adjacent dates in 1965 is anyone's guess, but the value of all recent proofs was quite inflated by speculative activity at that time.

1964

PHILADELPHIA
3,950,762

RARITY: Gems are common, even by the roll. The higher than usual number of cameo and deep cameo proofs reflects the large mintage for this date and the greater number of dies used. Rick Jerry Tomaska remarked "This is by far the most common date in gem ultra-heavily contrasted condition from 1950-67."[48]

POPULATION: PR RD = 285   PR RD CA = 138   PR RD DC = 112   TOTAL = 535
TOTALS   PR67 RD = 97   HIGHEST = PR69 RD (40)

VALUES:

GRADE	1965	1980	1995
PROOF	1.00	.85	——
PR65	——	——	1.00

VARIETIES: Four reverse doubled-dies are known, all of them quite minor.

COMMENTS: Despite a severe shortage of circulating coins the Mint managed to fill most orders for single proof sets, though many persons ordering multiple sets were disappointed. Countless 1964 sets still survive in their original packaging and in various states of preservation.

* * *

Though it achieved a tremendous mintage of proofs by contemporary standards the Philadelphia Mint could no longer provide this service to collectors in the face of such a severe, nationwide coin shortage. Director Eva Adams ordered a halt to proof coin production after the 1964 orders had been completed, and the presses used for this purpose were converted to the high-speed production of circulating coins.[49]

* * *

The debut of the Kennedy Half Dollar in 1964 pushed proof mintages to a record level that has been exceeded only four times since then. 1964 also witnessed the very peak of the frenzied speculative market in rolls and bags of modern coins. The following year brought an end to fine silver coins, an end to proof coins, an end to mintmarks and the collapse of the vast market run-up which had been building since 1959-60. The coin hobby suffered a huge hangover which drove many of the instant "numismatists" from the field forever and left legitimate dealers scrambling to restructure their activities back toward more traditional avenues of collecting.

1964 marks the highwater mark of popular coin collecting in general. Though most enthusiasts of the time knew little about what they were doing, it seemed that almost everyone in the country was made aware of the value of old coins and the potential profits to be gained with newly-released ones. Coin collecting figured in the plots of many popular television shows during the early 1960s, and the variety of coin albums available and the numbers sold have never since been equalled.

1964
EXPERIMENTAL

PHILADELPHIA?
(mintage unknown)

RARITY: Estimates of the number that exist range from 15 to 25.

POPULATION: These coins are of too recent discovery for extensive data to appear in the published population reports. As of January 1, 1996 PCGS had certified a single example as "Special Mint Set," NGC had certified four, designating them "Specimen," and ANACS had certified a single example as "Satin Proof." All of these designations are describing the same class of coin, but the conflicting terms emphasize the mysterious nature of the 1964 experimental coins.

VALUES: There are no published sales records for these coins since the time that they were correctly identified, so their value has yet to be determined.

VARIETIES: None are reported, but two die-states have been identified. These differ in the number and extent of polishing lines visible in the dies.

COMMENTS: Though the peculiar 1964-dated coins from cent through half dollar were tentatively identified by catalogers at Stack's in New York City as being possible prototypes for the special mint set coins of 1965, this interesting speculation prompted no further investigation when they first surfaced around 1993-94. It wasn't until the author was asked to prepare a *PHOTO PROOF* presentation on one of the half dollars that its special nature was acknowledged by one of the certification services, specifically NGC.

   It was the author's good fortune to examine two complete sets of these special strikings from cent through half dollar. While it was the opinion of this writer and the NGC grading staff that the dimes and quarters were not sufficiently distinctive visually to be certified as specimen strikes, all five denominations bore similar characteristics and were probably produced under the same circumstances.

   No documentation exists to prove what these coins really are or when and where they were made, but Stack's reports that they were consigned to their sales by a coin dealer who obtained them from the estate of a former Mint employee. Circumstantial evidence supports the notion that they were early experiments in a suitable replacement for proof coins, as the striking of proofs was suspended during 1965-67. These pieces were probably coined at the Philadelphia Mint in the Summer or Fall of 1965, at which time the 1964 date was still in use by authority of the Act of September 3, 1964. The application of mintmarks was suspended during 1965-67, so their absence on these coins does not preclude the possibility that they could have been struck at the San Francisco Mint. This facility produced the special mint sets of those years.

   Like all of the 1964 experimental coins the cents are extremely well struck, revealing sharp details and nicely squared inner and outer borders. They lack the brilliance of modern proofs and most closely resemble the satin proof Peace Dollars of 1921. Their entire surfaces are very smooth, the fields interrupted only by numerous shallow die-polishing lines which appear in broad swirls. These cents are included within the proof chapter of this book because they are presumed to have been prototypes for the special mint set coins dated 1965-67 which were themselves pseudo proofs.

   It's too soon to know whether a strong demand will develop for these great rarities. Their limited numbers will certainly discourage widespread acceptance, though a few specialists will seek them out.

1965
SPECIAL MINT SET

SAN FRANCISCO
2,360,000

RARITY: These coins are quite common. While they are far superior in condition to the ordinary cents of 1965, they will typically show a few scattered contact marks. Some cameo examples have turned up, but they're fairly rare, and no deep cameo pieces are known at all. Of the three major grading services, PCGS does not distinguish "cameo" specimens for Special Mint Set coins and NGC had not published its data for post-1964 cents in time for inclusion in this book. Thus the figures below are taken from the ANACS Population Report for January, 1996.

POPULATION:	MS RD = 62	MS RD CA = 10	MS RD DC = 0	TOTAL = 72
TOTALS	MS67 RD = 10	HIGHEST = MS68 RD (1)		

VALUES:	GRADE	1980	1995
	SMS	*4.00*	*3.00*

Values in italics are for complete five-coin sets.

VARIETIES: None are reported.

COMMENTS: These were coined early in 1966, as the Mint was finally catching its breath from all of the radical changes put into place during the previous year. The newly-reactivated San Francisco Mint had been producing planchets for use at the Denver Mint since 1964 but had only months earlier begun striking coins again. The limited capacity of this West Coast facility made it ideal for small press runs, and all future production of regular-issue proofs was confined to the San Francisco Mint.

The special mint set coins dated 1965 were struck singly on normal planchets but from polished dies. Those of 1966 and 1967 were struck on polished planchets, as well. They received no special handling within the mint yet were spared the abuse received by normal coins in the course of bagging and shipping. A poor replacement for true proof coins, these are nonetheless superior to currency strikes in a number of respects. They are more consistently fully struck, while they are less likely to show signs of extensive die wear or other technical flaws.

A few SMS cents of 1965 are prooflike, simulating the less brilliant proofs of 1936 and 1950, but most of this date have a satiny surface which resulted from the dies losing their initial polish. The desirability of these coins thus lies entirely in their limited mintage and their tendency to survive in higher grades than the regular issues. Although excluded from most catalog listings of proof coins, the author believes that the SMS coins of 1965-67 rightly belong in this chapter, as they were clearly produced as a limited issue of superior manufacture and intended specifically for collectors.

1966
SPECIAL MINT SET

SAN FRANCISCO
2,261,583

RARITY: Though their mintage was down from that of the disappointing 1965 sets, examples dated 1966 remain quite common. Most are in very high grades, but contact marks are not unusual. Cameo and deep cameo examples are quite rare, though not as rare as for 1965. Of the three major grading services, PCGS does not distinguish "cameo" specimens for special mint set coins and NGC had not published its data for post-1964 cents in time for inclusion in this book. Thus the figures below are taken from the ANACS *Population Report* for January, 1996.

POPULATION: MS RD = 54   MS RD CA = 29   MS RD DC = 0   TOTAL = 83
TOTALS   MS67 RD = 18   HIGHEST = MS68 RD (2)

VALUES:

GRADE	1980	1995
SMS	*4.25*	*4.00*

Values in italics are for complete five-coin sets

VARIETIES: None are reported.

COMMENTS: The SMS coins of 1966 were coined from polished planchets as well as dies, and they are more consistently brilliant and look almost as good as true proofs. Satin coins are the exception, though some may be found from dies which had begun to lose their polish.

　　Like the regular currency strikes the 1966 SMS coins were all struck between August 1, 1966 and the end of the year. The hard plastic holder used has ensured a high survival rate for gems.

1967
SPECIAL MINT SET

SAN FRANCISCO
1,863,344

RARITY: Gems are the rule for this issue, most coins being virtually indistinguishable from true proofs. Cameo examples are known, and their rarity based on the available data falls somewhere between that of 1965 and 1966. Of the three major grading services, PCGS does not distinguish "cameo" specimens for special mint set coins and NGC had not published its data for post-1964 cents in time for inclusion in this book. Thus the figures below are taken from the ANACS Population Report for January, 1996.

POPULATION: MS RD = 51   MS RD CA = 18   MS RD DC = 0   TOTAL = 69
TOTALS   MS67 RD = 19   HIGHEST = MS68 RD (1)

VALUES:

GRADE	1980	1995
SMS	*6.00*	*6.00*

Values in italics are for complete five-coin sets.

VARIETIES: None are reported.

COMMENTS: With the coin shortage essentially over by the end of 1966 there was no reason to not coin actual proofs. Thus collectors resented the continued production of pseudo proofs, especially since these sets cost nearly twice as much as the real proof sets last issued in 1964. This resentment, combined with a general malaise in the coin hobby, resulted in slow sales. Though hardly rare, the 1967 special mint set and its individual components have always enjoyed a premium over the previous two dates.

Given the mediocre quality of the 1968 proofs it may be said that the 1967 SMS coins are technically and aesthetically superior. The 1968 dies were frequently overpolished, resulting in coins having a soft, indistinct quality. The 1967 dies, however, were polished less vigorously and presumably less often. These coins feature sharper edges between field and device that make them better illustrations of their respective designs than the often muddy proofs of 1968.

1968

SAN FRANCISCO
3,041,506

RARITY: Gems are very common, though the poor condition of the hubs and dies used rendered them aesthetically unappealing in most instances. The value of this and most subsequent dates is so low that population figures are meaningful only with respect to the number of cameo and deep cameo coins certified. Non-cameo examples are simply not worth submitting to grading services.

POPULATION: PR RD = 21   PR RD CA = 44   PR RD DC = 65   TOTAL = 130

VALUES:

GRADE	1980	1995
PROOF	.85	——
PR65	——	1.00

VARIETIES: A very minor obverse doubled-die may be found.

COMMENTS: Most 1968-S proof cents were coined from overly polished and overly used dies. Low relief elements often appear diminished or detached from the main design, while the bust of Lincoln is not distinctly set off from the field. These deficiencies reflect hurried work and perhaps a lack of experience. In each previous instance when proof coinage resumed after a hiatus the first year's product was of disappointing quality, and 1968 was no exception.

*   *   *

As the first proof coins since 1964 and the first coins of any sort to bear the S mintmark since 1955, the 1968-S proof set was the object of intense anticipation and wild speculative activity. Issued at $5 by the Mint, countless orders were returned, and the value of this set was bid up to $15 by the following year. Once the novelty wore off, however, their value plummeted to as low as $2.50. For most of the 1970s, '80s and '90s the 1968-S proof set has hovered around its original issue price. The cent and the half dollar are of the most interest whenever these proofs are offered as singles, with the other three coins being difficult to sell.

1969

SAN FRANCISCO
2,934,631

RARITY: Gems are very common, with anything less being virtually unsellable. The new obverse hub introduced this year seems to have facilitated the the production of cameo and deep cameo coins, as the lower-relief dies wore more slowly.

POPULATION: PR RD = 28   PR RD CA = 31   PR RD DC = 82   TOTAL = 130

VALUES:
GRADE	1980	1995
PROOF	.85	——
PR65	——	1.50

VARIETIES: As unlikely as it seems there were proofs coined of this date from a broken die or cud variety. These are extremely rare, and no photo was available for inclusion in this book.

COMMENTS: The appalling appearance of the 1968 cents finally prompted the creation of a new obverse master hub for 1969. This was a vast improvement, and it may also have encouraged greater care in preparing the dies. The crude and excessive polishing so evident the previous year did not affect the proofs of 1969. These are typically quite appealing, though coins showing cameo contrast are rare.

* * *

The Mint's self-imposed production limit was reached in record time, and many orders were returned unfulfilled. Like the 1968-S proof set this one was the subject of irrational speculation even before the first sets arrived. Though no more common than later sets, and despite the fact that the 1968-69 proof sets contain a silver-clad half dollar, their value has just barely recovered from the tumble that they took when the initial speculation collapsed.

1970

SAN FRANCISCO
2,632,810

RARITY: Gems of the large date variety are very common, while small date proofs are scarce in any condition. The greater number of certified small date coins is merely reflective of their higher value. Cameo and deep cameo large date cents are scarce but still collectable, while small date cameos are rare.

SMALL DATE

POPULATION: PR RD = 86   PR RD CA = 38   PR RD DC = 13   TOTAL = 137

VALUES:	GRADE	1980	1995
	PROOF	37.50	——
	PR65	——	75.00

LARGE DATE

POPULATION: PR RD = 28   PR RD CA = 20   PR RD DC = 33   TOTAL = 81

VALUES:	PROOF	.85	——
	PR65	——	1.00

VARIETIES: Large date varieties include three minor doubled-dies and a tripled-die, both on the obverse. An even more interesting variety features small date over large date doubling.

COMMENTS: The small date proof is readily distinguished not only by the numerals 7 and 0, which are level to one another at their tops, but also by the diminished state of the word LIBERTY (see photos).

The two varieties of 1970-S cents caused quite a stir when discovered. They were naturally associated with the similar 1960 varieties, though they ultimately had much less impact on the hobby. Even so, the proofs of the small date have maintained a respectable premium.

Cameo proof authority Rick Jerry Tomaska wrote of an amusing though regrettable experience regarding this date:

The author [Tomaska] has rarely turned down the chance to buy a rare date cameo proof from the 1950-70 era. One of the few times an opportunity was missed occurred in 1983 when two 1970 small-date cameo ultra-heavy Lincoln cents were offered to him for $90 each. At the time, the price was considered too high. There are some mistakes one never forgets![50]

1970-S
Small date, Breen-2256   (Fivaz & Stanton)

1971

SAN FRANCISCO
3,220,733

RARITY: Gems are very common, though most are of the fully brilliant finish. Coins having light frosting on their devices are usually available, but deep cameo examples are quite scarce.

No figures are presently available from the certification services regarding the number of cameo and deep cameo coins they've examined. PCGS does not distinguish these features in its labeling, as many proofs of 1971 and later years are presumed to have at least some cameo quality. NGC does identify cameo and ultra cameo coins for these later years, but this data was not scheduled to be made available in time for inclusion in this book. ANACS also distinguishes modern cameos, but not enough data is presently available to be meaningful.

VALUES:

GRADE	1980	1995
PROOF	.85	——
PR65	——	1.50

VARIETIES: Three obverse doubled-dies may be found. Two of these are fairly prominent and reveal enough doubling to be desirable to non-specialists (see photos).

Two repunched mintmark varieties are also known; these are quite unusual for proofs.

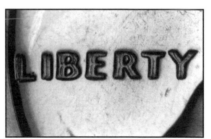

1971-S
DDO-1, Breen-2262 (Fivaz & Stanton)

COMMENTS: Beginning around 1971, the San Francisco Mint appears to have made a conscious effort to produce frosted proofs, known to collectors as cameo coins. While only partly successful this year, a greater degree and frequency of cameo contrast was achieved over the next couple of years. By 1973 cameo coins were the norm rather than the exception. Deep cameos became common a few years later. As a consequence, no premium is attached to 1971-S proofs having less than a deep cameo.

1971-S
DDO-2, Breen-2262 (Fivaz & Stanton)

1972

SAN FRANCISCO
3,260,996

RARITY: Gems are very common. Most examples show slight to moderate cameo contrast, but those having deep contrast are scarce.

VALUES:

GRADE	1980	1995
PROOF	.85	——
PR65	——	1.50

VARIETIES: Three obverse doubled-dies are known, one of these being common to all coins generated from a doubled master die. In *The Lincoln Cent Doubled Die*, John A. Wexler indicates that this feature appears on approximately 50% of the 1972 cents from all three mints. Though proofs are included, it's not certain whether this figure is true of them as well.

COMMENTS: The popularity of cent collecting is evident from the price maintained by this issue. Though $1.50 isn't much, it represents a disproportionate share of the value for a complete 1972-S proof set, which is often available for as little as $4-5.

1973

SAN FRANCISCO
2,760,339

RARITY: Gems are very common, as are coins showing light to moderate cameo contrast. Deep cameo coins are fairly scarce, though it's not certain how many buyers will pay a premium for such pieces at this time.

VALUES:

GRADE	1980	1995
PROOF	.90	——
PR65	——	1.50

VARIETIES: None are reported.

COMMENTS: The chromium plating of proof dies, previously experimental, became routine at about this time. Such protection against rapid wearing undoubtedly accounts for the greater proportion of cents struck from dies which retained their original frosting within the die cavities.

A new reverse master hub was employed for the cents of 1973. Its principal distinction is the much larger size of initials FG, which appear to the right of the Lincoln Memorial. This hub was used in 1973 alone.

*   *   *

Despite the greater quality of its product the U. S. Mint was losing customers throughout the 1970s, as the number of coin collectors continued its decline from 1964 levels. Also contributing to the lower mintages during this period was collector disappointment over the falling values of recent proof sets in the secondary market. Historically, the hobby had seen such coins only rise in value, though the speculative fever of 1957 and the subsequent "correction" resulted in a temporary setback. The proof sets of 1968-72, however, were priced fairly high at issue ($5), and once the initial excitement over the resumption of proof coinage had subsided the market could not sustain even this value. Collectors who had traditionally ordered a few extra sets for trading stock were less inclined to do so during the 1970s and later years.

1974

SAN FRANCISCO
2,612,568

RARITY: Gem proofs, virtually all of them cameos, are quite common. Deep cameos, however, would not become commonplace until 1978.

VALUES:

GRADE	1980	1995
PROOF	1.00	——
PR65	——	1.50

VARIETIES: None are reported.

COMMENTS: The first of two new obverse master hubs introduced in 1974 was even more attractive than that used since 1969. It appears that all proofs dated 1974-S utilized obverse dies taken from this hub (large date type). All proofs likewise bore a new reverse with the initials FG reduced in size from 1973 but larger than in previous years.

   1974 was the last year in which San Francisco coined cents for circulation bearing its mintmark. This resulted in a strong premium for these proofs for several years, though their value has since settled down to levels comparable to other proofs from the early 1970s.

1975

SAN FRANCISCO
2,845,450

RARITY: Cameo proofs are the rule for this date, and gems are common. Deep cameo coins form a minority of the proof mintage.

VALUES:

GRADE	1980	1995
PROOF	13.00	——
PR65	——	3.00

VARIETIES: None are reported.

COMMENTS: As the first proof-only cent from the San Francisco Mint the 1975-S issue was once the subject of frantic speculation; this is evident from its 1980 value. It is now valued at levels comparable to other proof cents after 1974, though this level is still at least twice as high as for earlier dates which do not possess such proof-only status.

———•••———

1976

SAN FRANCISCO
4,149,730

RARITY: Cameo gems are the norm for this date, while deep cameo coins are fairly scarce.

VALUES:

GRADE	1980	1995
PROOF	5.00	——
PR65	——	3.00

VARIETIES: None are reported.

COMMENTS: This was the highest mintage of proof sets ever recorded, as many collectors and non-collectors wanted souvenirs of the nation's Bicentennial. Unlike the quarter, half and dollar, cents were unchanged in their design and simply went along for the ride.

1977

SAN FRANCISCO
3,251,152

RARITY: Gems are very common, most of them cameo pieces. Deep cameo coins became slightly more available this year as the Mint continued to perfect the proofing process and the quality of its dies. Still, deep cameos form a minority of the available coins, but they don't bring very large premiums.

VALUES:

GRADE	1980	1995
PROOF	5.00	——
PR65	——	2.50

VARIETIES: None are reported.

COMMENTS: This was the last year before the San Francisco Mint began producing deep cameo coins on a consistent basis.

1978

SAN FRANCISCO
3,127,781

RARITY: Deep cameo proofs were the norm for this and all subsequent dates.

VALUES:

GRADE	1980	1995
PROOF	5.00	——
PR65	——	3.00

VARIETIES: None are reported.

COMMENTS: The depth of frosting on all relief elements is consistently greater beginning in 1978.

1979

SAN FRANCISCO
3,677,175

RARITY:	Dual-sided, fully cameo gems are very common.		

VALUES:	GRADE	1980	1995
FILLED S:	PROOF	5.00	——
	PR65	——	3.00
CLEAR S:	PROOF	——	——
	PR65	——	4.00

The 1980 edition of the Red Book did not distinguish these two varieties.

VARIETIES: Two different mintmark punches were used to prepare working dies. The old punch dated from 1968 or perhaps even earlier and had finally worn out, becoming at first partially filled and then completely indistinct. Both states are collectable and together comprise the majority of 1979-S proofs. A new punch was introduced for later proofs; it is clear and distinct and continued in use into 1981. The clear S variety is the scarcer of the two and commands a slight premium.

COMMENTS: This date received a boost in mintage because of the debut of the Anthony Dollar.

1980

SAN FRANCISCO
3,554,806

RARITY: Deep cameo gems are very common.

VALUE:	GRADE	1995
	PR65	2.00

VARIETIES: None are reported.

COMMENTS: The mintmark for 1980 was the clear S variety of 1979.

1981

SAN FRANCISCO
4,063,083

RARITY: Deep cameo gems are very common.

VALUES: GRADE   1995
FILLED S: PR65   1.75
CLEAR S: PR65   25.00

VARIETIES: The mintmark punch introduced in 1979 and used throughout 1980 began to fill, and it failed toward the end of the 1980 production run. It was replaced with a new punch of very similar style, and this was used to produce a small percentage of the 1981-S proofs. Though not really rare in an absolute sense it is popular with collectors and commands a strong premium.

COMMENTS: The U. S. Mint had already announced that no Anthony Dollars would be coined for general circulation in 1981, and orders for both uncirculated and proof sets were correspondingly high.

1982

SAN FRANCISCO
3,857,479

RARITY: Deep cameo gems are very common.

VALUE: GRADE   1995
               PR65   2.00

VARIETIES: None are reported.

COMMENTS: All of the proof cents coined in 1982 were of the brass alloy in use since 1962. There was apparently never any consideration of minting the new copper-plated zinc cents in proof during 1982. The obverse hub with large date (actually the small date type of 1974) was employed for all proof cents sold this year, as was a new mintmark punch. A trial run of proofs using the new small date dies was made at the San Francisco Mint, but these coins were subsequently destroyed.[50a]

1983

SAN FRANCISCO
3,279,126

RARITY: Deep cameo gems are very common.

VALUE: GRADE   1995
            PR65   2.25

VARIETIES: None are reported.

COMMENTS: As the first proofs coined with the copper-plated zinc composition, 1983-S cents are quite subject to discoloration. The replacement this year of the plastic proof set mounting insert used since 1968 with a fiberboard one exacerbated this problem. Only time will tell whether these coins can survive.

1984

SAN FRANCISCO
3,065,110

RARITY: As with all proofs since 1978 cameo coins are the norm, and these are readily available in gem condition. Deep cameo specimens are not particularly scarce.

VALUE: GRADE   1995
            PR65   4.00

VARIETIES: None are reported.

COMMENTS: A new obverse hub appeared for the cents of 1984. The only distinguishable change was a pronounced lowering of the relief on Lincoln's upper arm. This was intended to facilitate metal flow into the reverse die and reduce the often seen flatness in the motto E PLURIBUS UNUM.

A few years after the release of the 1984 proofs sets, customers began complaining that their cents had corroded. This was ultimately traced to the fiberboard used as a mounting. Storing coins away from moisture and temperature extremes should reduce such problems.

1985

SAN FRANCISCO
3,362,821

RARITY: Deep cameo gems are fairly common, though examples having less frostiness are not unknown.

VALUE: GRADE   1995
           PR65   2.75

VARIETIES: None are reported.

COMMENTS: The S mintmark was greatly enlarged for 1985. The mintmark was no longer punched into each working die but rather was punched into the master die for 1985 and *engraved* into the master dies for 1986 and later years. Thus all proofs dated 1985 and later will have mintmarks of identical style and placement within their respective dates.

1986

SAN FRANCISCO
3,010,497

RARITY: Cameo and deep cameo coins are readily available.

VALUE: GRADE   1995
           PR65   8.00

VARIETIES: None are reported.

COMMENTS: A new reverse hub was introduced for the coinage of 1986 and continued in use through 1989. It's barely distinguishable by its overall greater sharpness.

1987

SAN FRANCISCO
4,227,728

RARITY: Deep cameo gems are the rule rather than the exception for this and all subsequent issues.

VALUE: GRADE   1995
               PR65   3.00

VARIETIES: None are reported.

COMMENTS: Though the Director's *Annual Report* indicates that both master hubs were slightly modified this is not discernible from examining the coins.[51]

1988

SAN FRANCISCO
3,262,948

RARITY: Deep cameo gems are readily available.

VALUE: GRADE   1995
               PR65   4.00

VARIETIES: None are reported.

COMMENTS: None.

1989

SAN FRANCISCO
3,220,194

RARITY: Deep cameo gems are common.

VALUE:

GRADE	1995
PR65	4.00

VARIETIES: None are reported.

COMMENTS: None.

*   *   *

    Proof cents coined since 1983 are struck on planchets which receive an extra cleaning before being copper-plated. These planchets are also plated not once but twice. Such steps are necessary to combat the tendency of the copper plating to separate from the zinc base when receiving the second strike required for proof coins.[51a]

1990

SAN FRANCISCO
3,299,559

RARITY: Deep cameo gems are common.

VALUE:

GRADE	1995
PR65	5.50

VARIETIES: The biggest story of the year was the discovery of 1990 proof cents without the customary S mintmark. For more about this extremely rare coin see the following page.

COMMENTS: A new obverse master hub is barely distinguishable by the slightly larger initials V.D.B. at the truncation of Lincoln's bust. Even more subtle is the sharper lettering in the new reverse master hub.

1990 No S

SAN FRANCISCO
(mintage unknown)

RARITY: No more than 150 examples are believed to exist. As of January, 1996 PCGS had certified only three specimens, while ANACS had not certified any. The NGC figures for this variety were not available at press time.

VALUES:

GRADE	1995
PR65	1,900.00

VARIETIES: None are reported.

COMMENTS: It's hard to imagine that the mintmark could be omitted from a proof die without this error being caught, yet the same oversight occurred previously for the nickel in 1971 and the dime in 1968, 1970 and 1983! In fact, there were a few other instances of this omission not widely known to numismatists, as these mistakes were detected before any coins were released.

In all of the previous instances the mintmark punch was simply not applied to a particular working die. Since proofs dated 1985 and later have their origin in a master die bearing an engraved mintmark, the comedy of errors in 1990 was of much greater scope and should have been discovered in time to prevent the coins being struck.

A working die bearing no mintmark and intended for use at the Philadelphia Mint was instead shipped to the San Francisco Mint. It was duly sandblasted, polished and chromium plated, the normal preparation for modern proof dies. An unknown number of cents were coined before the error was discovered, and only 145 pieces were retrieved from sets already packaged but not yet shipped.

The first report of this error by a proof set purchaser was from Jim Cullen of New York on July 18, 1990. A press release from embarrassed Mint officials projected that some 3700 pieces were coined before the problem was discovered and the die pulled from production. David L. Karmol, assistant to Mint Director Donna Pope, later revealed that this figure was merely an estimate and that the number of S-less cents coined and released was unknown.[52]

The total population remains a mystery to this day, and the number of pieces extant is quite small. A figure in the range of 100-150 is probable, though many purchasers of 1990-S proof sets who are not in tune with hobby news may have such coins and not yet know it. Given the number of dedicated Lincoln Cent collectors this error coin will always be in tremendous demand. Listed at only $1900 this rarity seems a bargain, and it's quite possible that few if any examples are actually trading at that level.

1991

SAN FRANCISCO
2,867,787

RARITY: Deep cameo gems are common.

VALUE: GRADE   1995
PR65   6.50

VARIETIES: None are reported.

COMMENTS: None.

1992

SAN FRANCISCO
4,176,560

RARITY: Deep cameo gems are common.

VALUE: GRADE   1995
PR65   6.00

VARIETIES: None are reported.

COMMENTS: A new obverse master hub is readily identified by the peculiar addition of a long and irregular raised line to Lincoln's temple. This looks like a bulging vein, and it would appear for the next several years. The relief of Lincoln's upper arm was further reduced, as well. Changes to the master hubs of both obverse and reverse have come almost annually since this time, but they are virtually indistinguishable.

1993

SAN FRANCISCO
3,394,792

RARITY: Deep cameo gems are common.

VALUE: GRADE   1995
             PR65   6.00

VARIETIES: None are reported.

COMMENTS: None.

1994

SAN FRANCISCO
3,222,140

RARITY: Deep cameo gems are common.

VALUE: GRADE   1995
             PR65   3.00

VARIETIES: None are reported.

COMMENTS: None.

1995

SAN FRANCISCO
(pending)

RARITY: Deep cameo gems are common.

VALUE:

GRADE	1995
PR65	3.00

VARIETIES: None are reported.

COMMENTS: Due to an ordering period which extended into 1996 and to the several packaging options available for proof coins, the Mint has been slow to provide final mintage figures in recent years. The total number of proof cents issued was not available in time for inclusion in this book.

Notes to Chapter 8

[1]R. S. Yeoman, *A Guide Book of United States Coins.*
[2]*The Numismatic Scrapbook Magazine*, February, 1966.
[3]*Numismatic Scrapbook*, May, 1936
[4]*The Numismatist*, July, 1936.
[5]*The Numismatic Scrapbook Magazine*, December, 1937.
[6]*The Numismatist*, April, 1943.
[7]*The Numismatic Scrapbook Magazine*, June, 1943.
[8]*The Numismatist*, July, 1946.
[9]Ibid, October, 1946.
[10]Ibid, December, 1948.
[11]*The Numismatic Scrapbook Magazine*, March, 1950.
[12]Ibid, May, 1950.
[13]*The Numismatist*, August, 1950.
[14]*The Numismatic Scrapbook Magazine*, June, 1950.

[15]*Annual Report of the Director of the Mint for Fiscal Year Ended June 30, 1966.*
[16]Ibid, 1962.
[17]James Rankin Young, *The United States Mint at Philadelphia.*
[18]*The Numismatic Scrapbook Magazine*, March, 1942.
[19]Rick Jerry Tomaska, *Cameo and Brilliant Proof Coinage of the 1950 to 1970 Era.*
[20]*Annual Report*, 1928.
[21]Tomaska.
[22]Ibid.
[23]*The Numismatist*, March, 1912.
[24]Ibid, August, 1960.
[25]Ibid.
[26]Ibid, March, 1912.
[27]Ibid, January, 1932.
[28]Ibid, August, 1932.

[29]Walter Breen, *Walter Breen's Encyclopedia of United States and Colonial Proof Coins 1722-1977.*
[30]American Numismatic Association, Counterfeit Detection, Volume II.
[31]Breen, *Walter Breen's Complete Encyclopedia of U. S. and Colonial Coins.*
[32]Breen, *Proof Coins.*
[33]Ibid.
[34]Breen, *Encyclopedia.*
[35]Breen, *Proof Coins.*
[36]Ibid.
[37]Sol Taylor, *The Standard Guide to the Lincoln Cent.*
[38]Ibid.
[39]Tomaska.
[40]Ibid.
[41]Ibid.

[42]John A. Wexler, *The Lincoln Cent Doubled Die.*
[43]Breen, *Proof Coins.*
[44]Tomaska.
[45]Ibid.
[46]Bill Fivaz and J. T. Stanton, *The Cherrypicker's Guide to Rare Die Varieties.*
[47]*Annual Report*, 1962.
[48]Tomaska.
[49]*Annual Report*, 1964.
[50]Tomaska.
[50a]Alan Herbert, "Coin Clinic," *Numismatic News*, July 15, 1996.
[51]*Annual Report*, 1986.
[51a]Alan Herbert, "Coin Clinic," *Numismatic News*, July 2, 1996.
[52]Taylor.

Appendices

GLOSSARY

•

STATISTICS

•

REFERENCES

GLOSSARY

ALLOY – A mixture of two or more metals.

ANAAB – The American Numismatic Association Authentication Bureau is managed by the Association and maintains files on counterfeit and altered coins; in addition, it renders opinions as to the authenticity of coins.

ANACS – Formerly owned by the American Numismatic Association, it is now under commercial ownership and provides services similar to that of the ANAAB; in addition, it grades and encapsulates coins. The quantities of Lincoln Cents certified by ANACS for each issue in the Lincoln Cent series are included in the "Certified Population" data within Chapters 4, 7 and 8, where appropriate.

BASINING – Describes the process of preparing a working die for placement into the press. The die face is held against a rotating grinding surface of a predetermined concavity, or die-face radius. Successful basining allows for a smooth flow of metal into all recesses of the die during coining. This preparation is made at the mint of use, rather than being limited to the Philadelphia Mint where dies are initially created. As a result, coins struck at different mints may possess a unique character which identifies their origin nearly as well as the mintmark does.

BUSINESS STRIKE, CIRCULATION STRIKE OR CURRENCY STRIKE – A regular production coin, struck only once and intended for use in commerce.

COLLAR – The steel ring which surrounds the coining chamber between obverse and reverse dies. Modern coins are struck within a "close" collar in which the expanding edge of the planchet is forcefully restrained against the collar's inner surface. Lincolns were coined within a "plain" collar, as they have no design on their edge.

CONTACT MARK OR BAG MARK – A nick which appears on an otherwise uncirculated coin's surface from collision with other coins during the manufacturing or shipping processes.

CUD – A coin variety in which a portion of the die has broken away, usually as the result of a progressive die crack. This missing portion appears as a blank or filled-in area on the coin. A retained cud is one in which the dislodged piece of the die remains in place.

DDO – Doubled-die obverse. When a working die is not accurately in register between successive impressions from a working hub, a slight doubling or shifting of the image is imparted to the die. This will then appear on all coins struck from that die.

DDR – Doubled-die reverse.

DIE – A solid, steel cylinder which bears on one end a negative or incuse image of a coin design. Master dies are used to raise working hubs, while working dies are used to strike coins. In striking Lincoln Cents, the obverse die has been used as the upper or "hammer" die, while the reverse has been positioned as the lower or "anvil" die.

GALVANO – A thin, copper shell used as a mold for casting a duplicate of a coin design in plaster or other modeling compound. A newly-created coin design is modeled oversize by the sculptor and a layer of copper deposited atop it through an electrolytic or galvanizing process. This "galvano" is then used as a durable copy of the artist's model.

HUB – A solid, steel cylinder which bears on one end a positive or relief image of a coin design. A master hub is used to sink master dies, while working hubs are used to sink working dies.

JANVIER – Named after its creator, this reducing lathe or pantograph traces the contours of an artist's sculpted model and transfers its design in any scale desired to the face of a solid, steel cylinder known as a "hub."

MECHANICAL DOUBLING OR STRIKE DOUBLING – This occurs when one or both dies bounce back against the struck coin at the moment of striking or when one or both dies move laterally as they separate from the coin. The result is a slightly blurred or doubled image which is flat and shelf-like, rather than being contoured as with a true doubled-die variety.

MINOR COIN – A coin of small value containing no precious metals. The Lincoln Cent is classified as a minor coin.

MINTMARK – A small letter or symbol appearing on a coin which indicates its place of manufacture. Lincoln Cents coined at the Philadelphia Mint and the West Point Depository do not bear mintmarks. Cents coined at the Denver and San Francisco Mints bear D and S mintmarks, respectively. The exceptions are all cents dated 1965–67 and circulating S-Mint cents dated 1975 and later; these carry no mintmarks.

MINT SET – Known by the United States Mint (which produces it) as an Uncirculated Set, this typically consists of one each of the coins struck for circulation from each mint (sometimes non-circulating coins of ordinary manufacture are also included). Such sets have been offered for sale to collectors for the dates 1947-49, 1951-64, 1968-81 and 1984 to date.

NGC – The Numismatic Guaranty Corporation of America is a commercial service which authenticates, grades and encapsulates coins. The quantities of Lincoln Cents certified by NGC for each issue in the Lincoln Cent series are included in the "Certified Population" data within Chapters 4, 7 and 8, where appropriate.

OMM – Overmintmark, a variety in which one mintmark has been punched over another in the die. An example would D over S, abbreviated as D/S.

ORIGINAL ROLL – Coins are delivered to the Federal Reserve Banks (the Treasury and Sub-Treasuries prior to 1914) from the mints in bags or boxes, never in rolls. Thus, uncirculated rolls are wrapped by banks from freshly minted and delivered coins. "Original" rolls consist of coins which have been kept together since they were first issued and have not had the higher-quality pieces replaced with lesser ones by collectors.

PATTERN – A coin struck as a test of a new design or a modification to an existing design. Patterns are customarily for use only within the Treasury Department or for inspection by Congress, but examples have come into the possession of collectors.

PLANCHET – When a coin blank is first punched from metal strip by the punching press it has no raised rim. Its rim is applied by an upsetting mill, and the second-stage blank is then known as a "planchet."

PCGS – The Professional Coin Grading Service is a commercial service which authenticates, grades and encapsulates coins. The quantities of Lincoln Cents certified by PCGS for each issue in the Lincoln Cent series are included in the "Certified Population" data within Chapters 7 and 8, where appropriate.

PROOF – A coin made from specially prepared dies and planchets, struck two or more times to bring out all details. These are intended for presentation as gifts or for sale to collectors at a premium. Proofs of the Lincoln Cent have been offered to collectors 1909-16, 1936-42, 1950-64 and 1968 to date.

PROOFLIKE – Having some of the qualities of a proof coin. A prooflike Lincoln Cent will have brilliant fields from brightly polished or chromium-plated dies.

RED BOOK – The nickname given to R. S. Yeoman's *A Guide Book of United States Coins,* currently edited by Kenneth Bressett. Since 1946 this book has been published annually as a guide to retail values.

REDUCTION – The process by which an artist's oversize, sculpted model is scaled down to the size of the actual coin. A Janvier reducing lathe traces the model and transfers its image in any size desired to the end of a solid, steel cylinder known as a "hub." "Reduction" is also used as a noun to refer to the hub itself.

RPM – Repunched mintmark, a variety in which the mintmark has been punched two or more times in the die, not in perfect register. An example would be D over D, abbreviated as D/D.

SEIGNIORAGE – The profit accruing to the Treasury Department from the difference between the cost of manufacturing a coin and its resulting face value.

SMS – Special Mint Set. These sets of coins, one each from cent through half dollar, were issued in lieu of actual proof coins for the dates 1965-67. They are superior to currency strikes but inferior to proofs.

UPSETTING MILL – A rotary milling machine which compresses the edge of a coin blank and forms a raised rim on it. This facilitates the flow of metal into the coin dies during the striking process.

APPENDIX B

STATISTICS

TABLE 1: Laws Relating to the Lincoln Cent

Date of Law	Effect on cent coinage
April 22, 1864	Created the one-cent piece of .950 copper and .050 zinc & tin
March 3, 1871	Provided for the redemption of minor coins by the Treasury
February 12,1873	Reduced the tolerance for the legal weight of the cent and defined its legal tender value
January 29, 1874	Permitted coinage by the U. S. Mints for foreign countries and paved the way for numerous and unintended off-metal cents
June 22, 1874	Reaffirmed the composition of the bronze cent, defined the penalties for counterfeiting minor coins and established a legal tender limit for the cent of 25 cents
September 26, 1890	Limited design changes to not more than once in 25 years
June 11, 1896	Authorized the cleaning and reissuing of used minor coins by the Philadelphia Mint
April 24, 1906	Authorized the production of minor coins at the branch mints and provided funding for purchase of the required metals
December 18, 1942	Authorized the Treasury Secretary to alter the composition of the one-cent and five-cent pieces, such authority expiring December 31, 1946
September 5, 1962	Eliminated tin from the cent, which thereafter contained .950 copper & .050 zinc (until 1982)
September 3, 1964	Authorized the Treasury Secretary to maintain the date 1964 on all coinage until further notice (last 1964-dated cents coined December 29, 1965)
July 23, 1965	Prohibited the use of mintmarks for five years from the date of passage and made all U. S. coins (excluding gold) a legal tender in any amount
June 24, 1967	Restored mintmarks effective January 1, 1968
October 18, 1973	Permitted any U. S. Mint facility to produce coins (coinage commenced at the West Point Depository in 1974)
October 11, 1974	Authorized the Treasury Secretary to alter the composition of the cent without further Congressional action (not implemented until 1982)

TABLE 2: Specifications for the Lincoln Cent

Years	Composition	Diameter	Thickness	Weight Grains	Weight Grams	Specific Gravity
1909-42	95 Cu, 5 Zn & Sn	19.05mm	1.58mm	48.000	3.110	8.84
1943	Steel, Zn plating, .001" thick max.	19.05mm	1.58mm	42.500	2.754	7.80
1944-46	95 Cu, 5 Zn	19.05mm	1.58mm	48.000	3.110	8.83
1947-62	95 Cu, 5 Zn & Sn	19.05mm	1.58mm	48.000	3.110	8.84
1962-82	95 Cu, 5 Zn	19.05mm	1.58mm	48.000	3.110	8.83
1982-	97.5 Zn, 2.5 Cu *	19.05mm	1.58mm	38.581	2.500	7.17

* The figures shown for cents 1982 to date are net. These coins are actually struck from planchets which are .998 zinc and .002 copper with a pure copper plating applied.

TABLE 3: Mintage Totals for Circulating Cents

Date/Mint	Quantity	Date/Mint	Quantity	Date/Mint	Quantity
1909 VDB	27,994,580	1940-D	81,390,000	1970-S	690,560,004
1909-S VDB	484,000	1940-S	112,940,000	1971	1,919,490,000
1909	72,700,420	1941	887,039,100	1971-D	2,911,045,600
1909-S	1,825,000	1941-D	128,700,000	1971-S	525,133,459
1910	146,798,813	1941-S	92,360,000	1972	2,933,255,000
1910-S	6,045,600	1942	657,828,600	1972-D	2,665,071,400
1911	101,176,054	1942-D	206,698,000	1972-S	377,019,108
1911-D	12,672,000	1942-S	85,590,000	1973	3,728,245,000
1911-S	4,026,000	1943	684,628,670	1973-D	3,549,576,588
1912	68,150,915	1943-D	217,660,000	1973-S	317,177,295
1912-D	10,411,000	1943-S	191,550,000	1974 (P)	4,103,183,000
1912-S	4,131,000	1944	1,435,400,000	1974 (W)	128,957,523
1913	76,529,504	1944-D	430,578,000	1974 (total)	4,232,140,523
1913-D	15,804,000	1944-S	282,760,000	1974-D	4,235,098,000
1913-S	6,101,000	1945	1,040,515,000	1974-S	409,426,660
1914	75,237,067	1945-D	266,268,000	1975 (P)	3,874,182,000
1914-D	1,193,000	1945-S	181,770,000	1975 (W)	1,577,294,142
1914-S	4,137,000	1946	991,655,000	1975 (total)	5,451,476,142
1915	29,090,970	1946-D	315,690,000	1975-D	4,505,275,300
1915-D	22,050,000	1946-S	198,100,000	1976 (P)	3,133,580,000
1915-S	4,833,000	1947	190,555,000	1976 (W)	1,540,695,000
1916	131,832,627	1947-D	194,750,000	1976 (total)	4,674,275,000
1916-D	35,956,000	1947-S	99,000,000	1976-D	4,221,592,455
1916-S	22,510,000	1948	317,570,000	1977 (P)	3,074,575,000
1917	196,429,785	1948-D	172,637,500	1977 (W)	1,395,355,000
1917-D	55,120,000	1948-S	81,735,000	1977 (total)	4,469,930,000
1917-S	32,620,000	1949	217,775,000	1977-D	4,194,062,300
1918	288,104,634	1949-D	153,132,500	1978 (P)	3,735,655,000
1918-D	47,830,000	1949-S	64,290,000	1978 (W)	1,531,250,000
1918-S	34,680,000	1950	272,635,000	1978 (S)	291,700,000
1919	392,021,000	1950-D	334,950,000	1978 (total)	5,558,605,000
1919-D	57,154,000	1950-S	118,505,000	1978-D	4,280,233,400
1919-S	139,760,000	1951	294,576,000	1979 (P)	3,560,940,000
1920	310,165,000	1951-D	625,355,000	1979 (W)	1,705,850,000
1920-D	49,280,000	1951-S	136,010,000	1979 (S)	751,725,000
1920-S	46,220,000	1952	186,765,000	1979 (total)	6,018,515,000
1921	39,157,000	1952-D	746,130,000	1979-D	4,139,357,254
1921-S	15,274,000	1952-S	137,800,004	1980 (P)	4,653,915,000
1922-D	7,160,000	1953	256,755,000	1980 (W)	1,576,200,000
1923	74,723,000	1953-D	700,515,000	1980 (S)	1,184,590,000
1923-S	8,700,000	1953-S	181,835,000	1980 (total)	7,414,705,000
1924	75,178,000	1954	71,640,050	1980-D	5,140,098,660
1924-D	2,520,000	1954-D	251,552,500	1981 (P)	4,728,905,000
1924-S	11,696,000	1954-S	96,190,000	1981 (W)	1,882,400,000
1925	139,949,000	1955	330,580,000	1981 (S)	880,445,000
1925-D	22,580,000	1955-D	563,257,500	1981 (total)	7,491,750,000
1925-S	26,380,000	1955-S	44,610,000	1981-D	5,373,235,677
1926	157,088,000	1956	420,745,000	1982 (P)	7,135,275,000
1926-D	28,020,000	1956-D	1,098,201,100	1982 (W)	1,990,005,000
1926-S	4,550,000	1957	282,540,000	1982 (S)	1,587,245
1927	144,440,000	1957-D	1,051,342,000	1982 (total)	10,712,525,000
1927-D	27,170,000	1958	252,525,000	1982-D	6,012,979,368
1927-S	14,276,000	1958-D	800,953,300	1983 (P)	7,569,585,600
1928	134,116,000	1959	609,715,000	1983 (W)	2,004,400
1928-D	31,170,000	1959-D	1,279,760,000	1983 (S)	180,765,000
1928-S	17,266,000	1960	586,405,000	1983 (total)	7,752,355,000
1929	185,262,000	1960-D	1,580,884,000	1983-D	6,467,199,428
1929-D	41,730,000	1961	753,345,000	1984 (P)	6,114,864,000
1929-S	50,148,000	1961-D	1,753,266,700	1984 (W)	2,036,215,000
1930	157,415,000	1962	606,045,000	1984 (total)	8,151,079,000
1930-D	40,100,000	1962-D	1,793,148,400	1984-D	5,569,238,906
1930-S	24,286,000	1963	754,110,000	1985 (P)	4,951,904,887
1931	19,396,000	1963-D	1,774,020,400	1985 (W)	696,585,000
1931-D	4,480,000	1964 (P)	2,451,945,000	1985 (total)	5,648,489,887
1931-S	866,000	1964 (S)	196,630,000	1985-D	5,287,399,926
1932	9,062,000	1964 (Total)	2,648,575,000	1986	4,491,395,493
1932-D	10,500,000	1964-D	3,799,071,500	1986-D	4,442,866,698
1933	14,360,000	1965 (P)	301,470,000	1987	4,682,466,931
1933-D	6,200,000	1965 (D)	973,364,900	1987-D	4,879,389,514
1934	219,080,000	1965 (S)	220,030,000	1988	6,092,810,000
1934-D	28,446,000	1965 (Total)	1,494,864,900	1988-D	5,253,740,443
1935	245,388,000	1966 (P)	811,100,000	1989	7,261,535,000
1935-D	47,000,000	1966 (D)	991,431,200	1989-D	5,345,467,111
1935-S	38,702,000	1966 (S)	383,355,000	1990	6,851,765,000
1936	309,632,000	1966 (Total)	2,185,886,200	1990-D	4,922,894,533
1936-D	40,620,000	1967 (P)	907,575,000	1991	5,165,940,000
1936-S	29,130,000	1967 (D)	1,327,377,100	1991-D	4,158,442,076
1937	309,179,320	1967 (S)	813,715,000	1992	4,648,905,000
1937-D	50,430,000	1967 (Total)	3,048,667,100	1992-D	4,448,673,300
1937-S	34,500,000	1968-P	1,707,880,970	1993	5,684,705,000
1938	156,696,734	1968-D	2,886,269,600	1993-D	6,426,650,571
1938-D	20,010,000	1968-S	258,270,001	1994	6,500,850,000
1938-S	15,180,000	1969	1,136,910,000	1994-D	7,131,765,000
1939	316,479,520	1969-D	4,002,832,200	1995	6,411,440,000
1939-D	15,160,000	1969-S	544,375,000	1995-D	7,128,560,000
1939-S	52,070,000	1970	1,898,315,000		
1940	586,810,000	1970-D	2,891,438,900		

TABLE 4: Mintage Totals for Proof Cents

Date/Mint	Quantity	Date/Mint	Quantity	Date/Mint	Quantity
1909 VDB	420	1955	378,200	1976-S	4,149,730
1909	2,198	1956	669,384	1977-S	3,251,152
1910	2,405	1957	1,247,952	1978-S	3,127,781
1911	1,733	1958	875,652	1979-S	3,677,175
1912	2,145	1959	1,149,291	1980-S	3,554,806
1913	2,848	1960	1,691,602	1981-S	4,063,083
1914	1,365	1961	3,028,244	1982-S	3,857,479
1915	1,150	1962	3,218,019	1983-S	3,279,126
1916	1,050	1963	3,075,645	1984-S	3,065,110
1917	unknown	1964	3,950,762	1985-S	3,362,821
1936	5,569	1964 Experimental	unknown	1986-S	3,010,497
1937	9,320	1965 SMS	2,360,000	1987-S	4,227,728
1938	14,734	1966 SMS	2,261,583	1988-S	3,262,948
1939	13,520	1967 SMS	1,863,344	1989-S	3,220,194
1940	15,872	1968-S	3,041,506	1990-S	3,299,559
1941	21,100	1969-S	2,934,631	1991-S	2,867,787
1942	32,600	1970-S	2,632,810	1992-S	4,176,560
1950	51,386	1971-S	3,220,733	1993-S	3,394,792
1951	57,500	1972-S	3,260,996	1994-S	3,222,140
1952	81,980	1973-S	2,760,339	1995-S	
1953	128,800	1974-S	2,612,568		
1954	233,300	1975-S	2,845,450		

REFERENCES

BOOKS:

Alexander, David T. and Thomas K. DeLorey. *The Comprehensive Catalog & Encyclopedia of United States Coins*. Sidney, OH: Coin World, 1995.

Altz, Charles G. and E. H. Barton. *Foreign Coins Struck at United States Mints*. Racine, WI: Whitman Publishing Company, 1965.

American Numismatic Association. *Counterfeit Detection, Volume I*. Colorado Springs, CO: American Numismatic Association, 1983.

American Numismatic Association. *Counterfeit Detection, Volume II*. Colorado Springs, CO: American Numismatic Association, 1986.

Breen, Walter. *Walter Breen's Complete Encyclopedia of U.S. and Colonial Coins*. New York: F.C.I. Press, Inc. & Doubleday, 1988.

Breen, Walter. *Walter Breen's Encyclopedia of United States and Colonial Proof Coins 1722-1977*. Albertson, NY: F.C.I. Press, Inc., 1977.

Bressett, Ken & A. Kosoff. *Official A.N.A. Grading Standards for United States Coins*. Fourth Edition. Colorado Springs, CO: American Numismatic Association, 1991.

Carothers, Neil. *Fractional Money - A History of the Small Coins and Fractional Paper Currency of The United States*. New York: John Wiley & Sons, Inc., 1930.

Committee on Finance of the United States Senate. *Coinage Laws of the United States 1792-1894*. (reprinted) Wolfeboro, NH: Bowers and Merena Galleries, Inc., 1990.

Fivaz, Bill & J. T. Stanton. *The Cherrypickers' Guide to Rare Die Varieties*. Third Edition. Wolfeboro, NH: Bowers & Merena Galleries, Inc., 1994.

Kunhardt, Phillip B., Jr., Phillip B. III and Peter W. *Lincoln: An Illustrated Biography*. New York: Alfred A. Knopf, 1992.

Leach, Frank A. *Recollections of a Mint Director*. (reprint) Wolfeboro, NH: Bowers & Merena Galleries, Inc., 1987.

Manley, Stephen G. *The Lincoln Cent*. Muscatine, IA: Liberty Press, 1981.

Raymond, Wayte. *The Standard Catalogue of United States Coins*. New York: Wayte Raymond, Inc., 1934.

Reed, P. Bradley, editor. *Coin World Almanac*. Sixth Edition. Sidney, OH: Amos Press, Inc., 1990.

Taxay, Don. *Illustrated History of United States Commemorative Coinage*. New York: Arco Publishing Co., Inc., 1967.

Taxay, Don. *The U.S. Mint and Coinage*. New York: Arco Publishing Co., Inc., 1966.

Taylor, Sol. *The Standard Guide to the Lincoln Cent*. Third Edition. Sherman Oaks, CA: Sol Taylor, Ph D., 1983.

Tomaska, Rick Jerry. *Cameo and Brilliant Proof Coinage of the 1950 to 1970 Era*. Encinitas, CA: R & I Publications, 1991.

Vermeule, Cornelius. *Numismatic Art in America*. Cambridge, MA: The Belknap Press of Harvard University Press, 1971.

Wexler, John A. *The Lincoln Cent Doubled Die*. John A. Wexler, 1984.

Wexler, John A. & Tom Miller. *The RPM Book*. Newbury Park, CA: Lonesome John Publishing Co., 1983.

Yeoman, R. S. *A Guide Book of United States Coins*. Various editions. Racine, WI: Western Publishing Co., Inc., 1950, 1964, 1979, 1994.

Young, James Rankin. *The United States Mint at Philadelphia*. Philadelphia: J. R. Young, 1903.

PERIODICALS:

Annual Report of the Director of the Mint. Washington, DC: U. S. Government Printing Office. Various editions 1908-94.

The Coin Dealer Newsletter Monthly Summary. Hollywood, CA: The Coin Dealer Newsletter. October & November, 1980.

Coin World. Sidney, OH: Amos Press. Various issues as footnoted in the text.

Errorscope. Seattle: CONECA. Various issues as footnoted in the text.

Error Trends Coin Magazine. Oceanside, NY: Arnold Margolis. July, 1994 through June, 1996, inclusive.

Numismatic News. Iola, WI: Krause Publications. Various issues as footnoted in the text.

The Numismatic Scrapbook Magazine. Chicago: Hewitt Brothers (1935-67). Sidney, OH: Amos Press (1968-76) Various issues as footnoted in the text.

The Numismatist. Colorado Springs, CO: American Numismatic Association. Various issues as footnoted in the text.

Rare Coin Review. Number 108. Wolfeboro, NH: Bowers & Merena Galleries, 1995.

The Whitman Numismatic Journal. Racine, WI: Western Publishing Company, Inc. Various issues as footnoted in the text.

UNPUBLISHED MATERIAL:

Correspondence between V. D. Brenner and the Treasury Department. National Archives Record Group 104.

Martin, J. P. "Authenticating the Lincoln Cent." Colorado Springs, CO: American Numismatic Association, 1996.

It makes 'cents' to use only the best!

NUMISMATIC GUARANTY CORPORATION

As with any coins, the value of Lincoln Cents depends largely on their grade. When you buy a Lincoln Cent for your collection, you want to know that you're getting good value for your money and that the coin is correctly graded.

Who can I trust?

Trust in NGC, the most respected grading service in the numismatic hobby. In fact, NGC is **the Official Grading Service of the American Numismatic Association**. The ANA chose NGC over other grading companies to provide reliable and recognized services to its members. We've earned the ANA's trust, and we'd like to have yours.

What do I get?

David W. Lange
Director of Research

When your Lincoln Cents or other coins are submitted to NGC through one of its authorized dealer members, they will be evaluated by our expert graders and assigned a numerical grade which carries the weight of their many years of experience and their knowledge of the rare coin market. Sealed in chemically-inert and tamper-proof holders, your coins will carry their own 'credentials.' Just ask the consignor of the unique 1943-D bronze cent. That coin was certified and graded by NGC and realized a record-setting $82,500 when sold at auction.

What about PHOTO PROOF?

PHOTO PROOF is NGC's state-of-the-art system for creating full-color, digital photographs of certified coins. These are accompanied by an expert written analysis of each coin's qualities. Assembled into an attractive album and laminated for lasting protection, PHOTO PROOF permits you to enjoy the beauty of your coins at home while they reside safely in a bank vault. Through NGC's nationwide network of authorized member-dealers, PHOTO PROOF accepts all United States coins certified by NGC, PCGS and ANACS, as well as selected world coins.

Coins may submitted for grading and PHOTO PROOF services through any NGC-authorized dealer. Members of the American Numismatic Association may submit coins through the ANA. For information about NGC dealers in your area, call **1-800-NGC COIN**. For information about PHOTO PROOF, call **1-800-PROOF 67**.

**The Official Grading Service
of the American Numismatic Association**

P. O. Box 1776   Parsippany, New Jersey   07054

ABOUT THE AUTHOR

David W. Lange is Director of Research for Numismatic Guaranty Corporation in Parsippany, New Jersey. A prolific writer and researcher, Dave has authored two monthly columns for *The Numismatist* and has published more than one hundred feature articles for various commercial and non-profit numismatic journals. He is also a popular public speaker on a wide variety of numismatic subjects. His previous books include *The Complete Guide to Buffalo Nickels* and *The Complete Guide to Mercury Dimes*.